PIONEER TO THE PAST

Dr. and Mrs. James H. Breasted, and Charles Breasted at the age of eight, at the ancient temple of Amada in Nubia, upper Egypt, in 1906.

PIONEER TO THE PAST

The Story of

JAMES HENRY BREASTED

Archaeologist

Told by His Son

CHARLES BREASTED

THE UNIVERSITY OF CHICAGO PRESS
CHICAGO AND LONDON

The University of Chicago Press, Chicago 60637
The University of Chicago Press, Ltd., London

81 80 79 78 77 987654321

ISBN: 0-226-07186-3

To Martha
who called him "Dr. Pa,"
and whom he adored

August 26, 1908. I was thinking the other day what a secure possession the past is. The happiness and beauty that it had cannot now be spoilt or impaired: having had it one cannot be pessimistic either about this life or another.   *—Lord Grey of Falloden*

A comprehensive study of the ancient orient reveals to us the historic epochs of European man for the first time set in a background of several hundred thousand years. In this vast synthesis there is disclosed to us an imposing panorama such as no earlier generation has ever been able to survey.

This is the New Past.

He who really discerns it has begun to read the glorious Odyssey of human kind, of man pushing out upon the ocean of time to make conquest of worlds surpassing all his dreams—the supreme adventure of the ages.   *—James Henry Breasted, 1920*

The life of man has become a struggle between the *new* ideals of self-forgetfulness that arose but yesterday, and the deep-seated passion for power, which is as old as the human race itself and has thus far been so dangerously victorious over new-born conscience and character that we are faced with the grave question of the survival of civilization.   *—James Henry Breasted, 1933*

PREFACE

"I MUST work at top speed," my father said in August, 1925. "I am rounding sixty—there is little time left to me, the flow of resources I have tapped might be shut off, the Near East might catch fire again. I must make the most of every moment!"

After his death, a crowded decade later, everything came about as he had anxiously foresensed it would; and today his era, and even the immediately succeeding years during which this story was written, belong as much to the remote past as the ancient world he knew and loved so well. Yet the historic Anglo-American conquest of North Africa, together with Anglo-American collaboration in the military defense and occupation of Iraq and Iran lend a curious immediacy to this personal chronicle of a vanished epoch, and especially to his accounts of his Near Eastern travels in 1919–20. With the exception of France, the same dramatis personae are again—or should one say, still —facing the same political and ethnical problems which they failed to solve during the intervening twenty-five years; and just as in 1918, the opening moves in the final, decisive frustration of Germany's vast ambitions have been initiated in northeast Africa. In 1918 these moves spelled the end of her Berlin-to-Baghdad dream. This time they have made a travesty of her geopolitical plan for conquering the "heart-land" of Africa. Had they lived to witness it, neither Lord Allenby nor my father would have been surprised at this latest variation of an ancient theme: for each in his way understood better than most men the significance of the bridge-head between Asia and Africa.

The incidents in this story, including in its earlier portion the recon-structed conversations, the thoughts attributed to various characters, etc., are based either on original correspondence and journals, or on descriptions given me at various times by my father, by members of his family and by old family friends. Wherever my sources differed in important particulars, as they frequently did, I have followed those versions which seemed to be indicated by all the available evidence, or under the circumstances to be the most probable. My reasoning and conclusions cannot always have been correct; and for any resulting inaccuracies I must assume full responsibility.

The completion of this book adds a final punctuation mark to my father's abruptly ended life, and to what must always remain one of the richest chapters of my own. It is impossible to enumerate here the entire list of those to whom I am indebted for helpful information and constructive suggestions in an unaccustomed task which has occupied me for over four years. But I cannot take my leave of it without expressing my gratitude to Professor Harold H. Nelson, my father's old friend and one time student, and to Professor John A. Wilson, his successor as director of the Oriental Institute and also a former student, for their invaluable counsel; to Dr. Edith W. Ware— another of his ablest students, who for the last dozen years of his life assisted him in his researches and in the preparation of his books— for proofing and indexing this volume; to my friend, Maxwell Perkins, for his inexhaustible patience and helpfulness and his consummate editorial judgment in enabling me to reduce a two-volume manuscript to one; to my sister, Mrs. Bernhard L. Hörmann, and to my brother, James H. Breasted, Jr., for their careful reading of the manuscript; to Mrs. George Ellery Hale for permission to quote from Dr. Hale's correspondence with my father, and to Dr. Frederick H. Seares of the Mount Wilson Observatory, and to the California Institute of Technology, for placing biographical material at my disposal. Finally I wish to add that even with the generous aid of all the foregoing, this story might have remained unwritten but for the understanding and inspiration of my wife.

The publication date of this book promises to find me once more in the Near East, minutely involved in the latest episode of an ancient and endless story. As I travel again across those long familiar regions in which my father was so altogether at home, I shall often sense his presence, and be reminded of the words he wrote a few months before his death, regarding man's limited capacity for grasping the meaning of time: "We are like some frontiersman in the night holding up a torch over a dark stream and imagining that the circle of its hurrying current revealed by the torchlight is all there is to the stream. . . ."

CHARLES BREASTED

Washington, D. C.
December 1, 1942

PIONEER TO THE PAST

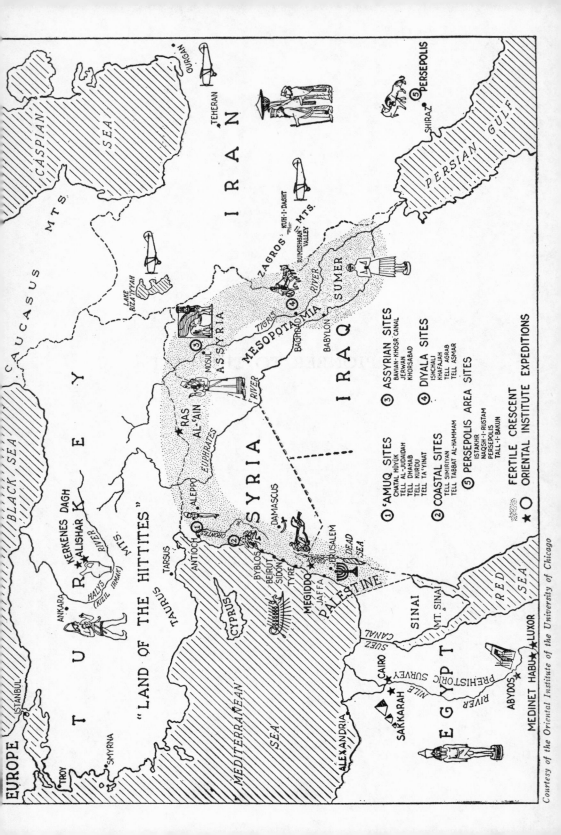

EUROPE

BLACK SEA

CASPIAN SEA

CAUCASUS MTS.

TURKEY

"LAND OF THE HITTITES"

TROY
SMYRNA
ISTANBUL
ANKARA
KERKENES DAGH
ALISHAR
HALYS RIVER (KIZIL IRMAK)
TAURUS MTS.
TARSUS
CYPRUS

IRAN

TEHERAN
GURGAN
PERSEPOLIS
SHIRAZ

PERSIAN GULF

ZAGROS MTS.
KUH-I-DASHT
RUMISHGAN VALLEY
LAKE RIZAIYYAH
TIGRIS RIVER
MOSUL
ASSYRIA
MESOPOTAMIA
SUMER
BAGHDAD
BABYLON
IRAQ

SYRIA
RAS AL-'AIN
EUPHRATES RIVER
ALEPPO
ANTIOCH
ORONTES RIVER
DAMASCUS
BYBLOS
BEIRUT
SIDON
TYRE
JAFFA
MEGIDDO
JERUSALEM
JERICHO
DEAD SEA
PALESTINE

MEDITERRANEAN SEA

SINAI
MT. SINAI
SUEZ CANAL
RED SEA

EGYPT
ALEXANDRIA
CAIRO
SAKKARAH
ABYDOS
MEDINET HABU
LUXOR
NILE RIVER
PREHISTORIC SURVEY

① 'AMUQ SITES
  CHATAL HÜYÜK
  TELL AL-JUDAIDAH
  TELL DHAHAB
  TELL KURDU
  TELL TA'YINAT

② COASTAL SITES
  TELL SIMIRIYAN
  TELL TABBAT AL-HAMMAM

③ ASSYRIAN SITES
  BAVIAN-KHOSR CANAL
  JERWAN
  KHORSABAD

④ DIYALA SITES
  ISHCHALI
  KHAFAJAH
  TELL AGRAB
  TELL ASMAR

⑤ PERSEPOLIS AREA SITES
  ISTAKHR
  NAQSH-I-RUSTAM
  PERSEPOLIS
  TALL-I-BAKUN

▨ FERTILE CRESCENT
★ ○ ORIENTAL INSTITUTE EXPEDITIONS

Courtesy of the Oriental Institute of the University of Chicago

HONORIS CAUSA

O N the morning of May 31, 1878, in the two-room red brick grade
schoolhouse at Downers Grove, Illinois, a slim thirteen-year-
old boy sat at a shabby desk, writing in a copy book. His lips
moved faintly—a habit they were never to lose—silently shaping the
words which his already competent pen set down in answer to a list of
questions chalked on the blackboard under the designation, "Monthly
Examination in Geography and Arithmetic for the Third Grade Grammar Department."

His brown-grey eyes studied the second question under Geography.
He was oblivious to the scratching of pens around him, to the voices
reciting elsewhere in the room, to the thick brown hair which sagged
over his forehead. The village bully had recently tied him in a potato
sack, whipped him across a barnyard until he tripped and smashed his
nose on the barn doorsill. Now the battered member, poorly set, lent a
certain attractive asymmetry to a very vital face.

Question II read, "Name the bodies of water you would sail on, in
going from Cairo [pronounced Kay-ro], Illinois, to Cairo, Egypt."

The youngster wrote, "Mississippi R., Gulf of Mexico, Florida Strait,
Atlantic Ocean, Strait of Gibraltar, Mediteranean [*sic*] Sea, and
Nile R."

Question III read, "Tell something about the Bedouin." He wrote
confidently: "The Bedouin are inhabitants of the deserts of Arabia
who look with contempt on the inhabitants of the towns. They are
wandering pastoral tribes, hospitable, but revengeful, and addicted to
plunder."

More than sixty years have passed since the youngster handed in
this examination paper, which lies before me as I write. Neatly entered
on the printed cover is the name "James Henry Breasted," whose "General Average" on that day was 88 and whose "Rank in Grade" was
"Fourth." Next comes the word "Remarks," followed by three blank

1

lines; and at the bottom, printed in capital letters, is the name "J. K. Rassweiler, Principal."

Apparently no "Remarks" occurred to Mr. Rassweiler about an average performance which rated neither censure nor praise. He had no more reason to suppose than did the boy himself that the answers I have quoted were written by a future Orientalist and historian whose name would become a byword for archaeological exploration and discovery, who would one day know the green plaid ribbon of Egypt and the lands of the ancient Near East as intimately as the prairie country of his Downers Grove boyhood; who would produce works to be translated into the leading languages of Europe and the orient; reap honors and renown, be consulted by soldiers and statesmen, and received by kings.

But though Jimmy accomplished all this and somewhat more, it left him incredulous, and at heart unchanged. Nearly fifty years after that morning in the Downers Grove schoolhouse, when a bewildering succession of honors had been conferred upon him, he wrote:

"All these things fill me with sudden apprehension, or seem like some grotesquely impossible dream—a case of absurdly mistaken identity—and I wonder who the other fellow can be for whom it was all without doubt intended. I felt the same way when I walked up in a scarlet robe before the Public Orator in the Sheldonian Theatre [when he received the degree of Doctor of Literature *honoris causa* from Oxford University in 1922] and listened to a lot of impossible nonsense in polished Latin, all of which was of course intended for somebody else. I saw a dusty, bare-footed youngster standing at the door of a cluttered smithy in a little village in northern Illinois, watching the big blacksmith shoeing his father's only horse. And here was a learned Oxonian in a similar scarlet robe, saying all these ridiculous things to this lad! Of course somebody would find out about it, and then the whole Theatre would burst into roars of laughter—I looked about me in anxiety, thinking it might occur at any moment."

For years I urged my father to write the informal story of his own human adventure. He was always surprised when publishers pled with him to produce such a book, astonished when they sent him substantial checks to bind their offers. He invariably returned the checks: the demands of his science, he said, took precedence over a book which was not essential and would entail "an unjustifiable interruption in his work."

In March, 1930, from the Mediterranean, I wrote him once again, entreating him to let me help him prepare his autobiography. He was willing to admit that "the long climb from the provincialism of a prairie village to the command of an archaeological 'firing line' stretching from the Black Sea to the Sudan," might interest the biography-reading public.

"But you would have to do it, my son," he insisted. "I doubt very much if I could ever bring myself to believe my life of sufficient consequence to write my own account of it. As I look back across the years, it seems to me that you have always been in this work since you were a tiny lad. Your whole life is woven into the picture wherever I look at it. You have toddled as a baby into every great museum in Europe, to greet your father in the late afternoon and take him home to supper. In older years you voyaged into Africa and played your games and amused yourself with the natives. In every temple on the Nile you watched your father toiling on ladders and scaffolding to save the curious records on the walls. It is impossible to think of any of the work I have ever done in America, in Europe or in the Near East, without you. I will yield to you about the biography, and do all I can to *help* you. If it is published while I live, it will be called self-advertising: it ought not to be printed until after I am gone."

But each passing year only added to the far-flung array of new scientific undertakings engendered by his unquenchable enthusiasm. He was far too preoccupied with recovering "the lost chapters of the human past" to waste precious time in recording his own. In the presence of what most men accept as old age, the tempo and productivity of his life merely increased until at seventy he died young, of a streptococcus infection which at any age would have been fatal. And of his half-promised autobiography, all that I inherited were his good intentions, and the unsorted mass of his personal papers.

The volume of these papers was in proportion to the scope of his activities. I marveled that his enthusiasm had steadfastly survived the years of hair-splitting philological research and the quicksands of academic drudgery. His ardor gleamed through the dullest stretches of such labor. As I slogged through the mass of written words into which his vital being had now resolved itself, I could almost hear his vibrant voice uttering the words I read.

Gradually I discerned in this residue of a brimming life, a story in the tradition of Mark Twain, William Dean Howells, Howard Taylor Ricketts, William Rainey Harper, and a whole sturdy procession of

American country boys who had wandered out of Main Street into the world.

This book is the story of one of these provincial country boys who became an Orientalist and archaeologist, and a pioneer to the past. It is much less a biography than the self-revelation of an intensely American scientist who viewed "the rise of man from savagery to civilization" as "the most remarkable phenomenon in the history of the universe as far as we now know it"; and who envisioned, and by his invincible determination achieved, the first laboratory in the world for the investigation, recovery and reconstruction of this epic development.

He was an extraordinarily captivating and persuasive person, especially in his maturer years, with a gift for winning the most intrenched opposition over to his own views. Hence, in our exceptionally close personal relationship and eventual working association, I felt that much of my usefulness to him, such as it was, lay in remaining as objective toward him as I could possibly be. I carried this so far that on several occasions of great spiritual travail he exclaimed, "My son, how can you be so impersonal in matters affecting both our hearts and souls?" Perhaps I was wrong, but it seemed to me then, as it does still, that one of us had to remain so. As editor of his story, with which my own is inextricably interwoven, I have tried as before to remain objective. But I am aware that herein, and in most of what I have attempted in this book, the result is but a faint suggestion of the vision.

When he was gone, the world of those whose lives he had touched paused for its moment of tribute, spoken in many languages and often from great distances. It seemed to me that of them all, none spoke more understandingly than a friend of my youth, Donald Culrose Peattie. "I loved him," he wrote, "for his beautiful voice, his smile and wit, something, too, peculiar to great American men, however cosmopolitan—some fundamental simplicity, integrity, saving sense of humor, personal accessibility such as we have idealized in, say, Lincoln."

I can only hope that at least something of these qualities, and of his indomitable enthusiasm for creative achievement and the pursuit of truth, will emerge as James Henry Breasted reveals himself in this story of an American prairie boy.

CHAPTER I

AN eccentric but engaging character named Thomas Garrison, of New Brunswick, New Jersey, possessor of a patient wife named Electa,* five daughters, one son, a tidy fortune, and real estate comprising, in addition to most of the "Jersey meadows," some pasture land just north of what is today Forty-second Street, Manhattan Island, was seized in the year 1853 by the epidemic urge to seek even greater opportunity in the West. The East seemed to him already moribund, while the West irresistibly challenged all his trading instincts.

So he sold at a loss the pasturage in Upper Manhattan, and all his other holdings, excepting the "Jersey meadows," which he let go for taxes; and with a household numbering seventeen persons, he joined the great westward migration.

Tom's only son was too young to be of much help in transporting this preponderantly feminine menage, and men were sorely needed. He was therefore quite pleased when the fiancé of his eldest daughter Harriet asked Tom's permission to throw in his lot with his prospective in-laws wherever they might go.

He was a nice young man, aged twenty-one, of Holland Dutch ancestry which had settled in New Amsterdam and the Catskills in 1637. His people were farmers, artisans and lawyers. He had just completed a three years' "apprenticeship at the Tin and Sheet Iron trade," with his uncle, who was a Master Tinsmith with a large establishment in Brooklyn. I have the young man's Account Book before me. For his first year, which began on St. Valentine's Day, February, 1850, he received $40.00, out of which he saved $6.45; his second year he received $50.00 plus $7.00 overtime, making $57.00, of which he saved $3.88; and his third year he received $60.00, of which he saved $9.37. Most of his evenings during his apprenticeship had been given over to reading, chiefly the dramas of Shakespeare and Plutarch's *Lives*. He had mem-

* Born in 1811, Electa (Walker) was a direct descendant (seventh generation) of George Soule, who came to America on the *Mayflower*, was the thirty-fifth signer of the "compact," and was listed as an apprentice to Governor Winslow of Plymouth Colony.

orized entire plays, and could quote whole chapters from the famous *Lives*. He was gently bred, well spoken, handsome, had an unfailing sense of humor, had learned a trade and the value of a dollar, and wanted to become a general merchant. Physically he was not robust, but on all other counts he seemed to Tom's appraising eye an admirable prospective son-in-law.

His name was Charles Breasted, and when in 1853 he married Harriet Newell Garrison and so became my grandfather, he must have broken at least one heart. For with his Account Book I found a little packet of Valentines, all postmarked Catskill, New York. Each carries a verse burning with appropriately restrained Victorian passion, all are written in the same spidery hand and enclosed in white envelopes embossed with intricate designs and sealed with diamond-shaped wafers imprinted with a bar of music and two or three significant words. I have often wondered what my biological status, if any, might have been had Grandfather Breasted heeded these *billets-doux*.

The glowing reports of friends who had settled there in 1848, led Tom Garrison to determine upon the Rock River Valley of northern Illinois as the Utopia where his dreams were most likely to be realized. But I cannot find in the record a chronicle of that westward trek, or any description of the wedding of Charles and Harriet. Suffice it, therefore, that Tom led his numerous family to Rockford on the forest-and-meadow clothed banks of the Rock River, and there secured a large tract of land in the center of which was a hill commanding the village and its environs.

On this hill he built what was then considered a luxurious house. It was of wood, painted white, and had a *porte-cochère*, high ceilings, French windows with green shutters. In interior finish it was anything but primitive. The doors, imported from the East, were of paneled mahogany inlaid with various other woods. The floors were parquet, the hardware heavy brass, and most of the furniture had come from England.

Behind the house Tom built a large stable and carriage house, with a fenced yard on one side. This yard became a fascinating and chaotic sanctuary for the diverse oddments which Tom's trading instinct could not resist collecting; and in the end, the graveyard of many of his fondest hopes.

His optimism and initiative were boundless. He had an exuberant faith in the future of the West and of Rockford in particular, and no land sale or auction was complete without his animated presence among the bidders, his solid figure clad in a long coat and a high black hat. For a time his acquisition of property was in chronically inverse ratio to his cash position. But his florid jocularity hid a canny trader with a Midas' touch, and presently the 'fifties found him recovering in Rockford what the 'forties had seen him lose in the East. He bought the largest interest in the water power from Rockford's first major dam, he bought timber tracts and quarries and small factories, and managed somehow or other to slip one of his restless fingers into every new pie.

Again and again he bought and sold merely for the sake of buying and selling, regardless of profit. When Rockford's wooden bridge, built of massive oak beams, was sold at auction as it stood, to make way for the first steel bridge, Tom bought it. He had to bear the considerable expense of tearing it down (the Rock River was broader in those days) and of carting the wreckage to his carriage yard where it was stacked in a great pile from which it was never removed. Dry rot and decay pocked the old beams, and after rains or the melting of snow, these cavities became little pools which trembled in the prairie breezes until they dried away. Grass and weeds, and even small bushes sprang up in the cracks. Field mice and barn rats, chipmunks and snakes found sanctuary among the jumbled mass of decaying timbers.

Tom Garrison's five daughters had the reputation of being exceptionally comely, and one of them, named Sarah Elizabeth, was considered a great beauty. Far from being resigned, like her mother Electa, she was fanatically rebellious and uninhibited. Being congenitally fearless, and having passionately espoused the cause of temperance, she had, before she was twenty years old, already become famous for storming saloons everywhere at all hours of the day and night, and with the aid of an expertly wielded hatchet, smashing everything smashable within each establishment before rolling its beer kegs into the street, and while their diabolical contents gurgled into the gutter, delivering herself of fanatically emotional attacks upon the proprietor and his astounded clients. She always signalized her departure with a shower of leaflets and tracts (written by herself, and printed at Tom Garrison's expense), whose fiery imprecations should have set ablaze the pools of liquor in her wake.

She met all objections to her conduct with the statement that she was "working for the Lord," and from the Canadian border to the Gulf of Mexico she was known as very devout and very "cracked." According to family history, "she was always dressed plainly in black, wore no personal adornment (not even a ring), long full skirts, a poke bonnet and shawl. Jewelry she condemned as 'works of the Devil,' and in several instances she buried valuable family heirlooms so that they never could be found and worn again." She was so beautiful and so incredibly strong that the chivalry latent in alcoholics, not to mention the discretion engendered by the sight of a lovely young thing gone holy berserk with a hatchet, protected Miss Sarah from the whaling she deserved.

Tom was a convivial soul, but he cherished law and order, and Sarah Elizabeth was a constant source of embarrassment to him. Deep down, he had a broad streak of prankishness, and he secretly admired the girl's leonine courage and superlative impertinence. The years passed, and one by one his daughters married, excepting only Sarah Elizabeth, who struck many sparks, yet herself remained unignited. But at last, when she was long past fifty, she went to Minnesota to work among the Swedes, met there a Swedish Lutheran minister named Cederholm, and to the unbounded amazement of all who knew her, married him. Time failed to mellow her virulent antagonisms and she was still relentlessly crusading when death subdued this intractable prototype of Carrie Nation.

Charles and Harriet were warmly welcomed in Rockford. For lack of houses, and often the time and means to build them, the majority of young newly married couples in frontier settlements lived with the parents of either the bride or the groom. So for the first few years of their wedded life these two experienced the incessant family surveillance attending their occupancy of a corner of the Garrison house on The Hill. That the young couple survived this ordeal was largely due to Charles's gracious amenability and sense of humor, and to the fact that he worked like a beaver. He formed a congenial business partnership, and set up his establishment for "Hardware and General Merchandise."

Before me lies a quaint business card which reads: "Day, Breasted and Co., Hardware Stoves and Cutlery, All Kinds of Agricultural Tools and Manufacturers of Tin Sheet Iron and Copper Ware, Main Street, Opposite the Post Office (West Side of River), Rockford, Ill. Particular attention paid to manufacturing and putting up Tin Eave Troughs and Lightning Rods."

Presently the business began to prosper, and Charles was able to establish Harriet in a pleasant little house of her own. She was a good wife, but a little vague. The fact that her children survived her initial innocence of the biological and practical facts of life was simply another evidence of the resiliency of Nature.

In practical matters she drove Charles to distraction. For instance, she had grown up to believe that anything made of iron was unbreakable. She had never learned to cook, and in the process of conquering this deficiency, she broke every item of iron in the kitchen equipment which Charles had selected with loving care.

His resources of humor were sorely tried while she gradually gained reasonable culinary proficiency. But she never became a good housekeeper. Whereas Charles was immaculate and neat in everything he did, she was careless and forgetful. He was integrity personified, while she was given to minor prevarication, more often harmless, but sometimes very irritating. He was of medium height, handsome, over-gentle and easily discouraged; she was petite, positive and doggedly tenacious. But her inexhaustible kind-heartedness equaled his, and her courage, on the whole, surpassed his. She loved fun, but had little sense of humor, and lived always in an anxiety of suspense as to what endearing nonsense or practical joke Charles would next foist upon her—a state of mind hardly alleviated by the birth in 1860 of her first child, a daughter, named May Garrison Breasted.

The beginning of the Civil War found Charles working so hard that his health began to break. "If I only labored when I felt well," he confessed, "I would not earn enough to buy my bread." All his friends enlisted while he anxiously awaited call before a draft board, which finally declared him physically unfit for active service. So he devoted himself even more feverishly to his business.

Meanwhile, Tom also continued to prosper. He had resisted the lure of gold in '49, and had never stopped upbraiding himself for his conservatism. Consequently, when he heard rumors in 1860 that gold and silver had also been found in Colorado, he vowed that this time he would be in the forefront and would make his everlasting fortune. He sold, sold, sold, liquidated, called mortgages, converted investments, he sold his water power, he almost sold his house on Garrison Hill. He equipped a bullock-drawn wagon train and set out for the treasure-larded mountains of Colorado.

While Tom was absent on this prodigal adventure, Harriet was preoccupied with her second child, a boy born August 27, 1865, and christened James Henry. At the same time, Charles's business developed so well that he and his partner transferred it to Chicago, where they bought a shop at State and Jackson Streets, on the site of what became The Hub Store. The new venture was immediately successful, but the effort it demanded of Charles finally broke his health so seri-

ously that Harriet brought him home to Garrison Hill in Rockford.
From its peaceful height he looked back hopefully to his partner to
carry on while he slowly regained his strength.

Thus it happened that little Jimmy Breasted's earliest memories
were of his Grandfather Garrison's house and of the romantic carriage
yard crowded with endless prizes. Through the long summer days,
Jimmy sailed imaginary oceans, crossed mountain ranges, routed
hordes of scalp-draped Indians. He swarmed over the weather-beaten
covered wagons which Tom had brought back from his first trip to
Colorado. The pile of wreckage from the old bridge became a forest-
covered, Indian-haunted mountain of solid bullion. At night Charles
would read to him—the Leatherstocking Tales, *Robinson Crusoe* and
Captain Marryat's sea stories, and Dickens's *Pickwick Papers*. From
Garrison Hill the boy looked down at the Rock River glinting and
winding between the billowing skirts of its wooded banks. He watched
it darken under summer clouds, turn sinister and pale with chattering
whitecaps before the autumn storms, and grow silent and immobile
in the prairie winter. Gradually it became a part of his life which
none of the great rivers of antiquity would ever equal.

The first tangible evidence of Jimmy's education which I have
found is a bill dated "Rockford, 1871, Jan. 17. Mr. Breasted, Dr. to
Mrs. Squire, for tuition for Master James, one term, $3.75. Rec'd Pay-
ment, (signed) Mary Squire." He was five years old and at the end
of his first year under Mrs. Squire's expensive and exclusive tutelage,
he was already in his Third Reader.

Charles's health had been improving, and his business seemed at
last to be leading him on to fortune. In the summer of that year (1871),
a group of leading Chicago business men decided to form a new
company which was to be one of the greatest hardware firms of the
country. Charles was invited to become a charter member of the corporation. The prospect of this reward for all his long, often heart-
breaking labors, thrilled him and filled him with self-confidence and
courage. Then, on the evening of October 8, the flimsy, sprawling,
tinder-built city of Chicago roared into flames visible almost as far as
Rockford. Charles's thriving business became ashes and twisted bits of
metal. The insurance companies could not pay. His partner skipped
his share of obligation. When a great firm was at last established, the
proffer of membership was not renewed. He was now a ruined, broken
man.

He and Harriet were still submerged in the gloom of desperation when the news reached Garrison Hill that Grandfather Tom had died suddenly under mysterious circumstances in that same October of 1871, somewhere near Central City, Colorado. The boys, as the saying went, had taken him. Some of Tom's executors did very well for themselves. Under their ministrations, his assets and resources dwindled and claims which were sold from his estate for hundreds of dollars, soon produced ore to the value of millions for their new owners. His associates, his lawyers and others were suspected of irregularities. But nothing was done about it and the Garrison fortune, too, was broken.

Then one winter day in 1873, the proud white house on Garrison Hill caught fire. The snow was deep and the Hill was beyond reach of the primitive fire department. The schools were closed so the children could watch the holocaust. After the first greedy roar of the flames had subsided, great hand-hewn timbers burned and smouldered for three days, until there was nothing left but an ugly black scar in the white snow.

Jimmy Breasted was sent to public school.

Jimmy Breasted grew up to be a curious mosaic of the most striking traits in his parents, his promoting Grandfather Garrison and his crusading Aunt Sarah Elizabeth Garrison. But while it was these who unwittingly determined his character, it was a person of no blood relation whose influence was to give him the initial impetus which was to determine his career. Her name was Theodocia and by a strange irony she was married to a man named John Backus.

These two old friends of the Garrison and Breasted families had been wealthy, but had sacrificed everything they owned on the altar of Seventh Day Adventism. Not long before the Garrison migration, a day had been set for "The Coming of the Lord," and like their fellow-believers, John and Theodocia had given away their entire fortune and their home, and in the flowing white robes constituting their only remaining possessions, had awaited Our Lord's coming. Instead of the Kingdom of Heaven, they had gained such broken-hearted disillusionment that Tom Garrison had kindly and firmly brought them West to begin life anew.

Few people guessed that "Aunt" Theodocia's gracious amiability and gentle gaiety courageously hid a quiet tragedy. She had been a very pretty girl who gave the impression of great vivacity without once losing her innate poise. She was deeply but not fanatically religious, quite unworldly, but endowed with profound human wisdom. When

handsome John Backus had courted her, it was in the flowery, sub-
limated manner of the day. It had been a relationship devoid of physiological fundamentals and when she had promised John Backus she
would marry him, she had capitulated to a romantic idealization with
whose actual physical being she was hardly acquainted. She adored
and craved children with all the passionate intensity of one who was
by nature intended to be a prolific mother. Only in wedlock did she
discover that what in courtship she had interpreted as chivalrous decorum and self-restraint, was in reality impotence. She was not in love
with John Backus, but it never occurred to her to think of herself as
legally entitled to divorce. The psychology of the day was that of noble
resignation.

There was something about the youngster, Jimmy Breasted, which
appealed to all her frustrated maternal affection. She took him into her
life as if he had been her own son. In many ways she guided and
helped him as his own mother was not able to do. "Pleasant Nook," her
brown frame house overlooking the Rock River, became the Mecca of
his summer vacations. To her delight he filled it with the voices of his
boyhood friends, he made it the starting point for canoe explorations
up and down the river, and in later years, the quiet haven where he
continued to teach himself ancient languages.

To Jimmy, Uncle John Backus remained always a vague, shadowy
figure. He was immaculately dressed, very kindly and hospitable, quite
successful in business—but as a personality always elusive, insubstan-
tial. When he died, he left Aunt Theodocia very comfortably off—but
childless, with the bloom of her life already faded. She became increasingly preoccupied with religion, quietly renouncing Seventh Day
Adventism in favor of Congregationalism. She identified herself with
many worthy causes, especially the Women's Christian Temperance
Union.

But above all, she found happiness in being the devoted mentor
and slave of her appealing small "nephew." He was constantly manifesting his admiration and love for her by grooming Dolly, her carriage
horse, and by mowing lawns, running errands, pumping the church
organ, and singing in the choir. But tacitly she relished especially the
unexpected excitements with which his volcanic pranks shattered the
monotony of her widowed life.

In the summer of 1873, when Jimmy was eight years old, Charles
used some of the small means he had salvaged to buy a seven-acre tract
in Downers Grove, Illinois, which he named "The Pines." Here he

built a little house which fronted on a tree-lined road called North Main Street, and here Jimmy passed a typical middle-western boyhood. He milked a cow, looked after a horse, weeded the garden, collected birds' eggs and butterflies, helped raise asparagus for the South Water Street Market in Chicago. He made furniture (more noteworthy for its workmanship—an aptitude inherited from Charles—than for its graceful appearance), he designed and flew kites better than any other boy in the village, and he learned to play the flute.

In the evenings he read the books in his father's small library. To the set of Shakespeare and Plutarch's *Lives* which he had acquired as a Tinsmith's Apprentice, Charles had added a considerable number of "accepted" works. Jimmy devoured them all, but none left a deeper impression than Layard's *Nineveh and Babylon.*

At "The Pines" the family lived the happiest, most peaceful years they would ever again spend together. There among his cherished trees and flower beds, Charles, especially, found solace from his recent misfortunes; and when Harriet gave him another son, whom she insisted upon naming after him, he was filled with joy.

But with his health, he had also lost the courage to attempt to re-establish a business of his own. He became the senior representative of a large stove company. Though he never spoke of it, he felt keenly the implications of his change of status from that of employer to employee, and at an age when most men who had labored hard and honestly were tasting of success. As he traveled to every corner of a large territory, he grew more and more melancholy, until gradually whatever vestige of personal ambition remained to him became submerged in his high hopes for his children, and particularly his promising older son.

"My early 'education' was wholly haphazard and without a pattern," wrote my father years later. "I attended the little red schoolhouse until I was fifteen, when my parents sent me to Northwestern [now called North Central] College at Naperville, Illinois. But my studies at this place were sadly interrupted by ambitions in chemistry and botany, which I thought might be furthered by serving an apprenticeship in a pharmacy at Rochelle, Illinois, belonging to my brother-in-law, a druggist named Walter Clement Powell. I served him some six months, and divided the following year between clerking in the village drug store at Downers Grove, and attending Northwestern College, where I began studying Latin."

During several summers he acquired a practical rudimentary knowledge of banking and bookkeeping, first by clerking, then by serving as paying teller in a small country bank. The whole banking system of America was at this time still in the heyday of unbridled license, and a bank which seemed flourishing one week would mysteriously evanesce the next. Clearing houses were distant, inadequate and functioned slowly, and the officers of remote country banks kept their fingers crossed while waiting for out-of-town checks to be cleared.

One day the president of Jimmy's little bank could not find the envelope of checks and drafts for the evening mail. It was traced to the mail tray, where it had apparently vanished. No one was suspected, but everyone was anxious and troubled, for the envelope had contained some substantial drafts. The bank was not insured against theft and the president was personally liable.

For several weeks the tension grew, until one afternoon when the village carpenter, at work enlarging the counters to add a new window, pried apart two sections of the old counter. Out dropped the missing envelope, intact. It was immediately mailed, but during the elapsed interval, three out-of-town banks had failed, and the checks against them rebounded, entailing a loss of nearly four thousand dollars.

Jimmy never forgot such lessons, and when much later in life he raised and became responsible for the expenditure of millions for scientific research, the business men and especially the bankers with whom he dealt were incredulous that a man of science should possess such a comprehension of business.

Though he later returned for further study and eventually gained the Bachelor of Arts degree at Northwestern College, he seemed for a time to be definitely headed for a druggist's career. For in 1882 he began attending the Chicago College of Pharmacy, and in 1886 graduated from it as a full-fledged registered pharmacist. Mr. Powell, who had meantime acquired a pharmacy in Omaha, Nebraska, now offered him a position as prescription clerk. Jimmy accepted it, and spent the following winter in Omaha, whence on election night, November 3, 1886, he wrote his mother a postal card:

"Trade has been good all this week, and has kept us pretty busy right along. This has been a long, busy day in the store. But I have spent the evening at home, playing the flute and reading, as Clem said there would not be much business election night.

"I find things come natural and the work is pleasant and does not seem irksome. But occasionally, when I go out in the sunshine, this glorious weather, I wish I might be outdoors a little while, as it is pretty dark and gloomy back of the ℞ case, so that we have to keep a gas jet burning constantly. I put up a shelf for the drug book today. Clem says I may leave the store every eve. at 8:30."

This picture of my father as a youth of twenty-one, standing behind the prescription counter of an old-fashioned, gas-lit drug store, with its glass vases of colored liquids in the windows, its medley of medicinal smells, its wall cases full of little drawers with porcelain pulls bearing enigmatical Latin abbreviations in black letters, has always possessed for me a curiously wistful and at the same time startling quality. He might so easily have drifted into the respectable oblivion of a pharmaceutical career.

I like to recall that Henrik Ibsen worked as a druggist's apprentice from the age of fifteen until he was twenty-one. Ibsen loathed the experience, but my father rather liked it. It made a lifelong impression upon him, and the practical chemistry it taught him proved to be of superlative use to him in later years. The crow's-feet of a physician's prescription never puzzled him, and he could himself prescribe standard antidotes and first-aid remedies. Among the little habits and precautions which this apprenticeship indelibly impressed upon him were two which by his example became reflex habits of my own: the first was to *read* the label on any medicine bottle or container before using its contents; and the second was, when pouring from a bottle, to hold it with the label *upward*, so that no stray drops might deface it.

Although Charles and Harriet were Congregationalists, their attitude toward the performance of week-day activities on the Sabbath was still rather orthodox, and at this time was evidently shared by Jimmy. Apparently he wrote his father a letter (which I have not found) expressing serious distress of mind because Mr. Powell made him sell cigars on Sundays. In this instance, Charles's usually adequate sense of humor seems to have abandoned him, for on November 14, 1886, he wrote to Jimmy:

"I notice all you said in a former letter relating to your feeling about selling cigars on Sunday.

"Advice on the question, as you are situated, is not easy to give. I am surprised that Clement should ask you to do anything that would cause you to do violence to your own conscience. I think I should in all candor say to C— that you could not willingly consent to do a thing that from your standpoint did not seem right or consistent, and that although you did not want to do anything at variance with his wishes, you could not sell cigars on Sunday without an earnest protest—and then, should he still insist upon it, do as little of the thing as possible."

In the spring of 1887, at his family's urging, he returned from Omaha to Downers Grove. "I thereupon tried to secure a position at Batavia, Illinois," he wrote, "in a combined grocery and drug store. The proprietor answered my application with a *post card* turning me down, so that everybody in Downers Grove knew it! After this I examined several drug businesses for sale in neighboring Illinois towns; until Father finally agreed to buy me a drug store on West Van Buren Street in Chicago. But in the midst of negotiations for its purchase, I suddenly fell very ill and returned to Rockford."

He abandoned everything in favor of convalescence under the loving ministrations of Aunt Theodocia. She tacitly regarded this interlude as her Heaven-sent opportunity to win him over to "the service of God," as she put it, for she was sincerely convinced that his greatest fulfillment lay in the ministry. For his own part he now experienced a complete apathy for the drug business. "I could never have anything to do with a business," he said, "which makes up bread and sugar into pills costing a fraction of a cent per dozen, and sells them for seventy-five!"

There is good reason to believe that Aunt Theodocia's insistent enthusiasm for the ministry may have influenced him more than he realized; but what finally precipitated his decision he described in a letter dated October 26, 1887, to his sister:

"Before I left Rockford I had an experience which was to me new and strange. On the third Sunday before returning home to Downers Grove, as I was sitting in the organ loft at the evening service with the chorus choir while Mr. Swift was preaching in his usual earnest manner, it suddenly flashed into my mind as if conveyed by an electric spark, that I ought to *preach the gospel*. From that time to this, this consciousness has *never left me*.

"I have not believed in special providences, and the idea was so new and strange that I thrust it from me and laughed at it, but day and night it was on me like an oppressive nightmare. I could hardly think of a verse of scripture but it was fraught with some occult message to me, and one followed me continually, 'The Lord hath need of me.'

"I fought all this for nearly two weeks, yes, *over* two weeks, with every power and faculty within me, but it was of no use and finally I gave up and said, 'Thy will be done.' Then came a struggle such as

I have never dreamed of; to which the first was nothing, *i.e.*, to tear out selfish ambition and ride down worldly desires. I was in a wild tumult, stirred to the very depths, I was like a tree bending to the ground before a mighty wind. But the calm came; and now, my dear sister, what have been my dearest hopes are dead ashes and out of them has sprung a new, a holier ambition. And though it has cost me more than in my best moments I ever imagined I could renounce, yet by God's help, I am now where I can say, 'I would rather be a useful man than a rich man!' and I am happier, *far* happier than ever I would have been, since I am accounted to 'spread His banner upon the mountain tops.'

"The world appears very beautiful now that I have a mission in it, and life has a new meaning. I begin studying in Chicago, at the Congregational Institute [Chicago Theological Seminary], next Tuesday. Do not think me inconsiderate in *one* particular: I shall be of no expense to father."

That autumn of '87, under the guidance of a fine old scholar, Dr. Samuel Ives Curtiss at the Chicago Theological Seminary, James plunged into the language and literature of ancient Israel.

One might have thought that to a young man with the nervous energy and vitality of a mustang, whose life up to this time had been wholly preoccupied with his own provincial present, the contemplative somberness of the remote world of the Hebrew Prophets might have seemed alien and forbidding. Instead, it broke the chrysalis of his provincialism and aroused an altogether new man, an eager, insatiably avid scholarly mind for which the mastery of Hebrew became a devouring passion.

To be near him and to guard his health against his consuming enthusiasm, Charles and Harriet sold the little farm at Downers Grove and moved into a small apartment not far from the Seminary. This touched him greatly, and he interrupted his studies long enough to build for them a complete set of window boxes which he filled with flowering plants from the garden they had abandoned for his sake.

His parents now saw little enough of him. His single-minded determination to master Hebrew was invincible. He wrote Hebrew vocabularies, verbs, declensions, phrases and passages on one side of hundreds and hundreds of small cards; and on the opposite side, the English equivalent. Wherever he went, he would carry several packs of these in his pocket and at mealtimes, on street cars and trains, in waiting rooms, whenever he could find two or three minutes, he would shuffle the packs and methodically run through them, first one side, then the other, incessantly disciplining his eyes to identify instantly the English or the Hebrew meaning. Whenever he made a mistake or found himself hesitating a moment too long, he would lay the unconquered card aside in a separate pack of "posers" for especially intensive drill. He would even wake up at night to run through this accusing pack. Then, when he felt convinced that his memory had inescapably imprisoned an elusive word, he would return the card to its regular pack. The pack of "posers" grew smaller and smaller as his competence increased, until his mind responded as easily to a Hebrew word as to an English one. With the same orderliness he attacked the Old Testament, until he could repeat whole Books, and instantly identify quotations and give their contextual and historical background. He began to *think* in Hebrew.

There was nothing new in this method, which almost every student of languages has used at some stage in his work. But no one ever employed it more conscientiously or persistently than James. By means of it, he eventually taught himself Greek, Latin, Aramaic, Syriac, Babylonian and Assyrian cuneiform, Arabic, ancient Egyptian, French, German, and a moderate facility in Italian.

Toward the end of his second year at Chicago Theological Seminary, a prize of one hundred dollars was offered as a reward for the student achieving the highest marks both in a written and in a public oral examination in Hebrew. Two of James's prospective competitors approached him privately and asked him to lend them in advance all or part of this prize. He expressed astonishment that they should turn to him when they had an equal chance to win the amount they needed without borrowing it. "You will certainly win it," they said. "If I do," he replied, "it belongs to my father."

Of the little community of people who knew of this contest, not more than a handful were much concerned with the outcome. But to James it loomed as a supremely important crisis in his life. The inner doubts which beset him and which he had not dared discuss with anyone, were not of his own ability to win a prize for proficiency in Hebrew but of his intellectual receptivity to the ministry which lay imminently beyond.

When the day arrived, spring was half-heartedly creeping into the vacant lots and back yards of a winter-sooted, unkempt Chicago, whose citizenry moved about their business, unaware of the grave considerations confronting a little group of incipient ministers of the Gospel.

The ease with which James raced through the written examination made him fearful of hidden catches, and he spent the remainder of the allotted time checking and rechecking his answers. Then he went quietly to his room and slept. He dined alone before reporting at the lugubrious chapel where the oral examination was to be held. To his surprise the pews were filled with people. He had hoped so much that Harriet and Charles could be present. But Charles was away on one of his plodding, hateful trips among the straggling towns of southern Illinois, and Harriet lay ill.

The young men drew lots for the order of their inquisition. James was last. He sat listening with sympathetic distress to the faltering uncertainty and the egregious errors of the four men who preceded him.

His own name was called. The questions and his answers came so quickly that he was startled, almost fearful at the words, "That will be all, Mr. Breasted." Surely they had been easier with him than with the others. The judges retired to confer, and there was a murmur among the audience.

The judges reappeared almost immediately, led by Dr. Curtiss, who said, "Because both his written examination this afternoon and his oral examination this evening have been without a single error, the judges have unanimously awarded the prize to Mr. Breasted, who will kindly step forward to receive it." As he handed the envelope to James, he added quietly, "I would like to see you in my office tomorrow morning."

James murmured his thanks, bowed to the judges, and as he turned to step down from the platform, many hands sought his. Among the upturned faces, he spied Aunt Theodocia's, her eyes brimming but smiling. "One of us *had* to be here tonight," she said. "You'll be going so far from this beginning, Jimmy!"

"I lay awake all that night," he told me many years later, "not because of the excitement of a modest victory, but because I intuitively knew what Dr. Curtiss would tell me the next morning, and that a grave personal decision lay before me, requiring courage and self-searching honesty. I dreaded it because I knew it would affect my whole future, and I lacked the experience and background for making it intelligently. I could look to my parents for unquestioning affection and blind faith, but not for the counsel I desperately needed. I felt dismally alone and inadequate, a feeling which has haunted me most of my life."

Dr. Curtiss greeted him with the gracious, paternal kindliness of a veteran scholar mindful of the exceptional promise of his ablest student. He rested his elbows on the arms of his chair, brought the fingertips of his outspread hands against each other, and came straight to the point.

"I have guessed, my young friend, that you are wavering away from the ministry. You are torn at the moment because the pulpit appeals emotionally to your imaginative and somewhat dramatic temperament. But intellectually, it confounds you with doubts which will only grow. You could be a successful preacher, but it would never satisfy you. You have the passion for truth which belongs to the scholar.

"You made a fine showing last night. You have it in you to make of yourself one of the outstanding Hebrew scholars of America. Hebrew would be only the beginning of a career in oriental languages, culminating, perhaps, in Egyptology—a vacant field. We have great need of Orientalists. The path is thorny, the positions are few, and the financial rewards are meager. But there is always a place for a first-rank scholar—and at best, scholarship is its own reward. If you decide upon this career, there is just one man under whom to continue your studies: Professor William Rainey Harper at Yale. He has already been told about you, and will give you every consideration. He is giving a course at Evanston next summer. I hope you will decide to make oriental languages your life work and will continue your studies under Professor Harper. Possibly he might eventually secure a fellowship for you. But whatever you do, I could not wish you greater success if you were my own son."

The older man's sincere tribute, his simple resolution of what through the endless night, and through months of driving concentration, had seemed to James an insuperable problem, was very disarming. His throat was disconcertingly tight and dry. He moved to a window which was murky and streaked with winter grime, and stared at the dismal frame houses across the way, dirty and colorless against a dead gray sky.

Dr. Curtiss's ancient swivel chair creaked as he rose and laid his arm gently on James's shoulder. "Something is giving you great anxiety," he said. "What is it?"

"Money. My family has lost pretty nearly everything, my father is almost an invalid, I may have to devote myself to supporting them—

and now you propose my going to New Haven to study under Professor Harper."

"Aren't you crossing bridges before reaching them? I've observed a good many young men in my day. I'm convinced you'll find a way, and that nothing will deter you in the end."

James thanked him earnestly, and they parted.

The decision he had so dreaded now confronted him. "The richness and fullness of life as I saw it at your age," he wrote me many years later, "were very much embittered by anxieties and complete unfamiliarity with the road I was attempting to travel. A single friend who knew the road, and could have put a reassuring hand on my shoulder from time to time, would have saved me years of suffering."

During his two years at the Seminary, James had faithfully lived up to his promise to be of no expense to his father. He had a fine tenor voice, could play the flute, and had organized a very successful quartet which was much in demand in this pre-movie era, when the public craved recitations, Swiss bell ringers, medicine men, evangelists, Chautauqua lecturers and church socials. Its average honorarium was ten or fifteen dollars an evening, of which each member received one-fourth. During his second year, James had occasionally supplemented these earnings by delivering Sunday sermons for a modest fee at outlying churches in the absence of the regular pastors, who used thus to find substitutes among the Seminary's abler students.

Up to this time, therefore, he had not burdened his father. But at New Haven, he would be unknown and friendless, and everything would be different. As he walked away from Dr. Curtiss's office, his heart was like lead. He was quietly certain of only one thing: no matter what sacrifices it entailed he must abandon the ministry and train himself as an Orientalist.

He was deeply concerned whether his family, and especially Aunt Theodocia, would understand this decision. The ministry was a calling they comprehended, but the word "Orientalist," which they had never even heard, would mean nothing to them. They would ask timidly if it was something by which he could earn a living, and it would be difficult to reassure them. To Aunt Theodocia, who regarded him as her personal contribution toward annihilating the wickedness of this world, his decision would come as a terrible shock. Only a short while before, she had written him in her usual vein:

"The young people [in Rockford] are going to continue the revival meetings, or secure the services of an evangelist. There has been a good deal of interest in the meetings, and quite a number of conversions—but I tell you, Satan is holding high carnival here. I never knew such an unceasing source of dissipation: two evenings last week at the Opera House was presented a play that was absolutely low and obscene—and the house crowded to overflowing—with people, too, who claim to be respectable, and some even members of the 'Christian Endeavor.'"

But whatever they said, he knew they would respect his decision, which he could not alter.

One afternoon later in the spring, James sat studying in his parents' apartment. The King James Version of the Scriptures and a copy of the ancient Hebrew text lay before him, both open at the same passage, the Hebrew of which he had just retranslated.

Suddenly he turned to his mother, who sat sewing by a window with her feet on an old carpet-covered hassock, and said quietly:

"Mother, I'm going to tell you something which will trouble you, and you must try to understand: I've decided that I cannot be a minister."

Her hands dropped into her lap and the bit of mending slipped to the floor. She stared at him with a look of grieved bewilderment.

"Let me read you this, Mother." He read aloud the translation he had just made of the Hebrew passage. "What I've just read is correct. Now listen to this," and he read the King James rendering of the same passage. "Do you see that it's full of mistakes which convey a meaning quite different from the original? I've found scores and scores of such mistakes. I could never be satisfied to preach on the basis of texts I know to be full of mistranslations. It's my nature to seek the sources of everything I study. The Hebrew writers fascinate me, I shall never be satisfied until I know their entire history and what forces created them. Dr. Curtiss knew this without my telling him, and has advised me to become an Orientalist and to continue my studies under Professor Harper at Yale. Somehow I *must* find the money!"

Harriet sat very still. She was not thinking of the disparities between the King James Version and the ancient Hebrew text. Like all her family, she had been brought up to respect the Scriptures as infallible, the one perfect thing in a sinful world. What little she had read of them had always had a very pacifying effect upon her, and the thought that they might contain errors, she shunned less from incredulity than from fear that the very roof beams of the structure of her simple faith might come tumbling down at this moment when she needed every mental and physical resource.

James picked up the mending from the floor and laid it in her lap, and took both her hands in his.

"You *do* understand what I've told you, don't you, Mother?"

"I understand the part that matters, Jimmy: we must fix things for you to study at New Haven."

Like Harriet, Charles had blind confidence in their son's judgment regarding a world of which they knew nothing. Aunt Theodocia, however, was less tractable. For the first time in her relationship with him, she was grievously disappointed in a decision of her nephew's. But she wisely sensed that it was unalterable, and therefore resigned rather than reconciled herself to it. She shook her head dubiously at the news that James intended to begin his work with Professor Harper at Evanston that summer.

As if in answer to her murmured prophecy that no good would come of this plan, a strange tragedy befell the family.

Charles, Jr., now twelve, had developed an elusive, unpredictable temperament—lovable, submissive and sunny at one moment, impish, rebellious and morose the next. He adored his brother Jimmy, yet on an extreme occasion in one of his recalcitrant moods had shattered every bird's egg and torn apart every moth and butterfly which for years Jimmy had gathered and with unending patience had deftly mounted in glass cases of his own manufacture. Only old Charles seemed to hold the key to the boy's heart, and could usually quiet his stormiest outbursts—though even he sometimes stood helpless. But the boy worshipped his father, and their relationship was like no other in the family.

One morning in the spring of 1890, when he had been playing "Run-Sheep-Run" and was out of breath and panting, the boy flung himself down to rest in some tall grass, plucked a stalk of Timothy and put the stem into his mouth. Still panting to regain his breath, he rolled over on his back, and as he did so, the head of the Timothy stalk was drawn, stem downward, into his windpipe. His convulsive coughing and breathing made it creep relentlessly downward, just as a spear of wheat will travel up a man's sleeve.

The child suffered horrible agonies. His coughing broke the Timothy head into its component seeds, which crept everywhere, deeper and deeper into his lungs. He could eat nothing, and while the attending doctors gave him morphine and whiskey, his family stood by, utterly helpless. His parents never left the child's bedside, and for a ghastly, timeless age of hot summer days and sinister nights they watched him steadily fading, until he died.

Harriet wept for weeks. Charles fell silent, and his gray hair went snowy white. . . . Several years later, when his father too had died, James found in his wallet an undated, unsigned penciled note, smudged and pocket-worn, which in a moment of quiet grief he had evidently written to his departed son:

"My Dear Little Boy—

"Oh, how my thoughts go out to you, and I wonder if you know how I miss you, and how often I seem to feel your presence. Sometimes it would seem as though your tender and confiding hand still nestled in mine, just as it used to during those hours of quiet and peaceful happiness we spent together at 'The Pines.'

"Those times are passed and gone forever, and now my strange little Boy lives only in my memories—but how deep, oh, how deep they are engraved on my mind, and I ask myself—'Shall I ever meet my dear Boy again?' God help me to believe I shall!"

It was a somber summer, and James refused to follow Harriet's urging that he should work under Professor Harper at Evanston, and leave them to grope their own way out of their deep sorrow. He stood by, doing all he could to re-inspirit them, and deferred to Harriet's solicitude over his disrupted plans only to the extent of one day's absence in Evanston in order to make himself personally known to the incredible, thirty-four-year-old human dynamo who was to be the first president of the already conceived University of Chicago.

"I'm gratified to see you, Breasted," said Harper in a stolen moment between classes, seminars, and lectures. "Sam Curtiss has told me all about you, and I'm counting on you to come to me at New Haven this fall. He tells me money is a serious problem for you. So it is for all of us! But I'm sure we can arrange something—jot me a line of reminder a fortnight before the term opens. Good-bye!" He held out his hand, and raced off to his next lecture, to appointments, conferences, and Heaven knows what else.

That was Harper: an enthusiastic, noncommittal expression of confidence that "something could be arranged," said with an infectious optimism and a personal warmth which sent the red blood of scholarly ambition surging through every young man who came into his magnetic field. So, in the near future, he would collect entire faculties, make eminent names of young unknowns, persuade the dying rich to make deathbed wills naming his new university as their sole legatee. He slept little, and without planes, good roads or automobiles, his public appearances in the course of a few months covered the entire country more thoroughly than the combined schedules of all candidates in a presidential campaign. He understood better than most men the virtue of patience, whether in sound scholarship or in the development of character, but in the execution of his dreams he rebelled incessantly at the brevity of each day and the fleeting inadequacy of the calendar.

That afternoon as James strode homeward along old-fashioned sidewalks of slate slabs and resin-sweating boards, unmindful of the summer heat, his head was high among the clouds of future achievement. Only when he neared home at dusk did he suddenly remember the grief it held, so that he felt curiously guilty, and was so solicitous of his parents' comfort that they sensed his subdued elation. They smiled, a little wanly—not, as he realized long afterwards, at the news of his day, but at the resiliency of youth.

It was characteristic of the provincial, eager young man of twenty-five who walked from the New Haven station toward the Yale campus one morning in September, 1890, carrying two heavy bags and a threadbare overcoat, that he hardly dared to stop occasionally for a moment's rest.

Harriet had juggled her household accounts, borrowed small amounts from this source and that, and what with a contribution from Aunt Theodocia, had eked out the sum of nearly forty dollars per month for James's year of study at Yale. Charles was worried because her financial intricacies were too much for him, and he couldn't determine just what she had done. She had once, against his better judgment, jostled him into investing in Florida orange groves with disastrous results, and was now probably squeezing third mortgages out of what little they had left. But he was too ill and exhausted to curb her, and let it pass, thankful that the boy was doing what he really wanted to do.

Meanwhile James was finding his place in the sun of Harper's indefatigable and ubiquitous attention. "If I can ever get fifteen minutes with him," he wrote, "I may learn more definitely about his plans for me, but you can form no idea of how he 'goes it.' Carries proof around in his pocket and reads it between classes—comes into class with his grip—at the end of the hour is out of the room in a jiffy—jumps into a waiting cab—is whirled away to the depot for his lecture in Boston, Vassar, or New York. The only time you can surely get him, when he is in town, is to make the round of his three studies at about 11:30 P.M.—then you can catch him, for he always walks down to the post office and mails his letters at midnight. This is all the exercise he gets—at 6 A.M. he is at work again."

The atmosphere of Yale, a name James had hitherto known only as a roseate legend, the diversity of his associates, the radiance of Harper's mind, the challenge of sharper competition, the romance of new experiences and new horizons, these filled him with a sense of exhilaration punctuated with moments of depression at the thought of his own deficiencies.

"I sometimes get a little blue," he wrote his father that January, "over my lack of college training, which of course can never be made up. Especially do I feel so among these Yale men. But when I look back on where I was three years ago—or even a *year* ago—it takes my breath away. If only there was a little money in it!—but a scholar never makes any money."

"Life is such a treadmill," his father answered, "when one is toiling, day after day, for the good of the body only. I have the same desire of reading good, solid books as I ever had, and I crave to get into some retired spot where my mind can absorb what I read. I am awfully commonplace, and know it full well. But I also know that I have a hungering after something more than the mere commonplace. I tire of these things, that a common ditch digger talks of and thinks of. So I am glad *my boy* can rise above my level, and I want to help him all I can."

James would meet his father's chronic melancholy with a cheery account either of the progress of his studies, or of some one of his infrequent ventures into "society."

"I had a little outing last night," he wrote on January 11, 1891. "Lester Bradner [who eventually became a leading Biblical educator of the Episcopal church], one of the post-grad. men, and a very nice fellow, invited me to his house for dinner. His Father and Mother moved to New Haven especially to be with him, as he is an only son, and oh, how I envy him! After dinner, Bradner told me he had an invitation for me to go out with him and spend the evening. I went, and I have never before spent an evening just like it.

"It was in an art studio, with four young ladies. I shall never forget the scene that greeted us as I entered—a large, high room, with raftered ceiling only dimly visible by the light of many candles here and there, and the flickering red glow of a broad-manteled fireplace.

"About the walls were numerous casts—the Gladiator, Mercury and the like, glistening white busts in many an unexpected nook and corner —while all the walls bore sketches in charcoal and colored crayon. A piano stood in one corner, reflected in the polished floor, which was covered here and there with sombre rugs. One or two ottomans were ranged about, and a guitar lay invitingly within reach. And in the midst of all, stood four young ladies in semi-evening dress, the ruddy firelight shining on their hair as they waited to receive us.

"I could not begin to tell you of it all—how we sang and talked, how they made chocolate for us, looking like priestesses of Minerva burning incense, as they bent over the shining brass service—till finally I found myself with one of them in a quiet corner on a settee, beside a little bookcase filled with tiny volumes in morocco and gold.

"She was very striking—her hair was done high in Colonial fashion, and she wore one of those petite high-waisted gowns much on the Colonial order, with short sleeves, wings over the shoulders, and cut low and square at the neck. She happened to mention Carlyle's *Hero-Worship* and we immediately found a kindred theme, and there we sat in the dusky light for an hour, going from favorite to favorite, and I found she was a young girl of ideas, the true offspring of New England culture, with none of its affectation.

"Alas, I can see how a few such evenings under that firelight, amid those surroundings, might be very dangerous indeed. It was my first experience with the annoying restrictions of Eastern conventionality, for when I sailed very close to the wind on the subject of receiving callers, the young lady informed me that she was not yet allowed to receive calls from gentlemen, which I told her I thought was a barbarous custom, and she agreed with me.

"Bradner and I did not get away until 12 м. and two other men who were there left with us. This morning I learned that the young lady is Senator Hawley's niece."

When Aunt Theodocia, to whom all his family letters were sent, read this, she immediately caught its familiar ring. "My dear boy, *don't fall in love* with any more girls," she begged. "Do you know that you are an idealist? You *don't really fall in love* as much as you *think* you do—'tis only an *admiration* for different styles of beauty—or rather, different forms of attractiveness. You are an idealist. When will you get down to solid rock?"

She was quite right. He was and always remained an idealist, though eventually an extraordinarily practical one. He was to understand humankind in historical perspective better than most men of his day. His failure to acquire a more personal knowledge and understanding of his coevals, especially of the opposite sex, was partly due to his innate detachment and partly was the price of his intensive intellectual development during the years since he had begun to find himself. His industry left him little time for the normal social relaxation, the casual banter and easy give-and-take which most of his associates took for granted.

His un-understanding of women was accompanied by an increasing susceptibility to them. His attitude toward them then, as later in life, was essentially sentimental, a quaint mixture of knightly chivalry and circumspectly torrid Victorian ardor, the effect of which he never properly gauged, and the volatility of which his victims usually discovered too late. His visits everywhere, particularly in Rockford, had left a growing number of casualties, and since it had usually fallen to his Aunt Theodocia to rehabilitate these stricken hearts, she had become very adept at recognizing the symptoms of any imminent, new onslaught.

No less idealistic was his attitude toward men. It was his nature as a matter of course to regard as high-minded gentlemen virtually all the university men with whom he was now gaining a widening acquaintance. The effect upon his associates of this trustful and generous attitude was to elicit a sublimation of their normal selves, so that faults which would have cried warning to more Philistine minds, were not revealed to him. It was impossible for him then, and continued to be so until too late in his life, to realize that his own attributes and capabilities could arouse the bitterest jealousies, or to conceive of the extremes of intrigue, meanness and duplicity to which presumably high-minded intellectual men would go.

Quite naturally, therefore, James attributed no ulterior motive to the unwonted cordiality and friendliness shown him by Robert Francis Harper, a younger brother of William Rainey's and a fellow-student in Semitics. He failed to perceive that Robert Francis, the antithesis of William Rainey, was deliberately ingratiating himself with a future colleague whose abilities he already had good reason to fear. Still less did James recognize in him the most virulent enemy he would ever have, who would do his utmost to ruin his career, and would teach him an unforgettable lesson in academic vindictiveness.

The progress of his work at Yale echoed, in a maturer way, his previous record. But the earnest young man who composed and solemnly read at his first meeting of the American Oriental Society (which he attended as a guest, not having joined because he felt he could not afford the five-dollar annual membership fee) a paper on "The Order of the Sentence in the Hebrew Portions of Daniel," now began to catch visions beyond the minutiae of syntax and philology, of worlds already ancient and rich in learning when the Hebrews were still nomads in the wilderness.

The innate historian in James had tacitly never accepted the fundamentalist belief that the Scriptures were the direct result of what forty years later he was to describe as "a spotlight of Divine Providence shining exclusively on Palestine." He had in fact already begun to discern what was to become one of the major theses of his career, that man himself had created the concepts he attributed to divinity, a spiritual achievement which seemed to him a far greater miracle. I cannot discover that he had read the *Spirit of Hebrew Poetry* by the German philosopher Herder, of which Van Wyck Brooks says: "Writing of the Jewish prophets, he [Herder] had abolished the distinction between the sacred and the secular, transferring to the credit of human genius all that had been ascribed to the divine. In the bards of Israel, all bards were glorified, a notion which, to the candid mind, far from drawing angels down, raised mortals to the skies. It recognized the creative powers of man." *

He became more and more aware that "incorporated in our magnificent legacy of Hebrew thought was a rich inheritance of cultural influences from much older neighbors, Babylonia and Assyria on the east and Egypt on the south"—and of these, Egypt enthralled him. William Rainey Harper watched the leaven working, and at adroitly timed moments, dropped suggestions and hints for the future. He himself was going to Germany to gather men and books for the University of Chicago, and was taking his entire family. Finally one morning, shortly "before the commencement of 1891," James wrote years later, "Harper overtook me as we were crossing the historic Yale Yard. He thrust his arm through mine in that friendly manner which so marked his intercourse with all his students, and asked me what I was proposing to do after leaving Yale. I told him I was hoping to go to Germany

* *The Flowering of New England,* by Van Wyck Brooks, p. 191.

to continue my studies in oriental languages, especially Assyrian, but I added a question which ran something like this:

" 'There isn't a single professorship in Egyptian in any university in the United States, and there never has been. Samuel Ives Curtiss once called my attention to this, and asked me why I didn't go into Egyptian. What do *you* think of this suggestion?'

"Professor Harper turned upon me with that quick, almost peremptory decisiveness of which he was sometimes capable, seized me by both lapels of my student jacket, and said:

" 'Breasted, if you will go to Germany and get the best possible scientific equipment, no matter if it takes you five years, I will give you the professorship of Egyptian in the new University of Chicago! Come to my office in North College tonight at twelve o'clock, and we'll talk it over.'

"I appeared at the appointed time, and he offered to give me in writing his pledge that I should have the post he had promised. But I refused anything in writing."

Once again, more stringently than ever, the bitter question of money arose to fill James with gloom. A number of his fellow-students were planning to continue their studies at Leipzig or Berlin or Göttingen. His parents would do their very utmost, they wrote him, to give him one more year at Yale. But the funds for sending him to Germany for several years on end—*that* was another problem beyond their almost exhausted means.

The pleasant practice of devoting a year or so to "polishing off" in some leading German university, which had grown out of the discovery of German learning by George Ticknor and Edward Everett in 1815, had become by 1890 not merely a thriving tradition in American graduate education, but a very determining influence in the life of any young man seeking an academic career. For a German higher degree had much the same ameliorative effect upon a young American's chances for a desirable academic post in his own country that a dress suit made by the very best tailor might have exerted upon his social acceptability. The possession of either implied that the owner had presumably been exposed to the right intellectual or social influences.

But a far more important consideration made him desperately eager to work there—the fact that the teaching and research center of the world for oriental languages, and especially for Egyptology, was Berlin.

"You have volunteered to help me here at Yale next year," he pled in a letter to his father. "If I could do as some men do, I would refuse it, and work my passage. There is a man here, a Swede, a great strong fellow, who preaches on Sunday, waits on table during the week, tutors on the campus, and so makes his way. But that sort of thing is an impossibility for me. I cannot do it.

"I have always dreamed of helping my father, much less have I ever thought of taking his hard-earned money when I know he needs every cent of it. I am often wretched when I think of it.

"I ran across a sentence in St. Augustine's *Confessions* which I want to send you. It was in reference to his departure for Rome to pursue his studies. He says:

"'Who did not extol my father, for that, beyond the ability of his means, he would furnish his son with all necessaries for a journey for his studies' sake—for many far abler citizens did not so much for their children.'

"And so, since you have been so kind as to offer to help me in Yale next year, do you know that it would not cost me *a cent* more to take the same year in Leipzig or Berlin?"

To which his father replied:

"I think the question of your future course will have to be left open for a time. You know our disposition is to do all we possibly can for you, even if it compels a good deal of sacrifice on our part; and we mean to keep it up. But you must bear in mind there is a limit to all things.

"I am, and always have been loath to make a promise unless I saw a reasonable prospect of being able to fulfill it. I have felt my age and bodily ailments more during the last six months than I have for a long time. It taxes the strength of younger men than I am, to carry heavy Gripps and keep on the move, going from town to town, and endure the nervous strain requisite to sell goods as times are now.

"You must pardon me for naming these things, but I am forced to, especially when there is a promise to be considered. I know you will appreciate all I say.

"P.S. What studies would you take up in Germany?"

Charles now fell seriously ill, a fact which Harriet minimized to James, lest the anxiety affect his studies. With spring drawing on, his whole future hanging in the balance, the uncertainty preying upon him, he turned again to his mother in a final appeal:

"For a man who owes as much money as I do, to think of increasing his debt seems very rash & foolish, & moreover is perhaps *impossible*. Yet can a man of my makeup stand on the verge of such opportunities, and not be shaken? These are golden bait, which I cannot see hanging *continually* before my eyes. I cannot dash it aside at one blow, & go to other work calmly, day after day, & say, 'When the time comes, I will reject it if necessary.' It is like holding a cup of water before a man perishing with thirst, and telling him that you cannot inform him until next week whether he may have any or not. The man would get along better if the cup were *taken away entirely*.

"Now, my dear Mother, all I wish to know is: Is there any way in which I can borrow enough money for this year without burdening father and you? I will turn 'Pleasant Nook' [which Aunt Theodocia expected to bequeath to James] over into your hands whenever it is mine—and may that be a long while—but I cannot let such an opportunity pass without at least telling you of it.

"And if I cannot go at all, Mother, I will finish my theological studies in America, and it will be all right. If you had not insisted on my pursuing what early studies I *did* follow, I would not *now* be where I am. I often & often thank God for a good mother, and I shall think of it as long as I live. Whatever shall be the outcome of these further studies, if there *are* any, will be owing to you."

When Harriet read this letter, death appeared to be hovering over Charles. "Your Father was too ill for me to read it to him," she answered. "I have taken care of him for nine nights, and most of each day. If his life is only spared, we shall be so grateful.

"He has talked so much about what he would like to do for you, and before he fell ill, tried to make plans to help you go abroad with Harper. Everything is so unsettled in his present state of health, that it is hard to make plans.

"But I *would make my plans to go.*

"The only thing I fear is, that you will overstudy in Germany. It does not seem possible for you to get a Ph.D. in one year without breaking down, but the year would do much for you. I think there *must* be a way for you to go—there surely will be if it is *best*.

"When he feared that he was dying, Father asked me for a piece of paper, and wrote you this little letter:

" 'My Darling Boy:
" 'May God *bless* and keep you. I feel safe to leave you in *His* hands.
" 'I am sure *He has* in the past ordered *all* your life and *not a part*

of it, but *all.* Be self-reliant, take the best possible care of your health, keep up good courage, and all will come out right.

"'How much we want to see you!

"'Your loving,
"'Father'"

Fortunately, Charles slowly recovered, and at last was able to write again:

"Well, my Boy, if it were my last act on earth, I should help you so long as I possibly could.

"The money question is a big one, but we will pull through somehow. You are going with Harper—that's settled, if we have to sell our furniture. Aunt Theodocia says 'Pleasant Nook' will have to be content with its old roof and shabby paint—so you see, there is earnestness in that. We shall have to forego a good deal, but it won't be so hard. Your Mother and I have great pride in trying to help you reach your degree in Germany.

"I need not tell you to stop giving oyster-and-champagne suppers!"

James saved the cost of a sleeping car berth by sitting up in a day coach from New Haven to Chicago, where he said good-bye to Charles and Harriet and Aunt Theodocia, feeling slightly like a young knight bound for the Crusades.

On the morning he was to leave, Harriet took him aside and placed a gold ring on the little finger of his left hand.

"Jimmy," she said, "you are going out into a world filled with temptation. If you are ever tempted to do evil, let this ring give you the strength to resist it."

He wore the ring until he died.

On July 30, 1891, with Professor Harper and his family and a small group of the former's students, he sailed for Germany on the steamship *Normannia* of the Hamburg-American Packet Company.

CHAPTER II

JAMES inherited from his father a quality of melancholy which lay always just beneath the surface of his life. Whether it was a reflection of delicate health, or the echo of some vague atavistic yearning, the lonely, nostalgic note of the western prairies ran through almost all the personal utterances of father and son. As they wandered through the present, they saw the past with Stevenson's "backward glance," and in retrospect invested even the happiest moments of youth with an aching sadness. "In spite of its exuberant joyousness," James wrote in later years, "all youth has always seemed to me to contain an element of deep pathos, because it is called upon to use wisdom which only years can bring and for which it cries out in vain."

More than forty years after his student days in Berlin, he wrote of them: "I shall never forget the dark shadow of uncertainty that always hung over me—uncertainty as to my own ability to make good, and about following a science of which there was not a single professorship or post of *any* kind in any American university! I used to look in the glass and shake my head dubiously, and it took all the courage I could muster *to stick.* For while the realization that my father had been apprenticed to a master tinsmith made me honor him, it left me with no confidence that I could ever become a scholar."

I suspect that memory deceived him, and that this "dark shadow of uncertainty" was only another manifestation of his chronic tendency to see the past "as through a glass, darkly." For after his death I found an old trunk containing every letter he had ever written to his family during his student days abroad; and from these there emerged a very cheerful, socially inexperienced and intellectually fire-eating young man who, far from being inhibited by uncertainty of any kind, was almost militantly self-confident.

At Yale he had been merely another young Middle Westerner. But the moment he stepped ashore at Cuxhaven one day in August, 1891,

34

he personified the patriotic, superior provincial given to hasty apprais-als, disparaging comparisons, and aggressive defense of everything American. He "profaned inwardly and outwardly" because "everyone on the ship had to be *tipped*—bed steward, bath steward, deck steward, table steward, 'boots,' musicians, etc., etc.—till I despised the whole business and thanked God I was an American!"

He ran the gantlet "between two long lines of staring, though jolly and smiling natives, through a wildly struggling mob of porters and tourists," to the Custom House "where some green-coated dutchmen, after sticking their beery-looking noses into our luggage, pasted blue labels on it, and let us pass.

"In Hamburg I could not conceive of the vast space of ocean which we had crossed." In one day he went everywhere, saw everything, until his mind was in a whirl of mingled amazement and amusement at this funny and in so many ways backward Old World he was entering for the first time. "One of the oddest sights on the streets of Hamburg is the milk wagons. They are simply a frame on two wheels, with the pails suspended below. A dog is harnessed underneath to pull the whole contrivance, and a man follows behind and steers. I have seen dogs no bigger than a black-and-tan, hitched to a cart as high as a man's chin! From the appearance of most of the proprietors, I should judge the dogs might run the business more successfully if their masters stayed at home.

"But only on settling down in Berlin do I begin to feel that I am in a foreign land, thousands of miles from home." His provincial loyalties came bristling to the fore. "The longer I stay here," he wrote after ten days in Germany, "and the more I see, the prouder I am of being an American. I feel six inches taller when they question me, and I say 'Ich bin Amerikaner!'"

The living habits of the Germans he found altogether exasperating—as for instance their national apathy to water, internally or externally. Without Aunt Sarah Elizabeth's militancy, Charles and Harriet had always regarded alcoholic beverages of any kind as wicked and had implanted in James the absolute conviction that their use, except medicinally in the most critical emergencies, spelled capitulation to the Devil. This was all very well in America. But in a land where beer was as much a staple food as bread, and *consommation obligatoire* was the rule, the observance of these homely precepts entailed a continual struggle between the intrenched forces of bibulous Evil and a lone young American rigidly addicted to water.

"You cannot get water to drink anywhere in Germany without enormous trouble," he complained. "After ten days here, I haven't yet been able to get drinking water without the greatest difficulty, and frequently I *could get none*. And in almost all table d'hôte menus, an extra charge is made when nothing alcoholic to drink is ordered."

Aunt Theodocia was dumbfounded when she read of this inexplicable drouth. "Now, I want you to tell me if there is *no* water in Germany," she replied. "What *does* it mean that one can get no water? What do they cook with? Have they no fountains in the city? I am sure God will leave no community without water!"

Because Professor Harper had never learned to speak German or to understand it orally (although he could read it easily), it was James who had found comfortable lodgings for him and his family in a short street just off the aristocratic Buelow Strasse.

"Here he and I used to sit in the garden for long hours at a time," James wrote many years later, "while I read simple German stories aloud to him, in order to accustom his ear to spoken German. I used to admire the tenacity with which he stuck to the task in spite of his insistence that he 'hadn't the slightest ear for spoken language.' He liked especially the tales of Tolstoi, translated into German, which I used to read to him over and over again, often repeating sentences which he instantly understood in print, but did not recognize when spoken aloud.

"In the midst of these reading sessions, he would sometimes rise from his chair, walk up and down very rapidly, and set forth with great volubility some new idea for the development of the University of Chicago, which at that time was still on paper, or rising as a vision in the mind of its first president. He used to sit for hours at his window, with pencil and paper, writing out the thoughts and plans in which his mind was so amazingly fertile."

Harper was eager to discuss the future of this proposed new institution with the leading men of Germany, and to persuade at least some of them to join its new faculties. At the same time he planned to purchase the nucleus of what was destined to become one of the greatest university libraries of America, and invited James to accompany him on his jaunts throughout Germany. James enthusiastically accepted, but added that "the whole university world in Germany travels Third Class—and besides, my means won't permit me to do anything else!" Harper grinned, and agreed that Third Class it would be. "And to help defray your expenses, Breasted, you can tutor my son in Latin." So they went off to Leipzig, Dresden, Göttingen, Frankfort, Munich, and a dozen other educational centers, and without a murmur of complaint, Harper sat on the hard and cushionless benches of the academically traditional Third Class.

They met men in every branch of science who were internationally known in the learned world, and whose names James had always unconsciously attributed to godlike beings upon some intellectual Olympus beyond the reach of ordinary mortals. It was therefore heartwarming to find them for the most part genial and unassuming humans, who received their American visitors most kindly in their book-and-paper-littered studies, or cordially invited them to afternoon coffee at their incredibly ugly suburban houses, always known euphemistically as villas.

When Harper took him to inspect a number of famous private libraries then being offered for sale by some of the leading booksellers of Germany, it seemed to him that he was personally witnessing an important event in the history of American education. For Harper expected to raise the funds to purchase the best of these for the new University of Chicago. It was exciting to watch an actual physical step in the steady westward expansion of learning.

But there was other history, too, in the making. Harper and James found themselves again in Berlin when Kaiser William II was holding his annual review of the German Army in commemoration of the twenty-first anniversary of the Battle of Sedan (September 1, 1870). Such a gargantuan display of military splendor, with all it implied of compulsory service, standing armies and competitive armaments, was as utterly alien to James as to any untraveled young American of his generation, and the spectacle fascinated him.

"By eight o'clock in the morning," he wrote, "the troops had already been arriving for two hours, and over the vast Tempelhofer Field, regiments were marching and counter-marching. New divisions in gorgeous uniforms and faultless order came onto the field in continuous motion, till the whole vast area was ablaze with one great glory of burnished helmets, bayonets shining in the sun, polished breastplates on the grenadiers, a forest of glistening lances borne by the mounted Uhlans and marked by the fluttering black and white of the Prussian pennant. They stretched away and ever away, till they were lost on the horizon.

"Nearby was the blazing red of the Kaiser's own regiment, and farther off the deep orange of the heavy Dragoons.* Batteries went dashing by at a hot gallop in dust and thunder. Whole squads of mounted buglers came on at a trot, giving their thrilling call. Officers and aides came riding furiously, buried in rich color and gold and silver cord, and finally, in the foreground, the carriages of the foreign embassies were attended to their places by mounted officers. It was a scene I shall never forget.

"At last the Army was drawn up in two tremendous masses stretching clear across the field, at one end of which, in a gorgeous group, were gathered hundreds of mounted officers. The continual restlessness of their impatient horses made an ever-changing, fascinating riot of mingled color.

"Then suddenly amid a clash of cymbals, came a company of cavalry in uniforms of pure white and silver cord, and behind them on horseback, the Kaiser and the Kaiserin. She was clad in pure white and he in the uniform of his regiment—blue, with red cord. They rode down the lines and clear to the end of the great field, then back to a tree in the center, where they stood at attention while the troops went endlessly by in inflexible regimental lines, and so marched from the field.

"As we turned homeward, we passed mile after mile of streets lined with an unending throng. Presently the Kaiserin came by with her escort, and the people shouted. A short time later came the Kaiser at the head of his regiment. I could almost have touched him from where I stood. He saluted the people continually, and the 'Huzzahs' were unceasing. He looked grave, and his face was almost melancholy. The consciousness of the great responsibility resting upon him showed plainly in his expression. No one could see him without conceiving a deep respect for him, and he has unquestionably won the confidence of his people. The papers in Berlin are much pleased at his removal of Bismarck—they like his pluck."

There were among the Kaiser's counselors a few who recognized that with his "plucky" dismissal of Bismarck, he had thrown overboard his Empire's supreme pilot, the guarding genius of its safety, and that now, as Germany moved toward her unpredictable destiny, the voice of statesmanship and reason would be lost in the intoxicating din of Tempelhofer Field. Of all this, James was later on to learn much more,

---

* In these descriptive details his memory was not altogether accurate; but since his errors do not mar or distort the general impression, they have been allowed to stand.

but even now he realized that what he had just seen was filled with disturbing implications. He left the crowds and returned through deserted streets to his quiet *pension,* and as he walked up the stairs, found himself repeating, as if it were an involuntary little prayer of thanksgiving, "Ich bin Amerikaner!"

The summer fled, Harper returned to America, and on the ninth of October, with several of his American fellow students, James "went up to the University and matriculated, and so much red tape I have never yet experienced!

"Along with about a hundred other young fellows, many of whom had upon their left cheeks numerous scars, and who wore across their breasts the badges of their different corps of the University societies, we found ourselves ushered into the awful presence of the University's officials and the Rector Magnificus. On the preceding day each of us had had to obtain a ticket which we had had to sign and to present simply for *admission* to this august tribunal."

The young men then passed under the scrutiny of innumerable frowning and guttural-voiced inquisitors, "filled out an interminable number of forms, and received in return the cards we had signed and submitted the day before. These omnipotent cards we are obliged under penalty of law to carry with us: They show that we are citizens of the University, they exempt us from arrest, or the slightest interference by the police, they answer as a passport, will carry us through the line of a military procession where ordinary citizens could not pass, and will procure us a rebate at theaters and concerts. And if we lose them, it will cost us 20 Mks!"

By virtue of these formalities and the prepayment of about twelve dollars in dues at the beginning of each term, James would for the next three years be known to the University's officialdom, to his professors, and to the local booksellers, as "Herr Kandidat der Philosophie Breasted, Hochwohlgeborner," or "Mr. High-and-Well-Born Candidate for the Degree of Doctor of Philosophy Breasted."

Custom now required that he don his most formal attire and call upon the professors under whom he was to study. So it was that he met for the first time the greatest Egyptologist of Germany, and perhaps of the world, in his day—and certainly one of the kindliest, most benign spirits of his generation—Adolf Erman, of French Huguenot extraction, short-statured, black-bearded, thick-bespectacled, infinitely good-humored, and loyal unto death. It was Adolf Erman's great-grandfather, Jean Pierre Erman who after the terrifying days of 1806, having been chosen at the age of seventy-one by the intellectual elders of Berlin to greet Napoleon the Great in the Royal Palace, had on that October 28 fearlessly interceded for his King and Queen. In addition to pleading for his sovereigns, old Jean Pierre had also unhesitatingly spoken his mind regarding many non-political subjects. At the close of the interview, he had seized Napoleon by the arm and said: *"Sire, ce bras est victorieux, il doit être bienfaisant."* ("Sire, it behooves this victorious arm to be beneficent as well.") That evening Napoleon remarked, "I met a man today who told me to my face the truth about myself!"

"Erman is very droll. He seats himself at his desk, and begins reading his lecture as if he were resuming where he had been interrupted ten minutes before. At the end of the hour, after taking his great, broad-brimmed hat and preparing to go, he continues to lecture, walks to the door still lecturing, jams the hat way down over his ears, delivers the final word, and closes the lecture and the door simultaneously by making a funny little bow as he backs out.

"And so the hieroglyphic war is on. Besides the work in Egyptian I have Coptic, Hebrew and Arabic. One is obliged to offer for his degree, *three* languages and philosophy. I will present Egyptian, Hebrew, and Arabic.

"I think that forty dollars a month, together with what I get from the Latin lessons [tutoring Professor Harper's son], will carry me through. It is remarkable how well I am—my memory was never so good, my power of acquisition never so rapid. I am now in the harness, and every minute must tell. Harper's last words to me alone were, 'Next to yourself, there is no man so concerned with your success as I am,' and whatever I can do to justify this confidence, shall not be wanting."

So began one of the most important periods of his life, a three years' struggle to win his spurs in Egyptology. It implanted in him the fundamentals of scholarship in what was then the highest Continental definition of the word, and subjected him to an intellectual discipline which became the keystone of his scientific career. The progress of his development was hastened by his aptitude for the German language which to the amazement of his professors he learned to speak and write like a native by the middle of his second year at Berlin University.

While he was thus striving for scholarly grasp of the ancient world, he could observe all about him the forces of modern history, which at times beat almost prophetically against the gates of the University itself. On a day in February, 1892, as he wrote his father that evening, "we were looking out of the University windows onto the plaza, when we heard cries gradually growing louder, till a great howling mass of humanity pressed their way into the square, crying 'Brod! Arbeit!' (Bread! Work!).

"We went down immediately, but found that the great iron gates of the University had just been closed. The mob now retreated toward the east, the police following with drawn swords. It smashed windows, plundered stores, hurled a policeman from a bridge into the river, had a bout with the Imperial Guards, and the uproar was tremendous.

"The vast machinery of the German Army will continue for many years to crush down this discontent, so that anything more than the breaking of windows is highly improbable. But in the next dozen years, the Army will be gradually permeated with socialistic principles, and *then will come the German revolution!* [the italics are his.] All is now quiet again, but one feels as if one stood in the midst of history in the making."

"Work has closed at the University and my first semester in Germany is over," he wrote in March. "It has pretty thoroughly initiated me into the methods of the German universities. I am ready to affirm that their great reputation is built up entirely by their *individual scholars*. Their methods as they affect the ordinary students, are simply abominable. After a semester or two, the wide-awake American student can stay in his room and do the work himself without going near the lecture.

"The exceptions are in studies like my own where the professor is often the sole textbook to be had and where the student must use the inscriptions and collections in the Berlin Museum. The *only* Hieroglyphic Grammar I have is a volume of lightning notes taken last semester. But to secure his degree the student *must* attend the lectures, and the signature of the professor must attest the fact of his attendance. The German students are glad to attend, for they know no other way of acquiring knowledge: most of them are simply jugs into which the professors are continually pouring information at a stupendous rate."

The German summer filled James with longing for Aunt Theodocia's hospitality. "What good times I have had at 'Pleasant Nook'! It almost seems like Heaven, as I look back upon it. I can hear the leaves rustle, see the sunshine flicker through the trees. I can see Dolly [Aunt Theodocia's ancient mare] stick her nose out and impatiently shake off the flies while waiting for the ladies to come out and drive off. I see the dining-room table—and visions of spring potatoes in cream, and pumpkin pie, and strawberry shortcake, come tempting my longing palate! Then I look up at the little window where I worked so hard many a long, hot summer day and I think of all I have built on the foundation laid then, and it seems very long ago and far away, and I am really homesick, and have to dig into my books."

This summer nostalgia was dispelled by an unexpected, idyllic experience unlike anything he had ever known before. Its prelude occurred on a Sunday afternoon early in August when he rode out to Südende (then a suburb of Berlin) on Lester Bradner's American-made bicycle, to call on Professor Erman, whom he found in the garden.

"The Professor," he wrote, "was delighted with the bicycle, declared it excellent, and asked if he might try to ride it. So we went out into a field where he said 'kein Mensch' [not a soul] would see us, I lowered the saddle to suit his shorter stature, and held the wheel while he mounted. Behold a Professor in the University of Berlin, Director of the Egyptian Museum, paddling vainly in the air in futile efforts to catch the pedals, and flapping out his elbows like Ichabod Crane, in desperate attempts at balancing, till the wheel shied crazily and the rider tumbled ingloriously to the turf.

"'Oh, what a 'fall was there, my countrymen!
Verbs and nouns and hieroglyphs fell down
While dusty pant-legs flourished over them.'

"When we came home, the Frau Professor made me tell her all about it, and I explained that the path had been too narrow. 'Yes,' said the Professor without a shadow of a smile, but with a twinkle in his eye, 'it was because the path was too narrow!'

"Then Erman produced a hammer and some nails, a roll of wire and some pliers, and we went to the summer house where we began putting up wire leaders and training the vines along them. Presently the maid appeared with coffee and cake, and while we partook of them, the Professor penciled on the edge of a newspaper a hieroglyphic inscription of Ramses II which had just been discovered on the rocks on the east side of the Sea of Galilee. It was probably Hebrew written in hieroglyphics, and the Professor wished to see if I could make any-

thing of this Hebrew transcription. But I could make nothing of it—
nor could he either."

Toward twilight when James was taking his leave, Erman drew him
aside and said with great friendliness: "Later this month I am going to
the Harz Mountains [about 125 miles SW of Berlin] for a fortnight's
holiday. I shall stay at the home of a Royal Forest Ranger and his wife,
who take paying guests. Herr Kurt Sethe [a brilliant student of
Erman's] and a few colleagues from other universities will foregather
there at their own expense—and I would be most happy if you also
would join me. You seriously need a rest, my American friend! And the
cost," he added thoughtfully, "is reasonable: your room and excellent
board for M. 3.50 [then about eighty-seven and a half cents] per day.
Will you come?"

James was astonished and embarrassed. Such an invitation was
uncommon enough between a German professor and students of his
own nationality, but when extended to a *foreign* student of less than
a year's acquaintanceship, it connoted exceptional respect and regard.
He calculated hastily that the fortnight's vacation, including railroad
fare, would cost him about twenty dollars. He remembered that he still
owed several dollars to a bookseller. "I have been saving for two
months to buy a big Arabic Lexicon costing 50 Mks or $12.50," he had
recently written his father. "I had to run a little in debt for it, but the
surplus on next month's remittance will more than settle the balance."
Now he was proposing to add to his debts. But something told him his
family would approve this extravagance, and that for once he must
forget economy and go.

"You *will* come?" Erman asked again.

When James, beaming with gratitude, said "Yes!" Erman was
jubilant. "*Das wird ja aber grossartiger Spass sein!*" ["That *will* be
magnificent fun!"] He shook James warmly by the hand, and his eyes
danced behind his thick lenses as he stood watching him pedal off
toward Berlin.

On a broiling hot day two weeks later, having changed three times
in seven hours to progressively funnier little trains, James and Sethe
found themselves walking with rucksacks on their shoulders, up a
steep little valley toward the Sonneberg in the Harz Mountains. "I
was explaining a game of baseball to Sethe," James wrote in his
journal, "when we saw Erman, alpenstock in hand and wearing a
broadbrimmed black hat, coming down the opposite slope to meet us.
He was full of kindly greetings and good wishes, and happily excited

over the discovery of a new and important inscription of the Sixth Dynasty [of Egypt], from which we have very little in written form.

"We rose out of the valley to a summit whence we looked off across the blue hills toward a gleaming little lake marking the university town of Göttingen. Off to the west, making a glorious sweep up in the clouds, lay the Brocken [highest point in the Harz]. There is an indefinable magic about these mountains with their misty silence, long reaches of sunshine on distant summits, shadowy valleys buried in unbroken pine forest. It is unlike our Adirondacks and Catskills and Berkshires. As we sat there in utter peacefulness, breathing cool air rich with sun-distilled pine scent, we could feel the beneficent spell of these heavenly mountains creeping over us, shutting away the prosaic world out of which we had climbed, and freeing us from all sense of time and anxiety and responsibility. We breathed deep and knew we were in Elysium."

In the silence Erman suddenly began singing an old German student song. The others joined in, and the forest re-echoed to their overflowing spirits. Soon the three of them rose to their feet and in rhythm with the song, began marching single-file along a path leading down into a little branch valley. At the head of this, against a steep slope, lay a small clearing in the center of which, surrounded by a flower garden, stood a peak-roofed house with wide eaves and plaster-and-beam walls decorated with gay-colored sixteenth century designs.

Everything about the place was spick and span and neat, and even the air had a quality of exceptional clarity and stillness. The almost stylized precision of the encircling pines (which the Royal Forestry always planted in rows), the glow of their branches and of the forest floor of brown pine needles wherever the slanting afternoon sun touched them, the richness of the shadows, the cyclorama of cornflower-blue above the mountain—all seemed transplanted from one of Humperdinck's operas.

The beauty of this scene, and the ingrained German sense of academic decorum in the presence of officialdom, silenced the trio as they reached the edge of the clearing. But their voices had long since preceded them, and the tall, broad-shouldered *Förster* (forester) "a royal officer of the Government who discharges the centuries-old duties of preserving the forest and the game"—was already coming forward to greet them, respectfully carrying his feather-garnished hat in hand. He was a genial, handsome fellow in his early forties, clad in a uniform of Lincoln green with buck-horn buttons. His tanned face was wreathed in smiles of sincere pleasure as he welcomed Erman and was presented to his two new guests. He led them into the house, where the equally genial Frau Förster took them to spotless rooms.

So began for James a fortnight in Elysium.

But the beauties of this sublime state did not consist alone of heavenly landscapes and charming companions. "You should see how they crowd food upon the table here!" he wrote. "At about seven A.M. we have coffee and home-baked rolls. At ten or eleven, the dinner table is covered with hot meats, cold roasts, chickens, pickled meats and delicious sausage of Frau Förster's own manufacture—huge rolls and yellow butter—milk and foaming beer. This is the regular and ordinary 'Frühstück'—really a second breakfast. Then at one P.M. we are called to a dinner of things innumerable—soup and several meat courses, vegetables and fruits!—the table groans under its load. And at four P.M., coffee again, with crumbly cakes and raisin-covered disks of sweetness. Finally at eight P.M., supper with an epitome of what we had left unconquered at dinner!"

And the cost of all this, together with a comfortable bed, boots blacked, buttons sewed on, clothes mended—was eighty-seven and a half cents per day!

Each summer the same little group of faculty men from various leading German universities returned to the Förster's house in this happy valley to spend their holidays with old colleagues and student friends, and to recapture their own youth as they surrendered again to the enchantment of a region which—to James—seemed Nature's reflection of the pleasantest and most appealing elements in German academic life.

Wherever he and Erman and Sethe tramped along the mountain trails, through brilliant sunshine, high clouds or occasional drenching summer storms, they sang and yodeled and sang again. Erman's fund of student songs was inexhaustible—it was no effort for him to sing fifty during a morning's walk. James would counter with the American songs that had helped him to earn his schooling, what already seemed a long time ago. Of them all, Erman was fondest of "Johnny Schmoker," "Michael Roy" and "Shoo Fly"—he became so obsessed with them as to insist that James write out the music and lyrics, which he learned by heart and remembered to his dying day.

Out of valleys hazy with the rosin-heavy fragrance of sun-warmed pines, where "the blue smoke of the charcoal burners rose slowly from the mountain-sides," they clambered up and up until they reached some mossy summit where they would lie down and feast their eyes on entrancing distances. Like so many boys in their 'teens, they played "mumble-ty-peg" and "duck-on-a-rock," became absorbed in following deer tracks, in catching the green-brown lizards which darted like lightning through the grass, or in watching large green caterpillars spin their silken webbing. It revived their antiquarian instincts to come upon "a sunken, moss-grown, abandoned road dating from the Middle Ages—for this region has been Royal Forest for centuries."

When they found a lovely brook, Erman proposed that they dam it up, and from bits of wood and a few pins, James made a waterwheel. "It really did look pretty in the brook—but these academic Germans, who have no mechanical ability whatever, thought this mill a wonderful piece of work. 'The Americans,' said Sethe, 'are simply born mechanical geniuses!' Then Erman took a trowel from a mysterious basket he had brought with him, dug from the brookside an assortment of ferns and mountain flowers which he carefully wrapped in damp moss and brown paper, packed in the basket, and carried to Andreasberg where he sent it by parcel post to his wife."

It was late afternoon when they turned homeward. The meandering white houses and red-tiled roofs of the village, banked against the hillside, glowed in a wine of sunlight distilled from the richness of the whole summer day. As they climbed the tortuous little streets, they saw far above them the serpentine procession of the village cows, each with a bell tinkling merrily as they moved slowly and carefully, and at steeper points, somewhat jerkily down their accustomed path. Their sleek bodies, swinging along with a ponderous rhythm, shone in the sun and cast long, fluid shadows. At the very last came the herder with a dog trotting beside him.

"In the door of every cottage stood the good Hausfrau," wrote James, "waiting to make certain that her own patient, slow-going beast would turn in at the correct narrow gate. As the tremendous bull passed us, Erman suddenly threw up his hands in the ancient Egyptian attitude of adoration. Sethe and I of course roared, and the villagers stared in astonishment. . . .

"I cannot make these Germans out. They certainly have deeps in their natures which are not sounded with a common lead—and yet they live, in spite of it all, so much in the body. One evening as we sat about the table after supper, the conversation drifted onto Hebrew, and between great gulps of beer, Smend * began to set forth the incom-

* An eminent Old Testament scholar, one of the guests.

parable beauties of the Psalter. He pictured the outcast, suffering, captive people, and always punctuating his words with more gulps of beer, he quoted many exalted passages in which the stricken nation poured out its struggling but immortal faith. It occurred to no one that there had been the slightest incongruity between Smend and the picture he had drawn. But I am learning more of German university life from the professorial side than I ever knew before, and I tuck away everything I hear."

On August 27, 1892—his twenty-seventh birthday—James wrote: "I derive no comfort from contemplating the progress I have made beside the years I have lived and the ideals I have tried to attain. But during these days upon the mountains, where the sky is nearer and the music of the pines seems to whisper of happy, useful years, and where silent, peaceful prospects breathe God's 'Benedicite', the future appears less uncertain and remote. When Erman comes to me with a question of Hebrew grammar or Old Testament history which concerns a review he is writing, then I *must* find encouragement in recalling how far away these men of learning seemed to me just *one* short year ago."

On the last day of August, the post-coach brought news which caused the Professor to pack his things hastily and hurry off for Berlin in a race with the stork. So James and Sethe also bade the good Förster and his wife farewell, and marched away into the eastern Harz. They stopped at castles and caves and historic sites, and finally came to Hildesheim, where Sethe also left him, to visit relatives in the provinces, and James found himself alone, lodged for thirty-five cents a day at an inn built in 1609.

Hildesheim was a mellow old town full of "winding streets, unexpected vistas, narrow lanes where the houses lean toward one another and converse confidentially. They are never guilty of being plumb. And in every doorway sits a funny old fellow with a visor cap who has just stepped out of a painting. Here, carved in a façade, is a row of Roman Emperors, all wearing burgher caps with a feather; there, a set of panels depicting the life of Samson, a worthy who is carrying two German gates of Gaza, and is himself rejoicing in a journeyman's round-about of knit worsted. Yonder he is slaying with a terrific jawbone, three Philistines in 14th century armor; and further on, he has fallen asleep with his head in the lap of Delilah who wears a dress suited to ladies of 'ong bong poing' and an apron I afterwards met in the next street!"

The following Sunday in Braunschweig (Brunswick), James attended the services in the Cathedral. "It is a pity that the true fire which burned in Luther," he wrote somewhat sententiously, "should have turned to cold ashes. The consciousness of religion as a spontaneous outgo of self toward the best things, an upward development growing *every* day, has completely disappeared in Germany. Religion is looked upon as a formal institution, subsisting by itself, and the fact that it is a *faculty of the human heart,* is forgotten. I heard a religion preached today which was as impractical as it was ineffective in touching the people. The pure Saxon face which looked out over black cassock and white bands, was aglow with an enthusiasm which might have had its roots in the sixteenth century, and since then had found no larger or more immediate reason for its inspiration. The German church is *dead.*"

He returned to Berlin mentally and physically revitalized, and plunged into his second year of work at the University. The superior and easily nettled young American of the year before was now much less conscious of being a foreigner. He already spoke German easily, the timeless fortnight of carefree companionship in the Harz had laid the foundation for at least two enduring friendships, the chronic feeling of being merely an outsider began to give way to an incipient sense of intellectual security and self-confidence. "What *they* can do, *I* can do," he had written in his journal. Nor had he ever been more sincere than when he had added his conviction that he could "make my own field of work like a sublime service for which the world will be my cathedral." From the friendly heights of the Harz he had caught a clearer vision of the scientific goal he had conceived for himself.

"Just one short year ago, I was painfully committing signs to memory through tedious, endless hours," he wrote that October. "*Now* I can read pages in a day—*then* things seemed somewhat dark and uncertain, *now* the reins are in my hands. Though it will be a very slow process, I no longer doubt that I can make something of myself. I must believe that I can, by and by, bring into the world a fact or two worth having. I begin to see that it is not so much the comprehensiveness of a man's *learning,* as his rational and careful method, which will bring reliable results, and I am very sure I *have* such a method.

"Yesterday, I heard Virchow's inaugural speech as Rector of the University. He is probably the greatest scientist who has held the place since Humboldt. His intensely interesting address touched German education in general, and disapproved of many features. One statement especially interested me: he said that many foreigners have come into the universities here without having had the benefit of the severe training of the German 'gymnasium,' and have done just as good work as the Germans. Something, he therefore argued, is wrong with the 'gymnasium.'

"Do not imagine that the acquirement of the routine fundamentals of such a science as I am pursuing is any pleasure. But after long months of toiling drudgery, there come times when the consciousness of growing intellectual power, of irresistible grasp, is so uplifting that a day of the intensest effort is gone like a moment.

"Such is coming to be my feeling as I work—a keenness of enjoyment that is inexpressible."

In 1886 Mrs. Mary Bannister Willard, a gracious and intelligent American widow—sister-in-law of Frances Willard, famous feminist and crusading leader of the W.C.T.U.—founded in Berlin the Home School for American Girls.

It was an era when finishing schools were very much the fashion, and they had sprung up like mushrooms in all the leading musical and cultural centers of Europe, especially in Germany. Like so many honey jars, they attracted the males from every nationality and profession—young American students, the secretaries of all the diplomatic corps, German and French and Russian officers, young Englishmen down from Oxford and Cambridge.

Among such schools in Berlin, none enjoyed more impeccable social prestige than the Home School for American Girls. Mrs. Willard's Friday receptions, usually in honor of some visiting American luminary, became the meeting place for the American colony. "I attend them once in two weeks," James half-apologized to his parents. "They are simply delightful, and I go in order to keep 'alive,' and in touch with people. The other evening Mark Twain was there, and I had an exceedingly pleasant talk with him—and with his daughter, who is quite a pretty girl"—and who subsequently married the famous Gabrilovitch.

James and his two friends, Bradner and Kent, were at this time giving well-attended courses in Biblical history and prophecy at the American Church in Berlin, and Mrs. Willard easily persuaded them to give similar weekly lectures to her charges, who were less intrigued, I suspect, by popular Exegesis than by the presence among them of three attractive and eligible young American males. "We three are awakening an interest in Bible studies," James solemnly informed his family. "The young ladies are quite industrious in preparation—so you see, we are not *merely students*. It is an excellent thing for us, too. We are kept in contact with people and life and popular thought, and most of all, *popular need*, and thus from the danger of drifting into dry scholasticism."

By curious coincidence, several of the young ladies for whom Aunt Theodocia had evinced such concern while James was at Yale, now began simultaneously to converge upon Berlin, prompted by a craving for the intellectual stimulus which only a sojourn in Europe—and especially Berlin—could gratify. He was soon more involved than ever in romantic complications which moved so rapidly from one little crisis to the next that letters with helpful counsel from Aunt Theodocia were always several crises too late. The extent of these entanglements was the more remarkable considering the little time he actually allowed himself from almost furious concentration on his work.

In the midst of these growing complexities, there had arrived at Mrs. Willard's School a handsome widow from San Francisco, named Mrs. Helen Watkins Hart, accompanied by four daughters, to all of whom she was determined to give every educational advantage obtainable with what remained from her late husband's fortune. She was aristocratic, courageous and genial, a democratized version of the Old World *grande dame*. She came of the Pitneys, who tended to predominate in New Jersey, and had behind them a proud record in the Revolutionary War. She herself had married an austere Virginian whose father had been mayor of Lynchburg for more than twenty years, and with him she had sailed around the Cape to settle in San Francisco before the railroads had reached the Pacific.

The four daughters were of as many temperaments, but had in common a strong family resemblance which ran to dark-haired, dark-eyed beauty, a nervous vitality, and a breezy and engaging Western sociability. The youngest, named Imogen, was a beautiful child of only six, and of the older sisters the most attractive was Frances. She was handsome, intelligent, a good listener, eager to learn, intuitive, and conscientious and proper to the point of prudery. At nineteen she was already a gifted pianist, and was studying for the concert stage.

Thanks to the little card certifying his citizenship in the University, James was entitled to student rates at the Berlin Philharmonic Orchestra and the Royal Opera. Tickets costing seventy-five Pfennigs were thereby reduced to forty Pfennigs or ten cents, and at such rates even his modest living allowance permitted periodic musical splurges in feminine company, especially when—as did Frances and most of Mrs. Willard's pupils—the young ladies paid their own way. When James casually mentioned to his family in December, 1891, that he had attended the Philharmonic with a "Miss Hart, a lovely California girl who is here studying music, and plays like an angel," they paid little heed.

But his father recognized the familiar danger signal when less than a year later, James wrote him: "We turned to the Thiergarten, now in the glory of Autumn leaf, and walked on and on, forgetting the flight of time. Miss Hart is like a sister to me—as kind and thoughtful as if I were her own brother. She listens patiently to endless tales of my work and my ambitions. You know, it is true of all souls: like the 'Ancient Mariner', they reach a state when repression is no longer possible, they must recite their tale of hope and longing and ambition, and will not be stilled until they have found someone who will listen. It was such a morning for me, and ere I was aware, we had reached Charlottenburg. Then we came slowly back to the City through the forest, having gone entirely around the great wood."

Ample precedents had caused Charles to mistrust his son's fraternal capacities in relation to young women, but he found comfort in the thought that history was bound to repeat itself.

It did, but not as he had anticipated. In November, 1893, Mrs. Helen Watkins Hart announced "the engagement of her daughter Frances to Mr. James Henry Breasted."

The ordeal of his Doctor's Examination was at last set for the 19th of July, 1894. Early that month he wrote:

"Erman speaks encouragingly [of my work], advises me to 'go to sleep' till examination time. But the suspense is intolerable unless I am constantly employed, and so I am grinding now chiefly to occupy my mind. I am very conscious of being on the homestretch with the goal still unattained, and I dare not relax for an instant."

Erman had noted the familiar nervous tension which afflicts almost every student approaching the finale of his long preparation for the doctor's degree, and with friendly concern had urged James for the sake of his health and scientific future to visit Egypt as soon as he had won his doctorate. "While you are there, you can help us by collating a number of inscriptions for the Dictionary," Erman added casually, knowing quite well how much encouragement his young American student would derive at this critical time from the proposal that he should assist the commission of the Royal Prussian Academy which had been appointed, and was being financed by the Kaiser himself, to compile the first comprehensive dictionary of ancient Egyptian ever undertaken.

Such an invitation to a foreigner was, in fact, an exceptional tribute, and his spirits would have soared but for the realization that he simply had not the money for a journey to Egypt. Once again he turned to his family with a plea for funds: "Apart from its usefulness for my studies, the Egyptian trip would be a replenishing of the man, and a lifelong inspiration. It would be a godsend before settling down to the grind at the University of Chicago." Furthermore, he added almost as an afterthought, now that he was engaged to be married, the Egyptian journey could also serve as a honeymoon.

Charles sent this letter to Aunt Theodocia, who wrote James:

"While I believe God would have used you to do a grand work for Him in the simple preaching of the Gospel, yet 'tis possible there may be a wider field of usefulness, upon which you have entered—that is, if there *can be a wider field* open to a man, than preaching the Gospel of the Son of God. I know there is more than one way of preaching it, and I do not know but the way in which you are being led is the best.

"If it is God's intention for you to open tombs long since closed, and unearth secrets and thoughts of ages gone by, to perfect His plan for the education of this generation, then shall we not consider it an honor conferred upon you? Though it *does* call for sacrifice and hard work from you, and for us who love you, we will offer it cheerfully, joyfully.

"I think you *ought* to go to Egypt.

"I have therefore sent your Father a draft for four hundred dollars, that he might forward it to you, and I will later send five hundred more. I do not like to raise any more money on 'Pleasant Nook' because the interest is so *imperative*. I know you will care for it just as soon as you can. But my dear Boy, you will have to get on your feet first. Meantime I will take care of the interest. Your Father feels just as I do, that the money thus expended is the best investment he and I ever made. We know you will pay it back a hundred-fold—you are paying it back now."

At last, on the evening of July 19, 1894, an unsigned cable containing only the two words, "PASSED WELL," informed Charles and

Harriet and Aunt Theodocia that the human investment into which for three long years they had unreservedly put all their resources of love, patience, hope and money, had paid its first substantial—if intangible— dividend. Then came an evening a fortnight later, when Charles read aloud to them, in a voice which he found it difficult to control, the following letter dated July 22, 1894:

"The long dreaded day is now three days past, and I do not feel at all top-heavy or inflated—only profoundly thankful and *glad* above measure for all your sakes at home.

"A formal card from the University summoned me to be at the Dekan's [Dean's] office at noon on the 13th, to be cited for examination. I found there five other men, among them Hancock [an American fellow student], and all six of us stood up in a row and were cited to appear before the faculty of Berlin University at 5:50 P.M. on the 19th of July. After receiving minute instructions, we all bowed low as if pulled by a string, and retired.

"I immediately went home and put on my dress suit and white gloves, and went about in a droschke to make the customary formal calls upon the professors who were to examine me—in this way each professor is formally invited to examine the candidate at the appointed date. I had never before seen Professor Zeller (Professor of Philosophy) —a venerable old scholar over eighty years of age, whose books are used the world over. He was very pleasant to me, and told me that if I could give an account of the Stoic School, he would require no more. Sachau (Professor of Arabic) was also very kind, and wished me every success. Professor Schrader (Professor of Hebrew) was equally courteous (Schrader is regarded as the founder of modern Assyriology).

"I then went home and crammed night and day on the Stoics. It was uphill business, but I learned *by heart* all that Professor Zeller ever had said about the Stoics, till I could grind it out with swing and rhythm, paragraph after paragraph, page after page, chapter after chapter, as I walked up and down my room. That was the reason I didn't write last Sunday. Maybe it was wicked, but I spent all the morning on the Stoics, and in the afternoon I read Hebrew.

"That evening I had a delightful visit at the Ermans—we played German games and romped outdoors in the long twilight, like a lot of children. I fell down heels-over-head, got covered with dust, everybody laughed, and all was merry as a marriage bell. Erman showed me a card from the University, summoning him to examine 'Herr Kandidat Breasted,' and Frau Professor whispered in my ear, 'I will squeeze my thumbs for you on Thursday evening (that is the German for 'wish you luck'), but you need not worry at all.'

"The days went slowly by. Though I did not become nervous at all, I seldom slept well, for I was working intensely. I woke very early on the eventful day, and went through the Stoic philosophers again from beginning to end before my second breakfast came in. I was thinking, as I sat at my eggs and tea, of the newspaper accounts of the last days of condemned criminals. 'The prisoner rose early and ate a hearty breakfast, etc.'

"Then I went to the Thiergarten and sauntered along its shady paths, thinking of the three years' work I had put in here in Berlin, unable to realize that the final struggle was really at hand. As I passed the little lake, it looked so tempting that I rented a skiff and sculled away under bridges and drooping water-side trees, till I found a quiet and secluded inlet where I stretched myself out along the thwarts, and so floated idly, looking lazily at the blue summer sky, and doing my best to think of nothing at all, at which I succeeded surprisingly well. When I returned to my lodgings, a delightful meal was served for me alone in a private room, so that no one should disturb me. Then I lay down but could not sleep a wink, and only tossed about feverishly till Fräulein knocked.

"I dressed and went up to Hancock's room, where I found him ready and bolstering up his courage all he could. We walked to the University through the Thiergarten and arrived just on time, finding the four Germans already there. We waited in an anteroom through which many of the Professors passed in entering the University Senate room.

"At six, a bell tinkled from the Dekan's table within, the door opened, the pedell [beadle] stepped out and called a name. One of the Germans rose and went in at the fateful door, and this was repeated till they were all gone and I sat alone.

"The bell tinkled again, I pulled myself together and answered to my name, stepping in at the little door, and after a bow to the Dekan, I was met by Erman who conducted me to a small table at one side.

"He sat quietly down, spread out a text for me, and asked me to read. I was very nervous, and though I *felt* very confident, I could not pull myself together as I wanted to. It was a Pyramid text, the most difficult of all hieroglyphics. Still, it had but one knotty passage. As we approached it, Erman watched with interest to see what I would make of it, and when I gave him the proper rendering, he expressed his satisfaction aloud. For the sake of appearances, he took on a brusque manner and to fill up the time kept up a volley of questions about many things as if they were entirely new, but with which he knew I was perfectly familiar. After my reading a passage from Papyrus Harris, he gave me a Coptic text.

"All this time the aged Professor Mommsen was walking up and down behind me, engaged in a quiet conversation with another colleague. Professor Erman's last question was on the form of a rare numeral, which I gave him correctly, but which he said was wrong. Of course I did not contradict him. Now he gathered up his books and left me, and returned shortly to sit and listen as old Professor Zeller came slowly in and sat down before me.

"The philosophy seemed to go very well, and the old gentleman graciously beamed when I was able to contrast Plato, Aristotle and the Stoics successfully. I made one small mistake, but as the rest was all right I did not care. By this time I was ready for anything.

"As Professor Zeller departed, good-natured Professor Schrader came in and laid two Hebrew texts upon the table. I was tired, as the strain was considerable, and he asked me of his own accord to sit and rest awhile. Then he began. His third question was on the relation of the Hebrew to the other Semitic languages. I was pretty much at home in that field, and so I began to give a sketch of *all* the Semitic languages, starting down at the south end of the Arabian Peninsula. I knew my man. Sachau never would have allowed a man to begin so far back, but Schrader offered no objection at all, and I preached away for ten minutes on a subject with which I was perfectly familiar. I had to give him a pentateuchal analysis and divide Isaiah, chapter by chapter.

"Finally he laid a chapter before me to read. They think it the proper thing in Germany to be able to pronounce Hebrew very rapidly. I started in like lightning run mad, and Schrader called out, 'Not so fast, not so fast,'—I cooled down and then translated the passage for him as if it had been German, and he retired, followed in a few moments by the dreaded Sachau.

"No one could have treated me more considerately and kindly. All went well. Without a moment's hesitation I was able to translate and read the Arabic he gave me. The time for the end drew near, and I was exulting, for I knew I had passed.

"Suddenly Sachau turned in his chair and hurled a poser at me: he asked me to give an outline of the critical history of the Koran. I sat dumb. I could read it as fast as if it were English, but I could not give its critical history. I faltered out a few words about one of the early Caliphs, and Sachau said sharply, 'I see you know nothing about it.' 'No,' said I, speaking frankly, 'I do not, Herr Professor.' It was the last question of the examination, and he rose and left me.

"I sat a few moments, feeling weighed down, for it was a bad miss, and then the pedell said, 'Herr Kandidat Breasted is at liberty to leave the room.'

"On going out, I found my five companions in misery, all walking nervously up and down the room, awaiting the results. Hancock was looking black, and said he had not done well in his major. Here, too, I found all my friends from the Museum, 'waiting to congratulate me,' they said.

"After about ten minutes, the bell tinkled again. The pedell appeared at the door, called a name, and one of the Germans went in, returning in a moment, holding a little card and looking happy.

"My name was then called. I stepped in, found the Dekan standing before the assembled faculty. I bowed, and he said, 'Herr Breasted, I have the honor to inform you that you have passed your examination *cum laude* (with praise).'

"It was the same grade Erman had received for his own Doctor's examination years before! He came forward, and with moist eyes, gave me a long hand grasp, then without a word stepped back again to his seat. I took my card from the Dekan's hand, somehow found myself among a circle of men who were all shaking my hand at once, and seemed as happy as I at the outcome.

"Hancock's name came last—poor fellow, I was sorry for him. He got 'sustinuit,' which means a bare scratch to come through. Then we feed all the 'supes' of the University, who stood about to bow and congratulate, and we came downstairs.

"As I stood in the great University gates, I could not realize it was all over. Within three feet of the spot where I had just been sitting to be examined, I had sat three years ago to be matriculated. We passed through the iron portal as I had done so many times before, but now for the first time with the dreaded ordeal behind me. As I stopped at the cable office to send you the good news there came over me a flood of recollections of years of toil, always with this distant goal in view, and I was filled with a deep sense of inexpressible gratitude for the happiness it would bring all my dear ones at home.

"Next morning I rose late, wandered in a dazed condition about my room, finally dressed, and only later when my eyes felt uncomfortable, remembered that I had forgotten to wash my face! I went to the Dekan's office again, and received my dissertation and papers. I enclose you my card—at the bottom you will see the predicate [rating] which my dissertation received: '*sollertiae et sani iudicii specimen probabile.*' It means 'an admirable specimen of critical skill and sound judgment.' It is one of the best predicates.

"On my way to the Dekan's office, I met Erman—his first word was that I was right on the Coptic numeral, in which he had corrected me. He told me Sachau reported me philologically first rate, but said I was historically lame! Everything else was good—so, that last miss with Sachau cost me a higher grade! Nevertheless, there is but one other American before me who has *cum laude* from Berlin.

"My next work is to autograph the thesis and get ready for the public exercises—this will take three weeks at least. But the test is passed, and there is no worry now."

True to the Victorian tradition of greeting glad tidings with tears, Aunt Theodocia and Harriet had wept throughout Charles' reading of this consummation of everything they had lived for during three long years. He had somehow managed to finish, but when the ladies, as he did so, began to sob outright, it was too much for him and he sought refuge among the flowers of the little garden which he had managed to acquire since James had gone to Germany. His own heart was very full, and at such times he liked to sit quietly among his flower beds, even though he could not see them in the darkness of the summer evening.

James was now technically a Doctor of Philosophy in Egyptology. But before the degree could be finally granted, copies of his dissertation (entitled *De Hymnis in Solem,* written entirely in Latin, the original copy in block letters with his own pen) had to be distributed among the faculty and officials; and on the morning of August 19, clad in a dress suit and white kid gloves, he had to appear on the platform of the University's great audience hall, and in a perfunctory ceremony spoken in Latin, had to defend his dissertation publicly against the pre-arranged "objections" of three of his fellow students. At last, with his own right hand clasped in that of the Dekan, he "took the oath of fealty to the University: 'To be a pure man, to serve the highest ends of scholarship, and to pursue and ever to declare the truth,' "—and was thereupon named a full-fledged "Master of Arts and Doctor of Philosophy."

CHAPTER III

AS the day in October, 1894, which Frances and James had set for their wedding, drew near, the thought of imminent marriage frightened her, and by way of temporizing, she reverted to a plan she had had before their engagement, for spending at least a year in study at some women's college in America. Such a separation, she told him, would be an ultimate test of their love, an enriching ordeal for them both, which would make their subsequent reunion all the more glorious.

James was somewhat bewildered by this decision, and by the prospect of visiting Egypt alone instead of on his honeymoon. But being by nature inclined toward *laisser faire* in human relations, he did not demur unduly.

Years later, from beyond a thousand other docksides, he was to remember the September morning when he brought her to the ship at Cuxhaven—the sudden burst of methodical, unexcited activity as the boat train crept to a halt in a great shed, the smells of caulking, fresh paint and new hawsers, the echoing splash of water pouring from a port in the black wall of the ship.

A steward took the hand luggage, and James hurried off to find the trunks.

But the trunks were not to be found. James's newly acquired title was invaluable: at the request of Herr Doktor der Philosophie Breasted, the trainsmen, dockhands, ship's officers, stewards and crew searched the ship and most of the Cuxhaven wharves as they never would have done for an untitled civilian. Still the trunks could not be found. At last the Freight Master, a heel-clicking Prussian official in a blue uniform with scarlet trimming and brass buttons, triumphantly brought forth a sheaf of bills of lading for the slow freight expected from Berlin during the next fortnight. Behold, one of these bore witness that the missing trunks had been dispatched by slow instead of fast freight, and were at that moment reposing on a siding somewhere between Berlin and Cuxhaven. It was to be hoped, said the Freight

Master, that the High-and-Well-Born Herr Doktor der Philosophie Breasted and the "gnädige Dame" this most-to-be-regretted and not-to-be-understood misdirection of "Grossgepäck" would graciously pardon.

Frances had ample clothing in her hand luggage for the Atlantic crossing, but apparently it occurred neither to herself nor to any one else that she might sail without two trunks which could easily have followed on a later ship. "Of course she could not sail without her baggage," wrote James laconically, "and so the steamship company sold her ticket, and we took the train back to Berlin."

I never knew whether they were happy or depressed during this curious, anticlimactic return journey. But I believe James was aware that it was leading him far beyond Berlin, to a point in his personal life from which there could be no retreat. As for her, whether because on quiet reflection she suspected that their engagement might not have survived a year's separation, or because her earlier fears had somehow been dispelled, she now abandoned all thought of returning to America in favor of early marriage.

But her hopes in this direction were somewhat over-sanguine.

"It is often almost impossible for an American to secure the papers necessary to make a . . . marriage valid . . . in Germany," said the Berlin correspondent of the *New York Sun and Record* in an article which appeared on January 5, 1895. ". . . [This] was illustrated [recently] . . . in Berlin, when the happiness of two young Americans hung . . . in the balance until German authorities finally consented to let them join hands and hearts. The young man was an Egyptologist, [who] hoped to take his bride with him [to Egypt]. . . .

". . . As there existed in the cautious German mind the possibility that [the bride] might have gone through the marriage ceremony on some previous occasion, it was necessary to publish the banns weeks beforehand . . . in the Berlin papers . . . [and] in the journals of her native American town. Both parties were obliged to secure certificates of the birth and baptism of themselves and their parents, and to furnish an epitome of the family histories down to date. . . .

"All the papers finally arrived and the couple repaired . . . [on October 22, 1894] with their friends and witnesses to the office of the legal functionary in whose hands their happiness reposed. The legal functionary, of course, had witnesses on his side—the Germans never transact any business except in the presence of witnesses. . . . Papers were produced. The bride told all about herself . . . the bridegroom told all about both of them. The mother of the bride assured the assembled company that this man was not insidiously defrauding her of her daughter. The company began to breathe more freely. . . .

"But the legal functionary was not going to let them off so easily. He . . . [suddenly] turned on the whole crowd, . . . asked them fiercely for their passports. Of course no one had such a thing about him, so the jaded bridegroom had to rush off in a droschke to secure as many as were necessary.

"The bride . . . by this time was almost in tears. . . . [But the passports were found] and the Americans . . . were finally made man and wife. . . . [Whereupon] they had . . . to . . . be married again by a minister who spoke English, shake hands with . . . [some] 500 friends, and catch the first train for Egypt."

James and Frances were married the second time in the English Chapel of the Empress Frederick in Berlin. Most of the American colony attended the wedding reception, and all the young hearts at Mrs. Willard's School beat faster at the sight of one of their number setting out with a handsome young husband for a honeymoon in Egypt.

Under the brilliant ministrations of Lord Cromer, the Egypt which James and Frances were now entering was just beginning to show definite symptoms of recovery from some two thousand years of depredation, persecution, enslavement and warfare. In the whole history of mankind, probably no population had ever endured a longer, more relentless oppression than the fellahin, the ancient farming class of Egypt.

Superficially the land and its brooding wreckage of prodigal ancient glories had changed little through the centuries. The Nile rose and fell and sought the Northern Sea with the same majestic rhythm it had observed through geological ages before men deified its murky, enriching flow, and nations struggled for possession of its superlatively fertile banks. But everywhere among its drowsy adobe villages beneath their eternal palm groves, which had harbored poverty and wretchedness such as only the greed of oriental despots knew how to inflict, profound changes were beginning to take place. By 1879 the blood-wet lash of the *kurbash* (rhinoceros rawhide whip) in the hands of the Khedive Ismail's tax collectors, enforcing a *corvée* tantamount to slavery, had wrung from the fellahin the utmost yield of their fields and the last ounce of their own undernourished strength. Starvation and pestilence had wasted village after village, provincial revenues had shrunk until the infinitely cruel, dissolute, shambling sovereignty of Egypt's foreign overlords stood bankrupt, and in 1882 England, with her eye on Suez and India, had by force of arms undertaken the rôle of receiver.

With the advent of Cromer, the faces of young Englishmen began to appear everywhere in newly organized government ministries and departments, and the chaos of the old order was beginning to resolve itself into the logical pattern of British administration under one of the ablest men the Empire has ever produced. The Turks and native officials who were thereby displaced or put under strict scrutiny and control, were bitter in their opposition and for once tireless, if only in their obstructionism. But for the most part, the native population welcomed the new regime, especially the fellahin to whom it spelled salvation.

British prestige was still in the ascendant. Commodities were incredibly cheap—in the country districts fresh eggs could be bought for as little as five cents a dozen, milk for three cents a quart, a turkey for twenty-five cents, a live sheep for a dollar. Craftsmen and artisans still followed traditional forms and techniques, happily without benefit of the alleged blessings of Western industrial civilization. The people still observed many habits and customs dating from Pharaonic times, and for the Europeans the daily life of Egypt had about it a medieval quality. In Cairo, the greatest city of the Moslem world, the carriages of the wealthy pashas and foreigners, drawn by superb horses, were still customarily preceded by barelegged *saises* (runners), their waists tightly bound with many colored silken scarves, who carried gold- or silver-mounted whips or rods with which they cleared the way for their lords and masters. Altogether it was a fascinating time to be in Egypt and to watch the passing of an era.

James had been so long submerged in Egyptian history that he felt almost as if in some previous incarnation he had lived among the scenes he was now beholding. From a thousand Egyptian inscriptions and Arabic texts he had pictured the clamorous actuality of oriental life with its extremes of drabness and beauty, disease and hardiness, its stenches and filth, its color and unconscious grace, its immemorial din of barking dogs, braying donkeys, wailing children, imploring beggars, chaffering merchants, pedlars calling their wares, muezzin chanting the call to prayer, fellahin singing to the rhythm of creaking well sweeps scooping Nile water into thirsting fields. His first reactions were nevertheless those of a tourist, and as the train neared Cairo, he "discovered the Pyramids on the horizon with such a shout that our native fellow voyagers started from their seats in astonishment."

"With our slim though united purses," Frances wrote many years later, "it never occurred to us to go to the already famous Shepheard's Hotel, or to the Continental Hotel. We went instead to the old Hotel du Nil [built in 1836] in the middle of the Mousky [the native quarter of the bazaars]. This seemed to us an oriental paradise. The balcony of our room looked down upon a beautiful garden surrounded by a high white wall and filled with tropical vegetation and tremendous palms, in the midst of which played a fountain. It was a cool, enchantingly peaceful oasis in the dust and turmoil of the native quarter. From an observation tower atop of the hotel, to which we mounted at sunset to look out upon the city so new and full of romance to our western eyes, we counted more than two hundred minarets.

"But even the Hotel du Nil was too great a tax upon our slender resources. We soon moved to a *pension* in an old Turkish palace in the Sharia Kasr el-Nil, where Professor Erman had stayed on his own honeymoon, a place kept by a strange, rather winsome though notoriously miserly little German widow named Frau Fink, who had lived in Cairo for thirty years without ever having been up the Nile."

Among the guests currently gathered at Frau Fink's cosmopolitan table were a gracious and well-born English widow named Mrs. Charles Smith (who sat on James's right) and her daughter Gracilla, a startlingly beautiful golden-haired girl in her early twenties. Between the lovely Gracilla and Frances sat a tall, dignified, exceedingly good-looking Coptic gentleman of sunburnt complexion, who was dressed immaculately in European fashion and wore a fez. His name was Salib (pronounced Saleeb) Claudius. He was very well educated, came of a proud old family, and was a good friend of the eminent British Orientalist, Archibald Henry Sayce, Professor of Assyriology at Oxford, who was then in Cairo. Claudius was a junior official in the Egyptian Post Office, and being a man of great ability and absolute integrity, stood forth like a shining light in the naughty world of Egyptian politics. He and James liked one another from the first, and quickly became good friends.

It so happened that when the fair Gracilla, only a few weeks earlier in Rome, had seemed on the verge of succumbing to the practiced blandishments of a proverbial Italian count, Mrs. Smith had hastily removed her from Italy to the presumably greater safety of Cairo—and had thereby pushed her exquisite charge from the frying pan into the fire. For handsome Salib Claudius, with his intelligent and appealing eyes wide open to the grave implications of his suit, had promptly fallen overwhelmingly in love with Gracilla. He informed James with disarming frankness and modesty that he loved her with all his heart and wished, she and God willing, to marry her. Mrs. Smith was desperate. She turned to Frances, begged her to exhort Gracilla to think wisely.

James recognized in Claudius a man whose love any girl should be proud to possess, and though fully aware of the traditional British attitude toward such a union, he was sincerely, albeit anxiously, impelled to wish him every success. For Claudius was a native-born Egyptian in the best meaning of the word. He was a Copt, and the Copts—whose very name stems from the ancient Greek "Aigyptioi," shortened by the Arabs to "Kupt"—not only became the earliest Christians of Egypt but are today racially the most direct descendants of the ancient Egyptians. Even the language of their orthodox church ritual is a last remnant of ancient Egyptian. "I thought, how strange that of all the myriad arts and all the teeming life where this tongue was once spoken," James wrote after attending his first Coptic service, "it has been preserved for five thousand years to be heard today only in praise of the one true God." That the Copts survived centuries of political and religious persecution, adhering throughout to their pristine faith when it would have eased their sufferings and bettered their fortunes to abandon it (as a considerable number of their weaker brethren did), must be attributed to their inordinate pride and their superior business ability. The Copts were at this time and remain today among the largest landowners of Egypt, and have their fingers in almost every profitable economic enterprise in their country.

Salib Claudius embodied the best physical and mental attributes of his people. No one at Frau Fink's table was therefore unduly surprised when Gracilla began to show symptoms of imminent and definitely pleasurable surrender to his quietly impassioned assault upon her heart.

Mrs. Smith perceived that her flight from Italy had been in vain, and confided to Frances that though she recognized his unexceptionably admirable qualities, she could not rid herself of a vague fear that Salib's conquest of Gracilla would lead only to some misfortune.

Altogether, Salib Claudius had much to occupy his mind. Yet he found time, and it afforded him evident pleasure to assist James and

Frances in making their preparations for a two months' journey up the Nile. William Matthew Flinders Petrie, already famous British Egyptologist, had written cordially urging James to spend a week with him at his two excavations—Coptos and Nagada, below Thebes—and advising him that by far the pleasantest and cheapest way to travel through Egypt was by boat on the Nile. Claudius strongly confirmed this counsel, adding that by embarking from Assiut, 235 miles upriver, they could not only charter a dahabiyeh (lateen-rigged native house-boat) at less than half Cairo prices, but they would save this long stretch of sailing against the tremendous current of an unusually high inundation. Through a friend in Assiut (and the definition of a friend in the orient is one who, among other things, is good for at least 60 per cent off the asking price in almost any transaction), Claudius secured a satisfactory dahabiyeh. James was able to write his father that "our boat, with bedding, linen, kitchen equipment, a crew of four sailors, captain and second captain, dragoman, cook and boy, and including all table and household expenses and hire of donkeys at all stops, will cost us $4.84 each per day. Some unavoidable purchases of equipment will bring the daily expense up to $5.00 per person."

Even this seemed to him a "dangerously heavy expense" which he felt justified in assuming only because "the boat will enable me to continue my studies without interruption." He was apparently never inclined to regard a honeymoon as in itself at least partly a justification of this extravagance.

Long afterward, Frances remarked with pride rather than regret, that "theirs had indeed been a scholarly honeymoon." Indeed, it was. She erred, I think, on the side of understatement. James was ebulliently romantic, but the habit of work, the driving sense that he *must* succeed, his consuming preoccupation with everything relating to a land which symbolized for him "the first emergence of the human spirit," the realization that many years might pass before he would again revisit Egypt—all this had the effect of translating their honeymoon into a one-man expedition fortuitously accompanied by a bride. For while they saw and did everything usually seen and done by tourists, and had a good time, work took precedence over play.

Every morning in Cairo, while the boat was being conditioned at Assiut, they would mount their donkeys and ride three miles to the Egyptian Museum, then housed in an old tinder-box of a "palace guarded day and night with fire engines." The Museum had been founded in 1858 by a French savant bearing the regal sounding name of Auguste Ferdinand Francois Mariette, whom the "retired" Khedive Ismail Pasha had appointed as his Conservator of Egyptian Monuments. Mariette, the son of a town clerk at Boulogne-sur-Mer, was a pioneer of Egyptology, and though more notable for his dynamic energy than his scientific infallibility, had been the first European with any semblance of historical training to tap the incredible wealth of Egypt's buried antiquities. During the thirty years of his activities, he had excavated enough treasures not only to make the Egyptian collection at the Louvre one of the best in Europe, but to start the Cairo Museum on the road to becoming at once the finest Egyptian collection and the most remarkable record of an ancient civilization anywhere in the world.

By far the most exciting experience with which James had yet met in his science was to find himself each day surrounded with original historical records of Egypt's past, most of which had either been translated inaccurately or not at all by European scholars. Here was a challenge to his keenest faculties, now hypersensitized by the realization that he was a lone young American Egyptologist pitted against the rather self-superior complacency of Old World scholarship. With a sense of elation he set about copying and translating the historical inscriptions which Erman had designated in the Cairo Museum.

The more he compared any existent translations by earlier scholars with the original inscriptions, the more mistakes he found. Although he did not realize it at the moment, this marked the beginning of his first major scientific project: he would himself eventually copy, translate and publish *every* known ancient Egyptian historical inscription—in the Cairo Museum, the museums of Europe and America, and on the ancient monuments and temple walls of the entire Nile valley itself. This ambitious undertaking was to require a decade of incessant labor before it was completed in four volumes.

Before leaving Berlin, James had received word from President Harper of his appointment as instructor in Egyptology at the University of Chicago at an annual salary of $800; and in addition of the appropriation of the impressive sum of $500 for the creation of an Egyptian museum at the University. While he winced at a salary appreciably lower than Harper had originally held forth, the fact remained that this was the first and still the only chair of Egyptology in America, and therefore worth some sacrifice. As for the proposed

Egyptian collection, Harper's instructions were characteristic: he was
to begin it at once, was to rely chiefly on the generosity of excavators, and to draw on this appropriation only as a last resort.

Had he been single-handedly assembling the Egyptian section of
the British Museum, he could not have taken his responsibility more
seriously. He first methodically listed the types of objects from each
age of ancient Egypt which an ideal museum collection ought to possess, then hunted for examples. Through the years he was to make the
acquaintance of every important antiquity dealer in Egypt; of a horde
of casual pedlars with endless stocks of "junk" which might contain
some pearl of great price; and of innumerable fellahin who frequently
found antiquities while digging among ancient ruins for fertilizer
(sebbah). For the fellahin had long ago learned that the detritus from
the ruins of ancient Egyptian towns made superlative fertilizer. It is
in fact exceptionally rich in nitrates and other chemicals invaluable to
agriculture which have been preserved because of the almost total
absence of rainfall. As a consequence many of the most important
archaeological sites in Egypt had in the course of centuries literally
been scattered far and wide, and plowed into the soil.

Genuine *antikas,* as the natives call them, were at this time not only
still incredibly plentiful but so cheap that the manufacture of forgeries
had not yet become one of the major industries of Egypt. James was
able to stretch the University's little appropriation to include a range
and quantity of items which the sharply increasing prices of the next
ten years would never have permitted. In addition, he persuaded Petrie
and a few others then excavating in Egypt, whenever they found two
or more similar objects, to donate one to the University of Chicago.

So, by wheedling material from excavators and additional funds
from people of means, he created the nucleus of a modest though representative collection. It had only slight intrinsic worth, and even in a
community still sparsely endowed with such synopses of human development, its value lay chiefly in what it taught him of dealing with
orientals and of securing for archaeology the enthusiastic financial support of some of his wealthy countrymen.

He worked so intensively at all these commissions that by late
afternoon his eyes needed rest, and he would take Frances on a bus-
man's holiday to visit the shops of antiquity dealers, or to pay his
respects to the various Government officials or private individuals in
some way related to Egyptology. On one of these occasions they called
upon Professor Sayce, who lived aboard "his own beautiful dahabiyeh,

the broadest boat on the river, a perfect little palace," as James wrote
to his father. "He has a generous fellowship from Oxford, but he
must have extensive means of his own to maintain a boat with such
rich furnishings and luxurious appointments."

Professor Sayce, James's senior by twenty years, became during the
eighty-eight years of his distinguished life not only one of the most
eminent Orientalists of his time, but a unique British institution in the
Near East, every corner of which he knew intimately. I vividly recall
my own first meeting with him in Cairo in 1905 when I was a small
boy of eight: he was a slight, genial little man with odd-shaped spectacles, who usually wore a Victorian black frock coat, a shallow-
crowned ecclesiastical black felt hat, and a standing collar, and had a
genius for keeping about his person precisely the trinkets and curiosi-
ties which would fascinate a small boy. The last time I saw him was
again in Cairo, twenty years later, when he was over eighty and, still
clad in his black frock coat and standing collar, was setting out alone
to travel overland across Arabia, and taking his peregrinations as
lightly as the train journey from London to Oxford.

He was known, trusted and honored everywhere by Europeans and
orientals alike, was forever being consulted, or called upon to act as
arbiter in disputes of every kind, remained always a bachelor, was
godfather to many of the children of his countless friends, and became
eventually an almost legendary figure. In many ways, he knew the
Near East better than Lawrence of Arabia himself, but there was
nothing of the military leader about this wise, gentle, kindly scholar.

"We sat on the upper deck and had tea in the cool afternoon
breeze. I presented him with a copy of my Doctor's dissertation and
we talked for a long time." Sayce knew every inch of the Nile for a
thousand miles southward from Cairo and had at his tongue's tip the
answer to every question James put to him. They talked of Egyptology,
politics, Cromer's reforms, and finally of their mutual regard for Salib
Claudius.

"He is showing high courage in his determination to win the hand
and heart of Miss Smith," said Professor Sayce. "He knows as we do
that from the moment he marries her, the two of them will be ostra-
cized from each other's communities. Yet I devoutly hope he will
succeed—for he has my friendship, and will have yours, I know, and
that of enough others like us to carry him through. Only, we *must*
stand by him—for I have a feeling he may one day need us rather
desperately."

At last the sun sank into the desert, and they regretfully took leave of the Professor, who graciously guided them ashore through the tangled moorings of the river craft, and stood looking after them as they jogged away on their donkeys.

So began a friendship which endured until the Professor ended his earthly travels.

On the morning of November 21, 1894, James and Frances boarded the train for Assiut, whence their dragoman, a young Copt named Habeeb Ibrahim, had sent word that the boat was ready. The engine whistled shrilly, tardy natives rushed for third-class compartments, the babel of shouting and general excitement redoubled as the train moved out of the station into a brilliant Egyptian morning.

It wound its way out of Cairo, rumbled across a steel bridge to the west bank of the Nile, and chuffed along the top of a dike past the Pyramids, luminous in the morning light, until it lost itself in the dusty iteration of palms and fields, canals and villages and the monotonous fertility of the Nile valley.

Everywhere the people stopped to stare at the train, shading their eyes with their hands. Men in breechcloths lifting water with well sweeps into irrigation ditches, black-draped women carrying children on their hips and great jars on their heads, little girls sitting atop of ponderous, mud-smeared water buffalo, old men on trotting donkeys, boys shooing birds from incredibly green ripening fields, all stopped to watch the train pass. Flights of pigeons rose and swept away, camels lifted their heavy-lidded, droopy-lipped faces and gazed cynically. A minor bedlam occurred at every station, with most of the local population and every chronic or train-time mendicant gathered on the platform to stare and jabber and shout, or to hold out withered hands and whine for baksheesh. Flies swarmed everywhere—insolent, adhesive flies that had fattened on sewage and the unspeakable, putrescent filth of the orient—flies that clustered on the open sores of diseased men and beasts, in black patches on the eyes of little children, and in hordes upon everything and everyone.

But James and Frances minded neither dust nor flies nor filth, and saw only beauty in the world passing their compartment windows. They seldom saw the Nile, for the flood plain is wide between Cairo and Assiut, but often they caught glimpses of the western desert gleaming and trembling beyond the lush vegetation of the valley. He sat with a map of Egypt spread out on his lap, noted the name of every station, and exclaimed as he recognized historic sites or temples whose inscriptions he had read with Erman in Berlin.

They drew into Assiut at twilight, weary, gray with dust, and glad to let Habeeb take them in charge. Nothing in the orient is ever done according to promise, and the *Olga,* as their boat was unpoetically called, would not be ready until the following morning. They dined pleasantly with the friend of Salib Claudius at a small European-owned hotel, and neither its hard mattresses nor the eternal barking of dogs kept them from sleeping soundly beneath a huge *moustiquaire* (mosquito netting), which had the same curious acrid smell of dust and stale starch as the lace curtains in all the Continental hotels and *pensions* they had ever known.

They admitted to themselves a certain childlike excitement as they walked to the river front the next morning for their first view of the *Olga.* She was a typical little dahabiyeh in a reasonable state of repair. She had an overall length of about fifty-five feet and a nine-foot beam. The galley was forward of the mainmast and the crew's deck. The higher, after portion of the boat contained a dining room, a dragoman's cabin, two minute "master" cabins each with one narrow berth, a bathroom with a much-dented home-made zinc tub, a toilet consisting of an orthodox seat over a removable box of sand, a dressing room and tiny after deck pierced by the rudder-shaft. The roof was a deck covered with an awning and furnished with easy chairs. Above the water-line the *Olga* appeared staunch enough, but as with most native-owned craft on the Nile, the condition of her hull was problematical. There was little about her to remind one of Professor Sayce's trim and patrician vessel.

But to two young Americans at least nominally on their honeymoon, she seemed little short of perfection. When Frances went aboard, while the crew stood at attention, she was entering her first marital home and beginning her first venture into housekeeping—for before her marriage she had never so much as boiled the proverbial egg. It was probably fortunate for James that her duties were light. Habeeb bought all the supplies, and the cook in his innocently unhygienic way prepared the simple meals.

There was not a puff of wind to fill the limp lateen sails when James gave the order to cast off for the first day's run. The reis (captain) ordered the sailors to rig a tackle block halfway up the mainmast, through which they ran a tow-rope, then set them to tracking the boat upstream. The men toiled slowly along the bank, shouting and singing in a rhythmic chorus as they called upon the Prophet and all the local saints to aid them.

"Whenever we rounded a bend, the sweep of the current would boil and surge under the bow, and we would barely move. Then, shouting more lustily than ever to the Prophet, 'Ya Mohammed, yalla, yalla, ya Zaid, ya Mohammed!' the men would tug and strain at the ropes till the veins in their necks stood out darkly and their backs glistened with sweat. Once more the mud banks would begin to creep slowly past.

"At intervals a long shoal would appear, extending out into the stream, and the boat would have to head away from the bank. The captain would now send more rope racing through the block and tackle, the sailors would break into a run to take up the slack. As they ran, the heavy wet rope would sometimes be swinging free in the air, again would drop with a hissing splash into the swift current, and would tremble and gurgle as it cut through the brown water.

"So we crawled slowly onward until at last we struck an impossible shoal and a hopeless stretch of current. The sailors now fastened their tow-rope to an anchor which they put into the felucca [small boat], carried up stream, and dropped into the water. Then they hauled the dahabiyeh up to this anchor, dropped a second anchor to hold the boat, and once more carried the first anchor forward. They repeated this until they could move no further. The river was too swift.

"Suddenly the surface of the downriver water darkened as the north wind sprang up merrily. The sails billowed and filled, and despite the current we moved swiftly upstream while the sailors shouted, 'Praise to Allah, praise to Allah!'"

At sundown of this first day, the wind fell and the *Olga* moored for the night. "As we were finishing dinner," James wrote, "Habeeb entered the little dining room, hesitated for a moment, then said deferentially, 'My Doctor,'—he always addresses me as 'My Doctor'— 'I would like to tell you about this dahabiyeh.'

"'Is there anything the matter with it?' I said.

"Habeeb nodded. 'I fear, my Doctor,' he said, 'our boat she have acquired some water.'

"He rolled back the matting from under our feet and lifted a plank: the hold was full to within a few inches of the floor!

"I summoned the captain. He gazed at the inky water with oriental imperturbability, then said, 'Allah has done this and there was no help for it. But at sunrise tomorrow I shall send for a diver to look for the leak!'

"By bailing all night long, the crew kept us afloat, and the first streak of dawn found a native diving again and again under the sides of the boat, checking every seam from bow to stern, and coming up each time blowing like a porpoise. Working entirely by his sense of touch, the water being much too muddy to see through, the diver discovered and repaired an uncaulked joint amidships, and after another half day's bailing, the hold was all clear again."

It was James's plan to travel continuously southward to Aswan at the First Cataract, about 580 miles from Cairo, and then independently of the north wind, to drift downstream, stopping wherever he chose at ancient temples and tombs. The little *Olga* therefore moved steadily southward, sometimes by laborious tracking but more often before the prevailing north wind, until she was lost among the endless array of white sails forever moving up and down the river, like flights of great exotic birds from inner Africa.

"I cannot realize, as we sail along, that I am really here in this ancient land," he wrote to Aunt Theodocia, "nor did I ever dream of making the journey under such enchanting conditions. Here am I with my dear wife, monarch of all I survey on this boat—I walk the deck and feel like a naval officer in one of Cooper's sea tales, for I have only to raise my hand and eleven men [the crew had been increased] are ready to obey my slightest word! It is truly a lucky combination of circumstances which enables us without exceeding my stipend for the journey, to travel like a king and queen, and permits me to continue my work amid all possible comforts. It seems like a dream!"

But in this dream he never for a moment forgot the grim economic realities which awaited him in America. There was his debt to Aunt Theodocia, and Charles's imminent retirement, and now his own married state, a home to be furnished, expensive scientific books to be bought for his work, and all these liabilities to be financed by himself whose only visible source of income as yet consisted of a salary of $800 per annum! He faced a long period of lean years during which he would have to supplement this salary by giving popular lectures, one of the very few sources of outside income possible for a university man. "If I could have four or five hours a day to devote to it, I could within a year produce a book on the religion of Egypt," he wrote. "But I cannot do this, I fear, with University Extension lectures to give. However, they will bring me 'popular' reputation, and that seems to be the chief requisite to 'success' in American education."

So, when he was not studying the passing country through his binoculars and checking his observations against those of earlier scholarly travelers, or collating inscriptions, or reading historical commentaries, he was assembling the lectures he would soon be giving in the United States.

Early in December, the *Olga* reached Luxor—"glorious Thebes"—where James could not resist stopping. "For three days, from dawn till dark, I never lost a moment copying inscriptions—and on one night at Karnak I copied by moonlight. The silver light streamed down through the broken roof of the vast colonnaded hall, splashing with bright patches the dusky outlines of the enormous columns. Figures are prosaic: but imagine a forest of 134 columns, the middle two rows sixty-nine feet high and twelve feet thick, with capitals eleven feet high; and carved upon them in deep relief the tall figures of gods and kings, with legends in hieroglyphic, and myriads of royal cartouches [oval rings within which were written the names of Egyptian kings]. I shall remember that evening until my dying day."

From Luxor they pushed on before a steady wind, past "mile after mile of palm-grown banks, with mauve and yellow mountains sometimes low in the distance, again rising bold and dazzling from the water's edge, often honeycombed with rock tombs, long since plundered, silent, empty." The limestone of lower Egypt had gradually given way to standstone, and now, as they reached Aswan, to an abrupt and grandiose extrusion of granite, the first of six cataracts between this point and Khartoum by which Nature, as if she had changed her original plan, had vainly sought to stem the one great river flowing from inner Africa into the Mediterranean.

"It was from Aswan that the granite for all the obelisks of Egypt was quarried and transported downriver," he wrote. "For thousands of years this place has marked the southern frontier of Egypt proper. The country beyond was inhabited by black people over whom Egypt usually ruled. On the rocks you will find the names of the Twelfth Dynasty Pharaohs (about 1994 to 1780 B.C.) or the rude scratchings of the Roman soldiers who for centuries were garrisoned here on this distant frontier of the Empire.

"It is a noble sight to watch the angry, foaming Nile rushing madly through a gateway blocked with a thousand black and glistening boulders." On the island of Philae above the cataract they wandered through the famous, almost perfectly preserved Ptolemaic temples, the ineffable loveliness of whose original coloring would so soon be engulfed and irretrievably destroyed by the construction of the Aswan Dam.

Everywhere from cliffs and the walls of temples and tombs, inscriptions beckoned to James—upon one island alone, "over 200 are cut into the rocks of a valley. I traced the high priesthood of the cataract god Anek through three generations of priests who had recorded themselves there. With a little search, this could undoubtedly be carried much further. Oh, for the time to copy and publish these inscriptions!"

He examined the ancient Nilometer and wished that he might excavate the ruins at the south end of the beautiful, palm-covered island of Elephantine (pronounced Elephanteenee), opposite Aswan. He climbed the mesa-like cliffs on the west bank of the river and looked longingly toward the southern horizon where Nile and desert faded into sky. But he could not linger. "This is the southern limit of our journey. Perhaps some day I shall return." Ten years would pass before he came this way again.

The little *Olga's* main yard was taken down and lashed above the awning and a small yard was rigged in its place. Great, crude oars, one to each man, were set out at either side of the crew's deck, and to the rhythm of an old river chant, the boat moved out into the swift current, northward bound.

"The oars fell with a splash, and after long slow strokes, rose dripping from their swirls. We drifted with the current past all the changeless life of the river, hour after hour, till the shadows of the western mountains drew across the valley toward the purple east, and the boundless brilliance of the Egyptian night, as if begrudging the day its twilight, filled the sunset sky with stars. Slowly we moved under a high bank to moor for the night, and the cliffs beyond sent back the startling echo of the heavy maul as the mooring stakes were driven into the soil."

Thus drifting, they came once more to Thebes, where James paid farewell visits to all its mighty ruins. On his last day he "visited the famous place [among the cliffs on the west side of the river] where in 1881 the royal mummies of the Eighteenth and Nineteenth Dynasties were found. The tourists never go there, and I was the first visitor in years, for it is difficult to get down the shaft, which is halfway up the slope in a narrow valley of glowing, amber-hued rock.

"Habeeb and a guide begged me not to go down, but I ignored their nonsense and stripped myself of all superfluous clothing. As I could not trust them to let me down safely into the thirty-eight-foot shaft, I stationed them behind some projecting rocks, made them lie down, brace their feet as in a college 'tug of war' and hold fast to the rope. With a candle and some matches in my pocket, I swung over the edge and, hand over hand, let myself down to the bottom.

"I lighted my candle and began crawling along a very low passage, rendered smaller still by pieces which had fallen from the ceiling. After two right-angle turns, the passage led 195 feet into the mountain. The air, heated by the suns of thousands of years, was suffocatingly hot, and the perspiration poured from me. Behind and before me was inky darkness, and a silence so deep that even the burning of the candle flame became loudly audible.

"Suddenly there was a rushing sound, the candle went out, and in the first instant of darkness, something struck me full in the face. It was only a bat, but match after match failed to strike, and though there was nothing to be afraid of, it seemed an eternity in that horrible blackness till the candle flickered again.

"The passage ended in a chamber about twenty feet square. Here the priest-kings of the Twenty-first Dynasty had concealed the bodies of the great kings of the Eighteenth and Nineteenth Dynasties. For even as far back as that time it had become impossible to protect their tombs against grave robbers. But here in this secret, rock-hewn chamber they had lain secure and undisturbed for nearly 3000 years, till modern natives—the descendants of those same early tomb robbers—in 1881 discovered them. The first indication that something extraordinary had been surreptitiously discovered was that the local fellahin were found to be selling gorgeous ancient ornaments. The already eminent Frenchman, Gaston Maspero, then 'Director-General of Excavations and of the Antiquities of Egypt,' investigated until he found this place. [The mummies, stacked in unceremonious piles, had been pillaged both in ancient times and by the natives who had recently found them. But even so, they represented a tremendously important find by which the Cairo Museum was greatly enriched.]

"Huge blocks had fallen from the ceiling till it was difficult to move about in the chamber (a small piece came down while I was there). A few years will see it completely choked. If I was not the last visitor, there will be few after me. I put the candle on a fallen block, and sat down for a few minutes while my mind tried to envisage the strange scene which took place here 3000 years ago—first when the workmen cut this shaft and chamber into the limestone mountain, next when the most trusted men of the priesthood secretly brought the mummies (which to them already seemed very old) to this hiding place. If these walls could give out the voices which once reverberated against them, if by some miracle the full knowledge of a single member of that trusted group could be imparted to us, what a superlative chapter in the history of human development it would make! My heart thumped at the thought.

"I took up my candle again, crept back along the passage to the shaft, and pulled myself up into the heavenly brightness and relative coolness of the outer world.

"We rode back at twilight over the Theban plain, past the great Colossi of Memnon, and along dykes among mist-covered fields until we reached the broad river and saw, gleaming across the black water, the bright outline of our boat. She was hung with gay lanterns, for it was Christmas Eve! Habeeb had prepared an 'illumination' for us, and hung the boat with palm fronds and tamarisk branches. I shall long remember this first Christmas of our married life."

He anticipated with tremendous eagerness his visit with Petrie who had begun digging in Egypt in 1881. The moment the *Olga* reached Nagada, a half-day's run with the current below Luxor, he jumped ashore and without waiting for a donkey to ride, hurried off on foot to find Petrie. His eagerness and the warm welcome he received made him oblivious to the long, tiring walk.

Petrie was a man of forty-one, slightly taller than James (whose height was about five feet, eight inches), with a genial face, kindly eyes, and the agility of a boy. His clothes confirmed his universal reputation for being not merely careless but deliberately slovenly and dirty. He was thoroughly unkempt, clad in ragged, dirty shirt and trousers, worn-out sandals and no socks. It was one of his numerous idiosyncrasies to prefer that his assistants should emulate his own carelessness, and to pride himself on his own and his staff's Spartan ability to "rough it" in the field. He served a table so excruciatingly bad that only persons of iron constitutions could survive it, and even they had been known on occasion stealthily to leave his camp in order to assuage their hunger by sharing the comparatively luxurious beans and unleavened bread of the local fellahin.

Petrie made good-natured fun of colleagues like Professor Sayce "who paid more attention to luxuries than to their science, and had the gout in consequence." It was never quite clear to those who endured his deliberately primitive regime why service to archaeology should necessarily entail the opposite extreme of rags, dirt, malnutrition, chronic dyspepsia and almost total absence of the most rudimentary creature comforts.

The fact remains that he not only miraculously survived the consistent practice of what he preached, but with all his eccentricities and despite numerous scientific theories not accepted by his younger colleagues, established in the end a record of maximum results for minimum expenditure which is not likely to be surpassed.*

He appeared pleased to see James, at once showed him what he was doing and all he had found. For several days James absorbed every detail of the technique of excavation, its supervision and cost. He learned that during the previous year, Petrie had paid "just five shillings a week for provisions for himself and his assistant," and that "to excavate the ancient city of Coptos, keeping seventy men at work for eleven weeks, had cost them £300 ($1500)."

Assignment of sites and permission to excavate then rested with a government "Committee of Antiquities" which met only once a year. The chief condition it exacted of an excavator was that he must give half of his finds to the government. But if a site proved unfruitful or worthless, the excavator had no choice but to wait a year for the Committee to grant him a new one. At this time the least promising sites were assigned to European excavators, while the richest sites were given to native antiquity dealers who were permitted to carry on haphazard digging solely for commercial purposes.

Responsibility for the incalculable loss to Egyptology resulting from this custom rested with the British, who as a government have traditionally neglected the cultural values of the lands they have ruled; with the French, who had arrogated to themselves the supervision of Egypt's antiquities; and with an unsavory individual named Emil Brugsch (brother of the great German Egyptologist, Heinrich Karl Brugsch), then in charge of the Cairo Museum. "Emil Brugsch is an unscrupulous adventurer," wrote James, "a bookkeeper who fled as an embezzler from Germany to America, went through '49 in California, came to Egypt when his brother [Karl] was in favor [with the Khedive Ismail Pasha], and though he knew absolutely nothing about science, was appointed to a position in the Antiquities Department. He married a woman from the harem of Ismail, and as every one is very cer-

* Sir Flinders Petrie died on July 28, 1942, at the age of 89.

tain, is now industriously stealing from the museum of which he is in charge."

This state of affairs was as discouraging to James, to whom it was comparatively new, as to Petrie, who had already been fighting it for some fourteen years. The more the latter saw of James, the more he sensed a rebellious kindred spirit who would not only be useful in the field, but could assist in America by raising funds for excavation. Petrie presently proposed that he and James should in the near future jointly share an excavation, dividing their portion of the finds equally between the University of Chicago and the British groups which Petrie represented.

"It would be great fun for a while, I think," wrote Frances, "but if we ever attempted an expedition, I should make many improvements and be at least tidy. This has been Mr. Petrie's life for at least ten winters—the summers he spends in England. He must have lost many of the niceties of feeling by so continuously 'roughing it.' I was sitting talking to him, when off came his shoe, right before me, while he shook out the stones. He wore no stockings and his dusty foot was exposed. I thought it a pity to be quite so careless in feminine company."

She laughed at herself in later years for such Victorian prudery. But at this time James ruefully admitted to himself that any joint enterprise he might undertake with Petrie could hardly survive her irrepressible missionary impulse to impose tidiness upon a man who would continue to expose his dusty feet and shake stones from his shoes before the Almighty himself. Petrie's proposal, however self-interested, was immensely flattering to a young Middle Westerner fresh from his doctorate; but he was mature enough to realize that a near-genius who had always run his own "show" would find intolerable the divided authority implied in a joint enterprise.

Though he bade Petrie good-bye without committing himself, this first glimpse of practical field archaeology had had the effect upon him of clarifying and confirming the conception of an ultimate scientific goal which had already been forming in his mind during those days in the Harz Mountains. He foresaw that his own most important work in Egypt would be the reconstruction of her ancient past rather than the recovery of the material remains of her civilization. Excavation seemed to him eminently worth-while but of secondary importance. Despite illicit or legitimate commercial marauding, Egypt's *buried* antiquities were reasonably safe and could wait. But the inscribed records on her

ancient monuments were exposed to weathering and vandalism, and
even since the days of the scientific expeditions of Napoleon and
Lepsius, had very perceptibly suffered. He was thinking in terms of
Mommsen's mighty *Corpus* of Latin inscriptions which was begun in
1854, by 1895 had hardly progressed beyond its preliminary stages,
and even today remains unfinished.

"I have tried to find some phrase which would sum up what I want
to do, or *can* do," he wrote to his father. "It is this: I want to read to
my fellow men the *oldest* chapter in the story of human progress. I
would rather do this than gain countless wealth."

As he clambered up steep, tawny cliffs into silent tombs, or
searched for inscriptions along the face of the desert plateau, or moved
through the jumbled wreckage of fallen temples and the twilit stillness
of those yet standing, filling his insatiable notebooks with swift, neat
copies of hieroglyphic records which for him were not remote and
silent but alive with all the surging immediacy of their time, he knew
that he was gathering the story of human progress in Egypt, as no one
had done it before him.

The provincial town of Minia, 150 miles southward of Caïro,
marked the geographical and budgetary limit of their downriver voyage by boat. One evening late in January, 1895, the *Olga's* crew disconsolately watched the northbound night train carry James and
Frances into the darkness.

Cairo had shed its off-season lethargy and was swarming with tourists and well-to-do foreigners who spent their winters in Egypt. On
the hotel terraces sat people from every part of the world, in gay
clothes, wide brimmed hats, smart riding habits. Even Frau Fink's
quiet establishment felt the pressure of the *haut saison* and could not
have received James and Frances had not Salib Claudius surrendered
his rooms and retired to a cot in a storage loft.

He would gladly have slept on the floor, so grateful was his state
of mind. For while James and Frances had been upriver, he had not
only won Gracilla's heart, but by his kindly patience and resourceful-
ness had transformed her mother's attitude of opposition into one of
fond regard and even of dependence. Mrs. Smith had exacted of Salib
only one condition, with herself to be the judge. She would take her
daughter back to England for three months during which no letters
were to be exchanged. If at the end of this period Gracilla's love for
him should appear to have lessened in the slightest degree, she would

forbid the marriage. But if the girl's love for him remained unchanged, then she would unreservedly welcome him as her son-in-law. This not only seemed eminently fair to Salib but caused him to walk among the clouds of a seventh heaven, for his faith in Gracilla was absolute.

She and her mother saw much of James and Frances during these closing days of their Egyptian honeymoon. Together the ladies wandered a last time through the bazaars where like every tourist since Herodotus, they bought brass finger bowls, trays, and pen-cases, folding stands of turned wood inlaid with mother-of-pearl, pottery, garish *tenta*, textiles appliquéd with bits of looking-glass—oddments of indifferent workmanship and smelling mustily of the orient—and which, out of their context, were certain to add an alien and depressing note to the cheerfullest occidental living-room.

During his Berlin years, James had taught himself classical Arabic and had learned by heart large portions of the Koran. Since his arrival in Egypt he had by diligent practice also acquired modern Arabic. It amused him now to take the ladies to the finest mosques in Cairo, and by asking the attendants in purest classical Arabic supported by generous quotations from the Koran, whether he might show "his family" the architectural beauties within, to be accorded marked courtesy and special minor privileges. "These Moslem attendants are greatly impressed by the obvious quality and orthodox limitation of my harem," James explained to the three ladies. "Old school Mohammedans, whether they possess one wife or the Koran's limit of four, never speak of them in conversation, but refer with delicate indirection only to 'their family'!"

When he took them to the great Moslem university of el-Azhar, and standing in the sun-flooded court surrounded by its countless slender columns, listened to the murmur and chant of pristine self-instruction by infinite and too often empty repetition, he was suddenly filled with the memory of his own boyhood and the red-brick grade schoolhouse in Downers Grove. Here before him as for a thousand years, old men and youths and little boys with ink-smeared faces were squatting in desultory groups and circles upon a vast expanse of polished stone. Some, sitting alone, were silent and deeply intent, others were swaying to and fro while reciting aloud, and others still were lackadaisical and distrait and not above asking for baksheesh, as in their several ways they responded to the rudiments or the profundities of medieval Arab learning which teaches that the earth is flat, the sun revolves about it, and the one true God is Allah.

They went at night into the middle of Old Cairo to watch meetings of whirling and howling dervishes. Salib Claudius took them to a Coptic and a Moslem wedding. And in a final *pour prendre congé* to the antiquities, they rose before dawn to spend whole days at some of the most impressive ruins in all Egypt, which are among the oldest cemeteries in the world—Sakkara and the pyramids of Dahshur, on the margin of the western desert south of Cairo.

Their honeymoon drew to its end. "It has cost almost inhuman effort, and a dreary separation from my family, to accomplish all I set out to do," James wrote to his father on his last night in Egypt. "Now at last it is finished. I have not yet gained financially, though we shall all have enough. But I have acquired the equipment for a great work."

The voyage of the *Senegal,* a shabby little nondescript of the Messageries Maritimes which carried James and Frances second class to Marseilles, was somehow like a portent of the struggle lying before them in America. She lumbered out of Alexandria harbor into a howling northern blast which churned the Mediterranean into a foaming tumult of blue-black seas, and wrenched an icy, stinging rain from clouds scudding before the gale like tattered caravans.

She passed through the Straits of Messina and Bonifacio in stormy darkness, and late on the fifth day, in a gloom of rain and snow "which smote into our very marrow," she crept past the dismal grim fortress islands of Pomègue and Ratonneau, and by some homing instinct found her way through a spiky wilderness of shipping to her dock in that pesthole of the Mediterranean, the harbor of Marseilles. To James, entering France for the first time in his life on a stormy evening late in February, this seemed by far the bleakest, most forbidding land he had ever seen.

They waited in the railway restaurant of the Gare St. Charles for what was gallantly called the Paris Express, which would take nearly twenty-four hours to cover the 500 miles. The air was heavy with cheap tobacco, *vin ordinaire,* greasy cooking and the acrid smoke of switch engines. They were ravenously hungry after the five retching days from Alexandria—even now the station seemed to heave and sway. But before they ordered a light meal, they carefully brought their expense accounts up to the moment, and determined how much they would have between them to carry them to London and Chicago. At ten minutes to ten, beneath a sign marked "Aux Trains," one half of a tall

double door with glass panels covered with dirty-white starched curtains into which were woven the initials "P-L-M" (Paris-Lyons-
Mediterrané), was flung open by a squat official in a mussy, unpressed
uniform, with a whistle on a brass chain around his neck, who nasally
announced as if intoning a mass, the imminent departure of the
Paris Express.

They sat up all that night and all of the next day. Through windows "thickly coated with shining frost," as he described it long afterwards, they "saw little of the snowy hills and frozen rivers of France,
so gaunt after the genial sun of Egypt. The French cars are heated only
by long cylinders of hot water laid on the floor, over which one is
constantly stumbling. Every three or four hours, with a horrible bang
and a cry of '*Attention!*' meaning 'Look out for your feet!,' new cylinders are pushed in. Fontainebleau, Melun—and at last, in the bitter cold
darkness, with passing lights making grotesque animated hieroglyphs
on the frosted windows, we entered Paris.

"Never in my life had I felt quite so miserable as when we finally
came to a halt in a cramped room under the eaves of a melancholy
little hotel. We crouched over a tiny grate in which a feeble flame
fluttered hopelessly against the freezing night air dropping from the
soot-ridden chimney. This return to Europe was a dismal awakening
from a heavenly dream.

"In the dim morning the sky seemed to rest on the very roofs
outside our single unwashed window, and Paris was hushed by the
merciless cold. I walked shivering to the Louvre [Museum], and as I
hurried toward the Egyptian Department—which of course I had never
seen—my teeth chattered until they almost re-echoed in the great halls
with their icy stone floors.

"Alas, the Egyptian Department was closed. In the shadow near
the entrance, a motionless uniformed figure stood on a small square
of wood, like a wax effigy from Madame Tussaud's. It suddenly stirred,
and informed me that the doors would not open until eleven.

"I decided to find the Conservateur of the Egyptian Antiquities.
The guard led me to a door in a remote corner, and in almost total
darkness I climbed an endless winding stone staircase until I was far
up under the eaves of the Louvre. Here in a honeycomb of tiny rooms
had once dwelt the servants, minor courtiers and infinite hangers-on
of the decadent French court, and here today, among their ghosts, was
housed most of the administration of the Musée du Louvre. In an
'office' lighted by candles and an oil lamp, I found the Conservateur

of the Egyptian Antiquities, Mons. Pierret—a dusty, musty relic of the days of the guillotine. But he was reasonable enough. In dreadful French (for he spoke no English), I explained my reasons for wanting to enter the Egyptian Department before eleven in the morning. He indulged in a few moments of official hemming and hawing, then gave me a pass permitting me the run of the place from nine o'clock onward.

"It gave me a curious feeling to move about the solitary halls of this vast old palace whose walls could recount such volumes of unwritten history. I could copy a tablet standing on a mantel upon which Napoleon had often leaned, or an inscription hanging beside a window from which this or that Louis of France was accustomed to look out upon his people.

"I worked in the Louvre for a solid week from morning till evening. I did spend an hour with Frances among the Asiatic collections, and ten minutes among the Greek marbles, to see the Venus de Milo. But I saw nothing of Paris and its environs, I learned almost nothing of the French, and moved like a mole through the wintry streets between a shabby little hotel and the Louvre. This was obviously not the way to broaden one's horizon or enrich one's cultural experience. It was, in fact, reprehensible and stupid. But I was trying desperately to make myself an Egyptologist according to a concept I had evolved alone and could not find words to impart to those around me."

"On the day before we were leaving [Paris] for England," he wrote to his father at the time, "I took the time to call upon the great Gaston [Camille Charles] Maspero. Scientifically he stands in France where Erman does in Germany. He received me cordially, talked delightfully for more than an hour about his books, his purposes, his youth and his present researches. I questioned him especially on his last book [*Les Inscriptions des Pyramides de Saqqarah*], which I had been asked to review. He told me that ever since he had begun it, when he was only eighteen years old, he had worked at almost no other subject. I began to wonder at my own brashness in having consented to review it.

"He was kind enough to ask about my own work, graciously giving me the opportunity for presenting him with a copy of my Berlin dissertation."

The instant liking which this meeting engendered between the young American plainsman and the eminent, old-school Frenchman grew into a long scientific friendship. Maspero immediately recognized the younger man's ability, and thereafter greeted with patience and magnanimity his youthful readiness to point out his senior's errors of scholarship or take issue with his scientific conclusions.

Three years in Germany had created in James a deep distrust of French scholarship, and particularly of French Orientalists. "Their methods are inclined to be slipshod," he said. "The most obvious details escape them, and they hide their distaste for the drudgery of solid research behind a façade of facile, sometimes brilliant, but too often inaccurate generalization." It astonished him that not even Maspero was free of scientific errors unworthy of his proven ability.

While there was a good deal of justice in this criticism, it was also true that James had not yet recovered from the intellectual myopia and the new-broom complex induced by the long struggle for a doctorate under German scientific discipline. He could not resist the youthful temptation to tick off, in his reviews of their books and in occasional footnotes in his own publications, what seemed to him the mistakes or the false contentions of his French contemporaries. This naturally made him many enemies in France, who accused him of having fallen completely under the influence of German scientific methodology, which they publicly derided because it failed "to see the woods for the trees," and privately despised because its meticulous, plodding, unimaginative attack was at once so reliable and so fundamentally alien to their own volatile temperament.

His views softened as the years mellowed his judgment, but with the exception of a very small group amongst whom, years later, Franz Cumont and Georges Bénédite stood pre-eminent, he never overcame his fundamental mistrust of French Orientalists. It was hardly surprising that France should have been slow to honor him. Only when he was sixty-five did the French Academy make him a corresponding member.

After Paris, the smoky gloom of London in March seemed to James and Frances supremely cheerful. The weather abated, coal was only sixpence a scuttle, and their dingy rooms in Bloomsbury near the British Museum were actually habitable. Though they were in England for the first time, they had the usual uncanny sense of having suddenly come home. The mere sound of spoken English was music, after four years among alien tongues. They roamed over London for a whole day without goal or purpose, reveling in the simple fact of being there. "I have stepped back into the world of Dickens, with its familiar streets whose names I can still hear you pronouncing as you read aloud to me when I was a boy," James wrote his father. "My most vivid memories seem to be of *Pickwick Papers* and *Master Humphrey's Clock*, and at every turning I feel I shall happen upon Sam Weller, winking at the pretty housemaid."

On their first Sunday they went to the great City Temple to hear a sermon by the almost legendary Rev. Dr. Joseph Parker; and to St. Margaret's in Westminster to hear the famous Archdeacon Frederic William Farrar. "They were among the most eminent preachers of the day," James said long afterwards, "and I listened to them with deep interest, both for what they had to say and for my own response to a calling I had abandoned in favor of the sequestered, precarious career of an Orientalist. I confidently believe that had I continued in the ministry, I could have preached as well as they. But when the services were ended, and the organ pealed somberly as I moved with the congregation back into the streets of London, I knew that I had no regrets."

Inevitably he was drawn to the Egyptian Section of the British Museum. On his first visit he "fell in with a large group of people listening to an impressive young gentleman in a silk hat and long black coat, delivering a lecture on the monuments. I fear I took a somewhat mean advantage of him by acting the part of an ordinary inquiring tourist. He made more mistakes in two minutes than I would have thought possible in a volume, and while at first I was content simply to listen to the new and astonishing facts in Egyptian history which he uttered, mischief finally got the better of me.

" 'The sarcophagus before which we are now standing,' said the young man, 'belonged to King Apries.'

" 'How is this known?' I asked.

"He flushed slightly and cleared his throat. 'Well, in the first place,' he said, pointing to a cartouche at the foot of the sarcophagus, 'here is the name of King Apries.'

" 'Oh, then your system of hieroglyphics in the British Museum is new and unusual. On the Continent and in Egypt, this King is called Amasis II.' Followed confusion in the British ranks, and a hasty retreat!

"But the young man was really not to blame: he was merely reciting what he had gleaned from the official descriptive label on the exhibit. During the next few days, I turned up innumerable similar blunders. So I went one morning to pay my respects to the Keeper, a pudgy, logy, soggy-faced gentleman named [Ernest Alfred Wallis]

Budge, whose hand when I attempted to shake it—he withdrew it half-shaken—had all the friendly warmth of a fish's tail. He gave me no greeting and stared at me morosely, finally remarking that he had 'heard of me.' I was a little nettled and asked him to accompany me for a moment.

"I showed him one of the most important monuments in the entire collection, so ridiculously labeled that it was evident those who had installed it knew nothing about it. Budge himself now showed that he was ignorant of it. With the temerity of youth, I followed it up with one similar instance after another. It was embarrassing to watch the gentleman's manner change under this barrage. He exuded attention and solicitude, pled the onerous duties of his office—the labels were old, put on before his time, etc., etc. But his own books, filled with egregious errors, belied him. The only Englishman who really knows hieroglyphic is Francis Llewelyn Griffith at University College in London. . . ."

"This was my first introduction to the great British Museum, which had always been held before me as the standard of solid reliability, a sort of scholastic Bank of England," he said thirty years later. "But its Egyptian Section, like the silk-hatted young lecturer and Budge himself, reflected the state of Egyptology in the world at this time. In the whole of Europe it numbered only a handful of *competent* followers, and even these often disagreed violently among themselves in fundamental matters of chronology, philology, archaeology and history. It lacked commonly accepted textbooks and spellings, and all the useful apparatus, the 'tools' and 'implements' of any long-established science. The creation of these, and the future of Egyptology as an accredited science, rested in the hands of a few novitiates. In America, Egyptology really did not exist at all—and here was I, proposing single-handedly to introduce it into a Middle Western community which for the most part did not even know the origin of the names Cairo, Illinois, and Memphis, Tennessee. I was blessed with ignorance of what lay before me—heartaches, derision, betrayals, battles with the bigotry of closed minds, relegation to the province of medicine men and county fair side shows. The future, as for all youth, loomed simply as an exciting adventure.

"As I wandered for the first time among the beautiful, peaceful Colleges at Oxford and Cambridge, I was less conscious of their being strongholds of a classical tradition soon to be attacked by a new humanism to which I would myself almost militantly subscribe, than

of their symbolizing the rich classical learning, the cultural opportunities and civilizing influences, the intellectual peace and security I
had read and dreamed about, but had never experienced. As I watched
the students, I wondered if they had the remotest inkling of their
enviable privilege. For here was something I had not found in
Germany. I could not define it, but it affected me deeply."

This visit in England marked the end of his student days. On March
13, 1895, he sailed with Frances to begin the "exciting adventure" of
assuming, with the humble rank of instructor, the first chair of Egyptology yet established in America.

CHAPTER IV

DURING the second half of the last century, while Chicago was expanding and ramifying like a giant octopus, there had sprung up on the ancient lake bottom immediately west and south of the town, a miscellany of scattered settlements and four-corners whose life cycle followed a typical American pattern. The four-corners would become villages, the villages suburban towns. The tentacles of the octopus would reach out and touch their fringes, then steadily engulf them until nothing remained to distinguish them from their inexorable captor save a few islands of unfrequented streets lined with old shade trees and friendly frame houses whose depressing architecture was softened but hardly redeemed by tidy lawns and flower beds.

Such an island was Englewood, some seven miles southwest of the city's business center. Like its many contemporaries, it had once lain among open fields and possessed a modest suburban identity. Its Union Station had since the beginning been a regular stop on the main lines of the New York Central, the Pennsylvania and the Rock Island railways: when the town council had granted these their rights of way, it had stipulated that in perpetuity, *all* their passenger trains must continue to stop at the Englewood Union Station.

The day would come when this dismal red brick, slate-roofed edifice, this pride of a pioneer era, with its winding ramp for horse-drawn vehicles, its marble-floored waiting room, brass spittoons and golden oak benches, would stand forlornly among freight yards and towering gas tanks, starving little factories and shoddy frame houses, a sooty monument to an identity lost in the oblivion of Chicago's ravenous and ugly growth. Yet here everything from fusty locals and milk trains to sleek ripplestreamed Limiteds would continue, though with growing impatience, to halt beneath an epitaph in gold letters on a black ground: ENGLEWOOD—Chi. 7 Mi.—New York 954 Mi.—Kan. City 510 Mi.

Month after month while James had been abroad, Charles had come and gone at this old station. He was determined that no matter

87

what it cost, his boy should have the best education to be had any-where in the world. Struggling against ill health, he had traveled his old rounds among the infinite little towns of Illinois and the surrounding Middle Western States. His catalogue cases had seemed to him to grow heavier and heavier as he carried them back and forth, almost two miles, between the station and his home—on foot, for he could not afford a carriage. He had found himself gradually succumbing to a mysterious, irresistible weakness which he had realized at last was simply old age descending upon him. Then there had come a morning in February, 1895, when he had started as usual through the snow for the station, and Harriet, watching him anxiously from the window, had seen him suddenly falter, put down his cases, and sink slowly beside them in complete collapse.

"I'm so ashamed of the old gentleman," he had murmured to her as she bent over him, "but I'm afraid he's played out, my dear!"

He lay for several critical weeks, disconsolately contemplating the implacability of the enemy which had finally defeated him. He found the strength to write cheerful letters to James, giving no hint of his plight. When he finally got on his feet again and looked at himself in the mirror, he saw a very frail old gentleman whose silver-white hair seemed now to signalize his dignified surrender to the inevitable.

"I think the time has come for you to stop traveling, Father," James had written him from Upper Egypt. "To me the dearest spot on earth is the home where you and Mother are, and at last I am daily drawing nearer to it. Though painfully small, my university salary, together with extension lectures, will keep the Englewood house going. Be sure of one thing, Father: barring enough for a suit of clothing and a few books, *everything I can earn* shall go toward running the home. What-ever comes, we stand together, and I shall have the joy of doing for you what you have so long done for me. Frances fully understands this."

Mingled with the emotions of profound gratitude and relief which welled up in Charles as he re-read these lines was the little chilling wonder whether Frances *would* fully understand. How wisely had his boy chosen? He would soon be able to see for himself.

But in the meantime, whatever the outcome, Charles knew that there was one step which in fairness to his long-time employers he *must* take. One morning without telling Harriet, he extended his customary convalescent stroll by boarding the newly completed cable-car line and riding into the city to call upon the president of his company.

The president, like everyone who knew Charles, bore him a real affection. The two men were of the old school who after twenty years of business association still called each other by their last names. When they had talked of friendly commonplaces for a time, the president said once more:

"I'm delighted to see you in such good health again, Mr. Breasted. We are greatly looking forward to your return—if you are so minded."

"It is most generous of you to say so," Charles answered. He took a letter from his pocket and gave it to the president. "I suspect you can guess its nature," he said with a wan smile. "Let me only add verbally what I could not write: I know at first-hand how bad business has been, I know that the firm has for a long time not required my services, and has continued them out of personal consideration for me and my determination to let my son complete his education. He has done this with honors, and will soon return home to his position in the University of Chicago. And now Old Dobbin will go to pasture. . . ."

Charles could not finish, but shook hands and left abruptly. The president stood for some time looking after him, then slowly opened the letter. It was in Charles's familiar neat hand and tendered his resignation, effective immediately.

Soon after James had gone abroad, Charles and Harriet had acquired by one of her characteristically involved transactions, a typical frame house on a typical street in Englewood. It was solidly built, unpretentious, contained twelve rooms, one bath, one toilet and such modern innovations as gas light and a hot-air furnace.

It embodied the usual ugly structural and decorative conventions of Victorian America. The front and back parlors, embellished on one side with high stained-glass windows, and separated by sliding doors, were lugubriously twilit even on the brightest days. Upon the walls hung large reproductions of several of Gustave Doré's illustrations for *Paradise Lost*; a picture of terror-struck stallions on the eve of a storm; and an array of pale sepia photographs of the family in their more proprietary Rockford days. The front stairs debouched in a crescendo of radiating golden oak fretwork which reached its climax in the entrance to the front parlor, a room reserved for Sunday use. The front door contained more leaded panels of stained glass through which to

anyone answering the doorbell, visitors appeared to be suffering from
a combination of the spotted plague and a sudden attack of St. Vitus's
Dance. The somber black walnut furniture, the hardware and the gas
light epitomized the knobs, cubes, beading, cornices, urns, swirls,
plush and antimacassars for which this period was so unhappily distinguished. A curious mustiness pervaded this humbler though no less
hospitable successor to the old mansion on The Hill at Rockford—the
subtle melancholy of slow disintegration, of departed heyday and
vanished prosperity.

Frances had written her mother from Egypt: "I rather dread going
to that strange house in Englewood, to be scrutinized and later discussed and appraised behind closed doors. I pray they will be kind to
me."

All her life afterwards she remembered the look in the faces of
Charles and Harriet and Aunt Theodocia as they stood, clad in their
Sunday best, on the familiar station platform that April morning when
she and James arrived at Englewood. It was the look of truly good,
selfless people, careworn and weary, upon whom Heaven had suddenly
opened its portals in a flood of such ineffable beauty and light that
their eyes glistened with tears of inarticulate happiness.

The old ladies took Frances in their arms and kissed her, then
Charles took both her hands in his and said, quite unsteadily, "We
are so happy and proud at having a new daughter—" and he too kissed
her. During the tearfully cheerful confusion that ensued, James finally
ushered everyone into the surrey which Charles had rented and was
driving himself for this triumphal occasion. The emotional tension
which for the moment had left everyone tongue-tied, quickly gave
way to general volubility, while the stable-fragrant vehicle jolted down
the station ramp and toward the house Frances had anticipated with
"dread."

As the carriage drew up in front of the house, and James jumped
out and hitched the horse to a ring held in the outstretched hand of a
little negro boy made of cast iron, neighbors stood on their front stoops
to watch the party's arrival. Soon they called in person to shake hands,
and to leave little tokens of cordial welcome—greetings, potted plants
and flowers, home-baked cakes, glasses of home-made preserves.
Everyone was so eager to welcome Frances, and the family was so
determined she should be happy, that her fears soon vanished.

Charles and Harriet had become so accustomed to disappointment and misfortune that for some time after James's return they were half-afraid lest their years of wishful thinking had merely conjured up his image, and that his corporeal self might still be residing in some remote place across the water. They felt lost and vaguely neglectful at the cessation of their Sunday letters to him, and of his to them. But there was no mistaking the physical reality of his presence. The house was ringing with his voice and newly alive with his laughter.

Frances was filled with wonder at the happiness James brought to those about him. "It is a joy to see Charles and Mother Breasted and Aunt Theodocia," she wrote her mother. "They are simply radiant as they watch James. I marvel that he is not completely spoiled, they worship him so—Aunt Theodocia follows him about like a shadow. But he is such a sweet-tempered, good person, it is easy to understand their adoration, which I share. Of evenings he plays the flute while I accompany him, and the old people simply beam with happiness. James is their world and their Heaven all in one. They might well be a little jealous of me, but were I their own daughter, they could not be kinder or more loving."

Charles said to Aunt Theodocia: "Jim is like a summer day full of sunlight after a shower, with a southwest wind blowing white clouds across a blue sky, and raindrops out of wet trees. If the dear Lord will only grant me a year in my Boy's company, I shall be ready to depart this life."

The Lord granted Charles his wish, and the cup of his happiness overflowed. He spent the long summer days in his beloved garden, and when James came bicycling home in the late afternoon from his new duties at the University, Charles would be busy with watering can and hose, filling the air with the cool smell of drenched lawns, wet loam, and of old-fashioned flowers glistening in the setting sun. The sounds of children playing, lawns being mowed, neighbors talking at open windows, and far-off train engines tolling and chuffing and whistling only deepened the peace of the garden as Charles would show James what he had done that day.

They went together that August on private expeditions to visit "The Pines" at Downers Grove; and to Rockford to see Aunt Theodocia whose waning strength confined her more and more to "Pleasant Nook." (She smiled as she observed their eyes noting how badly the house needed paint and the roof new shingles. "Their raggedness," she said, "is but a token of the joy my Boy's Berlin degree has brought me!")

Almost before they knew it, the idyllic summer was gone, the air had become hazy and pungent with burning leaves, then still and cold, and filled with falling white feathers which whispered among the withered stalks and uncouth sleeping shapes of Charles's garden. As he peered at it through frosted windows one gray and shadowless afternoon, he said to Harriet, "When the old gentleman's gone, Hattie dear, don't neglect the garden. He'll bless you from every blossom and chide you from every weed!"

"James is so devoted to children," Frances had written her mother in April, "that I think he would be very pleased some day to have a child of his own. But we both realize how happy and carefree we now are, and we do not want that added responsibility for a long while to come. So you need have no worry about me."

But this Victorian era had not yet wholly subjugated Nature, and her self-assurance was considerably shaken when Frances discovered in January that she was with child. When at last she told James, he seemed highly pleased, yet with just a little of the same genial detachment and masculine un-understanding he might have shown had she told him of a new dress she had bought. But Harriet was overjoyed and full of homely advice, while Charles was jubilant, though with a trace of wistfulness.

James had always been slow to apprehend the physical indisposition of those about him, but he now had good cause for appearing somewhat distrait. He had begun the long, slogging ordeal by which any academic career was either made or broken. A young instructor's advancement depended upon his physical and intellectual endurance, his ability simultaneously to teach classes, serve as office boy to his older colleagues, supplement his minute salary with outside income from writing and lectures, and above all, to carry on and publish significant researches in his special field. James overflowed with enthusiasm, and his whole being responded to the challenge confronting him. "Harper is full of plans for me, and I myself have enough schemes for twenty men," he wrote. "If *only* I can *earn* enough to care for all those who now depend on me—!"

The University of Chicago at this time consisted of President Harper's magnificent paper plans, a small but extraordinary faculty, and a few new, austerely Gothic buildings standing in irrelevant detachment among the marshy, willow-bushed terrain which had bordered "The Midway" of the first Chicago World's Fair. In two rooms on the fourth floor under the roof of one of these courageous structures called Cobb Hall, was housed the Department of Semitic Languages. "There was not even space for filing the photographs, much less for displaying the antiquities I had brought back from Egypt," James wrote. "These had to be stored among the jumble of mineralogical samples in the basement of the Geology Building." Amid the hurly-burly and travail of a great university's birth Egyptology was a supernumerary item of antiquarian bric-a-brac to be laid aside until the rest of the house was in order.

President Harper was then working 18-hour days, bidding against old-established institutions with their great endowments and usually higher salaries, for the services of the country's ablest men of science and letters; and cajoling Chicago's wealthier citizens into matching, usually on a 4-to-6 basis, funds provisionally pledged to the University by John D. Rockefeller. The pressure under which he labored and which in the beginning had been merely self-imposed, had gradually increased as he became more and more the victim of the awesome and irresistible genie he had created. For with supreme confidence in the invincibility of his vision, he had committed himself to appointments, buildings, equipment, unprecedented curricula and researches for which the money was not yet in hand. In the midst of all this he was lecturing, preaching, writing, rushing to conferences at a hundred points in the United States, and periodically to Europe; and, as James charitably understated it many years later, making "heroic efforts both to conduct the administration of the great new University, . . . serve as the administrative head of the Department of Semitic Languages, [and] . . . as a professor in that Department. . . . It was, of course, quite impossible for one man single-handed to carry all these responsibilities. . . . Though President Harper was indefatigable in his efforts to promote research, a Department of Semitic Languages with insufficient books, with no original monuments of any kind, and with no building, was necessarily very limited in research activities." *

The lack of a building was unexpectedly remedied when in the late spring of 1894, a generous widowed lady named Mrs. Caroline E. Haskell, desiring to commemorate her late husband Frederick, had "arranged to give [to the University] one hundred thousand dollars for building the Haskell Oriental Museum." † The cornerstone of this

* *The Oriental Institute,* by James H. Breasted, p. 27.
† *A History of the University of Chicago,* by T. W. Goodspeed, p. 297 ff.

edifice, which with its ponderous buttresses and graceless embellishments suggested a mésalliance between a bastard Norman chapel and a Germanic mausoleum, was laid on July 1, 1895. An inscription had been cut into each of the three exposed sides of the cornerstone. The first was in Greek and read, "He was the true light that, coming into the world, enlighteneth every man." The next was in Latin, reading, "Light out of the East"; and the third, in Hebrew read, "The entrance of thy words giveth light." The tenor of the principal address of the occasion, delivered by the Reverend Dr. John Henry Barrows, Mrs. Haskell's pastor, who was doubtless affected by the foregoing pervasive effulgence can be deduced from the following excerpts:

"I deem this a golden day," he said, "in the history, not only of the University of Chicago, but also of the University life of America. This, I believe, is one of the first buildings dedicated exclusively to oriental studies, those studies from which so much spiritual and intellectual light has come to mankind, and from which so much illumination is still further expected. . . .

"A century hence the Haskell Oriental Museum . . . will be surrounded by groups of academic buildings that shall repeat many of the glories so dear to Oxford. Two hundred years hence this University may be the crown of the world's metropolis. . . . We are pioneers of an immeasurable future, and the cornerstone that is laid today is a milestone in human progress. . . . All blessings on the generous benefactress whose gracious hand lifts this splendid structure toward the sky! All hail to the glorious and imperial future, rich with increasing spoils of learning and the multiplied triumphs of faith of which the Oriental Museum is a sure and golden prophecy." *

In accepting "the keys of Haskell Oriental Museum" at the dedicatory exercises one year later, President Harper concluded by saying that "I promise, on behalf of the University, that the building shall be sacredly set apart for the purpose indicated." † The purpose indicated was to include only a museum and the Departments of Comparative Religion and Semitic Languages. But to these was added the University's Baptist Divinity School, which from the moment the building was opened, and for thirty years afterward, absorbed so much room that the designation of "museum" could only be applied by courtesy to the small space so used.

* *A History of the University of Chicago,* by T. W. Goodspeed, pp. 298–299.
† *Ibid.,* p. 300.

James's keen disappointment at this was hardly alleviated by the title of "Assistant Director of Haskell Oriental Museum" (the Director was Robert Francis Harper), which sounded impressive enough to those unaware that he now presided over a few plaster-cast reproductions, and a small group of exhibition cases containing the little collection of antiquities he had brought back from Egypt.

When the antiquities dealers in America, notably the orientals among them, learned of James's museum appointment in an institution at the time largely supported by John D. Rockefeller, they besieged him with offers of collections and items of every description, at quotations usually based on the assumption that Mr. Rockefeller would be the vicarious purchaser, and that James would tacitly pocket a commission. Typical of these was the following letter from one Azeez Khayat, "Antiquarian from Tyre, Palestine," with a shop then on Sixth Avenue, New York:

"Dear Sir: Besides that my prices are the best and my prices are the lowest and this you will know by examination: for preferring to secure my collection I will be glad to offer you a commission of 25/100 this will be understood between you and me only and would be kept in secret. If I sell for $2,500 you keep $500 and send me $2,000 and in answer I will acknowledge the receipt of $2,500. By this way I sold to many museums."

In showing such letters to President Harper, James would remind him that his salary was still $66.66 per month. But his chances for an early increase were almost hopeless. The President was doing an unparalleled job of educational development, at a cost of what seemed to his Trustees appalling annual deficits. He was fundamentally a kind man who knew that to gain his larger objective he must be ruthless. "Have patience, Breasted," he wrote, "your time will come!"

But patience alone would not repay James's debts to Charles and Aunt Theodocia, or buy scientific books, or pay grocers' bills. He turned inevitably, even desperately, to university extension lecturing. He possessed a rich vocabulary, a handsome and dignified presence, and a dramatic—almost melodramatic—sense of presentation. In the history of the United States, their people had never been as ravenous as now for lectures on every subject under the sun, and James was much in demand. To the lectures he had written during his first Nile journey, he added many others. His facile memory quickly learned them all by heart, and his reputation as a lecturer was soon widely established.

While this deepened the resentment of Robert Francis Harper, who accused him of neglecting his University duties, it gratified the President, to whom it offered another excuse for temporizing in the matter of a salary increase. "You are fortunate, Breasted," he said comfortingly, "to have the opportunity for simultaneously buttering your bread and dispensing light regarding a little-known field!"

The University's faculty during the next few years was crowded with young men whom Harper had discovered and groomed in anticipation of their possible appointment to the new University of Chicago. Like James, they now struggled to reconcile their scientific hopes and dreams to the grim economic realities of the moment.

Life was perhaps a little less arduous for the men in the natural sciences because the latter, as James later expressed it, "required neither justification nor defense, whereas Egyptology was then commonly regarded by the public and the press as something bizarre, an oddity at a county fair, a fakir's imposition upon general credulity. I lectured in every part of the country, before every conceivable type of audience, in every imaginable sort of auditorium, primarily out of sheer necessity for earning money for food and clothing, but always with the realization that I must dispel a thousand superstitions and misapprehensions about antiquity in general and Egypt in particular. Often I traveled several hundred miles to earn twenty-five dollars and expenses, and only after years of barnstorming was this gradually increased to what was known among University Extension lecturers as 'F.A.M.E.'—'fifty and my expenses'! I was young and vigorous enough to derive a sense of exhilaration and inspiration from learning to know at first hand the face and the mind of my own people. More than ever I was consumed with the desire to devote my life to serving my countrymen by bringing to this New World the intangible riches and the lost beauties of the ancient past.

"But I was also trying to continue scientific researches, write books based upon them, keep abreast of my own field and in touch with my European colleagues, and teach University classes. It was not long before I realized that I was caught in a hopeless economic treadmill. The waves of depression which almost engulfed me were deepened by chronic enteric trouble and the loneliness of one-night stands in provincial towns. I began to understand as never before what my father had patiently borne for almost twenty years; and with my whole soul, like a man on the brink of intellectual extinction, I resolved to achieve freedom for myself and those dependent upon me. I determined at all costs to return to Europe for further scientific work, and I was even so bold as to hope that I might earn enough to take my parents with me."

In the spring of '96, when Charles began once again to cultivate his garden, he moved with a much slower step, and as his fingers touched the freshly thawed earth he loved so well, he seemed to feel its chill creep through his whole body. The days grew mild and balmly, but not even the warmest sun could dispel the strange cold numbness deep within him. He tired quickly, and sat quite still for long periods at a time, with a faint half-wistful, half-mischievous smile lighting his face, which wore a look of quiet expectancy. In the evenings, he talked happily to James of old times, of all the fascinating things they would see and do together in Europe, and of his imminent new grandchild. "If it's a boy," he said musingly, "perhaps we could call him Charles, after our little boy who left us," quite forgetting for the moment that the little boy had been named after himself.

With each passing day he seemed to grow wearier, until there came a morning late in June when he said apologetically to Harriet that the old gentleman felt too tired to leave his bed. A hush fell over the house, everyone tiptoed on the stairs, and even the children instinctively spoke in whispers. At last in the stillness of a hot midnight late in July, with Harriet and James holding his icy hands, Charles murmured something about "being so grateful to the dear Lord for this year with my Boy," and about "taking care of Harriet, and not overworking at the University—" and then slipped peacefully away.

While Frances remained at home and wept as her own father's death had never moved her to do, James and Harriet and feeble Aunt Theodocia buried him in the family plot at Rockford, overlooking the river.

On the evening of the thirteenth day of the following September, while Harriet stood by to comfort her and to assist the doctor, whose behavior seemed curiously unsteady, Frances lay in labor with her first child. The sound of her moaning reached James as he wandered through the house in a state of griping, helpless anxiety, and of remorse at the realization that he had been too preoccupied and unhelpful during these last difficult months.

Two hours passed, the moaning ceased, and the faint odor of chloroform drifted down from the upper hall. The tension became unbearable and James climbed the stairs, three steps at a time, and stood listening at the door of the room. The smell of chloroform was stronger now. The bathroom across the hall was cluttered with medical oddments hastily set down, and the jagged hissing flame of the gas jet was turned on full force. He stood for an unmeasurable time, waiting and listening. Suddenly there was a cry, the cry of a newborn child, and then silence. . . .

He could not remember, afterwards, just when he had become aware, first of the doctor saying thickly, "a pity, such a fine baby," and after he had gone, of Harriet putting her arms about him and resting her head against his breast; and finally, of Frances making no sound while her closed eyes ran with tears which wet his face as he knelt beside her.

It had been a boy, strong and perfectly formed. But the doctor had been intoxicated and in haste to reach another patient, and the child, which Frances never saw, died mysteriously a few moments after it was born.

"Don't pity me, my dear, 'tis not so very lonely," Aunt Theodocia had written James in the spring of his last year in Germany. "Very often, like Joan of Arc, I hear 'voices,' sometimes coming from the dear ones that are still on this side of Jordan, sometimes from those who have joined the innumerable host beyond. So you see, I have the very best of company—and I ought to improve, oughtn't I?"

The knowledge that she was helping James to win his doctor's degree, and the sense of participation in his life which she had gained from his letters, had enabled her to face with courage and equanimity the lonely evening of her life. It had required all the adroitness and wisdom she possessed to guide their relationship safely through these years of impetuous romantic entanglements toward the inevitable day when marriage would finally take him from her. She had seen enough of Frances to know that he had married a *good* woman: beyond this she preferred not to explore, for people, as she put it, were so often like Pandora's box.

She had tried to school herself to face philosophically the ironical fact that when four thousand miles of land and ocean had separated her from James, their relationship had been closer than it could ever be again when he returned to America with his bride and became absorbed in his career at the University, only a hundred miles from Rockford. The excitement of his homecoming, the wonder and comfort of his physical presence had sustained her during the precious weeks she had lingered in the Englewood house. Again and again she had slipped quietly into his little study, and while he pored over his books, she had lain on a couch and feasted her eyes upon him, striving to re-create within herself a breathing, sentient image which would abide with her through what remained of her now purposeless life. For she knew that she could not follow him into the world she had helped him to attain, and that henceforth she would seldom see him.

But the death of Charles, the onslaught of age upon her bodily strength, the consciousness of being a desolate old woman in an empty, lonely house had together so tried her spiritual fortitude that at last she turned to James in a gentle plea for help. "I wish I could look into your brown eyes," she wrote in a faltering, barely legible hand. "Please do not be hurt if I tell you that I miss from your letters the old-time tenderness so dear to my old heart. If you still have it, please give expression to it. I need it. I know I cannot see you often, but I want your heart to touch mine—always."

James was greatly moved by her appeal, which he answered from a full heart. But as he learned too late, his letter never reached her. For there had settled upon "Pleasant Nook," like vultures sensing prey, a pair of unctuous indigents from Texas named James Hervey and Hannah Bemis. Mrs. Bemis, a niece, was a sanctimonious and adhesive lady with executive capacities and broad sympathies which were singularly susceptible to the prospect of material gain. Her interest in her Aunt Theodocia's welfare dated from the receipt of news that she appeared to be entering her last illness. By the well-known expedient of peaceful penetration, Mrs. Bemis quietly took over the house, installed nurses of her own selection, controlled Aunt Theodocia's correspondence and even dictated the disposition of her estate.

Aunt Theodocia wilted rapidly under the leech-like ministrations of Mr. and Mrs. Bemis, who saw to it that for one inspired reason or another, none of her family was permitted to see her. The end finally drew near, and as they contemplated their work and saw that it had been good, they expressed their confident satisfaction by graciously permitting Harriet to stand beside Aunt Theodocia's bed at midnight of January 7, 1897, as she almost imperceptibly "joined the innumerable host" of her loved ones beyond Jordan.

In *The Rockford Register-Gazette* of January 30, 1897, appeared the following story:

"The will of the late Mrs. Theodocia Backus . . . was a surprise to

her many friends in Rockford. It had been the general impression
that the bulk of the property, including the homestead ['Pleasant
Nook'], would go to Prof. James H. Breasted of Chicago University.
. . . All the wills made by Mrs. Backus up to and including one made
last September, verified this. . . .

". . . The will admitted to probate was signed . . . about a week
before her death, the signature manifesting total physical collapse. By
this will the entire estate, . . . aside from mementos of associational
value, passed to the nieces and nephews of Mrs. Backus.

"One of the [principal] heirs, Mrs. Hannah Bemis of Texas, attended
Mrs. Backus the last five months of the latter's illness. Mrs. Bemis is
a very amiable lady. Among the many inestimable services to her aunt,
must be included the mechanical execution, if not the actual composition, of the will. . . .

"Although Mr. Bemis has compromised with his creditors a number
of times, in all his vicissitudes . . . he ever exhibited a commendable
fortitude. Mr. and Mrs. Bemis are to be congratulated on this testa-
mentary accession to their fortune."

James was both stunned at this ironical finale of a cherished relationship and shocked at his first direct encounter with the kind of
conniving depravity which had hitherto existed for him only in newspapers and novels. But what filled him with a sadness which time
never wholly dispelled was the fact that Charles and Aunt Theodocia
could not have lived to receive the interest on their human investment.
With a heavy heart he turned again to his work and to the complications of the somewhat volcanic family of which he had now become the
head.

The loss of her child had aggravated in Frances a tendency to
extreme nervousness, to moodiness, and to unpredictable outbursts of
querulous condemnation of those about her, followed always by fits of
abject self-deprecation and remorse.

Without household duties to occupy her, she had tried to find solace
in music and books. But in the end this had only saddened her and set
her to brooding. She yearned for old Charles, who had always had a
knack of keeping the family peace, and had filled the long hours of
James's absence with his kindly, endearing companionship. He had
given her a sense of usefulness by asking her to help him as he worked
in his garden or mended something in the house. Now that he was
gone, her black moods seized her more frequently and fiercely, until

they affected the whole household, and James would come home to find the air tense with anger, Frances locked in her room, and no one speaking to anyone.

He realized that if their marriage was to survive, not even the pinching, hounding need for economy must any longer keep him from giving her a home of her own, however small. So in the winter of that sorrowful year, he moved her into rented rooms on the top floor of a frame house near the University. The stairs were steep and in the heat of the withering summer which followed, the rooms under the roof became almost unendurable. But she was unmindful of any hardship, and a great calm rested momentarily upon her. For she was again with child.

On the night of September 13, 1897, a year to the day after the birth and death of her first child, I was born—if not, strictly speaking, in a trunk, at least as inevitably into the academic life as some children are born to the circus or the stage. And as might have been expected, I was called Charles.

CHAPTER V

DURING the year which had witnessed so many trials James had begun one of his most ambitious scientific tasks.

"In all the American universities at this time," he wrote in after years, "the study of the oriental languages was considered an end in itself instead of an incidental aid in the investigation of the ancient orient. I was filled with dread at the possibility of becoming a tuppenny, dry-as-dust teacher dispensing a smattering of oriental linguistics and philology.

"My salvation came in 1899 in the form of an invitation from the Royal Academy in Berlin to copy the Egyptian inscriptions of Europe for the Kaiser's great Egyptian Dictionary. The appointment carried with it living expenses but no salary, and my acceptance was made possible solely by the fact that I had gone barnstorming among the women's clubs and university extension lecture centers of America until I had saved enough money outside of my minute salary to enable me to return to Europe to associate with the men with whom I had studied, and to show them that at least I had not been standing quite still.

"In 1896 I had definitely launched upon one of the most arduous undertakings of my life, the plan for which had been steadily growing in my mind since my Berlin student days. I began the task of collecting all the historical sources of ancient Egypt, from earliest times to the Persian conquest, wherever they existed in the world; of translating them into English; and of creating thereby for the first time a solid foundation of documentary source material for the production of a modern history of ancient Egypt.

"To accomplish this was to involve copying the original texts both in Egypt and all the museums and private collections in Europe and America. The entire work occupied ten years, and the translations alone—not counting the copies of the original documents—filled ten thousand pages of manuscript."

The same Providence which was to protect us again and again in years to come, watched over us when in August, 1899—exactly eight

years after my father's first trip abroad—we sailed for Europe on the
steamship *Patria*. We had with us all his scientific manuscripts and
notes, and his working library of scientific books filled with his
marginal commentaries and emendations. On her next voyage the
Patria caught fire in the North Sea and sank with her entire cargo and
a heavy loss of life. We might have survived, but the labor of years
would have perished.

Now began a strange Odyssey in quest of every extant fragment of
Egyptian history. When my father had taken photographs and made
pen-and-ink copies of every ancient Egyptian relic in Europe bearing
so much as a lone hieroglyph of historical import, we scoured the
Mediterranean and Aegean world, and traveled southeastward to
Egypt and the northern Sudan, where he copied and photographed
every historical inscription along the Nile valley between Aswan and
Khartoum.

For years we lived as scholar gypsies in an unending succession of
dreary, grubby little hotels and *pensions,* in furnished rooms and apartments, in villas and inns and chalets, in tents and houseboats, trains
and ships—always with the same objective: to ferret out the history of
ancient Egypt. We were terribly poor. My parents skimped and denied
themselves in a thousand ways, often going hungry that I might be
properly clothed and fed (for years they habitually ordered only two
portions of food at the back-street restaurants we frequented, gave one
portion to me and divided the other between themselves). We crossed
and recrossed the Atlantic—seven times before I was five—and our
only home was under the roof currently sheltering our trunks and my
father's travel-scarred box of scientific books and the gray canvas-
covered telescopic case filled with his growing manuscripts. We belonged to a nomadic host of scholars and little academic families of
every creed and description from every civilized corner of the world,
who were enduring the extremes of economy and self-sacrifice in order
to pursue the particular segment of research, the scientific grail to
which their lives were literally consecrated.

The ubiquitous existence we led was possible only because life in
Europe, especially in Germany, was so very cheap. Even in Berlin, the
most expensive German city, a furnished four-room apartment, including kitchen and toilet but no bathroom, a convenience then usually
found only in private houses, could be had for seventy-five marks, or
twenty dollars per month. The wages of a *Dienstmaedchen* (maid-of-

all-work) were thirty-six dollars to forty dollars *per year*, while food and clothing were cheaper than in the country districts of America. At the same time, the incomes of most professional men, and the salaries of university professors in Germany, were by American standards inhumanly low. The average salary of most of the younger professors in universities like Göttingen, Leipzig, Heidelberg, Dresden, Rostock, Strassburg and others, were about $150 *per year!*

"Those of us who lived and traveled in pre-war [pre-1914] days," remarked James Truslow Adams in his review * of Clarence K. Streit's *Union Now*, "look back as to a golden age to the time when we went all over Europe—except Russia—with no passports, with stable currencies, and felt what we shall never regain: the sense of being a citizen of a larger world than merely our own nation." Whether or not it was a golden age, I know that the privations and inconveniences we then shared together as a family drew us closer to one another and to an approximation of happiness than did the comparative comfort and plenty of later American years.

The years of matching mind against mind which had passed since my father first landed in Europe, had taught him much about the fallibility of Old World scholarship. It no longer loomed as awesomely as in the beginning. But more than ever before, the experience of living in its midst and of pursuing pure research, was to him a high and exciting adventure—an adventure in the exploration of that vast river, the history of the ancient orient, which so long ago had mysteriously vanished beneath the Classical World.

"Behind all this preliminary work looms my history of Egypt," he wrote to his mother in the summer of 1900. "But before I write a history based on the original monuments, I intend to find out, to the last jot and tittle, *what the monuments say*. This is what the other fellows have not yet done. It is taking me years, but before I am forty, I propose to make myself the leading authority on Egyptian history. Had I been willing to compile a history out of the *books of Germans*, I could have finished it in six months. But I ask no odds of anyone, taking nothing second-hand from any middle man. I hope you will not think I am boasting: I have just been revaccinated, and perhaps this outburst is due to the virus!"

I was hardly aware that these years of my childhood were either lonely or in any way unusual. What few playmates I had were the

* *The New York Sunday Times*, Feb. 19, 1939, Sec. 6, p. 1.

children of my father's colleagues or the fleeting casuals one met on ships, or in public parks and squares under the baleful eyes of chattering English and French and Prussian governesses.

It was my bitter misfortune to have been born with pale gold, curly hair which my mother took great pride in training into long curls reaching halfway down my back. To add to this crown of thorns, which I wore until my fifth birthday when my hair was bobbed Prince-John-style, she dressed me in European sailor suits and hats. As long as we lived abroad, these afflictions passed unnoticed. But the moment we again set foot in America, every schoolboy and alley-rover who spied me—even little girls—would stop and stare at me with incredulous and mounting disgust which the young ladies vented upon me by jeeringly repeating the most contemptuous and humiliating epithet in their vocabularies, "SISSY! SISSY! SISSY!"; and the boys, by thrashing me, smearing my insufferable head in the mud, and sending me on my way with tears of anger and pain welling from my blackened eyes, while gore dripped from my battered nose onto my unendurable sailor suit. I derived little comfort from my mother's sympathetic indignation, or from my father's logical suggestion that I must learn to defend myself.

It was a childhood filled with the sunless days, the eternal rain and earthy smell of northern European winters; the clip-clopping on wet pavements of passing carriages whose fluid reflections moved at night across high ceilings; the odors of ships' corridors, and the creaking of their wooden cabins in Atlantic and Mediterranean storms; the shrill hysteria of Continental train whistles, and the bleat of the old side-wheeler ferries in New York Harbor; the spring fragrance of the Bois de Boulogne, of German forests and lilac-filled city squares, of English meadows, Tyrolean vineyards and Swiss orchards, of violets among Italian olive groves; the minor chant of pedlars drifting down into quiet oriental gardens from beyond tawny, flat-roofed houses and dusty palms stark against sapphire emptiness; the smell of burning autumn leaves in America, of roasting chestnuts in the towns of France, and the exotic scent of spice-filled coffee and strange commodities in the sun-slatted twilight of Eastern bazaars.

My recollections of that vanished world are steeped in the music of all the great classical composers, the melodies of old folk songs and the notes of my father's flute. For wherever we remained long enough, my mother would draw upon her small inheritance to rent a piano, at which she would practice as much as six hours a day. Her fingers were still nimble and charged with a fiery strength, but she played—as I

listen now in memory—with the passionate, almost desperate intensity
of one who already foresensed the inevitable slowing of their limpid
facility. The keys they caressed with such lyric gentleness or struck
into sweeping torrents of storming chords were the only ones capable
of opening, at least in part, the gates of the high-walled, shadowy garden of her self-imprisoned soul. There were times when she suddenly
stopped in the midst of some *molto espressivo* or *con amore* passage,
and I would open the door a crack, and see that her head was resting
upon her arms against the music rack, and that she was sobbing
bitterly. . . .

Of evenings, after I had had my supper, she would often accompany my father while he played the flute during a few precious
moments stolen from his desk. Through some friendly connection, he
had been able to secure for a trifling sum occasional lessons from
Emil Prill, *Kapellmeister* to Kaiser William II, a charming man who
was regarded in Germany as the greatest flutist of his day. I remember
vaguely that his life was filled with tragic bereavements, and that his
several children had died. One memorable day when my father took
me to call upon him, Herr Prill gave me an armful of their toys. My
father remonstrated, but he pushed them into my hands, saying, "Take
them, my little Karl!—my children dwell in you and in all childhood.
They will rejoice as I do in your happiness at what was theirs."

When we were not actually traveling, I usually saw my father only
from five o'clock until six on weekday evenings, and for a few hours
on Sundays. My whole day focused upon these gay, uninhibited
moments with him, which in every possible way I tried to inveigle him
into lengthening. I used to make miniature stages of cardboard boxes,
and with little Tyrolean carved wooden figures, and toy villages from
Berchtesgaden, I would set up for his edification tableaux depicting
scenes from the tales of Hans Christian Andersen, the Brothers Grimm
and the whole medley of Continental folk-lore and mythology I had
absorbed. But he was usually less amused by these creations than by
spur-of-the-moment games with my few toys, and by romps which left
me weak from the utterly abandoned laughter of childhood. To quiet
me, he would draw upon his inexhaustible fund of stories about the
Tailor Who Hadn't Enough Money To Buy Cloth For His Business,
and the Adventures which befell him when he closed his Shop, and
with a bundle on a stick over his shoulder went forth into the World.

Yet again and again during these times together, his eyes would
take on a faraway look, and he would seem to have forgotten my

presence entirely. This gave me always the same leaden sense of desolation as when I thought that in some crowded shop or station I had lost my parents. I would shake his arm or pull at his lapels until he rediscovered me. Then, when I had asked him accusingly where he had been, he would always answer, "Ich war in Nubien, mein Kind!" ("I was in Nubia, my child!"). It was a magic country, he said, to which he would one day take me: I could dig there in almost any spot and uncover the most fascinating treasures. This was enormously enticing— but even then I already vaguely understood that my mother and I shared his affections with this strange rival called Nubia; and I would fall asleep to the muffled thumping of his Hammond typewriter in the next room, as he resumed his incessant labors upon the manuscript which dictated the whole pattern of our lives.

We possessed few clothes and personal effects, but the quantity of our luggage was astounding. For though my mother spent most of her life in travel, she never learned the art of it, and was always obsessed by the fear that some emergency might befall us for which she had not prepared. She had a strange dread of insufficiency, whether of Castile soap, darning wool, hair curlers, dental floss, umbrellas, camels' hair blankets, hot water bottles, homeopathic remedies, or a hundred other sundries. As a consequence our luggage, which could easily have accommodated a small French traveling circus, suggested a cross between a private nursing home and the "notions" counter of an old-fashioned country department store.

Though I must have been less than four years old at the time, I can vividly recall my mother's triumphant satisfaction when she acquired a collapsible rubber-and-checked-cloth bathtub manufactured in England. It was a circular affair with vertically ribbed sides about one foot high, and when folded in its case, was no larger than a small pillow. At best it afforded only a "sponge bath," but the fact that it was portable, and that one could either stand or sit in it as one chose, was obviously a tremendous improvement over the still prevailing tin or zinc *Sitzbad.*

My father's baptism of this new contrivance revealed him to me for the first time as a fallible being whom sufficient force of adverse circumstance could actually topple from the grace of impeccable conduct. On that memorable occasion the room was filled with the warm, damp smell of "Lanolin" soap and new rubber, as he luxuriously scrubbed and splashed behind a screen, all the while humming random snatches from *Parsifal*. Finally he dried himself, donned his Yaeger robe and slippers, then grasped the sides of the tub and lifted it carefully toward the large waste jar. Suddenly one side of the sloshing thing began to slip from control. In his effort to ward off disaster he trod upon the soap, knocked over the screen, dropped the tub and fell face downward into the flood of slithering gray water.

As he lay for a shocked moment prone and inert amidst the rapidly spreading inundation my mother's sense of humor rushed to her tongue. " 'Save me, O God,' " she quoted with fair accuracy, " 'for the waters are come in unto my soul. I sink in deep mire, where there is no standing: I am come into deep waters where the floods overflow me.' "

"*Damn* the *damnable* thing!" bellowed my father.

Perhaps it was their context, or perhaps the fact that they were the first "swear words" he had ever uttered in my presence, which indelibly impressed them upon my memory.

It is interesting to me now to discern that while I was thus growing up in a world which was often confusing but seldom dull, my father was maturing and mellowing, and laying the solid foundations of his career. Each visit to another Continental seat of learning, each scientific congress or meeting he attended, added new names to the widening circle of what were to remain his lifelong acquaintanceships and friendships among the scholars of Europe. He began to acquire during these years a modicum of that fragile by-product of indefatigable labor and sound original research known as scientific prestige.

The Egyptian Dictionary Commission asked him in the autumn of 1899 to begin the copying of all the ancient Egyptian monuments in Italy, and his first visit to that country stirred him deeply. "The culture of this classic world is making a tremendous impression upon me, such as I had not thought possible," he wrote after a morning in the Museum of the Diocletian Baths at Rome. "It is a long lacking chapter in my education, and I am absorbing it like a famished man. A thousand wonders have made the ancient Roman world live for me as it never did before, but none of them more vividly than have the silent streets of Pompeii.

"I have looked into the courts and shops of houses where matrons sat and watched their children romping precisely as they do in every Italian town today. I have seen a bakery where the flour mills stand exactly as they were left, and have peered into the ovens from which modern excavators have removed the loaves that were overdone nineteen hundred years ago when the bakers fled before the deadly volcanic rain. I have passed along stone-paved streets deeply rutted by ancient chariot and wagon wheels, and have read upon the walls the painted posters of candidates for city offices, for which the elections were never held. I have wandered through charming villas whose colonnaded patios and flower-filled gardens embellished with bronze and marble sculptures brought or copied from Greece, smile again in the sunshine and resound once more to fountains whose water is drawn from ancient leaden pipes exactly like our plumbing of today, and all in perfect preservation. I have felt by turns awed and amazed and humbled by the practical and cultural contemporaneity of an unimportant provincial Roman town."

It was an arduous year of frequent migrations and hampering poverty. "The Italian railways are hideous—they check no baggage free, hence everyone carries at least one trunk with him into the *coupé*. When the luggage racks are full and the seats already contain twice the humanity they were designed to hold, you can imagine what fun it is to have a porter dump your possessions into this vermin-ridden melange of crying, dirt-smeared children, garlic-reeking men who spit all over whatever portions of the floor remain exposed, and smoke foul tobacco whether you are in a 'smoker' or not; and peasant women who are usually not only nursing their latest born with unabashed candor, but who continually test their own lactivity by squeezing their udders with complete indifference to the effect of the resulting parabolic jet upon the immobilized victims sitting opposite!

"I could work much faster when photographing the museum collections, and be saved a great deal of labor, if I could afford to use film rolls instead of glass plates. I can only load for twenty pictures a day, and I spend most of each evening in darkness, unloading and re-loading plate-holders—and if I happen to use up my twenty an hour before a museum closes, of course I lose this hour, and must turn to other work. Another inconvenience of being poor!

"What I could do if I could only find some one ready to invest a few thousands a year in my scientific work! I shall find him some day. Meanwhile I would rather struggle on all the rest of my life to make both ends meet, than do anything else on a king's income. I have worked so hard, I did not think I had much enthusiasm left, but I *have*. The universe is a big thing, but man is the most tremendous thing in it of which we know, and I am working away trying to restore a lost chapter to his astonishing biography. I used to talk in toplofty fashion about devoting one's life to science, etc., etc. I presume it read well. After my first year of it in America, I felt like the English infantry in Buller's first battle. Now I have had more than five years of real service, I am already gray, and I say: I propose to devote the rest of my life to science. If that means twenty-five years more of the same kind of thing, very well. I ask only a little more time in my study, and an occasional nod of appreciation from a friend or two—for appreciation is a pleasant and inspiriting thing. We Breasteds crave approbation, and failing of it, become despondent—like Dr. Johnson, who had no pleasure in completing his dictionary because all those who would have taken pride in his achievement were gone.

"I am now laying plans to copy not merely the historical, but *all* the inscriptions of Egypt and publish them. This will require $25,000 a year for fifteen or twenty years, and as soon as I have finished this commission for the [German] Academies, I expect to raise sufficient funds at least to begin. The only possible thing which could interfere would be the lack of money."

Before the end of this first year, "Their Excellencies, the Board of Trustees of the University of Chicago," received a formal communication from the Egyptian Dictionary Commission indicating that the latter "would recognize with especial thanks the University's relinquishment to them of the services of Prof. Dr. Breasted for another year." It was signed by "Erman, for the Royal Prussian Academy of Sciences at Berlin; Pietschmann, for the Royal Society of Sciences at Göttingen," and "Brugmann, for the Royal Saxon Society of Sciences at Leipzig."

From St. Petersburg, Russia, where President Harper happened momentarily to be, my father received a penned note in characteristic vein: ". . . I think we must . . . recommend that you be given leave of absence to do the work proposed, with your salary to continue at the rate of 2/3 the sum you are now receiving . . . or $1066 [per annum]. . . . I shall be in Berlin in ten days, and we can then eat sausage and settle the details. We have great things ahead of us now. Don't get so Europeanized that you will not want to work at home. . . . Can the University [of Chicago] be recognized in any way in connection with this work? Think of this!"

The details were arranged not over sausage but at a dinner with Ambassador Andrew Dickson White at the American Embassy in

Berlin. Harper promised him an increase in salary and a roseate future. Our wanderings were destined to continue.

Long afterwards my father wrote: "Next morning the President and several of his friends paid me a visit [at the Berlin Museum] to see the Imperial Egyptian Dictionary and to meet Erman and his group of scholars. As soon as we were alone again, he said to me:

" 'Breasted, please call a droschke and come with me—I have two errands, one of which needs you.'

"We drove first to an optician's where he bought a beautiful and expensive pair of binoculars. 'These are for Judson,' * he said. 'He has been working so hard during my absence, I want to take him something.'

"As we re-entered the droschke, he said, 'Do you remember where we used to live when we were all here in Berlin? I have forgotten the address. Please drive me there.'

"We drove across the city and down the Buelow Strasse into a familiar court, and stopped in front of the house he and his family had occupied in the summer of 1891. I waited for him to descend, thinking that he had some errand there. But he only sat quietly looking up at the window where almost a decade ago he had spent so many hours gazing at the dingy northern skies and seeing in them visions of the new university of which he was to be the first president. He did not speak, but sat for fully a quarter of an hour, staring musingly up at this window. Then we drove away in silence, and so far as I know he never visited the place again.

"It was always my impression that President Harper's early stay in Berlin had contributed essentially toward confirming his own conception of the function of a university—the prosecution of research. He had always at every opportunity stressed this view while teaching at Yale; and it had found its ultimate expression in his splendid dream that the University of Chicago should become the greatest *research* institution in the world. I believe this underlay his desire to see again the window through which his thoughts had soared so high; and I am certain it explained—with the exception of one subsequent strange and inconsistent interlude which he later deeply regretted—his consistent support of my own long years of research work in Europe."

President Harper now sailed for America, and we returned again

---

* Harry Pratt Judson, formerly professor of history and lecturer on pedagogy at the University of Minnesota, was then Harper's assistant, and was destined to become his successor.

to Rome, where my father interviewed "the Pope's Major Domo, His Excellency, Cardinal della Volpe, regarding a 'permesso' [to work on the Egyptian collections in the Vatican]. After long waiting in an anteroom, I was ushered into the presence of a splendid looking fellow in ecclesiastical robes, who received me very kindly. As my Italian was insufficient and the prelate spoke no English, we had to resort to mutually halting French.

"He asked me if I was officially appointed by the German Government. I said, not *directly*, but by the four Royal Academies, which are government institutions. 'And they appointed an American on such a mission?' he asked in surprise. (I have found it created comment wherever I have gone.) He said that he would do all in his power to assist me. Next morning I found my 'permesso' ready for me, a formidable document bristling with conditions intended to prevent publication of the material I was permitted to copy.

"My pass brings me in past the Pope's Swiss Guard, up many a staircase, through a court, up other staircases climbing the slope of the Vatican hill, till I reach the endless corridors (forming an L with St. Peter's) which are so long they diminish in the distance like a railway tunnel—and are lined on either hand with sculptures. Thence I go up a short staircase, past the marvellous torso of Hercules which Michael Angelo, when he could no longer see it, used to come and feel with loving fingers.

"All these vast passages and remote vistas are silent and deserted, and the echo of my footsteps is strangely loud, as I come at last into the sunshine of the beautiful Belvedere Court, the highest point on the Vatican hill. Here in the peaceful sunlight, with a fountain tinkling, I can look through a door at the right and see the glorious Apollo to which the court has given its name, occupying a chamber of honor by itself. Through another door I can see the Laocoon. I shall never forget the moments of silence I have spent before these as I go to and from my work. Beyond are several halls filled with the world's masterpieces, and then come the Egyptian halls.

"The interview with the Major Domo and these long walks through the Vatican palace have impressed me deeply with the wealth and power of the Pope—the reality and vitality of the papacy are here so visibly embodied that I have felt them as never before."

But it was Florence which my father regarded as "the most charming of all European cities. I enjoy it more than any historical center of art I have ever visited," a generous avowal for one so partial to Egypt.

"On my way to and from the Museum I pass a lovely Madonna and Child by Giovanni della Robbia; a moment further, the house in which (in 1500) Benvenuto Cellini was born. Though I pass them all four times each day, my delight in them never lessens. I have but to turn my head to see from my window what Ruskin calls the most beautiful piece of architecture in the world, Giotto's Tower. (Ruskin's *Mornings* is my ideal of how to use technical knowledge; it is of no use in the head of a scholar. No German could ever have written such a little book!) Five minutes 'round the corner in one direction is Santa Maria Novella with the Madonna of Giotto's master, Cimabue. Five minutes the other way is San Lorenzo, and in the adjoining chapel of the Medici's, the Night and Day, and the Twilight and Dawn of Michael Angelo—the dawn and noonday of Italian art.

"Years ago, when I was a boy, I read Mrs. Oliphant's *Makers of Florence*—and prompted by that book, I secured Vasari's *Lives of the Painters* from the Rockford Public Library, and devoured it. The romance of the Florentine story has always fascinated me, and now I revel daily in its rich memories and glorious associations. Sometimes it all seems a dream to me—to be engaged in a mission requiring work which is a constant pleasure. I am devoutly grateful."

From Florence we moved on to Pisa, Naples, Syracuse, Palermo, Genoa, Turin, Milan, Venice, Munich, Vienna, Prague; back to Berlin, Paris, Marseilles, Lyons, Brussels, Leyden, Amsterdam, London, Manchester, Liverpool—on and on we traveled, with scores of intermediate stops, and periodic voyages to America. My father's work acquired a steady rhythm and tempo, the telescopic manuscript case grew perceptibly longer and heavier, and his way of life and his personal comportment began to take on the quiet confidence and poise which comes from service under fire.

"I have compacted a peace with all my enemies, and have stopped fighting," he wrote to his mother. "I am even making overtures to Maspero! But I fear my German friends excepting Erman, Sethe and one or two others, are not as *sympatisch* as they used to be. I cannot abide their unreasonable hatred of the English, whom they hope to see whipped [by the Boers] in South Africa—just as they doubtless hoped we would be in our Spanish war. It is not they, but myself who have changed as I have come out into the practical struggle of life. They are no less kind and thoughtful than in the past, but they sympathize with tendencies to which I now realize I am fundamentally opposed. They are so unpardonably provincial—if I have any right to say so, who sprang from nothing else! But as I see it now, our life at Downers Grove was not *all* loss. For though there was little to stimulate one, and the 'cultural forces' were not powerful, the quiet life of the country worked its best for us. Yet I often wonder whence came the unquenchable ambition to grow beyond that little local world."

More than forty years later I wonder too, and have not found the answer. Though even as a child I was conscious of his incessant struggle, I was far too young either to understand its nature, or to realize that the fascinating and only world I knew, I owed to his unconquerable determination.

It was a world in which something unforgettable was continually happening. I remember the talk of Dewey and Manila, and of the Boer War. I remember a late afternoon in September, 1901, when my father was holding me in his arms as he stood on the deck of a ship nearing New York Harbor. A huge red sun was dropping into a glassy sea, and burning a path through intermittent tatters of fog. Our engines stopped, and the splash of water pumping from the side was loud in the stillness as we crept slowly abreast of the Fire Island Light Ship. There was no wireless then, and through a megaphone our captain reported his ship, while the passengers listened intently for the latest news from shore. I remember the silence, the moment of suspended movement, the hazy red path of the sun, and then a voice coming from the Light Ship: "President McKinley has been shot!"

I remember the death of Queen Victoria, the unprecedented mourning everywhere, and the sorrow which crept into people's voices, even in countries that disliked England. It was the end of an age, they said, which the future could never again equal. . . . Then I remember one October day in 1902, standing in the window of a London bank (a point of vantage for once probably won by my infernal curls), to watch the postponed coronation procession of Edward VII: and out of all the color and pageantry of that historic day, I still see more clearly than anything else the solid, speckled throng in the street below, doffing their hats to a column of officers and men newly returned from the Boer War, which had ended only that spring.

I remember later in Berlin standing beside my governess on the curb of a *chaussée* in the Thiergarten and watching the unhurried passing of an open carriage in which sat, like so many animated portraits, that same Edward VII in company with Kaiser William II, Czar

Nicholas and Emperor Franz Joseph. The sight of royalty and great folk and the gossip about them were common enough then so that without benefit of radios and newsreels even a small child like myself heard everywhere the jocose rumor that the Kaiser and the Crown Prince were nightly stumbling over one another at the stage door of the Royal Opera, as they vied for the favor of the beautiful American singer, daughter of a genial professional baseball player—Geraldine Farrar, to whom the crowned heads and all the capitals of Europe were paying romantic homage.

But to my young mind none of this could compare in importance and interest with such immediate personal experiences as being on a tiny ship in a horrible storm in the Tyrrhenian Sea, throughout which one had piteously entreated equally prostrated parents to "close one's stomach"; or the blessed relief of staggering ashore at Ajaccio on the Island of Corsica; or being lost in the Magazin du Louvre, and transformed by degrees from a terrified stray into a captivated and deliberately uninformative ward of the Paris Prefecture of Police while, in the absence of telephones, one's parents were on the verge of distractedly dragging the Seine; or feeding the pigeons in the Piazza di San Marco in Venice; or driving day and night in an open carriage from Botzen (Bolzano) over the Brenner Pass to Innsbruck; or watching sheep dogs, at an ancient country fair among the Lakes of England, obeying their shepherds with almost more than human intelligence by racing away like the wind to bring back tiny white specks that were sheep on a distant hillside; or standing beside one's father in the garden of a villa of Tiberius on the Island of Capri, with the sea incredibly blue and far below, and hearing him tell the story of the tragic death of the Emperor's little son. . . .

But perhaps even more vivid than any of these was the memory of the irresistible fragrance of chocolate which greeted one everywhere in the vicinity of a famous shop window in Berlin's Leipziger Strasse. This window formed one side of a white-tiled room filled with the shining machinery of a chocolate mill from which at frequent intervals white-clad attendants removed great mouth-watering masses of rich brown paste. On the rare occasions when I passed this delectable spot with my father, he would instinctively sense—I suspect because he experienced a similar assault—that my small stomach was in a state of convulsive yearning for just a taste of the heavenly stuff beyond the window; and with strict injunctions not to tell my mother what had spoiled my appetite, he would buy me a few pfennigs' worth of little chocolate disks covered with white sugar-beads that crunched deliciously. But in company with my mother or my governess, I was always forcibly led past this seductive shop with the invariable and irrefutable admonition that chocolate was much too *"verstopfend* (constipating)!"

I remember ships, countless ships, the repetitive rhythm of ocean crossings at every time of year—the black-hulled, white-trimmed ships of the transatlantic lines coming into Plymouth and Southampton and Liverpool, Cuxhaven and Hamburg, Havre and Marseilles; the white ships of the North German Lloyd, plying between Genoa, Naples and New York, their holds laden with citrus fruit and sulphur from Sicily, with wine, olive oil, silks, cheeses and macaroni from Italy; and the steerage of every westbound ship swarming with emigrants from the remotest corners of Europe.

In all the westbound crossings of my entire childhood, what untold thousands of steerage passengers I peered at, through the railings of the upper decks! They were always a source of deep concern to my mother. We seldom completed a voyage without her going to the aid of at least one stricken or desperately needy family—she would sometimes even take up a collection for them among her fellow passengers.

My father was no less sympathetic, but to him steerage represented a fascinating sociological phenomenon, "one of the great mass migrations of history," as he described it some years later, "with a crucial bearing upon America's development. Undoubtedly a certain amount of new blood is stimulating and beneficial. But what shall determine the proper amount? American industry's need for cheap labor? A House of Congress thinking of the nation's future in terms of the next election? Our theoretical sociologists? Inevitably we shall close our gates too late. It remains to be seen whether the creative contributions of the Schurzes, Steinmetzes, Michelsons, Pupins and their rare kind, and the solidity of the better farming and lower middle class elements from northern Europe, can offset the retarding effects of great unassimilable masses of Mediterranean and eastern European populations."

Today steerage is almost a forgotten word for the human cargo upon which all transatlantic steamship lines fattened for nearly two generations; a word once fraught with all the hope and promise of American opportunity, and with all the sufferings and tragedies, the births and deaths at sea, of beings who at best fared only passably in good weather, but in storms were crowded and tossed about like cattle

in their own verminous filth and blood and vomit, in the unspeakable
bowels of ships which vanished long ago.

If I have dwelt overlong upon them, it is because such memories
are the essence and all that remains to me of the pre-1914 world in
which my father evolved the pattern of his later career and I gained
my earliest, on the whole somewhat unhappy, impressions of life.

The effect of our mutual experience of that seemingly solid world
whose dissolution we were so soon to witness was to draw me the
more closely to him. For I cannot overemphasize the weight which my
father attached to community of experience as a cementing element
in all relationships. It was an attitude of mind which on the one hand
fortified his loyalty to my mother during the forty years of their married life, and on the other strengthened his attachment for his son by
virtue of all we endured together as a result of our own limitations
and frailties in coping with the extremes of her mercurial temperament.

The bonds which these early years forged between us, and the
seeds of the sympathetic understanding of his hopes and dreams which
they implanted in me, were one day to bring us together in a working
association such as is seldom permitted a father and son. Yet I was
never able to conquer nor he to understand the overwhelmingly
depressing effect upon me of the dead world which was his supreme
inspiration. He found it incomprehensible that the vast material
residue of the life of man on earth, neatly arranged in the tomb-like,
musty silence of a thousand museum halls and galleries and basements,
from which of late afternoons I had for years been taken to fetch him
"home," should gradually have filled me, even as a child, with an
unbearable sense of death.

Until I was a man grown and he saw that it was in vain, he tried
in every possible, however gentle way to persuade me to undertake a
career like his own. I would have had to be moulded in stone for him
not to have aroused my tremendous and permanent interest and curiosity. But not even the brightest fire of his genius for recapturing and
revitalizing the dead past could overcome my involuntary apathy for
it, or my profound predilection for the present.

There came a period of several months while we were in Europe
in 1902, when my father's daydreaming absences "in Nubia" became
almost continuous, until they finally culminated in a practical plan

—which he drafted and redrafted at least a hundred times—for archaeological exploration and research in the Near East, including his cherished project for copying and translating all the ancient Egyptian inscriptions in the entire Nile valley.

He sent it off at last to President Harper in America, who promptly approved it and transmitted it to Frederick Taylor Gates, "business and benevolent representative" of John Davison Rockefeller in New York. "He wishes to see you as soon as you come home," said Harper. "Please call upon him without fail."

This interview with Mr. Gates marked an important turning point not only in my father's scientific career, but in his social thinking as well.

Mr. Gates was a Baptist clergyman, a widely read, kindly man given to very decided opinions and possessed of an inflexible will, who was born in the town of Maine, Broome County, New York, in 1853. After being ordained at the age of twenty-seven, he had been called to one of the important pastorates of Minneapolis, where he had shown such an incisive understanding of the opportunities and problems of his denomination's educational enterprises, that he had been appointed Corresponding Secretary of the American Baptist Education Society. He had thus become closely involved in the development and execution of the Baptist-promulgated plan for a University of Chicago.

His grasp of what this great project should comprise, his ability to cut through mazes of detail and bring order out of accumulated confusion, the clarity and wisdom of his reports and recommendations, and his effectiveness, despite a native bluntness, as a diplomatic negotiator, had quickly brought him to the attention of Mr. Rockefeller who, with his usual genius for selecting men, had asked him to come to 26 Broadway. Mr. Gates accepted, and within a comparatively short time after coming to New York in 1893, was not only acting as his employer's representative in philanthropic and benevolent matters, but had become one of the more important members of his "inner cabinet" of advisers.

At this time not even the closest of these advisers was in a position to understand as did Mr. Rockefeller himself either the enormity or the uniquely paradoxical nature of the problem he was facing, a problem such as had never in remotely comparable measure confronted any other man in the history of the world: the judicious disposition of a fortune which was growing with unparalleled rapidity. He was acutely aware of the effect upon public opinion of what—as his proponents subsequently explained—he had deemed the only methods whereby, while momentarily enriching himself to an unprecedented degree, he could bring order out of chaos and accelerate what he regarded as an imperative and inevitable capitalistic and industrial readjustment in the United States.

My father definitely shared the public's resentment of the ruthless business imperialism which, according to press exposés and government prosecutions of the Standard Oil Trust's machinations, Mr. Rockefeller and his associates had purportedly been practicing for more than twenty years. Although he still believed in the *theory* of democracy, he had long since become convinced that the doctrine he had absorbed in the little red schoolhouse at Downers Grove, that all men were created equal, was, like socialism, "a sentimental contradiction of human experience." Like his father and grandfather before him, he was at this stage still a Republican who looked with a deep, inherited mistrust upon anything relating to or advocated by the Democratic Party (a stand from which by 1912 he was to veer so far as to vote for Woodrow Wilson). On the other hand, he unconsciously lapsed into Socialist platform phrases whenever he bitterly denounced "the shameless exploitation of our natural resources and the prostitution of the people's interests by the Republican robber-barons"—such as the railroad and lumber magnates, and the Standard Oil Trust.

He had found it increasingly difficult to reconcile these sentiments to his incumbency of a professorship in an institution which owed its existence to the success of business methods he so sincerely disapproved. His quandary was further complicated by the rumor that Mr. Rockefeller was definitely planning to give away during his lifetime the major portion of his personal fortune for humanitarian purposes. It was said that the carefully devised system of philanthropic giving which he had set up in 1890 was only the prelude to his gradual and large scale dedication to the public well-being of the wealth his detractors charged he had "wrested" from the people. Certainly there were many current developments, like the University of Chicago itself, which seemed to confirm this rumor. The amounts of his benefactions had already surpassed all precedents, and his wisdom in the selection of objectives had impressed even his most virulent critics.

The story of the creation in 1901 of the Rockefeller Institute for Medical Research was typical of his confidence in the judgment of his advisers, and of his own response to a cogently demonstrated universal need. From reading Dr. William Osler's *The Principles and Practice of Medicine,* written and published (1892) as a textbook but by instant public acclaim elevated to the rank of a classic, Mr. Gates had gained a vision of the realm of medicine as a vast dark continent beside which our present knowledge of it was as a grain of sand. He had given the book to Mr. Rockefeller with the solemn warning that it presented at once the greatest challenge and the noblest opportunity which had ever confronted a man with adequate resources to do them justice. From this had sprung an undertaking whose investigations were to benefit mankind in every corner of the world.

This story had made a very deep impression on my father. "As I walked the deck on our return voyage to America that year [the spring of 1903]," my father told me long afterwards, "I was full of daydreams about the plan which Mr. Gates wanted to discuss with me. But I could not shake off my anxiety as to whether or not I ought to see Mr. Gates at all, and kept reassuring myself that the ethical eccentricities of an ascetic capitalist who appeared to keep his business code and his religion in separate, water-tight compartments, were no concern of mine, and that it was obviously my duty to secure every penny I could for my university and my science. I was not cynical enough to condemn manifestly humanitarian benefactions as mere subterfuges for cloaking allegedly high-handed business practices. We have come a long road since then, and I can smile now at what seemed the momentousness of my final decision to see Mr. Gates."

As a result of this interview, Mr. Rockefeller contributed $50,000 to the University of Chicago for the support of archaeological field work in the Near East, and President Harper immediately organized, under his own direction, the "Oriental Exploration Fund."

It seemed to my father that at last the turn in his scientific fortunes had come, and that only the settlement of a few practical details intervened before he would return to Egypt to fulfill his most cherished scientific hopes. The elation this prospect aroused in him reflected itself in the enthusiasm with which he resumed his public lecturing, and the exuberance with which he greeted his colleagues. Word soon got about of the part he had played in securing additional Rockefeller funds, and what with his rather dramatic platform delivery, generally spirited bearing, and the frequent mention of his name in the press, he was locally becoming a somewhat public figure.

Scientifically he had already established an identity of his own even among a faculty numbering such brilliant if slightly older men as the physicist Albert Abraham Michelson, the biologist Jacques Loeb, the philosopher John Dewey; and men of his own generation like the young astronomer George Ellery Hale, Michelson's assistant Robert Andrews Millikan, and the bacteriologist Howard Taylor Ricketts (who discovered that the deadly Rocky Mountain fever was transmitted by ticks).

But to some of his colleagues it seemed as if the wine of early success had gone slightly to his head. Others merely envied him his long sojourns in Europe and resented what they appraised as his ephemeral popularity. The most outspoken of those who discounted Breasted's potentialities and staying powers was a young instructor in sociology, endowed with a caustic wit, and generally regarded as among the most promising younger men in his field. Unaware that his victim was within hearing, he had once remarked to a group of colleagues, "Breasted—up like a rocket, down like a stick!" It had hurt my father's pride at the time; but he later remarked "that perhaps a momentary ascendancy of pride over humility earned me this rebuke."

His critic, George Edgar Vincent (who had also been born in Rockford, Illinois, a year before my father), was to become progressively better known as president of the University of Minnesota and of the Rockefeller Foundation, and as one of the most brilliant lecturers and after-dinner speakers in America, than as a creative scholar. But twenty years later, when my father sought Rockefeller support for an increasing number of scientific and altruistic enterprises, notably one that elicited from Mr. Rockefeller, Jr., the proffer of one of the largest single gifts to which the latter had ever committed himself, he had no friendlier or stauncher supporter than Vincent.

At the moment, however, Vincent's remark seemed almost prophetic. For President Harper suddenly informed my father that the University's archaeological work in Babylonia was to take indefinite precedence over any plans for such work in Egypt. "I advise you to return to Germany," he said without further explanation, "to complete your assignment for the academies there, as well as the several books from your own pen upon which you are now engaged."

Thus almost casually the hopes of years were brushed aside. President Harper himself visited Constantinople to make the necessary arrangements, and in 1903 "the Sultan of Turkey issued a *firman* [permit] for the excavation of the ancient Babylonian city of Adab, called by the modern natives Bismayah." The Rev. Dr. Edgar J. Banks, a man of curious reputation, was made field director of the expedition, in association with the President's brother, Robert Francis Harper, to whose self-seeking intrigues my father realized too late these developments were in large part due.

As if to cap his discouragement, President Harper had also informed him that despite repeated promises, eventual publication by the University of his four-volume work, *Ancient Records of Egypt*—embodying the years of labor I have already tried to describe—would have to await a subsidy, the prospects for which appeared at the moment very dim.

Unable to understand these unexpected rebuffs, my father did his best to suppress a surging resentment at having apparently been "led on" for years, only to be suddenly deserted by his old teacher and friend whose change of heart so contradicted his hitherto unbounded optimism and enthusiasm. He was unaware of the sinister pathological enemy against which the President was already tacitly struggling.

One evening as he stood with his arms raised against a window through which the setting sun shone full in his face, my father said quietly to my mother, "Perhaps the little President has turned the tables because he feels that I have tried to move too fast at the expense of Robert Francis. But I have only to wait—you will see, his brother will defeat himself!"

That autumn of 1903 we returned disconsolately to Berlin, where he found some comfort in being warmly welcomed back by his German colleagues, and in resuming the familiar routines of his work. But he was heartsick and greatly disturbed, and tried to lose himself in completing the books which alone, as he now realized more clearly than ever before, would earn him the right to achieve his scientific goal in his own way. It had greatly encouraged him that Charles Scribner, the New York publisher, had shown a kindly interest in his *History of Egypt*.

"In a letter which is a model of courteous consideration," my father wrote to his mother, "Mr. Scribner expresses the desire that they may be 'privileged' to examine my *History* when I return. I can only hope he does not expect a definitive history of Egypt to prove as fascinating as the latest summer novel! After doing purely scientific work for so long, I have found it hard to strike the right style for such a book. I believe I have it now."

But moods of deep discouragement continued recurrently to afflict him. "Eduard Meyer [the eminent historian of the Ancient World, successor to the great Mommsen] and I dined together the other night to talk over some particular points in Egyptian history.

"He sweeps the whole field of the orient down into Greek and Roman times, including also the history of these two peoples. I sometimes long to stretch my wings over such a field as that! If I could have foreseen my career twenty years ago, I should have done it. But now I lack the equipment, and it is too late to get it. The career of man down into Christian times—*that* is a fascinating study! As it is, I only get him started with all the material arts and a long experience in government, organization and law: and there I have to leave him—I can only study his early progress while regarding him in the mass. I cannot follow him into the ages of the development of the individual, when he discovers the worth of himself as a soul. This leaves unused in myself capabilities of comprehension and sympathy which I long to employ. I wonder if we get another chance somewhere else to do it all over again in the light of what we have learned here."

Month after month the clatter of his typewriter began at half-past seven in the morning and continued far into the night. On Sundays we sometimes joined typical family excursions of the Ermans, the Sethes, the Eduard Meyers, the Heinrich Schaefers or other colleagues, on long walks in the Grunewald (near Berlin), which usually included a late luncheon at some Gasthaus (inn) deep in the forest, where in fair weather the tables were set out of doors, and—outdoors or in— were laid with bright checked cloths, and with a pungently beery cardboard coaster at every place. Once the meal was over, the men would invariably talk shop over quaint steins of Muenchner, and the women would discuss their children. And on the twilight walk through the forest back to the railway station, there would often be singing of the old student songs led by Erman, who never failed to render a duet with my father of his old Harz Mountain favorites, "Shoo Fly," "Johnny Schmoker" and "Michael Roy."

If my father "rested" during a weekday, it was usually to visit the Berlin Museum to confer with fellow Egyptologists regarding abstruse questions arising from his work on the great *Aegyptisches Wörterbuch* (Egyptian Dictionary) project. Sometimes this involved visits to other museums in Germany, and such excursions, albeit they were busmen's holidays, at least had the virtue of a change.

There was one classic occasion when he and Erman and Sethe, after a day in the Egyptian section of the Leipzig Museum, were still deep in a philological discussion as they hurried aboard what they thought was a Berlin express, to discover themselves an hour later actually on a "Bummelzug" ("jerkwater" local or milk-train) on a spur line running in exactly the wrong direction. At the next way station they learned there were no more return passenger trains to Leipzig that night, but that if they were willing to travel as *corpses,* they could with special tickets board a freight train due shortly. With many appropriate and hilarious quotations from the Egyptian *Book of the Dead* they availed themselves of this unique offer. But when three decidedly animate "corpses" clambered out of a box car far out in the Leipzig yards, they were promptly arrested by the station police and led before the Stationmaster who accused them of criminal conduct. Erman and Sethe, despite their much higher rank in the Prussian official hierarchy, were humbly resigning themselves to these charges when to their awed gratification and astonishment their American member, in fluent and flawless German, not only refuted the pontifical Stationmaster, but reduced him to a state of abject apology.

But at best it was a slogging, unexciting life relieved very occasionally by little discoveries which served as comforting oases to punctuate the long barren intervals between. In February, 1904, my father wrote: "Schaefer [another former student of Erman's, who later became Director of the Egyptian Section of the Berlin Museum] and I have made a startling discovery: in a list of Palestinian towns, which an Egyptian king Shishonk (called Shishak in the Old Testament) states he captured, we found a place called 'The Field of Abram.' This is the first mention of Abraham in any ancient monument outside the Bible. Otherwise the work goes on quietly as before. I am terribly weary of the struggle to finish my books."

But one never knew what might prove to be grist to one's mill. At a farewell dinner given that February by Eduard Meyer before his departure on his first trip to America, my father sat beside Professor Felix von Luschan, "one of the greatest anthropologists of our time. He has just returned from Egypt, where he has found prehistoric flint implements, the work of human hands, embedded in geological deposits older than the Nile itself, showing that man lived and worked there several hundred thousand years ago. This is all very valuable for my history."

Just twenty-one years later, my father was to stand on the Mound of Megiddo in Palestine and read a weather-worn cartouche containing the name of King Shishonk, inscribed on a fragment of stone unearthed by the workmen of an expedition he himself had organized to excavate this historic place. And at the same time, another expedition of his own creation, the Prehistoric Survey in Egypt, would not only confirm but amplify with extraordinary new evidence the earlier conclusions of Professor von Luschan.

But I am anticipating.

A letter dated February 24, 1904, from President Harper in America to my father, contained the casual sentence: "I have been having a slight attack of appendicitis but am fully recovering."

On March 28 he wrote again: "As you have by this time learned [from the press], another attack of appendicitis came on and I was taken to the hospital and the operation performed. I will not go into details, but it is perhaps sufficient to say that it is much more serious than was anticipated. I was able [nevertheless] to be present at all the important meetings of the German celebration [referring to an official visit to the University of Chicago of a delegation of eminent German scholars, including Eduard Meyer, and the conferment upon them of honorary degrees]. We have had a great time with the Germans. I think they are more than satisfied. It has been the greatest event in the history of the University. . . .

"[My family] and myself will leave . . . in July for Berlin . . . to spend six months. . . . Will you give me some advice [on the best way to live there]? I shall hope to see a good deal of you. Pardon the brevity of this letter. I may write again more fully a little later."

It was the letter of an indomitable man in constant pain, who already knew that he had cancer and not long to live, but whose magnificent vitality and courage drove him to make plans for the future as vigorously and intrepidly as he had always done.

I can still hear the clatter of exclamatory conversation which swept through Berlin in February, 1904, when the Russo-Japanese war began, and the sound of my father's voice as he read aloud to my mother from the leading German papers, especially the old *Lokal-Anzeiger*. The whole of Germany, and above all the Army high command, gloated over every Japanese victory. For the sinister shadow of Russian rivalry had been stretching farther and farther across the path of Germany's Berlin-to-Baghdad ambitions; and this first major rehearsal of Japanese naval and military strength augured ill for the future of England's power in the Far East—and possibly India as well.

"I am fascinated by the Russo-Japanese war," my father wrote to his mother that June. "Neither the average American war correspondent nor his editor at home has the slightest idea of the historical significance of the Japanese successes. The fate of a continent and the supremacy of a race is being decided every day. Already it is evident that whatever the eventual course of this war may be, Russian domination in eastern Asia is gone. To future centuries looking back upon it, the triumph of the Japanese over the Russians will be as significant as that of the Greeks over the Persians at Salamis or Marathon.— Please excuse this lecture, Mother: there is no charge—it went off by itself!"

I cannot find Harriet's response, if any, to this rather oracular declaration. But while her comprehension of the significance of Salamis and Marathon and the nascence of Japanese power in Asia may have been vague, I know that her son's invariable assumption that she understood all these things warmed her heart and filled her with pride in his command of knowledge she could never hope to possess.

That spring Eduard Meyer had persuaded us to move from our gloomy Berlin *pension* to rooms in Gross-Lichterfelde, a pleasant suburb where he and his family, by curious coincidence, lived in the Mommsen Strasse, named after his renowned predecessor at the University of Berlin.

Gross-Lichterfelde was far enough removed from the already feverish expansion of the city to have retained the *Gemütlichkeit* (genial, friendly intimacy) of a small provincial town, where people moved with a comfortable tempo, and where even the construction of a new house, and the ancient ceremony of affixing little flags and a bouquet or a flowering branch or shrub to the highest point of the roof-tree on the day that this was finished, was still a matter of genuine personal interest to the local populace. The streets ended in peaceful, gently undulating meadows and wheat-fields interspersed with little copses of aspens, lindens and birches glowing with fresh new leaves, and of dark pines mottled with fresh light-green needles; the air was full of birdsong and the rich fragrance of intermittent showers.

In the congenial detachment of Gross-Lichterfelde my father attacked the final portions of his *History* and his *Ancient Records of Egypt*. This might have been an interlude of ideally sequestered rural peace had it not been for the sense of pressure under which he worked, and his anxiety for the future. He was on the verge of completing the great task he had so long ago set for himself, and like a climber nearing a peak which had seemed to him always to be receding, he now strained toward it desperately, utterly obsessed by the determination to finish.

His only interruption each day continued to be the brief interval before my supper hour, when he read aloud to me from *Robinson Crusoe* or *Peter Simple* or the Leatherstocking Tales; or strolled with my mother and me along an unfrequented country road past fields where I could find Prussian-blue corn-flowers nodding among the grain; and along a stream overhung by weeping willows from which, on red letter days, he would make me willow whistles. But whatever we did, however gaily he played with me, one had only to look into his eyes to know that his inner thoughts were still among his books.

So much that I could not then comprehend now stands out with sharp significance.

At the edge of the town, for instance, just where our favorite lane entered the open country, stood the famous *Kadettenanstalt* (military academy). Despite great trees, the buildings were angular and grim, with sentry boxes at the doors, and at the gates in the surrounding walls. We reached the place always in the late afternoon, and at this hour we would usually see staring out at us from the windows, all of which were barred, the pasty-white, shaven-headed, leering faces of what seemed more like trapped animals than young human beings. Often they would only stare silently as we passed. But again, they would shout and shriek and spit at us with hateful derision; and on one occasion, when I had foolishly lingered in order to vent my childish anger at them, the whole gruesome dormitory-ful, as if suddenly gone mad, burst into uttering and enacting the foulest obscenities. I was terrified, afraid to tell my parents what I had seen.

These caged animals were to become officers in the Imperial Army which during that baking August a decade later would almost engulf Paris as the first step in Germany's proposed conquest of the West. There were other *Kadettenanstalten* in Germany, some worse, few better than this one, but their product varied little.

During his student days my father had been aware that tremendous social forces were at work in the great German nation beyond his immediate little academic world. But while he deplored what we had seen at Gross-Lichterfelde, he did not yet recognize it as symptomatic of the very social forces which would one day destroy the apparently imperishable world of German science and learning.

His eventual realization of all this was to plunge him into years of deep spiritual anguish. But in that summer of 1904 he looked upon

Germany as the land of his scientific salvation. "For no one in America, least of all the University of Chicago, appeared to care whether or not I ever returned," he wrote years later. "President Harper's rebuff still rankled, and I could see no hope of ever bringing my archaeological plans to reality. The only words of encouragement and appreciation I had yet received had come from my colleagues in Europe, particularly in Germany." Adolf Erman and Eduard Meyer had read large sections of the manuscripts of the two major works he was now completing, and had approved them so unreservedly that he felt alarmed lest the finished volumes should disappoint these high expectations.

One placid Saturday afternoon of that July, Meyer invited him to come in for a cup of coffee in his garden. "I would like to discuss with you certain confidential questions," he said in his message, "for which I would entreat your sympathetic consideration."

The Meyers lived in a villa whose typical ugliness was softened by a large and pleasant garden, which for once did not suggest the melancholy landscaping of an average German cemetery. There were whole areas of lawn upon which in summer one was actually permitted to tread, and at the back there were great elm trees from the tallest of which hung a high rope swing. Even the inevitable summer-house and rock garden seemed designed rather for the delectation of the living than as memorials to the departed.

Here in nice weather could usually be found—schoolwork and household duties permitting—the Professor's several sons and daughters (what with neighbors' children, I was never quite certain of their number), and his shy, pink-cheeked, buxom Swiss wife Rosina, who often asked me to join her brood at play. The girls attended their dolls, Frau Professor did knitting and mending, and the boys—by whom I was tolerated as an onlooker—spent every weekday hour they could spare, not to mention whole vacation days and their entire savings, on lead soldiers of which it seemed to me they possessed untold thousands. Over this ménage Eduard Meyer, a wiry, inflexible giant with a brown beard, massive head, thick gold-rimmed spectacles, frock coat, bull-of-Bashan voice and Olympian laughter—at heart a kindly and engaging human being—ruled with a hand of iron.

On this particular afternoon, however, Meyer was mellow and genial. With his mouth full of Rosina's coffee cake he told stories and joked with everyone until the garden re-echoed with his laughter. After a time he motioned to my father, and the two men wandered off to a secluded path where they walked slowly up and down while Meyer smoked a cigar.

In unwonted low tones he began asking my father the most searching questions regarding his future, his scientific hopes and expectations, and his probable earning capacity in America. My father answered warily, wondering what had prompted his friend thus to interrogate him as he had never done before regarding personal matters.

Meyer stopped suddenly and faced him. "You wonder, perhaps, why I appear to pry into your private affairs," he said. "It is not that I am curious, although I must admit that what you have been good enough to tell me, interests me greatly. It is that I have been asked in the strictest confidence to ascertain your attitude in the event that a some future time those in authority should consider offering you an appointment to a professorship in some leading German university."

He spoke only in general terms, and referred noncommittally to Berlin, Leipzig, Heidelberg, Göttingen. "No vacancies in your field exist anywhere at this time," he added, "but if the idea should attract you I have reason to believe its fulfillment would probably be only a matter of patience. Let me assure you that all your friends here in Germany would warmly welcome you! There is no hurry. Give the matter long and careful consideration, and whenever you wish, you can discuss it further with me—or with Erman, who is of course also familiar with the situation. And now let us speak of other things!"

"I tried to be as casual as I could," my father recalled long afterwards, "about a proposal which touched every loyalty and every instinctive tie of my life. I sensed that no matter who 'in authority' might have requested him to speak to me, my beloved old friend and teacher, Erman, must have played a large part in bringing it about.

"As we sauntered back to the summer-house and I took my leave, my mind was spinning with questions. What would President Harper, with all his respect for German science, say to this?—what would my colleagues in America say? Where lay my duty—to my family, my science, my country?—how could I best serve them? It seemed to me at the moment utterly unthinkable that even if I were to accept a professorship in Germany, I could ever renounce my birthright as an American: but how would years of residence there affect me? Where would my sympathies lie if she became involved in war against England or France?—or even the United States?—and would my son grow up as a German subject? What of my old mother and all those dependent upon me in America? Extension lecturing might be hateful, but without it my family and I could never have survived—and in Germany this source of income simply did not exist. Could we possibly subsist even on the highest professorial salary then obtainable in Germany?

"The proposal was in the nature of an honor, a reward for years of hard work acceptably done. I confess it grieved me and hurt my pride that it had come from Germany rather than from my own country. I knew in my heart that I could never accept it, and yet the debate with myself continued for days and weeks on end."

I remember so well that debate. In the midst of it he received a similar "feeler" from a colleague at the University of Vienna. During those weeks our afternoon walks grew longer, and late at night in my sleep I heard the low drone of my parents' voices in the next room as they thought their way aloud, back and forth again and again over the same ground, with my father in the end always returning to the same simple conclusion. "Putting everything else aside, Frances," he would say, "we are, above all, Americans!"

Early in September he called upon Meyer and with all the tact he could muster explained to him that for reasons wholly beyond his control he could not accept, were it offered to him, the honor of a professorship in a German university. Meyer took this decision in good part—having so recently been widely honored in America, he could hardly do otherwise. As for Erman, he fully understood. He put his arm through my father's and said somewhat wistfully, "I did not dare hope we could win you away from your own country. But I am glad that you now know the feeling about you here."

A few days later we boarded a ship for America, and during an equinoctial crossing my father wrote the last words of his *History of Egypt*. "A whole segment of our lives is invisibly embodied in this book," he had written to his mother. "I have been too long and too deeply submerged in writing it to judge whether it makes good reading or bad. I know only that no one in my field has ever striven more conscientiously to be accurate. It is my own work, based throughout on my own study of the original sources—as I was from the beginning determined it should be; so that whatever its undoubted faults, they too are mine alone. I have only one *great* regret—that I could not have copied *all* the extant inscriptions along the entire Nile valley before completing both the *History* and the *Ancient Records*. But I can honestly say that excepting for any modifications this might have entailed, it is the best I could do. I shall feel strangely lost when these incessant companions of the last ten years have gone to the publishers."

He spent the last day of the voyage in fingering through the mass of manuscript pages, making final minor changes and corrections. From time to time he murmured, "I wonder, Frances, I wonder . . ." At five o'clock the next morning, as we were entering New York Harbor, he wrote the concluding sentences of the book, and that afternoon, delivered it himself to Mr. Scribner.

Within a fortnight Mr. Scribner sent him a contract and a gracious assurance that his firm would esteem it a privilege to publish *A History of Egypt*.

Once he had returned to his University, it seemed to him that for years he had been moving in a great circle which had now closed. His books were finished, his mission for the Egyptian Dictionary Commission had been fulfilled; and therewith President Harper's arrangement permitting him to spend at least half of each year in Europe would automatically terminate. There was no telling when he might again be granted such opportunities for almost uninterrupted pure research. Once more he resumed the old routines of teaching and extension lecturing. But everything he attempted was now rendered doubly arduous by the bitter enmity and hatred of Robert Francis Harper.

The progress of President Harper's grave illness had prevented his intended visit to Germany that summer. Instead, he had worked more furiously than ever to complete a whole array of unfinished projects and to set in motion as many more which he had been merely contemplating. Opposition to his ambitious schemes and to his Napoleonic disregard of their cost had grown rapidly of late, but he was going down with his colors flying.

From time to time during this strange climactic period of his ebbing life he received ugly news about the Bismayah expedition. A serious disagreement between the Reverend Dr. Banks and Robert Francis Harper had developed into a smouldering, irreconcilable hatred, until finally the two men, who shared the same mess and the same tent, had ceased speaking to one another, and the morale of the camp had suffered accordingly. Since no member of the staff was an experienced excavator, the "scientific" work of the expedition had amounted to little more than promiscuous probing and loose pillaging for loot in an historic site rich in important antiquities. At last Robert Francis returned to America, followed shortly by the Reverend Dr. Banks, who left the enterprise to be run for a second season by the expedition's draughtsman.

Presently the Turks learned that a large number of the expedition's more valuable finds from the first season had disappeared from their country without being declared. The government demanded their immediate return; and when Robert Francis and Dr. Banks both disclaimed any knowledge of them, it severely reprimanded the University of Chicago, and canceled its concession. The expedition ended on June 1, 1904, under what might have been called, scientifically and financially speaking, a cloud.

From this abortive Babylonian venture Robert Francis returned angry and resentful. He vented his spleen by inflicting upon his colleagues, and especially upon my father, the sort of galling petty affronts and studied insults which a vindictive Upper Form bully in an English public school might have dealt his fag. With death already hovering over him, President Harper was too preoccupied with all he was determined to finish to heed his brother's behavior, and even delegated to him his own duties as head of the Semitics Department. Having thus become my father's acting chief, Robert Francis tried, by every badgering, dispiriting device his vengeful mind could conceive, to goad him into resigning from the University of Chicago.

For a time he almost succeeded. The pace of these last years and the fixed habit of overwork had seriously affected my father's health and left him gaunt and prematurely gray. He had often enough engaged in verbal battles with other scholars over scientific questions, and in the course of his career thus far had gained numerous enemies among them. But never before on either side of the Atlantic had he incurred such a virulent personal enmity—one which he only now realized must have begun when he and Robert Francis were students together at New Haven.

Then came a final blow which left him on the verge of a nervous and physical collapse.

At President Harper's express desire, he had submitted to the University of Chicago Press the ten thousand manuscript pages of his *Ancient Records of Egypt*. Now the President informed him that he had been unable to find the funds for their publication, which would have to be indefinitely postponed.

My father volunteered to find the necessary donors himself, and made only two requests: that if the book was published, he be permitted to dedicate it to his father; and that once it was in print, the original manuscript be returned to him.

"I am heartsick," he wrote. "After ten years of unremitting service to my science in compiling what must for some time remain the standard reference work of Egyptian historical sources, if only because no other yet exists, my reward is the privilege of finding the money to publish the results!"

But in his discouragement he had forgotten the tenacity of President Harper's will. The fate of the Babylonian expedition might have deterred a lesser man from further ventures into Near Eastern archaeology. To the President it was merely a challenge to clear the record by engaging the University in some other archaeological enterprise the scientific value and conduct of which would be beyond reproach.

In the spring of 1905 he suddenly said to my father that "the coming autumn seems a propitious time to begin your proposed epigraphic survey of Egypt. You will be given leave of absence to undertake this project, which will be financed with the unexpended balance in the Oriental Exploration Fund. You may devote yourself to this work without concern over the publication of your *Ancient Records*: I believe I have now found the money for it."

Once again my father clambered up out of the slough of despond, and began to make his way back to the world of all his daydreams. But he was not jubilant. "Apparently I must accept as one of the invariable ironies of my life," he said, "that an opportunity to render a major service to my science must always find me too worn out with seeking it, to do it justice!"

CHAPTER VI

M Y father's characteristic bonhomie, and the self-assurance he consistently showed and genuinely felt in his profession, hid a lonely man of few intimate friendships, who looked upon his personal life as a failure.

As a result of long separation and the diverging tastes of maturity, the attachments of his boyhood and youth had largely atrophied; while from his years at New Haven and in Germany, almost the only American friendships which had survived the following decade were with William Horace Day and Lester Bradner—and as it was, he now seldom saw these two. He craved and delighted in human companionship, but my mother's jealousy of those who were attracted to him in a world to which she felt unequal had led him to submerge himself more and more in his work.

At the University of Chicago he formed only two close friendships. The first was with George Stephen Goodspeed, an idealistic human being of rare sympathy and warmth, as well as an ancient historian and comparative religionist of great promise. They shared each other's scientific views, fought each other's battles, and together often played an equally mediocre game of tennis. Then, in February, 1905, when my father's future loomed blackest and the fellowship and counsel of his beloved friend would have been as sunlight in a darkling world, George Stephen Goodspeed died.

Since the death of Charles and Aunt Theodocia, he had suffered no comparable bereavement. He seldom spoke of it, and betrayed his grief in curious little ways, such as never playing tennis again. Long afterwards he confided to a little note-book a reaffirmation of his gratitude "that work can so engross the mind as to make it unconscious of its pain, until time can transmute bereavement into inspiring memories. For the future I find no other hope, nor any solution of the Mystery, beyond this courage to look up undaunted, and to believe the struggle worth while for its own sake."

The other friendship which began during this period was with

134

George Ellery Hale. It was to become the greatest of his life, but was yet still too young to permit his turning to Hale for solace in his loss. Only some twenty years later did the two men outgrow their mutual shyness of discussing personal matters, or of expressing to one another their inner feelings, or even of calling one another by their first names.

But the development of their friendship was very natural. Both men were utterly devoted to the pursuit of truth, shared the same scientific creeds, the same conception of the place of scientific research in a civilized world. By somewhat different spiritual experiences they had arrived at the same reverence for the forces of Nature, which found no difficulty in reconciling science and religion. In their boundless intellectual curiosity, in the play of their imaginations, in their vision of the unlimited potentialities of the human species, whatever its eventual fate as a result of cosmic processes; and in their sensibility to the indefinable loneliness of service on the frontiers of knowledge—in these and a hundred other ways, their two minds reacted with extraordinary similarity.

Their backgrounds, on the other hand, were in marked contrast. For George Ellery Hale, as the son of well-to-do, cultivated New England parents, had been born (at Chicago on June 29, 1868) into a Middle Western version of the New England tradition whereby the sons of merchant princes often devoted themselves to the pursuit of science, arts and letters. From the outset he had been able, without thought of expense, to pursue whatever course of training he had deemed necessary or desirable, and to go abroad for further study whenever he wished.

Looking back upon the beginnings of his scientific interests when he was only a small boy, Hale wrote in 1933: ". . . I . . . made the discovery that simple instruments sufficed to reveal new and wonderful worlds, hidden from the unaided eye. Here was the origin of a life of research. . . ." From a Beck microscope and the wonders of infusoria collected from neighborhood ditches, he progressed quickly to astronomy. At fourteen he built his own telescope, and from this point onward the pattern of his brilliant career as an astrophysicist, rather than an astronomer, had developed with perfect logicality and astonishing speed.

In 1892, just as my father was beginning his studies in Berlin, President Harper had appointed young Hale as associate professor of astrophysics in the new University, for which Hale immediately envisioned an ambitious astronomical observatory. Harper was enthusias-

tic enough in his moral support but warned him that the University
neither possessed the funds nor knew where to raise them for such an
obviously expensive undertaking.

Hale's indirect retort was to turn upon Charles T. Yerkes, a tough-
skinned Chicago traction magnate from whom Harper himself had
failed to secure a gift for the University, those gentle yet irresistible
persuasive powers which during the next forty years were to enlist
untold millions of dollars in the service of science. Mr. Yerkes first
succumbed to the extent of giving the funds for the purchase of lenses
for a forty-inch telescope (at that time the world's largest); then, after
flatly refusing to contribute another penny to the enterprise, gave the
money for the telescope mounting, and finally for the observatory
building itself. Hale next persuaded other Chicago citizens to donate
appropriate land at Williams Bay, overlooking Lake Geneva in southern Wisconsin; and in the autumn of 1897 the Yerkes Observatory was
completed and dedicated. Hale, only twenty-nine and already internationally recognized, was its first director.

His struggle to find funds to maintain this enterprise, to direct its
researches, and to carry on his own, taxed to the utmost a physique
which at best was never robust. But no sooner had he solved these
problems than he began dreaming of new scientific conquests.

The story of his creation of the Mount Wilson Observatory in
California, and of the long series of imposing undertakings which
followed, should make his biography one of the most fascinating in
modern science.

It was hardly strange that my father should have been so strongly
drawn to this ingenious, charming, altogether modest, apparently invincible young man. Their paths had crossed infrequently. Yet it was typical of Hale that whenever they had met, he had never failed to mini-
mize his own activities and to astonish my father with questions
revealing a remarkably intimate acquaintance with the nature of his
work.

"No summary of Hale's many interests would be complete without
some reference to the fascination that Egypt always held for him,"
his colleague Frederick Haley Seares wrote after his death. ". . . The
story is bound up in his friendship with . . . Breasted and is to be read
in the hundreds of letters of the two men to each other over a period of
more than twenty years. The correspondence is most remarkable. Each
man was the confidant of the other. . . . Hale's dreams for new telescopes and [new enterprises], . . . besides striking summaries of his

own work on the sun, went into his letters; and from Breasted there came fascinating accounts of the 'recovery of the lost story of the rise of man,' diversfied by paragraphs in which with a flash of genius some intricate matter would be set forth in all clarity. . . .

"The association was a valued thing in the lives of both men. . . . Hale's historical sense was intensified, his synthetic view of events broadened; and in the evolutionary sweep of civilization he found the sequent of things beginning within the atom of the physicist. Breasted's instinctive approach to archaeological problems [was] through the methods of [natural] science. . . . Moreover, in certain respects the two men were alike. They had the same buoyant enthusiasm, the same imaginative grasp on broad fundamental problems, the same driving force to accompany great ends. . . ." *

He had already established what was to remain his lifelong residence in California and had taken with him several of his ablest Yerkes colleagues. Thus began a long hiatus in his relationship with my father, while their careers were preoccupied with activities which were eventually to bring them together again in a friendship and correspondence that only death would interrupt.

But throughout that summer of 1905 Hale continued vicariously to exert a powerful influence upon my father. For when he had learned that a doctor had advised my parents to take me to the country for the summer, he had quietly arranged for our occupancy of one of the houses at the Yerkes Observatory left vacant by staff he had taken to Mount Wilson.

Perhaps memory deceives me, and the heat of the summer of 1905 was merely average for the Middle West. Often since then I have sweltered in tropical climates, but I can still feel its withering days and nights, when not even the hour before dawn brought a faint stirring of air to ease one's pounding heart and breathe a hint of coolness into walls and floors and beds baking with fever heat. Our white frame house became overrun with ants, the woods luxuriant with poison ivy; all day long the parched, motionless countryside rang madly with the screeching whine of seventeen-year locusts, all night with the din of whippoorwills, katydids, and the frantic hum of gnats and mosquitoes.

The house looked out upon a great parched field that seemed under the pitiless sun to have become fluid and to be splotched with pools of dancing blue-white water out of which rose the tan brick, gray-

* *George Ellery Hale, The Scientist Afield,* by Frederick H. Seares, *ISIS,* No. 81 (Vol. XXX, 2), May, 1939, p. 260 ff.

terra-cotta trimmed mass of the Yerkes Observatory, with its one large
and two smaller gray domes stark against the cloudless sky. It was a
curious structure, partly grotesque, partly impressive, a utilitarian
mixture of Mesozoic reptile and oriental mosque. Its halls were always
cooler than the outer air and filled with the odor that clings to all
observatories, a blend of the aromas given off by electrically driven
machinery, physics laboratories and photographic darkrooms. The daylight hours I spent within this place, and above all, those superlative
occasions when a gracious and gentle New Englander, Edwin Brant
Frost—Hale's successor as director, and a friend and student contem-
porary of my father's in his Berlin days, whom a cruel and ironical fate
was soon to afflict with blindness—permitted us to view the heavens
through the large telescope in the mysterious gloom of the great dome
which rumbled like distant thunder as its opening was turned toward
the appropriate blue-black segment of starry sky—all these made a
profound impression upon me. Never since then have I entered an
astronomical observatory without a sense of having lingered for a
moment at a way station to infinity.

But for my father the Observatory was something more than
impressive, it had a very personal significance. It embodied all the
earlier hopes and struggles, the trials and disappointments of his
friend Hale who, even with the advantages on his side which the
natural sciences enjoyed as opposed to the humanities, had had to
fight for years for the right to extend the frontiers of his science by
means of this great piece of physical equipment. It stood now as
a monument to his patience and tenacity, to his gift for translating
dreams into realities. To my father it was an inspiration to go forth and
do likewise. . . .

By day from Mondays to Fridays all through that grueling summer,
he taught classes and prepared for his imminent expedition to Egypt;
and in the evenings, and during weekends at Williams Bay, he read
proofs and made indexes for his *History*, his *Ancient Records*, and
a popular book he had somehow managed to write in odd moments for
Underwood & Underwood—a total of six volumes. Proofs bulged from
his pockets, distended his briefcase. He read proofs wherever he
went—at mealtimes, or walking to and from his classes, or in crowded
day-coaches as he sat on filthy, acrid-smelling plush seats beside un-
closable windows which belched soot and noise and dust.

On Friday afternoons when the train chuffed into Williams Bay,
the end of a spur line, the wealthy citizens of Chicago with summer

homes on Lake Geneva would emerge from their parlor cars and go aboard their steam yachts, or don long linen coats for a dusty ride in magnificent, today incredible, open automobiles, all bound for the even greater Victorian magnificence of rococo wooden summer palaces. My father, roused only by the thumping and banging of seats being turned back by the conductor, would always be the last to clamber from his day-coach, clutching proofs and a fountain pen in one hand, a suitcase in the other. Sometimes I would be waiting for him. But more often he would climb into a horse-drawn stage and for twenty-five cents be carried along the two miles of rutted, unpaved main road to the crest of a ridge where the Observatory road branched off. Here I would meet him, and carry his suitcase as we walked another half mile to our house, while he asked how my mother was, and what troubles we had had *that* week.

Visiting us were my Grandmother Harriet and a pretty young girl. Harriet was now a slim little old lady clad all in black, who subsisted on memories and on idolizing her son James so completely and with such a plaintive solicitude as to keep my mother—what with the inhuman heat, no maidservant, and all the cooking and housework to do—in a state of constant irritation. The pretty girl was Imogen, youngest of the Hart sisters, who had been a child of six when Frances and James had first met in Berlin. Now seventeen, gay and carefree, with a lilting laugh and dancing brown eyes, and not above playing with me, she seemed to my eight years the embodiment of everything desirable in an aunt. It did not trouble me that she was what my mother called irresponsible, or that except for the few hours during weekends when she helped my father in proofreading, she was forever darting away down a path into the woods leading to a summer colony of gay people whom my mother strongly disapproved—largely, as I now suspect, because of her own somewhat puritanical mistrust of gaiety, and because they apparently did not toil as she did. Her overserious, slightly evangelical efforts to instill in the girl a sense of responsibility beyond her years merely created tearful scenes and more frequent escapes down the path into the woods.

My father was seldom spared a recital of the week's grievances and mishaps, including my own misdemeanors. Having listened patiently, and as often as not suffered the consequences of defense or palliation, he would quietly revert to reading his proofs.

So passed the summer of 1905, under the strangely potent shadow of George Ellery Hale's observatory. Early that October we sailed again for Europe, where he expected to leave my mother and me while he led his first scientific expedition up the Nile.

In Berlin my father fell gravely ill, so ill that we despaired of his ability to carry on. But when we had given up hope, his old invincible vitality reasserted itself, and shaking from fever and weakness, he dragged himself from his bed and resumed final preparations for the project of which he had dreamed so long. Later, in his official journal, he wrote almost apologetically that an eminent bacteriologist at Berlin University "forbade a man in my state of health to undertake a journey in tropical Africa without either a physician or at least my wife. I have therefore brought her and my son with me, of course at my own expense."

He knew quite well that to include my mother was to risk the success of his first expedition. I was still too young to sense the apprehension which filled his mind as we stood on the deck of a ship late one afternoon in November, 1905, and drew into Alexandria Harbor. I was aware only of the indefinable fragrance of the off-shore desert wind, and of the excitement of entering for the first time the land which had always dominated my family's life.

The bedlam of landing and the train journey to Cairo under a starry sky were for me like witnessing the actual performance of a play which had been read to me again and again. Sentiment led my parents back to the old Hotel du Nil deep in the native quarter, which seemed to me straight out of the Arabian Nights. But ten years had not lessened the pressure of economy which soon led as before to the *pension* of old Frau Fink. Personal misfortunes had greatly aged and embittered her, and though in a smarter neighborhood, her establishment was now much smaller. My parents looked hopefully for familiar faces but found none.

"What has become of Salib Claudius and Miss Gracilla Smith?" they asked her.

She shrugged her shoulders. "I scolded him for falling in love with her in *my* house," she said morosely. "He went away, and married her, and God punished them. I have not seen him since he left my house." She would say no more.

While my mother occupied herself with final purchases and preparations against improbable emergencies, my father took me everywhere on his business and to all the places and sights about which he had told me ever since I could first understand speech. We went deep into old bazaars smelling of incense, musk and sewage, watched native shadow theaters, listened to Arab storytellers, took off our shoes and entered all the great mosques in Cairo. We made the rounds of the antiquities dealers, and as my father with deft hands thoughtfully examined the medley of ancient objects laid before him, I became acquainted with a person I had never seen before—a dispassionate expert, as I realize now, in whom artist, historian, critic, detective and disingenuous trader were momentarily merged behind an inscrutable face which not even the canniest oriental could be sure of reading correctly. Even today in memory I have difficulty in reconciling the impersonal authority of this stranger to the Illinois prairie boy who happened to become an Egyptologist. . . .

We went up to the Citadel during the paradoxical Fast of Ramadan (the month in the Arab lunar calendar during which from the moment at dawn that a *good* Moslem can distinguish a black thread from a white, until sunset, he is forbidden to eat, drink, or smoke), and I heard for the first time the far murmur, then the exultant human roar as the sunset gun ushered in another night of feasting in the greatest Mohammedan city in the world. We rode out southeastward of Cairo to the cathedral-like quarries in the brown Mokattam Hills whence came the facing stones of the great pyramids of Gizeh; and to the ridge nearer the river, on which stand the round, tower-like remains of the windmills which Napoleon erected in 1798 to grind flour for his army. And of course, though I had to be lifted from almost every tier of enormous blocks to the next, we climbed the Great Pyramid.

He took me to Sakkara, the last ancient place in Egypt he and my mother had visited ten years before, and here in government excavations being conducted by a colleague of Petrie's named Quibell, I saw for the first time antiquities actually being uncovered and removed from the ground. . . . That night in the white flood of a full moon we rode back on donkeys along the irrigation dykes across the fields to catch the last train for Cairo. As we came among the palm groves overgrowing the site of ancient Memphis, he told me very simply the history of this place and of the colossal granite statue of vain old Ramses II which we passed, now lying ingloriously on the ground. When he had finished, we drew up for a moment, and listened to the night—palm leaves overhead stirring dryly, and in a neighboring village, dogs barking, waterwheels whining. Suddenly he said, "Boy, some day when you are very much older and your father is gone, you'll remember that once as a little fellow you rode with him by the light of a full moon through the palm-covered ruins of ancient Memphis!"

So I do—as if it had been last month's instead of a full moon more than thirty-five years ago. . . .

One morning we paid a courtesy call at a severely plain building in a high-walled tropical garden overlooking the Nile. (It was no coincidence that the Kitchener-built Kasr en-Nil Barracks, a few hundred yards downstream, also discreetly overlooked the river—a strategic advantage in the event of native uprisings.) British sentries guarded the gates, and the place wore an air of importance all the greater for being, architecturally speaking, understated.

This was the official dwelling of Consul-General Lord Cromer which later, as the British Residency, was to house a long series of High Commissioners for Egypt and the Sudan. As we entered the main gate, the sentries came to attention. "Whether or not they have any right to be here," my father said to me in a low voice—and a little grudgingly, I thought, "these people signify law and order in Egypt!"

At the *porte cochère* entrance a *bawab* (doorman) clad in Turkish white pantaloons, short gold-embroidered crimson jacket, and a tarboosh, respectfully addressed my father as "pasha," ushered us into the hallway where another servant led us to the visitors' book. My father signed his name, laid cards with corners appropriately turned down, on a silver tray, and we were returning as we had come, when the gorgeous doorman indicated the presence of someone behind us. We faced about, saw standing beside the visitors' book an extraordinarily handsome elderly gentleman with a gray moustache, who carried himself with the unconscious ancestral dignity of a Raeburn portrait.

He came forward and greeted my father in a most friendly manner. "I'm Cromer," he said. "It is most kind of you to have called—and high time we became acquainted. I've just ordered a copy of your newly announced *History of Egypt*, and a letter from Lord Lansdowne asks us to help you in any way we can. You must tell us what you need!"

My father thanked him cordially, and added, "I need at least six additional well-trained staff members for an expedition without the money to pay them!"

Cromer laughed, and the talk turned upon the difficulty of training young novitiates on his own staff, just out from England, to understand the peculiar problems of administering modern Egypt. "The first text-book I now put into their hands," he said, "is the official report which your General Leonard Wood has written of his military governorship of the Moro Province in the Philippines. I consider it a model, both as a report and as a summary of the considerations which should guide any conscientious official in the administration of protectorates."

With a kindly proffer of future hospitality, and a handshake even for me, he turned and disappeared into his office.

This unexpected meeting helped to modify, if only slightly, the deep, righteous resentment which the British administration of Egypt had roused in my father, and in a host of other scholars and laymen, by flinging the mighty Aswan Dam across the Nile just below instead of just above the Island of Philæ, and thus dooming to destruction the loveliest architectural relic of Ptolemaic times. The controversy between those who deemed this sacrifice unnecessary and the engineers responsible for selecting the site had been a *cause célèbre* in which Egyptian agriculture, the national treasury, and what my father called "the fundamental Philistinism of the British government" had finally triumphed. "Mais, il y aura plus de champs de cotton," said Pierre Loti at the close of his book, *La Mort du Philæ,* and even the complacent British Foreign Office had winced slightly. But the incident, like the waters mounting above Philæ itself, was closed.

Except for this gigantic harnessing of the Nile flood, some lesser barrages, and a new sugar factory here and there, the face of Egypt had changed little since my parents' honeymoon on the river. But a highly romantic and portentous chapter of Empire history had been written, whose economic and political consequences were eventually to affect, among others, such diverse matters as the war of 1914, American cotton production, and the science of Egyptology. I believe that its effect upon the last of these deserves brief mention here, both for its inherent interest and its bearing upon my father's later activities.

In 1822 Mohammed Ali, an Albanian adventurer who had made himself master of Egypt, conquered the Sudan in hopes of reviving his empty treasury. His conquest proved to be only another liability; and the ensuing sixty years of Turkish graft and injustice rendered the already poverty-stricken Sudan utterly destitute, and ripe for rebellion under the insanely militant leadership of a religious fanatic named Mohammed Ahmed, who called himself the Mahdi of Allah—"one who is guided aright by God."

The initial victories of this self-appointed Messiah, who regarded all foreigners as Turks and promised in the name of Islam to exterminate them from the world, included the annihilation of an Egyptian force of over 10,000 men sent against him in November, 1883, and the surrender of the brilliant Austrian, Slatin Pasha, then serving Egypt as governor-general of the Sudanese province of Darfur. The Mahdi's almost mesmeric influence now spread like brush fire among the tribes.

At this point England, following Cromer's counsel, ordered the still insolvent and chaotic Egyptian government to evacuate the Sudan, a precarious task which was entrusted to a veteran of earlier Sudanese service—General Charles George ("Chinese") Gordon. What followed is familiar history—the Mahdi's siege of Khartoum, begun in March, 1884; England's procrastination; and Gordon's incredible defense until his tragic death on January 26, 1885, two days before the arrival of the British relief expedition. Like many others at the time, my father felt that Gordon had been the victim of Mr. Gladstone's obtuseness, and delighted in quoting Henry du Pré Labouchere's remark: "I don't object to the old man keeping a card up his sleeve, but I do object to his asserting that God put it there!"

In June, when the British had withdrawn northward again and his victory was virtually complete, the Mahdi suddenly died, and his gory mantle fell upon a successor even crueler, if possible, than himself—Abdulla el Ta'aisha, whom he had long since appointed Khalifa. During the next ten years, while Abdullah's rule of terror remained almost undisputed, Cromer quietly set the Egyptian economic house in order; and by 1896 had brought Egypt so far that England could enlist her co-operation in a reconquest of the Sudan before some other European power should attempt to gain control of the sources of the Nile.

That year Kitchener began the carefully planned campaign which culminated in his destruction of the Mahdist forces at Omdurman on September 2, 1898. The death of Gordon was thereby avenged, the Sudan reconquered—but as so often before, the Khalifa had once again eluded capture. Then at dawn on November 25, 1899, at Umm Debrekat south of Khartoum, the Khalifa and all his chiefs, surrounded in a surprise attack, knelt upon their prayer rugs and as they calmly faced their God of blood, were shot to death by a British flying column commanded by a young Colonel Francis Reginald Wingate; and the last vestige of Mahdist power had been broken.

Sir Reginald, as he became for his deeds, succeeded Kitchener as

governor-general of the Anglo-Egyptian Sudan and sirdar (commander-in-chief) of the Egyptian army; and from his white-washed
mud-brick palace at Khartoum, ruled like a king over a territory about
one-fourth the size of Europe. When my father in 1906 led his little
scientific expedition into the Sudan, Sir Reginald (again at Lord Lansdowne's request) accorded him "every possible courtesy and assistance." But again I am anticipating.

While Kitchener's campaigns had been steadily extending British
control along the vast belt between Cairo and the Cape, France had
looked on with increasing anxiety and imperialistic envy. Finally, in a
badly timed and feebly executed effort to counter this progress, she
had dispatched a little contingent of 120 Senegalese soldiers under the
command of a Major Marchand, to hoist the tricolor on the banks of
the White Nile.

Kitchener met him at a swampy, fever-infested spot called Fashoda,
and probably saved him from annihilation by the dervishes, who had
already attacked his force once and were then preparing a *coup de
grâce*. To the accompaniment of flowery exchanges of courtesies and
expressions of mutual amity, and the presentation of a supply of
excellent French brandy to replace the Major's exhausted stock,
Kitchener impressed upon him the impropriety, meaning the unequivocal impossibility, of raising the French flag within the dominions of
the Khedive of Egypt. But while the Major was susceptible enough to
these amenities to agree that the *impasse* could best be settled by
diplomacy, he could not disregard his orders, and continued to fly the
French flag. Kitchener countered by posting the British and Egyptian
flags, and a force to guard them, at a point farther south, and took his
leave.

Only after long, often crucial negotiations had made clear the
untenability of the French claim, was Marchand ordered to withdraw,
and the Fashoda incident—as it was thenceforth known—closed. But
injured French pride was not mollified until the signing of the Anglo-
French Declaration of 1904, whereby Britain recognized French control
of Morocco, and France recognized British predominance in Egypt.

This agreement contained a clause which directly affected my
father's science, and again drew his ire at what he considered another
flagrant instance of British governmental Philistinism.

The French had always held that the great array of savants whom
Napoleon had carried with him on his abortive campaign to Egypt
(not to mention Champollion, the decipherer of hieroglyphic writing,

and the many others who had followed later), had by their scholarly industry established the scientific priority of France in that country. Hence they had insisted upon the inclusion of a clause providing that for the 30-year duration of the Anglo-French Declaration, the post of director-general of the Egyptian Antiquities Department (under whom also fell the administration of the great new Cairo Egyptian Museum, completed in 1902) should be held by a Frenchman. With its traditional apathy for the cultural values in the countries under its political domination, His Majesty's Government had welcomed the opportunity of conceding as a sop in return for more profitable advantages, a responsibility it had at no time desired.

Some twenty years later, this clause was to play an important part in blocking an unprecedented American philanthropy. But at the moment it appeared as nothing more than the formalization of an arrangement already long in effect. For Gaston Maspero, who had held if not actually created this position in the early 'eighties under the Khedive Ismail, and had resigned it to resume his professorial duties in Paris, had been reappointed to it in 1899 by the Khedive Abbas II.

My father was therefore confronted by an old friend when we called one morning upon the Director-General of the Egyptian Antiquities Department, to secure an official permit to photograph or copy all the inscribed ancient monuments of Upper Egypt.

Maspero sat in an office crowded with open boxes of recently excavated antiquities, some of which had come from the government's own excavations but most of which represented the fifty per cent division it required of all foreign excavators. I was entranced. Here, like treasure in a cave, was everything imaginable, all the things my father had told me I myself could perhaps dig up with my small shovel! This was my very first tactile encounter with ancient objects not formally laid out under glass cases in museum halls. I could actually touch objects fresh from their long burial in tombs and in the wreckage of vanished towns, the personal possessions of human beings who had lived thousands of years ago.

While the men talked their shop, I moved about among this haphazard, exciting display—the household and funerary effects of ancient Egyptians—wooden cooking utensils, pots and pans of baked clay, bits of wooden furniture, beads, cosmetic jars and "vanity" boxes of ivory and alabaster, fragments of colored textiles, rolls of linen mummy cloth, ushabtis (little blue *faience* mummy-like figures put into tombs as "proxies" to represent the deceased's servants), alabaster vases, pottery sherds inscribed with household accounts, a miniature wooden boat painted in natural colors, upon which stood little wooden sailors who had held their oars in the same position for over three thousand years. Under a table I came upon several packing boxes filled with green-coated copper coins, and a smaller box of what appeared to be little silver coins.

At this point I must have exclaimed, for Monsieur Maspero came over to see what so interested me. He found me peering at the silver coins. "Ah, my young man, would you like to have some of them?" he asked. I was dumbfounded, and looked appealingly at my father, who dashed my hopes by saying quickly, "No! No! Under no circumstances —you must not even think of it, Monsieur Maspero!"

But Monsieur Maspero not only thought of it, he scooped up a handful of the little silver coins and said irresistibly, "You may choose six!" This time I avoided looking at my father, and did as I was told. The fact that I was simply speechless seemed to delight Monsieur Maspero all the more. He leaned over, scooped up a handful of the copper coins as well, and poured them into the pockets of my sailor suit. "Ce jeune homme doit se faire archéologue!" he said, patting me on the shoulder.

I can remember nothing more of this visit except the wonderful weight in my pockets as I walked home in a trance beside my enormously embarrassed father. . . . One day some twenty-five years later, when I came upon them again in an old family cabinet of miscellaneous antiquities, it occurred to me that four of the six little silver coins might make a pleasing set of cuff links for my father. I took them to a well-known firm of jewelers, and presently received a letter from its director, apologizing for their inability to execute my commission. "When our silversmith found the coins to be peculiarly susceptible to heat and immune to solder," he wrote, "he tested them for their silver content and discovered they contained almost none. We thereupon submitted them to a leading numismatist, who has informed us that they were probably struck in Alexandria during the reign of Emperor Aurelian, about A.D. 270, when provincial Roman coinage became debased until its content of precious metal was almost nil. The chief value of your coins would seem to lie in their tangible evidence of the decadence of governmental integrity during the decline of Rome."

After a quarter of a century, I could still hear old Maspero's laughter!

On the eve of our departure upriver, my father in accordance with Continental custom paid his respects to his numerous European colleagues then in Cairo, a rite to which with few exceptions I was again an involuntary party. They were all very kind to me, and I behaved reasonably well; for I was already a veteran at enduring eternities of my elders' cigar smoke and scientific shop talk. Conversations during such visits were usually so far beyond my understanding that I hardly listened to them. Gradually, however, they lodged in my subconscious mind a miscellany of archaeological lore, scientific and historical facts, geographical information and curious personal experiences which for me invested my father's world with a quality of enthralling romance in complete contrast to those other aspects of his work that repelled me.

But among all these rather stuffy archaeological visits, one in particular made a lifelong impression upon me.

Toward sundown one afternoon, both my parents took me to call on kindly Professor Sayce aboard his dahabiyeh. He seemed tremendously pleased, even moved, at seeing his old friends again. Across a silver tea service he beamed reassuringly at me, as the talk reverted to the days before my own brief time. For almost to the day and hour, ten years had passed since he and my newly married parents had sat on this same deck, and just as now, the shore, the overhanging palms and the river craft moored all about, had been set aglow by the rippling reflections and the ineffable glories of the Egyptian sunset.

The beauty of his boat, his perfect understanding of a small boy's appetite, and the antiquities he gave me "to add to my collection," would have been memorable enough. But it was the sequel he told us of the story of Salib Claudius and the lovely Gracilla which none of us was ever to forget. Its effect upon my parents was profound. For like Professor Sayce, they now felt almost responsible for what had befallen a romance to which from the beginning they had given their friendliest encouragement.

Soon after my parents had left Egypt in 1895, Mrs. Smith had taken Gracilla to England for the stipulated three months' separation. The girl had strictly obeyed her mother's wishes, and had uttered no complaint. But her health had betrayed the strain, and it was obvious that far from having undergone a change of heart, she was more than ever in love with Salib Claudius, whose manifestly sincere cablegram on the ninety-first day of their silence showed clearly that his feelings for her had only deepened. Most of Gracilla's relatives threatened to disown her if she insisted upon consummating this marriage, but Mrs. Smith now felt in honor bound to give it her consent—though she could not rid herself of a certain strange foreboding. Gracilla eagerly gathered her trousseau, and with her mother sailed for Egypt, where her reunion with Salib was so joyous as to allay for the moment all parental fears.

Before their wedding day, Salib said to Gracilla, "Please understand that when you have become my wife, you will have lost none of your freedom. You shall go and come as you choose, you shall visit your people in England whenever and for as long as you desire. This is my promise."

They were married in Cairo, once in a quiet Church of England ceremony attended by Professor Sayce and a little group of mutual friends from the English colony; and a second time in a Coptic ceremony attended chiefly by Salib's numerous relations, and again by loyal Professor Sayce. Everyone was especially kind—for everyone, as did Gracilla herself in a vague way deep in her heart, understood the implications of such a union. . . .

In the ensuing years, Salib rose rapidly in the postal service of his government. He was appointed postmaster of progressively larger provincial towns, and everywhere acquitted himself admirably. Those who knew the pattern of such things, said that without doubt he would one day become postmaster-general of all Egypt.

Meanwhile Gracilla with genuine enthusiasm gradually adjusted herself to wifehood under conditions for which nothing in her earlier life had prepared her. She acquired Arabic, familiarized herself with a whole new world of ancient customs and social usages, learned to keep house with native servants, to buy in the local provincial markets, and to dispense the hospitality expected of the wife of a locally important Egyptian government official.

In due course she bore Salib two daughters—each time, at his firm insistence, at an English-run hospital. They were charming children— though they had inherited their father's sun-tanned complexion, and for all they betrayed of her Nordic blonde beauty, their mother might have been a Circassian. As time went on and the little girls grew old enough to talk, she realized that despite an English "nanna," they were more quickly learning to speak Arabic than English.

She realized, too, with a pang, that she herself had been seeing less and less of her own people—and not only of her own, but of Salib's as well. Subtly, almost imperceptibly, many of their old pre-marital friends had fallen away: not deliberately so much as on the usual, half-wishful assumption by the English that she now belonged to his people, and by the Egyptians that he had gone over to hers. Her love for Salib had grown steadily deeper. He was the most considerate human being she had ever known. Yet in a way she could never impart to him, she was lonely, and desperately hungry for her own people. The homesickness she had so long stifled, welled up within her. . . .

A day came when Salib was appointed postmaster of Alexandria, the port through which passed most of the mails between Egypt and Europe. It was an important promotion—only Cairo now stood between him and the postmaster-generalship of Egypt. Gracilla was very proud. For the moment she forgot her longings in the little excitement of moving to Alexandria, into a pleasant villa not far from the sea. But once the household had resumed its usual routines, her old thoughts crowded back upon her. She formed the habit of accompanying the children and their nurse to the wide seashore, solely that she might watch the ships moving in and out of the harbor, or crawling along the horizon to and from Port Said and the Suez Canal. Some of them, she knew, were always bound for England. . . . At last the longing to go home surged up irresistibly. She decided definitely to go to England with her children for a generous visit. She would be a better wife for having done this. She had never reminded Salib of his promise. It made her happy to realize there would be no need to—the mere voicing of her wish would be his command.

When she told him of her plan early in the spring, he said simply, "I have long known this was in your mind. It is right that you should go, and I shall arrange everything. You must stay in England until you can no longer resist coming back to me!"

He engaged passage on an English vessel, and on the sailing day saw his little family aboard in his official steam launch. He generously tipped the purser and those who would serve them, asked the captain to make certain that throughout the voyage they lacked no possible comfort or kindness. . . . Never once since their marriage had he referred directly to the difference in their blood. But his consideration of her at all times, and especially in public on occasions of parting or reunion, had told Gracilla more plainly than words that he never for a moment forgot it. It was she who asked to be kissed good-bye. . . .

He made a handsome figure in his red *tarboosh*; standing in the bow of his launch beside the white crescent and green field of a fluttering Egyptian flag, and waving to Gracilla and the little girls as their ship gained speed at the opening of the breakwater, and then veered north-eastward into the purple-blue Mediterranean, bound for England.

Two months passed, the blistering Egyptian summer drew on, and all the legations in Cairo, the families of the wealthier upriver foreign colonies and of Cromer's Anglo-Egyptian civil servants, every foreign national, Levantine and native Egyptian who could afford the time from his duties and the high seasonal tariff, fled from the merciless heat and sought the benign coolness of the Mediterranean. Some sailed north to France, others crossed to the pine-clad slopes of Mount Troödos on the island of Cyprus, a few went up among the giant cedars in the High Lebanon above Beirut. But a vast number stopped in Alexandria, where every available house and room in the city was rented. People spent their days beside the languid sea, and of evenings crowded the open-air restaurants and cafes.

But Salib went about his work as always, dining alone at night in the quiet English club of which, as a mark of exceptional esteem, he had been made a guest member. Afterwards he would walk home to his empty house, and write his daily letter to Gracilla.

Her own letters for the first fortnight had been almost daily, but gradually the intervals had lengthened. All her family, she wrote, had been reconciled to her marriage, and in their eagerness to make amends, had begged her to pay them lengthy visits. This incessant hospitality, which she had thought it best to accept, had left her little time for letters. She knew he would understand, and share her pleasure at this happy change. She repeated again and again that in future she would not revisit England without him—he must obtain leave of absence and accompany her. For she missed him constantly, each day would bring her twice the happiness if only he were beside her. He was so kind and generous, she said, to have granted her this sojourn in England.

Salib understood, and took great comfort in her happiness. But his aching loneliness for her grew until it required all his self-control to keep it from creeping into his letters. The longest summer he had ever known slowly gave way to early autumn, visitors began to depart upriver again, and still she made no mention of the date of her return.

At last he could bear it no longer. In a letter which was the more moving because it was written with the natural simplicity and dignity, and the utter sincerity which characterized his whole life, he laid bare his heart, confessed his desperate, pent-up loneliness, and expressed the fervent hope that since without her his life was as a desert, she would soon return to him. Lest he should reconsider his action and destroy the letter, he carried it himself to the main post office, asked a night clerk to cancel the stamp, and himself placed it in a pouch leaving on the morrow for England.

When he found a cablegram lying on his desk, early one morning a week later, he was at first afraid to open it, then ashamed of his own lack of faith and courage. He slit the envelope, unfolded the message: she was overjoyed by his letter—it dispelled the little mutual reticence their long separation had created—she was hurrying back to him by the quickest route—by rail to Marseilles, thence by a French steamer to Alexandria—she could hardly wait. . . . As he read and re-read the cablegram, he experienced a sense of relief and happiness such as he had known but once before in his life, on the day when Gracilla had promised to become his wife.

He had only one small regret—that she was not returning on an English ship. Long experience had taught him that the French were undisciplined and inefficient at sea.

On the great day when the ship was due, he filled the house with flowers, bought toys for the children, some pretty trinkets for Gracilla. His launch lay ready at the government quay, awaiting only the harbormaster's signal that the ship had been sighted. He had not been surprised when the local agent of the line had reported her several hours late in leaving Marseilles—she should have arrived at dawn of this day, but now was due toward noon.

Midday passed, the afternoon dragged on. At four o'clock when the autumn sun was lowering rapidly, the harbormaster reported the ship on the horizon but moving very slowly. The afternoon wind died down and the sea turned glassy smooth. Salib boarded the launch, put off for the entrance of the inner harbor and waited there as the French ship with unwonted slowness approached the outer breakwater.

He peered at her through his binoculars. There was something strange about her—she was not flying the proper signal flags, all her portholes were covered, her railings were not lined with passengers eagerly gazing toward the low shores of Egypt and the white and amber houses of Alexandria glowing in a late sun which set windows aflame and filled the sky with purple and mauve. He could see no signs of life whatever, not even the crew.

Her bow made no ripple as she crept past the outer breakwater. Instead of continuing toward the inner harbor, she moved slowly inside the outer breakwater about a mile distant, swung gradually toward it, and stopped. There was a far rumble and a splash as her anchor dropped into the sea.

It was now dusk. Salib ordered his launch to approach the ship which save for a few glimmering lights, still appeared as if deserted. He drew abreast of the bridge, but no one looked over the side. He hailed the captain, and no one answered. After a long interval, the first officer came to the railing of the hatch-deck, and cupping his hands, said angrily in French:

"The captain requests you to cease molesting this ship, and to return to the harbor and summon the chief of police of Alexandria. He will permit no one aboard, nor confer with anyone but the chief of police."

Behind the outward calm of a ranking official performing a routine duty, Salib struggled desperately to control his cold, frantic fear as to the meaning of all this for Gracilla and their children.

"I am Salib Claudius, postmaster of Alexandria," he answered in somewhat guttural French, without a trace of emotion. "Your ship is anchored in Egyptian waters and carries mail which it is my duty to safeguard. Under the laws of Egypt I have the right to board your ship, and if the captain hinders me in the execution of my duty, he will be criminally liable. In the name of the Khedive of Egypt, I demand to come aboard!"

The officer made no reply, and disappeared. After a long delay, he reappeared, this time on the bridge. His tone was now more respectful.

"The captain has consented that you alone, unaccompanied by any member of your staff or crew, may come aboard," he said. "But when you draw alongside, your boat must fasten no lines to his ship, and must stand clear while awaiting your return!"

A lantern appeared at the rail of the hatch-deck, and a rope ladder was lowered. While his sailors steadied the launch with boat hooks as best they could, Salib climbed aboard the ship. He was met by the captain who saluted him and without a word, motioned him to follow.

Preceded by the first officer with the lantern, they climbed to the first cabin deck, and halted before a door. The captain took a ringful of heavy bronze keys from his pocket, selected one, unlocked and swung open the door, stood aside for the others to enter. As Salib stepped over the high sill into a long passage, dimly lit by a few widely separated bracket lanterns, he noted that the stale reek of unwashed humanity, uncleaned lavatories and rancid cooking was even stronger than usual—evidently all doors had been locked and the passage unventilated for many hours.

Having carefully relocked the door, the captain led the way past a number of short side-corridors, all identical and lined with cabin doors facing one another, until he reached a corridor approximately amidships. Here he stopped again, selected another key, unlocked a cabin door, pushed it open. Taking the first officer's lantern, he entered, and stood waiting for Salib.

With the opening of the door, Salib became conscious of a horrible odor, felt himself growing ill and faint. But he controlled himself, and stepped in. The captain held the lantern over a berth covered with a sheet which he drew back.

In a jagged welter of dried and blackened blood, her throat cut from ear to ear, lay Gracilla.

As the ship had been on the point of sailing, its entire crew had walked ashore in response to a sudden general strike of the sort for which Marseilles has always been notorious. Unwilling to lose time, the line had adopted its usual expedient of combing the city's foul back streets for a pick-up crew *sans* seamen's papers, with no questions asked. It was well aware that the majority of the men thus acquired consisted of escaped or recently discharged criminals.

One of these, assigned as a waiter in the first class dining room, had noted that a middle aged American lady at his table was bedecked each evening with an extraordinarily rich array of jewels. Knowing that the ship was to reach Alexandria Harbor before dawn of the sixth day, where he could escape by swimming ashore, he had ascertained the lady's cabin number, armed himself with a razor which he had stolen from the ship's barber, and on the last night, taking advantage of the general disorganization and the absence of a regular night watch, had crept into her cabin to steal her jewel case. He had been unable to find it in the total darkness, and in his impatience and haste had made a noise which awakened her and caused her to cry out. To silence her, he had in his anger cut her throat.

Or so he thought. But by mistake instead of entering the cabin of the jewelled American lady, he had stepped into the one adjoining, which belonged to Gracilla. Her first shrieks awoke fellow passengers, but before they could reach the corridor, he had disappeared.

The captain had immediately reduced the ship's speed, ordered his officers to confine all passengers to their own quarters, put the entire crew in irons, seal all port-holes. Gracilla's body was left exactly as it had been found, for under French law it could not be removed except by authority of the police. It was soon discovered that the dining room waiter of the American lady's table was missing, but in his bunk were found his neatly folded uniform, property of the line, and lying upon it a slightly blood-stained razor belonging to the ship's barber. Certain that the waiter was the murderer, and was still aboard and being protected by fellow criminals among the crew, the captain had personally examined every man, and with his officers searched every inch of the ship from anchor chain bulkhead to rudder post.

But it had all been in vain. Then as a climax to his baffling failure, faced with the certainty that his line would make him the scapegoat of its own guilt, and the possibility, if not of a prison sentence, of relegation to the oblivion of tramp steamers for the rest of his life, the captain had been confronted by the one man in all the world he had least wanted to meet. The irony, at this critical moment in his life, of being outranked in authority by a native Egyptian government official who was also the husband of the murdered Englishwoman, filled him with a vindictive anger that expressed itself with Gallic cruelty by subjecting Salib to a horror which in that one night turned his hair snow white. And as if this were not enough, it was later discovered that even as Salib was being led into Gracilla's cabin, the murderer had leapt overboard and escaped.

A fortnight later in Cairo, the American lady died of nervous prostration.

Salib begged Mrs. Smith to come and take his little girls to England until he could gather up the pieces of his shattered life. She came at once, and was a great comfort to him while he closed his house and resumed the simple ways of his bachelorhood. Her departure for England with his children on an English ship was like a tragic echo of that other day when he said good-bye to Gracilla—he saw them aboard in the same launch, waved to them as they sailed out of the harbor. Not long after they had reached England, the care of his children fell to others. For Mrs. Smith also died—of a broken heart, it was said.

My father had personally selected every item of equipment for this first expedition he had ever undertaken.

From America where makers of foodstuffs had not yet learned to pack for export, he had bought only "Triscuit" as bread (and even this was packed in thin pasteboard instead of hermetically sealed tin boxes); a few revolvers and rifles; some Ingersoll watches, cheap candy, wool sweaters, and jackknives, to give as baksheesh or to use for occasional trading with natives for chickens and sheep.

Most of our tinned food came from England—excepting tinned butter (terribly salty) from Denmark; and tinned milk and pure chocolate for emergency rations from Switzerland. Bottled water came from France; from Germany, Nuremberger Zwieback, camp equipment, glass photographic plates packed in sealed cartons enclosed in hermetically soldered tin cases. A large mahogany camera with a great bellows (which in this day of compact instruments would seem incredibly clumsy), using eight-by-ten-inch glass plates, had been superbly constructed in Vienna by Kurt Bentzin, one of the ablest camera builders of his day, and fitted with lenses by Carl Zeiss, who then produced the finest in the world. There was equipment against every emergency—tools, medical supplies, even dental instruments and gutta-percha for temporary fillings. My father had learned a great deal, especially negatively, from Flinders Petrie.

I have never forgotten the care with which he examined every article for its practicality and durability, the logic of his final choice, the orderliness of his lists, the clarity of all his instructions. Not until long afterwards did I realize what a difficult, creditable performance this had been for a scholar whose experience in such matters, except for an epigraphic honeymoon on the Nile, had been largely confined to philology and history. His example was always before me when years later I myself became responsible for fitting out many similar enterprises. But these were never again attended by the same exciting sense of anticipation which marked this first venture for which he had waited so long.

Everything had finally converged upon a vacant native shop in a narrow, unpaved street off Sharia Kasr en-Nil in Cairo, where on an evening early in December, 1905, I sat atop of an empty crate and watched him and his two assistants—an American civil engineer named Victor Persons, and a German photographer named Friederich Koch— checking the last of the more than one hundred wooden cases containing the gamut of a small expedition's needs for a six months' season.

In the dusk outside there passed a vague procession of natives, foreigners of many nationalities, push-carts, donkeys and camels with riders or loaded with packs, and ragged little urchins who held out filthy hands and whined for baksheesh. Within, the room was hot, the air thick with the pungent dust of excelsior and straw, and the odor of pinewood cut from northern forests. As my father and his helpers moved about, their shadows rose against the high walls of the dimly lit room like huge and grotesque genii. His earnest face was absorbed in lists held close to a lantern. An oversight might mean weeks or months of time lost upriver, awaiting forgotten equipment—and he had already waited too long. When he was positive everything was in hand, he straightened up wearily, ordered the last of the boxes sealed.

The December evening of our departure was not one of the three each week when the Luxor train carried sleeping cars, for we could not afford such luxury. In a downpour of rain—which loyal Cairo residents, like Southern Californians, always assure visitors is most unusual—we climbed sopping wet into a second-class compartment, and in company with three poker-faced Levantine gentlemen, sat up all night.

The winter rains of the Delta seldom extend far south of Cairo, and dust soon enveloped us in a choking shroud. The clatter of the train and the snoring of our companions induced a blessed semi-stupor finally broken only by the explosive opening of the door into the passage, and a guttural voice shouting, "Dee nex' stashone LUUK-SORE!"

We pushed up slatted shutters, through darkened glass saw groves of leaning palms beyond irrigation-chequered green fields, smoke hanging low over adobe villages, flashes of the river touched here and there by a morning breeze like warm breath on gun-metal—the ruins of Karnak casting long shadows—dykes, houses—and the train drew into the station. Begrimed as so many newly exhumed, slightly animate antiques, we emerged stiff and bleary-eyed into the glorious morning brilliance of Luxor.

To my father Thebes was one of the most inspiring sites of the ancient world. On his first visit it had surpassed his most colorful pre-conceptions, had remained ever since one of the favorite haunts of his daydreams. Now that he was within an hour's donkey ride of it, he could hardly wait.

He hurried us to a shabby hotel facing the Nile, then aboard a creaking ferry, already laden with jabbering natives, donkeys, crates of distraught chickens, some naked little girls herding four sheep and a family of geese. Sitting astern reading Baedekers as calmly as if in a peaceful French cathedral, were two green-veiled, seamy-faced English ladies convoyed by a possessive dragoman.

As our Noah's ark neared the west bank, a boarding-party of piratical donkey-boys, alternately reviling and pummeling one another, and shouting at the tops of their leather lungs the names and virtues of their respective mounts, waded out to capture our patronage by the immemorial oriental method of attrition. The moment the ferry touched the shore, their onslaught took on a lunatic fury. Even the English ladies, placing markers at "Section B, The West Bank at Thebes," looked up with impassive interest. Suddenly, in a cloudburst of sonorous Arabic, my father stunned the milling assemblage: "May ten thousand wild asses," he shouted, "bray for ten thousand years over the graves of your ancestors." In the silence following this dreadful curse, we chose our donkeys and trotted off across the Theban plain.

A sea of green stretched away toward a mountain of golden-brown limestone rising mesa-like above the jumble of temples and tombs at its base—the city of the dead of ancient Thebes. In his eagerness my father gradually drew far ahead, but when after some time he reached two gigantic seated figures of stone, the Colossi of Memnon now standing alone among the fields, he dismounted and waited in order to show me the one which each morning, as the first level rays of the sun touched its weather-worn, battered surface, gave out a strange melodic sound. He recalled how he and my mother had heard it on a morning eleven years before; and then with his arm resting on my shoulders, stood silent for some moments, as if hearing it again across the years of his struggle to re-achieve Egypt.

He was thinking less of the past, however, than dreaming of the future. With his first expedition hardly yet in motion, he was already planning another similar but more ambitious undertaking. As we wandered through the neighboring ruins—the huge temple of Medinet Habu, and the Ramesseum—he was so preoccupied with making copious entries in a note-book, he quite forgot his family. Years later he wrote of that day:

"My inexperience, and the inspiration of Thebes after so long an absence, perhaps inclined me to be oversanguine. But it seemed to me obvious that any successful effort to record and interpret this extraordinary place must be on a scale commensurate with its magnitude. I decided on that morning to do everything in my power to carry out, on a greatly expanded basis, a plan I had conceived during my first visit, for the publication of *all* the monuments, tombs and buildings of ancient Thebes."

It was a day which twenty years later we would both remember well.

With boyish eagerness he led us in and out of countless tombs belonging to nobles and grand-viziers, through chapels and temples on whose walls he showed me endless portraits and scenes of kings and queens with long-familiar names. He knew the exact location of every inscription, every figure, took delight in pointing out his favorites—a succession of Amenhoteps and Thutmoses; Ikhnaton—a dreamer, he said, born over a thousand years before his time, who was the first man to believe in one supreme God; a beautiful, brilliant, incredibly energetic lady named Hatshepsut, with an uncommon flare for architecture and intrigue, who confused me somewhat because apparently she should have been born a man, was for some time married to a king who was also her half-brother, and finally became a *king* in her own right! He was inclined to resent a pair of boastful kings named Ramses One and Two who seemed to be everywhere, with a penchant for vast statues of themselves. Before one of these, hewn of granite brought from Aswan, which stood in a forecourt of the Ramesseum and now lay among the ruins in enormous tumbled fragments, my father recited for me—while we ate a lunch of dried dates and native bread—Shelley's *Ode to Ozymandias*.

By the time he had led me through Queen Hatshepsut's lovely temple of Deir el-Bahri, set in a vast bay of cliffs, where he showed me the famous wall reliefs depicting treasure brought back to her by a fleet of ships she had once dispatched through the Red Sea to the Land of Punt, far south toward Ethiopia, the shadows had begun to lengthen again across this strange ruined city of the ancient dead. My mother and I both begged for mercy: our legs and eyes ached, and what with sitting up all night in an Egyptian train, we had had our fill for one day of hieroglyphs and royal profiles and the acrid stench of bat-filled tombs. With a laugh he said that our patience would now be rewarded—and asked us to follow him on foot up the steep trail leading over the mountain to the Valley of the Kings' Tombs!

Only the magic of that name could have sent me scampering after him—up and up, until the temples below grew as small as the models I had seen in museums, and the whole valley of the Nile from horizon to horizon lay spread below us. Even my mother forgot her weariness at seeing it again. He pointed out to me the ruins of Karnak far across the river, and from a still higher rock, showed me the gap in the mountains of the eastern desert through which passed the ancient caravan route between Thebes and the Red Sea. On very clear days, he said, one could sometimes see faint wisps of smoke rising from invisible ships.

We turned now and followed the crest until we looked down into a barren valley already steeped in twilight by the great cliffs which closed its western end. Jackal trails rose from it here and there, and disappeared over the high rim of the desert plateau above. Even to a small boy who had as yet witnessed death only in the shape of unwrapped, withered mummies irreverently displayed in museums, this silent, lonely place seemed a fit habitation for departed kings.

He had told me again and again of the forty and more great slanting shafts cut hundreds of feet into the solid rock at the bottom of this valley. They ended sometimes in a room, sometimes in a vertical well, in which had been placed the sarcophagus and mummy, and the richest personal belongings of a king. Each king had tried to insure his eternal rest in the hereafter by having his tomb made with the utmost secrecy and designed with false passages, impenetrable bulkheads of granite, deep, wide pits to serve as impassable moats, and other ingenious devices to thwart rapacious posterity or even contemporaries. A few tombs, including that of a young king named Tukenkhamon, had never been found by modern excavators. But the known ones had all been robbed in antiquity, he said, by the remote ancestors of the modern natives whose little adobe villages we had seen clinging like birds' nests among the ancient wreckage along the foothills of the mountain.

Though I found all this *mechanically* fascinating, I could never understand what he meant by "hereafter"; nor why kings, especially, should have taken such tremendous trouble about their tombs. But as often as I asked him, he merely smiled and pinched my cheek, and said that one day I would discover the answers for myself. . . .

As we clambered down into the shadows, we saw in the distance a great motionless cloud of dust, and in the stillness heard the rhythmic minor chant of native workmen singing, the shouts of their foreman upbraiding the laggards in a circling procession of small boys carrying away baskets of rubbish from an excavation.

This was an archaeological enterprise being conducted by an old friend of my father's, a retired elderly American lawyer and financier named Theodore M. Davis from Newport, Rhode Island, who had been visiting Egypt since the '80's. We soon came upon him, standing with two or three other gentlemen, looking on with obvious excitement as his men dug at the entrance-shaft of a tomb they had discovered only a few hours earlier. He was smoking cigarette after cigarette, intermittently leaving the group to pace nervously back and forth, oblivious to the white dust which lent an eerie quality to the twilight of the place.

He seemed very pleased at my father's unexpected arrival, at once confided to him how much he hoped this might prove to be the first tomb of a king, intact and untouched by ancient robbers, ever to have been found in Egypt by an authorized modern excavator. But in the debris from the deepening pit—limestone chips made by the chisels of ancient stone cutters, detritus from the Valley slopes—the workmen were already finding the ushabtis, alabasters, beads and other intrinsically valueless objects which warn an excavator that he has long since been anticipated by tomb robbers who tossed them aside in favor of richer plunder.

In the group beside Mr. Davis was a black-haired, black-eyed young English artist of medium stature who was one day to achieve unparalleled world renown. He had come out to Egypt a dozen years before as an archaeological draughtsman, had gradually been drawn into excavational work under both British and French auspices, and in 1899 had been appointed by Maspero as Inspector-in-Chief for the Monuments of Upper Egypt and Nubia, with headquarters at Thebes. His name was Howard Carter, and it had been at his suggestion and under his personal supervision that Mr. Davis had in 1902 undertaken the systematic exploration of the entire Valley of the Kings' Tombs.

Carter's Egyptian career had been anything but humdrum. In 1898 Loret had discovered among the cliffs facing the Nile the tomb of Amenhotep II. It had been robbed in antiquity, and subsequently, in an effort to protect them from further robberies had been used by the decadent priesthood of the Twenty-second Dynasty as a cache for the mummies of a whole group of kings. Most of the mummies were removed to the Cairo Museum, but the body of Amenhotep II was left in its sarcophagus. A guard was installed and the tomb was opened to visitors. One day a year or so later, gunshots were heard, the guard fled, and the tomb was rifled.

Though the chief guard had been absent, Carter held him responsible, immediately dismissed him, rounded up all suspects, forced the return of the loot, and brought the men to trial in Luxor. As this was unavoidably before a native court, the case dragged on interminably.

Despite flagrant obstruction of justice and repeated threats upon Carter's life, the suspected parties were proven guilty beyond the slightest doubt. But the native judge finally declared them innocent, dismissed the charges. Meanwhile the enemies Carter had made among influential local natives whom he had deprived of their usual "cut" from the proceeds of such plunder, brought about his transfer to the Inspectorate of Lower and Middle Egypt, with headquarters at Sakkara.

One day a party of drunken Frenchmen without the required official entrance permits demanded admission to the Serapeum (at Sakkara). The native guard dutifully declined to admit them, a Frenchman struck him, a general fracas ensued in which other guards joined. This was at full tilt when Carter arrived on the scene, remonstrated, and was met by insults. He thereupon ordered the guards to protect themselves, and a Frenchman was knocked down.

It was not surprising, in view of the peculiar relation of the French to the ancient monuments of Egypt, to which I have earlier referred, that a casual group of French tourists should have succeeded in covering their own drunken misbehavior under the charge that the honor of France had been insulted.

On their return to Cairo they lodged a formal complaint against Carter. The French Consul-General demanded an apology. Carter insisted he had only done his duty, refused to apologize, finally had to resign. Maspero was genuinely distressed, begged Carter's friends to persuade him to reconsider, and reassume his post. But he remained adamant, and though penniless, returned to private life.

He somehow made his way back to Luxor where the reis of the guards, whom Carter had dismissed, now took him into his house, fed him, gave him money, tided him over until he had painted some pictures to sell, and was finally employed by Mr. Davis as draughtsman for his work in the famous Valley. The added familiarity he thus gained with the place doubtless contributed to the later course of events by which his name was to become forever associated with the Valley of the Kings' Tombs.

Though the sky was still luminous, the night which in Egypt banishes the day with tropical suddenness had transformed the Valley into a chasm of fluid darkness. Mr. Davis ordered the foreman to fetch a lantern, and to spread out on a cloth upon the ground all the newly discovered small objects for examination by my father, who searched eagerly among them for any that might be inscribed with the name of the occupant of the tomb. On an alabaster statuette he found the name of Merneptah-Siptah, a Nineteenth Dynasty pretender to the throne of Egypt, whose brief rule had lasted only from 1215 to 1209 B.C. Three days later, after we had gone upriver, this identification of the tomb was confirmed—but to Mr. Davis's bitter disappointment, it too had been robbed in antiquity.

We made our way by starlight out of the Valley, and from the crest of the ridge saw the distant lights of Luxor. As we descended toward the river plain, I remember the warmth which rose from the sun-baked limestone cliffs through the chill of the desert night; then the familiar rich fragrance of irrigated fields, the odors of musk and aromatic smoke drifting from groups of shapeless figures gathered about small fires before wattle huts as they guarded their crops; the sounds and smells of farm animals munching, off in the dark; the muffled clatter from our donkeys' feet, whose dust was constantly in our nostrils; and overhead, stars beyond anything I had ever known.

From a great way off, through the torpor of exhaustion which engulfed me, I could hear my father saying animatedly to my mother, "Frances, I could so readily be attracted to the sort of work Davis and Petrie and the others are doing—it's no trick to raise money for excavation—it captures the dullest imagination. But what I'm doing is equally important, perhaps more so—only it holds no appeal for men of means, and there are too few of us doing it. But I shall find the money, and it shall be done—you'll see!"

I remember nothing more of my first day at Thebes. For apparently, sitting up in the saddle, I fell asleep—as soundly as all the kings in the Valley behind us.

From Luxor we hurried southward to Aswan, stowed the little expedition aboard a passably waterworthy dahabiyeh (named the *Mary Louise,* which all the river folk pronounced *Amir el-Wuz*); and on Christmas Day, 1905, embarked for Wadi Halfa.

My father now entered upon another period of scientific drudgery at a self-appointed task the importance of which, he knew, would be recognized by scarcely a dozen men in the entire scientific world. As for the general public, the meticulous recording of long-known, steadily perishing, and largely unpublished historical monuments *above* ground had about it almost none of the excitement and fascination popularly associated with digging for *buried* ancient treasure. But he was more than ever convinced that however much the excavations of men like Petrie, Davis, Quibell and others might contribute to Egyptology, he himself could render it no greater service than to copy while they were still legible the historical records on the ancient monuments of Egypt.

Just as ten years before, he constantly scoured both margins of the Nile valley with his binoculars and everywhere inquired among villagers for inscriptions. He had devised a new method of recording which, though simple and obvious enough, had never so far as he knew been employed before: Herr Koch would photograph an inscription, make blueprints from the negatives, which my father would then collate with the original, thus combining the accuracy of the camera lens with that of the expert epigrapher's eyes.

Whenever reliable natives reported they had seen "writings" somewhere in the desert, we would make sorties into the rocky desolation beyond the river. The "writings" would usually prove to be crude, prehistoric rock-drawings of wild asses, ostriches, ibexes, dogs, giraffes, and—if they happened to be in the eastern desert along ancient trade routes to the Red Sea—of boats equipped with oars, and perhaps even with masts and sails.

It was on such an excursion that we crossed a battlefield where Kitchener's troops had annihilated a great force of Dervishes. I never forgot the startling sight of white skeletons lying in the desert just as they had fallen, often in the grotesque distortion of death agony. Some were half-covered with drifting sand that hissed against them in the wind, while from many there still fluttered little tatters of the sky-blue, hand-loomed cotton cloth which all the Mahdi's followers wore. I picked up on this battlefield the timing mechanisms of several exploded British shells, which for years remained among the proudest trophies of my younger travels.

Whenever we moored near a village, all the halt and the blind, the sick and the injured who could be carried or led, would gather on the river bank beside the boat and beg to be cured—for the impression persisted among them that every white person was a doctor. Ninety-five per cent of the population suffered from some form of highly infectious ophthalmia, predominantly trachoma; while to the other diseases especially prevalent in the orient were added most of the ailments and injuries afflicting humanity in general. My mother was indefatigable in doing what she could for these sufferers, and in extreme cases my father would interrupt his work to draw upon his pharmaceutical knowledge for such remedies as our modest medical supplies would allow.

The sight and reek of filth, blood, suppurating sores, leprosy, and the like often caused Herr Koch to grow faint and sometimes inhibited even my mother; so that it frequently fell to my father, Mr. Persons, and in a modest way myself to render first aid. It was a rigorous, often gruesome schooling—and sometimes heartrending, as when a weeping father would come hopefully leading by the hand his little boy, a handsome child, with one eye running from its socket down his cheek, the result of being accidentally struck by a stone from another boy's rope sling as the two were frightening birds from a field. All this set my mother to dreaming of one day equipping and staffing several hospital boats which would minister to the ills of every village in the Nile valley beyond the reach of the few existing missionary infirmaries—a dream she was never able to realize even in part.

My father intrusted to her the duties of expedition housekeeper. She fulfilled these with a conscientious perfectionism which kept the little household in a state of chronic ferment and on several occasions provoked open mutiny among the Nubian servants and crew. She had a habit, whenever domestic crises occurred, of writing notes to my father, even though he might be in the very next room; and as far back as I could remember, I had been their involuntary bearer. How often that winter I brought such missives to him as he sat at his work, and watched the emotions in his face as he read them and with a sigh either slipped them into his pocket or jotted down a reply which I solemnly carried back to her! Again and again her messages would send him hurrying to the boat to retrieve the peace she had such a sad genius for dispelling. . . .

As we sailed, or with sweeps and current moved from one ancient place to another, the detached existence and the daily labors of the little group aboard the *Amir el-Wuz* gradually took on the indefinable rhythm of the river which incessantly murmured and tinkled against her hull. For long periods nothing marred the brooding beauty of the great valley. The sun rose and set like a vast bird of paradise. Unbelievable nights of full moon echoed with the far-off barking of dogs, the whining of water wheels, and with the immemorial chanting of sailors aboard black-hulled, silver-sailed boats.

Then again the spell would be harshly broken when for a fortnight at a time nerve-racking, howling sandstorms would hide our world in a deep, faintly amber twilight. Palm trees would bend their streaming heads before the gale like suppliant hags. Dust and grit penetrated everything, even watertight watches, and the emulsion on photographic plates resembled emery paper.

Beside such storms, other annoyances seemed unimportant. Sometimes, with a high, shrill hum of almost deafening volume, like myriad tuning forks, clouds of gnats would engulf us, as thick as tar smoke and so tiny no screens could exclude them. Occasional scorpions and tarantulas would drop onto the deck from overhanging trees; and when we moored near native cargo fleets, roving swarms of ugly, vicious rats that defied poisoning or capture, and attacked one when cornered, would overrun our boat.

But week after week the work continued. Sometimes my father and his two assistants would be working high up on a rocky promontory overlooking a great stretch of the Nile, where three thousand years or so ago an official of an ancient Pharaoh had perhaps sat for many days, counting his sovereign's cargo ships as they brought tribute or imports from inner Africa—ebony, ostrich feathers, ivory, captive animals, pygmies, and the like. A combination of boredom and vanity often led such a man to carve on the rocks an inscription which in the neat hieroglyphs of a practiced scribe set forth his rank and station, his honors, the year of his Pharaoh's reign, and the date when he had sat counting the royal ships. Frequently he would add a few casual comments or facts of extraordinary interest and new historical significance. Despite the great lapse of time such inscriptions, especially if carved on granite, would often be as sharp and clear as if cut the day before.

Again, the men would have to work for days at a stretch in the suffocating blackness of the inner chambers of rock-hewn tombs or in the windowless storage rooms of temples, where the air which had never been changed was not merely hot but stank unspeakably from untold generations of bats hanging in regiments from fouled ceilings. Here all photographic adjustments had to be made by candlelight, for such commonplace modern equipment as electric dry-battery flashlights were still not yet practicable for the field. The bats would beat out the candleflame or fly into a burning magnesium tape during an exposure.

Under conditions like these, the men worked for forty days in the great rock-hewn temple of Abu Simbel with its four gigantic statues of Ramses II facing the rising of Re, the sun god. Only one item in the task of recording this huge place was a great inscription or stela just outside the temple to the south of the facade. It described "the marriage of Ramses II and the Hittite princess Manefrure," my father wrote in his journal in January, 1906. "It is an enormous document of forty-one lines, each about eight feet long, [a total of] 328 feet of inscription! Only about one third is in good preservation. The sunlight is so dazzling that there are no shadows, and the badly weathered parts cannot be read by day. It is therefore necessary to copy it by lamplight, either under canvas or at night. Sixty years ago Lepsius copied and published the few upper lines then exposed [above sand drifts], and comparatively recently Bouriant made a copy of the remainder which he published very inaccurately and incompletely. Hence no usable edition exists."

He worked at this inscription uninterruptedly for over fourteen days, usually till late at night, sitting on a tarpaulin-covered scaffold of ladders and planks. Toward the last, when he reached the bottom lines which were in a trench created by our clearance of drifted sand, he had to hang head-down, alternately holding a kerosene lamp at various angles to secure a reading, then entering the latter in his transcription.

At this point the twice-weekly Sudan government steamer arrived with its usual party of Thomas Cook & Son tourists. They were soon straggling about the temple, led by a bumptious dragoman who in an ecclesiastical drone of guttural, ungrammatical English delivered himself of astounding hyperboles of historical misinformation.

As they neared the scaffolding a dowageresque, black-satin-clad English lady could not resist drawing back the canvas and peeping through her lorgnette at whatever was being screened from public gaze. When she beheld a purple-faced gentleman hanging more or less inverted, with his head in a trench, copying chicken tracks in a notebook by the light of a kerosene lamp, she was obviously surprised and disappointed.

"Fancy," she said with deprecating amazement, "fancy earning one's living doing *that* sort of thing!"

He was accustomed enough to such ineptitudes from impervious English and American tourists. But during the ensuing months he was inclined to share the lady's reactions.

On January 22, 1906, he wrote in his journal: "Through the *London Times* we have just learned of the death of President Harper. [The end had come actually on January 12th, but no one had thought to cable my father.] I have put the flag at half-mast with my own hands, and it will remain so during the rest of the voyage."

The little President had broken many promises to him, had often hurt him cruelly and apparently needlessly; and despite their old student-and-master association at New Haven and in Germany, had never extended to him the hospitality of the President's house at Chicago. But the fact remained that he had created for my father the first chair of Egyptology in America, and in his mercurial way had been a friend. Now he was gone—and with him the only restraining influence which even as a dying man, he had continued to exert upon his brother Robert Francis.

My father had not yet overcome the sadness and anxiety these developments had caused him, when one morning in March he received a copy of the first volume of his *Ancient Records of Egypt.*

"I have just turned to the dedication page," he wrote to his mother from Amada in Nubia. "I have had some black days in my life, but this is one of the blackest. I want you know what was on that page when I left America after approving the complete final proofs:

To the Memory of
My Father
CHARLES BREASTED
these volumes are
Dedicated

"For eleven years I toiled on this monument to my father. Without my knowledge they have removed his name and inserted those of three strangers. As I feel now, it is a matter of indifference to me when the other volumes appear, or whether they *ever* appear.

"The three names belong of course to those who gave the publication funds. They are in no way responsible. If I had no family dependent on me, I would resign from an institution from which I have suffered so much." (Only some months later did he learn that the University of Chicago Press had destroyed the manuscript whose margins for more than a decade he had filled with countless annotations and references for his own future use.)

He became very grave, seldom smiled, now threw himself into his work with a kind of quiet desperation. By the end of March, at a place called Gerf Husein, some fifty-four miles south of Aswan, the north wind suddenly dropped, and the temperature in the cabin of the *Amir el-Wuz* sometimes reached 140°. But still the work continued, until on April 3, 1906, he was able to state in his journal: "We have now finished [copying the historical inscriptions in] all the pre-Ptolemaic temples of Lower Nubia (between the First and Second Cataracts). Besides these temples, numerous historical stelae and graffiti have been copied and are ready for publication. Thus *all* the pre-Ptolemaic monuments of Lower Nubia are included and completed in this winter's work."

Just before reaching Aswan again, he received a sheaf of reviews of his *History of Egypt.* Typical of the more generous group was that of the *London Times Literary Supplement,* which appraised it as the most accurate, authoritative work yet produced in its field. Among the few unfavorable notices was one in the *American Historical Review,* which deprecated his having based his work entirely upon the researches of the German school of Egyptologists; and another in the Chicago *Record-Herald,* which characterized his style as that "of a high-school sophomore."

But it was the reviews in the scientific journals of Europe, with a total circulation of only a few hundreds, which anticipated his future standing in the scientific world. Of these, the English reviews were cool but most favorable; those of the French—whose jealousy in Egyptology was all but insuperable—were surprisingly friendly; while the Germans rated the book as a new classic.

"I had an eerie feeling," he wrote, "that they [the reviews] were discussing the work of a stranger unknown to me. We forget so quickly how much life-blood a long task has cost us! If only my father and Aunt Theodocia could have lived to read these tributes to them, and to hold in their hands the book they helped me to write!"

The expedition disbanded at Aswan, and at the end of April we sailed northward again, stopping briefly in Sicily. To come suddenly from the tawny barrenness and the hot winds of the Sahara into the Mediterranean spring in full bloom was like a benediction.

At Taormina, roses and wild flowers and lush grass were growing everywhere amidst one of the most enchanting of all Greek ruins. "I am sitting in the upper arcades of an ancient theater," my father wrote to his mother. "More than two thousand years ago, when plays were being performed in it, Greek ladies and gentlemen in their white robes strolled here during intermissions. As they discussed the performance or exchanged news and gossip of the day, they could look out through these marble arches at a magnificent coast of capes and headlands green with olive and almond groves and vineyards, and fringed below with snowy surf which merged into the bluest sea the sun ever shone upon; while southward, beyond the stage, snow-covered, smoke-plumed Etna—just as today—made a vast sweep upward, as if to draw the whole of Sicily toward the highest heavens. I think this is probably the most beautiful spot in the world—and many share this opinion who are far more traveled than I."

The ruins of Greece and Rome mellowed by some twenty centuries of Mediterranean sun, rain and greenery, and standing often among surroundings of ineffable loveliness, have about them an appealing quality of friendly familiarity and of belonging to our own past which is seldom conveyed by the strange alien beauty of ancient Egyptian ruins. The classical Mediterranean was one of the strongest of the broadening influences which led my father to become ultimately a historian not of Egypt alone but of the entire early world. At the moment, however, I understood only that his spirits were visibly rising, and that his eyes were beginning to twinkle again as they had not since before our summer at Williams Bay.

It will be recalled that in April, 1906, Vesuvius had on very short notice indulged in one of the most serious eruptions in its history, which blew off the old crater and formed a new one hundreds of feet lower and vastly larger. When we crossed to Naples we found many of the city's streets and roofs still covered with a deep layer of ashes, and huge piles of it lying everywhere, which hordes of laborers were gradually shoveling into an endless procession of clumsy two-wheeled carts.

Pompeii had received a much scantier rain of ashes than Naples, so that we were able to wander at will through the ancient town. Nothing my father had ever shown me from the ancient world had so enthralled me.

My mother and I noticed that he continually looked up at the new crest of Vesuvius, which against the lambent Italian sky appeared utterly peaceful and innocent. In the recent eruption, lava had over-flowed and destroyed a great portion of the *funicoláre* which used to run up to the old crater; and the government had announced that anyone who ventured up on foot did so at his own risk. Altogether the mountain presented a challenge which he was obviously finding it impossible to resist. Presently, with a mischievous expression, he left us, to reappear shortly with the triumphant announcement that he had secured horses and a guide, and that early next morning we would climb Vesuvius!

The day of our ascent—May 28, 1906—dawned cloudless and perfect. But no sooner had we mounted what proved to be decrepit, bony, underfed nags, than from Vesuvius there rose straight toward the zenith a vast column of slowly writhing smoke approximately a mile thick, and as black and viscous-looking as boiling pitch. Our guide, our innkeeper, and the *padrone* from whom my father had rented the horses begged us not to go on this day. But my father pooh-poohed them, and off we went.

We rode for several hours across great lava streams which had burst from fissures in the slopes of the mountain and flowing toward the sea, had inexorably pushed before them or engulfed and covered all vineyards, houses, and villages in their paths. At several points the lava was still perceptibly moving—glass bottles or objects of soft metal when dropped into cracks would melt before one's eyes. Soldiers stood guard at villages to prevent pillaging while the former inhabitants tried to salvage whatever they could from their smoking, crumbling houses.

The mountain at length became too steep for our pathetic Rosinantes, and we dismounted to climb the rest of the long way on foot. The slope appeared solid enough, but with every step we sank almost to our knees in volcanic ashes so hot that we could not stand still, and in self-defense continued clambering upward. Far above us the sinister column of smoke, still churning and boiling upward, had reached the higher atmosphere and begun to spread in a vast dark fan.

The sun on our backs and the heat burning our feet and beating up into our faces soon made us terribly thirsty, and we longed for just a small spot of shade. At last, near the crest of the crater, we spied a huge boulder which had been blown out by the volcano. We hurried toward the patch of shade it cast—but when we reached it, found the entire precious area occupied by a gigantic drunken Italian who rose up when our guide woke him and threatened us with a knife. So we contented ourselves with standing on some harder ground, and as it was now midday, sought comfort in what food we had brought with us. The innkeeper had forgotten to include drinking water. I can still feel the peculiar, dull ache created by the granular dryness of a hard-boiled egg immovably lodged like so much crushed stone at the base of my young throat.

But these discomforts were forgotten when we reached the very edge of the crater. Behind us lay the crescent of the glinting Bay, tipped on the south by Capri and on the north by Ischia, with Naples spreading away from the far edge like a collar of ivory lace. In front of us we peered down through a twilight of smoke and vapor toward the beginning of the world. From the invisible depths came such a booming, grinding thunder that our efforts to speak became so many soundless grimaces. The guide became frantic with anxiety as we stood on the very edge, segments of which were continually breaking off and slipping into eternity. Now and again the smoke would clear slightly and we could see masses of tremendous stones and vast, tattered blobs of lava shooting upward and out of sight. What little wind there was momentarily blew away from us, and this deadly rain fell on the opposite slopes of the mountain.

The guide now broke into actual sobs: he would never desert us, he said, but if we had no regard for our own lives or his, would we not for the sake of his wife and *bambini,* leave the crater and descend the mountain?

This appeal moved my parents as none of his others had done. We looked a last time into the crater, and while he uttered thanks to the Virgin Mother, we started down the mountain. We were about halfway down the steepest slope, when the wind changed and freshened, and the column of smoke began to creep nearer and nearer until the choking sulphurous blackness engulfed us like a sudden midnight. The four of us clung together. We could hear a deep thunder, and all about, the thud of falling stones. We breathed only by tying handkerchiefs across our faces. At last it grew lighter, and we saw that we were as blackened as chimney sweeps. The wind veered once more, the smoke lifted, and as the lowering sun glowed across the Bay, we found the horses again, and at sunset reached the inn—which had no bath!

We were told later in Naples that we could not possibly have ascended Mt. Vesuvius on May 28, for that was the day of another serious eruption when a rain of ashes and great stones had fallen upon the town of Torre del Greco, which the government had placed under martial law and ordered evacuated!

CHAPTER VII

HARRY PRATT JUDSON, the new president of the University of Chicago, personified the reactionary conservatism of a Board of Trustees whose patience had been exhausted by William Rainey Harper's splendid disregard of budgets in favor of the most brilliant men he could gather from either side of the Atlantic. In understandable deference to Mr. Rockefeller, Sr.'s righteous resentment at having had to make up deficit after deficit, the Trustees had selected a man who would be altogether "safe." My father was therefore the more surprised and relieved when that summer of 1906, President Judson informed him he intended to carry out President Harper's written promise that the Oriental Exploration Fund would finance the Egyptian Expedition for at least another two seasons of work in the Nile valley.

He began at once preparing for a second campaign, this time along the upper Nile in the northern Sudan.

Messrs. Persons and Koch did not return to the field, and my father engaged as their successors two men who could hardly have been more dissimilar. One was a great six-foot-four, happy-go-lucky, good-natured, inordinately boastful, tawny-haired and bearded Russo-German photographer in his middle thirties, named Horst Schliephack, who had been photographer on the German military expedition to Pekin after the murder there of the German ambassador in 1900. The other, a short, wiry, *pince-nez-ed* English Egyptologist of about the same age, named Norman de Garris Davies, was an excellent copyist and draftsman with a quick temper and a militant sense of the superiority of everything British, who had once been a parson in Australia.

That October all of us met in Cairo, and for a fortnight "from dawn till dark," wrote my father, "I have had my head in packing boxes. Our needs for this campaign are more complex: large sums of money in gold, silver, and small change (the gold we carry in leather belts worn under our clothes, the silver and small change is packed in a special 'treasure chest'); endless supplies properly distributed to dif-

173

ferent points between Khartoum and Wadi Halfa; a felucca, and a cargo boat fitted with temporary living quarters; camels wherever we cannot travel by boat. . . ."

Because the journey through the cataracts of the upper Nile would be too arduous for us, he firmly decreed that my mother and I would remain in Cairo: perhaps later, should it prove feasible after the expedition had again reached easier country, he might send for us to join him. She found poor comfort in this half-promise when at last a white train carried him into the darkness beyond the Cairo station. By the light of the street lamps as we rode in a carriage back to our *pension,* and again when we reached our now spiritless room and she lighted an oil lamp, I could see her tears.

I tried in vain to comfort her, and during the long weeks of waiting which followed, loneliness like an illness settled upon her. While her life revolved entirely about the arrival of my father's letters, the tedium of mine was somewhat relieved by attendance at a German Lutheran parochial school which at the time was regarded by the European colony—including, curiously enough, the English—as the best European school in Cairo.

Here I met children of a dozen nationalities, but all of us were made to speak German. I soon learned that the offspring of the diplomatic corps looked down their noses at those of the commercial colony. As the only American and the son of a scientific man I was tolerated, though with unconcealed curiosity, by both groups.

We sat in rows on long, well-polished benches at scarred desks, in my case too high because I had been flatteringly placed in an advanced form of pupils older than myself. The boys sat on one side of the room, the girls on the other. In front of us on the wall above a blackboard was a large, pale green-and-yellow map of "Das Vaterland"; and, above this, a photographic portrait of Kaiser William II in full military regalia with all medals and honors.

Our master, a youngish German with a pale face set in a sneer, always wore a dingy black frock coat and frayed striped trousers and carried a wide, flat rule with which he resoundingly slapped the faces of any German children who gave poor recitations. They accepted this as a matter of course. For the rest of us who failed to satisfy his requirements (among whom I seldom failed to be included), he employed subtler punishments—sarcasm, extra assignments, ignominious periods of standing face-to-wall before the class.

Of afternoons my mother and I walked everywhere in Cairo, until we were recognized in the bazaars and along the main thoroughfares as residents, immune to tourist-mulcting. We often saw Lord Cromer in his handsome carriage, or the Khedive Abbas II attended by scarlet-and-gold-jacketed, white-pantalooned servants; or watched the afternoon opening of the Kasr en-Nil Bridge and the river boats moving up and down; or the rugger matches and the drilling of British troops on the parade ground beside Kitchener's Barracks. At sunset we listened for the Citadel gun, and to the muezzin chanting from a hundred minarets. After supper she read aloud to me.

The repetitive effect of all this was almost hypnotic. It seemed to me we had lived thus for years. Then one afternoon I returned from school shaking with dengue, and all sense of time deserted me. For long days and nights while I tossed with fever, my mother for some reason read me Longfellow's collected poems—amongst which *Evangeline* and *The Legend of Hiawatha* still stand out in my memory as infallible opiates. When the fever seized her also, our spirits went into total eclipse.

But the weeks which passed so slowly for us were crowded with new experiences for my father. His daily journal of his first campaign had been pedantic and stilted. That of his second was from the outset full of verve and enthusiasm. Not only was the Sudan more exciting than Egypt, but for the first time in his life he found himself without domestic hindrance in charge of an exploratory project in a great sweep of wild country the records of whose ancient history had never before been systematically surveyed. The prospect challenged and thrilled him.

The following summary of his explorations is quoted from journals and letters written under the rigorous conditions of expedition life ranging from desert camps at night to a felucca racing down the turbulent cataracts of the upper Nile.

"The two hundred miles between Aswan, at the First Cataract, and Wadi Halfa, at the foot of the Second, comprise a stretch of country so difficult that a railway has never yet been attempted. At Aswan therefore the expedition boarded one of the regular stern-wheel Sudan government steamers which bridge this gap.

"Five hundred miles south of Wadi Halfa the country gradually changed from the desert, which flanks Egypt on either hand, to heavily grown savanna plain with no trace of plateau, or to sparsely grown steppe with great patches of bare gravel. At length we crossed the

Atbara, the Nile's only tributary—it was full to the brim, though it runs dry in summer. The bridge we passed over was furnished by American steel mills on a rush order from Kitchener, which the English mills could not fill quickly enough. Forty days after receipt of the cabled order, the bridge, ready for assembly, was on a ship in New York Harbor!"

First objective of the expedition were the pyramids and ruins of Meroë, situated in the desert about 150 miles northeast of Khartoum and some two hours' caravan journey east from the Nile.

"Davies and I immediately began key-plans of the pyramids, which are in three groups, the eastern, the middle, and the western, each containing about thirty. He took the eastern, I the middle group. There must have been two flourishing dynasties here to have left such imposing tombs as these. They were the immediate ancestors of Queen Candace, whose eunuch was converted by Philip, as narrated in the Book of Acts. We now know that this land, long supposed to have been the source of Egyptian art and civilization, actually received its culture from the Egyptians and finally continued as an independent state of wealth and power long after Egypt had politically perished.

"My bedroom is the chapel of one of these pyramids, and I wake every morning with a fat Ethiopian monarch, some relative of Queen Candace, looking benignly down upon me, as he waves the palm branch he has been holding for over 2,000 years.

"The first capital of Ethiopia was at Napata, just below the Fourth Cataract, where we have yet to work. There in the days of Isaiah, and often the object of his philippics, reigned Shabaka ('So,' as mentioned in the Old Testament), Shabataka and Tirhaka, the first and last being mentioned in the Old Testament. Napata was more exposed to attack from the North and was finally forsaken by the Nubian kings in the sixth century B.C., when they established their capital here at Meroë, where we are now working. Then began the long line of kings and queens in one of whose tombs I am now writing, and it continued until the early Christian centuries, as we see in the incident of Philip.

"Our first practical problem here has been sterilized water. One drinks perpetually in this scorching sun, in which the thermometer goes up to 130° or 140°! Luckily the air is so dry that a felt-covered flask kept wet on the outside furnishes a really cool drink in the worst heat of midday. One of our camel drivers spends every hour of daylight going to and from the river carrying four sheepskins of water each trip. Our supply is assured, but such water! Even when strained, it is so full of mud as to be almost unusable for photography. We filter and then boil it for drinking, but after it has sizzled and been churned all day in a vile sheepskin under a broiling sun on a camel's back between the river and our camp the taste is disgusting. We put in lime juice (supply going fast!) and make tea of it to disguise the flavor of ancient mutton, but it still comes through very distinctly.

"These pyramids are the sole remains of a great age here on the upper Nile. The people who built them, though still understanding Egyptian and using hieroglyphics on their monuments, nevertheless spoke their own Nubian language, which today remains their native tongue—though all the men also speak Arabic. The Ethiopians wrote this language in a system of writing not yet deciphered, of which there used to be many examples here at Meroë. But most of these have been carried away, some even by Lepsius to Berlin. We have as yet found none.

"We are in the very heart of the region fought over by the English several times in the last twenty-five years, but today the people here are friendly and harmless.

"The pyramids are in a sad state. They are very much smaller and are built with much steeper sides than those of Egypt; and as the core (within the shell of good masonry covering the outside) consists largely of loose rubble, they can be easily ruined. Not one of them has retained its apex.

"A hundred years ago they were ransacked by one Ferlini, an Italian who found a rich hoard of jewelry belonging to a Nubian queen. This was purchased by Lepsius and is now in Berlin. They have been visited by others—by an Englishman named Hoskins in 1822; by the Frenchman, Cailliaud, at about the same date; by Lepsius in 1843; and, two years ago, by representatives of the British Museum.

"Lepsius was the only one who carried away an intelligent record and account of the place. Excavation and exploration have now long since ceased to be treasure-hunting. Mariette and Schliemann dug for treasure only. The conscientious scientist of today knows that an exhaustive record of *everything* stationary or movable found on the spot is the supremely important thing, including especially all inscriptions, reliefs, decorations, and the like, *in facsimile.* The search for fine museum pieces is mere commercial treasure-hunting. Ferlini's find of jewelry has been the ruin of this place. As far back as Lepsius' day an attempt on the part of Osman Pasha to penetrate these pyramids for treasure was avoided only by the wise appeals of Lepsius himself.

How often other native officials have attacked them, it is impossible to say.

"Imagine, then, our disgust at finding that someone has very recently been doing so-called 'excavating' here. Whole pyramids have been removed, till the interior has become a crater. Well-preserved chapels have in several instances been carried off block by block. The debris of the dismantled pyramids has then been thrown out over the fragments and blocks of fallen chapels, which we might have put together again had they not been thus hopelessly covered up. Huge excavations have been made under chapels and pyramids, so that they are sure to tumble in after the rains of a few years. Such shafts, galleries, and yawning holes have here and there been covered over or shored up from below with railway ties. These last are to my mind unmistakable evidence that the guilty parties were closely connected with the English government of the Sudan, probably Budge and Scott-Moncrieff of the British Museum. Nevertheless we may be able to save a large proportion of the records. I have had men at work for days clearing encumbered chapels and rebuilding others.

"It all keeps one going unceasingly. Hassan [the head servant] wants to know where to put the men next. Schliephack wants another list of negatives to be made, with limits of each chalked on the wall. Davies wants soft pencils & having forgotten to pack his ink bottle, wants to borrow my fountain pen bottle; the cook wants to know what we shall have for dinner, some native clamors for his pay, or Hassan needs money for eggs, or the camel drivers strike! Yesterday Schliephack exposed negatives all day, using the wide-angle objective, without computing that the great diffusion of a wide-angle lens demands five or six times the exposure of the ordinary objective. So a day's work was lost, and a lot of plates were spoiled when our supply at this place is already badly short! Our provisions are also low. In Cairo Davies packed one vegetable box full of celery, thinking it was peas, and also gave us an excess of jam. So we lunch on jam and celery and dine on celery and jam! What with this sort of thing, the heat, the copying, and a full scientific record of all that is going on, one is too tired at night to write a journal.

"Though we are constantly turning over stones and moving rubble, we have not seen a scorpion or a serpent. We are also surprised to find no flies here, nor any mosquitoes. But every day about noon, a cloud of gnats blows into the chapels and makes life intolerable until evening; and often at sundown, huge swarms of enormous grasshoppers, a handbreadth long, fly in from the river, often rising 200 or 300 feet into the air. The bats are very numerous and troublesome—one of the pits dug by the eminent Budge is just before my door, the bats swarm into it, and when the wind is right, the stench is intolerable. The birds are numerous—hawks, vultures, and now and then an eagle; but most of them are unfamiliar to me. Gazelles appear often on these black standstone hills.

"One of the joys of staying here is the dust, especially when there is a high wind at night. One wakes with his hair full, and clothing and papers deluged. It is inches deep on the floor of one's room. When the pillow falls off the end of one's headless cot in the night, and all clean pillowcases have been sent to the boat which we shall not reach for three weeks; or when toothbrushes or stockings drop into it, or the wind blows one's towel around in it half the night, one's temper becomes somewhat frayed. Our great consolation is to erect a rubber bathtub in this sea of dust and have a glorious bath in two quarts of muddy Nile water perfumed with the odor of long-dead mutton!

"*November 5, 1906:* The most important observation of our stay here has come out this morning.

"Ferlini avers that he found the Berlin jewelry in a chamber *at the top* of a pyramid. This has always seemed strange, and is an arrangement which was never employed in Egyptian pyramids. The Sirdar [Sir Reginald Wingate] spoke to me about it when we recently met in Cairo and said that he did not believe this, though he added that it was very strange the burial chambers could not be found.

"It is evident that in spite of all their deep shafts and long galleries into and under these pyramids the British Museum people failed to find the burial chambers. The reason is that Ferlini was right: this morning I found a window and other conclusive evidence of a burial chamber at the *top* of Pyramid 22! It was doubtless Ferlini who completely demolished all the others—which explains why the pyramids have all lost their tops.

"*November 7, 1906:* I spent the morning photographing the architecture of the East Group of pyramids. As I was passing the chapel of Pyramid 6, a block covered with fresh dirt caught my eye, for through the dirt glimmered a cartouche! It proved to be an offering tablet with a royal inscription running all around it. While Davies's back was turned our native workmen had thrown out among the rubbish the funerary dining table of a king whose name proved to be Ergamenes, known to the Greeks and the Ptolemies. I shall send this monument to the authorities at Khartoum and ask them to give it to Haskell Museum. The inscription is well done, and royal monuments of this age are very rare.

"Grasshopper in the soup tonight—of course he was served to me! I crunched on him for some time, supposing he was a piece of dried herb. But finding him invulnerable, I pulled him out, still intact, but very dead!

"*Noon, November 10, 1906:* We have finished making ground plans of the pyramids and chapels of Meroë and recording all extant inscriptions. It is a great satisfaction to be carrying away—for the first time it has ever been done—as much of the record of an entire age and people as has survived in the wreckage of a great kingdom which began planting its over 100 pyramids here in the sixth century before Christ, and existed down into the Christian age."

Traveling by caravan and train, the expedition on November 11 reached Naga, some fifty miles southwestward, "a group of five temples, and three great ruins which presumably were once the palaces of the kings and queens who were buried in the pyramids at Meroë. One's wonder continually grows that a town with such buildings could have arisen in the desert 2,000 miles up the Nile. But this part of the desert is middle ground in the transition from the arid Sahara to the fertile regions of the Sudan to the south. In the summer it rains here, and this is now caught in reservoirs by the natives, just as must have been extensively done in antiquity.

"On our way to Naga we stopped at the dwellings of some neighboring *Bisharin* [a widely distributed tribe of nomads]. The men were all away, and an impressive, aged woman came out to meet me, doing a solemn reverence as she advanced. I gave her my gun to hold and took several pictures of the curious skin tepees in which they lived.

"The women, clothed only from the waist down, were handsome and well-proportioned. They generally drew up a loose end of their garments and threw it about their shoulders as I approached. Their children, brown and chubby, were clean and fine looking. I offered several of the women money to let me photograph them with their babies, but they refused, perhaps because they did not understand Arabic. I tried to enlist the old woman in my favor, for she spoke a little Arabic; but she finally waved me away with a face so solemn and with such commanding gestures that I felt hypnotized and compelled to obey.

"This old lady would not even look at my money. Nearly ninety years ago, when the Italian, [Giovanni Battista] Belzoni, visited lower Nubia where we were last winter, the natives had never seen money and refused to take it. I am wondering if perhaps these Bisharin far out in the desert are also ignorant of the use of money. Often by barter and exchange one can get along without it. But in most places it is essential, and it is because there are no centers on our route from which to secure a supply that we have had to carry with us a 'treasure chest' containing cash for our entire winter's needs.

"*November 14, 1906:* We are at work at 6:00 A.M., and the sun is long down before we stop. I spent yesterday on a ladder, copying from a glaring wall upon which this fierce sun was beating in full force; and I rose this morning with one eye swollen shut. Even with dark glasses, I sometimes find work on a sunlit wall impossible.

"Today at sunset I climbed the neighboring mountains to make a bird's-eye view plan of the entire place. It was most impressive to look down upon these dismantled buildings, worn and weather stained, framed in the silent desert. I have never before seen such a landscape— rambling expanses of straw or pale-green vegetation separated by black and forbidding mountainous hills of desolate rock stretching on and on to the distant skyline. And yet this country furnished the economic basis for a city with five temples and a number of palaces. We have copied and photographed all the records now surviving here. Together with those we secured at Meroë, they comprise all that survives of the history of Nubia as an independent nation.

"*November 15, 1906:* After a caravan march of five hours we have reached the Nubian palaces of Mesawwarât, a mass of ruins lying in exactly the same kind of country as the temples of Naga. But there are unfortunately no inscriptions here to tell us what great ruler built this enormous complex of palaces, consisting of three colonnaded buildings, one of which is a temple with standing colossi of the king before it, in Egyptian style. The largest colonnaded building is of imposing proportions, and may have been a banqueting hall. Its rich and ornate columns, a bizarre mixture of Egyptian, Nubian, and Greek, are of a style which has never been studied. The masonry, a white sandstone which weathers red, is of the finest character.

"There has never been a large camera within these walls, and I soon had Schliephack at work exposing plate after plate. With a small camera I recorded the remarkable architectural details, while Davies made a sketch plan, beginning with the beautiful banqueting hall, at the rear of which I found the records of previous expeditions here:

Cailliaud in 1822, Linaut a little later, and Lepsius, the last, in 1844. We shall be much too busy to add a record of our own—and, alas, the times have changed!

"As I write, we are camped under the stars in one of the courts of this vast palace of the Nubian kings. The night air is soft and warm, and all is quiet save the distant voices of our servants and camel drivers, seated round their flickering fire. I should be glad if more of my notebook could be incorporated into these hasty jottings, written in the evening when I am very weary, by the unsteady light of a lantern with a broken globe, amid a constant bombardment of bats and of clumsy grasshoppers which leap into one's face, eyes, and hair!

"Tomorrow we shall see blessed 'pater Nilus' once more and shall not be obliged to part company again till we leave him for the season."

From Mesawwarât the expedition returned from the desert to the railway line. Schliephack with servants and equipment went downriver to Abu Hamed, while my father with Davies went upriver to confer with officials at Khartoum, where they arrived on "the greatest of Moslem feasts, Bairam, when they celebrate the close of their month of daylight fasting. We had no proper clothes in which to attend the Governor-General's levee at ten o'clock in the morning, but we stood outside and saw the great sheiks from Darfur, Gondokoro and the central African provinces of the Sudan coming in gorgeous raiment to pay their respects to their ruler.

"The Governor-General's palace stands on the same spot as that of Gordon, in which he perished. I have never seen a more impressive sight than the brass band of raven black Sudanese soldiers in spotless white uniforms, standing in the lovely palace garden and with their shining instruments serenading their immediate ruler. An hour later he himself issued from the palace where he had been receiving, walked over to the neighboring square, where hundreds of black women and children were gathered, and distributed to them Bairam gifts of money and grain. It is all very different from poor Gordon's day— sanitary work, hospitals, the Gordon College, and much else which the British are doing to uplift a once hopeless country.

"I visited Omdurman, seat of the Khalifa's misgovernment and greatest of markets for the products of central Africa. The town stretches for miles along the river front, but with the exception of the heavy walls around the Khalifa's quarter, it is all wretched low mud houses. The dismantled tomb of the Mahdi, whom the Khalifa succeeded, still stands but is rapidly perishing.

"*Abu Hamed, November 19, 1906:* We are now encamped at the head of the Fourth Cataract, which is about 135 miles long.

"A military officer who lived in the days of Egyptian Empire's greatest expansion placed in a quarry near Cairo an inscription which long escaped notice in modern times. It states that he erected boundary records for the Pharaoh in the Upper Euphrates country, fixing the Empire's northern boundary; and also in 'Karoy,' fixing its southern boundary. That 'Karoy' is the Fourth Cataract region can be proven from the known monuments. We must therefore explore the islands of the Fourth Cataract as the most probable place for the erection of these boundary landmarks. We shall thus be doing for the Egyptian Empire what Mommsen so long labored to do for that of Rome.

"I hardly look for success. But to make the attempt, we must have some kind of boat in order to search the islands, while our camel caravan with our main supplies moves parallel with us along the bank. As the islands are often miles long and sometimes lie several abreast, we shall frequently find it difficult to work around them.

"From Abu Hamed we shall follow the entire 600-mile westward swing of the Nile. We shall be able to travel by boat the 400 miles from the foot of the Fourth Cataract to the foot of the Third; but from the head of the Second Cataract, a wild stretch, we shall have to caravan again for some 135 miles to Wadi Halfa, where we began work last year.

"The owner of the only felucca suited to our purpose is asking an exorbitant price for it. The Mamur (governor of the district) is under instructions from the Sudan government to help us and promises to bring the man to reason. As an extra precaution, the Omdeh (mayor) of Abu Hamed is sending for the only other available boat from a village fifteen miles upriver."

While awaiting this alternative boat, he fell to thinking again of the future and of his dream of copying and recording not merely the historical but *all* the ancient monuments of the entire Nile valley, beginning with those lying in the 800-mile stretch between the First Cataract and the Mediterranean. President Harper had promised his expedition $7,000 per year for three years—an inadequate sum for field work alone, without providing for the cost of publishing the results. Under the University's new president he could not hope for an increase —he must look to himself to raise additional funds. It seemed to him that the only remotely possible source of further support to which he could address himself from the wilds of the northern Sudan was

26 Broadway. On November 20 he wrote a letter to Mr. Gates, presenting certain general proposals, and posted it himself at the railroad station in Abu Hamed. On the 22nd he continued in his journal:

"Until almost dawn this morning I labored with Zubeir, owner of the felucca we want, trying to bring him down from his asking price of £25. But he remained adamant and in disgust I went to bed. Then the Omdeh, who labored with him for several hours more, came and woke me to say that Zubeir would accept £14! I got up again to give him his money, could not find him anywhere in the town—and this morning he went back on his word, now asks £20! Meantime the other boat is on its way. It is now early afternoon, the camels are being loaded. A man comes in to report that he can see the boat coming around a bend. When it arrives, the unspeakable Zubeir—who as I write squats beneath the palms before our tent—will probably agree to my terms. If so, he will receive much less than £14!

"*Later.* The other boat leaks like a sieve, will not do in water like the cataracts below us. So while Zubeir sits in triumph under his palm trees, the Omdeh once more belabors him with arguments. Thus is business transacted in the orient!

"*Still later.* He finally accepted my offer of £15 for his boat. A crowd of curious natives surrounded us as I ceremoniously counted out the gold into the hand of the Omdeh who with equal ceremony passed it to the now crestfallen Zubeir.

"The boat is about twenty feet long and eight feet wide, heavily built of acacia wood, can carry between four and five tons and is very steady. At last, after buying two heavy palm fiber tow ropes from the native market, we cast off, the Omdeh coming with us.

"The reis stood at the helm, and the oars were constantly kept going to avoid the frequent rocks on which we might have crashed to pieces instantly in the strong current. The Omdeh perched himself in the bow and never taking his eye off the river, warned the reis to steer this way or that. When we reached the worst stretch, he took the helm himself.

"We passed the first rapids immediately opposite Abu Hamed without trouble and came into smooth water again. The river is a stately stream here, often nearly a mile wide, dotted with many islands alive with birds sitting among the rocks or perched in the trees. I only wish I knew more of them. It is a splendid sight to see a huge blue heron poised motionless on a low rock, with long beak close to the water, ready to snap the next fish.

"At dusk we drew in under a high sandy bank on the east shore, where Hassan soon joined us with the camels all in good order. We shall sleep ashore in a little natural garden hedged in with thorn bushes, where I now write sitting on a camp-cot overlooking the broad moonlit river. These superb nights amply compensate for the heat of the day. There is a cool, lambent softness in the air, as if one were enveloped in a magic element not of this earth but derived from some new and youthful world. The stars come twinkling out so subtly that before one is aware they are all blazing with tropical brilliancy. The silvery sheen of the moon floods all the palms and the wide river from which floats up the faint roar of heavy rapids in the distance.

"My first scorpion today! I found him on my trouser leg and flicked him off a little too gently—he fell somewhere among our cargo and is still in the boat!

"*November 24, 1906, en route through the Fourth Cataract:* The natives of the Fourth Cataract region are real Arabs, of a tribe called Monasîr. They pushed in here from the east some generations ago and displaced the Nubians. They have been a bad lot in times past.

"When Gordon was beleaguered in Khartoum he sent [Lt.-Col. J.D.] Stewart with dispatches of vital importance downriver in a little steamer accompanied by two other boats. He cautioned him to stay always in midstream, especially when tying up at night. Stewart made the trip at about this time of year, and I marvel that even shallow-draught steamers managed to get through such water as we have just passed. There must be greater depth than is apparent—but they must also have done some daring and skillful steering!

"Stewart was deceived by friendly assurances from these treacherous Monasîr who suddenly rushed him and his party, murdered them all, secured the dispatches for the Mahdi. The latter thereby learned from Gordon's own pen the exact predicament of his garrison and his own estimate of how long it could hold out without assistance.

"We have now reached the island of Um Duêma where the wreckage of Stewart's boat lies—it is on the north side of the upper end of the island, surrounded by scores of great jagged rocks. The woodwork has entirely disappeared. She was heading south: toward the north lie the boiler, nearly upside down, two cylinders and steam chests, the shaft of the starboard paddle-wheel with its hub, and some fragments. Southwest of these is the shaft of the other paddle-wheel and a large complex of plate iron which may have been the armored wheelhouse. We found rivet heads in great numbers so firmly imbedded in the

crevices of the neighboring rocks that we extracted them with difficulty.

"While we were examining these melancholy evidences of Stewart's
fate, the men of the tribe who killed him and perhaps some who themselves had a hand in the deed, came out to see us. I believe the story
they told me of his having been enticed from his steamer must refer to
his forsaking it after the wreck. They said he was separated by strata-
gem from the other boats, which were driving with the stream—probably he had no choice but to go ashore. In any event his reis obviously
took the wrong channel. Yet even so, had the steamer survived a few
shocks more or had she not grounded completely, she would have
passed safely, for a few rods farther on the channel is clear. Apparently
a wrong quarter-turn of the helm one way or the other decided the
fate of Stewart and possibly also of Gordon and Khartoum.

"These Monasîr are now quite friendly—I talked with them about
their crops and the fishing—I had a revolver under my coat and a gun
in my hand, but there was nothing to fear for they are now thoroughly
pacified. The head of the principal family who was the ringleader in
the Stewart business perished, the tribe was decimated and badly punished, and they are now as docile as the Egyptian fellahin.

"*November 26, 1906:* This morning Gumar the cook pulled a huge
scorpion out of his bed!

"Just above an island called Boni the reis failed to keep a sharp
watch, we crashed on a rock in midstream, sprang a bad leak. As we
raced onward, I managed to shoot our first goose—a needed windfall.

"The shores are now huge and irregular black granite rocks, rising
fifty to seventy-five feet from the water, which is here very swift, winding in and out between small islands and alternating promontories.

"We have found that we cannot possibly search these rocky headlands for inscriptions from the *land* side, as they usually have deep,
swift water at the base, passable only in a boat. We are therefore
obliged wherever possible to select the main channels, and scan the
rocks on both sides with binoculars. Our eyes are very weary, for we
have been doing this all day, often amidst racing rapids where we
would rather have watched for the main chance in case of a crash!

"Our camp tonight is in a little bay such as constantly recur between
these headlands and cliffs—little 'pockets filled with alluvium supporting luxuriant fields of waving durra [millet]. One finds them far
in the heart of the cataract, hidden among the intricate network of
tortuous channels; and behind them is always a little group of mud

huts or mere wattle shells, sheltering a few families whose sole support is drawn from the soil of such little rock-bound plots. These people are indeed far removed from the great modern world, and probably
none of their children has ever seen a European. The men are fine
looking, but weak and slight. The young women are very graceful,
often handsome. They are shy and usually avoid us—though one day
as I was sitting writing at the entrance of our tent at Abu Hamed, a
willowy young girl passed us on her way to the river only a few feet
below us, removed her clothing and leapt into the stream. She swam
like an eel.

"*November 27, 1906:* This afternoon we entered the worst rapids
we have yet encountered. The cross-currents and rip tides were terrific,
often meeting in midstream and forming a powerful backwater upstream. The water piled up behind huge rocks like a peak roof and
shot down each side, forming a line of heavy breakers extending
obliquely across our course.

"The voice of our reis rose above the roar of the water as he
shouted his orders, now encouraging now warning, again calling for a
quick stroke on one side and back water on the other, never changing
his mind or his orders, but making instant decisions at every critical
point. At one moment when the oars had lost control of the boat, he
quickly swung the tiller and shot us over into a backwater in midriver,
where we stopped as suddenly as if we had been gripped in a vise.
We lost our dangerous momentum, gained a few seconds' breathing
spell. In these cataracts such backwaters are often veritable havens of
refuge—though wherever they are met on each side by the down-going
current, they are surrounded by an inferno of raging water, twisting
in yawning whirlpools. A constant danger was that in avoiding one
rock, we would strike another below it. At one time this seemed certain, but the men pulled for dear life, two men at an oar, with the reis
fairly screaming the rhythm to keep them in stroke—and we *just* grazed
past!

"My words cannot convey the blood-tingling exhilaration of such
splendid moments when the boat darts with a bird's swiftness down
the tumbling, surging river.

"At sundown we came into quiet water, stopped at a tiny village
where we found an empty house which some men and women working on a near-by threshing floor told us we might use—a welcome protection, for our tents are with the caravan. Though even in winter the
temperature rises here at midday to 90° or 95°, the second half of

the night is bitter cold. Gordon remarks in his journal that the Dongola desert is 'bitter cold' at night, and we are finding it so.

"I talked with the people on the threshing floor about their life now as compared with the days of the Mahdi and the Dervishes. They said they were much happier, for the Dervishes used to take away all their grain, chickens and sheep, while today the English take only a few piasters.

"*November 28, 1906, evening:* Today I had a reckoning with our obstinate camel drivers who have been incessantly troublesome and mutinous.

"The English have built a narrow-gauge railway from Abu Hamed northwestward around this cataract to Kareima at its foot, but the intervening rugged country forced them miles away from the river. At a place called Shebebêt, however, they were obliged for the sake of water to run a siding down a wadi to the river. There is of course no station, but I found a native in charge of the water tanks; and while an expression of comprehension that they had been hoist on their own petards began to dawn in the faces of the onlooking camel drivers, I induced him to send our boxes by the next train up to the main line and so to Kareima. Then I sent the camel drivers away utterly crestfallen without their usual baksheesh!

"*November 29, 1906:* When we were almost within sight of the Hagar es-Salâma, 'the Rock of Salvation (or Safety),' so called by the natives because it stands at the end of the dangerous water in the Fourth Cataract, we again crashed upon a rocky head, took water, and the hull sprang another serious leak! But we can now hear the roar of the last rapid we shall be obliged to run. Tomorrow we shall reach Kareima.

"*November 30, 1906:* We have passed the Hagar es-Salâma, have emerged at last from the cataract region with all its islands and rapids, and entered the broad reach of unbroken river down which we are now floating to Kareima, less than two hours distant.

"It has been a fascinating journey through the Fourth Cataract. But we have found neither the record marking the southern boundary of 'Karoy' nor any other inscriptions. Our disappointment is not lessened for having been anticipated!

"*Later:* We have gained our first glimpse of the pyramids on the west shore, the tombs of the earlier Nubian kings against whom Isaiah declaimed in the streets of Jerusalem. Seven miles farther down river on the east shore rises the majestic table-mountain of Gebel Barkal, at the foot of which are the temples and pyramids of this same family of kings. Here they had their residence, here Tirhaka of the Old Testament lived and built his temple which we shall copy and I hope excavate. This is classic Napata, possibly the Noph of the Old Testament.

"*Kareima, evening:* We are sleeping tonight in the deck-house of a boat prepared for us at my request by the Sudan government, on which we shall travel the 400 miles from this point to almost the head of the Second Cataract.

"Hassan reports that the leaky felucca I refused to consider at Abu Hamed has just sunk, drowning four native women!"

Lying at the upriver entrance to the rich province of Old and New Dongola, the little commercial town of Kareima—consisting of mud-brick houses, a few native shops, a market, and some government ware-houses—presented a cross-cut of the Sudan. Along its busy waterfront, which included a small shipyard, clustered swarms of lateen-rigged native boats or giyassahs. Some were under construction or under-going crude repairs, but the majority were loading and unloading a medley of cargoes—Dongola dates and grain, gum-arabic from the Sudan, timber from northern Europe, great unglazed earthenware jars from Lower Egypt, bolts of cotton cloth from Manchester, tins of kerosene from America, burlap-covered bales from India and China.

Milling about in the town and squatting along the waterfront were crowds of coal-black Sudanese, "fuzzy-wuzzy" Dervishes, Bisharin, Nubians, Berbers, handsome old sheikhs from divers desert tribes. Like the Bisharin, many of all these wore their hair in small tightly braided plaits, heavily oiled and smelling of musk. Naked black children with shaved heads and dusty bodies ran squealing in and out of the crowd through which cursing drivers prodded over-burdened camels and donkeys; while scrawny yellow dogs howled from the roofs, and itiner-ant sheep and goats added their inept baa-ing to the general din, and their pellets of dung to the acrid dust underfoot. The odor of Kareima was the odor of African humanity—warm, pungent, fetid, aromatic, unpleasant yet strangely stirring, and once breathed, never forgotten.

The lone English resident of this place presided over the shipyard. Here he had fitted out for the expedition a giyassah about fifty feet long and twelve feet abeam, by overlaying the after half with plank-ing and erecting upon it a wooden framework covered with reed matting and tarpaulins. When this boat was found to be inadequate, another somewhat smaller one, similarly equipped, was added; so that with the battered felucca, the expedition possessed a little fleet of three river craft.

My father now decided that with sufficient living accommodations on board, and with less arduous country ahead, his family might join the expedition for the remainder of its current campaign. From the moment my mother read his instructions to proceed at once via Abu Hamed to Kareima, her health underwent abrupt improvement, as if some melancholy spell had suddenly been lifted from her.

On our journey southward we were passed from one kindly British official to another, last of whom was the director of the Sudan railways, at the moment inspecting the Abu Hamed-Kareima narrow gauge line, a dreary run of 145 miles which a twice-weekly train took almost ten hours to make. He invited us to lunch in what he called his "private saloon," and was greatly mystified when my mother, being unacquainted with this Anglicism, politely declined because "she felt it undesirable for a small boy to be taken into a *saloon!*" We were nearing Kareima before her scruples had been allayed and we joined him in nothing more sinister than a very primitive official private car.

It was starry-dark and very cold as the train crawled to its final halt. My father flung open our compartment door, lifted us down. Some of the crew, with a lantern among them, stood respectfully distant. The muffled crying of a child here and there, and the high-pitched howls, descending into full throated barking, of near-by dogs being answered by remoter brethren, only deepened the general stillness as we trudged through the town, picked our way down the river bank and boarded yet another in the unending series of our transient homes.

The three of us slept in what by day was the mess room. My bed was a camp cot suspended by wires from the ceiling beams above my mother's cot. I soon grew accustomed to the patter of larger rats just overhead as they scurried across the matting-and-canvas roof. Sometimes a sharp blow would send a loiterer skyward and with a splash into the river. But he always returned; and *nothing* we could do would keep the little brutes from taking possession of the boat between sunset and dawn. "It was a very carnival of riotous rats," wrote my father in his journal. "They danced and galloped across the roof in a constant tattoo, they dropped through a window onto my bed so that I would be awakened by one sitting on my face! They invaded the kitchen, rattled about among tins and frying pans, even managed to gnaw holes in theoretically unattainable bags of dried beans suspended from the ceiling, so that their contents poured onto the floor with the sound of heavy rain!"

Messrs. Davies and Schliephack were militantly independent bachelors, and resented the inhibiting presence of a woman and an ubiquitous small boy, especially when my mother was again made expedition housekeeper. Gradually the nervous tension bred by sandstorms, personal idiosyncrasies and the unpredictable minor crises of expedition life increased until it flared and crackled—as my father later put it —"like an overcharged Leyden jar." It was a peculiar little household. But such was my father's patience and forbearance that the personal equation seldom impeded the expedition's scientific work.

The volume of this grew rapidly. For as we moved away from the Fourth Cataract and deeper into territory once thickly populated and highly developed by the ancient Egyptians, the number of their ruins greatly increased. Sometimes we employed between fifty and a hundred men to excavate temple courts buried in rubbish and drifted sand; or to reassemble like jigsaw puzzles the reliefs on fallen walls; or to relocate and record by modern methods the inscribed monuments mentioned by earlier visitors like Lepsius, Cailliaud and others.

Disintegration and destruction of monuments had since their day progressed at a startling rate, for reasons everywhere evident. For example, "one morning on our way to work at the Barkal temples," my father wrote, "we came upon a typical scene—a group of natives grubbing out blocks of temple masonry to lay over the body of a dead man about to be buried in the cemetery of the neighboring village. We stopped them, though they were disinclined to obey; and I promptly sent a report to Colonel Jackson, British governor of Old Dongola province (and one of the principal figures in the Fashoda incident). I presume the mounds of this cemetery cover hundreds of inscribed stones which have thus disappeared since Cailliaud's visit. The governor summoned all the head men of the near-by villages, and his inspector read them the 'Antiquities Ordinance' enacted by the Sirdar, decreeing one year's imprisonment and a heavy fine for removing such stones."

The marvel was that any ancient Egyptian monuments were left at all, for such destruction and dispersion had been practiced both by the ancient Egyptians themselves and for several thousand years thereafter by the Greeks, Romans, Copts, Turks and Arabs, not to mention frequent European vandals. My father was only too aware that in the face of such a tradition, decrees threatening imprisonment and fines were almost futile; and that his little expedition must redouble its efforts to record every significant hieroglyph before it should be lost forever.

The superlative fertility of the stretch of Nile valley now called Dongola which ever since prehistoric times has made it a fat prize of contention is due to broad flood plains of inexhaustibly rich silt so deep that during the low-water season the fields lie as much as forty feet above the river. As my father described it in his journal, "year in and year out the natives here raise three crops a year of maize, millet, wheat, barley, lentils, beans and some sugar cane—much of the time in the same ground, though they practice rotation of crops to a certain extent. As for date palms, one district alone contains more than 180,000—they are taxed by the Sudan government at two piasters or ten cents each per year.

"The necessary water for irrigation (which being silt-laden, continually revitalizes and enriches the soil) is raised twenty to forty feet from the Nile to the level of the fields by the animal-power bucket pumps called sakiahs which are used from the Mediterranean to Khartoum. An endless, openwork palm-fiber belt to which at one- or two-foot intervals are fastened heavy earthenware jars, passes over a large *vertical* wooden cogwheel geared to a still larger *horizontal* cogwheel with a projecting pole pulled round and round by blindfolded oxen, camels or donkeys. For miles along the river banks of Old Dongola these sakiahs are distributed at intervals of often no more than 100 to 150 feet. They are deliberately never greased so that their proprietors may know at a distance whether or not they are functioning. The resulting doleful creaking, groaning quaver from several score sakiahs simultaneously audible from both banks somewhat resembles the interminable tuning up of a symphony orchestra too vast and dispersed to achieve a common pitch. On moonlight nights (over half the time in these latitudes) they are operated continuously, and there is no escaping their din."

But as we approached the headwaters of the Third Cataract the fields gradually grew narrower until they gave way altogether to the barren sandstone cliffs and tawny drifts of the inexorable Sahara. Occasional extrusions of black granite, rounded and polished like heaps of gigantic ripe olives, hinted of wilder country to come. Crocodiles and uncouth water lizards lay sunning themselves on shoals and sandspits. Birds were everywhere—wild ducks and geese flew over us constantly, their underwings more brilliant than those I had seen in Albrecht Dürer's drawings; and often great clouds of migrant cranes and storks wheeled and circled far overhead.

To relieve our monotonous diet of tinned foods my father went hunting as often as he could for geese, duck and snipe, taking me with him as retriever. On one such occasion, amidst wild cataract country, he shot three large geese on the wing. They dropped into a swift current which swept them down a channel always just out of reach. Suddenly they were caught by a whirlpool, and in our eagerness we dropped our pith helmets, stepped into the water and had almost touched the birds when the main current snatched them away again. We waded across, clambered on over high rocks, and at last after a long chase, salvaged them as they swung round and round the margin of another great whirlpool.

We were gone so long that my mother came in search of us. In the sand beside a wild rapid she found our helmets, and alongside them, our footsteps disappearing in the water. The roar of the rapids drowned out her shouts. When we returned as we had come, we found her in a state of hysterical grief from the natural assumption that we had perished in the river. To the end of her life she never wholly recovered from the shock of this experience. . . .

As we drew nearer the Cataract every bend and headland revealed enchanting hidden backwaters with little crescent beaches fringed with thorn and castor bushes, and overhung by palms, acacias and tamarisks. Occasionally, like those in the Fourth Cataract, such places sheltered little patches of soil cultivated by a few Nubians, living in wattle huts, who stared at us as we drifted past. Except for the fact that probably none of them had ever beheld a white child before, they were never surprised to see us: for by that mysterious way in which a native in Khartoum would know of a happening in Cairo before the European had learned it from his clicking telegraph, these remote, isolated people had for days been informed of our whereabouts and almost hourly progress.

We never ceased marveling at their ability to converse with one another across great stretches of water. Again and again in places where the Nile had suddenly widened to a breadth of almost two miles, so that we would have to inquire locally regarding possible inscriptions or ruins along the farther shore, we would watch a man address a friend so far away on the opposite bank as to be a mere speck wholly out of earshot. He would stand at the very edges of the river perhaps ten feet above its surface, and cupping his hands some four inches in front of his lips, would talk into the water at an angle of about 45°, in a loud voice but without shouting. At intervals he would stop to listen while the distant man evidently replied in kind. But we who stood close by heard no sound. Presently the exchange would end, and he would tell us in a matter-of-fact way what he had learned.

If all this interested my father enormously, it was utterly fascinating to me. I forgot almost immediately what they had tried to teach me at the German Lutheran school in Cairo, but I can still recall as if it had been yesterday every detail of our sojourn in the Sudan.

By the tenth of January, 1907, we had reached an island called Tombos at the head of the Third Cataract. "On the black granite boulders of the east shore, opposite this island," wrote my father, "are engraved the triumphant memorials of Thutmose I.

"Here a vast dam or ridge of black granite boulders and headlands sweeps out of the far horizon of the eastern desert and directly across the channel of the river in an imposing rampart causing the obstructions to which the first bad rapid of the Third Cataract is due. Thutmose I, issuing here at the head of the cataract in the initial Egyptian conquest of this region, found this the proper place for commemorating his achievement. Five triumphal stelae adorn the boulders of the east bank.

"The largest of these, containing 18 lines of inscriptions, is an invaluable historical document containing what is at once the earliest mention of the river Euphrates in an Egyptian record and the earliest evidence of Egyptian expansion thither.

"The inscription is on a huge conical boulder 25 feet high which since the monument was engraved has fallen backward and on its side at an angle of 45°, making photography exceedingly difficult. But by spending a day building special equipment for double-tilting our big camera downward and sideward we secured perfect negatives which are the first facsimiles ever made.

"On the island of Tombos itself I found a new and unknown inscription of a prince and viceroy of Nubia, probably in the 20th year of Thutmose IV. It gives a list of the things he sent back to the palace [at Thebes]: 'perfumes, ivory, ebony, carob wood, panther skins, khesyt wood, incense of Mazoi.' This last item is an interesting reference to a tribe of Nubians who lived on the road from the head of the Fourth to the foot of the Second Cataract, and hence received the aromatic gums of the south and east, which they passed on in trade to

Egypt. Such commodities then took their names from the last people who immediately furnished them to Egypt.

"*January 11, 1907:* This morning I took on a local reis to act as our pilot through the headwaters of the Third Cataract. The wind proved favorable and we cast off early.

"The first rapid, called Hannek, is a cataract in itself, resembling those in the Fourth Cataract. At only one place have the waters been able to force through it a passage of any navigable depth—a narrow, sluice-like channel or mill-race which the natives call a 'bab' or 'gate.' The gates in the successive granite ridges are not opposite each other but are staggered; so that in shooting through one, there is great danger of being wrecked on the next ridge below.

"The method used by these Nubian reises in navigating such difficult waters is most interesting. They wait for a strong wind against the current, which is fortunately the prevailing north wind of the Nile valley. They then drift with the current to the head of the cataract where they hoist all sail. With the wind directly astern, their craft now begins to move slowly upstream; whereupon the reis loosens the sheets, spilling enough wind so that she moves slowly downstream, until she reaches the first rocks. Since she moves down much more slowly than the current, she still has plenty of steerage way. If he is opposite a 'bab,' he lets the boat slowly down stern-on till she passes safely through the gate. But the instant he has dropped through it he must haul his sheets tight again to prevent crashing into the next line of rocks and wrecking the boat.

"To aid him in thus maneuvering for position two enormous sweeps are shipped forward, each manned by two sailors. Simple as all this may sound, it is nevertheless thoroughly exciting—and today when one of our sweeps broke amidst the rapids, a spice of danger was added.

"The strain on rudder and rigging is heavy—many times today the reis struggled in vain to throw the heavy tiller, and shouted for help to bring it around. The current is terrific, and our nerves were exhausted from the tension of watching the boat hovering above the jagged reefs, every rope aquiver, the sails straining to burst, and the roaring water piling under the bow and threatening to demolish us on the rocks below. Often we would hang thus for several minutes, with the rudder but ten feet from the hungry rocks, when a lull in the wind would have meant total wreck.

"Our two reises showed great caution, judgment and skill in bringing us through—much more than I had thought possible—but my heart began to beat normally again only when I saw our boats emerge intact at the foot of the Hannek rapid.

"*January 12, 1907:* This has been a discouraging day. The north wind rose all night, by morning was blowing a gale the power of which increased hourly until by noon it was a hurricane. Had we not been under the lee of a high shore, our deckhouse would have been carried away.

"At midday a few inches of our badly battened mainsail escaped from its housings. The wind seized it instantly—the men scrambled frantically up the yard, but before they could reach it, the blast had wrenched out the whole upper half of the great canvas and ripped it across the middle like tissue paper. By desperate efforts of our combined crews the pieces were gathered in and housed before the whole sail had been torn to tatters. The huge canvas looked like an enormous serpent as it was brought down this afternoon, and under the protection of the river bank a beginning was made in repairing the damage.

"By two o'clock the storm had reached its worst. There were no clouds in the sky, but a gloom of driving dust and sand hid the sun and threw a ghastly grey light over the great river which was lashed into a heavy sea of strangely white rolling waves as the current fretted and fought its way through the stubborn masses of granite. The dust and sand sifted into our porous cabin and settled upon papers, notebooks, and photographs at a rate which not only made work impossible but endangered our negatives.

"*January 15, 1907, in Kagbar rapid:* This is the most dangerous rapid of the Third Cataract. Here again a colossal granite dam runs diagonally across the Nile, and at a distance of half a mile presents the appearance of an artificial work. The river has broken through it in the middle but in so doing has merely created a wild and impassable chaos of boulders and tumbling water.

"At one end of the dam, however, there is a mill-race such as I have described, about fifty feet wide, running at a zigzag much like a backward Z. It is very irregular, broken by numerous islands and boulders, and a tremendous current rushes through it.

"The population of this region is scanty and I could secure only sixteen villagers to supplement our own crews, making a total of twenty-six men. But the villagers were accustomed to the task before them, and confidently leapt into the rapids, swimming from island to island till they reached our boats lying at the head of the passage. With two ropes from the bow and one from the stern, they first let the larger boat slowly down, stopping often and swimming to the next island below to throw a bight of the line around some convenient boulder further down."

At this point my father ordered my mother and me into the felucca. With us went the "treasure chest" containing the expedition's gold and silver cash; the most important records and photographs; and a few of our own most essential belongings. While he remained on board we were taken to a small rocky island to wait until the boats had passed through the most dangerous rapids.

"When we reached the worst rush of water, where there was a sudden drop of several feet," he wrote, "it was impossible to hold the larger boat. The men were obliged to let her drive while the heaviest line was kept running around a bow-post on which it was slowly tautened and finally choked as the boat reached the greatest drop. But no boulder suitable for fastening the line on shore could be found, and as it tautened it dragged the fifteen men who were holding it headlong down a sand bank. They clung to it frantically and just as they were being pulled into the furious water, they brought the boat to a stand-still in the lower angle of the Z—where we still lie, with the surging, roaring water under my elbow as I write. It was the narrowest escape we have yet had.

"The sheikh of the villagers now told me he must go home with his men, but would come again in the morning to bring down the other boat. I differed with him, and after the usual oriental palaver they finally went back for the other boat and brought her alongside of us. But they refused to take us out of the last reach of the Z. After another long talk, I peremptorily ordered them to take through the smaller boat, though it was now late afternoon and the wind had risen again.

"They reluctantly obeyed but in trying to break out the mainsail got the sheet hopelessly tangled with the towline, with the result that the men holding the latter on shore were completely tired out, at the critical moment dropped it too soon; so that before the wind could fill the sails, the current seized the boat, swung her about, drove her into some rocks, then swept her down broadside-on. Yet by some miracle, despite striking several hidden rocks in the channel, she issued at the lower end without being wrecked!

"All this so demoralized the crews and so delayed us that as dusk drew on I made no attempt to carry the bigger boat through. I promised the villagers baksheesh for every man who appeared before sunrise the next morning."

My mother and I were now allowed to come aboard again. The journal continues:

"We went to bed with the roar and rush of the lower 'bab' directly under our beds. The wind had again risen to a gale which, as the boats lay, was directly offshore. It was difficult to sleep, but I finally dropped off, only to be awakened by a familiar sound even louder than the tumult of the rapid. Above the wind howling through the rigging I could hear the sharp crack of loose canvas.

"I ran out on the deck, saw the mizzensail whipping wildly in the gale. It had been badly housed as usual, the wind had ballooned it, and as the reis had neglected to throw out a stern hawser, the pressure of the gale had been quite sufficient to carry the stern far out into the fearful tide of the cataract. If the forward moorings gave way, we should be broken to pieces in an instant on the rocks a hundred feet below us!

"I shouted down the forward hatch, had the crew out in a jiffy, woke the old reis in the stern, and the lot of them somehow managed to house the sail without its being torn to tatters. But against the storm all of them pulling together were unable to drag the stern back to the bank.

"By the following noon the wind had abated enough to enable us to pass safely out of the lower 'bab'; but it was still a gale, and when the natives cast off the ropes we were blown across the river at high speed. As we neared the east bank the reis, instead of killing our motion by heading into the current and then again into the wind, merely rounded into the shore where we struck heavily on a hidden rock, then by good fortune immediately came to rest on a sand bank.

"Hearing a sailor exclaiming about water in the boat, I looked down the forward hatch, saw a torrent gushing into the hold which contained our entire winter's supplies and all our negatives! The crew at once obstructed this hatchway with their own chests of clothing and bags of millet flour. Luckily we had two other hatchways—at the point of my revolver I ordered several sailors below, and the boxes began coming up rapidly.

"We formed a line, passed everything quickly ashore. Ten minutes from the time we had struck, the hull had filled to the deck, but all our hundred boxes were safely on the river bank.

"As I write, the latter presents a ludicrous picture! The most difficult stores to save were our boxes of Triscuit which is our only bread and is packed American-style in flimsy pasteboard cartons.

"To prevent the boat from tipping over into the current we fastened lines from our two mastheads to a palm high up on the rocky shore.

"Tonight (January 16, 1907), the lower corner of this little room is nine inches under water and we are careening so badly that dishes will not stay on the table. The north wind continues to blow steadily, and with the waves rolling over our rail, the boat looks truly like a wreck. We are between 160 and 175 miles from Halfa where our campaign closes for this winter. We need the boat for at least another fortnight—to leave it *now* would be a catastrophe for our winter's work, even if we could secure camels here, which is very doubtful. Schliephack ripped his hand on a piece of strap-iron while handling boxes, cannot work in the dark room. Everything is at a standstill. Altogether, it is the most serious setback we have experienced this year.

"*January 17, 1907, just below Kagbar Cataract:* I sent at once for help from a village three hours distant, but no one appeared. It was obvious we would have to work out our own salvation.

"With all available man power tugging at the ropes from the mastheads we managed to right the boat a few inches. Next we plugged the hole in the hull from the inside with canvas rags, then set all hands to bailing. After hours of alternate bailing and hauling, the water in the cabin disappeared, the boat began to right; and the problem was to careen her sufficiently to reach the hole from the *outside*.

"A piece of extraordinary good luck now befell us. A number of natives appeared among the palms. I thought of course they were the help I had summoned. Instead, they proved to be members of a surveying party but half an hour away, led by two young Englishmen who were caravaning from the Second to the Fourth Cataract, making a survey in anticipation of the raising of the Aswan Dam! A message quickly brought them to us.

"Their men were from Shellal [just above Aswan] and quite familiar with such repairs as we were attempting. They found a wreck near by, pulled out timbers from it, laid them under our keel, and by putting plenty of men at the tackles, drew the boat up several feet onto the timbers, exposing the hole. A patch I had prepared was now tacked over it, the Englishmen secured from their stores a tin of water-cement with which we filled the hole from the inside, covering this in turn with a heavy board. The result is almost watertight and the very slight leakage can be bailed out twice a day.

"We rewarded the two Englishmen each with a cake of American maple sugar which they had never tasted before and greatly fancied! I gave the foreman of their men a sovereign with which to buy a sheep. But presently a messenger brought a note from the Englishman in charge saying that on second thought he believed he had followed a wrong principle in allowing me to reward his men for merely doing their duty, and he was therefore returning the money!"

As we reloaded our cargo we congratulated ourselves that at last we would be rid of the pestilence of rats. But we had no sooner settled on board again than despite every precaution against them they mysteriously reappeared, as arrogantly and numerously as ever!

"*January 21, 1907, Dulgo:* For hours before we reached it as we drifted slowly downstream against an ever-increasing north wind, we could see the three only remaining standing columns of the temple of Sesebi opposite this place.

"Upon our arrival I noticed that all three columns bore reliefs of Seti I, as Lepsius says they do. But I noticed also that on all three columns a deeply cut sun-disk penetrated through and interrupted Seti's inscriptions.

"I could not fathom this, but finally conjectured it might be the work of Ikhnaton (Amenhotep IV) which had been covered with stucco and re-sculptured by Seti I. But no temple of Ikhnaton is known south of the vicinity of Thebes (500 miles north from here), so that this was a hazardous guess.

"I worked on, when suddenly behind the form of Amon on the column I saw dimly through the rough chisel marks of intentional expungement, the lines of the well-known figure of the great heretic. A dozen other unexplained peculiarities in the reliefs of Seti I were now immediately explained, and I could discern the figure of Ikhnaton on each of the columns, worshiping the sun-disk. This meant much: it meant the first discovery of a temple of the great reformer in Nubia; it meant the sudden extension of his sun-worship temple 500 miles farther south; it meant the possibility of identifying this place with the Nubian city founded by Ikhnaton and known as Gem-Aton, a hitherto unnoticed reference to which I had found at Barkal.

"New visions of the importance and power of the great reformer rose before me as through the defacement by his enemies I saw his figure emerging on the columns of his first known temple in Nubia.

"Unfortunately the wind blew so viciously as to make photography on a ladder almost impossible. But a discouraging day which had carried us only six miles northward, had brought us the most important discovery of the winter.

"*Gurgot, January 25, 1907:* This inexorable north wind has no mercy on us. One feels like Van Der Decken trying to round Cape Horn. It has been blowing fourteen days, but for the last nine days has raged without a moment's cessation. For two days we have been unable to move from this spot.

"Yesterday morning when I found that again we could not move, I sent the unwilling crews ashore to the ropes and made them track the boats. They made twenty-five yards, then the wind stopped them completely. They could not budge the larger boat another inch. We tried to secure more men from the neighboring village across the river but found only feeble old men, women and children—the able-bodied men are all either in Egypt or elsewhere in the Sudan. Not even the one sakiah in the village was running.

"At noon today the wind quickened again into a furious gale which buried us in vast clouds of dust and sand like ashes from Vesuvius. There is a pungent odor of dust in the air, it grates between one's teeth, one's ears are full, one's eyebrows and eyelashes are laden like the dusty miller's, it sifts into all boxes and cupboards, penetrates between glass negatives, ruins chemical solutions in trays in the dark room.

"Amenhotep III's great temple of Soleb is only thirty miles away. We could reach it on good camels in a day, but to face this storm on the open desert would put out one's eyes!"

Despite the gale we reached Soleb on January 30th. A sufficient portion of its high walls and columns were still standing to occupy the men from dawn till dark for ten days, before we struggled onward another thirteen miles against the howling north wind, to a temple at Sedëinga on the island of Sai.

"Amenhotep III erected the temple of Soleb to himself as a god," wrote my father, "and several times he appears on its wall reliefs offering to *himself* as a god. He built the temple at Sedëinga for the worship of his queen, Tiy, as a goddess.

"On a fallen block Davies found the name of this place, heretofore unknown, written in a rectangle signifying: 'Fortress of Tiy. Thus this royal pair, the most splendid in the history of Egypt, became the patron divinities of their great Nubian province, much as a Roman emperor was worshiped in his foreign dominions. Only one column stands in this small temple of Queen Tiy, which does not approach the temple of Soleb for splendor. The fallen superstructure so encumbers the place that it is impossible to trace the ground plan. But this solitary column—which fortunately bears the dedication to Tiy—is splendidly fluted and strikingly resembles a Greek column of a thousand years later."

With each day's progress the river was becoming wilder, the rapids more frequent. We were drawing into the headwaters of the Second Cataract which only our felucca could navigate. In anticipation of the moment when we would have to abandon the two larger boats and continue northward by caravan, my father had arranged with Colonel Jackson that some thirty-three camels were to be sent from Wadi Halfa to meet us in this region. On February 15 we finally came ashore at a place called Kosheh and in the face of a sand-blasting gale from the north we transferred our cargo to the backs of the waiting camels, and by caravan began the last stage of our journey.

Close to the next inhabited village downriver, called Firka, we saw "a sizable deserted village of the Dervishes from which they had been driven by Kitchener's advance. The bodies of the slain still lie scattered in the streets and within the ruined houses.

"On the river bank at Firka two huge hippopotamus heads were hanging from a tree. They were killed here recently by the villagers. As far back as 1823 a hippo seen by Hoskins at Tombos above the *Third* Cataract was said by the natives there to have been the *northernmost* of his race and the only one they had ever beheld. Hence the appearance of these two beasts at the head of the Second Cataract is very remarkable. They must have been caught by the swift current at high water and carried down through the cataracts.

"This 135-mile stretch of country known as the Second Cataract was the first serious barrier to the southward progress of civilization in the Nile valley, and is strategically most important. The Egyptians had a canal through the First Cataract as early as 2000 B.C., and by about the same time had conquered the lower half of the Second. The forts—built in the days of Abraham—which guarded this old frontier still survive. The gold mines of Nubia and the rich traffic with what is now Dongola and the Sudan constantly lured the Kings of Egypt southward, but it was 500 years before they overcame the Second Cataract wilderness and added to their kingdom another 400 miles of this remarkable Nile valley.

"Today we passed two camel caravans laden with merchandise, including many cases of Standard Oil petroleum in 5-gallon tins, on their way to the country above this cataract! Such has been the means of transport here for thousands of years. Records dating as far back as 2500 B.C. tell us that a caravan of 300 asses penetrated this region (the camel was unknown in ancient Egypt).

"Short stretches of clear river channel here alternate with long reaches thickly studded with rocks. Fierce rapids and dangerous cataracts recur every few miles. The shore on either hand offers little or no foothold for vegetation—the territory of the rare villages is hardly sufficient to maintain them—and for miles at a time the stream winds on between desolate black rocks rising sometimes to a stately height. The cliffs on the west side are clothed on their southern slopes with drifts of bright yellow sand dropped by the north wind—they stretch up shadowy clefts and gorges in long sunlit sweeps like the snow on the crests of the Alps. When this dramatic intermingling of black and gold is slashed by the sky-reflecting river fringed with the green of palm groves, the scene is beautiful beyond words. But when the beholder turns his back on the river, there is nothing in the forbidding prospect to gladden the eye—the awful desolation of tumbled rocks stretches on and on to the horizon."

Travel by camel caravan is far less a romantic than an arduous, tedious business. For generally speaking, there is a much greater difference between a pack camel and a fine riding camel than between a pack horse and a beautifully bred riding mount. The camel's motion being far more complex than that of the horse, the opportunity for continuous, and for those unaccustomed to it, diabolical discomfort is several times multiplied. The animals we rode differed from their freighted brethren only in that they appeared slightly less moth-eaten, and bore carpet-covered wooden saddles more impressive looking but hardly more amenable to the human anatomy than the pack frames of the others. A good riding camel can easily do thirty or forty miles a day. With our beasts we looked upon twenty as excellent, upon twenty-five as a record.

The drivers' consistent cruelty to their beasts was often too unbearable to watch. They prodded and beat their flanks and hindquarters with sharp sticks and cudgels until open sores developed wherein would gather maggots and great, bloated, grey-green leeches which the men seldom removed, since it was easier to control an animal in this condition! Sometimes a camel would rebel, go berserk, and despite its load would dash off into the desert at astonishing speed, to be recaptured only with the greatest difficulty. This behavior was not due solely to the innate cruelty of most of their keepers, but to the fact that camels are among the most treacherous of animals and can never be trusted or tamed. There is an Arab legend that only the camel knows all the hundred names for Allah, and hence is so contemptuous of man.

I still shudder at the recollection of a gruesome scene I witnessed on the outskirts of Kareima, of a naked shaven-headed little Sudanese boy leading by a rope halter one of the largest camels I had ever seen, which for no apparent reason he was periodically beating unmercifully with a cudgel. When the boy spied me he stopped to stare, and as he did so the snarling camel towering behind him suddenly opened wide its great jaws, dropped and closed them over the child's skull, crushed it like a black ostrich egg. . . .

But far less tolerable than pack camels was the incessant flailing of the north wind. Even with kerchief-masks the sand blast cut one's face like infinite minute razors. Nothing one could apply would heal the bleeding cracks in one's lips and the corners of the mouth, and on knuckles, joints and finger tips. The blast gradually gave one a curious fever, tautened one's nerves.

Each night we camped in tents surrounded by the burbling, grumbling, eternally complaining camels. Water for washing was brought from the river in the usual evil-smelling sheepskins. Sand gritted in our food, in all our belongings, seemed to permeate our whole existence. All of us were weary, but there was no illness among us. Even my mother accustomed herself to this life—though as always, even when riding a camel, she dressed in the same Victorian clothes she habitually wore in Europe and America.

"*February 21, 1907:* A long march over the worst section of caravan track we have yet met has brought us to Kummeh," wrote my father.

"Below Ambugol and above Attiri the Nile winds till its wild and precipitous gorge reminds one of the fjords of the Norwegian coast. At Doshât the narrow tortuous trail high up along the face of the cliffs is like a pass in a miniature range of the Andes—at many points a false step would have sent the camels 200 feet down into the river below.

"As we began ascending this difficult gorge, the sheikh of the drivers raised a weird cry which rang along the valley, and the other camel drivers took it up far down the straggling line of the caravan, till the mountains resounded. They were repeating the name of their patron sheikh, a holy man named Abd el-Kâder whose tomb is at

Halfa. They hoped thus to keep their camels from stumbling. Their invocation was effective and it was with great relief that I saw our heavy negative-boxes come safely down out of the pass.

"This place marked the southern frontier of the Middle Kingdom Pharoahs in the days of Abraham. Here still stand the fortresses— Kummeh on the east and Semneh on the west bank of the river— by which they commanded the narrowest point in the entire Nile. In each fortress is a temple of the Empire. The one on the east bank has been used for centuries by the natives as a dwelling—in fact, until quite recently, when the government at my request evicted them. The almost ceaseless wind deluges us with reeking clouds of the dust and filth which lie three feet deep on its floors. If we escape contagion we shall be thankful.

"*February 22, 1907:* This morning our baggage lay under drifts of sand like snow after a storm. In the Kummeh temple work was torment —the wind, whirling in furious eddies through the roofless halls, buried us in the foul residue of generations of native life. We look and feel like coal miners, but much dirtier—for coal is *clean* by comparison. The temple is surrounded by the squalid houses of the tiny village. Goats run about on the roofs baa-ing at us, and babies with fly-ridden eyes cry in our ears as we work.

"On the rocks under the walls of the fortress are the records of the Nile levels made by the Twelfth Dynasty Pharaohs, nearly 4000 years ago. They are of remarkable interest, since they average some twenty-five feet higher than the water ever rises today.

"From the felucca as I was crossing to the west bank, I could see clearly the gap through which the river here flows. A huge dam of granite three hundred feet thick, and thirty to fifty feet above present water level, lies directly across the bed of the river. In one place there is a gap only a hundred feet wide, and through this narrow but enormously deep breach pours the *entire* Nile!

"It is easy to understand why the Twelfth Dynasty Pharaohs sagaciously chose this easily guarded place as the southern frontier of their kingdom. The forts on each side completely commanded the stream, and no boat could descend the narrow gap without the consent of the garrisons.

"The west fort is an enormous structure with a moat fifty feet wide, carefully built of unhewn granite. The main walls, with towers projecting far beyond the curtain walls, show a thorough knowledge of defense strategics. In one corner of this fort, Thutmose III built a temple of superb workmanship. In it Lepsius sixty years ago discovered the frontier landmarks of Sesostris III (Twelfth Dynasty).

"There are many graffiti on the cliffs of both shores—they line the road leading up to the east fort and are for the most part the work of idle soldiers and scribes. One's imagination can easily picture a scattering of loafing guardsmen from the garrisons sunning themselves here, and inscribing the rocks with scrawls which in many instances appear as fresh today as when they were cut 4000 years ago.

"*March 2, 1907:* While at work on the ancient Nile levels recorded on the west shore I came upon an almost invisible record of Amenhotep I, placed on a rock by his viceroy Tura. We have known that he invaded Nubia, but this inscription is the first evidence of his invasion ever to have been found in the region itself. It is dated in the king's sixth or seventh year and is the earliest record of the Empire yet discovered in Nubia.

"We have also found proof that the high levels of the Nile recorded here almost as early as 2000 B.C. give the *actual* level of the water. The highest of these is some thirty feet above the maximum Nile of today."

During the night of March first the north wind again became a tempest which continued through the following day. In the morning of what was to be our last day at this place, while my father was standing on a ledge of granite cliffs above the camp, collating Davies's copies of some graffiti, he slipped, lost his balance in the terrific wind, and pitched headforemost more than twenty feet down onto some rocks below.

By some miracle he was not killed. I remember seeing him come reeling into camp, bleeding and stunned. We gave him brandy, disinfected and bandaged his ugly lacerations, tried to persuade him to rest for the remainder of the day. But he quickly regained his composure and resumed work. "We finished the excavation of the temple in the east fortress this afternoon," he wrote that night. "It brought us three inscriptions on the pillars and doorposts, and two stelae, all the work of Nubian viceroys. Tomorrow, having been here nine days, we take to the camels again!"

On March 3 his journal continues: "We left Kummeh this morning, soon came abreast of a lofty island called Uronarti which is crowned by the remains of a huge Twelfth Dynasty fortress like those at Kummeh and Semneh. I had just despaired of crossing to this island because the felucca had not yet arrived, when a native appeared and offered to take me over on a float consisting of two long, cigar-shaped bundles of reeds exactly like those so often depicted in ancient Egyptian wall reliefs. I accepted, boarded his precarious craft and sat down virtually in the water. Holding the raft with his hands, he propelled it across with his feet. He was a powerful swimmer and except for the inevitable wind which created surprisingly high waves, we went along very well.

"Besides the barracks of the troops, the fortress contained a small stone temple or chapel of one room, built by Thutmose III. It was at this place some years ago that my friends Steindorff, Schaefer and Borchardt, pushing up by camel from Halfa, found a duplicate of the boundary stela of Semneh.

"Tonight we are only a day's march from Halfa where our work began last year.

"*March 5, 1907:* This morning I was detained by the sheikh and the camel-*owners* among our camel-*drivers*, who demanded to know for how many days they were to be paid.

"I shook them off twice, but the third time took out my daybook and gave them the total it showed. They looked very dark, told me they expected to be paid from the time they left Halfa to go south to meet us. As the caravan was costing nearly $15 a day, this meant a serious increase in the total charge. No compromise was possible: I told them I would not pay it, and that if they wished they could go and leave us in the cataract desert. Knowing we had plenty of provisions they thought better of it, and obeyed orders when told to strike the tents and load.

"The long baggage train finally disappeared through a defile to the north, and we followed on the most wearisome march we have yet had. Late in the afternoon we descried on a high rock on the other shore the tomb of the holy Abd el-Kâder to whose efficient protection we owed the safe passage of the precious plate-boxes through the difficult pass of Doshât. Then above the northern palms appeared the minaret of the distant mosque of Halfa; and presently we could discern as a faraway speck on the opposite shore the temple where our work of the previous campaign had begun over fourteen months before.

"At Halfa we were 1000 miles up the Nile. From a point nearly 1000 miles still *farther* up, beginning with the southernmost ancient monuments in the Nile valley—that is, nearly 2000 miles from the Mediterranean—the expedition has this year carried the work of exploration and recording down to our last year's 1000-mile starting point.

"The notebooks and negatives produced by the expedition's two campaigns will when published make a complete corpus of the monuments of Nubia in about sixteen folio volumes. There remain to be done next year the historical inscriptions in the 800-mile stretch between Aswan and the Mediterranean, including the temple of Philae.

"At sundown on March 5, 1907, we rode into Halfa, pitched our tents for the last time beside the steamboat landing; and the following day embarked on a freight steamer for Aswan."

Twelve years before, he had stood on the cliffs opposite Aswan and looking off toward the southern horizon had silently prayed that he might some day push far beyond this point to the southernmost reaches of ancient Egyptian power. Now at last his wish had been gratified. But though in future he was several times to revisit Wadi Halfa, he was never again to set eyes upon the fascinating, arduous country beyond.

The fat mail pouch which greeted him at Aswan contained a diverse assortment of letters.

For instance, an official communication from the Sudan government at Khartoum stated that their inspector of antiquities had just discovered, cut in unsightly prominence on the temples at Naga and Mesawwarât, the legend:

H. SCHLIEPHACK

1906.

They respectfully begged to inquire if an individual of this name was not a member of the University of Chicago's expedition.

"When I had cooled down sufficiently to do so without unseemly wrath," my father wrote of this incident, "I peremptorily discharged Herr Schliephack in writing, as is customary in Germany. He refused to be discharged, proceeded to seize as security the most valuable optical equipment of the expedition, worth probably $1000; and to *write* me that he would deposit it for safekeeping with the German Consul in Cairo!

"I summoned him and said: 'I have your written admission of having taken property not belonging to you. If you return it immediately you will receive the kindest treatment. If you do not, I shall put this letter in the hands of a magistrate, and yourself behind bars!"

"He saw what a fool he had been, surrendered the equipment, and departed. I could make no other amends to the Sudan government than to inform it of the man's dismissal."

There was a letter from Mr. J. A. Ramsey, secretary of the "Ramsæy Family Association of America" at Topeka, Kansas. "I notice from press reports that you have unearthed an account of the marriage of Ramses II," wrote Mr. Ramsey. "There is a tradition that our name originated with the Ramses. My theory is that some of their descendants went north and west. I would like to know if in your research you have found out what became of them, and whither you think they went. A man named Pharaoh Ramsey lives in Kentucky at the present time, which is to say the least a strange coincidence."

But everything else was forgotten when he came upon a letter from Mr. Gates acknowledging the general proposals for further work in Egypt which my father had sent him from Abu Hamed.

"Before replying," said Mr. Gates, "I should like [to have] such a bird's-eye view of the financial part of the undertaking as will disclose the whole cost.

"I have not mentioned the subject to Mr. Rockefeller and so I feel at liberty to inquire of you whether, in case I should secure from him the necessary funds to complete this work, the [resulting] volumes . . . could be suitably dedicated to him as the patron of the enterprise. . . .

"I will confess this much—that the idea of perpetuation of all the monuments of Egypt for all time in this way is to me an alluring thought, as it is to you. . . . How far, however, it may attract Mr. Rockefeller we can only learn when we can place before him, in a reliable and final way, the financial estimates."

My father's spirits and hopes soared again, and for several weeks in Cairo he was wholly preoccupied with reducing the dreams of years to practical, easily comprehensible terms and figures: an itinerary and a plan of work covering fifteen years; a publication program providing for 100 folio volumes, each in an edition of 300 copies, a complimentary copy to be given to every great library in the world; estimates from Cairo shipyards for a floating laboratory on the Nile; and a total budget of $455,000.

On a hot day in May we sent off by registered mail from the Cairo general post office a bulky white linen envelope sealed with red sealing wax. As he methodically put away the registry receipt he said to me, "Well, my son, whatever comes of it, I may as well hang for a goose as a gander!"

Once again we traveled northward, this time through most of classical Greece, thence to Smyrna, up the coast of Asia Minor, and one morning at dawn into the southern end of the Dardanelles where my father showed me "on the Asiatic side, about three miles inland, the large conical mound marking the ruins of Troy where we could easily discern with a glass the heaps of rubbish from Schliemann's and Doerpfeld's excavations."

One of the chief reasons for our visiting Constantinople was my father's desire to examine in the museum there the magnificent alabaster sarcophagus which some authorities thought might have belonged to Alexander the Great. But for me the place was rendered unforgettable by the prosaic fact that one afternoon while my parents were at tea with President and Mrs. Gates at Robert College on the Bosporus, the son of the prime minister of Bulgaria, then a student there, gave me most competently my first lesson in American baseball, especially in the art of batting, while a little crowd of Turkish and Balkan youngsters looked on!

By June we had settled again in Gross-Lichterfelde outside of Berlin. On the evening of the 13th he wrote to his mother:

"It makes my heart rejoice that you are still here with us to read these lines, and that I am not condemned to feel with Dr. Johnson as his honors came to him, that all those to whom he would have told them, and who would have rejoiced in them, were gone.

"This evening at dusk on our return from a walk in the fields I was told that two gentlemen had called and left a card for me. I found lying upon my desk Prof. Erman's card, on the back of which was written in lead pencil the following:

'Socio epistolario Academiae Regiae Berolinensis hodie electo ex animo gratulamur.
Ad. Erman   Eduard Meyer'

"I could not believe my eyes as I read:

'To the corresponding member of the Royal Academy of Berlin this day elected, heartiest congratulations from
Ad. Erman   and   Eduard Meyer'

"And these two men, once my masters and now my friends and colleagues, had come in person to give me this news! I cannot tell you, dear Mother, what a pleasure it is to sit down and write *you* of it first of all. To be elected by vote a member of the body where von Humboldt, Mommsen, Virchow and Helmholtz have sat—it is unqualified recognition from the greatest body of scholars in European science, and is the greatest honor Germany or Europe can bestow upon a foreign scholar. I can never expect anything higher.

"I can't believe it yet as the card lies here before me. Charles inquired if he wasn't a member too, but his mother told him 'No'—like the Irish sergeant's wife—'only me and your father!'

"How I should have loved to have Father know of this!"

A few days later he wrote her again: "I have received a formal letter from the secretary of the Academy informing me of my election. The Emperor signed the appointment—it went through without the least opposition, which is not always the case.

"There are two classes of members in the German Royal Academy: the first is called the philosophical-historical class; the second, the natural science class. In America there are two members in the former group—Prof. William James, the philosopher of Harvard University; and—I leave you to guess the other member! In the natural science class there are four members in America: Prof. Simon Newcomb, the great astronomer of Johns Hopkins University; Prof. Edward Charles Pickering of Massachusetts Institute of Technology; [Alexander Emanual] Agassiz; and Josiah Willard Gibbs of Yale.

"I must confess great surprise at finding that among the Americans there are no other philologists, Orientalists or historians. With one exception they are all much older than I, and none of them happened at the very beginning to cut out as big a piece of work as I did— a piece of work about which nobody knew anything till it suddenly all appeared within a year, and was therefore likely to make an impression. So it has come about that the maturer and more deserving men have been overlooked in favor of a man who made a kind of hundred yards' dash."

Later in July, accompanied by his old master Adolf Erman, he formally took his place in the Academy for the first time, at a meeting which included an illustrated lecture by Eduard Meyer and was attended by the Emperor. My mother and I were permitted to sit in the visitors' gallery, whence we looked on when at the close of the lecture my father was presented to the Emperor who congratulated him upon his assistance to the Egyptian Dictionary Commission, his various scientific accomplishments and his election to the Academy.

"For the first time in my career," he wrote later that day, "I have a feeling of quiet confidence in the future, of freedom from being always on the scientific defensive."

Hardly had he expressed this "feeling of quiet confidence in the future" when he received two blows in rapid succession which almost wholly destroyed it. The first was a letter from Mr. Gates, reading in part:

"We have concluded that we are not prepared to recommend to Mr. Rockefeller the taking up of this monumental work involving such great expense and covering so many years. We recognize in you the one man in the world who is qualified to do this work, but we think . . . it should be done by the Egyptian Government . . . and not as a private enterprise. . . ."

A few sentences dictated by an ecclesiastical old gentleman sitting in a lofty building overlooking New York Harbor had put an end to his great hopes. He had all along tried to steel himself against this outcome, yet in the back of his mind had unconsciously thought only in terms of success. The plans he had so carefully prepared in Cairo had embodied everything he had come to believe as a scientist and historian and all the practical experience he had gained in the field. But to Mr. Gates at 26 Broadway they had been merely another item in a daily assault of pleading letters from a host of dreamers like himself in every corner of the world.

Such a wave of exhaustion now overcame him that we went for a brief holiday in Switzerland, at a small inn on the Bürgenstock across the lake from Lucerne. The mountain meadows were thronged with crocuses, fruit trees were in bloom, snows were receding to the higher peaks and northern slopes, every brook and stream was singing, summer had re-conquered the Alps. We took long walks, climbed high ridges where my father sat for hours at a time, his arms around his knees, gazing at pine-clad distances reminiscent of his student days and of our sojourns in the Austrian Tyrol. He soon responded to the tonic effect of all this beauty, and though with something less than his old enthusiasm, began to think aloud new plans for the future of his work.

Then at the end of July, without warning or explanation, arrived cables from Robert Francis Harper (who had become head of the Oriental Exploration Fund) and President Judson, terminating the

Egyptian expedition, and as if to soften the blow, granting him a year's leave of absence.

In his dazed astonishment he turned to an old friend and colleague, Ernest De Witt Burton, who was one day to become president of the University of Chicago:

"I have many times risked my life for this work on the Upper Nile," he wrote, "and my reward is a vote of 'no confidence.' A contract providing for three years' work in Egypt and signed by the president of the University and the committee of the Fund for which I myself raised the principal, has been broken without reference to me. I am seriously considering immediate resignation from the University of Chicago. But before I take this step I would be deeply grateful for your judgment and advice."

Professor Burton replied that the University's action had been forced upon it by the attitude of Mr. Gates, "a man of wide reading, decided opinions and strong will. He has been reading books on Egypt and on Assyria and Babylonia, and has come to the conclusion that Egypt's contribution to the civilization of which we are the heirs is much less important than that of Assyria and Babylon. Having made up his mind that further work in Egypt is a waste of money, he has requested that excavation in the former regions be resumed. I have no idea whether he is right or wrong, but this is his conviction. Could *you* have seen him face to face at the proper moment you might have convinced him that he was wrong.

"Since its financial support depends upon his word, the committee of the Fund had no choice but to accept his judgment. They have interpreted your three-year appointment to work in Egypt not as an inviolable contract but as an instruction, subject to modification as altered circumstances seemed to require it.

"I hope you will accept this disappointment as unavoidable, and will find a way to publish the valuable results of the work already done. As for your immediate course, on this I have no doubt: don't think of resigning! Come home, resume your place and work at the University. If there is any trace of feeling against you here, it is only that you have been so intensely interested and absorbed in your own special work that you have not thought a great deal of your department or of the University—a feeling which, if it exists at all, you can easily dispel by your personal presence. You have made a splendid record. There are years yet in which to work. Come home, my dear friend, and work with us!"

Professor Burton's understanding and conciliatory letters finally dissuaded him from resigning, but his spirits and physical condition remained at low ebb. For nothing could persuade him that Mr. Gates's sudden loss of interest in Egypt was merely the spontaneous result of recent reading in Babylonian and Assyrian archaeology. He was convinced that the shadow of Robert Francis Harper's hatred had once again fallen like a blight across his career.

The Sudan had taxed his strength far more than he had realized and what with the anxiety and the heavy burden of paper work which these unexpected developments had caused him, he was struck down by bronchial pneumonia and serious complications. He lay ill for several months in a small hotel in Lucerne, and was twice at the point of death. My mother nursed him night and day, and I helped her as best I could. It was a grim time, filled with the mists and rains of the Swiss autumn.

At last when he began to convalesce I often walked alone in the surrounding country; from a young watchmaker named Gübelin on the Schweizerhofquai I learned much about the construction and assembly of watches; and on one occasion I was solemnly arrested for fishing from the old covered bridge across the river, with a hook I had made myself.

When he was strong enough to travel we returned to Berlin whence in November, 1907, he wrote to his mother:

"It does me more good than any medicine to be here again among the familiar scenes—it is the only spot on this side of the water where I feel at home. I look up with genuine affection at the windows of the room in the old university where for three years I heard Erman lecture. Just down a narrow side street is the telegraph office from which on an eventful evening nearly fourteen years ago I cabled you that I had passed the doctor's examination.

"When I think how often during those student days, with my arms full of books, I used to trudge past the door of the Royal Academy of Sciences, a few hundred yards down the Linden, I cannot credit my senses that I now have a seat there myself. I refer to it again only because this has been a very welcome encouragement. For I have felt like an office boy looking for a job, and have often found it difficult to convince myself that I have ever accomplished anything. Not till I returned here to the old scenes, and again laid eyes on the books I had written did I feel somewhat reassured."

But he could not seem to regain his old vigor, and the doctors informed him he must spend at least a year of convalescence in a favorable climate like that of Bordighera on the Italian Riviera. At the combined insistence of my mother and his colleagues, he agreed to go; and presently we had established ourselves in a minute villa, appropriately named "Villa Modesta," overlooking the Mediterranean on the steep slope just east of the Citta Vecchia at Bordighera, on the estate of the widow of Charles Garnier, architect of the Paris Opera House. The rental with everything furnished including uniforms and headdress for the servants was $35 per month; while the *combined* wages of a cook and parlor maid, both exceedingly pretty, were $3.50 per week!

Each of the two floors of the Villa Modesta opened onto a little garden filled with olive and tangerine trees and beds of flowers. We bought fish directly from the nets of fishermen on the pebble beach below. The pretty cook was affianced to a young florist who kept the house filled with flowers.

As my father grew stronger we explored the mountainous hinterland with its fortified villages whose walls were still pocked with cannon-ball holes made by Mediterranean pirates when a century earlier they habitually raided this littoral for slaves. We visited most of the Roman remains along the coast from Ventimiglia to Genoa. I read insatiably from a little library left to the town of Bordighera by a long-time British resident—I used to curl up in water-carved niches among rust-colored igneous rocks overhanging the sea, and while friendly lizards scurried about in the sun, and likely as not a mirage of the Island of Corsica hung upside down along the southeastern horizon, I reveled in a patternless *divertissement* of everything from Cooper's Mediterranean sea stories to Thackeray's *Pendennis*.

By day my father worked at an abridged version of his *History of Egypt*, of evenings read aloud to my mother beside a fire of olive logs. The wash of the sea lulled us to sleep. Altogether the months we spent in this place were amongst the happiest which as a family we were ever to know.

Our return to the University of Chicago in the spring of 1908 was an ordeal for my father, whose state of mind was that of a man who had somehow failed in midcareer. His health was still so precarious that had he known he was beginning a twelve years' exile from Europe and above all from Egypt, I believe he would have suffered a spiritual and physical collapse. As it was, he survived on a diet of tenuous hope.

After the blows which the University's administration had dealt him, he had anticipated an unfriendly reception. But even his former critics recognized that adversity had tempered his earlier aggressiveness and dramatic intensity, and without quenching his inner fire had invested his manner with a new, quiet gravity and poise. To his considerable surprise he was warmly welcomed by everyone—excepting of course Robert Francis Harper whose enmity had now become a psychosis of sadistic persecution.

Whatever encouragement this prevailing amity might have afforded him was vitiated, however, by familiar economic problems. The care of the Englewood household had largely devolved upon him. The cost of living in America was very much higher, while his salary remained the same; and in the autumn following our return my mother had given birth to another son. The old, griping anxiety of insufficient income began hounding him more persistently than ever—and as always in the past he turned again to public lecturing far and wide.

During the next few years he filled lectureship after lectureship, from Maine to Georgia, from the Atlantic to the Pacific. He had the curious experience of returning to New Haven and addressing a packed auditorium not far from a theater in which Eva Tanguay was playing to a poor house. He lectured in Omaha where, as he wrote my mother, "I revisited what had been Clement Powell's old drug store in which I worked as a youth of twenty-one. I seemed to be suddenly translated into another world. The store was now occupied by a dingy family liquor shop, the whole neighborhood was time-stained and rapidly becoming little better than a slum. It made me shudder. I am still wondering how I ever escaped it twenty-five years ago!"

Though he appeared to lecture with all his earlier fire and enthusiasm, any exhilaration and dramatic release this had in the beginning afforded him had long since given way to a sense of relentless economic pressure, of cold dread of the first day of each month which chronically nullified the slightest gain of income over expenditures.

"The strain on health and the discouragement of all this are intolerable," he wrote. "I am lionized to nausea at every corner, but my check-book is as impotent as before. *Why* isn't it all of some practical use in securing me a post where I can continue my scientific work without incessant financial anxiety?"

About 1910 my mother inherited a moderate sum of money from a gay and gout-ridden old uncle named Benjamin Hart who had lived in Paris in a luxurious house which stood, somewhat ironically, in the *rue Galilée*. His spreading white moustache, pointed beard, gleaming eyes, broad-brimmed Western hat and loud tweeds had for more than a generation been a familiar sight in every leading Continental watering place. His legacy to her would probably have been appreciably larger had she and my father not indignantly refused on a certain occasion to dine with him in company with a piquant lady whose abode by happy coincidence not only adjoined his own, but as if to emphasize the general spirit of neighborliness, was connected with it by a door on an upper story.

Knowledge of these things had come suddenly and with a dreadful shock to my mother. "Thinking him suffering and alone, I had really begun to cherish some sentiment for Uncle Ben," she afterwards wrote in her diary. "But alas, it was like casting pearls before swine!"

Personally I had always rather fancied Uncle Benjamin—he used to send me a hundred francs at Christmas and on my birthday. But after that bitter time, the nature of which my ears were presumably too young to hear, he never did again. Of course I did not dare breathe that I was sorry.

Quite understandably, he changed his will following this estrangement. But what may have seemed to him a punitively reduced bequest was nevertheless sufficient to enable my parents for the first time in their lives to free themselves from landlords and the treadmill of rental payments. They used Uncle Benjamin's legacy, supplemented by a mortgage, to purchase a plot of ground near the University, and in 1912 to build a house. My father himself planned the interior; and Howard van Doren Shaw, an eminent American architect in his day and an old friend, designed its exterior after the villa of the poet Ariosto which still stands in a narrow street in Ferrara, in northern Italy.

On either side of Ariosto's door hung a great wrought-iron ring, to hold torches at night, while the entrance steps were at each end shielded from passing carriage wheels by a "sugar loaf" of stone. It seemed to my fifteen years that our house, some four centuries later, standing well back from a street already lighted at night, hardly needed such provisions. But both Mr. Shaw and my father were enamoured of the Renaissance, and took the greatest delight in reproducing these archaic embellishments, including an inscription in third-rate Latin by the poet himself, who had had it executed in terra cotta letters across the entire façade of his house. In ours it was happily confined to a marble plaque above the entrance. *"Parva, sed apta mihi, sed nulli obnoxia,"* it read, the many "seds" giving it a curiously legal sound, *"sed non Sordida, parta meo sed tamen aere domus"*—which Mrs. Shelley translated thus:

> " 'Tis small but fit for me, gives none offense,
> Not mean, yet builded at my own expense."

If the total effect of all this was rather distinguished, it was also somewhat unexpected and perhaps a little precious—and to my unsolicited way of thinking at the time, very disappointing. For I had always hoped that one day we would inhabit a Georgian or a Southern Colonial house, and never became reconciled to our irrelevant emulation of Ariosto. It lacked what my family needed above all else—the quality of sunlight.

For the first time my father now possessed an adequate study at home, and could with magnificent impunity drive nails into any wall in the house he chose. But he soon discovered that his hoped-for emancipation from rental payments and landlords was only a snare and a delusion—he had merely exchanged them for interest on a mortgage, and for personal responsibility for obsolescence, repairs, taxes. As for his study at home, it was to prove in the end the last stronghold of his Victorian wishful thinking. For the old familiar problem of managing a household, rearing children, and keeping them and herself presentable on an insufficient academic budget tended to make each day for my mother a scaling of Mt. Everest.

She could never grasp, for instance, that servants existed only by reason of the limitations she so deplored; and through our kitchen passed a succession of heterogeneous domestics all of whom, with a persistence unshaken by experience, she struggled to induct into the highly individual ways of her housekeeping. At a certain point in their emotional reactions, which long practice had taught us to predict with considerable accuracy, her pupils would usually erupt from our employ. Of the two or three who were obdurate enough to survive this discipline for as much as several years, the most memorable was a mad, sun-struck old Irishwoman whose unexpectedness fascinated my mother —as when on the morning in August 1914 that my sister was born, she poked her frizzled head resembling a caricature by "Boz" into the door of the natal room and said heartily, "Manny, manny hoppy returrns av th' day, M'om!"

The fact that everyday life was for my mother such a constant struggle caused my father the profoundest distress of mind. Yet by his own admission he "had not the courage to face the reality"; and as always, with a fine Victorian chivalry, he attributed to their relationship whatever it may have lacked. When household duties and insufficient practice had stiffened her fingers until she could no longer find solace and escape in the keyboard of her piano, he strove to bring her other, compensating interests. Evening after evening, year after year, while she did the family mending, he read aloud to her—Hamerton's *The Intellectual Life;* Mahan's three great works on The Influence of Sea Power; biographies of Agassiz, Disraeli, Huxley, Thackeray, the letters of Carlyle; and many, many others. The sound of his voice gave her a comforting sense of proximity to his mind, stimulated her powers of comprehension just as her music used to do. But when it had ceased, when he had inserted a marker, closed the book and risen from his chair to lock doors and windows for the night, she gradually sank again into the quicksands of tomorrow's household anxieties.

Almost twenty-five years later, I found the following undated entry in her personal diary, which soon after making it, she had interrupted and never resumed:

"Nowhere in these pages have I recorded that among my husband's trials and problems the greatest has been my peculiar temperament (for which I am not *entirely* to blame, for I inherited my strange disposition from my father). Not even my intense love for him has helped me to conquer it. I can never undo the harm it has caused him. Remorse will be to the end my punishment. Whatever I am that is worthy I owe to him. God helping me, I will make a little happier what remains of our life together!"

She tried desperately to do so, and by her very desperation largely failed.

Nevertheless he was able to write and in the spring of 1912 to deliver at Union Theological Seminary in New York the Morse Lectures, which were published under the title, *Development of Religion and Thought in Ancient Egypt"* * and were regarded by critics as the ablest, most penetratingly thoughtful work he had yet produced.

As for me, I had re-entered what in my case was ironically misnamed the School of Education, a part of President Harper's laboratory for the training of teachers. From this point until close onto my graduation from the University of Chicago a dozen desultory years later I

* Charles Scribner's Sons, New York, 1912.

never overcame my quandary as to the meaning of this whole undisciplined experience, nor the over-aggressiveness with which I attempted to cover the lack of self-confidence it bred in me.

The psychology of boys' gangs, their preference for inflicting a bloody nose to accepting an apology; the repeated theft—condoned as mere "swiping"—of my books and few personal belongings from my school locker, the casual way in which my schoolmates usually treated their elders, the absence of little Continental amenities and courtesies, yet the peace and calm of most of their homes compared to my own— these were only a few of the things which profoundly puzzled me. For I had never become really acquainted with my own people, or learned to play with my American coevals. The price of my years of interesting if involuntary travel was a desolating sense of loneliness, and an overwhelming yearning for the Europe and the Mediterranean where after our gypsy fashion I had been at home. In America I was *abroad.* . . . I found refuge again in books, which on summer days I often carried to the highest eastern turrets of the newly built William Rainey Harper Memorial Library whence I could look off at the blue Lake and the mirage-lifted shores of Michigan. Even the rising and falling drone of trolley cars clanging through distant sun-baked streets was a reminder of travel and escape.

In August, 1912, my father wrote in an intermittent, curiously impersonal journal which he had reticently begun in 1908:

"The field of my life work is the early civilization of the whole Mediterranean Orient, including Israel. I selected Egypt as a base of operations for two reasons: first, it has left us the most plentiful monuments; and second, it possesses the most highly refined and developed civilization of the early orient—it was like Greece in the Classic World, Italy in the Renaissance. From the beginning of my career I looked forward to the systematic collection of the surviving historical material of the entire near orient, which I linguistically command. I am the first to appreciate the enormity of the task.

"William Dwight Whitney introduced comparative philology into America, a field now represented in every large American university. The study of the Mediterranean orient must be introduced in the same way—but must be transformed from a primarily philological to a primarily historical discipline—one in which art, archaeology, political science, economics, language, literature and sociology, in short all the categories of civilization shall be represented and properly correlated.

"Just as Charles Elliot Norton for the first time articulated the story of art in its course from nation to nation, so the histories of the individual nations of the Mediterranean orient properly woven together into one whole, will present to a new generation of American students the human career as it rises behind the classic age. This can be made, and must become, one of the most important cultural courses in American universities.

"For seventeen years I have striven toward this end. During all this time I have earned between a third and a half of my income outside of the University. In a few days I shall be forty-seven years old. Yet in spite of incessant application and some measure of success, I am still in constant financial anxiety, still obliged to lecture at every opportunity. I cannot afford to attend scientific meetings in other cities, or to extend hospitality to visiting scholars. Since my return to America I have had no time for scientific research. My health is breaking down. Life has become a problem of maintaining my family—and I cannot even do that.

"I am in the last ditch!

"Under these circumstances I am again approached by a hard-headed New England neighbor, Henry Hoyt Hilton, a senior partner in the great publishing house of Ginn and Company, who has repeatedly asked me to write an ancient history for the high schools of America, to supplant gradually the ancient history of Myers which has an enormous circulation but is seriously out of date. Hilton assures me that besides being 'a great educational opportunity,' it means an additional income for me of at least $5000 a year and doubtless eventually more. They will advance me royalty to prepare the text of the book, and will agree to my radically new ideas for illustrating it sumptuously.

"I have always refused to turn aside from research to undertake pure popularization—thus far without having gained the time and strength for the former which the benefits of the latter might have brought me. How *can* I better rid myself of outside lecture trips from which I return completely exhausted, than by closing with Ginn and Company?"

Even at this point he could not bring himself to sign a contract committing him to at least another three years' separation from his own researches while he laboriously produced a book as new to his experience as the vast audience of American boys and girls for whom it was intended. Having essayed every other means of persuasion, Hilton now sent him a copy of every ancient history textbook currently in use in the high schools of the United States. "It has occurred to me," he said casually, "that you might be interested to see for yourself what this country's children are being taught about the ancient world."

It was some months before my father found time to examine them. When he did, their effect upon him was precisely what Hilton had anticipated. With only two or three exceptions the orient was either cursorily passed over or elided altogether in favor of the traditional detailed treatment of Greece and Rome, the two cultures which the student was led to believe constituted ancient history. Almost without exception the summaries of preclassical oriental history were so filled with misstatements, inaccuracies, flagrant errors, false conclusions and general misinformation as to leave him at once astounded and righteously aroused.

"The hidebound classicists have done more to kill Ancient History than any other cause," he wrote. "These moss-grown brethren must learn that there is such a thing as the *human career as a whole!*" To Hilton he said: "I will write an ancient history textbook for you on condition that I be allowed to devote *one-third* of its pages to the early orient!"

No sooner was the contract signed than Ginn and Company asked him to produce first a short ancient history for a volume in collaboration with his old friend James Harvey Robinson of Columbia University, to be called *Outlines of European History*—destined to become one of the best-known school texts of America. Without benefit of an initial full-length presentation from which to make an abridgment, he found it enormously difficult to produce at the outset an abbreviated work embodying his concept of the rise of man. When the first draft was submitted to a selected group of America's outstanding teachers, they unanimously agreed that while beautifully written it was far too mature for children of twelve.

Having supposed that he had erred on the side of over-simplification, he was terribly cast down, almost humiliated to discover that he did not yet know how to write for children. But he was determined to learn, at once began rewriting the entire manuscript.

The result was a minor classic, accomplished once more, however, at the cost of his health. On June 1, 1913, he wrote in his journal: "When President Judson learned that I had been very ill again and was deeply discouraged, he urged a long vacation which I told him I could not afford. A few days later he informed me he had available a fund 'for special purposes' which I was to use. Never before has the University shown me such solicitude!"

This generous arrangement enabled him to visit for the first time the Big Horn Mountains of Wyoming, an experience which deeply stirred his mind. As the westbound train crossed the great plains, he wrote to me:

"I can already feel the fascination of this open, broken country with its vast and expanding reaches framed by bold and noble buttresses soaring so splendidly, they seem like Nature's Statues of Liberty.

"I should call these grasslands a 'steppe' like that of southern Russia or northern Arabia. Such regions in *other* lands have played a great part in history. Men have always detached themselves from settled society and roamed them as wandering shepherds. Whenever anything has seriously disturbed their shepherd life they have overflowed from their pastures back again upon the civilized urban communities.

"So the Huns and Goths and Vandals and other Germanic tribes left the Russian steppe to overwhelm the Roman Empire. So the shepherds of Arabia under Mohammed's successors nearly girdled the Mediterranean and brought the Moslem call to prayer within sound of Bordighera churchbells on the Italian Riviera, where you remember we found Arabic words like echoes of the desert across a thousand years, still audible in a north Italian marketplace. So the Hebrew nomads left their pastures on the east of Jordan to forsake their wandering lives; and it was the rugged, sturdy character of these people in conflict with the settled life of the Palestinian towns which in a social struggle of centuries brought forth the Hebrew prophets and their dreams of a righteous ruler, a Messiah, ushering in a golden age of social justice and personal righteousness.

"I should not want to live here—in spite of the distant prospects it must be a cramped and meager life. But it is a magnificent country in which to dream, and to catch visions of the broad earth as the shaping and fashioning power in the moulding of this tremendous social complex which it has been bringing forth through the historical ages. It stirs again the exulting sense of being not only a part of the vast process, but also of putting forth a hand to help it on.

"*That*, my son, is wherein we are a new age—the first age to realize the process, and that man may put forth his own hand to the lever which controls an infinitude of possibilities not even faintly suggested by the present!"

From a camp high in the Big Horn Mountains he continued:

"Amid this vast panorama of beauty one can discern with awesome clarity the natural forces which are still in operation exactly as they have always been. We see but an instant in an eternal process, are ourselves socially and individually a process. And what we work out *today* as experience and as vision is as valid for ourselves and for future men as any chapter of revelation penned by seer or prophet of old. *All* is part of this infinite process and all is divine, or none.

"I am happy and content in such a conception of life, deeply and reverently grateful for this brief glimpse—content, too, when it is done, to go out like a spark forever. Only let me live to the full, and as I merge for my little moment with these eternal forces, grant me a fleeting sense of the meaning of immortality!"

That August, when he had returned considerably improved, he wrote in his journal: "On July 1st my salary was advanced $500, making it $4500 a year! Perhaps in another two years, when I am fifty, I may be released from financial worry, and may even be able occasionally to revisit the orient!"

During these years the old friendship between my father and George Ellery Hale had been revived as the latter repeatedly traveled between California and New York in his effort to secure financial support for his many scientific projects. Despite all his own responsibilities he was always enthusiastic regarding plans for research in the orient. "You may count on all the assistance I can give in extending your investigations," he wrote again and again. "But you must not overestimate my powers," he would add, "for I have only dreamed as yet, and may be able to do little more!"

Hale looked upon excavation as the surest bait for attracting financial backing which could later be induced to support less appealing archaeological enterprises. While contemplating these possibilities his tireless mind had recently conceived of a scheme for probing deep into the alluvial flood plains of the Nile and into the river bed itself for possible ancient ruins and major objects which during several thousand years might have been buried under silt.

"For instance, the Nile once flowed close to the Temple of Karnak," he wrote my father in July, 1913. "Is it not probable that valuable inscribed objects may have been thrown into the river either by despoilers or merely in the natural course of loading and unloading barges, or building and expanding the great temple? Might we not strike some evidence of them by probing with a special drill? I feel sure that if sculptors' studios existed at Tell el-Amarna during its short life, there must have been many on the Plain of Thebes. Those are words to charm with, and we must get below the Nile deposits on that glorious Plain!"

It was again characteristic of Hale that he contributed more to the advancement and recognition of humanistic research in the United States than any other American natural scientist, and in fact with only a few exceptions, than the American humanists themselves. He was at this time full of plans both for a building (to be erected either in California or in Washington, D. C.) to house the National Academy of Sciences, and for expanding the latter's membership to include the humanities. He discussed these proposals at length with my father who, while himself not yet a member, was peculiarly aware what benefits they implied for the field he had so aggressively championed throughout his career. "Our conversations," he wrote Hale, "have quite restored my enthusiasm for research in America. I owe you a great deal!"

During the spring of 1914 Hale plied him with many fundamental questions which he answered in a series of letters from which the following condensed excerpts are quoted:

"The chief obstacle to the natural scientists' recognition of research in the humanities is the distrust they feel toward it. But the methods which aroused such distrust are now long since antiquated. Archaeological research, for example, is in close touch with the methods and results of natural science. Palaeolithic archaeology is furnishing the geologist with a sequence of forms in human industry which enable him to date natural formations by means of the artifacts contained in them just as if the latter were fossils. At this point you cannot draw a sharp line between geology and archaeology. As the period of time under investigation goes on and man advances, the two sciences of course part company. Social processes begin to emerge which are studied exactly as in natural science, with this difference: we are not able to *repeat* the experiment. But this limitation likewise attends many fields of research in natural science, such as astronomy or geology.

"Presentation of this undeniable progress in the methods of the humane sciences may have more effect on a body of natural scientists than a plea that the humanities need assistance to achieve improved methods. Nevertheless humanistic research in the United States sadly needs organized assistance and representation.

"Its expeditions in foreign fields, for example, are very much handicapped as over against those of European countries which receive every help from their home governments. The following incident illustrates the advantages gained by official representation through an academy: When for lack of funds our work of recording in Nubia stopped some forty miles above (south of) the Aswan Dam in territory where the existent monuments were perishing owing to the backwater created by the great Dam, quick action was imperative. The Royal Academy of Berlin at once secured an appropriation from the Prussian Government, purchased our entire field equipment, and adopting our field methods, continued the work and photographed and recorded the tremendous mass of inscriptions on the Temple of Philae. Had the humanities in America possessed a center of influence like the National Academy of Sciences, I am inclined to think we should have been able to complete this work ourselves."

The two men kept one another constantly informed not only of the progress of their efforts to "educate" the leading philanthropic foundations and certain wealthy citizens to the financial support of each other's plans, but especially of their encounters with any new "hopefuls." Typical was a letter my father wrote Hale in July, 1914:

"Mrs. Henry Fairfield Osborn last March arranged on her own initiative for me to lunch at her home with Mrs. Edward Henry Harriman and Mrs. Elizabeth Milbank Anderson [who created the Milbank Foundation and] who recently gave two million dollars to Barnard College. Mrs. Anderson proved to be interested in some of my plans, but as I was meeting her for the first time, I did not have the courage to put up to her the large Nile plan [which had failed to win the approval of Mr. Gates]. I only proposed to her the establishment of an Oriental Institute in some American university, with an endowment of $200,000.

"She expressed much interest, but said she was now involved in a great enterprise in New York City—the daily feeding of 30,000 breakfastless and lunchless children! This seemed a sizable contract and I did not push my interests further. [Not long afterwards] she invited Mrs. Breasted and myself to go up the Nile with her next winter as guests on her dahabiyeh. Mrs. Osborn informs me Mrs. Anderson is enormously wealthy. I believe a winter on the Nile would give me an opportunity to convince such an intelligent woman as I find her to be, of the necessity for saving the records there. She must know that pressure would be involved in such a trip. Would she expose herself to it unless she expected to respond?"

On August 4, 1914, he wrote in his journal:

"The news of the appalling war in Europe has banished the Nile journey with Mrs. Anderson and all the hopes I had dared to base upon it. Yet how utterly trivial and insignificant such personal dreams and ambitions appear in the horrible light of this conflagration!

"Today I finished reading page proofs of my part of *Outlines of European History*. Those who have read it say it will be a great success. But what drudgery, all for the means to pay household bills! And now instead of reverting to research I must slog away at the large ancient history for Ginn and Company. I wonder whether I am capable of convincing a skeptical new generation of schoolchildren that the same processes which are destroying the European world of my generation lifted mankind from jungle savagery to what we hopefully call civilization?"

With that blistering August of 1914 he entered the somberest, most disillusioning and thoughtful years his already overserious career had yet experienced. He looked on helplessly while the forces he had observed as a student began to engulf the old academic Germany which had trained him and been the first to recognize and reward his subsequent labors. He was shocked to find his loyalty to these old German academic associations and friendships condemned as pro-Germanism by colleagues whose dispassionate, peace-time detachment had given way to hysterical bitterness and hatred; and was humiliated to find that his own powers of cool reasoning were themselves no longer immune to such corrosive influences. Like almost every other great American university, Chicago seethed with differences of opinion and sentiment to the point where old friends would pass one another without speaking.

It seemed to him that he was watching the preposterous, futile destruction of everything upon which his life had been built—the human relationships, the idealistic values, the fine freedom of roving minds in the unboundaried world of scholarship. Never before in his darkest moments had he suffered such anguish of mind. It was therefore hardly strange that he should have dismissed as no longer relevant or important, and as no more than a fortuitous reminder of an ugly forgotten dream, the news that on August 5 in London Robert Francis Harper had died.

The wide correspondence he had for so many years carried on with colleagues in Germany was presently reduced to that with his beloved old master Adolf Erman, who wrote in November, 1914: "I have always cherished my old friendship with you as something unto itself. I pray with all my heart that despite profound differences of opinion, despite any future strife between our two peoples, this old bond may only draw us more closely together. And I pray that everyone in our field of science may be guided by the ancient maxim: *in necessariis unitas, in dubiis libertas, in omnibus caritas.*"

As the War drew on, death one by one took the sons of my father's European colleagues, youths I had known and played with as children: Peter Erman; the sons of Eduard Meyer, whom I had so often watched as they campaigned with lead soldiers in the garden at Gross-Lichterfelde; the sons of George Adam Smith, and of so many British friends; the son of Gaston Maspero.

On August 31, 1915, Maspero wrote my father in English from Paris: "The death of my son on the 17th of February dealt me a new blow. Until now I felt considerably younger than my age: I cannot tell you how suddenly I olded.

"Jean came back from Egypt to take his place in the French army on the 1st of August. He was very heavily wounded on the 23rd September, at Cheppy in Argonne, and returned to the front the 31 of January: the 17th February, he received a ball full in face, while leading his section at Vauquois, and died outright. . . .

"Though we grieve so much on his death, his mother and I, we feel consolation in the fact he helped defeat the invasion, when it was really dangerous. When the final victory comes to us, as it will in the end, then we may weep on him and be mortally sad that he is no more amongst us to rejoice in it: *il a été à la peine, ça sera grande pitié qu'il ne soit pas a l'honneur.*

"I oblige my mind to work as in ordinary times, not to feel my loss too much. You will see very soon in the *Receuil* a part of my recent work. Meanwhile I thank you for your kindly words."

In July, 1916, my father received a black-bordered, printed notice (in German) from Adolf Erman and his wife Käthe which read: "On the morning of July first there fell with seven of his comrades on the Western Warfront our beloved, promising son who was our happiness and joy—Johann Peter Erman, non-commissioned officer in Reserve Field Artillery Regiment No. 40 and Knight of the Iron Cross."

"Peter was with us at home only a few days before he fell," Adolf Erman wrote my father (again in German) soon afterwards. "He had become a man almost overnight. After the monotony and frightfulness of war he seemed inexpressibly happy to be breathing again the clean, friendly air of civilization and home. They tell us that when he returned to active duty he was still in his happy mood, and that he whistled and sang as he served his gun himself during the seven days' continuous shrapnel fire which brought about his death. When a boy has spent twelve years in school and two years in the war with never an opportunity to fulfill the rich promise he held within himself, the fact that he died a hero's death is empty comfort. It is so unnatural that boys of twenty like Peter should die, and the old like ourselves should live on.

"I bury myself in my researches, and crave to live only long enough to leave the *Dictionary* completed, and perhaps see the world once more at peace. But news of the war has become so sinister, my dear old friend, I begin to fear that you and I may never meet again in this life. Now that it appears almost inevitable that your country also will soon be at war with ours, Käthe and I both wish to tell you once more from our hearts how much we have always loved the Breasteds, and come what may, always shall. Once more, while yet there is time, let me assure you that my affection and loyalty will endure to the end of my life. When this Deluge of Evil has at last receded, may those of our children who remain alive be reunited, and may they carry on the friendship of their parents!"

Like these colleagues, my father too tried to lose himself in his work, and in preoccupation with the remote past wherein one already knew the worst which had befallen every age and nation, and one was untroubled of such anxiety for the future as rendered the present almost unendurable.

On August 14, 1916, he wrote in his journal: "*Ancient Times* was published today. I feel like a convict suddenly set free after years of weary labor and bondage."

That year he attended the annual meetings of the American Historical Association and met for the first time its current president, Colonel Theodore Roosevelt. Their immediate mutual liking for one another soon developed into warm friendship which often drew my father to Sagamore Hill, and was reflected in the Colonel's enthusiastic review of *Ancient Times* in *The Outlook* for February 14, 1917.

At about this same time my father received, to his considerable astonishment, a letter from Mr. F. T. Gates which read in part:

"In the midst of reading your *Ancient Times* I am irresistibly moved to express my gratitude to the Author. My business, my correspondence, my friends and my family are all being neglected while I give first place to your book.

"It meets my want, answers innumerable questions on my lips for years, is written in a fascinating style and for the first time gives me some measure of the debt we owe to ancient times, and enables me to distribute the debt with a reasonable degree of justice to the ancient nations. Every page and every paragraph is full of interest to me. The illustrations with their lucid explanations are not less valuable than the text. This is a book to read, to re-read and to read still again, and to commend to every lover of books, of men, and of the story of human progress—which ought to be the soul as it is the only worthy theme of History. Thank you in the name of multitudes of high school youth and their parents for this truly great book."

These were the words of a man who had once held that nothing good could come out of the land of Egypt; had forbidden the University of Chicago to continue its investigations there; and had not only shattered my father's most cherished scientific hopes, but so crushed his spirit that for a time he had even considered permanently abandoning his scientific career.

While Mr. Gates's unexpected enthusiasm on the whole reflected the majority of opinion, there were inevitable exceptions. The die-hard classicists, and those teachers of ancient history who had been trained in the tradition that the cultures of Greece and Rome were the result of some divine spontaneous combustion, found it difficult, often impossible, to accept the author's revolutionary re-appraisal of the importance of the orient in the development of civilization. It was only to be expected, too, that the fundamentalists everywhere, especially in the southern States, should resent his evolutionary approach to history, an attitude which received curiously antithetical expression in 1925 at the famous "Monkey Trial" of a young biology instructor named J. T. Scopes who had committed the crime of teaching evolution in Tennessee. Clarence Darrow, who defended him, cited *Ancient Times* in substantiation of the truth of such teaching; while William Jennings Bryan pilloried the book as a consummate example of the kind of iniquitous falsity which he insisted was destroying American religious faith.

Nevertheless *Ancient Times* was soon generally accepted as a classic in its field, and steadily achieved a sale which at its height, in its various editions and abridgments, approached 120,000 copies per annum.

The production of the book had necessarily taken its author further than he had ever before ventured into geology, palaeontology, anthropology and the whole pre-history of Europe, the Mediterranean, Africa, Asia, and the orient. It had illuminated and invested with a new perspective his long-cherished, ever-maturing plan for a definitive history of civilization. "In the whole range of writing," he wrote me, "I have found nothing so inspiring as the life of vanished generations of men when we have marshaled them one after another, until there is disclosed to us a deep vista of the human past issuing from the midst of the geological ages. It stirs my blood and is the moving inspiration of all the work I do."

There was an interesting if modest analogy between the production of *Ancient Times* and of Sir William Osler's *The Principles and Practice of Medicine* (see p. 120). Each author undertook his writing reluctantly and under duress; neither appreciated upon its completion the potential influence of the volume he had compiled; and both books were eventually directly responsible for eliciting large—in the case of medicine, enormous—financial support from the same source. In his *Life of Sir William Osler* (vol. I, pp. 340–341), Harvey Cushing quotes Osler as having written on a flyleaf of an interleaved copy of his *Principles* "the following statement of how the book had been written: 'On several occasions . . . I was asked . . . to prepare a work on Diagnosis, and had half promised one; . . . but [I had] continually procrastinated on the plea that up to the 40th year a man was fit for better things than text-books.'"

But whereas Osler's book had appeared when he was forty-three, *Ancient Times* was published when its author had turned fifty-one. "I have only some fifteen years left," my father wrote on his fifty-first birthday, "in which to accomplish the work of half a dozen lifetimes!"

It was several years before he discovered that nothing he had ever done, least of all the abstruse researches he had so reluctantly interrupted in favor of the ungrateful task of writing a high school textbook, had been of greater service to his science. For *Ancient Times* was something more than a contribution to the education of untold thousands of school children in America and England—and, as respective translations appeared, in China, Japan, Malay, Palestine, Syria and

Iraq. Its implications made it at the same time perhaps the most force-ful and convincing statement of the case for humanistic and especially archaeological research which had yet appeared. At a singularly appropriate moment it served to acquaint the boards of the leading philanthropic foundations of the country with the untouched oppor-tunities for recovering the story of mankind's struggle to achieve civilization. It was undoubtedly among the strongest influences which, together with the enormous popular interest later aroused by the discovery of Tutenkhamon's tomb, helped to secure for Near Eastern archaeology such unprecedented financial support as to enable my father to set in motion enterprises and projects on a scale far exceeding his most sanguine earlier hopes.

But in 1917 all this still lay in the future; and when, that April, America declared war on Germany, the future of such scientific endeavors appeared indefinitely remote. "I shall have to wait until after the War before they can dream of undertaking my plans," he wrote later that month, after conferring with the officers of the Rocke-feller Foundation and the Rockefeller-created General Education Board. "But I believe I have their attention, interest and confidence. They will grow accustomed to my plans, and I believe I shall see them carried out some day—at least as a foundation for younger men to build on."

One day soon after America's entry into the First World War, Colonel Theodore Roosevelt, on his way from the Pacific Coast to Sagamore Hill, stopped off in Chicago to discuss a certain matter with my father at an early morning meeting which I was privileged to attend.

The hallway leading to the Colonel's hotel suite was guarded by "plain-clothes" men who passed us quickly from one to another until we reached an ornate sitting room into which he immediately stepped from his bedroom. He had only just dressed and breakfasted. He beamed, his eyes danced, he radiated electrical energy and captivating geniality, said "Simply dee-*lighted* to see you!" exactly as he was so famous for doing—but I can still remember my astonishment at his short stature as he shook my hand. He was in fact quite a small man. Yet from the first moment of meeting I somehow completely forgot the fact, and always thereafter found myself thinking of him as an impos-ing figure.

Waving his hand deprecatingly at the stuffy near-grandeur of the sitting room, he led us into the bedroom. "It's much cheerfuller!" he said. The bedclothes lay just as he had tossed them aside upon getting up. He motioned my father to a chair, himself sat down on the bed, asked me to sit beside him. He began at once to question me about my age, bents, interests; told me with evident enjoyment how his son Quentin had recently "fibbed" about his age in order to enlist in the United States Air Service, and only a few weeks later had appeared in the sky over Sagamore Hill at Oyster Bay, and flown in great circles about the house. "He wanted to allay any fears I might have had about his ability to fly at such a tender age," said the Colonel with a grin.

Then he turned again to my father. "Only wait—your son will be doing something similar one of these days! For we are truly at war. Think of it!—think of the irony of our having been led into war within thirty days of the re-inauguration of a President who got himself re-elected on the slogan, 'He kept us out of war!'—and who knew, even during the campaign, that our entry was inevitable!"

He rose as he spoke, walked up and down between us, and with a characteristic gesture of the right hand, added: "I believe it will go down as one of the greatest ironies of American history!"

He sat down again, and became very businesslike. "This is the question I wanted to discuss with you: I am trying to persuade the President to authorize me to raise a division of troops under my command, for service abroad, in a region with which you are peculiarly well acquainted. I have already selected my chief-of-staff in the event I succeed—he is probably waiting outside, for I invited him to join us in this discussion."

He went to the door, spoke to an attendant, and in a moment a fine looking Army officer entered. The Colonel introduced us.

"This is Captain Steele who went up San Juan Hill beside me."

After a few friendly exchanges the Colonel fetched from an attaché case a map of the Near East, spread it out on the bed, and the three men bent over it as he continued talking.

"I'm convinced the War will be won in the Near East—by blasting the Germans' Berlin-to-Baghdad dream. After reading your *Ancient Times*, I was impelled to re-read the description in your *History of Egypt* of the strategic importance of Kadesh in the control of northern Syria, and of Ramses II's battle with the Hittite king, Metella, who almost defeated him, and really ought to have done so. I studied detailed maps of the whole region, and it seemed to me obvious that if control of Kadesh once spelled control of northern Syria, then surely the seizure today of Alexandretta, followed at once by a northeastward thrust cutting off the Baghdad railway, would simultaneously strike the Germans and the Turks at the most vulnerable point in their flank, isolate their southern forces, and by achieving control of Syria and Palestine, destroy the Berlin-to-Baghdad plan. I fully realize that a single American division couldn't turn the trick alone—but covered by the British Mediterranean fleet, and assisted by a force of Australians, it would almost certainly be successful.

"All this seems so obvious that of course it must long have been in the minds of the British and the French. Hence I want to ask you, Professor Breasted, whether in your opinion I have analyzed the strategic situation correctly, and whether this would be the very best possible use to be made of my division—and if so, why hasn't it already been done?"

"I believe you are correct in every particular," my father answered, "including the inference that such a plan has long been in the minds of the British. I have been told confidentially that at the very beginning of the War they proposed precisely such a plan to the French, who replied that they would construe any British move into Syria as an act unfriendly to France. The matter was therefore dropped. I can't understand why the French should be so blindly jealous of British activity in Syria. But *you* are popular with the French, and an American expedition under your command would be a guaranty of ultimate withdrawal, even if the Australians assisted you, for we obviously have no colonial ambitions."

There followed a long discussion which touched upon ancient and modern politics, history, imperialism, science; upon hunting and exploring in Africa, Asia and South America. I sat enthralled. After more than two hours, a secretary anxiously reminded the Colonel of another appointment before train time. As we rose to leave, he said to my father, "If this thing goes through, I shall need to confer with you further—and meanwhile you must both come to stay with us at Sagamore Hill!"

But of course it never went through; and when years later I visited Sagamore Hill, it was to stand at his grave.

In the midst of the Second World War it is curiously difficult for me to recapture the emotional quality and tension of that first one, and especially of a morning in October 1917, when I stood among a group of men—all of us naked as God made us—in a medical examining room of the U. S. Army Post at Columbus, Ohio, and solemnly took the oath of enlistment "for the duration."

For my father, the implications of my enlistment were at once sad and ironical. It signified for him a final break with the Old World: his son would now face the sons of his former German colleagues in the battle for civilization itself.

"How different from mine, twenty-six years ago, will be your departure for Europe," he wrote me in camp. "I went as a raw western boy, seeking the culture and the science which only Europe possessed; while you go as a soldier of the new world, to protect civilization from destruction by the very nation which had the most to offer me.

"I am proud that you have felt the call to go. I know you will not flinch, will always do your duty. But whenever you honorably can, avoid danger. Think of your father, and never run a risk unless it is your duty to do so.

"I cannot grapple with the fact that you are no longer at the desk in your room. I thought I knew something of loneliness and renunciation, but I am only just beginning to learn. Your old father salutes you in humility and unworthiness!"

He sent me—bless him!—the little German dictionary he had used as a student—he had had it rebound, and had written on the fly leaf, "Dictionary of the Enemy's Language."

At Camp Devens in Massachusetts I fell gravely ill, underwent a major operation. A few days later my regiment sailed for France. For months I lay in the Base Hospital, staring out at snow-laden pines and a wintry sky as limitless as the sense of futility which engulfed me. Patients came and went, departing more often on foot, but sometimes in a long wicker basket. I could never decide which were the luckier.

Early in the spring of 1918, with an honorable discharge in my pocket and an open mastoid wound in my head, I crept ingloriously back to civilian life. "Will you give my hearty regards to your son Charles?" Colonel Roosevelt wrote my father. "He is entitled to exactly the same credit as if he had received his wound in action in France!"

That was characteristically understanding and kind—for Quentin was already gone, killed in action over France.

When the wound had healed and the army had accepted me for re-enlistment, my papers were cancelled by the Armistice. My father was full of gratitude, and of plans for our future together. But I was utterly disconsolate, and found no solace even in the Colonel's brave and generous words.

The advent of peace found my father trying to reflect, at least outwardly, the optimism which a war-wracked, hardy-perennial world was daring to feel again. For the War which had so blighted his plans and hopes for the advancement of humanistic research had afforded his colleagues in medicine and the natural sciences an unparalleled opportunity for demonstrating once again the practical and vital relevance of research in these fields.

During his twelve years' exile from Europe and the Near East he had never for a moment relaxed his efforts to enlist for his science the financial support of wealthy individuals and of every conceivable philanthropic foundation; and to overcome "the inertia of the humanities which for generations," as he ruefully put it, "have been preoccupied with nothing more important than the history of the dative case." But thus far he had struggled in vain. The interest in his plans which the several great Rockefeller foundations had earlier evinced had apparently lapsed into apathy. The failure of Mrs. Elizabeth Milbank Anderson's health had finally precluded the long contemplated Nile journey from which so much might have resulted. Even after twelve years' effort he had been unable to secure either from the University of Chicago or from any other source the money for publishing the results of his first two expeditions in Egypt.

And now that the defeat of the Turks had thrown open the countries of the ancient world as never before to scientific exploration and archaeological investigation, he stood helpless for lack of funds.

His profound discouragement was hardly alleviated by the fact that under President Judson's negative administration the exhilarating spirit of educational and scientific pioneering created by President Harper had steadily given way to an atmosphere of resigned stagnation. It was Judson's proudest boast that he had not only kept the University within its budget but had ended each year of his administration with a substantial balance. The antithesis of Harper, he wholly lacked the latter's gift for inspiriting his associates and arousing in the citizenry of Chicago and the whole Middle West a sense of pride in and financial responsibility for their great new University. He possessed on the contrary a curious genius for rebuffing the natural enthusiasm of creative scholarship, and for alienating financial support.

He was convinced that any deliberate effort to befriend the daily press could result only in permanent loss of the University's academic dignity. The idea of a Department of Public Relations, which Harper's attitude had already anticipated and which is today a matter of course in almost every American educational institution, would have been to him sheer anathema. The cumulative effect of this policy was to isolate the University so effectively that the greater part of Chicago's inhabitants altogether forgot its existence; and to enable other universities to carry on increasingly successful forays among Harper's concentration of great minds, which in twenty-five years had made the University of Chicago one of the three greatest research institutions of America.

Faculty members who attempted to ameliorate this situation by seeking on their own initiative to enlist financial support outside of the University to further their researches, were reprimanded and reminded that "the solicitation of funds was strictly a prerogative of their president." The plea of Nobel Prize physicist Albert A. Michelson for a moderate extension of his outgrown laboratory was opposed on the ground of unnecessary luxury, and was finally successful only when Michelson defiantly circumvented the president.* My father had himself combatted this attitude too often not to realize that no matter how friendly his personal relations with Judson, whatever he might accomplish in the interest of his own field would be despite and not because of the president.

Nor could he hope for improvement in any other American institution. The Department of Oriental Languages and Literatures at Chicago was anything but brilliant, but the fact that such studies had been consistently neglected elsewhere in the United States had left it without any serious American rival. His own scientific destiny was therefore inextricably identified with that of an institution which he felt had requited his loyalty with broken promises and inadequate pay. No academic honors or prestige he had gained in the outside world could assuage the sense of rebellion and wounded pride which this bitter realization had aroused in him.

He was heartsick of the obstructionism and littleness, the bickering and quarreling of university departments and administrative offices

* It was in the resulting expanded laboratory that Robert Andrews Millikan, and subsequently Arthur Holly Compton carried on experiments for which they also were respectively awarded the Nobel Prize in physics.

filled with sterile minds. At the age of fifty-four he felt prematurely old and weary, a pedant shackled to the stultifying iteration of teaching and academic routine. In his own eyes he was a failure whose star stood in the East whither he could not follow.

By February 1919, having reached a state of hopeless discouragement, he determined to make a final effort to secure the funds for seizing an opportunity which would almost certainly never come again. He decided to address a plea—the first of the kind he had ever sent him—directly to his friend, John D. Rockefeller, Jr. It was a matter of public record that because Mr. Rockefeller, Sr., had indicated he would make no more gifts to the University, his son had in deference to this decision declared that he personally would make no further gifts to it during his father's lifetime. The chances of success therefore appeared hopelessly remote. But with nothing to lose, there were immeasurable new scientific frontiers to be won.

He wrote Mr. Rockefeller, Jr., a letter accompanied by a verbal blueprint for the organization at the University of Chicago of an Oriental Institute, ". . . a laboratory for the study of the rise and development of civilization . . . [which began in] the ancient lands of Western Asia, . . . the unexplored areas of history.

"The materials out of which we can recover and put together . . . [the] lost chapters [of the career of early man]," he wrote, "lie scattered among the buried cities of the Near East. This whole region has just been delivered from Turkish misrule, and for the first time in history the birth-lands of religion and civilization lie open to unobstructed study and research. In the entire history of knowledge, this is the greatest opportunity that has ever come for the study of man and his career.

"In confronting such a situation as this, the individual historian, fettered by a program of university teaching, and without the funds or the time for work in the ancient world, is of course absolutely helpless. I am . . . enclosing herewith a plan of work devised to meet this situation . . . [and to] enable us to follow among early men just those processes in which you are so interested at the present day.

"Let me explain.

"You are today one of the great forces in . . . social, economic and industrial history. The very principles of justice and fair treatment which you are so admirably applying . . . first grew up in the minds and hearts of men in that ancient world of the Near Orient around the eastern end of the Mediterranean. The noblest task in the study of man is to recover the story of the human career, which culminated in the emergence of a religion of divine fatherhood and human brotherhood. . . .

"It is evident that the opening of Asia Minor, Syria, Palestine, Mesopotamia and Babylonia to modern business and to enlightened exploitation in mining, railroad-building, manufacturing and agriculture, means the rapid destruction of the great ruined cities and buried records of early man, with which these lands are filled. They must be studied soon before they are lost forever. . . .

"The university teacher is as unable single-handed to cope with a situation like this, as would be the astronomer to study the skies without his observatory or his staff. . . . A laboratory containing all the available early human records in systematically arranged archives is as necessary to a study of man's career as is an astronomical observatory with its files of observations and computations in the study of the career of the universe. . . . The methods and the equipment of natural science should be applied to the study of man. . . .

"While the Oriental Institute might accomplish much in suggesting and encouraging excavation, its plan does not contemplate supporting from its own budget any costly excavation campaign. Its budget is therefore a modest one. It could be set going for about $10,000 a year."

At the same time he earnestly besought Mr. Gates, still senior watchdog over Rockefeller benefactions, to support this plan.

"*Your powerful influence,*" he wrote, "*. . . will settle the question for or against [it]. . . . Will you not save the enterprise and put it on its feet?*

"It is very distasteful to me to appear at all in such a crusade for funds. But do you not think I ought to do it, rather than to rust out during the last fifteen years of my life, thousands of miles away from the human records I ought to be saving and using?"

When more than two months had passed without so much as an acknowledgement of these letters, he said: "I find it impossible to admit defeat—yet I suppose there is no other name for it. I shall not try again. For by the time I could summon the courage for another attempt, I would be too old to do justice by success if it came. Whether I can philosophically revise the whole plan and content of my life work remains to be seen."

CHAPTER VIII

ONE morning early in May, 1919, my father was sitting at breakfast reading his mail and as usual evincing his academic sales resistance by segregating all advertisements and flinging them across the dining room into a great Sudanese basket reserved for this idiosyncrasy, when his eye fell upon an envelope bearing an old-fashioned drawing of The Homestead at Hot Springs, Virginia.

This, he thought to himself a little resentfully, would be another personalized letter from some effusive managing director brimming with cordiality, inviting him to spend the sort of vacation for which he had never had either the time or the money. He was about to crumple it and toss it unopened into the basket, when curiosity got the better of him, and he slit open the envelope.

I remember so well hearing him suddenly exclaim in a low voice, "Good Lord—at last!"—and then after a pause, "Oh, if I were only ten years younger!" His face wore a look of mingled sadness and elation, as he handed me the following letter from Mr. Rockefeller, Jr., dated May 2, 1919:

"I owe you an apology for not having replied earlier to your letter of February 16th. . . . The pressure of many other things and absence from my office must be my excuse.

"I am greatly interested in the project which you have in mind. . . . I fully agree with you that the present opportunity should be availed of as fully as possible. . . . Because I believe that no one is better fitted to lead in this enterprise than yourself, I shall be happy to finance your project on the basis of the annual expense outlined [$50,000 at the annual rate of $10,000] for a period of five years, through the University, in whose name and under whose direction it would, I assume, be your wish to have the enterprise carried out. . . ."

A confirming letter to President Judson ended with the precautionary warning that the pledge "should not be construed to imply any commitment on my part towards the enterprise beyond the five years' period."

To my father these letters were like a reprieve from the slow hemlock of endless frustration. He had kept his flag flying because, as he once wrote his mother during his student days in Berlin, "I am a proud fellow, proud as Lucifer, and my pride and my will, will carry me through almost anything."

But now suddenly, in the shape of a few typewritten paragraphs which he had *almost* consigned to the wastebasket, had come emancipation and the beginning of a great scientific adventure.

Upon learning of Mr. Rockefeller's gift, Mr. Martin A. Ryerson, then president of the University's Board of Trustees, pledged himself personally to contribute an additional sum for the first year, gave assurance that the University also would appropriate a similar amount. Nor did the implications of Mr. Rockefeller's letters escape President Judson, who even committed himself to secure further supplementary funds.

My father at once set about organizing a reconnaissance expedition with a staff (which was to meet him in Cairo) comprising a colleague and four younger men, with himself as leader. Its purpose was to determine what archaeological sites in the Near East could profitably be investigated or excavated; and to "secure by purchase at least a share of the ancient documents of all sorts which during the War had been accumulating in the hands of antiquity dealers both in Europe and the Near East." As soon as they learned of his imminent departure, a number of leading American museums desiring to expand their collections of Near Eastern art, sent him substantial letters of credit to cover such purchases in their behalf.

For years, through all the seasons, he and I had taken late afternoon walks along the shore of Lake Michigan, and always the talk had turned to his dreams of exploration and excavation in the orient, and to the future journeys we would surely make together. We would look off eastward—always eastward—across the water, and watch the great ore boats hull-down on the horizon of this tantalizing, un-salty sea, with its fickle moods and its dissatisfying smell of fresh-water marsh life. On days when the wind stood northeast and the sky was washed clean as a Wedgwood plate, the sunlit dunes of Michigan, floating miragelike beyond the farthest water, became for a nostalgic moment a southeastern Mediterranean coastline where Nile and Sahara greeted the sea, and the ships of the world threaded the needle's eye of Suez.

There was one journey above all others which we had promised to make together: to Egypt, up the Nile to Victoria Nyanza, eastward to Mombasa, by small steamer across to Karachi in northwestern India, up the Indus River to Alexander the Great's farthest east; back again to the Persian Gulf and north to Basra, up the Two Rivers, across the Kurdish mountains to Trebizond, where the remnant of Xenophon's Ten Thousand had cried, "The sea! The sea!" when in 400 B.C. they had beheld the Euxine (Black) Sea; thence to Istanbul, and by the Orient Express back to old haunts in Western Europe.

But this was to remain always an unfulfilled dream. The journey he now faced promised to be the most important he had ever undertaken. There was about it only one regret—that we could not make it together. Because he knew that at times it would be unavoidably dangerous and that something might befall him, he asked me to remain at home to look after my mother and the two younger children.

We were fully agreed on the wisdom of this decision. But if the prospect of his going depressed my mother, it spelled for me one of those disappointments which to youth seem almost irreconcilable. His realization of this impelled him despite a tremendous burden of work and the most difficult field conditions, to capture in his letters and journals and so to share with us his adventures during the anxious year of his absence.

He sailed that August for England, in London found it impossible to secure transportation to the Near East.

Ahead of him was "a waiting list of over 500 especially recommended personages, over and above the great body of officers in uniform, civil officials and troops of the line, who must take precedence over these 500. The Peninsular & Oriental Line is allowed only ten berths for civilians on each ship."

Western Europe was too preoccupied with its own rehabilitation, and the United States was too remote for either to be really aware that their so-called peace had hardly penetrated the Near East, where the war was still sporadically continuing, and where Wilson's Fourteen Points had imbued the Arab world with high hopes for an independence which Britain and France between them were to resolve into a mirage.

Because of constant fighting in Transjordan, one could not reach Mesopotamia by traversing the 850 miles directly overland from Cairo to Baghdad. Instead, one had to follow the two long sides of a triangle with its apex at Bombay, a distance of over 5000 miles. To the American Embassy in London, American archaeologists rash enough to venture into this still chaotic part of the world were a nuisance to be deliberately impeded rather than encouraged. "Our Embassy at this time has no interest whatever in assisting American scholars in the service of science," he wrote. "The fate of this venture will depend entirely upon the attitude of the British Government at home, and of their Army high command and their political officers in the field."

So he hurried from one lethargic Government office to another, waiting on the slow reflex-reactions of outer-office clerks, checking the infinite details of transport, food, permits, visas, equipment, and seeking above all the benediction-in-principle of the highest authorities in the Empire.

He was just beginning to make progress, when all the railways of the British Isles called a general strike, and England philosophically took to its feet, or salvaged ancient vehicles, until the crowded streets and country roads resembled a pageant of the history of transportation.

But the tide turned when he rediscovered the potency of that "open sesame," that recipe for surmounting the insuperable, that infallible lubricant for accelerating the ponderous machinery of the British Empire—the letter of introduction. He had forgotten how seriously the English regarded such missives until, somewhat reluctantly and by way of experiment, he had presented one or two of the many which had been generously urged upon him by influential British friends.

Typical was a staccato note of introduction from the eminent archaeologist and Orientalist, Professor D. G. Hogarth, Keeper of the Ashmolean Museum at Oxford, to Sir Edmund Allenby, who had recently been made High Commissioner for Egypt and the Sudan and was then on leave in England, awaiting his viscountcy. Allenby replied at once, enclosing *two more* letters—and so it went. From London to Bombay, through No Man's Land among the sworn enemies of England and France in northern Mesopotamia, and across the Syrian Desert, his road was paved with similar letters of commendation.

Their number was augmented again when his old friend Lord Carnarvon (patron of Howard Carter) invited him and his still older friend and colleague, Alan Gardiner, an Englishman whom he regarded as the ablest technical Egyptologist of the day, for a stay at Highclere Castle in Hampshire, "one of several great Carnarvon family estates—13,000 acres in this one.

"The Earls of Carnarvon are a branch of the ancient Pembroke family, prominent in English history. Highclere Castle—a tremendous house, portions of which are a thousand years old—is full of fine paintings of the Carnarvon ancestors, many of them by Gainsborough and Sir Joshua [Reynolds].

"Carnarvon himself is very friendly, democratic and unpretentious, but has never taken any part in public life, and is not popular in England. He goes about in ill-fitting clothes—always with a dog, and always in a jovial mien. He has wonderful horses, and is an ardent photographer of great ability. He is devoted to Egypt, and through Howard Carter has been excavating at Thebes for years. But his really good mind flits incessantly from one subject to another, unable to follow any one of them through."

My father and Gardiner "were in conversation on a terrace in the last rays of the afternoon sun, when Carnarvon returned with his guests from the races [at Newbury], and sent for us to join them in the library—a magnificent room of tremendous dimensions, embellished with many rare old paintings, works of art, and historical curios. These last include the office desk and chair of Napoleon I, the right arm of which is scarred with the scratching and whittling he habitually did with his pocket knife while discussing important matters with his callers!

"We found the room filled with guests moving about between sumptuous silver tea services, and chatting of the races as they drank their tea and nibbled their cakes and scones. Amongst them were Sir Valentine Chirol, member of the Royal Commission on Indian Public Services; and Sir William Garstin, for many years one of the leading British officials in Egypt, and the man who is chiefly responsible for the destruction of Philae. I was determined, however, to feel no prejudice!—and Garstin was most friendly. I suspect my liking for him may have been influenced by his seeming to be greatly impressed by my views on the strategy of Great Britain's position in the Near East, especially in Egypt and Suez! He and Chirol asked me to let them write on my behalf to Sir George Lloyd, Governor of Bombay Presidency.

"Garstin was an intimate friend of Kitchener, and confirms what I have long known, that K. urged the occupation of Alexandretta as the first step in the attack on Turkey, and Grey [Lord Grey of Fallodon] would not let it be done for fear of trouble with France who threatened to turn against England should the latter set foot there. The feeling against France, in view of the incalculable cost of such deference to her foolish sensitiveness, is very strong on the part of those who really know. Garstin, incidentally, has had access to all the papers concerning the sinking of Kitchener's ship, which according to every indication was caused by a mine."

Back in London, he found an invitation from H. G. Wells to stay with him at Easton Glebe in Essex. Wells was "writing a universal history, for which he says he has 'stolen a lot from Breasted and from James Harvey Robinson,'" and wanted him to read the sections on the Ancient Orient.

Fellow guests were two "grizzled proconsuls of the British Empire"—the great African explorer, linguist and naturalist, Sir Harry Johnston and his lady; and Sir Sidney Olivier (who became Lord Olivier of Ramsden, and Secretary for India in the Labor Government).

"Wells is keen and penetrating, jolly and democratic. As he himself told me, his father was a professional cricket player, and his family were quite uneducated people." The men talked of science and Empire, religion and history, and during the first evening the whole party played at the inevitable charades in "Mr. Britling's" barn.

Next day they walked "to the neighboring estate of Lady Warwick —Wells says she is 'an unusually intelligent woman for her social class!'—and visited the big glass houses where she keeps a lot of monkeys. Sir Harry named all the various breeds for us, but was not content till he had entered their cage to play with them. Three of them climbed to his shoulder, knocked off his hat and sat on his head. One, a female, showed him the deepest affection. She insisted on parting his scanty locks in a solicitous search for invisible cooties, and occasionally seemed to capture one, which to our unspeakable delight she would hold up in triumph."

At odd moments he ran through the earlier chapters of the new universal history which Wells had given him to read. They had a curiously familiar ring, and he was a little startled to discover that with his usual urbanity Wells had adopted the method and illustrative scheme of *Ancient Times,* applied its historical approach also to a treatment of modern times, and given to the completed work the title, *The Outline of History.* A series of volumes by James Henry Breasted and James Harvey Robinson was entitled *Outlines of European History.*

Nevertheless, when Wells's *The Outline of History* appeared, my father wrote: "I enthusiastically favor anything which will arouse 'the man in the street' to become interested in the history of mankind.

Wells has done it admirably, and if I have helped him, he is more than welcome."

Soon after his return to London, the railway strike suddenly ended, and a cancellation on the fabulously crowded Orient Express made possible a sailing from Venice.

At last, on November 1, 1919, after a twelve years' exile, he landed again in Egypt. "A thousand memories and associations throng to my mind as once again I see and hear and feel old Egypt all around me— the rich Egyptian sunshine, palms nodding in the Nile breezes, the mournful, eerie cry of kytes as they wheel in great, slow circles against the luminous sky."

The years had wrought dramatic changes and differences. A letter from Allenby, written in his own hand from the King of England's castle at Balmoral in Scotland, "was magical" in obviating customs and all other retarding formalities; while another from Arthur James Balfour to his successor, Lord Curzon of Kedleston, had moved the latter to request "His Majesty's High Commissioner for Egypt and the Sudan . . . to accord you every assistance in his power as regards your proposed journey from Egypt to Basra."

"What with the cordial cooperation of Mr. Hampson Gary, Diplomatic Agent of the United States in Egypt, I have no anxiety about our journey," my father commented. "But to bring all this about has taken no end of nerve and effrontery on the part of a backwoods boy from the Illinois prairies."

NOTE TO THE READER

[The narrative from this point to the end of Chapter VIII is entirely drawn from my father's journal-letters. For the sake of clarity and simplification, quotation marks are omitted and editorial comments are enclosed in brackets.]

I am trying to do the work of several men [he wrote on November 10]. I spend hours a day looking over the materials in the hands of dealers. It is endless—each stock is like a museum which has to be gone over. I have also begun going through the basement magazines of the great Cairo Museum itself, where there are vast masses of things doing nobody any good, of which I am trying to secure a few for the University of Chicago. In addition I must spend as much of each day as I can, copying the unpublished inscriptions among the Museum's displayed collections; keep up a heavy correspondence, and maintain all the essential, unavoidable social and official relations.

When the Allenbys arrived from England, they invited me to a dinner at the Residency. It was very pleasant, not a bit stiff and formal, despite the numerous important official personages present. Lady Allenby is most charming, natural, unaffected, animated and interested—asks intelligent questions, leaves no one neglected.

After dinner, Allenby to my great surprise led me to a chair apart from the company, and seating himself, began to take up a remark I had made referring to Clemenceau's *bon mot,* "Le bon Wilson avec ses quatorze points et le bon Dieu qui n'en a que dix." He continued to talk to me for the rest of the evening, without interruption or addressing a single word to his other guests.

Only a few months ago Allenby dealt the final annihilating blow to the leading oriental Empire [Turkey], which had ruled the Near East for about six centuries. He is at the moment the greatest man in the East, virtually king of the territory from the frontiers of India to Greece and Inner Africa. The quiet, matter-of-fact way in which he spoke of the momentous events wherein he played so great a part, his directness and unquestionable sincerity, made a profound impression on me, the more so because the simplicity of his manner at first quite veiled the greatness of the man.

"My impression of Wilson differs from yours," he said. "To me he seemed a man of conviction, with a good deal of strength and courage. I heard him tell the Peace Commissioners what he had come for, what he expected to see done, and that he insisted it be done. I had to deal with him in the matter of Syria and its future, . . . when I was asked to come to Paris to confer with the Peace Commission before the Peace Treaty was ready. President Wilson asked me what would happen if Syria were at once turned over to the French. I told him it would immediately result in a terrible war with the Arabs, which would . . . spread far into Asia and set the world on fire again.

"Wilson said to me, 'Will you state these opinions before the Peace Commissioners?' I replied that I could not do that, but would be glad to answer any questions put to me. The next day he asked me the same questions in the presence of the Peace Commissioners, and the French—including Clemenceau—heard me make the same answer.

Wilson then asked me how the wishes of the peoples of the conquered areas of the Near Orient might be ascertained. I told him, by asking the people openly and directly, to which he replied that a commission should be sent out for this purpose.

"Later, when I was called to Paris *after* the conclusion of the Peace Treaty to discuss with Clemenceau the future disposition of Syria, I could talk with the latter very frankly because I have known him for a long time and we are good friends. I said to him: 'You must believe me when I tell you that there is absolutely no occasion for all this French sensitiveness about Syria. *We* don't want it, [and] shall be glad enough to get well rid of the responsibility. We are quite ready to retire our troops as fast as you can move yours in, but when this transfer has taken place, we want peace in the whole region. Your people out there have been deliberately *trying* to stir up trouble and excite pogroms, in order to give you a chance to take possession of territory you want. You know it is going on, and it *must* be stopped!'

"Clemenceau replied, 'Yes, I think you are right!' 'Well, then,' I said, 'if you think I am an honest man—and I think you do—then shape your policy accordingly.' Clemenceau responded, 'It isn't as simple as that! I do believe *you* are an honest man, but I do not believe that the British nation is honest, and I do not trust them.'

"This is the situation," Allenby continued, "as I am now withdrawing my troops from Syria. Fortunately, the French have appointed an excellent man to assume control there—General Gouraud, a man often wounded in the present war, and lacking one arm.

"I am leaving for Beirut tomorrow so that he and I can ride together through the streets—you know," (Allenby's eyes twinkled) "for public consumption—so that they will understand that they can't hit Gouraud without hitting me. But a much more important reason for my going is to urge him to concede one thing to avoid trouble: to let me keep my troops in the northern Buka'a [the valley between the Lebanon and Anti-Lebanon mountains]. If my posts are removed and replaced by French troops, I fear there will be a serious outbreak, for the commander of all the [Syrian] Arabs has openly said he would not submit to French control, and that he would fight us too if we support a French mandate over them. . . . Of course I could not let such defiance pass. . . . I sent troops at once to arrest him, take him to Haifa. I expected a violent outbreak over my taking this action against him, and for the last twenty-four hours, while awaiting the trouble, I have been in an awful funk—my worst in the entire War,

I think! I ran a great risk. But nothing has happened, and I am very glad I did it for the sake of the French. Under Gouraud, however, I look for improvement, in spite of the unfortunate memories left by Picot."

J.H.B.: "Wasn't Picot the man who fled from Beirut at the outbreak of the War without destroying his confidential correspondence, so that the best friends of France among the Syrian natives were incriminated, and numbers of them were shot or hanged?"

"Yes. You can therefore understand the resentment of the Arab leader whom I have just arrested."

I cannot now recall what shifted our conversation at this point to the battle of Megiddo, but Allenby evidently took pleasure in talking of it.

"When they gave me a peerage, they wanted me to add 'Armageddon' to the title, but I refused to do that. It was much too sensational, and would have given endless opportunity to all the cranks in Christendom. So I merely took Megiddo."

J.H.B.: "Probably only the Orientalists know that it is identical with Armageddon, and the public will never discover the identity."

"Quite true," he answered, "and if such titles are to be used at all, Megiddo has had its appropriateness.

"You know, I went straight through the Pass of Megiddo, and at the crest I sent the infantry through to make a hole for the cavalry. They found a few battalions of Turks in possession of the height, killed thirty or forty of them, and captured all the rest. The cavalry got through the hole, and went forward with orders not to do any fighting, but to ride across the Plain of Megiddo and get astride of every road leading north, along which the enemy could retreat. I wanted to get old Liman von Sanders [the brilliant German general who commanded the Turkish Army in the Dardanelles and Palestine campaigns] and for three hours we had him bagged, with no possible way of escape.

"Then some of our men across a road to the northwest were summoned to help some comrades, and got into a fight which for a short time drew them off. Evidently von Sanders heard of it at once, for he slipped by in his automobile and escaped. I got my 'lie' out first and reported that von Sanders had at once fled northward as we advanced. But von Sanders got out a wireless which was probably nearer right than my dispatch, saying that after severe fighting, he had retired. Indeed, he *did* get together some of his clerks—his personal following—and he gave us a jolly good scrap before he got out of the net.

"Curious, wasn't it, that we should have had exactly old Thutmose's experience in meeting an outpost of the enemy and disposing of them at the top of the Pass leading to Megiddo! You see, I had been reading your book and [George] Adam Smith [*Historical Geography of the Holy Land*] and I knew what had taken place there."

J.H.B.: "Unfortunately we have too few in America who know the Near East or realize the obligation of the civilized world to keep order there."

"That is true, your country is at present behaving very badly!" he said with an engaging smile.

At that moment Lady [Gilbert] Clayton, who had sat on Lord Allenby's right, by rising gave the signal for all to go. Lady Allenby came forward to her husband and said, "I have asked Mr. Breasted to go with us to Abu Roash." He responded at once, "How would you like to go? Do you ride?" I said, "Yes, but I presume *not* after the rules of the approved British School—though if need be, I can still pick up my hat off the ground!" He assured me I would not be called on for any stunts, and bade me a very kindly goodnight.

You can now understand the complicated military and political situation we shall encounter when we leave Mesopotamia and come westward into French territory. I made no preparations for dealing with the French authorities, for I had expected that the British would be in control throughout the whole region until after our journey was over.

The War has indirectly affected the price of Egyptian antiquities. For a growing spirit of defiance, the knowledge that foreigners attach great value to the survivals from Egypt's past, and the possession of unprecedented amounts of money, have led the wealthier inhabitants to buy antiquities as never before, on a speculative basis. Through competitive buying, men of means like Mr. J. P. Morgan, Lord Carnarvon and others have inevitably played into the situation, so that Egyptian antiquities will increasingly command the high prices such men have been paying. I have therefore been delving into the collections of the antiquity dealers here in Cairo. Most unexpected things turn up, and the quest is fascinating.

For example, while keeping the doors of his shop tightly closed, one of the oriental rug merchants a day or two ago secretively showed me two stone statues of sitting figures. They represented an Egyptian noble whose name and titles were inscribed on the edge of the seat or base.

Twenty-five years ago, in my student days, I had read ten contracts inscribed on the walls of the tomb of a great noble at Assiut, which were intended after his death to provide him with gifts of plentiful food, drink and mortuary tapers on all the chief feast days of the Egyptian calendar. Now, these things were to be delivered not only to his tomb, but also to three statues, portraits of himself, one in the temple in the town, one in the temple outside the town, and one at the foot of the long stone stairway leading up to the [ancient] cemetery of Assiut. The contracts were written in the days of Abraham, some 4000 years ago, and the statues provided for in the contract had been lost and forgotten these thousands of years. But here before me, pulled out from under the rug-dealer's dusty counter, were two of these very statues, with the great Egyptian feudal baron's name still plainly legible on the side! The native asked an exorbitant price for them, and they are still slumbering under his counter.

I have also been devoting days and days to an enormous collection of antiquities belonging to a wealthy Syrian Jew named Nahman, who is cashier at the Crédit Foncier, and lives in a former gambling casino!

At the end of one of my recent visits to him, when I was dusty and tired and it was time to go home to dinner, he brought in a mass of torn and fragmentary papyri. As I went wearily and rather indifferently through them, I came upon a roll containing 16 columns of beautifully written Greek, each column about as large as the page of an octavo printed book. It was all in a fine *book* hand, and evidently a roll from an ancient library, not merely business documents like the other papyri at which I had been looking.

I examined it carefully, and saw at once that it was filled with numerals, written of course with Greek letters. Then I noticed the words, "from the Lion to the Virgin," and among many gaps in the worm-eaten papyrus, I recognized the words "to the Archer," then "star," "moon," "observations"—it was evident that I held in my hand an old Greek treatise on astronomy, which the character of the writing showed might be as early as the Third Century before Christ, and *might* have come from the lost Alexandrian library. It might well have been written by a member of that group of Greek scientists to which Euclid and Archimedes and Eratosthenes belonged. It made one's fingers fairly tingle!

One day I was in the shop of a particularly hard-headed Levantine with the Italian name of Tano, of whom I had bought a good many things. He told me he had a papyrus which was *very* fine, but as usual I discounted his glowing description. This papyrus, he said, was just across the street at the rug dealer's (where the statues were stowed away under the counter). After some parleying, he brought a mysterious box back to his own shop.

I thought of the ragged, tattered masses of papyrus which I had handled at Nahman's—the kind of thing we always expect when we hear of papyri just out of the ground. For usually they survive only as worm-eaten fragments, rarely showing any resemblance to a roll. And when the natives do find a complete, intact roll, they usually divide it by breaking it in the middle, like a stick!

So when Tano after carefully locking his shop door, began to open his box, I was only moderately interested. As the lid came off I saw a lot of mummy cloth bandages lying under it, and said to myself, "Of course—the usual mess of tatters!"

But when he removed the mummy wrappings, he uncovered a beautiful brown roll of papyrus as thick, fresh and uninjured as a roll of new wall paper!

It was difficult to maintain a "poker face" as he laid it on the table and giving it a fillip, exposed a perfectly intact bare surface before the beginning of the writing. It was the first uninjured beginning of a papyrus I had ever seen, as well as the first roll in such perfect condition that one could still unroll it exactly as the original owner had done.

And then came the writing!—an exquisitely executed hieroglyphic copy of the Book of the Dead, with wonderfully wrought vignettes, one of the finest copies to have come out of Egypt for many years!

Tano now wanted to go no further, lest he should injure the roll. I said: "If you wish to do business with me, I must see all of it!" So he unrolled, while I steadily rolled up, a constantly changing sequence of lovely vignettes done with wonderful delicacy and detail. Among the many chapters, I saw one toward the close of which the scribe had added a remark that it [probably the original from which he had made this copy] had been found in the day of Menkure, the great Pharaoh who built the third pyramid of Gizeh, nearly 2000 years before this [the scribe's copy of the] papyrus had been made.

Great beads of perspiration stood out on Tano's forehead. It was a long and painfully delicate task, for the roll was about thirty-five feet long! But at last I had seen it, and it was rolled back without mishap.

I knew that at this juncture I was in no state of mind to bargain with a canny oriental. Pleading weariness, I went home without saying a word about buying the papyrus.

I waited two days, doing much thinking. Lord Carnarvon's agent was due very shortly, and probably old Tano knew it. And after him there was Budge of the British Museum, and both of these men would want it, and outbid me if they could. So I was bound to move at once. As I write, the beautiful papyrus is safely packed in a tin tube in my trunk, Tano has 500 Pounds,* and both of us are happy.

Major-General Percy Hambro, Quartermaster General of the British Army in Mesopotamia, writes me cordially that he will arrange all transport as soon as we reach Basra, and will give us the privilege of buying our supplies as we need them from the British Commissary Stores. This means plentiful, cheap, good quality food wherever we may be in Mesopotamia. A staff officer from the Residency here in Cairo is under orders to secure our transportation from Egypt to Babylonia by way of Bombay. I must say these Englishmen have treated me splendidly—I have found universal cordiality, kindness and readiness to help.

This uncertain period of waiting for transport is trying, but I have more to do each day than I can possibly finish. Two days ago Nahman again sent word he wanted very much to see me—the old fox likes to show me things. He had some, of course, but he wanted especially to tell me about the collection of an old Swiss gentleman, Mr. André Bircher, whose house in a little side street off the Muski [the old street —now demolished—and district of the bazaars] I remembered having visited years ago.

It is an ancient house, some 450 years old, with wonderful old Saracen carvings and antique glass in the openwork of the fretted stone windows. Here André Bircher has lived for nearly fifty years, and in a little office just off the spacious court below, has carried on an importation business which has reputably netted him a fair-sized fortune. He has been buying antiquities for nearly forty years and has accumulated an immense collection which is looked after by an elderly woman, a Madame Serveux, who acts as curator. After serving

* Contributed by Mrs. Elizabeth Milbank Anderson for the purchase, as a gift to the University of Chicago, of what was christened the "Milbank Papyrus."

us oriental coffee in the afternoon light coming through the wonderful ancient glass and shimmering over a fountain in marble mosaic in the floor, he left us to go back to the office where he has spent half a century, and Madame Serveux showed me the collection. To look systematically through it is an immense job, for it contains over 17,000 numbers!

I am in the Museum the bulk of the day, grinding my eyes out on new fragments of royal annals like those on the Palermo Stone [the earliest known list of ancient Egyptian year-names and kings, covering a period of some 700 years, beginning about 3400 B.C.—so called because it is in the Museum at Palermo, Sicily]. I have made some good finds on these Cairo fragments—a whole row of kings of a united Egypt *before the dynasties,* all wearing the double crown, which none of the Frenchmen saw! I showed them to Petrie, who was very much pleased, as they corresponded to his Dynasty O.

At lunch today [December 15] at the Residency, before the excursion to Abu Roash, we talked of the present situation in Egypt, and from Allenby's quiet unconcern you would not have imagined that only three hours earlier, an attack had been made on the life of the Egyptian Prime Minister. He made some wise remarks about the danger of mere school learning such as the little Egyptian effendis get, without any real knowledge, and admitted that the English were very much to blame for this. I told him about Booker T. Washington's ideas of training for such people, and suggested that a series of Tuskegees up and down the Nile would be of great value. He agreed.

As we drove off after lunch, two men in khaki on swift motorcycles swung into their prescribed positions exactly one yard to the left and right, and one yard to the rear of Lord Allenby's car, and rode thus all the way out to the Pyramids where horses were awaiting us. I soon found myself astride of one of Allenby's big Australian chargers which he had ridden in the Palestine campaign!

I had never ridden so powerful a horse. He *was* a handful! The animals had not been exercised for a day or two, and were full of ginger. Mine was pulling hard as we started off at a rapid canter along the desert north of the Mena House [near the Great Pyramids of Gizeh]. Being a great cavalry officer and a superlative horseman, Allenby promptly noticed my discomfort, stopped the whole company, and had his A.D.C. loosen the curb and let out the curb reins. Though it was easier after that, I had all I could do to manage the animal.

Allenby led the way around the little village of Abu Roash, five miles north of Gizeh, then out into the desert where after a time we turned south until we stood looking up a vast artificial causeway leading from the desert level to a high promontory dominating the whole landscape. Here stood the substructure of what had been the Pyramid of Dedefre, successor of Khufu (Cheops). It is a remarkable sight. We rode up this causeway, soon coming to fragments of granite, which is not native north of the First Cataract, and at length we reached the top and stopped in the midst of a great stone-yard where mighty blocks of granite had been cut into shape for the pyramid. Allenby was very much interested, asked many questions.

After tea back at the Residency he showed me the new map of Jerusalem as it has just been laid out to protect entirely the old walls and city from encroachment by any modern buildings whatsoever.

[While awaiting accommodations for Bombay, my father re-visited various districts of Upper Egypt, and was amazed to discover the changes which had taken place in the economic life of the country since he had last seen it in 1907.

The wealth which cotton and sugar had brought to the larger land-owners suggested] the rise of a local nobility like the feudal barons who built their tombs at Benihasan, 4000 years ago. It is a new Egypt which we who knew it before can hardly conceive.

Imagine a whole group of fellahin with an income of as much as £E4000—practically $20,000—per year! The price of cotton is at the moment so high that it pays about £E100, or nearly $500 an acre per year. Hence if a farmer owns 40 acres, his income is nearly $20,000 a year—and many a native hereabouts has 40 acres. Quiet and stately old *omdehs* [mayors, or head men] in little towns of Upper Egypt you never heard of, are making as much as $50,000 a year.

There are 40 million dollars' worth of cotton now on the docks at Alexandria, guarded by British troops till shipping can be found for it; and the present crop is bringing in a total return of $500,000,000 (five hundred million) dollars to the Egyptian landowners and farmers.

[At Luxor, 450 miles southward from Cairo, news had preceded him that he was buying antiquities, and he was "waited on by rows of finely dressed natives who with oriental blarney" addressed him as pasha—or basha, as they pronounce it. He visited first the house of an old dealer named Yussuf Hassan, whom he had known since 1895.]

Nahman had told me in Cairo that Yussuf Hassan had bought from a village dealer at Keneh near Luxor, four splendid prehistoric and early dynastic stone vases of white and black mottled stone, one of them bearing the name of a very early king. Coffee came in and we talked of old times, and of everything else but the real subject which each of us knew was in the back of the other's head.

He brought out a great bronze statue of Osiris, over two feet high, much oxidized, but incrusted with semi-precious stones and overlayed with gold, most of which were gone. He showed me also a lovely bronze mirror, with a Hathor head on the handle. I took it to the window and under the oxidization I could just read the faintly visible hieroglyphs spelling the name of the great queen Ahmose-Nofretere. I was holding one of her toilet mirrors in my hand! Old Yussuf knew it was valuable, and despite the best I could do to preserve the poker mien of my buying face, I must have betrayed gleams of interest as I realized that I was holding in my fingers a mirror which over three thousand four hundred years ago had reflected the image of this famous and beautiful queen of the East! He wanted £E300 ($1500) for the mirror and the Osiris statue together!

Thereupon he rummaged in a crazy old safe built into the thickness of the walls of his house, and brought out one treasure after another. Among them were a lovely little hand and foot carved with marvelous refinement in deep blue lapis lazuli—part of a wondrous statuette wrought by some forgotten master living at the imperial court when Egypt was ruling the whole eastern Mediterranean world, and Thebes was the great capital of the East.

And so I could go on indefinitely. Suffice it that I secured these things and many others for the University. But what I wanted most to see were those archaic stone vases, one bearing an early royal name. When I asked Yussuf if he had any early stone vases he looked quite uninterested. So I in turn developed complete indifference toward all the prehistoric stone vases in the world, and bidding old Yussuf a cordial farewell, I departed.

Next morning I went over to pay him and make arrangements for packing the things I had bought. When this had been completed and the eternal coffee had been drunk and we had discussed everything in the universe except archaic vases, I rose to go. We went to the door and there at last old Yussuf finally asked me quite casually if I would come upstairs and see some "things." I replied that I was very busy and had not the time. Then he could not conceal his anxiety to have me see these "things"! So after he had warned his harem to keep out of our way, he went up.

On a divan in an upstairs room were six prehistoric and early dynastic vases, one of them almost as large across as a bushel basket. They were cut of black and white mottled stone, possibly diorite— exceptionally hard—and were of the very best workmanship. It was evident that old Yussuf thought more of their size than of the inscription which one of them bore. I turned it around to find the inscription, much obscured by the mottled color of the stone.

I had to assume an ostentatious indifference, and carry the vase casually to the window, where I discerned the inscription—a delicately traced palace front, and surmounting the palace the figure of the royal Falcon, the earliest of the royal titles of the Egyptian King; and below it, a little lost in the intricacies of the mottled surface, I saw to my delight the name of Menes, the first of the dynastic kings of Egypt, dating from about 3400 B.C. I was holding in my hands a piece of palace furniture of the earliest sovereign in the world of whose history we know anything at all—who ruled 5300 years ago!

The ensuing jockeying I could not begin to recount. Old Yussuf says he paid Girgia, the Keneh dealer, £E500 for these vases, and J.H.B. tells him he paid far too much, etc., etc., etc. Yussuf says he is proud of the high price he paid, that he has made all the dealers in Egypt very jealous by outbidding them, including his wealthy old competitor in Luxor, Mohammed Mohasseb (who owns nearly a thousand acres of land from which he derives an annual income of nearly $100,000).

I am dealing with shrewd men not in need of money, who know when they have stuff which cannot be duplicated, and to whom the profit from such traffic in antiquities is but a fraction of a much larger income.

[He finally closed his numerous bargains with the Luxor dealers, including old Yussuf, and returned to Cairo on the morning of December 24, 1919. On Christmas Eve he wrote:]

Three weeks ago I cabled President Judson, asking him for $5,000 more for antiquities purchases. Today [December 24] I had a cable from him: "Sending twenty-five thousand more." I wonder what has happened! And a cable from Mr. Charles L. Hutchinson [then president of the Art Institute of Chicago] reads: "Spend ten thousand more." Had I known this purchasing work would be so heavy, I would

have brought a secretary. For the listing and invoicing is very burden-
some, involving detailed vouchers and expense accounts for something
approaching $100,000.

I have been at work in the Cairo Museum on the magnificent gold
incrusted coffin of Ikhnaton [the first monotheist], endeavoring to
recover its inscriptions which are of the greatest interest. I rejoice
that I am not puzzling my brains over the unspeakably bad copies of
Daressy, but have before me the sheet gold on which the original
inscriptions are charmingly incised.

I was told by the Museum authorities that nothing had ever been
done about the body of Ikhnaton, since its examination by Elliot Smith
[a leading British physiologist, who had studied hundreds of ancient
Egyptian skeletons and mummies for ancient evidences of present-
day pathology]; and that it lay in a packing box in a storage magazine.
I was shown a rough box under a table, and on opening it, I found the
bones of Ikhnaton.

It was a strange experience to lift his skull from the box, and
endeavor to imagine all it must once have harbored. I turned over
the lower jaw and found that one wisdom tooth was still embedded in
the gum which had partially shrunk away and exposed it. The teeth
were powerful and in splendid condition, except that someone had
recently let the skull fall and had broken the lower front teeth. I have
persuaded the Museum authorities to set an anatomist to work on the
body, and it will soon be properly prepared and restored to the coffin
down the front of which, wrought in a band of sheet gold, runs
Ikhnaton's mutilated name, followed by the words: "The Beautiful
Child of the Sun (Aton), who lives here forever and forever, and is
true in the sight of earth and sky."

I have also spent a wonderful day among the tombs and pyramids
of Sakkara. As I looked about, I wondered where my faculties of
observation had been slumbering in all my former visits, for now I was
seeing so much more than ever before. If my health and strength are
spared, I shall be able to improve my *History of Egypt* immensely,
and also to write a preliminary book on the *Origins and Early History
of Civilization* which will go far beyond anything now available.

The Royal Air Force has shown me hundreds and hundreds of air
views of Egypt, Palestine and Syria, but practically nothing of use to
us archaeologists. The Air Commodore gave orders to his flyers to

make special photographs for us of the whole margin of the Desert from Gizeh to Dahshur; but I wanted to take some of my own. He informed me that the regular charge for flying a civilian was £E20 ($100) an hour! When Allenby learned of this he said it was absurd—the purpose was scientific work, and it must be done without charge!

I promptly received an official order, and went out to Heliopolis whither my R.A.F. ship was being flown from the airdrome at Helwan [twenty miles south of Cairo]. The young officers were inclined to regard my experiment as a joke but I was not in the least disturbed, and waited until a speck rising over the southern horizon grew into the ship which circled and landed just in front of us.

The pilot asked me to don a fur-lined helmet, fur-mounted goggles, a pilot's huge leather overcoat, and a large pair of heavy gauntlet gloves! I looked like Peary in the Arctic! Then the young officers assisted me into the cockpit, and the pilot, after telling me he had fastened a notebook and a pencil over my seat for writing him my instructions, disappeared over the top of his covered perch.

We went slowly down the field, swung around and with a tremendous roar, rushed back into the wind. As the young man put on full power, we lifted and went off over the roofs of the hangars and the buildings of New Heliopolis.

It was impossible to utter a word in the crashing noise of the engine and the roaring vortex behind the propeller. I opened my mouth to find myself gasping and choking, and quickly realized that one could only breathe through the nose. The pilot had a glass windshield, but the observer was not protected in any way except that he sat deep in his cockpit. I began seriously to wonder whether I could stand two hours of this.

We climbed rapidly, headed directly westward across the southern apex of the Delta. Then the full splendor of it all broke upon me, and it was thrilling beyond words. Five thousand feet below was spread the green carpet of the Delta, with the misty wilderness of the desert visible for a hundred miles to the east and west. At this point the pilot wrote me a nice little note, asking how I felt and if he was headed correctly. Before I knew it we were sailing over the margin of the western desert, and I was looking obliquely down on the ruined pyramids of Abu Roash and the vast causeway up which I had ridden with Lord Allenby only three weeks ago. It had seemed a long ride up that causeway then, but now it looked like a child's sand bridge on the seashore!

I had the camera all ready for the first shot. But when I lifted it above the edge of the fuselage, the blast crushed the bellows into the field of the picture. No matter what I did, I could not prevent it, and had to make the exposure with much of the view thus cut off The five miles from Abu Roash to Gizeh were passed in less than as many minutes, and we hovered over the Great Pyramid.

The pilot veered and banked the machine sharply so that as we tilted far over to one side the camera was somewhat protected. My eyes now looked five thousand feet straight down upon the Gizeh group—a wonderful and uncanny sensation. Then came Zawiyet el-Aryan and Abusir, Sakkara and Dahshur, and far to the south, Lisht and the Fayum.

As we passed the grand pyramid group at Dahshur I turned and looked northward along a magnificent thirty-mile line of pyramids with the giants of Gizeh towering in the background—a vista I shall never forget. I snapped the camera twice on this, hoping devoutly that the bellows might not have spoiled the pictures.

Now I had to reload the camera. The air was very lumpy and we kept dropping with a sickening fall into air pockets. This had been going on for nearly an hour and I was getting groggy. But I stuck to my pictures and to studying the terrain as we moved from one great pyramid cemetery to the next, grinding my teeth and swearing I was not going to give up. Alas, it was all of no avail—I leaned over the edge of the cockpit, and surrendered a very good lunch to the Sahara. The pilot tactfully refrained from further correspondence about my health.

I was unashamedly grateful when we turned northward and sailed away homeward. I tried to continue with the camera but I was pretty seedy. Nevertheless, as we swung northward I shall never forget the panorama of the eastern desert illuminated by the low afternoon sun behind us. It was in marvelous contrast to the rich, glowing green of the valley in the foreground, behind which the desert cliffs and ranges rose in one yellow sand-drift after another.

At Gizeh we turned northeastward, sailing over Cairo and the Citadel at 6000 feet. A few moments later the pilot shut off almost all his power, the awful roaring and terrific wind blast ceased, and with our first really pleasant sensation of buoyant flight we spiraled downward until we glided onto the landing field and the wheels regained the ground so gently that I was hardly aware of it. My first flight was over. We had been up nearly two hours—and they now told me that on the first trip they rarely keep anyone up more than twenty minutes!

[At last the British Residency reported it had secured passage to Bombay for him and his party on the P. & O. steamship *City of Benares,* sailing on February 18 from Port Said.

When he bade the Allenbys good-bye, the High Commissioner took him into his office to write him a promised letter to Feisal, momentarily King of Syria.]

Allenby was clawing about amongst the drawers of his desk, and was dropping half-whispered expletives as he failed to find writing paper, when he came upon some typewritten sheets clipped together, which he passed over to me, saying, "That is confidential, but you ought to know it."

My eye fell on a big rubber-stamped mark "SECRET," then on the heading: "*Armée Française en Syrie,*" and I quickly found myself deep in a report from French Headquarters. It is evident that the whole middle section of the Fertile Crescent from Baghdad to Aleppo and Damascus is on fire, and a concerted effort is being made by the Turks and the Arabs to throw the French into the sea. I fear we shall not get far from Baghdad, but we shall run no risks, and whenever it seems too hazardous to go further, we shall return by the route we came.

While I read this report, Allenby wrote me a kind note to Feisal. When he had finished his letter, he said to me, "You know, I told old Clemenceau this was coming [referring to the French report], and when he asked me why, I said, 'Because you are so unpopular,' and when he asked me why again, I said, 'Because you keep your religion exclusively for export, and when you take a territory, you at once turn it over to your Catholics. That's the first reason. The second is that a Moslem woman is never safe whenever your army is around.' Though Clemenceau and I are old friends, he didn't like that very much!"

He handed me the letter, and bade me an earnest good-bye and *bon voyage.*

[When I myself revisited Cairo two years later, and paid my respects at the Residency, Lord and Lady Allenby each told me that they had only with the greatest reluctance and anxiety complied with my father's request for transport and other facilities; for the High

Command in Mesopotamia had reported conditions there as so dangerous that they had not expected to see him alive again.]

As I write [aboard the S.S. *City of Benares*], I am passing through the Suez Canal for the first time in my life.

Arrangements for packing of antiquities purchases scattered in four places in Luxor, and in six places in Cairo, with different kinds of packing required by varying conditions and sorts of objects; full invoices to be submitted to the Cairo Museum for clearance of these purchases; lists for the packers, lists for the consular invoices, lists for the shippers, accession lists; endless bills to pay with a constant eye on my budget; calls on the men who could help us in Asia; correspondence with diplomatic and government officials, etc., etc., etc.—all this, known only to me and necessarily done by me, made the last weeks in Luxor and Cairo pretty much a nightmare. I still have a huge mass of work to clear away on this voyage, but I fear we shall reach Bombay before I have finished.

[February 19:] If you will take the map in my *History of Egypt*, you will see the copper mines marked in Sinai, and will understand what an epic-making bridge-head this region has been. As we left the 100-mile Canal and passed down the Gulf of Suez, we had on one side the fine jagged ridges of the desert east of Egypt, and on the other the great rock masses which rise skyward above the desert of Sinai. The highlands along the Egyptian side are broken now and then by wadis through which the earliest Egyptians reached the Gulf of Suez. The greatest of these is the Wadi el-Araba.

Along the low shores afforded by these wadis, the Egyptians built the first ships that sailed the Red Sea. They were thus perhaps the earliest—certainly among the earliest—men to navigate salt water.

At noon today we had Mount Serbal and Gebel Musa rising grandly behind the rock-bound coast of Sinai. It was good for the soul to hear the First Officer devoutly explain to a passenger, that yonder was Mt. Sinai where "the Sermon on the Mount was delivered!"

A little north of Serbal is the Wadi Maghara, where the earliest known copper mines still survive, and all about them the inscriptions of the earliest kings who ever carried on such an enterprise. It was from these operations that Europe first received her knowledge of metal.

The Red Sea was to me intensely interesting. When I was a little fellow in the tiny red brick schoolhouse at Downers Grove, I used to look at the Bab el-Mandeb on the map, at the south end of the Red Sea, and to wonder and wonder how such far-off lands and places looked and how it would seem to be there. Even to an old-timer such as I have come to be, it is very far from a matter of course to pass through this famous Strait. For here were the desolate rocky islands so long infested by Arab pirates, the scene of many an adventure of our friend Sindbad. One of them, the Island of Perim, is held by a British garrison and is used as a large and important coaling and oiling station, although it is entirely without water, which has to be obtained by distilling sea water.

The African side of the Red Sea is the Land of Punt, which the first Egyptian ships began to visit some 5000 years ago, and here lived the fair fat queen who was visited by the fleet of Queen Hatshepsut which is so beautifully sculptured and painted on the walls of the Temple of Der el-Bahri at Thebes.

Apart from the American commercial men—one of the coarsest and most vulgar lots I have ever come across, who spend most of their time in the smoking room playing cards for drinks—there are some interesting people on board. One of them is a big, ponderous, florid-faced Briton named Major Pratt-Barlow. He is very taciturn and modest, but we have at last induced him to talk. He was Chief Liaison Officer between Allenby's Headquarters and the famous Colonel Lawrence.

Lawrence was a student of Hogarth's in archaeology at Oxford, who went to the Near East and became familiar with the Arabs and their life. He rapidly gained intimate acquaintance with Arabic dialects, and with the most prominent Arab leaders. The latter all liked him, and he had a strange and unprecedented influence over them. When the War broke out and it was evident that the Arabs only needed proper leadership to rouse them against the Turks, the English sent Lawrence out to undertake this task.

What followed reads like romance. This young Englishman roused all Arabia, and marched with the Arab leaders at the head of thousands of desert tribesmen on Allenby's eastern flanks as he advanced northward against the Turks. After reaching the head of the Red Sea at Akaba, he left the bulk of his Arabs behind, and advancing northward with only a thousand of his best men, flanked the Fourth Turkish Army on the east of Jordan, and cut all the four railway lines which connected the Turks with their northern base at Damascus. In probable danger of being overwhelmed by a sudden onslaught of the Fourth Turkish Army—some 20,000 strong—he maneuvered so cleverly that he kept out of harm's way, while constantly harassing the discomfited Turks, until he had their whole Fourth Army on the run. He killed about 5000 of them, took about 8000 prisoners, and scattered the rest completely. His triumphant entry into Damascus reads like a story from the Crusades.

While Lawrence was operating on the *east* of the Jordan valley, Allenby's Army was pushing north on the *west* of it. Lawrence cut the only railway line of retreat open to the Turkish forces facing Allenby, enabling the latter to capture, cut up and destroy practically the whole Turkish Army in Palestine. He took some 90,000 prisoners, and in addition killed a great multitude.

Major Pratt-Barlow has in his attaché case the original manuscript of Lawrence's confidential report to Allenby, covering his own part in the foregoing campaign. The French are so insanely jealous of Lawrence's power and influence among the Arabs, that the British have not published his report for fear of offending them. It is a pity, for it is an extraordinary document. Barlow has given me permission to make an abstract of it.

Lawrence subsequently wrote a book of several hundred thousand words, recounting his work in the Near East. I was told in London that one day he was carrying the manuscript in a bag on a train in England, and on arriving at his destination, did not discover until after leaving the station that the bag he now held in his hand was not the original but an exact duplicate of the one he had had on the train— identical even to labels, and marks of wear and age. The question arises as to who would have had reason to suppress his book—and Major Pratt-Barlow, who told me the story, answered the question without hesitation.

The bitter feeling I have found here between the English and the French has surprised me greatly. There is open talk of a future alliance between England and Germany, whenever English public opinion will permit. They call France the bully of Europe, and they are sick and tired of kowtowing to the French. France on the defensive was magnificent, but France victorious is thoroughly disappointing.

[In a chapter omitted from *The Seven Pillars of Wisdom* and published in May, 1939, Lawrence said of his campaigns with the Arabs: "I had to join the conspiracy, and, for what my word was worth, assured the men of their reward. In our two years' partnership under

fire they grew accustomed to believing me and to think my government, like myself, sincere. In this hope they performed some fine things,
but, of course, instead of being proud of what we did together, I was
continually and bitterly ashamed.

"It was evident from the beginning that if we won the war these
promises would be dead paper, and had I been an honest adviser of
the Arabs I would have advised them to go home and not risk their
lives fighting for such stuff." *

Under these circumstances he considered himself unentitled to
honors, all of which he declined, and in his discouragement he sought
sanctuary by enlisting as a private soldier, first in the Tank Corps, then
in the Royal Air Force.

On the day this omitted chapter was published, G. B. Shaw was
quoted by the British press as saying that "with regard to the Arabs,
at first Lawrence thought they had not been well treated, then he felt
they had been given rather more than they could manage, and finally
he gave the impression that it didn't matter either way. The truth is
that Lawrence had no political sense at all. He was like G. K. Chester-
ton: he was a great boy who never grew up." †

There is good reason to believe that he never grew up and that, as
is so evident in the limited edition of *The Seven Pillars of Wisdom,* at
least one of the causes of his reputedly mysterious influence over the
Arabs lay in their characteristically ready response to the turbulent
adolescence of which he remained always a prisoner.]

Under a blistering midday sun we steamed into crowded Bombay,
where not a bed was to be had in any hotel. But by dusk I had found
five vacant cots in a public building which during the War had been
used as a hospital and owing to the shortage of hotel space had now
been turned over by the Government to Thomas Cook & Son to be
run after a fashion as a shelter for travelers.

Our cots were among at least fifty others in a huge open room
about 50 feet long. The night was hideous—men coming and going
till daylight, indifferent that others were trying to sleep. There was
nothing to allay the withering heat save a filthy shower bath at daybreak, and some vile tea brought by an unwashed native boy.

Recurrence of serious trouble in Mesopotamia has compelled the

* *Oriental Assembly,* ed. by A. W. Lawrence, Williams and Norgate, 1939,
p. 143.

† *New York Herald Tribune,* May 24, 1939.

British to reinforce their garrisons on the Tigris and Euphrates, so that space on ships has suddenly been absorbed again. But at last, after hounding steamship company offices and the British Embarkation Officer, and refusing to be put off, I have secured berths for our party on a ship sailing tomorrow.

This morning I drove out along the beautiful waterfront of Bombay, past the Towers of Silence to Government House, to hand in letters which Sir Valentine Chirol and Sir William Garstin in London had made me promise to deliver to Sir George Lloyd, the Governor of Bombay Presidency.

The sea was washing the sands below, palms nodded in at the windows, and scarlet-clad native attendants made splotches of brilliant color against masses of tropical foliage, as I sat and waited in this paradise of a garden office at Malabar Point. Soon one of these gorgeous displays entered to tell me H.E. was awaiting me. I was led across a superb garden to a young A.D.C., who presented me to the Governor of sixty million orientals.

Sir George Lloyd is probably under 50, looks much less. His manner was informal and engaging as he led me to a sofa, where he sat down with me, expressed great interest in my mission, and asked many questions about my work.

The talk quickly turned to the world situation. He seemed anxious to justify British stewardship in India, and charged me with messages for my countrymen.

"In managing the public revenues of 60 million people, how many white men do you think I am able to put over the task?" he asked.

He held up two fingers. "Just two," he said, "and the native personnel is practically worthless. We are absurdly understaffed, and endeavoring to carry on heavy responsibilities in a very exhausting climate. My private secretary, who brought you in, has been serving out here for twelve years with only three months' leave in all that time. I myself have been on duty for six years without leave. We are very weary of our heavy load, and believe that if the United States understood the nature of our task and of our motives in carrying it, they would come in and help. I wish you would tell your people this!"

As I was leaving, I referred to the tragic collapse of Wilson's statesmanship, and Lloyd reminded me of Frederick the Great's dictum that "the most brutal conceivable punishment for a guilty people whom he wished to chastise, would be to put them under the rule of a philosopher!" This was an infelicitous answer for an Englishman, but I fear the United States have laid themselves open to such barbs.

[It was not until several years later, when Lloyd had succeeded Allenby as High Commissioner for Egypt and the Sudan, that my father discovered the disingenuous nature of this disarmingly engaging diplomat, whose aggressive ambitions for the Vice Royalty of India were destined for defeat.]

Along the southern coast of Persia, desolate pale-gray cliffs rise directly from the sea, and the coastal ridges westward of Jask are flanked by distant mountains 6000 to 10,000 feet high. The entire littoral is a desert except where occasional transverse rifts in the mountains have permitted the rains to wash down a little alluvium in which have sprung up a few lonely groves of trees and clusters of tall palms. I could understand why Darius had failed in his great effort to make Persia a maritime nation, and why Alexander the Great's terrible march westward along this very coast on his return from India had cost him a large part of his army.

This noon we entered the Strait of Ormuz, where the ship left the coast of Persia and headed straight northwest for Ras (Cape) Mussendom on the projecting coast of Arabia. The backbone of this Cape is a north-and-south ridge of great mountains dropping abruptly to the sea, and continuing northward in a straggling group of craggy islands extending many miles out into the Strait.

A week after leaving Bombay we have sighted the light at the mouth of the Shatt el-Arab, the stream formed by the united Tigris and Euphrates as they flow into the Persian Gulf.

The sixty-mile stretch from the mouth of the Shatt el-Arab to Basra—which did not exist in ancient times but has since been laid down by the river—seems to be one vast palm plantation—at first we could see the desert beyond, but soon it receded behind an ocean of palm tops. The Shatt el-Arab is an imposing river of pale fawn-colored, very dirty water. Every hundred yards or so an irrigation trench leads back among the palms, alternating with larger ditches and occasionally extensive canals. The many sailboats resemble those of the Nile, but the smaller feluccas are long and narrow and turned up at both ends like the kaiks of Constantinople and the Venetian gondolas.

At Abadan, where their pipe-lines come down from the Persian mountains, we passed the huge tanks, the docks and far-reaching works of the Anglo-Persian [now Anglo-Iranian] Oil Company. Their general offices are at Muhammera, a little further upstream. The Sheikh of Muhammera has long been a protégé of the English. Their arrangements with him would have prevented the Germans from reaching the Persian Gulf with their Baghdad Railway. British policy in Iraq, just as in Persia, is largely determined by oil.

In a few days it will be seven months since I left home. It seems a century. I am grateful for the responsibilities and the pressure of work which keep my mind mercifully preoccupied. Yet even in the busiest moments—in banks and consulates, on docks and boats, in custom houses and hotel lobbies—thoughts of my home and my loved ones sweep over me and shut out everything around me, and there is an ache that will not be quieted.

Basra itself is a vast military camp extending for four miles along the Shatt el-Arab, with native and English shipping stretching practically the whole distance in mid-stream or along the docks. This place marks the first lap of our Western Asiatic campaign.

The new railway from Basra to Baghdad passes right through ancient Ur of the Chaldees (modern El-Mukaiyar), our first important stop. From there we shall zigzag by car and boat and caravan from place to place, keeping near the Euphrates and the railway line in order to use them as much as possible.

[On March 14, 1920, he wrote from General Nepean's Headquarters at Basra G.H.Q. of the River Command:] A Lieutenant-Colonel Venning came on board, brought me cordial letters from Major-General Percy Hambro in Baghdad, and from General Nepean, in charge of the River Command, extending from the Persian Gulf up both sides of the river to Amarah. In a few minutes we were bowling down a concrete automobile road between miles of palm trees among hundreds of military, administration, and store buildings, with an enormous radio installation towering over everything.

We finally drew up in front of a buff-colored brick building with many oriental awnings, facing the River. Colonel Venning took me to a spacious guest room, and invited me to join the Staff Mess. He showed me a file of papers, dispatches and orders concerning our expedition, and the arrangements for our advance from here to Baghdad. Everything possible was being done for us.

In the Mess Room hung a large autographed engraving of the

Kaiser in hunting costume—the familiar one we have so often seen in Berlin. When I expressed surprise, the young officers told me we were sitting in the German Consulate. I sit writing these lines in a German chair at a German table, and I shall sleep in a German bed!

The job of preparing for our caravan trip would have been utterly impossible had I not been supplied with a car. All stores and equipment are classified by kinds and are in scattered depots usually miles apart—tents in one place, oil stoves in another, field candlesticks somewhere else, tableware and kitchen canteen in a remote warehouse, camp equipment in the officers' store, provisions in a different canteen; and so on for everything. And my driver is a turbaned East Indian who knows almost no English!

The Indian troops to which this driver belongs had a great deal to do with the conquest of the region we are about to go through. The authorities insist that we shall not go anywhere without an escort either of such men, or of *shabana,* the native Arab police who are already very smart and keen on their job.

[Ur Junction, Babylonia, March 18, 1920:] I sit writing in a freight car, in which I slept last night on a field cot. Not far away, looming high against the setting sun, is the temple tower of Ur of the Chaldees, the traditional home of Abraham.

Ur Junction—what would Abraham say to that!—consists of a group of tents, a mess house, quarters for the army officers in charge, a post office, and three tents in a row serving as a railroad restaurant. It lies on the new main line from Basra to Baghdad over which the first train passed shortly before our arrival, and which we are the first archaeological expedition to use. There is a little branch line running from here up to Nasiriyeh, and hence the name, Ur Junction!

It required only a little manipulation of the official wires to produce two Ford vanettes in which we were soon rolling along the desert at twenty miles an hour. Before us in the early morning sun lay the ruins of our first Babylonian city—chiefly the temple tower of the Moon-God of ancient Ur, and adjoining larger buildings such as the palace of the ruler and its administrative buildings which form a nucleus at one end, beyond which some low mounds mark the houses of the unpretentious town. There is none of the architectural grandeur of the Egyptian buildings with their vast stone superstructures and magnificent colonnades. For there was little or no stone in ancient Babylonia, and everything had to be built of burned or unburned brick. Still, I found

it very impressive to be standing in the first ancient Babylonian city
I had ever visited. The bricks of the temple tower lying all about are
marked with the name of Nabonidus, the father of Daniel's Belshaz-
zar; while the older lower court of the tower contains bricks bearing
the title of Urnammu, who lived in the twenty-third century B.C.,
almost 1700 years before Nabonidus.

We next drove to ancient Eridu (sixteen miles south of Ur Junction,
today called Abu Shahrein), once on the Persian Gulf but now some
150 miles from the nearest shore line. It was strange to be riding
across desert over which once rolled the waters of the Persian Gulf,
and to cover in an hour and a quarter a distance for which a caravan
would have needed a full day!

[From Ur—which Sir Leonard Woolley later excavated with brilliant results—the party zigzagged northward, traveling alternately by
railroad, Ford vans, river launches and horseback, visiting one ancient
historical site after another, many of them unidentifiable.] Often we
searched in vain for an inscription—especially a brick stamped with
a dedication which might reveal the name of the place. We wandered
far and wide among mounds which in the rain would become morasses
of sticky mud. Usually we could find no inscribed material on the
surface of the ground. It was strange and tantalizing to look out over
a once populous city, and endeavor to re-people its vanished houses
with the life that once flourished here and had now passed away,
leaving not even a name to give it identity. Doubtless excavation
would in most cases have disclosed it.

[At a modern town called Kalat es-Sikkar, roughly midway between
the Tigris and Euphrates, the local British Political Officer (as the
civil administrative officer of a district or region is called), a Captain
Crawford, "aged 26, with a wound in one leg not yet entirely healed,
a bullet through his stomach, and part of his right hand shot away,"
joined them on March 23d in a ride to a great ancient city mound
now called Tell Yokha.]

Captain Crawford had horses assembled on the west side of the
river [Shatt el-Hai], and we rode off southwest for Tell Yokha. Five
of the neighboring Sheikhs had signified their desire to ride along with
us, and to these were added five Arab guards armed with rifles, so that
our cavalcade numbered 16 horsemen.

At the first group of over 100 dark, camel's-hair tents which we
encountered, there was a strong mud fort with tall rounded towers,

intended as a place of refuge for the tribes when one of the incessant tribal wars was on. The sheikh came out to greet us, accompanied by a servant bearing coffee—the never failing symbol of hospitality. As we rode on, two more sheikhs from a turbulent tribe which had been recently bombed by British airmen, came in and assumed a friendly attitude.

All around us on the plain were the distant mounds of unknown ancient cities. One of the Arabs who could read, gave me their current names and I have recorded them all with the correct Arabic spellings. About 1:30 P.M., having been in the saddle nearly five hours and ridden twenty-three miles, we came among the vast mounds of Tell Yokha. I had galloped on ahead, with Captain Crawford following me, so that we were far in advance as we began ascending the mounds, which were encumbered with great sand dunes that had drifted in from a stretch of desert four hours' ride to the north.

A strong north wind was driving the sand into our eyes, and visibility was difficult. Shelton [one of his staff members] had managed to stay pretty close, and now joined us. A moment later he touched my sleeve and said, "Who are all these?"

Looking where he pointed, I saw a body of thirty or forty Arab horsemen sweeping up the slope directly upon us. Crawford was fifty paces away and did not see them. I walked over to him, asked him to look around. His face never changed and with the utmost composure he asked our own Arabs who these horsemen were. They replied, "They are the Beni Ghweinin."

In a moment the riders halted, drawn up in a line like a platoon of cavalry on parade. The Beni Ghweinin had recently been bombed by British airmen, their sheikh, named Mizal, and many of his followers had been outlawed—and these were the men before us a hundred paces away!

Crawford was splendid. He folded his arms and quietly contemplated the horsemen. We had five rifles and they had thirty or forty. We were completely at their mercy.

Four sheikhs dismounted, left their horses in the line and came forward to us. The sheikhs in our party introduced them, and they all stepped forward and kissed Crawford's right shoulder, at the same time dropping from their heads their rope-like *agalas* [headdress] arranged in coils over their headcloths. To let the *agala* fall down to the shoulders is a token of complete submission. It was quite evident that this had all been arranged beforehand by the sheikhs who accompanied us. Crawford told Sheikh Mizal that he must come with him [Crawford] to Kalat es-Sikkar and afterwards to Headquarters at Nasiriyeh, to make his formal submission there and stand his trial for his misdeeds.

Mizal was not expecting this and the palaver which followed was long and interesting as one sheikh after another took up the word. Mizal did not assent, but rode with us to the tents of his tribe. Throughout a two hours' ride eastward toward the river, the Arabs shouted, raced at wild speed, caracoling their horses in wide curves, and brandishing their rifles.

On our arrival we were taken at once to the *madhif*, or guest tent of Sheikh Mutlaq, Mizal's brother who is now sheikh in his stead. The big, black tent, open on one side, was carpeted with gay rugs, and at the right were cushions where Crawford and I seated ourselves. The rest of the party sat on our right, then the sheikhs who were with us, and then the notable men of the tribe. Tea and cigarettes were at once brought in and passed by Sheikh Mutlaq himself.

Four men now appeared carrying between them an enormous tray heaped high with boiled rice on which lay two whole roast sheep. It was set down in our midst, together with a smaller tray of rice, numerous roast chickens, pieces of roast mutton, bowls of clabbered milk and generous piles of Arab bread. As we fell to, the leading sheikhs gathered around the big tray, and bevies of dark hands began carrying the food to a great circle of dark faces.

The food was really well cooked and delicious, but I shrank inwardly from drinking clabbered milk from a bowl the outside of which under the rim was caked with deposit from legions of Arab mouths. But being hungry and thirsty (for we had had nothing to eat since early morning), I shut my eyes and drank. Circle succeeded circle around the big tray, until finally it was carried out to the women and children. At last there remained only the skeletons of the two sheep among a scattering of rice.

There was now a stir in the assembly, and suddenly where the big tray had just been, appeared two holy men (*sayyids*), accompanied by Sheikh Mizal. All three knelt before Crawford. Mizal at once prostrated himself with his forehead to the ground, and with words of contrition begged forgiveness while the two holy men interceded in his behalf. An Arab is a very proud man, and it was an extraordinary sight to see a sheikh thus humiliate himself before his whole tribe.

Along the open side of the tent, the tribesmen thrust anxiously forward with expectant faces whose contrasting features and highly varied types defied description. Other sheikhs also pled for Mizal, but Crawford was quite unyielding. The sheikh, he said, must ride with him to Kalat es-Sikkar and afterwards stand trial at Nasiriyeh.

The scene continued thus for half an hour. This imperturbable young Englishman, sitting here unarmed in the midst of a wild Arab tribe who outnumbered us fifty to one and could have slaughtered us all in a few minutes, swayed them like a king.

As he concluded the interview by rising and going out to his horse, the whole tribe surged about us. All at once they opened a passage, and five women passed rapidly up to us. They were Mizal's four wives and his mother, who had come to plead for him.

I mounted my horse and rode out of the throng to snap a photograph of the extraordinary scene. As I rode away I found Mizal's mother and one of the wives at my elbow, wailing out appeals for the outlaw. We all rode off rapidly, Crawford looking back at intervals to see if Mizal was following. But his people were evidently advising him not to go, and we saw no more of him.

Another two hours' ride, the last half hour in darkness making the network of canal trenches and embankments treacherous, brought us to the river where after some delay we found Crawford's launch. We had been in the saddle nearly nine hours, had ridden nearly forty miles.

[On March 31 he reached the ruins of ancient Babylon, where a German expedition led by the eminent Professor Robert Koldewey had excavated during the fourteen years preceding the First World War.]

I am sitting on the balcony of Koldewey's deserted house as the sun sets and the evening light settles over the quiet Euphrates, with a bright moon sailing over the palms.

We have had a wonderful afternoon examining the enormously extensive ruins of Babylon. One of the things which interested me most was the bridge-head and the piers of the ancient bridge once connecting Babylon on the east side with the city's suburbs on the west side of the Euphrates. The river has since shifted westward at this point, and its former bed is now so dry that one can trace the scanty remains of the piers in midstream. Though only from the sixth century B.C., it is the oldest known *dated* bridge of which parts still stand.

I spent a morning in the Festival [or Procession] Street—the pavements of this gorgeously adorned street of Nebuchadnezzar's are some thirty feet higher than the floors of the Assyrian buildings which lined it. This is because he raised the palace quarters high above the level of the Assyrian restoration which followed the complete destruction of Babylon by Sennacherib, Emperor of Assyria, who, weary of constant rebellion on the part of vassal Babylon, utterly destroyed the city and turned a canal over the wreckage.

His successors restored the venerable city, and a generation later after the destruction of Nineveh [612 B.C.] and the fall of the Assyrian Empire in 606 B.C., Nebuchadnezzar, the brilliant young king of a revived Babylon, raised his vast palace over the Assyrian restoration of the city, and crowned the whole with the famous "Hanging Gardens." It was all done in the time of the Babylonian captivity of the Hebrews, after Nebuchadnezzar had destroyed Jerusalem in 586 B.C.

I also examined the Ishtar temple where, according to Herodotus, every woman was obliged to sacrifice herself. Wonderfully interesting is a tremendous and massive mound at the extreme northern edge of the city, still called by the modern Arabs, "Bab-il" or "Gate of God," which preserves the venerable name of the ancient city. We do not know what this vast foundation supported, but the natives and uninformed visitors call it the "Tower of Babel."

It was fascinating also to look over the scanty remains of a Greek theater erected by Alexander the Great's successors after his death, which you remember took place in Babylon in 323 B.C. For such ruins mark the extraordinary interfusion of East and West which had already been going on for some time, and culminated in the western spread of Christianity, an oriental religion.

I returned alone through the palms growing in thick groves where once stood the crowded houses of the great city. A native with his son and three donkeys came up behind me and insisted on my mounting his own donkey. We chatted as we rode on through the palms, talking of his crops, of his children and of his little blind daughter.

"Sahib," said he, "we are very glad the Turks are gone, and the English are here. The Turks were very bad. They hanged us, and they cut off our hands if we did not let them steal our crops and our sheep. Oh, yes, Sahib, things are much better now!"

Eyeing my wrist, the little boy said to me, "The Sahib carries *two* watches, one on each wrist!"

He had discovered my wrist compass.

[The expedition reached Baghdad on April 6 where my father was the guest of Major-General Percy Hambro, Quartermaster-General of the British Army in Mesopotamia.]

Hambro is a prince of a man. Though independently wealthy, he has spent 27 years in the Army, and despite serving in France throughout the War, has come out to one of the hottest regions on the globe (to which he cannot bring his wife and children) to help his nation carry a huge new burden of responsibility.

Being deeply interested in antiquity, he gladly joined me in a visit to Ctesiphon, 25 miles down the River, on the same bank of the Tigris as Baghdad. This was the residence city of the New Persian Kings, which they built after their sudden and remarkable rise to power soon after the overthrow of the Parthians in the third century A.D. All that remains standing is a portion of the great White Palace, a marvelous building of burned brick with a vast Throne Room crowned by a gigantic arched roof—the greatest arch in Asia today.

I am a fairly hardened observer of great buildings, but I found this magnificent hall simply overwhelming. One's pygmy figure seemed like some contemptible little insect gazing up at the sky, as one crawled along under this colossal crown of arching brick masonry! Without any wooden centering to support the masonry such as all western builders are always obliged to use, this vast arching roof was flung out over the colossal void as if it floated buoyantly on the atmosphere, till it had been keyed into place and the whole enormous hall had been covered. No other architectural relic of the past, except the great pyramids of Egypt, has filled me with quite the same consciousness of human achievement. . . .

I have come upon very important antiquities among the native dealers in Baghdad—especially a large six-sided baked clay prism, eighteen inches high, bearing the Royal Annals of Sennacherib.* But many obstacles lie in the way of its purchase—the owner's exorbitant price, an export permit from the government, etc.

Later: Hambro has just stepped into my room to tell me that he has invited Gertrude Lowthian Bell to be our guest at dinner this evening— she is an Englishwoman who, like Lady Hester Stanhope, has been out here among the Arabs for some 25 years. He added: "Tell your wife that an English general who knows without being told how the Arch of Ctesiphon was built, says you are looking very well." It is true. Before we went out there, he explained to me his idea of how the vast arch was put up, and he was quite right. He is therefore qualified, I think, to report on the exterior of an archaeologist!

* This historical treasure is now on exhibition in the Oriental Institute Museum at the University of Chicago.

[The meeting with Miss Bell—explorer, administrator, archaeologist and author—began a cordial friendship which ended only with her death in 1926. She was set down as a virulent blue stocking by her enemies, of whom her brilliance, bluntness and almost masculine aggressiveness made a good many. But far truer is the statement that she "was one of the most remarkable women of her time," whose political and diplomatic influence was such that she was frequently referred to as the "unofficial Queen of Mesopotamia." Those who have read *The Letters of Gertrude Bell*, edited by her stepmother, Lady Bell (1927), are aware of the richness of her adventure-filled life.

At this particular time, she was Oriental Secretary to Colonel (later Sir) Arnold T. Wilson, then Civil Commissioner, or tantamount to king of Mesopotamia. To my intense regret I have been unable to find a journal-letter of my father's describing his excursions in company with Miss Bell, Major-General Hambro and General Haldane, then Commander-in-Chief of all the British forces in Mesopotamia, to various archaeological sites in the environs of Baghdad. Her energy was incredible, and she ran her male companions ragged. On one historic occasion when sunset found the party's two cars still far from Baghdad, she sprang on the running board of General Haldane's car and over the Commander-in-Chief's protests, ordered the drivers of both cars to push on at high speed farther out into the Babylonian plain to the tents of a recalcitrant Arab tribe whose sheikh she had befriended, and who was now restrained from molesting these gentlemen of the Army only by his personal loyalty to and trust in this amazing Englishwoman.

She insisted that the party must enter his tents and partake of his proffered tea and cigarettes, the acceptance of which he at once construed as a flattering and deliberately planned gesture of friendship from Great Britain. In the dim glow of a brazier, the sheikh failed to observe that the Commander-in-Chief was all but apoplectic with stifled indignation—and from that day forward he and his tribe became devoted allies of the Empire.

During the last three years of her life, Miss Bell served as Honorary Director of Antiquities in Iraq.]

This morning [April 12] I received my first home letter in nine weeks. It makes an immense difference to me as I take the trail again this afternoon for the trip up the Tigris. I hope you may never be in a situation where letters mean so much. All this is part of the price to be paid for results. My compensation lies in the conviction, right or wrong, that it is service to science—nothing great or brilliant, but the best that I am able to offer, and done at a cost to be measured only by the extreme sensitiveness, loneliness and almost morbid love of home with which I am unfortunately encumbered.

[Late that afternoon, the expedition boarded the new "Mesopotamian Railways" and started for Mosul, near the site of ancient Nineveh on the upper Tigris. The roadbed had been completed only as far as Shergat, something over 180 miles north of Baghdad, which the train took nineteen hours to cover! From the Military Rest Camp at Shergat, my father wrote the following day:]

One could feel the difference in the air as we passed from the dead alluvial flat of the parched Babylonian plain only 100 feet above sea level, to the uplands north of the prehistoric shores of the Persian Gulf. The air now became fresh and invigorating, and the country was clothed in a pale green mantle of succulent steppe grass several inches high. Its dewy morning fragrance recalled to me a thousand old associations.

At intervals we could see the Tigris between us and the eastern highlands, from which a long spur extends northwest, directly across the course of the river. Long ago the latter cut through the northwestern reach of this spur, leaving the elevated tip as an isolated height on the west side of the stream. On the summit of this elevation, the men of Assur some 5000 years ago built their earliest home, a fortified town called Assur, from which the Assyrians took their name. Assur became a kind of Rome of the early orient, from which its warlike people spread until eventually they dominated the whole Near East. It was fascinating to me to see it all for the first time.

The indolent train suddenly swung around a headland and disclosed to us the ruins of this first Assyrian capital.

[The journey from the railhead at Shergat to Mosul, some eighty miles, had to be made by automobile and wagon train over a dreadful road.]

Rest camp below Shergat: My typewriter is mounted on a provision pannier, and I sit writing on a camera trunk while we wait for our convoy.

As I look through the tent door down upon the broad river plain of the Tigris, it vividly reveals to me the sources of material life on which the men of Assur depended for centuries, while they were beginning the development of a great nation on this height commanding the plain. I had no adequate idea of it when I wrote about the place in my *Ancient Times*. It is an indispensable element in history writing to be acquainted by *actual contact* with the lands of which you write.

I have just been watching a long train of 125 wagons, manned entirely by East Indians, deploying from their night's camp and winding slowly away across the plains toward Mosul. Two such trains totaling 250 wagons, constantly moving between Shergat and Mosul, complete the transportation link between Baghdad and Mosul, the northernmost limit of British control on the Tigris.

Beyond Mosul everything is unsafe, for the Arabs here are not as well under control as in Babylonia. A big Rolls-Royce armored car fitted with a machine gun will head our column.

Assur was entirely excavated by the Germans in a twelve years' campaign completed a few months before the [First World] War. It is the only place in this Assyro-Babylonian world which has been wholly cleared, and the Germans have published the results in a series of volumes which are models of what such work should be. The slopes of their great excavation dumps are now grass-grown, but in many places their shafts, tunnels and lateral trenches look as fresh as if made yesterday. I followed the ancient city walls—from whose crevices were growing blood-red anemones, like little red poppies—down the watercourse and along the Tigris waterfront, then climbed up into the city. Here the Germans had cleared and recorded everything down to the native rock, where they found the oldest settlement yet discovered in this northern region—archaic remains reaching back to about 3000 B.C.

All members of this German expedition were given commissions at the outbreak of the War, and served here until the collapse of the Turks. As we descended again from the city walls, we found several hundred unexploded Turkish shells lying beside excavated gun emplacements—part of the ammunition supplies abandoned by the Turks in their final retreat from the place.

From Assur we drove northward about eighty miles up the Tigris to Nineveh, Assyria's later and most splendid capital, just across the river from Mosul.

We soon rose to the breezy and spacious Assyrian uplands, grass-grown and carpeted with far expanses of wild-flowers in every hue of the rainbow. The hills began to show outcroppings of coarse alabaster, or a stone very much like it, which the Assyrians used in finishing and adorning their palaces. This hilly and broken steppe was flanked by ranges of the Persian mountains, rising to 10,000 feet. As we moved northward, we had before us the dim contours of the snow-clad range to the north of Nineveh.

After a four hours' drive over this highly varied and interesting country, we climbed to the crest of a massive ridge from which we suddenly looked down upon Mosul on the west side of the winding Tigris, with the widespread mounds of Nineveh on the opposite shore. Our eyes could follow the lines of the ancient walls, within which lay fields of grain and at one end, the little village of Nebi Yunas ("Prophet Jonah"), perched on the great platform where once stood the palace of Esarhaddon.

In four hours we had driven practically the whole length of ancient Assyria before it was more than a little kingdom stretching for 80 to 100 miles along the Tigris, and we had passed from its earliest to its latest and final capital. The journey had been one continuous demonstration in the economic and historical geography of the early East, and I had learned more in these four hours than I had gained at home from the most intensive study of local topography through maps, photographs, and the descriptions of other travelers.

[From Mosul, where he was the guest of General Cecil Fraser, in command of the region, he wrote on the evening of April 15:]

A wonderful day at Nineveh!

The prospect northward from this high palace area of Sennacherib and Assurbanipal reminds one very much of the view in Lombardy from Turin to the encompassing ranges of the snow-covered Alps. The Persian mountains rise on the north and east, purple and blue in the hazy distance, and above the gaunt *arêtes* [sharp ascending ridges], a procession of gleaming snow peaks marches among great trooping clouds. What a situation for the imperial city of the Assyrian conquerors!

Around me is an endless carpet of daisies under a blazing sun, but across them plays a cool south breeze such as must once have proven as refreshing to Sennacherib among the palms of his terraced palace gardens as it is to us on this very warm day of 1920 A.D.

The vast palace platform must be at least twenty-five acres in extent, and today's waving fields of wheat probably cover almost half of this spacious area. It is perforated with frequent shafts made by the old-time so-called "excavators," when excavation consisted solely of grubbing for museum exhibits. But the whole of great Nineveh awaits systematic and long-continued investigation like that at Assur.

From below the palace platform clear out to the distant walls of the city stretch wide fields of grain and vegetables. This lower area, once covered with dwellings, markets and bazaars, has evidently been cultivated for a long time, doubtless for centuries—perhaps from the days when Xenophon saw the place as a complete ruin two centuries after the fall of the city in 612 B.C.

At sunrise on April 17th we crossed the Tigris once again on the tedious and precarious old ferry, to visit Khorsabad, our last historic site here in the north.

The ferries are large, clumsy, heavily timbered boats open at one end for the entrance of horses, donkeys, and crazy old Turkish coaches comically askew and threatening instant collapse. The old sheikh of the ferry sits at the open shoreward end of the boat, and receives from every entering passenger a fare which varies according to his financial status or momentary inclination. Crowds of shouting orientals all the while swarm up and down the river bank like so many ants, overflowing into the boats and from the boats again inundating the shore—a multitude of lunatics, all shrieking directions, advice, orders, messages to friends, abuse, billingsgate and revilings of your father and your father's father, your mother and your mother's mother—vileness which would cause the speakers' instant arrest in any civilized community, but to which every one here—including crowds of women—listens with the utmost unconcern.

Water carriers are filling their jars or waterskins with the filthy river water, a group of convicts with heavy shackles on their legs come pushing a cart bearing a metal tank which they fill with water for the public offices and then drag up the steep slope, prodded by riflemen following close behind. Higher up the bank is a line of curious earthenware stills, with fires under them, tended by a native who watches the distillation of arrak, a wickedly intoxicating beverage. And beyond stretch the bazaars, where artisans and merchants are selling every known commodity of the East.

Once across the Tigris we turned northeastward on the "road" to Khorsabad—a rock-strewn, almost impassable trail—and by noon had covered the fifteen miles to the tiny modern village now perched on the palace platform of the northernmost residence of the Assyrian King, Sargon II, who came to the throne in 722 B.C.

[Some seventy-odd years ago,] Botta and Place, both of whom were French Consuls at Mosul, excavated this palace platform and took away everything of value. While it seems to have been completely gutted, I learned from the sheikh of the village that the Frenchmen did not excavate the great gates of the city [which was about one mile square]. Just below one of these gates, near the southern corner of the city, I found a large building—which also had not been excavated by Place—and still in position under a few inches of soil, a mighty stone paving block about five by ten feet in size, bearing in stately cuneiform characters the annals of the great King. They are of the greatest importance, for Sargon came to the throne during the Assyrian siege of Samaria, whence he sent the so-called Ten Tribes away as captives. The excavation of these gates alone would bring a fine return in museum monuments—but in the meantime, this particular block will of course be broken up and sold in fragments by the Arabs!

[Torrential rains driven by hurricane blasts and accompanied by "thunder suggesting the spacious mountain wilderness across which it was rolling down upon us from the snowy north," delayed the return to Baghdad. News from the south was ugly: bridges were washed out, the Arabs had undermined the railway at several points and were shooting into the rest camp below Shergat.

Nevertheless on April 20 the expedition left Mosul as part of a convoy of twenty cars which crawled through the deep mire and had to be pushed by man-power across wadis wherever the bridges had been swept away. Repair crews were constantly mending broken wheels and springs. But the wearied convoy finally reached Shergat, a train got through from the south, and the party boarded it for Baghdad whence on April 25th from the house of Major Bowman, Iraq's first Director of Education, my father continued:]

Our plans are suddenly undergoing an altogether unexpected change which promises to fill our return journey with new interest and excitement.

Yesterday General Hambro showed me some sketches of wall paintings just discovered by the British officer [in command of a troop of the Black Watch, General Arthur Wauchope's regiment] stationed at Salihiyah on the upper Euphrates in the course of digging trenches. The Civil Commissioner proposes that I go out to examine these paintings for him, and bring back full records before they suffer damage.

(As the British military frontier moved northward from the Persian Gulf, the country was transferred as fast as practicable to civil authority under a British Governor called the Civil Commissioner, who is momentarily virtually king of this immense Tigris-Euphrates region. The "Political Officers" we have been meeting during our journey are his local representatives.)

Now, Salihiyah is approximately 250 miles upriver, or about half-way to Aleppo! This has suggested the feasibility of our avoiding the long, wearisome journey back as we came via Bombay, by pushing straight on across the desert to Aleppo and the Mediterranean—a saving of almost 5000 miles!

The Political Officer in the Salihiyah region is Lieutenant-Colonel G. E. Leachman, a well-known explorer and student of the Arabs who has been among them for years. His name appears repeatedly on most of the recent maps of North Arabia. He will receive me at some point part way up towards Salihiyah, and let me know as to the possibility of continuing on to Aleppo.

A curious combination of events may perhaps make possible our crossing of the Syrian Desert. Salihiyah is right out in the fighting— the extreme outpost of the British occupation of the Upper Euphrates. When I first proposed a trip up the Euphrates to the military men, they were unwilling to let me go even as far as Anah, far below Salihiyah. But the discovery of the wall paintings and the lucky fact that my arrival happens to coincide with very important negotiations between the British and the Arabs regarding the Anglo-Arab boundary, has induced the authorities to *send* me there!

You may have read in the press that the Arabs had seized Der ez-Zor, the uppermost British post on the Euphrates. The Civil Commissioner revealed to me how this came about: His Majesty's Government in council with Arab representatives in Europe, agreed to give up Der ez-Zor into the custody of the new Arab State—but H.M.G. entirely forgot to notify their own authorities in Mesopotamia of this change! When the Arabs went to take over Der ez-Zor, the British officials, not knowing of the new arrangement, resisted, and were captured and imprisoned.

The Civil Commissioner then added: "In strictest confidence, let me explain the exact situation on the Euphrates: No one but the Commander-in-Chief—not even General Hambro—knows that I am about to evacuate Salihiyah, and even Anah, and turn them over to the Arabs. These places are both so far from our bases that it is better to hand them back to the Arabs.

"While you are in Salihiyah, Maulud Pasha, the Arab Governor of Der ez-Zor, will be holding a conference with Colonel Leachman to arrange this transfer. The Arabs will be on their good behavior. If Leachman suggests that they show their good will by furnishing safe conduct to an American party as far as Aleppo, it is highly probable that Maulud will cordially agree to do so. There is some risk, but it is a very favorable opportunity. Only, you must not delay!"

When I saw General Hambro about transport, it was very awkward to be unable to explain to him why the overland trip to Aleppo might be feasible!

Syria is supposed to be absolutely cut off from Baghdad by hundreds of miles of hostile country. When we first reached Iraq, via India, no one dreamed that it would be possible to return to the Mediterranean overland. We are putting our heads in the lion's mouth, but I am taking every precaution. I shall go beyond Salihiyah only if Colonel Leachman advises me to do so. General Haldane thinks we shall get through all right—he and Miss Bell hope we shall return soon to undertake excavation, for which they promise every possible help.

The Arab Governor of Aleppo, Nadji Beg Suwedi, is a native of Baghdad, where his wealthy and aristocratic old father still lives. I called on the old gentleman and mentioned casually our imminent overland journey to Aleppo. He said at once, "I will give you a letter to my son!"

Meanwhile the purchase of some of the most valuable ancient historical records ever to have been brought to America, awaits reply to a cable I sent to President Judson a fortnight ago. I asked for $50,000 more!—a piece of effrontery for which he may blame me. But we must have this amount if we are to take advantage of an extraordinary opportunity.

Good-bye, my dear ones! I know you trust me to see my duty and to meet it faithfully. God bless you all! Should anything happen to us in the desert, I shall be thinking only of you.

[On April 28, with the sun rising behind them, a string of seven dusty Model "T" Ford vans chugged westward out of Baghdad, crossed the Euphrates on a bridge of boats above Fallujah, and headed northwest.]

Toward sunset of the second day, all traces of the road disappeared —we had lost the trail, and before us stretched the endless desert. The last gleam of sun faded into twilight which was suddenly transformed into moonlight and across the level river flats we saw Bedouin camp-fires. We avoided them, but invisible eyes were doubtless watching us as the cars drew up for the night in a circle wherein we set up our field beds. Each of us stood watch for an hour and thirty-six minutes; and a little before 5 A.M., we were up and away again.

[On the night of April 30, he wrote:] With the automobiles around me, I sit again in misty moonlight, looking down across a half-mile of desert to the Euphrates, the murmur of whose full flood I can faintly hear. The others are all asleep, and I am keeping the first watch of two hours. I write by the light of a carefully masked globe candle, and every fifteen minutes make the round of the camp with my gun in one hand, a shillalah in the other.

This afternoon one of the Indian drivers stalled his engine on a short hill, let his car run back out of control, smashed a rear wheel. After two hours' hard work no one could remove the old wheel. So we abandoned this van, carefully dividing its load among the six remaining, already overloaded cars.

Because we were paralleling the Euphrates, we were obliged to cross all the ancient drainage channels flowing into the river. We plunged into wadi after wadi, only to climb painfully up the other side over rough and jagged rocks.

Suddenly with an ominous grinding sound another car stopped, and the driver reported trouble in the differential. Meanwhile against orders, three of the drivers had pushed on ahead and disappeared over the top of a desolate ridge on the distant northern horizon. It was an hour before we could signal them to turn back again—the infidels would have carried away all our food and bedding, and left us in the desert!

They were ugly and sullen as they drove up. One of them who had been offensive before, not only came back at a pace which sent his load skyward at every bump, but as he angrily rejoined us he collided seriously with one of the other cars. I stepped over to him, drew back and gave him a first-class smash in the jaw. His reactions were numerous and audible, but thereafter his behavior improved. I warned the others that any who might be similarly inclined, would go into the guardhouse at the next post if they didn't cease their deviltry, and they all promptly quieted down.

As I jiggle away at my journal by the light of a masked camp candle, I hear voices faintly from the trail just beyond a great cliff: a caravan is passing, trying to avoid the Arabs by moving at night.

[From dawn till dark the little string of Ford vans clattered on, through dust storms, across desolate, roadless terrain, again along good military roads, until they drew up at Anah,] a beautiful, palm-shaded village straggling nearly five miles along the Euphrates, filling the narrow strip between the cliffs of the desert plateau and the river below. Most of the houses had been wrecked by the explosion of a huge ammunition dump placed here by the Turks and blown up by the British after their capture of the place. The ground was littered with large-caliber shells—a number of over-curious Arabs who had tinkered with them had been abruptly gathered unto their fore-fathers!

At Anah we joined a convoy of 34 vans for the trek to Abu Kamal, one of the last British strongholds here in the northwest. There were many rumors of trouble with the Arabs, and as we swung our machines into line, the Colonel in command greeted me cordially, told me to keep constantly with the big convoy: their *shabanas* [police escort] had been fired on the day before from across the river. The Arabs of this region happen to be excellent marksmen.

Leachman greeted the convoy at Abu Kamal, took us at once to the Military Headquarters where we were welcomed by the Commanding Officer, General Cunningham, who had recently beaten the Arabs here in a first-class battle. For lack of accommodations anywhere, Leachman made us set up our field beds in his own office.

Next morning the General asked me to drive with him the twenty-seven miles upriver to Salihiyah to see the newly discovered paintings in which he was greatly interested. A rifleman sat beside the driver. Our road crossed the scene of the recent fighting, and the General pointed out to me on the surrounding high cliffs the positions of the British guns which had decimated the Arabs.

This vivid picture of current imperial history was still in my mind as we drove into the ruins of Salihiyah—ancient Doura—a tremendous stronghold of the late Roman Empire on the Euphrates—in the midst of which were now pitched the tents of British East Indian troops.

A body of these troops under a sergeant was placed at my disposal and everything was made ready so that we could devote the entire following day—May 4th, the last day before the British withdrawal from this region—to clearing and recording a group of wall paintings which was to prove of the utmost importance in the history of Byzantine art.

This morning [May 4] at Abu Kamal we bade our British friends good-bye, and moved on to Salihiyah where we dismissed our faithful British Army Ford vans. Drawn up beside our camp were five *arabanahs* (springless native wagons)—three for our baggage, and two for ourselves—which I have engaged to carry us from Salihiyah to Aleppo.

Leachman gave us a native police escort which will accompany us tomorrow for about ten miles to the last British frontier guard post. Turki Beg (or Bey), a border friend of the British, will send some horsemen to meet us at this point and conduct us upriver until we are joined by another contingent of horsemen from Meyyadin, the first border post in the Arab State, who will take us on to Der ez-Zor.

We immediately set to work on the paintings. The one originally found by a British officer was on a high wall, and depicted in many colors a life size group of eleven people reverently absorbed in worship. With our East Indian troops we now excavated further, and found some additional paintings. Although they are in a sanctuary which has every appearance of being Christian, they do not contain a single unmistakable Christian feature. One of those we uncovered shows a Roman officer standing before an altar with fire burning upon it, and conducting worship for a group of Roman legionaries behind him. His name and title have been inserted by the artist in Roman letters before his figure, thus:

IUL. TER.

ENTIUS. TRIB.

If I had a glossary of the thousands of Roman officials now known, it is possible I could find this Julius Terence, Tribune, and thus date the building at once. It must have been built either just before the official recognition of Christianity by the Roman State under Constantine, or during the reversion to the pagan gods under Julian. For the above group of people are standing before three statues of oriental gods and two figures of goddesses of fortune whose names are written in Greek alongside their figures. This scene of Roman legionaries at worship is the easternmost representation of Roman troops thus far discovered.

The huge fortress with its surrounding ancient city—whose name, Doura, I found in a Greek inscription in one of the paintings—was part of the Eastern Roman Empire in the third or fourth centuries of the Christian era. The sanctuary was visited by many people, and the painted walls are covered with scribblings, scratched in chiefly by Greek visitors in ancient days. I regretted that there was no time to copy all these—but they were in a rapid, cursive hand, very difficult to read. While my colleague Luckenbill took photographs, the younger men made a ground plan of the place, and I spent the day in making as full notes as possible on the paintings and inscriptions.

When we had finished, I suggested to the young British Officer commanding the Indian troops, the wisdom of covering the wall paintings with rubbish again, to protect them from destruction by the Arabs. He at once gave orders that this be done, and before the British withdrew, everything was again safely buried.

[Later study of the extraordinary paintings at Salihiyah, or Doura-Europos, as the Romans apparently called it, showed them to be "the first of the oriental ancestry of Byzantine painting as yet found in the Near East," the direct antecedents of such Byzantine mosaics as those in the Church of San Vitale at Ravenna in northern Italy. When Syria became a French Mandate, Salihiyah came under the jurisdiction of France, whose Académie des Inscriptions et Belles-Lettres, in association with his old friend Professor Franz Cumont, the great historian of religion, shortly afterwards asked my father to collaborate with them in excavating the place. But the Oriental Institute was then not yet equipped to undertake such operations, and he declined the offer in favor of Yale University, which sent out an expedition headed by Professor Mikhail Ivanovich Rostovtsev. Unfortunately before these arrangements materialized tragedy befell the paintings: heavy rains settled the debris with which they had been re-covered, until the heads of an entire row of eight figures were exposed, and "strolling Arabs, practicing the barbarous iconoclasm which they regard as prescribed by the Koran, smashed and disfigured all these faces. The only record of them in any state of completeness remained in Luckenbill's photographs and my notes!"]

As I was working away at the walls, with the wind whirling dust and filth all over me, a young British officer suddenly appeared and handed me an envelope, saying, "A wire from below for you, Professor!"

The sun was just setting, and tipping with golden light the tents of the outermost forces of the greatest of modern empires in a stronghold of the greatest of ancient empires.

I opened the message. It was a cable from Chicago, relayed from Cairo via Bombay to Basra, telegraphed to Abu Kamal, telephoned by the Army to Salihiyah, and finally handed to me in this ancient Roman fortress on the edge of the ancient world. It read: "President Judson cables quote you may draw immediately for twenty five thousand dollars unquote."

That was pretty heart-warming news, after a day's grubbing in the dirt and grime for a few details in the long story of this great Eastern world!

I wish President Judson could know the benedictions I call down upon him tonight, as I sit at my little typewriter beside my camp bed, while the full moon pushing up the eastern sky sheds a wonderful light over this grand old Roman stronghold.

[On the evening of May 5 from Meyyadin on the Upper Euphrates, he continued:] This morning at dawn our little train of five *arabanahs* wound slowly out of the old Roman fort and bore due west into the No-Man's-Land between the British Empire and the new Arab State. Just as we were pulling out, Turki Beg's five riflemen joined us in accordance with Leachman's request, to guard us until we had been taken over by the Arabs. When our road dropped down from the high plateau to the level of the river plain, we stopped to fill our drinking water tank, which was still half-full of chlorinated water—we trusted that this would disinfect the river water!

An hour later a motor car overtook us, followed by a Light Armored Motor Battery machine, commonly called a "Lamb" after the initials of the organization. It was Leachman and a fellow officer going out into No-Man's-Land to meet the Arab representatives headed by Maulud Pasha, Governor of Der ez-Zor (to whom Leachman had given me a letter), to arrange for the British withdrawal from nearly a hundred miles of Euphrates country to the vicinity of Anah. There was but one time for our adventure, and that was *today*: we were at the critical spot at the exact moment when the negotiations were being carried on.

Leachman had advised me from the outset to fly an American flag on our wagons. At Meyyadin we drew up in a *khan* [quadrangular inn or shelter for caravans], and were at once surrounded by a crowd of natives. One of them proudly took our flag and held it aloft on its crude staff while a police officer led the way to a house where a room had been prepared for us. Here I immediately hung the flag from our window, for now we were truly in the hands of the Arabs, with Leachman miles to the rear.

[Less than three weeks later, Lt.-Col. Leachman was murdered by the Arabs in the desert outside Fallujah, near the spot where the expedition had spent its first night after leaving Baghdad.]

I had hardly hung out the flag when one of the soldiers appeared on the roof outside our door. My servant Ali whispered to me that he had come to receive his baksheesh for accompanying us. As I had surmised, our so-called protection would have to be purchased. I asked the soldier if he and his companions were accompanying us tomorrow. He replied that they were to take us to Der ez-Zor. So I gave him three rupees for himself and two for each of his men. That was about $5 for one day's safe conduct by the Arab State. We shall pay at least that for the next ten days, all the way to Aleppo!

My companions on this expedition are all such fine fellows that I feel almost ungrateful for craving an occasional snatch of peace and privacy. There is never a moment's quiet, for of course the party is incessantly around me—and when I am not doing something for them, or making their arrangements, the natives besiege me. For instance, the drivers have just come up to demand money: I gave them 250 rupees, they went off to the bazaar. But rupees are not accepted here in Meyyadin. So during another half-hour of oriental palaver I had to compute in Turkish gold the amount due them, and send them off a second time.

I much need a bath, but as the only available water has to be brought a very long way from the Euphrates, this luxury must be indefinitely postponed. I can only hope for enough filthy water in which to shave before we "dine" on our first hot meal today, which Ali is now cooking over a wood fire.

We had no sooner tumbled into our field beds, dead for sleep, than the soldier who had brought us to these lodgings, knocked at the door and announced that his chief, the Arab army officer in command of Meyyadin, was waiting below and desired to pay his respects. I longed to take the wish for the deed, but of course invited him to come up.

He was a pleasant fellow who presented me with a picture post-card displaying Haroun al-Rashid receiving the ambassadors of Charlemagne, showed me his commission with his photograph on it, gave me his card bearing the name of Ahmed Nadji, followed by a number of titles in Arabic. I was appropriately edified by all these exhibits. He said he had telephoned (God save the mark!) to his chief, Maulud Pasha at Der ez-Zor, who would be ready to receive us. He apologized profusely for the plain accommodations given us, said it was absolutely all they had, and laughingly referred to the great hotels in America about which he had somehow heard. I asked him a few searching questions about his country's problems, which he answered intelligently and with un-oriental brevity. He had the good sense to observe that our eyelids were leaden with sleep, and saying we must be tired, gave us a friendly goodnight.

In any Arab town the night from twilight till dawn is one unbroken pandemonium from legions of barking, yapping, howling dogs. They run the gamut from high-pitched, staccato yelps or minor whines, down through every note to the deep booming and re-echoing raucous basso of a thousand empty wine vats being pounded in a cooper's yard. The noise rolls over the town in frantic waves as one group of savagely barking mongrels answers another, and if the bedlam dies down for an instant, it quickly breaks out again. A large cat began to forage among our provisions, and a soldier searching for one of his fellows began hammering at the door of our house, shouting to wake the dead. Sleep became a pearl of great price.

At dawn there was a clatter of horsemen in the street below. A body of cavalry with several field guns were on their way to take possession of the territory newly evacuated by the British. Our friend Ahmed Nadji of the evening before was at their head. He looked up, and seeing me at the window, waved his hand and shouted good-bye— in English!

As we rode out of Meyyadin, there was only one horseman accompanying us—one rifle instead of the five who rode with us yesterday! And this single symbol of protection promptly relinquished his horse to our servants, climbed into one of our wagons, and was soon rapturously snoring on top of our bed bags, with his rifle stowed away below!

But near Der ez-Zor a troop of armed horsemen joined us, and we made quite a procession as we drove through the marketplace. Swarms of children ran alongside, and curious townsmen thrust their heads out of the bazaars and fairly into our wagons, as they examined us and our outfit.

We drove to the *serail,* where an Arab officer took my letter from

Leachman to Maulud Pasha, and then, with half the town accompanying us, led us to the "hotel," which was nothing more than an ordinary
khan with shopworn urban trimmings.

I had hardly entered my comical little room when Ali appeared at
the door, looking ridiculously doleful: some Arab ruffians had waylaid
him, and finding no money on his person, had playfully stolen his cap
and breeches! Would I by the grace of Allah give him forty rupees to
replenish his wardrobe at the bazaar? I ran through my accounts,
found I owed him more than this, gave him his forty rupees; and with
a grateful smile he hurried away to re-clothe his extremities.

I had just sat down again to my typewriter when an orderly
appeared with an invitation to dine with the Pasha. I conveyed my
acceptance in Arabic properly garlanded with the flowery compliments so dear to orientals, and was again reverting to my typewriter
when two soldiers brought in a fine-looking, richly clad old sheikh,
wearing a huge silver-hilted sword. The sheikh desired to furnish us
with a guard to Aleppo. I asked him if he came from Maulud Pasha,
and the soldiers answered that he did not. I explained to him that I
must see the Pasha before I could make any such agreement, whereupon the sheikh stalked out, very angry.

This of course started one's imagination: Where did the old villain
live, and would he be on the road waiting for us? But I could not risk
offending the Pasha by employing a guard furnished by some one else,
and thus slighting this figment of an Arab State!

And so as a matter of important etiquette, I first called on Maulud
Pasha. He was at his desk in the *serail*—a young, fine-faced Arab clad
in desert attire which appeared incongruous behind an office desk.

A number of natives waiting on divans watched us curiously, lis-
tened attentively to our greetings and my story, and especially to the
Pasha's long oration in the finest Arabic, on the state of the new Arab
Kingdom and the difficulties confronting it.

I asked the Pasha whether it was proper for me to call on Nadji
Beg Suwedi and discuss with him our journey to Aleppo. He replied:
"Most certainly! Nadji Beg is probably himself returning to Aleppo
tomorrow morning, and would be glad if you would accompany him.
Besides, I shall send some of my own soldiers with you."

Then the Pasha sent a messenger for Nadji Beg, who promptly
appeared, expressed great pleasure at receiving the letter from his
father in Baghdad, graciously confirmed what the Pasha had said,

adding only some apprehension lest our wagons should be unable to keep pace with him: he expected to make the trip to Aleppo in four days.

The news (which I had given out with Leachman's permission) that the British were withdrawing nearly a hundred miles southward, raced from lip to lip among the populace of Der ez-Zor, until we were looked upon as almost its official bearers. When I returned to our lodgings, I found Arab sheikhs, Army officers, Government officials —young men and old men of every description—all waiting to discuss with me the political future of the Arabs, and the destiny of the new Kingdom of Syria. With childlike eagerness they sought information regarding the intentions of the British, toward whom they bore a growing resentment and mistrust.

I plied them with questions in Arabic, French and English, and soon found myself favored with a hundred conflicting confidences concerning the domestic and international ambitions of the Arabs, and immersed in the infinite complexities of Near Eastern politics. The air of my room was solid with smoke and heavy with the musky odor of oriental bodies and the tobacco-and-coffee reek of guttural throats. The one invariable *leit-motif* throughout their confusion and uncertainty was always their hope of assistance from America, and their complete confidence in our ability to help them.

At dinner with Maulud Pasha, attended by his officers and staff, I listened again to endless protestations of admiration and affection for America where they begged me upon my return to intercede in their behalf.

I tried as best I could to explain to them America's own difficulties, but failed to make any impression upon them whatever. We were so tremendously powerful, we had such unlimited wealth, ours was the land of liberty and human rights, where all men were treated justly and fairly: surely we could secure—or help to secure—the same things for the Arabs who had so long endured despotism.

Maulud Pasha had been the first Arab officer to go out with Lawrence, and while he expressed appreciation of the latter's services and of the fine qualities of the English, he said quietly that just as the English necessarily serve their own state and people, so he must likewise serve his. As the evening progressed, the Pasha and his guests became increasingly frank. I confess I was greatly surprised at their expressions of deep-seated resentment toward the British, and of unconquerable determination not to permit their domination. They told me the detailed personal histories of Feisal, so recently proclaimed King of Syria; of his father, the King of the Hejaz; and of his brother Abdullah, whose proclamation as King of Iraq had been immediately disallowed by the British.

The Pasha was pale, and his refined spiritual features showed suffering. On my noting that he ate scarcely anything, he confessed that he had just been through a long sickness and was only that day out of his bed. I took my leave of him with sincere regret and with a curious feeling of anxiety at the importance which he evidently attached to our visit.

Because our safety would be guaranteed all the way to Aleppo by Nadji Beg's presence, I was eager to join him promptly on the road as we had agreed. So I roused our party at 3:45 A.M. But the scoundrelly drivers had made a night of it in the town, came staggering in at 6:00, mounted their boxes and went immediately to sleep. We crawled along at two and a half miles an hour, and Nadji Beg completely outdistanced us.

Toward noon we passed the tents of a large tribe of Bedouins known as the Al bu Sarai, whose sheikh, Ramadhan Beg Ibn Shallash, sent out a messenger urging us to join him for coffee. At this time I knew only enough about Sheikh Ramadhan to make me suspect it would be wise to accept his invitation.

The sheikh's entire story was later given me by General Waters-Taylor, Chief Intelligence Officer of the British Imperial Staff in the Near East. Ramadhan was an officer in Lawrence's army, and during his active service there had suffered a facial disfigurement (a part of his nose was shot away) which made him flatly decline to be photographed. After the Armistice, Feisal gave him large sums of money to carry on propaganda on his behalf in the North among the Kurds and the Turks. It was then discovered that Ramadhan was carrying on propaganda in the interests of Mustapha Kamal, the renegade Turk who is head of the rebellious Young Turk Party in Asia Minor and is leading a powerful army there. Thereupon Feisal recalled Sheikh Ramadhan and afterwards made him Governor of Der ez-Zor, where he led the Arab seizure of that place, including the imprisonment of the British officers, of which I wrote from Baghdad.

The sheikh gave us a cordial welcome at his big, black *madhif* [guest tent], and asked warmly after our welfare and that of America. "For we Arabs all love America," said he, "and without America, the English and the French could not have won the War."

"Well," I said, "the War is over now!"

The sheikh looked at me shrewdly, and said, "Between the Arabs and the English?"

Thereupon there was a loud murmur of approval from the old men and from a score of wild looking Arab riflemen who sat around the big *madhif*. We chatted most amicably, the sheikh assuring me again and again that the Arabs loved America. His words were comforting as I looked about me and realized that we were alone in this Arab wilderness, without a soul who could have raised a finger to help us. He and his tribe all spoke approvingly of our American flag, the first they had ever seen.

When coffee had been passed around twice, I suggested that we be allowed to take a picture of the assembled Arabs. They all assented with evident pleasure, for the Arabs love to be photographed. But because of his disfigurement, the sheikh himself refused to be included.

As we crowded back into the tent, a huge Arab raised a massive tent-pin mallet over my head. For an instant I thought we were in trouble, but the Arab explained that "*that* was what he would do if I were an Englishman!" He smote the ground several times with all his strength, repeating that *that* was how he would treat the English if he had the chance!

As I thanked the sheikh for his hospitality and took my leave, he informed me he had an important letter he wished to send to "a newspaper in Aleppo," and that he knew he could trust an American to deliver it. I assured him he could. One of his servants fetched the letter, which the sheikh handed over to me, and all the Arabs stood watching me in silence as I laid it carefully in my wallet. Only much later, when I learned that Ramadhan had again been flirting with Mustapha Kamal's Turks (this time apparently in the interests of the French), did I understand his not having used Nadji Beg, an official of Feisal's government, to carry his letter to Aleppo.

Then the sheikh accompanied us to the *arabanahs*, and ordered one of his riflemen to accompany us to the next *khan*.

[From a *khan* in a village called Kishlak Sabkha on the Upper Euphrates, he wrote on the evening of May 8:]

Despite my best efforts, we have been unable to catch up with Nadji Beg who at the end of each day has always been just one *khan* ahead of us. We have been making over four and a half miles an hour, and are now about 130 miles from Aleppo and something over 400 from Baghdad, which we left ten days ago. By getting up at three in the morning and contenting ourselves with cold food all day, we should reach Aleppo in three days from this point. These pre-War Turkish springless wagons are made for orientals, sitting as they are accustomed to sit, cross-legged on the floor. The owner furnishes a few rugs and cushions, and by adding some of your own bedding you can lie down and make yourself reasonably comfortable. But the rough road keeps knocking you violently about, a pretty wearisome business when kept up day after day from 3 or 4 o'clock in the morning till evening!

As I was writing the foregoing words, the aged sheikh of the Sabkha Arabs named Suwan, came in with a note left this morning by Nadji Beg, asking us to take the old fellow along—I suppose for our protection. He is an intelligent old chap, and shares the prevailing Arab affection for America.

At five this morning, when we had already been up for an hour, old Sheikh Suwan appeared at my door. We *had* to find a place for him in one of our passenger wagons, for to put him in a baggage wagon would mortally have offended all the Arabs of his tribe, who gathered to bid him farewell! We had no choice but to put him in the same wagon with Luckenbill and myself.

The old chap of course sat cross-legged, and soon began to spill about promiscuously, gradually spreading over the whole wagon. When his knees were not in my ribs he was sitting in my lap, or on my typewriter, or in the lunch basket. It is amusing enough in retrospect, but toward the end of twelve actual hot, dusty, flea-ridden hours it loses its humorous aspect!

A few miles outside of Sabkha we passed a large group of Bedouin tents a hundred rods from the highway.

"My tents!" said Sheikh Suwan. "Come in and have something to eat!" But the other wagons were already far ahead, and I declined.

A handsome boy whom the sheikh introduced as his nephew, now appeared running beside our *arabanah*, and told me with great glee that he too was going to Haleb (Aleppo) with us and his uncle. This was protection with a vengeance!

An hour later at a group of huts which the sheikh called Mazar, we stopped to feed and water the horses. Here, he said, his territory ended.

A fine looking Arab splendidly attired, carrying a new Mauser rifle and mounted on an excellent horse, suddenly rode up and was introduced by the sheikh as his son, Rakaan Ibn Suwan. "He has come riding after you," said Suwan senior, "to see you safely out of our lands, and to wish you safety and health!"

Rakaan greeted us cordially with the same gestures and expressions of amity toward America to which we have grown so accustomed: the Arabs hold up one first finger with the thumb turned in toward the palm, and then doing the same with the other hand, they lay the two first fingers together, and say: "Thus are the Americans side by side as brothers."

He asked me why no *American* rifles had ever appeared in Arabia, although the Americans do everything by machinery. Thereupon I unlimbered my typewriter, and while a crowd of curious Arabs gathered about, I typed the name "Rakaan" on a leaf torn from my notebook, and gave it to him. He said at once, I must also write my own name with his, which of course I did. He was profoundly interested to know that the Americans wrote in this way, and he put the sheet carefully away in his mantle. They were still more astonished when I told them there were houses in America with fifty windows, one above the other! Many were the grunts and the "By Allahs," which greeted this information. Rakaan assured me that if any Americans ever came that way again, he would be wholly at their service. He kissed his father's hand and laid it against his forehead, and with many an "In Peace" and "In the safety of Allah!" we left him, gazing after us.

I am now much amused at my apprehensions before we entered Arab-ruled territory. An Englishman would be in the gravest danger here, a Frenchman more so. But Americans may now travel where they like in Arabia, for the Arabs know we are not looking for some advantage out of them. Everywhere they utter the same sentiments: "We Arabs love the Americans, we would like to live with them like brothers. We hope they will come here to help us." The one thing that might befall us would be robbery by highwaymen—but I can recall such occurrences even in America!

I have seen no Bedouin tents on the plateau we are now traversing. It is only the beginning of May, and the winter rains have just ceased, but the ground is parched and dusty, the grass withered and brown, and all the Bedouins are down on the river plain of the Euphrates. The color of the soil in the river valley is exactly like that of the desert plateau—a dusty, faded terracotta, the color of the Missouri River at flood-time. Thus far I have not seen a single square foot of *black* soil anywhere in Western Asia. There is no contrast as in Egypt, between the tawny desert and the rich black loam of the flood plains. Even the richest and most productive soil is of this same light color, which Americans would at once misjudge as very poor and clayey.

As I write [in the *khan* at El Hammam on the Upper Euphrates, late in the afternoon of May 9], we are preparing to spend the night in a filthy hole beside which a pigsty would be palatial! Nothing I have ever seen approaches it—our life in the Sudan was luxury and cleanliness compared with it. An English report on the Baghdad-Aleppo route, made before the War, says of this place: "Bad *khan*, 1908." I shall not go into details, but would like to add: "Worse, 1920!"

The *khan* is entirely full, and old Sheikh Suwan will have to sleep on the floor beside me. He has just wandered in, and would have wrecked my field bed completely had I not tactfully enthroned him on a duffle bag, where he is contemplating my typewriter with much curiosity. His nephew sits at my other elbow. My only privacy is derived from their ignorance of English.

[From the *khan* at Nahr ed-Dahab on the afternoon of May 11, he continued:] Yesterday I got everybody out at 3:00 A.M., and the caravan off at 5:00 for a stage of forty-five miles, the longest we have yet made in a single day.

This carried us from El Hammam to Meskeneh, where the Euphrates begins to swing eastward toward the Persian Gulf. From Meskeneh we rose to the Syrian upland, and as the river and the road parted company, we looked back for the last time on the Euphrates. We had entered the Mediterranean East: a new chapter in our experience and exploration was about to begin.

We thought we had struck the worst of all habitations at El Hammam, but this *khan* of Nahr ed-Dahab which means "golden river"!) sets a new "low."

The only second-floor room in this hole is already occupied. We are down among the horses and their attendant mess. The rustic flavor would be bearable but for a swirling wind which picks up all the dried horse droppings in the *khan* and with fiendish accuracy deposits them on ourselves and our belongings. My field bed is already deluged, my bag is full. A delicious touch was added to this bouquet of flavors and aromas when the drivers thoughtfully set a leaky petroleum tin on top of my bed-roll.

Especially effective and penetrating is the smudge from the burning dung, the only available fuel. The disconsolate Ali has just carried a huge tray of it past my door. Our dinner is being cooked *over* it, and thanks to the wind, quantities are being cooked *in* it as well. To add to our domestic comforts, swarms of crickets infest the place and enormous black beetles as large as silver dollars come droning in and plop down alongside our camp light like so many flying toads.

You can form no conception of the filth of these people. Our drivers sit in the dung heap around the *khan* court. Here they eat with the greatest enjoyment. They drink out of buckets in which they have just watered the horses. They use the same buckets for washing down the sweat-begrimed animals, omitting no part of their anatomy. Then they swab off the beasts with their own bandana handkerchiefs which they afterwards spread out on the horses' backs to dry.

They sit at dinner and sleep all night—stretched out on the horse droppings in the yard—on the same cushions and rugs upon which we ride all day in the *arabanahs*. We are simply alive with fleas, and existence is one long scratch. You incessantly feel them crawling all over you, and resign yourself to misery as best you can.

But all this is a minor incidental to exploring in Western Asia. Tonight in this execrable den of filth (which we have christened "The Golden River Hotel"), we are only twenty-five miles from Aleppo!

Later: The drivers were so anxious to reach the end of our journey that they woke Ali soon after 1:00 o'clock [the following morning, May 12] and he called Luckenbill and me to tea at 2 A.M. I not only heard our escort of soldiers tramping about overhead but *felt* them— for with every step they shook down a shower of filth and vermin from the blackened ceiling above my bed. We were so glad to be leaving this foul den that we quite forgot the difference of an hour and a half in time between Baghdad and Aleppo—we were actually getting up at about 12:30 A.M.!

When I stepped out into the court of the *khan,* all the other wagons were gone. The stars twinkled with marvelous brightness. A half-moon hanging just above the western horizon threw a ghostly light over the huge court, and our wagons made long, broken shadows across the litter and filth of this desolate caravanserai. All at once the place was beautiful, and the spirit of the never-changing East seemed to brood over the long arcaded court of this station through which the life of the orient had so long ebbed and flowed.

A ruddy light came through a door by the main entrance, and as I stood in the silence of the night listening to the munching of the horses, the low sound of voices reached me faintly. Our drivers were sitting inside, earnestly talking with the *khanji* (the keeper of the *khan*). The scene was like some old Dutch painting of the kitchen of a wayside inn, with the coachmen gossiping with the landlord. The candlelight behind them brought out in illumined silhouette the weather-beaten, glistening features of their rugged faces enveloped in the smoke of cigarettes at which they puffed almost rhythmically.

I walked through the great gate of the *khan* and looked down across the silent Syrian Desert touched here and there by the fading moonlight. Beyond lay civilization and home, and behind me, the great Arab wilderness of the Tigris and Euphrates through which we had come. In a few hours we should be safely through this adventure—in a few weeks I could embark for home!

Over there in the dark wagons was a trunk filled with nearly a thousand old Babylonian and Assyrian documents of the greatest value—some wonderfully cut cylinder seals, some sculptures, and a bronze statuette from the archaic Babylonian age of which only a few exist. Better still, in another trunk beside my cot in the terrible room which I had just left, was a six-sided terra-cotta prism eighteen inches high, bearing in fine cuneiform the royal annals of Sennacherib. It reports among all his other achievements the campaign against Jerusalem which called forth the greatest oration of Isaiah—the campaign in which he lost a large part of his army through a terrible plague, rendered classic in English literature by Byron's poem, *The Destruction of Sennacherib*. This piece alone costs 19,000 rupees, nearly $9500, but there is nothing like it in any museum in America.

As I stood there in the moonlight, I forgot the years of struggle to bring about this venture, the hardships of our journey, the filth of this oriental *khan*. I was suddenly filled with renewed courage, with confidence in the future, and with gratitude that we had been able to secure these historical treasures for America, and for our own university.

[That afternoon the rickety wagons trundled into Aleppo, whence he wrote:] It would be impossible to convey my feeling of deliverance as I entered our hotel and ordered a *bath!* From head to foot I am one mass of red blotches—but I believe that actually I am now no longer entertaining a single flea.

We have come almost 600 miles from the northern reaches of Babylonia, up the Euphrates valley to the heart of Syria. We are the first non-Moslems to have crossed this Arab State since it was proclaimed.

[He at once cabled to America news of the party's safe arrival. The French authorities, sensing a reflection upon their ability to control this region, completely censored the messages which were never received. But the single innocent word, "Greetings," telegraphed to General Hambro in Baghdad, went unintercepted and elicited from him the prompt reply, "Elhamdulillah," the Arabic for "Praise to Allah!"

He omitted from his journal that he reached Aleppo with a raging fever and so seriously ill he could hardly muster strength to deliver Sheikh Ramadhan's letter, and find the American consul, a Mr. Jackson, who immediately summoned the best available medical attention. He recovered sufficiently to continue the journey, but the malady—which not even the Rockefeller Institute for Medical Research was able to identify—afflicted him intermittently for years. Long afterwards it was discovered that he had acquired, probably somewhere along the strenuous trek from Cairo to Aleppo, a rare dysentery amoeba.]

Mr. Jackson gave us the first news of the mandates here in the Near East: Mesopotamia to Great Britain, without condition; Palestine to Great Britain on condition that there shall be room for a Jewish State; Syria to France; and Armenia to the United States. I would consider it dangerously unwise for the United States to assume the responsibility for the defense and maintenance of Armenia.

The Turkish border is only seventeen miles north of us. I am eager to examine the ruins of ancient Antioch [east of Aleppo] and Mr. Jackson tells me that by putting us in charge of an old native friend, a bandit who lives in Aleppo and controls all the country between here and the Gulf of Alexandretta, he could get us "safe conduct"! One of the most important places I came to see in western Asia is ancient Carchemish,* about seventy miles N.E. of Aleppo on the Euphrates, just above the point where we had to leave the river. But all this region is entirely out of the control of the Arab government.

News has come this morning that a French force of 3500 men sent to relieve a besieged French garrison at Aintab, just north of the

* Before the First World War, T. E. Lawrence served as a young archaeologist on the staff of a British expedition which excavated Carchemish under the directorship of D. G. Hogarth.

Turkish border, has been beaten back. Two young Americans doing relief work there were shot down on the highway, and twenty more Americans are without food, protection or way of escape. To embarrass the French the Arabs will if possible cut the railroad south of Aleppo (they have just cut the line connecting Damascus and Haifa, on the coast by Carmel).

Under these conditions I consider it my duty to get our little expedition as quickly as possible out of this war zone. I have asked Nadji Beg Suwedi to give us safe conduct by railroad southward to the great mound of Kadesh on the Orontes, just south of Homs; thence to Baalbek and near-by Rayak, whence a little cogwheel railway will carry us across the Lebanon Mountains to Beirut on the Mediterranean.

[The Governor immediately approved this itinerary, placed a railway freight car at the party's disposal, and for their protection assigned them a guard of Arab soldiers.

My father had never before seen Kadesh where in the thirteenth century B.C. Ramses II had beaten the Hittites in one of history's major battles; but years before, he had analyzed its strategy in a treatise * which had found its way into most of the military reference libraries of the West.]

It is a privilege [he wrote on May 15] now for the first time to look out upon the places mentioned in Ramses' war records, and to recognize point after point over which I worked at such a disadvantage without having seen them. I can now well understand how this great rich valley between the snow-clad Lebanons must have excited the greed of Ramses II and the other Pharaohs who so repeatedly plundered this region.

[I have spoken of the mysterious way in which natives in widely separated places like Khartoum and Cairo have always been able within a few hours to communicate news to one another. While this was an old story to my father, he was nevertheless startled when as the train reached the ruins of Baalbek at twilight on May 20, two Bedouin accosted him and asked him bluntly whether he had delivered the letter which Sheikh Ramadhan Beg Ibn Shallash had given him to take to Aleppo. He realized now even better than before that day and night the Arabs had been watching every step of his journey from Salihiyah and Meyyadin onward—and he speculated to himself what might have befallen him and his party had he for any reason failed to deliver the letter.]

* See also his *A History of Egypt,* p. 427 and ff.

[Shortly after midnight of May 20, the expedition reached Beirut and heard once more the wash of the Mediterranean along the rocky shore below the American University. Here he stopped with his former student and old friend, Professor Harold H. Nelson, who long ago had made his doctorate under him and was now a pillar of what had become one of the most influential institutions in the whole Near East. Two of its alumni were members of Feisal's cabinet at Damascus, and the college was "doing its best to avoid being compromised by the political activities of its graduates scattered over this entire part of the world and vehemently demanding independence."

Professor Nelson, who knew every corner and a host of the habitants of Syria, was permitted by the college to join the expedition during its Syrian explorations. He guided the party northward along as much of the ancient Phoenician coast as was still under the control of the Arabs.

My father's first visit to Jebail, ancient Byblos, "oldest city of the Mediterranean of which we have any knowledge, whence the Egyptians brought cedar in the thirtieth century B.C.," reminded him of what he had written of this place in *Ancient Times*: "The Greeks received from abroad *papyros,* designating the Egyptian paper on which they wrote, and we remember that this word has in its English form become 'paper.' Much of the papyrus used by the Greeks was delivered to them by Phoenician merchants from Byblos. The Greeks often called papyrus *byblos* after the Phoenician city from which it came. Thus when they began to write books on rolls of such paper, they called them *biblia.* It is from this term that we received our word 'Bible' (literally 'book' or 'books'), once the name of a Phoenician city."

On May 27, his last day in Beirut, he conferred with General Gouraud, High Commissioner of France in Syria.]

He asked me when I was expecting to come back for archaeological work in Syria. I answered, "Not until all is quiet and safe here." This was not a wholly diplomatic answer, but I could not dissemble. I mentioned the discontent of the Arabs, and Gouraud replied, "The power of France will subject them. *Il faut se subir!*"

This was a soldier's answer. His business is force. But French subjection of unwilling Syrians among whom are many educated men who understand something of what self-government means, smacks of Germany's subjugation of the Belgians. Conditions just now in French Syria are terrible, public safety is far worse than under the Turks, corruption and bribery are just as common. The only difference is that it now costs more to buy what you want from a civil official than it did under the Turks!

[From Beirut the party recrossed the Lebanon mountains to Damascus, where he was formally invited to attend a meeting of the Chamber of Deputies of the new Arab (Syrian) State, and was consulted by "a stately Syrian named Riza," the Chamber's President.]

Discussion was quiet, orderly and interesting: the old turbaned sheikhs favored enforcement of completely centralized government with no local independence; while the younger men in European clothes and red *tarbushes* (fezes) pled for local autonomy and wide local liberty.

A deputy who—as Nelson told me—had flunked out of the American University at Beirut, then matriculated at Columbia in New York and graduated easily, said to me:

"Why did the United States enter the War? Was it not to protect the small nations?"

I said, "We went into the War to beat the Germans!"

"Well, if that is all," he answered, "then you have simply enabled other nations to do what Germany would have done had she won!"

In the light of Syria's experience, this statement was difficult to refute!

[When Feisal, then still King of Syria, heard that my father was in Damascus, he asked the American Consul, a Mr. Young, to bring him to his house for an interview.]

Feisal has a palace also, but prefers the informality and simplicity of his own house, to which we were driven through the narrow streets in his car, with a terrible noise of exhaust and siren. Young aides took us to a rear balcony overlooking a luxuriant garden filled with richly laden fruit trees overhanging a sparkling fountain. Below us spread the houses and minarets of Damascus.

The King stepped quietly out on the balcony, greeted us as any European would do, sat down and began talking with us in French—which he speaks even more haltingly than I.

Conversation was quite commonplace until I brought up the situation of the Arab State. He said bluntly that his present unhappy position between French and English aggression, the one in Syria, the other in Palestine, was America's fault! The Consul and I both demurred, but failed—I think—to alter his feelings.

I then told him of our journey from Baghdad. He asked me particularly about conditions in Iraq, and the feeling of the people

about their rulers. I was very careful in what I said about their attitude toward the British, but spoke unsparingly regarding the feeling
there toward his own brother, Abdullah, who claims the kingship over
Iraq, just as Feisal has gained it over Syria. I told him frankly that
the hero of Iraq was not his brother, but the great Sheikh Ibn Sa'ud
(a superb Arab who some years ago led his people across the desert
and captured Mecca. He is a Wahhabi, one of the sects of Puritan
Moslems who do not revere the saints, will not tolerate the sacredness
of tombs, not even that of Mohammed at Medina, or of revered objects
like the sacred Black Stone at Mecca. They do not even allow smoking,
so universal among Moslems.)

Feisal did not take offense at my frankness, and when the audience
closed, invited the Consul and myself to dine with him a few days
hence.

Later: As I write the sunset gun has just boomed and muezzin
cries float over the city from all directions, for it is again the Fast of
Ramadan.

The dinner with King Feisal [on May 31] was this time at the
Palace. The good Consul had not been using his dress clothes for so
long that he was late, and I think we were a little tardy at a King's
dinner!

We passed through three anterooms in succession, filled with innumerable sentries, aides-de-camp, adjutants, chamberlains and attendants, amongst whom we were introduced to the King's younger
brother, Zaid Pasha, regent in the King's absence in Paris, and to
Nuri Pasha, his chief general, who seemed little more than a boy.

The King immediately came out of his private apartments and
greeted us with noticeable weariness, though very courteously. On
account of Ramadan, he explained, it was necessary to have dinner
early, so we went in at once. He motioned me to the seat on his right,
which I was reluctant to take, since Uncle Sam was officially present,
but of course I could not demur.

The dinner was simple—about what one would find in a fair hotel.
It ended with the famous Damascus pastry and really luscious fruit.
I avoided politics and we talked of other things, ancient and modern,
and especially of his possible visit to America. It was all pleasant and
friendly enough, but unrelieved by a single flash of the wit he had
taught us to expect of him—like his sly remark during his recent visit
to England, that the nations of the West and the Peace Commission

resembled a caravan. In the Near East, a caravan is always led by a donkey!

After dinner he led the way to a balcony overlooking the palace gardens and the entire city. There was a full moon, and below us lay Damascus, a sea of silvery houses, minarets and gardens. At my side stood the founder—perhaps—of yet another new dynasty in the long history of the orient.

Because the King seemed worn and weary with the Fast of Ramadan, we took our leave early, and drove back through the moonlit streets.

When we entrained for Haifa early the following morning, we experienced at first hand some of the problems confronting the new Arab State.

Of the two first-class compartments reserved for us on the train, one had been pre-empted by Syrian Army officers, and the other by a group of Bedouin in full desert regalia. These Bedouin were relatives of Sheikh Nuri Shaalan who took a distinguished part in Lawrence's campaign which destroyed the Fourth Turkish Army along the very railway line we were traveling. One of the party was a black Sudanese. All of them said they did not see why Bedouin should vacate for mere Turks—they apparently regarded all wearers of European clothing as Turks! One of them threatened to plant a dagger in the train official's bosom if he attempted to enter the compartment. All the officials available could not free the compartments for us. The Bedouin had a note from the King!

Had there been time, *we* also might have procured a note from the King—but as it was, we had to retire ignominiously to the third class, where a harem [women's] compartment was vacated for us!

Everybody is in mortal fear of the Bedouin. Their services in the War make them a strong group as opposed to the townspeople and the educated modern class, and they terrorize the towns much as did the cowboys of a generation ago on our own frontier in the West.

Vermin-infested natives tried to climb in with us at every station, were kept out by the considerate train official. The paymaster was also on our train, and held it half an hour at each station to pay two or three employees their wages, then engage them in a leisurely conversation!

The railroad runs directly southward from Damascus, and was

built by the Turks as part of their Mecca line which they call the Hejaz Railway. At Deraa, where a line branches off toward Haifa and the Mediterranean end of the Carmel Ridge, the bellicose relatives of Sheikh Nuri Shaalan climbed out. They had themselves no doubt participated in Lawrence's campaigns, and I would have been glad to talk with them—but they shouldered their packs and marched off toward the desert.

From Deraa we swung westward down the beautiful gorge of the Yarmuk River which flows into the Jordan just south of the Lake of Tiberias (Sea of Galilee). When we reached Samakh at the south end of Lake Tiberias, we had dropped nearly 3000 feet from Damascus, which is over 2260 feet *above* the sea, to Lake Tiberias, 680 feet *below* sea level.

Near Samakh we saw hanging from a telegraph pole beside the railway line the body of one of the Bedouin who had been cutting the Haifa-Damascus line! He had shot two Jews, resisted arrest, and been properly quieted by the Indian troops sent to bring him in. Such methods are possible in Palestine, but the Arab State [of Syria] cannot treat the Bedouin in this way. At Muzerib I saw the wreckage of one of the airplanes which Lawrence said were shot down by the Turks at this place.

From Haifa on the coast, we drove along the northern edge of the Carmel Ridge toward Megiddo, the fortress commanding the middle path across the Ridge. These Carmel hills form the first transverse barrier which an army met when advancing from Egypt to Asia. The first battle ever fought there of which we have any knowledge, was that of Thutmose III in the early fifteenth century B.C. For 3300 years since then it has been the great battlefield between East and West, down to Allenby's victory over the Turks on the same ground. The New Testament name of the place is Armageddon—which means simply "Mount (*har* or *ar*) of Megiddo."

[At Haifa, Professor Nelson turned back to Beirut, for it had become evident that due to the prevailing turbulent conditions, further exploration in Palestine and Syria would for the moment be impossible.]

When Major-General Sir Louis Bols, formerly Allenby's Chief-of-Staff, and now Commander-in-Chief of the British Forces in Palestine learned that I had reached Jerusalem, he asked me to lunch. He is one of the finest men in the British Army—Allenby has often said in public that it was Bols who suggested the plan of the final and the decisive battle with the Turks at Megiddo.

The British Headquarters are in a magnificent hospice which the Germans built on the Mount of Olives—a large and showy stone building with a lofty tower. In the court are two high niches containing life-size bronze statues of the German Emperor and Empress in the attitude of adoring saints. The building also contains a sumptuous Byzantine church with a large ceiling fresco showing the same two august personages enthroned side-by-side. The Emperor holds in his right hand a large model of the building.

I went up to the tower, from which one can see the whole region from the misty blue mountains of Moab in the east, the Dead Sea and the Jordan Valley, to the desolate ridges of the Judean highlands in the west. From no other place in the world is such a view obtainable, for the point of observation is some 2600 feet *above* sea level, while the lower Jordan Valley and the surface of the Dea Sea are 1300 feet *below* sea level; so that in relation to *sea level* it is the deepest chasm known to us in the earth. The surface of the Dead Sea, about 15 miles from the observer, is thus nearly 4000 feet below him. On his campaign through here, Allenby one day puzzled the War Office in London by reporting that "two of our bombing planes, flying 600 feet below the sea, today bombed the enemy's camp!"

The scene is not only geologically fascinating but arouses the religious emotions of one's childhood, as one stands on the Mount of Olives looking out over Bethany, the hills of Bethlehem and Tekoah, the home of Amos, the Valley of Kedron near which was Gethsemane, and behind it Jerusalem itself, with a Moslem mosque where once the Temple stood.

After lunch I took General Bols into a corner and told him what I knew of Arab hostility to the British. I had chaffingly remarked that the Arabs did not want the French because to get what they wanted they had to pay them twice as much as they had formerly paid the Turks; and they didn't want the English because they couldn't get what they wanted at any price!

Bols asked me with great earnestness whether I thought Feisal was really in control of the Arabs. I am confident that in this question lies the chief English difficulty: they have long been subsidizing Feisal, and make no secret of it. But while all that is supposed to have ended, I would be willing to wager that on the quiet they are still subsidizing him, and are anxious to know whether in holding Feisal loyal, they are also holding the Arabs.

I told Sir Louis I could not answer his question, and did not think anyone could, but that the sheikhs with whom I had talked had shown little enthusiasm for Feisal. Our conversation then turned to the situation in Palestine, where the position of the English seemed to be growing steadily worse. The Arabs of the desert on the east, and the Moslems of the towns are deeply disaffected, and trust none of the Allies.

"Consider their grievance," said General Bols. "When practically everybody at the Peace Conference had agreed to give Syria and Palestine a plebiscite, and to send out an international commission to ascertain what their people wanted, Clemenceau suddenly said, 'If this is done for Syria, it must also be done for Mesopotamia.' Miss [Gertrude Lowthian] Bell and others representing English interests in Mesopotamia vigorously protested. As a result first France said she would send no commission, then Italy, and finally Great Britain. Although it was by this time entirely futile, President Wilson sent out the Commission representing the United States to go through the country and study the situation.

"What shall we then think of a government," the General continued, "which after such a beginning, solemnly promises the people of Palestine that they shall have a *British* government, and proceeds to give them a *Jewish* government in a country only 10 per cent of whose population are Jews!"

He is quite right. The money of wealthy Jews everywhere is inundating this country, and is augmented by the money of western Christians who are caught by the idea of restoring the Jews to their Promised Land. Almost none of these donors themselves come, or want to come to Palestine—they are vicariously patriotic through subscriptions; with the result that the Christians and Moslems forming ninety per cent of the population of this ancient land, have been suddenly subjected to the supremacy of a Jewish minority.

But the British feeling is the smallest part of it. The appointment of a Jewish High Commissioner [Sir Herbert Samuels, an exceptionally able and gifted administrator] by the British politicians at home is not a blunder of merely political consequences; it is almost certain to kindle a conflagration of the most serious proportions. Within the last few weeks strong anti-Jewish demonstrations have already been made, many Jews have been killed and many more wounded.

And the Commander of the British Army in Palestine asks a passing American archaeologist, How could anything else be expected?

The evening before I left Jerusalem [June 8], General Waters Taylor [Chief Intelligence Officer of the Imperial Staff in the Near East] called on me, asked me to tell him of Sheikh Ramadhan's letter, carefully jotted down in his notebook the dates I gave him, then said: "Count de Caix [an important member of the French diplomatic corps in the Near East upon whom my father had called in Beirut, only to be informed that he had left for Paris] had not left for Paris when you were in Beirut—he had probably gone to Aleppo to get Ramadhan's letter!"

We tried to conjecture what it may have contained, and to what tribe belonged the Bedouin who had cross-questioned me at Baalbek.

Next day Waters Taylor and I traveled in the same train from Jerusalem to Cairo [a 300-mile journey which then took nearly fifteen hours]. During the day's long and intensely interesting conversation he gave me among much else, the history of Sheikh Ramadhan (which I have already mentioned) and of the present situation in Syria, Palestine, Egypt and Iraq.

Once again in Cairo, I called at the Residency on expedition business, and when they heard we had come overland from Baghdad, they said they must tell Lord Allenby, who sent out word he would like to see me at once and asked me to a lunch intended for a lot of diplomats and soldiers—Waters Taylor was there, General Congreve, Commander-in-Chief of the Army in Egypt; Brigadier-General Ronald Storrs, Military Governor of Jerusalem; etc., etc. Allenby made me talk about our journey.

After lunch we wandered out upon a broad balcony at the rear of the Residency where Allenby fed a plateful of small raw fish to a comical, serenely smiling Marabout (stork), while General Congreve talked to me about conditions in British territory in Western Asia. I expressed grave apprehension regarding Palestine if the present British policy were continued. Then Allenby joined us and drew me into his office.

In his direct way he led at once to what was on his mind, saying: "Look here, Congreve has just suggested to me that H.M.G. ought to hear what you know of Western Asia. I wholly agree. Would it be possible for you to go home by way of England and have a talk with the Prime Minister and the Foreign Minister?"

I told him that although after great difficulty I had finally succeeded in engaging passage for the United States, I would be glad to do anything I could to bring the facts before the Government in London. He sat down and with his own hand wrote two notes, the first to Prime Minister Lloyd-George, the second to Lord Curzon, Minister for Foreign Affairs.

He then called in his A.D.C. and said, "Tell G.H.Q. I regard it as very urgent that Professor Breasted should be given passage to England at once, if possible on the same ship on which Lady Allenby is sailing."

Turning again to me, he added, "I've repeatedly warned the people at home that their present policy is steering straight for trouble. But they won't listen to me. Perhaps they will take it from you!"

So I left him, clearly troubled by the outlook—I had walked into the Residency to attend to a minor routine matter, and had come out charged with an errand which might conceivably have something to do with saving Palestine from civil war, and the whole Near East from another conflagration.

On my passport they put the big Diplomatic Visa, with the seal of His Majesty's High Commissioner, which means that my baggage goes in and out of every port and station on the way to England without examination or delay. My visions of a quiet, restful trip home have vanished. But I could not have refused to go.

[On the afternoon of June 15, he boarded the special train on which Lord Allenby was escorting Lady Allenby to her ship at Port Said on her return to England for the summer.]

At the request of Colonel Allen, U. S. Military Attaché, I prepared this morning a full statement about my recent journey for dispatch to the War Department in Washington. On my way to the station I picked up at a dealer's the official cylinder seal of King Snefru, builder of the first great pyramid just preceding Gizeh; and also another seal belonging to a great official of King Menkure.

Along the entire length of the Cairo station platform, a sumptuous red carpet runner had been laid down, which expanded into an ocean of red beside the train itself. I was joined in the drawing-room compartment of the High Commissioner's car by Dr. Llewellyn Phillips, the leading physician in Cairo, who had inoculated us all for cholera last February. He was going to Port Said to see the little daughter of General [Sir] Gilbert Clayton, Internal Adviser to the Government of Egypt. (Clayton's two little daughters were with their mother at Port

Said when one of them was suddenly taken ill with a strange infection and died forty-eight hours later. Clayton had this morning buried the little girl at the English cemetery in Cairo, when a telegram arrived from Port Said, saying the other child was similarly affected, had a temperature of 106! These are the unsung sacrifices of service to the Empire.)

A few minutes later, Clayton appeared on the platform and came into the train, direct from his first little girl's funeral. With the usual English reserve and self-command, he engaged in conversation with us, and no one would have known there was any trouble.

The entire station was deserted, for no one was allowed to come in. Presently Lady Allenby appeared, coming down the long red carpet alone. Her husband soon followed, conversing animatedly with General Congreve. As Allenby came forward to greet me, Congreve said to me, "I am very glad you are going on this errand—but, I say!—you seem to have scared Gouraud to death! He seems to be frightened out of his wits." I asked him to explain, but he insisted he was only joking, and would say nothing more. I am sure he had just received some private intelligence which he finally decided not to impart to me.

Even though the car windows were fitted with bluish glass, and large electric fans were running, the trip was very dusty and hot. At every stop a guard of Tommies climbed out and patrolled each side of the entire length of the train. No one was allowed to come near. As we reached the twenty-five or thirty-mile stretch between Kantara and Port Said where the railway runs beside the Suez Canal, we passed our ship, the *Mantua,* steaming along only a hundred yards from our train.

During dinner Lady Allenby said to her husband, "You must tell Dr. Breasted of the curious coincidence of our visit a fortnight ago to the battlefield of Megiddo."

"You know, for you have very fully written of it," Allenby said, "how Thutmose III crossed the Carmel Ridge, riding through the pass to meet the enemy in a chariot of shining electrum. We had your book with us, and we had just read the account of it, so we knew the dates: Thutmose went through on the 15th of May over 3,000 years ago, and on the same day I took Lady Allenby for the first time to see the battlefield where we beat the Turks, and like Thutmose III, we also went through in a chariot of shining metal—for our machine had wheels of aluminum and was all covered with polish metal. So she saw the scene of our victory on the anniversary of the earliest known battle there, and also approached it in a chariot of glittering metal. I wanted her to see it, for as I have told you before, I took my title from there —Allenby of Megiddo—because it was a cavalry operation which broke the Turkish line, and I am a cavalry officer."

Later, after we had boarded the ship and he and the A.D.C.'s had settled Lady Allenby in her cabin, he came to my quarters and having satisfied himself that everything was satisfactory, strolled with me toward the gangway for a last word on the nature of my errand. He quite embarrassed me with the kind things he said, and I told him so.

"Well," he said, "you must live up to the reputation I have given you!"

I purposely misconstrued him, saying, "You mean on board this ship?"

"No, in London!" he responded. "All joking aside, it is of the highest importance that the facts you have told me should be plainly brought before the Prime Minister and Lord Curzon, and you have an opportunity to do a very important piece of work—for they do not understand that Arab feeling, once so friendly to us, is now stale and hostile toward us. Or that the Arabs and the Christians are now united against the Jews, and that the present policy is aggravating this anti-Jewish hostility to a dangerous degree. Do not fail to make this clear to them as you have done to me. And above all, tell them what you have told me of the danger of Arab union with Bolshevism in the north."

It was now long after midnight. Above the shouts of men, the clanging rattle of chain hoists, the crunching of avalanches of coal, the smell of coal dust—the quiet stars looked down with serene indifference. I went up to the top deck beyond the dust and noise, and walked there for some time, supposing I was alone. But as I rounded a deckhouse, I suddenly met the Allenbys having a last little stroll together. A few minutes later, in the glare of great electric lights, his launch pushed off from the side of the ship, and as he stood waving at his wife, the boat glided away and disappeared in the darkness.

As I contemplated the responsibility he had placed upon me, I had a depressing sense of complete inadequacy—a pedagogue meddling minutely in the vast game of the imperial powers. I have terribly "cold feet," and can only hope for at least a hearing in London. The spectacle of England and France plotting against each other in the Near East has cured me of any vestige of such idealistic visions of international amity as I may still have been cherishing when I left America.

[On June 16 he wrote from the S.S. *Mantua:*]

It seems quite impossible that I am really embarked for home—on a heavenly Mediterranean summer morning, and a wonderfully blue sea! And before me ten whole days with no responsibilities, no telegrams, no packing cases, no checkbooks, no antiquity dealers, no Arabs, no palavers—only fresh sea air and sunshine and rest on a summer sea!

Just ten months ago I reached London, outward bound, and now the circle has closed again. Scientifically I have not accomplished a great deal. But in the matter of museum pieces, and the practical foundation necessary to establish our work in the newly organized Near East emerging from the Great War, I am quite satisfied. It is also gratifying to learn that the Milner Commission has put into its report to H.M.G. all the recommendations they requested of me regarding the antiquities of Egypt. [The Milner Report was eventually scrapped.]

But whatever the journey has yielded has been, I fear, again at the cost of health. My head throbs, I am alternately full of fever, chills and vertigo—probably due to malaria, for despite precautions I was badly bitten by mosquitoes in two malarial regions through which we passed.

[As a possible partial solution of the servant problem in the United States, he had brought back with him the expedition's little Iraqi cook, Ali, who had become "as devoted as a faithful dog." Ali no longer had any ties in Iraq, for his family had all died of privation during the War. He continued, of course, to wear his native dress, and made a quaint picture when upon their arrival in London my father] took him for a walk along the embankment and showed him Waterloo Bridge and the Obelisk, whose base was still deeply scarred and disfigured from German bombs during air raids in the War. Ali was greatly interested when I showed him the Houses of Parliament and told him they were the seat of government. He said, "You mean the house of the Sultan?" Otherwise his reply was always, "Na'am!" meaning "Yes!"

We walked to the Foreign Office, where I delivered Allenby's note to Curzon; and into famous old Downing Street, where I handed the porter at dingy No. 10 the note to Lloyd George—who, as I learned, was absent at the Spa Conference.

Lord Curzon has a reputation for devastating rudeness, but in almost an hour's conference with him, I found him the personification of courtesy and thoughtfulness. He immediately discarded his usual austere official reserve, and made no effort to hide his eagerness to hear what I had to say. I summarized our journey through Iraq and across the Syrian Desert; referred to the incident of the letter from Sheikh Ramadhan which probably reached the Count de Caix; described the Sheikh's probable relation to Mustapha Kamal; summarized what I had told Feisal, Bols, Waters Taylor and Allenby, prophesied imminent disaster if the French continued their present policy of intimidation in Syria, and murderous inter-racial strife if the British adhered to the Balfour Declaration in Palestine.

I was about to end with an expression of doubt as to whether what I had told him had justified my imposition upon his time, when he startled me by throwing back his hands and exclaiming, "My God—to think that at such a time His Majesty's Minister of Foreign Affairs should have been ignorant of the facts you have brought me!"

At this point there was a commotion somewhere below, outside the building. A secretary entered quickly, layed a chit before Curzon, who nodded without looking up. As I rose to go, he stepped from behind his desk and said:

"In the Prime Minister's absence at the Spa Conference, I am under promise to interview a labor delegation which has already been waiting more than an hour and refuses to be put off again. It is with the greatest regret that I must therefore close our interview in which you have given me facts and views of the most critical value. Even if—as I fear —they have reached my Government too late to forestall imminent catastrophe, they will nevertheless fortify us in any eventual modification of our Palestinian policy which circumstances may force upon us."

He thanked me in behalf of his Government for what I had done and for what it implied of Anglo-American amity, and we parted.

[For the first few moments after reaching Whitehall again, he walked rapidly, still exhilarated and buoyed by the apparent importance of everything he had returned to London to tell Curzon. But now that it had been told, the sustaining sense of elation suddenly left him like the receding effects of a drug, and weariness engulfed him. The great Government buildings of the British Empire looked inscrutably down upon him, careless of his little *sortie* across a segment of currently troublesome Empire terrain. The interview had set his head to throbbing again with fever, and he surrendered to the leathery gloom of an antediluvian taxi which trundled him back to his hotel and the sumptuous and lonely suite engaged for him by the Foreign Office.

Next day he dashed "back to Paris where I have got track of an ancient Babylonian King's golden diadem bearing a long inscription. I hope to get it!" But the price was exorbitant and he failed. His return to America with Ali ended his journal letters.]

The year of my father's absence had been a serious trial for my mother. The blank weeks of waiting between his letters, the dread of every cablegram, the lengthening months of anxiety, and above all the deep, unabating pain of separation from one who embodied her world and was her reason for living—these had cruelly aggravated the strange neuroses which had always enslaved her.

She had constantly followed his progress with pins on a map, had kept a log of his journey on a calendar, and each evening had subtracted one from the total number of days before his promised homecoming. She had thought of little else.

But as the day of his return had drawn nearer, the possessive nature of her affection for him had become more and more intensified, and her profound involuntary jealousy of all he had seen and experienced without her had grown until it had consumed her and made her—as usual—physically ill. On the July afternoon when he was to arrive, she lay anguished in a darkened room.

I stood alone on the platform as a long, dusty, sun-baked train screeched to a halt among the same sordid tangle of tracks and antique railroad architecture labeled Englewood which for so many years had witnessed our family partings and reunions. In the distance I saw him climb down, followed by the small figure of white-clad, turbaned, impassive Ali. The porter dragged out a mass of battered duffle bags and luggage from which, even through the acrid smell of hot brakes and Pullman vestibules, there rose an indefinable aroma of the orient. The conductor waved to the engineer and swung aboard. In a crescendo the train thumped and rumbled past, and in the sudden silence we faced each other.

He had aged and grown thinner, and around his eyes were the little wrinkles men get from staring across great distances under a glaring sun. He was tanned and weatherbeaten without looking healthy. But he was at home again, and I thanked God. He asked about my mother. She had been suddenly afflicted with one of her "sick headaches," I said, and was bitterly disappointed that she could not have come with me. He looked at me gravely for a moment. I could see in his eyes the never-say-die Victorian vanquishing the realist. The responsibilities he had placed upon me such an interminable, exacerbating year ago, were his again; and for the fraction of a moment he was wondering—I knew—whether coming home did not perhaps demand greater courage than the rigors of the field. . . .

The year of reconnaissance had greatly clarified his vision of the project to which he now hoped to devote what with uncanny prescience he correctly anticipated as the fifteen remaining years of his life. He was travel weary and still fever-ridden, but too aware of the enormity of his task and the brevity of the time left for its accomplishment, to stop for rest.

By way of signalizing his return, the University invited him to be the principal speaker at the Convocation which closed that Summer Quarter. It so happened that on this same occasion I was to receive my delayed college diploma. Knowing that he had thus far failed to win me to his calling and that I was about to take wing into a world of my own, he composed an address, entitled *The New Past*, which was at once a statement of the responsibility of American science for "the recovery and reconstruction of the career of man," and an appeal to American youth to enter this field of research.

On a sunny September afternoon I sat among rows of capped-and-gowned students in a crowded auditorium, and listened to his splendid voice uttering with swinging cadences his melioristic credo of the rise of man. Only he and I among all that audience knew that he was making a final appeal to his son. As I looked up at his earnest face I was terribly torn between affection for him and the rebellious urge of pulsing young blood to escape the grim drudgery, the gloom, the atmosphere of all-past-and-no-future with which in my immaturity I had come to associate the career he envisioned.

"A comprehensive study of the ancient Orient," he said, ". . . reveals to us the . . . historic epochs of . . . European man for the first time set in a background of several hundred thousand years. In this vast synthesis . . . there is disclosed to us an imposing panorama . . . such as no earlier generation has ever been able to survey.

"*This is the New Past.*

"Lord Acton has well said that 'next to the discovery of the New World, the recovery of the ancient world is a second landmark that divides us from the Middle Ages and marks the transition to modern life.' . . .

"What was the ancient world . . . to which Lord Acton refers?

. . . We listen now not only to the voices of Cicero and Socrates, of Isaiah and David, as did the men of the Renaissance, but also to the voice of Sennacherib in the proud story of his victories, to the voice of Cheops telling in terms of colossal masonry architecture the triumphs of the first great organized state, to the voice of the earliest smelter of metals singing in the tinkle of his primitive anvil the song of man's coming conquest of the earth, to the voice of remote and long-forgotten aeons heard now only in the message of ever more carefully wrought stone implements, to the voice of geological ages muttering in the savage gutturals of incipient human speech which we seem to hear resounding through prehistoric forests re-echoing to the first inarticulate utterances of . . . creatures about to become men. . . .

"Such a vision of the New Past, just beginning to dawn upon the minds of modern men, has values as yet all unproved. . . . He who really discerns it has begun to read the glorious Odyssey of human kind, disclosing to us man pushing out upon the ocean of time to make conquest of treasure unspeakable, of worlds surpassing all his dreams— the supreme adventure of the ages. . . .

"I have seen the ruined capitals of the ancient East slumbering under their gloomy mounds at sunset, and many a time as the sun arose and dispelled the shadows, it has seemed as if the banished life that once ebbed and flowed through those now rubbish-covered and dismantled streets, must start forth again. With a regret so poignant that it was almost physical pain, I have realized the years that must elapse before these silent mounds can be made to speak again and reveal all the splendid pageant . . . which transformed our father-man from savagery in some remote cavern where at most he could count five by the aid of his fingers, into a godlike creature who reached out to the stars on those Babylonian plains and made the first computations which have at length enabled us to plumb the vast deeps of the universe. . . .

"The inspiring task which confronts America in the Near East cannot be achieved without the aid of a new generation of young Americans who are willing to spend the years necessary to gain the training and equipment without which the work cannot be done. . . . It will be a life of some sacrifices. Those who elect to undertake it must set their faces to the East, feeling a deep reverence for the life of man on the earth, and highly resolving to devote their all to this new crusade. To such spirits . . . the recovery of the unfolding life of man will not be a toilsome task, but rather a joyful quest, the modern quest for the

Grail, from which arduous journeys and weary exile in distant [oriental] lands will not deter us. For . . . we know what the first crusaders could not yet discern, that we are returning to ancestral shores. And in the splendor of that buoyant life of the human soul which has somehow come up out of the impenetrable deeps of past ages and risen so high, . . . [we] shall find a glorious prophecy of its supreme future."

His words moved me deeply, filled me with a vague sense of disloyalty for failing then and there to stand up and announce firmly my enlistment in this "new crusade."

But I could not—I simply could not.

Afterwards, during a quiet evening walk, I told him so, as kindly as I knew how. He put his arm through mine and said he understood; that in whatever I chose to do I would have his blessing, and the best training to be found anywhere in the world; and that for my own sake he hoped I would not waste precious years in trial and error as he had done.

He never failed me—nor gave up the secret hope that eventually I might still become an Orientalist.

That July of 1920, a French Army had driven Feisal out of Syria; and during the ensuing year uprisings occurred throughout the country which culminated in an attempt—nearly successful—to assassinate General Gouraud. This was the prelude to years of recurrently bloody struggle between France and her Syrian Mandate; while from the moment Great Britain announced the appointment of Sir Herbert Samuels as High Commissioner for Palestine, the Arabs of that Mandate began the long series of angry protests which, fomented by the Balfour Declaration, were to grow at last into country-wide murder and rebellion.

What followed is history which my father, like scores of other intelligent men who could read obvious portents, had prophesied to the British Government. In May, 1939, just nineteen years after his conference with Curzon in London, His Majesty's Government cut the Gordian knot by renouncing the Balfour Declaration in a White Paper which, far too late, terminated a tragic experiment in irreconcilable economics, sentiment, politics and creed.

Both England and France were guilty of bungling, procrastination and bad faith in their diplomatic and political treatment of the lands they had freed from Turkish misrule. But even at their worst, the

Allied Powers represented a revolutionary improvement over the Turks, whose former dominions were now accessible as never before to Western commercial and scientific enterprise.

This state of things happened to coincide with the beginning in America of that Baron Münchausen decade following the First World War which witnessed an accretion of excess income, especially by the great private fortunes, the like of which we shall probably never see again. All the elements were ripe for a brief Golden Age for those so-called idealistic projects, institutions and pursuits which depend upon prosperous times for their existence. Among these none possessed more potential appeal than archaeology, which needed only a champion and the impetus of a timely discovery to arouse public interest and enlist financial support on an unprecedented scale.

But in 1920 the United States was well advanced into its first post-War depression, and such developments still belonged to the future. My father shared the general conviction, however, that prosperous times were in the offing, and at once began preparing for their advent. What he had seen in the Near East had convinced him that if he hoped to bring into actual being the great research organization which had so long been taking shape in his mind—a laboratory of which the newly created Oriental Institute was only the beginning—he must secure sums beyond anything he had heretofore dared to think possible.

He took up with George Ellery Hale the feasibility of attempting to raise, from a combination of private donors and philanthropic foundations, a working endowment of $5,000,000. In reply Hale outlined a campaign of fund raising, but emphatically advised against attempting to achieve such an amount in one lump.

"You would perforce become a mere administrator," he wrote, "with no time . . . for your own [research] work. . . . I can speak from the heart . . . because I have refused [administrative posts] through my desire to carry on research personally—and even now [I] find almost no opportunity [for it], . . . though the [Mt. Wilson] Observatory requires far less administrative work than the vastly greater project you have in mind. . . . Your own health is none too good, and I can say from experience that the worry of making effective use of large sums of money . . . breaks one down. The one important thing . . . is the preservation of your health and the conservation of your time for your own researchees. (*Verb. sap.!*)"

Insofar as it pertained to fund raising, my father heeded Hale's sound advice. But in the matter of health, each man remained as incapable of following the other's periodic solicitous counsel as of practicing his own preaching.

In October, 1920, my father wrote me at Harvard (whither for reasons which now seem very remote, I had gone for graduate study in the history of the English drama under George Pierce Baker):

"I have submitted to the President and Board of Trustees of the University of Chicago a plan for the logical and natural expansion of the Oriental Institute. What I am now proposing is almost beyond my strength to cope with: at least one field expedition to work in each of the cradle-lands of civilization at the eastern end of the Mediterranean; all these expeditions to be responsible to an administrative, scientific headquarters at Chicago, where their findings would converge and gradually become the source for writing the greatest drama ever conceived—all the greater because it would unfold a tale of actual facts —the story of the most remarkable phenomenon in the history of the universe as far as we now know it, the story of how man came to be what he is.

"My blood simply tingles at the thought of what such a laboratory could accomplish! Perhaps it will come about, and in time for me at least to lay the foundation for younger men to build upon.

"But if it does not, I shall not be cast down. I have made up my mind that this is the last time I shall try to carry out these larger plans. For I feel some confidence that in the fifteen years remaining to me I can carve out single-handed, here at my desk, a piece of work foreshadowing what *might* be achieved by such a laboratory; and that even with our present state of knowledge, what I have done for Egypt I can at least begin to do for the whole group of civilizations from which ours is descended."

Meanwhile he continued to organize new research enterprises, among them the first comprehensive dictionary of cuneiform, which he called the Assyrian Dictionary Project, patterned after the great dictionary of ancient Egyptian at Berlin and the English dictionary at Oxford. He began also a research task of his own which for the next ten years was to occupy every moment he could spare from his other responsibilities—the translation of what he discovered to be "the earliest known scientific document," the Edwin Smith Surgical Papyrus belonging to the New York Historical Society, which asked him to undertake its publication.*

* This remarkable papyrus was purchased in 1862 at Luxor, Egypt, by Mr. Edwin Smith, an American who resided there for more than twenty years, beginning in 1858; and in 1906 was presented by his daughter to the New York His-

With the end of the year 1921 he reached a definite turning point in both his personal life and his career.

At the close of that November, in her eighty-fifth year, Harriet fell asleep for the last time. Even in her younger days she had only vaguely understood the nature of his work; and during the latter years when with inexhaustible patience he had in his gratitude tried always to tell her about it (in the same simple words with which he used to tell me stories in my childhood), she had been too ill and frail to do more than relish the sound of his voice and the warmth of his presence. She had had no need to understand his work: her instincts had long ago told her that he had justified a hundredfold whatever sacrifices she and Charles and Theodocia had made for him. This realization filled her with a profound contentment and peace of mind which in her final sleep banished the years from her face, until she looked like a young girl again. He laid her beside Charles in the cemetery at Rockford, overlooking the River; and returned to his work "with that added sense of loneliness," he wrote, "which one feels on suddenly becoming the oldest generation."

That winter was my family's last in their cherished replica of Ariosto's villa. Homesickness and the alien climate had finally driven mad the tragi-comic little Ali, and he had had to be deported to his native Iraq. What with her failing health and the scarcity of servants, my mother no longer felt equal to the burden of managing the house. So, with a heavy heart, my father put it up for sale. On Christmas Day, 1921, he wrote me:

"I look about my dismantled study and realize that this is the end of my home at a time when most men can look to the spiritual shelter and peace of theirs. Of the three great things which constitute a man's life—his home, his friends and his work—the last must for me henceforth largely take the place of the first two. I am always thankful for work, which does not destroy feeling nor render it callous, but is like a faithful friend who gently leads one into a lovely garden of consolation and noble interest where aches and anxieties are soothed into sweet forgetfulness."

torical Society. In 1920 Dr. Caroline Ransome Williams, one of my father's ablest former students, while engaged in the study and publication of the Society's Egyptian collections, came upon "a large and beautifully written papyrus in a stately ancient book format," and brought it to his attention. "It was found to be . . . not only the earliest known surgical treatise but at the same time the earliest document in the history of science." Printed by the Oxford University Press, it was published in 1930 as Vols. III–IV in the Oriental Institute Publications Series issued through the University of Chicago Press.

CHAPTER IX

M Y FATHER'S visit to Egypt in 1919–20 had impressed him more than ever "with the dire need of epigraphic work * to save from destruction . . . [the] fast-perishing written records.

"[For example,] in forgotten storage in the unfloored basement of the Cairo Museum lay beautifully painted wooden coffins bearing precious . . . texts which were submerged in [Nile] water whenever there was an inundation above the normal level. . . . [While] the need for copying the records still surviving on the tomb and temple walls . . . gave me the greatest anxiety, . . . the resources of the Oriental Institute were still too limited to undertake such work on the great temple buildings, [hence] I cherished the hope . . . that [we] . . . might . . . save and publish the Coffin Texts." †

The significance of these in the history of man's developing ethical consciousness he described thus:

"The religious documents of Egypt are of commanding importance [because they disclose] to us . . . man's earliest surviving ethical ideals. The Egyptian Book of the Dead has become, in title at least, a household word in the Western world. The Book of the Dead, however, is but a *late* group of religious documents, compiled out of similar but far older material. Because of the excessively corrupt state of the manuscripts, existent translations of the Book of the Dead are of little or no value. In order to build up a sound original text, its older constituent elements must be completely collected and carefully studied and compared.

"The oldest body of literature yet known in any language is a large group of religious texts employed for the benefit of the later kings of the Pyramid Age or Old Kingdom (about 3000–2500 B.C.) and for

* As used in modern archaeology, the term "epigraphic work" refers to the recording of ancient inscriptions for the sake of their preservation, study, etc.

† *The Oriental Institute,* by James H. Breasted, University of Chicago Press, 1933, p. 37.

their exclusive use engraved in their pyramids in the cemetery of Memphis. They are therefore termed the Pyramid Texts. These include literature which had descended from an older period at least as far back as the thirty-fifth century B.C., while the latest of the Pyramid Texts are a thousand years later than that date.

"With the extension of a blessed destiny in the hereafter to include less exalted folk than the kings, the nobles began to record excerpts from the Pyramid Texts in their tombs and upon their coffins. After the twenty-second century B.C. the barons of the Feudal Age (the Middle Kingdom) were more and more interested in having such literature available after death. The popularization of a blessed here-after not confined to the kings produced many pictures of happiness for humbler folk in the next world. Much of the resulting body of religious literature concerning the life beyond the grave probably owed its origin to the Feudal Age, though some of it was older. Such texts, then, form a mortuary literature suited to the *people* of the Feudal Age, whereas the Pyramid Texts had been intended for the king only. Much of this later body of mortuary texts passed over into the Book of the Dead, which therefore consists of selections from a humbler and more popular mortuary literature.

"The position of the Coffin Texts both chronologically and socially is between the Pyramid Texts and the Book of the Dead, though they are quite like the latter in character. Hence they contribute essentially to the understanding of both the other groups.

"These forerunners of the Book of the Dead, including copious extracts from the preceding Pyramid Texts, were written on the inner surfaces of the heavy wooden coffins of the Feudal Age. Every coffin-maker in the towns up and down the Nile Valley was furnished by the priests of his town with a local version of these utterances. Before the coffins were put together the scribe in the maker's employ filled the inside surfaces of the cedar planks with pen-and-ink copies of such texts as he had available. The work was commonly done with great carelessness and inaccuracy, the effort being to fill up the planks as fast as possible. In the same coffin the scribes might write the same chapter two or three times; in one instance a spell is found no less than five times in the same coffin.

". . . It is now quite evident that the moral sensitiveness of the early Egyptian has made his religious documents the earliest literary expression of man's ethical consciousness. In the Coffin Texts we find the first clearly outspoken convictions of moral responsibility in the life hereafter. They therefore mark one of the most important stages in the evolution of civilization." *

He "therefore decided [during the winter of 1921–22] that the first project of the Oriental Institute in Egypt should be the formidable task of copying the thousands of surviving lines of Coffin Texts in the Cairo Museum and [together with those in the museums of Europe,] preparing them for publication." The University granted him a year's leave of absence in which to inaugurate this undertaking and attend to many other scientific matters in Europe and Egypt.

At about this same time the French government, through the Académie des Inscriptions et Belles-Lettres, invited him to attend the centenaries of Champollion's decipherment of ancient Egyptian hieroglyphic writing, and of the founding of the Société Asiatique, to be held in Paris in July, 1922. And later that spring he received a penned letter from the Registrar of Oxford University which read: "The University . . . intends to celebrate, on October 24 next, the Tercentary of the Camden Professorship of Ancient History, by the admission of Scholars distinguished in Ancient History to the Honorary Degree of Doctor of Letters. I am directed . . . to invite you to attend a Convocation to be held . . . at Oxford [on that day], in order to receive the Degree of D. Litt., honoris causa."

He arranged for his family to accompany him during this year abroad, which was to include, beginning that November, a dahabiyeh journey up the Nile as far south as Abu Simbel. This would be a rather heavy responsibility, he wrote me: would I lighten his load by taking charge of the family's travels till the end of the Nile voyage?

His letter found me in North Wales, absorbed in a first attempt to write a play. My transition from George Pierce Baker's precious "47 Workshop" at Harvard to the windswept isolation of a minute sixteenth century cottage atop of one of the craggy, rust-colored, high-meadowed mountains overlooking Cardigan Bay and the Irish Sea, is of no relevance to this story beyond the fact that for the first time I had a sense of doing what I had always wanted to do.

When I wrote him, begging off, he replied in his most appealing vein that he had made his plans on the assumption of my help without which he must give them up. Knowing that I should not, I surrendered. On my last night in the cottage I burned the manuscript, which de-

* *The Oriental Institute*, by James H. Breasted, University of Chicago Press, 1933, p. 150 ff.

served no better fate. But I realized as I did so that in the heap of crinkling black flakes edged with smoldering glow had vanished a freedom I had never succeeded in defending against my affection for him— a freedom I might be long in regaining.

Late in June my family left the Ariosto house for the last time, and sailed for France; and as their ship touched Plymouth on the Fourth of July—Independence Day, I reminded myself—I came aboard.

"It is thirty-one years," my father had written in his journal during that Atlantic crossing, "since I bade my parents good-bye and sailed for Germany to study oriental languages. Thanks to textbook royalties, I am for the first time in my life leaving America without financial anxiety—and for the first time leaving behind me not one of those to whom I owe everything, including such incidental recognition as these years have brought."

The summer was a continual reminder of the transformation his life had undergone. As he moved about in Paris from one to another of the many official meetings and social functions commemorating Champollion's historic achievement, and the founding of the Société Asiatique (which he was obliged to attend as an official American representative appointed by the Department of State), he noted that "everything was characterized by the inevitable politics, the tinsel and glitter, the dramatized hospitality, and at the same time the unexpected bursts of graciousness and warm cordiality with which the French imbue such occasions as naturally as they breathe."

He stood one afternoon before a meeting of the Académie des Inscriptions et Belles-Lettres and read a paper on his findings at Salihiyah. "I remembered again," he wrote later, "my first visit to Paris and the Louvre Museum, that bitter winter of 1895. The intellectual stature of the men now sitting before me had then seemed awesomely great, and the scientific world which they inhabited very remote indeed. Except for grayer beards and heavier figures, twenty-five years had hardly altered them. It was their *minds* that startled me—somewhere during the interim, most of them had ceased to expand, and premature, inflexible old age had settled upon them like a blight."

For the first time since 1907, he re-visited Germany and met his old colleagues again. He found them "the same loyal friends I had always known—all save Eduard Meyer, who sent me a message through Erman that 'he had nothing against me personally, but that he could have no intercourse with an American!' "

His research on the Edwin Smith Surgical Papyrus had revealed many words wholly new to Egyptology, which together with a large number of familiar ones in unusual contexts investing them with unaccustomed meanings, required several weeks of daily conferences with his colleague and one-time fellow-student, Kurt Sethe, now an eminent authority and professor of Egyptology at the University of Göttingen.

When they were nearing the end of this intensive work, my father invited him and his family—excepting Frau Sethe, who was gravely ill—to join us on an automobile excursion of several days to their former haunts in the neighboring Harz Mountains. He and Sethe found old familiar paths, they sang again and reminded one another of that sublime August of exactly thirty years ago, the full flavor of which they might almost have recaptured but for the absence of Erman whose failing sight and strength had kept him in Berlin.

My father ordered for his old friends the best that was available of everything—which was easy to do, for the mark had already fallen to over 3000 to the dollar. But at the final midday meal together on the last day of our outing, when everything should have been at its gayest, the Sethe family suddenly fell silent, and one saw that their eyes were brimming. When my father, surprised and troubled, asked them what had happened to sadden them so, they smiled as best they could and said it was nothing, only the effect of much happiness coming to an end.

The day after their return to Göttingen, Sethe was noticeably subdued when he joined my father for their usual period of work together. Finally he said: "Forgive us, old friend, for our behavior yesterday. We ought not to have gone on your excursion, which you meant so kindly. America is a land of such plenty and so untouched by the War, that you would find it difficult to understand the effect upon us when you ordered as a matter of course, all sorts of dishes—*meat, good* bread, *butter*—and plied us with *second* helpings of everything which for years we have disciplined ourselves to do without. It is for lack of the very things which you take for granted, that my wife is now in her last illness!"

During the weeks that my father consulted the Egyptian Dictionary in connection with the Surgical Papyrus, "working in the familiar, gloomy, dungeon-like rooms filled with cold-storage air antedating the Franco-Prussian war," he saw much of old Erman who soon put him *au courant* again with the great project for which twenty-five years ago he had labored so long and we had traveled so widely. He found his "admiration stirred by the quiet perseverance with which throughout the War my old colleagues had continued their work on the *Dictionary,* and in the face of inflation and the most discouraging post-War conditions, are now planning for its publication."

With his visit to Oxford in October, 1922, to receive his honorary degree (an experience he described in a passage quoted toward the beginning of this book), one of his most memorable sojourns in Europe since he had first beheld it in 1891 came to an end; and once again, this time with his entire family, he returned to Egypt.

None of the three books Howard Carter published on his discovery of Tutenkhamon's tomb made any mention of an incident which was virtually the determining factor in bringing about his superlative find. He personally described it to me, and when I asked him why he had omitted it, merely shrugged his shoulders.

In the summer of 1922, he said, soon after he had returned to England from still another unsuccessful season of excavation for Lord Carnarvon in the Valley of the Kings' Tombs at Luxor, his patron summoned him to Highclere Castle to discuss the question of whether they should continue this expensive and thus far fruitless task. Carnarvon rather dreaded the interview which as it then seemed to him could end only in a decision even more saddening for Carter, if possible, than for himself.

He had in mind the fact that throughout his career in Egypt, Carter's one great hope had been "to dig in The Valley." When their association in excavation had begun in 1907, "it was in the joint hope," as Carter later recalled,* "that eventually we might be able to get a concession there." The latter was then and until 1914 continued to be held by Mr. Theodore M. Davis; and during the interim, Carter "dug [for Carnarvon] with varying fortune in other parts of the Theban necropolis." † The concession had in that year become available to

---

* *The Tomb of Tut-ankh-Amen,* by Howard Carter and A. C. Mace, George H. Doran Company, 1923, 2 vols., p. 117.

At this point let me anticipate the reader's quandary by noting that soon after the discovery, the spelling "Tutankhamen" was adopted and given out to the American press by the Egyptian Section of the Metropolitan Museum of New York. It differs slightly from "Tutenkhamon," which my father and many other Egyptologists had been using for upwards of 25 years, and which simply for that reason is used in this book. The difference is due partly to the arbitrary individualism of a younger generation, but largely to the fact that Orientalists and field archaeologists in the Near East have never unanimously agreed upon a consistent system of transliterating ancient or modern oriental languages into English.

† *Ibid.,* p. 117.

Carnarvon only because Mr. Davis in his discouragement, after finding nothing for several seasons, had relinquished it. The Valley, he had insisted, was dug out. Even "Sir Gaston Maspero," said Carter, "[then] Director of the Antiquities Department, who signed our concession, agreed with Mr. Davis that the site was exhausted. . . . However, . . . we were quite sure that there were areas, covered by the dumps of previous excavators, which had never been properly examined." *

Despite the duties in which the First World War involved him, Carter had been able during those years to excavate intermittently in The Valley. To make absolutely certain that not a square inch of its floor and slopes should escape his examination, he made a large-scale map of it upon which he subdivided the entire terrain into convenient sections; and as his excavation of an actual area progressed and he had completely satisfied himself that it contained nothing of value, he checked off the corresponding sections on the map. The real campaign began in the autumn of 1917. But the results consistently failed to justify the expense and effort they had involved, until by the spring of 1922 Carnarvon had about concluded that Davis and Maspero had been correct, and that the only sensible thing to do was to abandon further digging in The Valley.

Carter also anticipated their interview with anxiety, for he better than anyone knew that thus far the record warranted no other conclusion. His one hope resided in a simple plan which he proposed to lay before Carnarvon.

When they finally met at Highclere, Carnarvon reviewed the history of their work, expressed again his appreciation of the years of effort Carter had given to it; and with genuine regret, stated that in view of the post-War economic stringency, he would find it impossible to support further this obviously barren undertaking.

In reply Carter said that their consistent failure to find anything had not in the slightest weakened the conviction he had held for years, that The Valley contained at least one more royal tomb, probably that of Tutenkhamon, the existence of which was strongly indicated by circumstantial evidence. He granted again that perhaps even this problematical tomb might have been robbed in antiquity—but there was always the possibility that it had not!

Carter now laid before him the familiar map which showed, season by season, the record of their probing and excavation. At first glance not a single square meter of Valley floor and slopes appeared un-

* *Ibid.*, p. 118

checked, but Carter reminded him that just below the entrance to the tomb of Ramses VI there remained a small triangular area, clearance of which they had postponed for some later, off-season time because it would temporarily prevent visitors from entering the foregoing tomb. In this area he had noted the foundation remains of a row of crude stone huts, evidently built by ancient tomb workmen, which he would have to remove in order to probe the terrain beneath them.

Now, said Carter, only when this triangle had been cleared would he feel that their work in The Valley had been absolutely completed. He therefore wished to propose that Carnarvon grant him permission to undertake one more season's work at his—Carter's—own expense, using Carnarvon's concession, and the same workmen and equipment he had employed for years; and if at the end of this final season he found nothing, he would of course, and with a good conscience, agree that they should abandon The Valley. But if on the other hand he should make a discovery, it should belong to Carnarvon exactly as under their long-standing arrangement.

Carnarvon was by nature a sportsman, and Carter's proposal appealed to him as eminently fair—in fact, as too generous. He would agree, he said, to another and final season of excavation; but it would be at his own, not Carter's expense. They shook hands upon it and that autumn Carter returned to Egypt for what was to be his farewell season in the Valley of the Kings' Tombs.

"Would he find the missing tomb of Tutenkhamon?" my father later wrote of this extraordinary quest. "The tombs of all the great emperors had long ago been found. But at the end of the Eighteenth Dynasty there was a gap caused by the fact that the revolutionary Pharaoh, Ikhnaton (Amenhotep IV), after annihilating the old gods, especially Amon, and introducing the exclusive worship of a sole god, the sun-god Aton, had forsaken Amon's imperial city of Thebes and built for himself a new capital at Tell el-Amarna, some 228 miles downriver. There he had established the earliest monotheism, and there he had made his tomb. Dying without a son, he was succeeded first by one and then another son-in-law.

"The second of these sons-in-law, Tutenkhaton ('Living Image of Aton,' as his name signified), was unable to maintain the religious revolution against priestly opposition. The priests of Amon at the old capital forced him to return there and resume the worship of the old gods, especially Amon. They obliged him even to change his name by inserting Amon in the place of Aton. He became Tutenkhamon, 'Living

Image of Amon,' and his wife, the princess Enkhosnepaaton ('She Lives by Aton'), was likewise constrained to renounce the name her great father had given her, and to become Enkhosnamon ('She Lives by Amon'). Tutenkhamon reigned for only a few years somewhere between 1375 and 1350 B.C.

"During the season of 1907–1908, Mr. Davis's workmen had found a cache of large baked clay jars containing funerary equipment consisting mainly of bundles of linen but including many of the things used in funeral processions. He dismissed the discovery as unimportant, and it might have been forgotten altogether had not Herbert E. Winlock of the Metropolitan Museum noticed that seal impressions in the closures of the jars, and a marking on one of the pieces of linen contained the name of Tutenkhamon. This, together with other indications, made it credible that the King himself lay buried somewhere in the Valley of the Kings' Tombs.

"The astonishing revolution which Tutenkhamon had survived had carried the art of Egypt to a level of beauty surpassing anything before known in Egypt or anywhere else in the early Orient. If the missing tomb existed at all and had escaped the post-Empire robbers, perhaps it might contain some of the artistic splendor of this remarkable period. Who could say?"

As in previous years, we sailed from Cairo almost continuously southward. On November 26 we stopped for an hour at Luxor only for provisions, without ourselves even stepping ashore, before pushing steadily on to the temple of Abu Simbel which we reached one evening just as a sunset of Sahara rose-quartz was giving way to the white glory of a Nubian moon. By December 7 we had returned again to Aswan, at the foot of the First Cataract, where a large sack of accumulated mail was brought aboard.

Among the letters was a note from Lord Carnarvon, written as he was hurriedly departing for England, expressing great regret that before a messenger could reach my father while we had stopped at Luxor on November 26, the day of "the opening of a tomb or cache which Carter has found," we had sailed southward beyond his reach. "I wish I had known earlier [that you were arriving], for I might then have persuaded you to stop a day and behold a marvelous sight. Still, there is another sealed door to be opened, and I hope I shall then have the pleasure of seeing you there!"

"He did not say what it was," my father wrote soon afterward, "for he knew I would understand that Carter had found what might be the tomb of Tutenkhamon!"

When we reached Luxor again a few days later, Carter was absent in Cairo. There were vague rumors in the town that he had discovered a tomb, but the press had not yet received the full story, and the name of Luxor had not yet been spread to the remotest corners of the earth.

My father was eager to see the exact location of the find, and on the day before Carter's return we visited the Valley of the Kings' Tombs, approaching it by the usual road which enters it from the river flood plain. As we neared the mouth of The Valley, we passed on our right the one-story adobe houses in which Carter had lived all through the years of his fruitless quest. I thought back to my boyhood visits to this strange burial place of ancient kings, and to my first meeting with him on the day when Davis's workmen had uncovered another royal tomb which like all the rest had been robbed in antiquity. But now at last Carter had apparently earned his reward.

Immediately below and slightly to the right of the entrance to the tomb of Ramses VI, we came upon a freshly excavated pit which had been walled on three sides with newly laid, unmortared rubble. In the middle of this pit there was a pile of debris topped by a crude slab of limestone upon which had been hastily drawn with black paint the coat of arms of the house of Carnarvon. Guarding this pile of debris sat a Mr. Callender, one of Carter's assistants, a loaded rifle across his knees. Three trusted native carpenters were busily constructing a small shack for housing watchmen, protecting equipment, and the like; while at intervals along the rubble retaining walls stood native soldiers, also guarding the place with loaded rifles. An occasional passing tourist would peer perfunctorily into the pit and in the gleaming hot sun would note chiefly the huge beads of perspiration upon Mr. Callender's uncovered and balding head. At this particular moment of calm before an unparalleled deluge of world-wide publicity, the scene of Carter's discovery was singularly unimpressive.

Next morning, on his return from Cairo, Carter came directly from his train to our boat, where for two hours which flew like as many minutes, he sat telling us the story of his find.

He had reached Luxor on October 28, he said, and by the morning of November 1 had made up the payroll of his old workmen, and was ready to begin trenching southwards at the northeast corner of the entrance to Ramses VI's tomb. By late afternoon of the 3rd his men had again laid bare the foundation stones of the row of ancient workmen's huts beneath which he had never probed. When he arrived at the "dig" the next morning—the 4th—he found the men impatiently awaiting his arrival: for, a little more than two feet under the very first hut they had attacked, they had come upon a step cut into bed rock; and in accordance with the rule always observed by well-trained workmen on every archaeological excavation, they had stopped their digging pending the arrival of their chief.

"Think of it!" Carter exclaimed at this point in his story—"twice before I had come within two yards of that first stone step! The first time was years ago when I was digging for Davis, and he suggested that we shift our work to some 'more promising spot.' The second was only a few seasons ago when Lord Carnarvon and I decided to reserve clearance of this area for a time when we wouldn't interfere with visitors to the tomb of Ramses VI."

Another day's work laid bare more steps and the rectangular opening of a descending stairway passage; and presently, the upper part of a doorway sealed with rubble which in turn had been covered with mortar wherein had been made many seal impressions. Very carefully, without destroying any of the latter, he broke a small hole at the top by which he was able to determine that the space beyond was filled with the same kind of limestone chips and debris which his men had been removing up to this point.

He now re-sealed this hole, ordered the men to re-fill the entrance passage up to the former surface level, posted a strong guard over the place. His excitement allowed him little sleep that night, and early the next morning he hurried to the telegraph office in Luxor to send Carnarvon a cable (which Carter showed my father), reading, "AT LAST HAVE MADE WONDERFUL DISCOVERY IN VALLEY; A MAGNIFICENT TOMB WITH SEALS INTACT; RE-COVERED SAME FOR YOUR ARRIVAL; CONGRATULATIONS."

Later that day he took further precautions against robbery by having his workmen pile additional debris over the site of the discovery, and by posting a squad of Egyptian soldiers at the spot. On top of the heap of debris he had his workmen place some of the large stones which had composed the ancient workmen's huts; and on one of these stones he had himself daubed an approximation of the Carnarvon coat of arms.

With his daughter, Lady Evelyn Herbert, for years his companion on his visits to Egypt, Carnarvon made the journey to Luxor as quickly as he could. In anticipation of their arrival on November 23, Carter had re-excavated the pit; and by the afternoon of the 24th, Carnarvon and Lady Evelyn had witnessed the clearance of sixteen steps, as creamy white as if they had just been cut, leading down to the new completely exposed sealed doorway.

"It was toward midday of the 25th," Carter continued, "that Lord Carnarvon and I would have been especially grateful for your presence, for we had spent the morning in carefully studying and photographing the seal impressions which had been made while the mortar was still soft, immediately after the door had been blocked shut in antiquity. We noted that the upper part of the doorway was covered with one set of seals, and that at the bottom there was evidence of the tomb having been broken into and subsequently re-sealed and stamped with another set of seal impressions. It appeared certain that the tomb had been broken into in antiquity!"

The next stage of the work was to remove the blocking of the door in sections, with a minimum of damage to the seal impressions, so that they could be more carefully studied by my father and others at a later time. By the afternoon of November 25, the blocking of the first doorway had been completely removed and the workmen had begun clearance of a descending passageway beyond it.

November 26th—when we had stopped briefly at Luxor, and Carnarvon's messenger had failed to reach us in time—proved to be what Carter called "the day of days." All morning the clearance of the descending passage continued, and by mid-afternoon, at a distance of thirty feet from the first doorway, the workmen now came upon a second one, almost identical in the matter of seal impressions and evidence of having been broken into in ancient times. With Carnarvon at his side, Carter now made a small opening in the upper left hand corner of this sealed doorway. As a test for any possible deadly gases, he inserted a lighted candle. It only flickered in a rush of hot, musty air which had been pent up for almost thirty-three centuries! Next, he broke away a little more of the rubble closure, and inserting an electric flashlight, leaned forward and looked through the opening.

As Carter spoke, his imagination recaptured the emotion of that first moment, and his voice failed him. He paused for a moment, and then remarked that he had been similarly moved when he stood peering in at the ineffable wonders of the first chamber, and thought back over the long barren years which had led up to this unbelievable consummation of all his hopes. We understood—for as he sat describing in a low voice what he had seen in those first moments, we too found ourselves deeply stirred.

He did not yet know the extent of the wealth he had found. On the back of an old letter which he pulled from his pocket, he hastily sketched as much of the ground plan of the tomb or cache as he could remember, and while doing so, described briefly some of the treasure and its location in the antechamber. The stark simplicity of the room and the total absence of decoration or even of any finish on the walls might indicate that this was a cache where the King's funerary treasure had been hastily hidden at his death, which must have occurred in politically troublous times; and that the actual burial of the King might have been performed elsewhere.

Some years before as Chief Inspector of Antiquities for Upper Egypt, Carter had supervised the installation of an electric generator in the Valley, and of lighting in most of the tombs. He was therefore now able to set his men to work connecting the foregoing system with the new find. But this was only one detail among a thousand important problems confronting him. He and Carnarvon immediately arranged an official opening of the tomb, to which important personages from the Egyptian government and the British administration in Cairo were invited, including the Cairo correspondent of the London *Times*. Immediately after this Carter once again re-sealed both doorways with very heavy timbers, re-filled the entire pit with debris, and took further precautions to safeguard the area. Carnarvon and Lady Evelyn Herbert hurried back to England to make countless arrangements necessitated by the discovery. Carter himself went to Cairo to gather all the cotton batting, collodion, paraffin and other preparatorial equipment and preservatives available there on such short notice; and to have built a massive grated steel door for installation in the entrance to the first chamber.

"We shall now re-excavate the entrance," Carter said, "install the steel door—which was shipped on my train—and make many other preparations which will consume three days. On the third day from today, please cross the river as if on a routine visit to the Theban temples, climb the mountain as if for the view—and then drop down into The Valley. Plan to reach the tomb at three o'clock in the afternoon. Bring with you a complete change of underclothes—the temperature in the tomb is still such that after only a brief stay in it, one comes forth dripping with perspiration!"

Thereupon with an abrupt good-bye he climbed into his waiting felucca and soon disappeared on the west bank of the river.

On the third morning thereafter we did exactly as he had told us, casually crossed the river, mounted donkeys and rode to the great temples and ruins along the margin of the western desert. Presently we left our donkeys at the foot of the cliffs, and as if merely to get the view, ascended the old familiar trail. With no one following us or aware of our errand, we continued climbing to the crest of the great ridge, thence descended at once on the other side.

At the entrance pit of the new find we were met by Howard Carter and his assistant Mr. Callender; and Mr. Harry Burton, expert photographer, and Mr. A. C. Mace, field archaeologist, respectively from the Metropolitan Museum's Expedition at Thebes and Lisht, the services of whose entire staff had been lent to Lord Carnarvon by the Museum. Also awaiting us and their first view of the tomb were Mr. Winlock, Field Director of the Metropolitan Museum Expedition, Mrs. Winlock and one of their daughters.

The appearance of the entrance pit had changed greatly since our earlier visit. The little shack had been completed, the entrance passage to the tomb had been cleared of the tons of protective debris, chairs had been placed at the head of the stone stairway, and everything wore a purposeful, businesslike air.

To relieve the curious tension of the moment, we exchanged perfunctory commonplaces, while the men took off their coats. Carter now stepped to the head of the stairway and said, "Are we ready? Come, please!"—then turned and began the short descent.

My father and the other gentlemen followed him down the sixteen steps which ended in an inclined passage. The place was not deep—not more than forty feet from the open air to the grated steel door now installed in the final entrance. In front of the latter had been hung a white sheet upon which a flood of radiance from behind cast shadows of the steel bars in silhouette. All my life I shall remember the picture of that little group of men as they stood waiting with glowing eyes while Carter paused with his left hand at the upper corner of the white sheet, then suddenly drew it away.

Through the steel bars we saw an incredible vision, an impossible scene from a fairy tale, an enchanted property-room from the opera house of some great composer's dreams. Opposite us were three couches upon which a king had lain, all about were chests, caskets, alabaster vases, gold-embellished stools and chairs—the heaped-up riches of a Pharaoh who had died some three thousand two hundred and fifty years ago—before Crete had passed her zenith, before Greece had been born or Rome conceived, or more than half of the history of civilization had taken place. In the brilliant light, against the white limestone wall, the colors of all these things were vibrant yet soft—a medley of brown, yellow, blue, amber, gold, russet and black.

Carter stepped forward, unlocked four large Yale locks, removed several steel chains and smaller padlocks, then swung open the barred gate. Not even the harsh rattle of steel against steel could break the spell upon us all; and when Carter said to my father and Winlock, "Will you not enter?" they were reluctant to move lest everything vanish like a mirage.

Still hesitant, they went in very slowly, followed by Carter. The former two stood for some time as if transfixed, their incredulous gaze taking in the entire room. When at last they turned and looked into Carter's face, one could see tears in the eyes of all three men—even for Carter, to whom it was no longer new, the experience was overpoweringly moving. Words failed them, and by mutual instinct they all shook hands and laughed a little sheepishly as they rubbed their eyes, and my father and Winlock began examining the wealth about them.

"I could only utter one exclamation of amazement after another, and then turn again and shake Carter's hand," my father wrote afterward. "Emotion struggled with the habit of years to observe and to understand, a struggle in which my critical faculties were for the moment completely routed. All about us lay a totally new revelation of ancient life, transcending anything we had ever known before. Here was the magnificence which only the wealth and splendor of the Imperial Age in Egypt in the fourteenth century before Christ could have wrought or conceived—and as it at first seemed, with everything still standing as it was placed there when the tomb was last closed. Never was anything so dramatic in the whole range of archaeological discovery as this first view of what must surely be Tutenkhamon's tomb.

"Against the rear wall of this first chamber—which was about 14 feet wide and approximately 26 feet long—and extending almost its entire length, were placed head to foot three magnificent couches all overwrought with gold. As one faced them they were breast high—his majesty probably required some sort of portable step when he climbed into bed. The couch at the right was made in the form of a standing panther, the creature's head and legs forming respectively the bedposts at the head and the supports beneath the couch. The middle couch had the form of a mottled cow with four horns, while the third couch at the left was a grotesque typhon-like hippo with mouth open showing the grinning teeth.

"Under the couches were chairs and caskets, chests and boxes. On the inside of the back of the finest of these chairs there is a representation of the King and his Queen standing together. The work is executed in gold and silver with incrustation and inlay of semi-precious stones in bright colors. In art and craftsmanship it is one of the finest pieces of work now in existence from any age of the world.

"In a corner at the right I knelt before a lovely casket containing part of the royal raiment. The outside of this casket was painted with scenes in miniature, representing the Pharaoh and the royal suite engaged in hunting and in war—a dying lion clutches with his mighty paw at an arrow which has entered his open mouth and hangs broken from his gnashing teeth, while his wounded jungle comrades lie about him in postures of pathetic suffering. The marvelous refinement of detail, especially the depiction of the hairy manes, reminds one of similar work by Albrecht Dürer.

"In the left corner of the front wall lay the dismounted wheels and other parts of a number of royal chariots. Like the back of the royal chair, and fully equal to it in art and craftsmanship, they were adorned with sumptuous designs in gold and with incrustation of semi-precious stones. The wheels bore traces of having been driven over the rough streets of Thebes. They were therefore not show pieces especially prepared for the King's tomb, but vehicles intended for actual use—and nevertheless, adorned like this! Not vulgar and ostentatious magnificence, but the richness of matured and refined art, formed the daily environment of these great rulers of the Nile in the fourteenth century before Christ.

"The splendor of Nineveh and Babylon seems now but a rough foil for setting off the civilization of Egyptian Thebes, which could boast such craftsmen as had produced this royal furniture—men quite worthy to stand beside Lorenzo Ghiberti and Benvenuto Cellini. I felt the traditional 'culture values' of the ancient world shifting so rapidly that it made me fairly dizzy!

"I aimlessly fingered notebook and pencil. Of what use were notes made in such a state of mind, with myriad details and whirling thoughts crowding to be recorded all at once? There, between two of the couches, stood four alabaster vases carved with open-work flowers growing on each side and forming the handles. No one had ever seen such vases before. Yonder was a casket of jewelry, and under one of the couches lay a courtier's magnificent baton with a superb handle of gleaming gold, the designs being done in filigree and lovely chevrons made up of tiny spheres of gold, laid—scores of them to the inch—on a background of sheet gold.

"Just beyond this casket was a door in the back wall of the chamber, opposite the chariots and accessible only by crawling under the left-hand couch. Carter handed me a portable electric light, and I crawled under the tall couch to peep through the door. It had originally been sealed with masonry like the other doors, and like them had been broken through at the bottom. Beyond this breach, I could see a second room which Carter had christened 'The Annex.' This was so filled with royal furniture, it was impossible to enter the place without injury to its contents.

"Leaning against the wall to the right, and immediately beside the door as one entered the antechamber, was a large, now brown and desiccated bouquet of what on the burial day had been exquisite, gay-colored flowers.

"Farther to the right, and facing each other like silent sentries on either side of a still unopened sealed doorway in the right end-wall of the chamber, stood two life-size statues of the King, each resting upon a reed mat. Each wore a regal kilt overlaid with gold, a crown of gold, and massive golden sandals. From the forehead of each rose a royal asp of shining gold, each held in its right hand a baton of gold, and in its left a golden staff. The statues themselves were of oiled wood, blackened with age. In spite of their sumptuous gilding, oxidation had invested the royal figures with something of the 'somber livery of the burnished sun' under which the King had lived.

"A second glance had quickly dispelled my initial impression that the royal tomb equipment had never been disturbed: evidences of disturbance and robbery were unmistakable. Openwork designs in heavy sheet gold which had filled the spaces between the legs of the finer chairs had been wrenched out and carried away. The chariots had suffered similarly, and when the robbers had finished with them, they had thrown the parts aside in disorder. They had also left the inner or 'Annex' chamber in great confusion. One of two shrines under the right hand couch had been broken open, and when the robbers found that the statuette of the serpent goddess within was not of solid gold, they had troubled neither to reclose the tiny double doors, nor to open its companion shrine of identical design and size, upon the doors of which the clay seal remained unbroken.

"As the robbers left, they found in their way a common couch for ordinary household use. They tossed this hastily aside—possibly as they hurriedly escaped from the tomb, where they may have been interrupted at their work—and it still lies on top of the couch resembling a cow, with one of the cow's horns sticking through the plaited thongs which had been tightly stretched across the couch frame. The marauders must have taken with them many vessels and other objects made entirely of gold.

"It was now important, besides being a 'Sherlock Holmes' task of unusual interest, to determine who these early tomb robbers were, or at least to gain some rough approximation of the date when they forced their entrance. The holes they had made in the two outside doorways to the tomb had not been large. Carter had of course carefully preserved the plaster with its precious seal impressions, which had covered the masonry closure. When I mentioned this problem to him, he urged me to return the next day for an intensive study of the seals."

As Carter had forewarned us, the air in the tomb, heated by almost thirty-three centuries of Egyptian sun, was insufferably hot. But so exhilarating had been this amazing experience that when we emerged into the cool air of the oncoming twilight we were unaware of being utterly wilted and weary, and conscious only of a sense of elation and of moving in a dream as we returned in the dusk over the cliffs and across the plain and the river to Luxor. I kept remembering that evening years before when as a small boy almost dead for sleep, I had ridden home along this same route from my first visit to The Valley.

The next day (November 18) my father returned to examine the seal impressions in the plaster which had covered the first two doors to the Tomb—the sections of plaster were now stored in a neighboring tomb which Carter was using as a workshop and laboratory.

"The ancient officials who had made the seal impressions had unfortunately neglected to use enough dust on the seal," my father wrote. "The plaster had consequently stuck to the seal, and when it was pulled away, the plaster under it had come away with it, leaving an almost or totally illegible impression. But as the same seal was used many times it was possible to read the four different seals on the two doors by combining the impressions of each. Three of the seals con-

tained the name of Tutenkhamon, and the fourth was that of the cemetery administration, and not necessarily post-Empire. The re-sealing
after the robbery had not been marked with the name of any post-
Empire king. These facts in themselves seemed to confirm that we were
dealing not with a cache merely containing the King's mortuary furniture, but with the *tomb* of Tutenkhamon.

"There still remained to be studied the seals on the unopened
doorway guarded by the King's statues. Carter asked me to return
again the following day, to examine this doorway.

"As I rode across the Theban plain the next morning, my mind was
absorbed with the problem on which we were engaged. If Tutenkhamon's tomb had really escaped the post-Empire robbers, who could
have robbed it under the power and wealth and efficiency of the great
Pharaohs of the Empire—rulers who were quite capable of protecting
the tombs of their ancestors?

"At Carter's house I found him with a mass of telegrams and
letters from all sorts of people who were trying to gain a glimpse of
the wonderful tomb. When he had disposed of these as best he could,
we rode together up the wild and impressive Valley. Under the
brilliant morning sun the rocks and cliffs glowed with a fabulous light,
a splendor worthy of the sepulchres of Egypt's greatest dead, the 'Sons
of the Sun,' as the Pharaohs called themselves.

"A mountain of sunlit limestone rose above the tomb of Tutenkhamon. We descended into the ante-chamber, and as the sound of our
footfalls ceased, we stood for a moment in the silence in which the
King had slept for over thirty-two centuries.

"I turned to the sealed door at our right. The floor before it was
encumbered with small objects which it was unwise to move before
the preliminary record of the conditions in the tomb had been made.
To bring my eyes close enough to the seal-covered mortar, I had to
stand on the ancient reed matting on which the two statues of the King
had so long ago been placed.

"Carnarvon and Carter had decided at the very outset that the
tomb had been robbed under Ramses IX, and Carnarvon had published a statement to that effect in a letter to the London *Times*. But
it was inconceivable to me that *post*-Empire robbers could have left
so much untouched treasure in the tomb. I now said so to Carter; and
when he replied that there were no robberies known in the royal
cemetery before the close of the Empire, I showed him that the seal
which he and Carnarvon had read as 'Ramses IX' was actually a seal

of Tutenkhamon; and that both the other sealed doorways, covered with scores and scores of seal impressions, bore only the name of Tutenkhamon or of the cemetery administration.

"I also reminded him that the tomb of Thutmose IV, which Carter himself had excavated, had after a robbery been restored by Tutenkhamon's almost immediate successor, King Harmhab, who had left a record of this pious deed on a wall of Thutmose IV's tomb. If another royal burial had suffered robbery soon after Tutenkhamon's death, might not the same robbers, I said, also have entered *his* tomb? At this point Carter exclaimed, 'My God, I never thought of that!'

"He repeated these words when I further recalled to him that the huts of the workmen who excavated the tomb of Ramses VI were built directly across the mouth of Tutenkhamon's tomb, showing that the latter had been covered over and forgotten long before Ramses IX's reign and the post-Empire robbers of the latter's time!

"Carter now left me to myself and as I became absorbed in the detailed examination of one imperfect, almost illegible seal impression after another, I began to hear strange rustling, murmuring, whispering sounds which rose and fell, and sometimes wholly died away.

"These sounds were evidence of the melancholy changes already taking place around me. For the air in this chamber had remained absolutely still and undisturbed for over three thousand years, until Carter had entered it. Now the incoming outside air was altering the temperature and the quality of the atmosphere in the tomb. Physical and chemical changes were being accelerated, and the wood in the furniture was adjusting itself to new strains, with resulting audible snapping and fracturing. All this meant that the life of the superlatively beautiful things around me was limited: a few generations more, and even in the protection of a museum, the objects not of pottery, stone, or metal will steadily deteriorate.

"Looking down upon me on either hand in quiet serenity, as I puzzled over seal impressions made but a short time after his death, was the benign face of a ruler who had dominated the ancient world in the days when the Hebrews were captives in Egypt and Moses, their leader and liberator, had not yet been born. Only the brilliant rays of the electric light suggested the modern world into which these amazing survivals from the remote past had been so unexpectedly projected.

"As I sat copying the 150 or so seals, a curious incident occurred. I happened to glance up at the face of one of the statues of the King—and as I did so, he clearly and unmistakably *winked* at me!

"For a moment this was strangely disturbing, but I quickly found the explanation. Attached to a virtually invisible filament hanging from the King's eyebrow in front of his eye, was a tiny piece of the dark pigment which had been used in coloring the statues and was now dropping off in small iridescent, shiny, mica-like flakes. In the faint movement of the air from the doorway, the suspended flake had caught and reflected the light in a manner exactly resembling a wink!

"This incident and the continuing sounds put me in mind of the story I had just heard of an occurrence which had taken place soon after Carter's return that October to his house at the mouth of The Valley.

"Before leaving England he had remarked to his friends that he was tired of living alone in Egypt, as he had done for nearly thirty years. They had assumed he was about to take unto himself a wife. But all that he acquired was a canary bird!

"He hung the bird in its cage from the ceiling of the portico in his house. There are no song birds in Egypt, and the carolling of the canary was very pleasant, especially for the natives who had never heard anything of the kind before and who came flocking for miles to hear it sing. They all said, 'The bird will bring good fortune!' Not very long after this, Carter uncovered the first step of the flight of stairs leading down to the tomb of Tutenkhamon.

"When they heard of the discovery the natives said, 'We knew it would be so—the bird has done it, the bird has brought him to this tomb!' And they promptly christened it 'The Tomb of the Bird.'

"Word soon spread through the villages of the region that a statue of the King stood guard on either side of a sealed doorway to what must of course be the burial place of the King himself. And on the King's forehead, they said, just as on his statues, would be found the sacred cobra with his hood spread and his tongue darting out and threatening to poison the King's enemies, exactly as the ancient Egyptians believed it did.

"One day soon after the discovery Carter sent an assistant to fetch something from his house which happened to be empty, the servants having gone to the weekly market at Luxor. As the man approached the house he heard a faint, almost human cry. Then all was silent again—even the bird had stopped singing.

"Upon entering, he looked almost instinctively at the cage and saw coiled within it a cobra holding in its mouth the dead canary.

"News of this spread quickly and all the natives now said, Alas, that was the King's cobra, revenging itself upon the bird for having betrayed the place of the tomb—and now something terrible will happen!'

"There was obviously nothing sinister or occult about the presence of a cobra in the cage. But as I sat there between the two already legendary statues of the King and heard the strange noises all around me, I could not help recalling this story.

"I continued working until I had examined every seal impression from the top of the doorway to a point near the bottom where the small objects and the reed matting interfered. It was already evident that this mysterious unopened doorway contained the same seals I had found on the other two doors; and in addition, fifteen impressions of a new seal (which did not appear on the other two doors) containing the name of Tutenkhamon himself. Whatever robbery had occurred had not been post-Empire.

"The hole made by the robbers at the bottom of this doorway was obviously much too small to have permitted the removal of anything but quite small objects. Almost certainly, therefore, the body of the only Pharaoh of the Empire which may have escaped the destruction of post-Empire disorder and lawlessness, lay beyond this doorway.

"Carter invited me to return from Cairo to Luxor as soon as he should have cleared the antechamber and have made ready to open the burial chamber.

"On the morning of February 14, 1923, as I sat working on the Coffin Texts in a long skylighted gallery which had been assigned to us in the Cairo Museum, I received a telegram from Lord Carnarvon summoning me again to Luxor; and by the middle of the following morning I found myself once more seated before the mysterious sealed doorway.

"The antechamber had been cleared, which greatly facilitated a re-examination of all of the 150 seal impressions. Again the evidence was unequivocal. Every seal belonged to Tutenkhamon's reign. The robbery must have been only slight and cursory, and must have occurred very soon after his burial.

"The next afternoon, February 16, in the presence of Lord Carnarvon and Lady Evelyn Herbert, several high officials from the Egyptian Government and various notable representatives of England, France and the United States, Carter with the assistance of Mr. Mace broke open the last sealed doorway. For three hours the little group sat utterly enthralled while the men methodically removed stone after stone, until they had revealed a great catafalque or shrine built of wood covered with sheet gold and inset with plaques of blue faience—the outermost of a series of shrines within the last of which the King lies buried.

"When we opened the doors of this first catafalque or shrine, we found that the seal on the next inner shrine was still unbroken. The evidence of the seals on the doorway to the burial chamber was thus corroborated.

"The floor of the burial chamber, which was approximately 12 feet wide by something under 20 feet long, was about four feet lower than that of the antechamber. Carter's subsequent measurements showed the outermost shrine to be about 17 feet long, 11 feet wide and 9 feet high; so that it almost completely filled the burial chamber. When Carter permitted us to enter, two at a time, we were therefore barely able to make our way between this outermost shrine and the walls of the room over to the farther right hand corner where another doorway, in this instance unsealed, opened into what Carter called a store chamber. This room, approximately 10 by 12 feet in size, contained a great array of chests (most of them with their seals still unbroken), furniture, models of ships, and above all, a miniature shrine exceeding in beauty and quality even the loveliest things we had seen in the other rooms."

Carnarvon asked my father to make translations of the seals on the shrines and chests, and so far as possible of the inscriptions on the furniture and other objects which might possibly yield immediate information regarding Tutenkhamon's death and burial and perhaps his reign.

"He also formally requested me," my father added, "to do all the historical work involved in the discovery and its eventual publication. Although this was a staggering assignment, I agreed to undertake it. He appeared to be quite pleased and relieved—reactions which I told him frankly I could not share! At the same time, Carter asked me to his house for a conference during which he formally made the same request, stating that he would confirm the arrangement in writing."

The discovery of Tutenkhamon's tomb—the most romantic and thrilling story of archaeological exploration and discovery since Schliemann's revelations at Troy and those of Sir Arthur Evans in Crete—

broke upon a world sated with post-First World War conferences, with nothing proved and nothing achieved, after a summer journalistically so dull that an English farmer's report of a gooseberry the size of a crabapple achieved the main news pages of the London metropolitan dailies. It was hardly surprising therefore that the Tutenkhamon discovery should have received a volume of world-wide publicity exceeding anything in the entire history of science. Almost overnight Carter and Carnarvon became international figures.

Their fame brought with it a host of unaccustomed and extraordinarily harassing problems. Carter was suddenly faced with the most enormous and difficult task which had ever confronted a field archaeologist, and with an inundation of visitors such as Egypt had not experienced since the Persian invasion. All day long a continual procession of messengers brought him sacks of telegrams, notes, letters and messages from hundreds upon hundreds of individuals entreating **or** demanding the privilege of viewing the tomb.

The seasonal volume of mail at the Luxor post office was doubled and trebled. The telegraph office at the station was completely buried under a deluge of newspaper despatches. Tourist shops quickly sold out their stocks of cameras and films, and of books on the history of Egypt. The two leading hotels of Luxor set up tents in their gardens, where many guests were fortunate to be accommodated for a single night on army cots. Each day the hordes of visitors swarmed across the river and into The Valley, where they gathered around the pit at the opening to Tutenkhamon's tomb and lined the path along which, once the work of removal had begun, the contents were carried to an incompleted tomb set aside as a workshop and preparatorial laboratory.

Carter, by nature nervous and high-strung, was now working inordinately long days at top speed under an inhuman strain, and his normally quick temper became tried in the extreme. Carnarvon himself was less actively involved in the work of salvaging the contents of the tomb, but he too suffered the inescapable tribulations which the discovery had thrust upon him. In their effort to ameliorate a situation unique in their experience, both men committed errors of judgment, the consequences of which were to extend far beyond the discovery itself.

By far the most complicated and vexatious of all their problems was that of coping with the press of the entire world. From the beginning Carnarvon had favored the London *Times*. Over Carter's emphatic protests, he presently entered into an agreement with his friend, Major John Jacob Astor, chairman of the London Times Company, Ltd., whereby the *Times* was given a world copyright on all news, pictures, etc., from the tomb. Under this arrangement the *Times* sold its Tutenkhamon news to all newspapers which cared to buy it, and turned over any profits over and above expenses, to Carnarvon to help defray the cost of the work on the tomb.

The net effect was to give to the London *Times* what seemed to the rest of the English-speaking press an unearned and continuing "scoop" on a story which belonged to the history of the entire civilized world. Whether justly or unjustly, the *Times* gained for itself widespread editorial condemnation and resentment both in England and the United States. The resulting feuds and enmities affected even the scientific men in their relation to the tomb, contributed to the growing misunderstanding and eventual breach between Carter and the Egyptian government, and played a definite part in the legal battle and the various other complications in which the tomb presently became involved.

All this was in itself unfortunate enough. But the discovery had created still another serious problem toward which Carnarvon's attitude, however justifiable on legal grounds, also resulted in regrettable consequences.

As stated in an earlier chapter, permission to excavate a given site in Egypt was granted by the Department of Antiquities to accredited individuals and institutions in the form of a concession, renewable annually. Carnarvon's concession to excavate in the Valley of the Kings' Tombs contained among other stipulations the following:

"8. Mummies of the Kings, of Princes, and of High Priests, together with their coffins and sarcophagi, shall remain the property of the Antiquities Service.

"9. Tombs which are discovered intact, together with all objects they may contain, shall be handed over to the Museum whole and without division.

"10. In the case of tombs *which have already been searched* [the italics are mine], the Antiquities Service shall, over and above the mummies and sarcophagi intended in Article 8, reserve for themselves all objects of capital importance from the point of view of history and archaeology, and shall share the remainder with the Permittee.

"As it is probable that the majority of such tombs as may be discovered will fall within the category of the present article, it is agreed that the Permittee's share will sufficiently recompense him for the pains and labor of the undertaking."

Because the tomb of Tutenkhamon was unique in the history of Egyptian archaeology, and despite the fact that beyond question it *had* been "searched"—an ambiguous phrase presumably meaning "entered and robbed in antiquity"—the Antiquities Service contended that *everything* it contained came under the heading of "objects of capital importance" which the government had reserved the right to retain. On the other hand, Carnarvon held that as stipulated in Article 10, the Service was contractually bound to share with him a large portion of the tomb's contents.

Just as Carter had flatly disagreed with him over his arrangement with the London *Times,* so he now disagreed with him over this knotty question of a division of a portion of the tomb's contents to which, he contended, Carnarvon should unreservedly renounce any rights or claims whatsoever.

"This painful situation," my father wrote on March 12, 1923, "resulted in such strained relations between Carter and Carnarvon that a complete break seemed inevitable. Alan Gardiner and I succeeded in pouring oil on the waters, but in so doing we both fell from Carter's good graces. The man is by no means wholly to blame—what he has gone through has broken him down."

Finally Carnarvon one day called upon Carter at his house to discuss the various matters upon which they could not seem to reach an agreement. Carter was on the verge of a nervous breakdown, and his patron's usual good nature had for once deserted him. Bitter words were exchanged, and in anger Carter requested his old friend to leave his house and never to enter it again.

Soon after this, an insect, probably a mosquito, stung Carnarvon's face. When he shaved the following morning he slightly cut the small welt raised by the sting, and for several succeeding mornings his razor scraped off the little scab which had formed each day over the original cut. He neglected to apply a disinfectant; and one morning an ordinary—which is to say, unspeakably filthy—Egyptian fly settled upon the tiny wound just long enough to infect it.

Carnarvon thought nothing of it, and went about as usual until he became aware of a high fever. He casually called in a doctor who instantly ordered him to bed and to follow a strict diet from which alcohol was absolutely excluded. But he still refused to take the matter seriously. Genially disregarding these instructions, he continued his former diet, supplementing it each evening with a bottle of the favorite vintage he had had sent out to him from his cellars at Highclere Castle.

Carter called to see him, and the two men were reconciled. But Carnarvon never crossed the former's threshold again. He was taken by train to the cooler climate of Cairo, and though attended by his personal physician who had been summoned from England, his condition grew steadily worse. Ever since an almost fatal automobile accident which he had suffered many years before while touring in Germany, Carnarvon's health had been greatly impaired. He was therefore the more susceptible to the present infection, which soon weakened his system until pneumonia set in; and from this on April 5, 1923, at the age of fifty-seven, he died.

The press attributed his death to an ancient curse, and sensationalized this superstition until it became a legend inseparably identified not only with the names of Tutenkhamon, Carnarvon and Carter, but with all the other dramatis personae and the entire history of the tomb episode. What could better explain, for instance, the untimely death in September, 1923, of Carnarvon's younger brother, Colonel Aubrey Herbert? Or the story of Carnarvon's friend, an eminent X-ray specialist who arranged to come to Luxor with equipment for making an examination of the sarcophagus before it was opened, to determine whether it contained the King's mummy—and who died en route to Egypt? Or the lingering illness and eventual death of Carter's foremost collaborator, Mr. Mace? Or of the English trained nurse who attended Carnarvon when he died—and within three years afterwards, having married a rubber planter in Tanganyika, herself died in childbirth? Or of Richard Bethell, only son of Lord Westbury, who during the second season following the tomb discovery, served as Carter's social "doorkeeper"—and whose sudden death in 1929 was followed three months later by the tragic death of his father?

It is as useless to argue with individuals who believe in the "curse" theory as with the press with its "morgues" crammed with Tutenkhamon "curse" stories which during that mad era of the 'twenties sent circulation soaring until for reader interest, archaeology was editorially rated second only to murder and sex. Since people believe what they enjoy believing, it is futile to remind the "curse" addicts that of the men who had any active connection with the tomb, a number were already elderly, and several had for a long time previously been in frail health. Contrary to tourist bureau propaganda, the climate of Egypt is not benign and Riviera-like but tropical and sinister. The salvaging work on the tomb and its contents was enormously exacting and trying, and lasted for some eight years. Whatever befell those who were involved in any phase of the Tutenkhamon discovery merely reflected mortality averages which are a commonplace to every insurance actuary.

Apart from his brief visits to Luxor in connection with Tutenkhamon's tomb that season, my father worked intensively in the Cairo Museum on the Coffin Texts project, which he described as "the *most* formidable task I have ever undertaken." At the same time he continued his research on the Edwin Smith Surgical Papyrus; his study of the Palermo Stone (see p. 254); wrote the section on the Egyptian Empire for the *Cambridge Ancient History;* and the manuscript of a volume on the Salihiyah paintings which he entitled *Oriental Forerunners of Byzantine Painting.* Before the heat of the early Egyptian summer came on he sent his family back to America; and in their absence worked even longer hours. By mid-April he was tired and could hardly have been in a more receptive frame of mind or have felt more gratified and encouraged than when he received a cablegram from George Ellery Hale, congratulating him upon his election to membership in the National Academy of Sciences (it was Hale himself who had proposed his name), and conveying an invitation to meet him in Florence for a visit with Mr. James W. Ellsworth at the latter's historic Villa Palmieri. He eagerly accepted this invitation.

"The Villa Palmieri," he wrote after his arrival there, "is where the Boccaccio tales were staged and by way of contrast, where Queen Victoria spent two vacations when the Villa belonged to the Earl of Crawford. Mr. Ellsworth, the present owner (the father of Lincoln Ellsworth, the Polar explorer), has modernized the house only to the extent of electric lights and luxurious plumbing, and has transformed the whole estate into a veritable paradise.

"He is at once a kindly, generous host, and a crotchety, eccentric old gentleman full of inflexible rules—his guests must be absolutely punctual for meals, are forbidden to smoke even in their bedrooms, and the like; and for infractions are scolded like children. On the other hand, when their visits end he insists upon presenting each guest with a ticket to his destination, even though this be as remote as the United States. His one great hobby is clocks of every age and description—he has about sixty in the Villa Palmieri, and at least a hundred in an ancient castle which he owns at Lenzburg in Switzerland. They are all kept running, they all strike, and as there are often several clocks in one room, the resulting din is to say the least startling!

"Hale and I have adjoining rooms in the oldest part of the Villa, which dates from 1259 A.D.—the rest of the house dates from 1350 and later. We breakfast together on a balcony overlooking the glorious gardens; and presently, with the song of the nightingale in our ears, we march up and down, thinking out loud to each other, exchanging experiences, plans and projects innumerable, and dreaming our dreams together. It is an inspiring experience—our spirits take wing and soar into other worlds."

It was one of these flights of practical imagination on Hale's part which brought about an unforgettable experience, described by my father in a letter to my brother:

"One moonlight night, led by Hale, we visited the government observatory which stands on the hill overlooking the city of Florence. Close by on the next hilltop is the villa where Galileo lived the last ten years of his life, imprisoned by the Roman Catholic Church for having made such discoveries as it believed were not in harmony with its religious views. We could even see the window of the room he occupied.

"We mounted into the dome of the observatory where we were received by Signor Abetti, the director, who had studied with Hale at Mount Wilson, and also at the Yerkes Observatory at Williams Bay, where years ago I had met him.

"Hale had asked Signor Abetti to bring up from the museum in the town Galileo's two telescopes and attach them with metal clamps alongside the eye-piece of the observatory's own 12-inch telescope, an old-fashioned instrument perhaps 20 feet long. You can imagine how tiny they looked—approximately 40 inches long, with lenses only about an inch in diameter!

"Now followed an experience such as none of us had ever had before—for so far as we know, no one since Galileo's time had looked at the skies with his telescopes. Through them we saw the mountains on the moon, the curious 'handles' on Saturn, and the four moons of Jupiter which he discovered (I believe some 8 or 9 are now known); and we could share his own wonder and amazement as he realized that his eyes were the first ever to have beheld these marvels.

"Apart from his desire to afford us an inspiring experience, Hale had arranged all this for an altruistic purpose. The Italian government had begun the construction of a new and more modern observatory, but lacked the money for its completion. Having already contributed as much as he could from a memorial fund left by his father for the support of science, Hale was bringing his inimitable persuasive powers to bear on Mr. Ellsworth in order to secure from him the rest of the required funds. Now, in the dome of the old observatory where we were standing there was a unique and most curious clock which Mr. Ellsworth was eager to possess. It was of no scientific value to the observatory, and Hale had suggested to Signor Abetti that its presentation to Mr. Ellsworth at the right moment might induce the old gentleman to help finance the new observatory. This proposal had filled Signor Abetti with great hopes, but at the same time with dread of jeopardizing his position by thus disposing of government property. Hale assured him that he would personally assume all responsibility.

"As usual, Hale's strategy succeeded. We were on the point of leaving the dome when Mr. Ellsworth announced that he would contribute the money for the completion of the new observatory on one condition, that he should be given the curious clock which he now saw before him. Hale and Abetti exchanged glances, and the latter, swallowing hard, assured Mr. Ellsworth that the clock was his for the asking. What a genius Hale is, and what an evening this had been!

"We came out again and looked over at the villa where the heavy hand of a blinded priesthood had imprisoned one of the world's greatest scientists, and as we drove home through the moonlight we were all too deeply impressed to say very much."

The pattern of their lives never again allowed Hale and my father another such idyllic period together of mutual freedom from workaday cares and scientific responsibilities as this stay in Florence had permitted them. It had been a communion of their spirits, a sublimation of their friendship, that made a permanent impression upon them both. As long as they lived they never ceased referring to it in their correspondence, and always with nostalgia. It marked, incidentally, the beginning of their addressing one another by their first names.

To Mr. Ellsworth's great chagrin, both men surreptitiously bought their own tickets to their next respective destinations. My father, bound for America, traveled to London where the Royal Asiatic Society of Great Britain, of which he had recently been made an honorary member, was celebrating its one hundredth anniversary.

On July 19 he wrote from London: "Yesterday at a reception given by the Lord Mayor at the Mansion House, Lord Chalmers, President of the Royal Asiatic Society, drew me into a corner and said, 'You are to be taken to the King tomorrow morning!'

"So this morning, in company with my old friend, A. V. Williams Jackson, Emile Sénart, President of the Société Asiatique of France, and the Norwegian Orientalist, Sten Konow, I was driven to Buckingham Palace. Guard mount was just taking place, with much music and ceremony all of which we appropriated to ourselves as we passed through the lines of stunningly uniformed guardsmen. Lord Chalmers met us at the door of the Palace, led us across the great court and through the entrance of the King's apartments, past the grand staircase up which the lucky ones go to make their curtsies at levees.

"Presently great doors were opened, and we were ushered into the King's [George V's] presence. He was dressed in a dark gray Prince Albert suit, and came forward to meet us with the utmost simplicity and cordiality. We remained standing, of course, while with much animation and interest he engaged each one of us in conversation. When he came to me he asked at once about Lord Carnarvon and said that he wished there were time for us to talk at length about the tomb of Tutenkhamon. I was much impressed with his quiet self-possession and keen intelligence, and I shall always cherish the memory of my one meeting with the gracious and kindly gentleman who is the King of England."

During my father's absence in Egypt, President Judson had retired, and in July, 1923, was succeeded by Dr. Ernest De Witt Burton, who at the age of sixty-seven brought to the presidency such vigor and splendid vision as the University had not known since the best days of William Rainey Harper's administration. Hardly had Burton taken office when he was once again involved in a critical development in my father's affairs.

Mr. Rockefeller's original five-year pledge for the support of the Oriental Institute was to end in June, 1924. In anticipation of this, my father in the autumn of 1923 presented to him a plan for the permanent development of the Institute on a budget of $50,000 a year. This proposal, as he wrote Hale, "greatly surprised Mr. Rockefeller who stated that he had several times written [President Judson] that he did not expect to continue his contributions [to the Oriental Institute] after the first five years. None of these statements had ever reached either Burton or me. The Institute had been allowed to come within a

few months of the end of its support without my being informed of the
fact or given an opportunity to meet the crisis."

The letters from Mr. Rockefeller, it appeared, had simply been
pigeon-holed, together with an unacknowledged pledge of an additional $25,000 for the purchase of certain antiquities, of which my
father had also never been informed.

At this critical point he was suddenly stricken with an attack of
acute arthritis which, as he wrote me, left him "little better than a
cripple. It is not easy at my age to acknowledge that one is down and
out, but I seem very near it. Such an ordeal just at this time is little
short of a tragedy for me, and I have moments of indignant protest
and rebellion. But then I look up at the driving autumn clouds and am
filled with peace, and with wonder and gratitude that I have been given
a place in this marvelous universe, where I can at least pick up a few
pebbles and pluck a flower here and there. If I suffer, it is only by
virtue of those cunning laws without which the whole would be
unthinkable. Whatever happens I am ready to bow my head and give
thanks. On the other hand, I am *not* piously resigning myself as utterly
down and out. I cannot walk to my office: but I am going to Egypt
again, if I go on a stretcher! I shall play the game as long as there
is any strength left in me—I am playing for a big scientific stake and I
must win!"

Ignoring the advice of his doctors, he accompanied President Burton to New York to confer with Mr. Rockefeller, who as a result wrote
them in due course "agreeing to support the Institute for an additional
year at $50,000, and stating that he would take up *de novo* the question
of a second five-year pledge."

Having gained at least a reprieve for the laboratory he had fought
so long and hard to establish, my father now not only set out for Egypt,
but despite his condition made plans for undertaking that winter a
journey of archaeological exploration into the Sinai Peninsula, which
he had been contemplating for years. For several days before boarding
his ship in New York he was Mr. Rockefeller's house guest.

"The night before I sailed," he later wrote George Hale, "Mr. R.
went up with me to my room, and leaning against the foot of the bed
while he made me sit down on account of my lameness, he told me
he had made his decisions as to the Institute: he would support it for
a second period of five years at $50,000 a year. He would not be inter-
ested in furnishing a permanent endowment or building (I had asked

for a $750,000 building), because he was supporting a *man*, not a recognized branch of science, and . . . [because my successor] might regard the work very differently if it was permanently endowed. He said he was quite convinced of the worth of the work I was doing, was interested to support it, and wanted to tell me [this] as soon as possible, so that I could go on with my plans.

"I feel much encouraged. In five years more we shall get on so far that they will not be willing to see us shut up shop."

From his ship as he traveled eastward through the Mediterranean he wrote to my mother:

"I have just finished *The Life and Letters of Walter H. Page.* Here was one of the greatest Americans thrown up by the vortex of the [First World] War. The radio this morning [January 13, 1924] announced the death of Page's former teacher, Gildersleeve of Johns Hopkins, at the age of 93!

"Page was a fellowship man at Hopkins under Gildersleeve, who to be sure gave the youngster a valuable acquaintance with Greek literature and thought. But when it came to researches, Gildersleeve set him to investigating the detailed history of a Greek adverb from Homer onward! That is the kind of thing our classicists have been steeped in, and in spite of Gildersleeve's great services to learning and research (his students hold professorships all over the U. S.), he never contributed anything toward a broader view of ancient Greek life as a chapter in human development.

"When I am gone, there will not be much to say about me, for my students will never be scattered through all the leading universities of the country. But at least it can never be laid at my door that I taught and studied the ancient languages as an end in themselves, forgetting that they are merely a means of recovering the content and significance of ancient human life for us of today. It is the *life* of ancient men which I am trying to recover and to picture to the men of today, because I believe it will enrich *our* lives. In spite of Gildersleeve's eminence and scholarship, poor Page couldn't shackle his soul to the dreary career of a Greek adverb, and he left Johns Hopkins to mingle with modern life."

On reaching Egypt, he went at once to Luxor at Carter's request, to assist him again in an advisory capacity in the many complex problems involved in the removal of the shrines from the burial chamber of Tutenkhamon.

I now rejoined my father who had asked me to take practical

charge of his projected expedition to Sinai. Since our previous year's Nile voyage together, I had served as a journalist in America and England and in this connection had (with my father's knowledge) arranged with Mr. Victor F. Lawson, then publisher of the *Chicago Daily News*, and with the *Christian Science Monitor*, to cover for them, in disregard of the London *Times* monopoly, the further developments which we anticipated in the Tutenkhamon story. We were all agreed that Carnarvon's contract with the *Times* was eminently unfair to, and legally not binding upon, the rest of the press. But to protect my father from involvement, it was understood that initially I would file my cabled dispatches over an assumed name. I informed Carter in confidence of these arrangements. He replied that whatever I did was my own affair, and that he would forget what I had told him.

When my father revisited The Valley for the first time after his return to Luxor, "Carter called off the men working in the tomb of Tutenkhamon," he wrote, "and spent the whole morning going over the situation with me.

"He is still far from the point where he can open the sarcophagus. He has lifted the roofs of the first three of the four shrines. These roofs were in sections joined together by heavy tongues alternately of wood and bronze. To take them apart was exceedingly difficult—the tongues penetrate at least six inches into each section on either side of a joint, and are often pierced at right angles with invisible bronze pins.

"The four shrines (which we have numbered from the outside inward) are fitted one within the next, like a nest of enormous Chinese boxes. Between the first and second shrines there was a broader space which was occupied by a heavy frame of gold-covered wood supporting a beautiful pall of black linen studded with golden rosettes, like a night sky spangled with stars. The roof of the fourth or innermost shrine was made as a single piece, over three meters—over nine feet —long. It must weigh many tons, for the shrines are massively built of especially heavy wood ranging from a minimum of two inches to almost five inches in thickness.

"It is extraordinarily interesting to reconstruct the approximate order of events after the King's body, sumptuously encased in a close-fitting coffin, had been lowered into the sarcophagus to the accompaniment of solemn ceremonies.

"The tomb must then have been turned over to the cabinet-makers, carpenters, mechanics, engineers and their foremen, who with their numerous slave helpers stood waiting outside amidst the gorgeous array of glittering golden shrine sections. In order to allocate every piece to its proper position in the tomb, a foreman had hastily scratched or written in black ink on each section a catchword such as 'front,' 'back,' 'north,' 'south,' 'middle,' 'second,' etc.; and these indications are as legible today as when the ancient craftsman put them there 3250-odd years ago.

"There must have been a diverting exchange of compliments between the chief of the cabinet-makers and the chief architect of the tomb when a group of slaves carried the first section down the entrance stairway to the antechamber, and it was found to be much too large to go in! The stonecutters were quickly summoned and ordered to cut out the lintel at the top of the stone doorway, and also the steps leading down to its threshold. But when the shrine sections were by this means admitted to the *ante*-chamber, it was found that the largest of them were too big to be introduced into the burial chamber! Here followed another exchange of salutations between the officials, and another attack by the stonecutters!

"Amidst this confusion the engineers proceeded to lower the parts of the innermost shrine into the burial chamber, only to find that they had mis-read or overlooked the cabinet-maker's marks. The shrine now stands with the entrance door facing the wrong way. One can imagine the chief cabinet-maker with laborious dignity climbing down to read the marks, and finding 'south' at the north end!

"There the thing stood, still in sections to be sure, but 'wrong end to.' Between the sarcophagus and the walls of the room there was not enough space to permit of turning the sections around. To do this they would have to be lifted out again—and they weighed tons and tons. It was at last agreed to leave them as they were, and today we find the word 'south' still at the north end.

"In the course of these troublous events, someone discovered that the chief cabinet-maker had marked the third shrine with the word 'second,' and the sections of it had been let down too soon. One hesitates to contemplate the remarks of the chief engineer who had to pull them out again!

"By this time the staff must have been much demoralized—the chief cabinet-maker may even have washed his hands of all responsibility and called off his men. In any case, the beautiful joinery of the woodwork at the corners of the third shrine was barbarously hammered together by clumsy mechanics.

"When Carter and I opened the doors of the third and fourth

shrines and beheld the massive stone sarcophagus within, I felt for the first time the majesty of the dead Pharaoh's actual presence. As we explored with a flashlight the space between the still standing side walls of the second and third shrines, we found lying there exactly as they were left on the day of his burial, several of the King's bows with a supply of arrows, and beside them a long object which we did not at first recognize. This last proved to be one of the Pharaoh's large ostrich plume fans which his slaves bore on his either hand when he went abroad in his palanquin or sat in state on a high throne. It was a handle some five feet long, surmounted with a sumptuously wrought half-disc of gold from which once radiated the long plumes forming the fan itself. But these had crumbled to gray-brown dust which lay in little heaps under the now naked ribs of the plumes. It suggested the scenes of oriental splendor in which it had been used at the Pharaoh's court."

My father had succeeded in defying the arthritis which that autumn had threatened to end his active career. But even before his arrival in Luxor he had begun to feel again the same feverish malaise he had experienced upon reaching London after his reconnaissance journey through the Near East in 1919–1920. This condition now grew worse. Each afternoon a fever returned to plague him with an aching throat and with alternate chills and periods when his blood burned in his veins and throbbed in his head. He assumed that he was suffering a recurrence of malaria acquired somewhere in Iraq, but laboratory tests by the attending English physician failed to identify or quinine to allay the malady. The doctor ordered him to bed where he remained for more than six weeks throughout which with clocklike regularity the fever continued to return every noon and to recede in the early hours of the morning. He was permitted to get up only when Carter urgently required his presence at the tomb for consultations. On such occasions, with a linen mask over his mouth and nostrils to guard against dust, he would make the ten-mile round trip to The Valley in an open carriage (which had to be ferried across the river), to return utterly exhausted and shaking with the fever.

But while awaiting completion of Carter's preparations for the opening of the sarcophagus, he persisted in his work on the Edwin Smith Surgical Papyrus, and continued to make plans for the expedition to Sinai Peninsula and for new Oriental Institute projects now possible as a result of Mr. Rockefeller's extended and increased support. One morning before the usual daily visitation of fever, he dictated to me a letter to his former student and old friend, Harold H. Nelson at Beirut, outlining the immediate organization and inauguration of "The Luxor Epigraphic Expedition," and inviting him to become its field director. So at last was born the enterprise which on that day in 1905 when he and I had stood together looking up at the Colossi of Memnon on the Theban plain, he had determined to make one of his chief scientific goals. It was to become in its time the largest archaeological enterprise in Egypt as well as the largest of all the Oriental Institute's projects.

These efforts to carry on his normal work were hardly facilitated by the fact that Luxor was again thronged with visitors of whom a larger number than ever brought him letters of introduction or on their own recognizance sought his attention, usually in the hope of his gaining them admission to the tomb of Tutenkhamon. With few exceptions they failed in this, yet he somehow succeeded in giving almost every such caller the impression of having experienced some little hospitality or courtesy at his hands.

At the same time he was being more and more frequently interrupted by visits from Carter and his various collaborators, in their concern over the fact that the growing stream of official government visitors to the tomb and the government's increasingly unreasonable demands were rapidly bringing their work in The Valley to a virtual standstill. My father's room and mine on the ground floor of the Winter Palace Hotel became the clearing house for most of the complications and difficulties which now began to overtake Carter and his discovery.

Luxor was also filled with the correspondents of the leading papers and press associations of America and Europe, all aggressively trying to nullify the London *Times* world copyright. They habitually divided their time between The Valley and the terrace of the Winter Palace Hotel, hoping for some new rumor or inadvertently dropped crumb of news which could be expanded into a cabled dispatch. Presently a number of them, including the London *Times* correspondent, received from their home offices clips of dispatches date-lined Luxor and signed by George Waller Mecham, which had begun to appear in the *Chicago Daily News* and the other American papers then subscribing to its foreign news service. Mr. Mecham, their editors commented, often seemed to have access to fuller information than the London *Times* itself: it might pay to make his acquaintance.

Night after night, somewhere between midnight and four in the morning, I wrote Mr. Mecham's dispatches, took them in a carriage through the streets of sleeping Luxor to the government telegraph office in the railway station, where I filed them with a drowsy, tarbooshed effendi. Occasionally I would encounter here some of the other correspondents, particularly Valentine Williams of Reuter's, the ablest and most attractive of them all, who wrote very successful detective stories as a hobby but who failed to identify Mecham until subsequent developments rendered further anonymity unnecessary.

Despite his condition, my father was absolutely determined to carry out his proposed expedition into the interior of Sinai. We were going, he said quietly, even though the doctor forbade it, and he had to be carried!

Early in February there arrived in Luxor a cultivated and pleasant-spoken professor of English literature named La Fleur, from one of the Canadian universities—a frail man, tall and slim, with a pointed brown beard and a quick sense of humor. Quite by chance he was given a room directly alongside my father's. We met him, were much attracted to him. He had letters to Howard Carter, which I delivered for him. Soon after his arrival he fell ill with influenza from which he was just beginning to recover when he received an invitation from Carter to come at once to see the tomb. He was still abed with a fever but being loath to miss such a rare opportunity, he got up and visited the tomb.

That night he became desperately ill with pneumonia. The muffled sound of his hacking cough echoed along the white, high-ceilinged hallway, and was audible in my father's room. Our English doctor attended him—a very ill man, he said.

At about three o'clock of the second morning I was sitting at my desk writing my daily cable-dispatch. My room door stood open. Suddenly I realized that the coughing had grown much fainter and less frequent. I stepped down the hall to La Fleur's door and listened. The coughing had stopped, everything was still. The doctor came out, closed the door softly after him, answered my questioning look with a slow nod, and wearily went off to make arrangements.

As I stood waiting in the stillness, I thought: there is something especially sad about dying alone in the night in this strange country, beside the great, ageless river, in a hotel crowded with unknowing fellow humans. I wondered whether La Fleur's final silence had awakened my father—and it swept over me again that we *must* prevent his attempting the journey to Sinai.

The doctor returned with two native servants carrying a long wicker basket in which the four of us bore La Fleur away. Afterward the doctor and I packed his things. When we had finished, he said abruptly, "We must keep your Pater from going on that journey—he might start, but he would never return!" Then he went off to catch an hour or so of sleep before the morning train arrived with its usual quota of sick tourists. I finished my dispatch, and when I took it to the telegraph office, the air was cold, the stars were already fading in another desert dawn, and life was beginning to stir again in the towns and the villages, and across the fields and along the river.

The early morning sunlight was flooding my father's room and he had finished his breakfast abed when the doctor and I entered to plead with him again. He lit a cigarette and was just beginning a little prepared speech, when my father interrupted him.

"I know quite well what you're about to say." He smiled at us both. "You two gentlemen are in league against me and I ought not to yield to you, but—" and he turned to me and added with quiet gravity, "I think I appreciate your concern a little better after what occurred last night." He nodded toward La Fleur's room. "I heard our friend's silence. We'll abandon the Sinai venture—but only temporarily!"

The Department of Antiquities was at this time under the Ministry of Public Works which was currently headed by a stolid Egyptian named Morcos Bey Hanna, who in the recent course of his political career had been tried and convicted for alleged treason. For this he had served a prison term which, far from stigmatizing him, had merely invested him with an aura of martyrdom, so that he had thereafter resumed his career with his prestige definitely enhanced. Judged by the abysmal standards of Egyptian politics, he was far better than most of his contemporaries. His mistakes in connection with the work on the tomb were attributable to an understandable dislike of Carter and a total and pardonable inexperience of everything implied in this unique discovery.

But one could not so charitably condone the attitude toward the Tutenkhamon affair of the Director-General of the Department of Antiquities, Mons. Pierre Lacau, a handsome and scholastically able French Jesuit and Egyptologist with a great beard, magnificent brown eyes and a torrential volubility which was exceeded only by his bureaucratic futility as an administrator. While admitting that no one in the world could have been carrying on the work in the tomb more efficiently or faithfully, Mons. Lacau interfered with Carter at every turn, and in disregard of his proverbially difficult temperament deluged him with an endless stream of arbitrary instructions relating to every phase of the work from the question of communiques to the press and the exact number of visitors and the times when they were to be admitted to the tomb, to government surveillance of his scientific collaborators.

Despite this obstructionism Carter was ready by February 12 for the opening of the King's sarcophagus. My father was by this time so weary and unwell that his doctor joined me in urging him not to make the effort to leave his bed for another visit to The Valley. But nothing could have stopped him. He went, and by February 14 had recovered sufficiently from the hectic events of the previous forty-eight hours to write, as he lay abed, the following description which, as he put it, was "likely to be the only available record of the observations and impressions of an eye witness" to the opening of Tutenkhamon's sarcophagus:

"I reached the tomb late on the morning of February 12th," he wrote, "and sat down to rest in the shade and quiet of the little sunken area at the head of the entrance stairway where I had so often sat with Carnarvon but one short year ago. I could hear Carter at work on his final adjustment of the tackle in the burial chamber below.

"At one o'clock he and Callender came out, tired and dusty. Carter looked ill, said he felt so. We walked together down to Tomb Number 41 [an incompleted tomb which Carter and his staff used as a dining room and meeting place] and sat down to lunch. I looked about me: the same group was sitting in just the same order as when we lunched with Carnarvon on the memorable day almost exactly a year before, when the burial chamber was opened. But now Carnarvon's chair at the head of the table was occupied by Carter who was at the moment busy with a batch of correspondence and papers. One of these was a communication from Morcos Bey Hanna, decreeing the tomb program for the next two days.

"Carter said again that the whole affair had made him ill. When I examined the document myself, I found it prescribed the identical program which the Minister and Carter had amicably agreed upon a few days previously: it was simply offensive in phraseology.

"A few minutes before three, we walked to the tomb where we found awaiting us Mohammed Pasha Zaghlul, Under Secretary of State for Public Works, representing the government, with a group of the invited archaeologists. Presently we were standing in the limited space still available at the north or right end of the antechamber, which was now filled with the cumbrous roof sections, cornices and doors from the four burial shrines.

"Here the entire end wall had been broken out across the full width of the antechamber. We looked down into the burial chamber as if it had been the short end of an L, the floor of which was 4 feet lower than that on which we stood. The tall sarcophagus was below us, its lid not much higher than our feet.

"Around three sides of the sarcophagus the detached walls of the four shrines were leaning four deep, like sections of stage scenery, against the walls of the burial chamber, leaving barely enough space for a person to pass by moving sidewise. The foot—for us the *right* end —of the sarcophagus was clear, so that there were some six feet of space between it and the wall. On the side toward the antechamber where we stood, we leaned with our elbows on the top edges of the detached shrine walls, and looked down on the thin granite lid of the sarcophagus.

"A crack across the middle of the lid had caused trouble. But by prying it up sufficiently to insert angle-irons on each long side, and fastening timbers across each end, Carter had secured it in a cradle at the head and foot of which he had rigged a multiple chain hoist, each fastened to an ingenious scaffolding. Since the lid was unexpectedly light—it weighed no more than 1¼ to 1½ tons—the raising promised to be an easy process.

"There was a few minutes' delay while Burton adjusted the movie camera. The intense heat was increased by two enormous electric light bulbs. Everyone stood in hushed expectancy, a silence broken only by an occasional low cough or the rustle of our slight movements.

"From where I stood I could see on the opposite wall of the burial chamber, beyond the heavy timbers of the scaffolding, a painting of Tutenkhamon's successor, King Eye, in the act of concluding the burial services over the body of the departed young Pharoah. The painted Pharoah on the wall seemed to me at that moment to take on a strange reality. I felt a puzzling sense of unworthiness as I looked up at him. Why did he seem so calmly superior? On my left and looking down upon the sarcophagus of his ancient ancestor, stood a representative of the government of modern Egypt. He beamed upon the preparations below with an expression of smug assurance and sluggish curiosity and the general air of good-natured inefficiency so characteristic of the modern Egyptian. Over on the wall stood Eye, still calmly extending his censer, still burning the last incense to the soul of his departed predecessor.

"When the movie camera was finally ready, Carter took his place at the hoist nearest the King's feet, while Callender stood at the other hoist. Carter now gave the word, the hoists began to click, and we heard the faint rhythmic buzzing of the movie camera.

"The sarcophagus lid trembled, began to rise. Slowly, and swaying uncertainly, it swung clear.

"At first we saw only a long, narrow, black void. Then across the middle of this blackness we gradually discerned fragments of granite which had fallen out of the fracture in the lid. They were lying scattered upon a dark shroud through which we seemed to see emerging an indistinct form.

"The ropes at the ends of the cradle were stretching, and when the hoists had been drawn up as far as the low ceiling of the burial chamber permitted, the granite lid was swinging not more than twenty-two inches above the sarcophagus. Carter turned a flashlight into the interior and announced that the burial was supported upon a golden bier in lion's form.

"Burton now set up the camera first at the foot, then at the head of the sarcophagus and made a record of the undisturbed interior.

"There followed a complete silence which had in it something of the oppressiveness of intervals of sudden stillness at funerals of our own day. In the midst of this, and reminding one for all the world of the routine efficiency of modern undertakers' assistants, Carter and Mace stepped quietly forward to the head of the sleeping figure and loosening the shroud on either side, slowly and carefully rolled it back off the head toward the feet.

"The once white linen was scorched and blackened as if by fire, and in some places it crumbled in their fingers. Under it was a second or inner shroud, less dark and discolored, and beneath this, half revealed and half concealed, lay the King. Through the veil of the shrouding linen we could recognize the contours of his arms crossed at his breast, could see the profile of his face, and above it, at the forehead, an irregular prominence as of the projecting royal insignia.

"I was only dimly aware of Carter's and Mace's efforts to lay the tattered shrouds across the foot of the sarcophagus. For there at last was the King who had slept thus in the silent heart of the mountain for some three thousand two hundred and fifty years.

"He had hardly begun his long sleep when the darkness of this place had been filled with the apprehensive whispers of the ghouls who robbed it and were forced to hurry out before they could reach the royal body.

"So those who had laid him to rest had last seen him lying—a youth unable to cope with the forces of a revolution not of his making. So he lay at rest when his girl-wife, Ikhnaton's third daughter, stepped down into this burial room for the last time. Was it perhaps she who then took from a waiting servant's hand an exquisite ivory writing palette, and placed it between the forepaws of the splendid sentinel jackals guarding in the innermost doorway, just where a year ago we found it lying? It had been brought from the palace of Amarna, and had been made in the days of power and splendor when the great state temples and the palace chapels were echoing for the first time in human history with hymns in praise of the Sole God. And now the hostile priesthoods of the old gods, who perhaps had caused her husband's death, had swept away all the glory of the new faith, and the young King, her husband, had perished in the downfall of her father's great dream.

"Did she then perhaps with her own fingers gently draw over him the shrouds beneath which he had ever since lain asleep—and then, standing exactly where I was standing, had she turned and looked back upon him again for the last time? And in a final gesture of affection and grief, had she perhaps placed beside the entrance of the ante-chamber a bouquet of delicate wild flowers—just where we had found it standing?

"And as she went forth again to face the struggle for the preservation of her venerable house upon the throne of Egypt—a slip of a girl pitted against two of her father's ablest servitors—one, a crafty old courtier, the other, a sagacious and powerful man of affairs who held the army in his hand—did she wonder whether the great Hittite Emperor, to whom her couriers were already speeding across the mountains of western Asia with messages she had written beseeching his intervention and offering herself in marriage with one of his sons, would bring about her salvation?

"All these momentary fancies and many more went thronging through the mind of an Orientalist as he looked down for the first time upon the undisturbed burial of an ancient oriental sovereign who had died in the dawn of man's first spiritual emancipation.

"Carter and Mace were now investigating the inner shroud. Presently, beginning at its lower end in the region of the knees, they rolled it slowly upward. The shroud being double, the King's figure, as they progressed, was still covered with the nether fold. When they reached the top of the head, they began to roll the under fold downward toward the feet.

"As they did so, we suddenly saw the gleaming gold of the vulture's head and the up-reared cobra on the King's forehead. We saw his eyes, which seemed to look out upon us as in life; and soon the King's whole figure was revealed to us in all the splendor of shining gold. His gold-covered arms and hands were crossed upon his breast; in his right hand he grasped a crook or staff, wrought of gold and colored stones; in his left, he held the ceremonial flagellum or scourge, also of gold. His figure was swathed in the gilded plumage of a protecting goddess.

"What we saw was the outer coffin, some seven feet long and thirty inches high, cunningly wrought by the sculptor with the aid of the lapidary and the goldsmith, into a magnificent portrait figure of the King lying as if stretched out upon the lid like a crusader on his tomb slab in some European cathedral. His face bore a striking resemblance to the wonderful figures which had guarded the sealed doorway of the burial chamber. The hands and the insignia they bore were wrought entirely free and in the round, and the eyes were inlaid of black and white stone. No anthropoid coffin lid heretofore known can approach it as a work of art.

"It did not occur to me till afterwards that as the King lies with feet to the east and head to the west, the Vulture, the Goddess of Upper Egypt, is on the Upper Egyptian or south side, and the Cobra, the Goddess of Lower Egypt, is on the Lower Egyptian or north side of the royal forehead. This is of course intentional.

"There are probably several inner coffins within the last of which lies the embalmed body of the young King—the size of the sarcophagus and the outer coffin does not favor the conclusion that he was a mere child. But this and other important questions can be settled only when the coffins themselves have been opened.

"I looked at my watch—scarcely an hour had passed since we had entered the tomb, yet we came away with a sense of having glimpsed the era and the last rites of Tutenkhamon!"

Early the following morning Carter burst in upon us, intensely excited and carrying dossiers of papers from which he had extracted a telegram from Morcos Bey Hanna, peremptorily forbidding him to admit into the tomb of Tutenkhamon the wives or families of the collaborating scientists, as he had planned to do on this morning of February 13. The Minister had underscored these instructions by despatching an additional force of police to the tomb, so that if any American or English ladies invited by Carter had appeared, they would have been forcibly prevented from entering.

The scientific and technical men affected by this order answered it by unanimously refusing to continue their work.

Carter, fuming and pacing nervously up and down my room, dictated while I typed at least a score of different versions of his proposed announcement of the closing of the tomb, each one, as his anger ebbed, a shade less vitriolic than its predecessor, until under the pacific influence of my father and the group of eight or ten American and English scientists who had gradually joined us, the following finally met his approval and was posted on various bulletin boards in Luxor:

February 13, 1924.

NOTICE

Owing to the impossible restrictions and discourtesies on the part of the Public Works Department and its Antiquity Service all my collaborators in protest have refused to work any further upon the scientific investigations of the discovery of the tomb of Tutankhamen.

I am therefore obliged to make known to the public that immediately after the Press view of the tomb this morning between 10 A.M. and noon the tomb will be closed and no further work can be carried out.

(signed) HOWARD CARTER

Accordingly, after the press view, Carter locked the tomb. Because he assumed that his difficulties with the government would be settled within a few days, he left the coffin lid suspended exactly as when it had first been raised.

The government now forbade him to re-enter the tomb pending his agreement to resume work within forty-eight hours on the government's terms, and warned him that his failure to do so would result in cancellation of their authorization to Lady Carnarvon. Carter countered by applying to the Mixed Tribunals in Cairo to have himself appointed sequestrator of the tomb, which he asked Morcos Hanna's permission to re-enter in order to lower the sarcophagus lid. The government refused his request, charged him with carelessness for having left the sarcophagus lid suspended, cancelled Lady Carnarvon's authorization, and indicated it would formally take over the tomb on February 22.

Throughout these developments he was constantly in our midst, reviewing his grievances and seeking counsel which for the most part he was nervously too exhausted and emotionally too upset to follow. The scientific men agreed that however injudicious and temperamental his behavior had been at times toward the Egyptian government, the latter's treatment of him had been so inconsiderate and unjust as to have forced remonstrative action upon him.

On the morning of February 22 I went to The Valley to witness the government's seizure of Tutenkhamon's tomb. As I sat waiting on the familiar wall above the entrance, I thought of the irony of what was about to happen.

Since I had first met him in 1905 near this very spot, Carter had spent most of his career searching for this tomb. Its discovery was not only his own supreme achievement but had brought Egypt greater prestige and hordes of visitors than anything which had befallen that country in modern times. He had sacrificed health and large financial returns as a result of his insistence upon personally superintending almost every phase of the removal and preservation of the objects in the tomb. He had quarreled with his old friend Carnarvon because of his belief that the entire find should remain in Egypt. And now the same soldiers he had had posted to insure the tomb's safety were marching up and down before me, under orders to prevent his access to it. "The arrogant, self-conscious, sweepingly victorious Nationalists at the moment in unchallenged control of the Egyptian government," as my father described them, had in fact already dispossessed Carter —the imminent ceremony was merely a gesture of political bravado.

Toward two o'clock the government's representatives, led by Mons. Lacau, arrived at the tomb, accompanied by several native locksmiths sweating under a great load of tools, most of which were irrelevant. While the members of the party disposed themselves about the entrance and lawyers attached to the Ministry of Public Works made copious notes on every step of the procedure, Mons. Lacau read aloud a letter from Carter in which he refused to surrender the keys to the tomb.

The locksmiths now set to work and despite superlative clumsiness and many bleeding fingers, succeeded within less than an hour in sawing through the padlocks on Carter's outermost door to the tomb. They experienced somewhat more difficulty with the steel grated door to the antechamber, but by mid-afternoon the rape of the locks had been completed. It was found that the sarcophagus lid had not fallen but that the rope had stretched until the lid with its supporting cradle almost rested again on the sarcophagus. The party next proceeded to the tomb used by Carter as a preparatorial laboratory, broke its locks and formally took possession.

The sun was setting as I rode back along the Valley to Carter's house where I found him waiting for news of the day's developments. He looked disconsolate and worn but was quite calm and evinced no rancor as I described the latest in the long series of strange episodes which had attended and had finally deprived him of the greatest archaeological discovery in the history of the orient. As I was leaving, he thanked me and said, "Tell your father I am going to Cairo where I have retained legal counsel to fight the government in the Mixed T ʾunals until they appoint me sequestrator of the tomb!"

The government had now created a curious and complex legal situation. The discovery had transformed Carnarvon's concession into a contract presumably committing the government to a division of the tomb's contents: with his death, Carnarvon's executors therefore found themselves legally bound to sue the Egyptian government for his Estate's interest in the contract.

To the Egyptians in general the significance of Tutenkhamon's tomb was entirely political and financial. It was further proof of their past and present glory, it offered a superlative excuse for another burst of crowing over their newly acquired independence. Most important of all, it contained golden treasure and attracted great crowds of tourists to be bled of their cash. This was something the Egyptians could understand; whereas the proper salvaging of the objects in the tomb, the solicitude of the entire scientific world, and the legal rights of the discoverer and his late patron were wholly academic matters which they neither comprehended nor cared about.

Two days after reaching Cairo, however, Carter telegraphed my father—who was still fever-ridden and confined to his bed in Luxor—that the Egyptian government, the Carnarvon Estate and he himself desired him to act as mediator in an effort to settle the case immediately by friendly conferences out of court, before it came up for trial in the Mixed Tribunals.

The doctor agreed that a shift northward to the slightly cooler climate of Cairo was more likely to benefit than harm my father. So he accepted the rôle of mediator, and we returned to Cairo.

The conditions under which he was expected to effect a friendly out-of-court settlement were hardly auspicious. Carter had wisely summoned from California, where he was sojourning in his retirement, Carnarvon's chief executor, old General Sir John Grenfell Maxwell. The General's long military career had included a generous period as commander-in-chief of the British Army in Egypt where even the extremist and anti-British factions held him in warm esteem. But Carter offset this advantage and added to the general confusion by retaining in behalf of the Carnarvon Estate a reputedly able English lawyer named F. M. Maxwell—the man who only two or three years previously had publicly prosecuted for treason and had demanded capital punishment for Morcos Bey Hanna and a number of his political associates!

My father drew up and submitted to the government a set of reasonable conditions under which Carter should be permitted to return to his work on the tomb; and to allow for their consideration, got the lawyers on both sides to agree to a postponement of the trial. The government countered with conditions of its own in the form of a new authorization to Almina, Countess of Carnarvon.

At this point Carter, so overweeningly confident of a complete victory that he spurned a compromise, declared the conditions of the proffered authorization unacceptable and against everyone's advice including his lawyer's, withheld his consent to further postponement of the trial.

"He lost all control of himself and became very high-handed and arrogant," my father wrote. "He appears so overcome by his misfortunes as to be incapable of major decisions. I would withdraw from this thankless assignment but for the vital importance of a just settlement to the future of science in Egypt and the Near East."

Negotiations were broken off and the hearings now began in the suit of the Carnarvon Estate vs. the Egyptian Government. They immediately precipitated verbal exchanges so bitter that near-riots occurred in the court room. At the same time the vernacular Nationalist press scathingly denounced the plaintiffs.

During the first hearing the government suddenly agreed to accept my father's conditions providing Carter would renounce any claims in his own behalf to any of the objects in the tomb. He had of course never made such claims, and though correspondingly incensed by this demand, was persuaded by my father to sign a brief statement of renunciation.

The government now stated that before it would accept the mediator's conditions, the lawsuit must be withdrawn. Carter rightly refused to do so without a written guarantee that the government would thereupon accept the conditions.

The trial was proceeding when the government indicated for the third time that it would accept the conditions providing Almina, Countess of Carnarvon, and the executors of the Carnarvon Estate would in turn renounce *their* claims to a share of the tomb's contents. My father got Sir John Maxwell to sign a letter addressed to Morcos Bey Hanna, renouncing "all claims to the antiquities found in the tomb," calling the government's attention "to the enormous value of the discovery to Egypt," which had gained it without cost, thanks to the services of Howard Carter and the Metropolitan Museum staff; reminding it of "the large number of duplicate objects in the tomb," and suggesting "the appropriateness of . . . recognizing . . . the above services . . . by presentation of some of these duplicates to the British Museum and to the Metropolitan Museum in the name of the Countess Carnarvon."

When my father on March 11 met with the Egyptian government's representatives, a complete accord appeared to have been reached by all the parties on every point involved in the litigation. Pens were poised for affixing signatures to an agreement whereby Carter was immediately to resume his work on the tomb, when Abdel Hamid Bedawi Pasha, one of the government's legal counsellors, hurried into the conference room to report that Mr. F. M. Maxwell while addressing the court late on the previous afternoon, had referred to the Egyptian government as having broken into the tomb of Tutenkhamon "like a bandit!" and that as a result of this insulting language, the government was breaking off all further negotiations, effective immediately.

At this point my father, utterly disheartened, handed his resignation as mediator to Sir John and Carter, who declined to accept it and insisted upon his making still another effort to reach a settlement. He reluctantly agreed on condition that he be permitted to give to Morcos Bey Hanna a note stating that "I wish to disassociate myself absolutely from the use of the word 'bandit, and to express my profound regret that such language should have furnished the just occasion for the termination of our negotiations."

Sir John and Carter both approved this note. Mr. Maxwell hesitated for a time but finally agreed to it, and even accompanied my father to the door of the Minister's home when he delivered the missive in person that same evening.

To have been publicly characterized as a bandit by the very Englishman responsible for his recent imprisonment had roused his Excellency to an apoplectic fury of righteous resentment. While my father listened patiently, Morcos Bey Hanna strode up and down the room, uttering a tirade against the haughty injustices of the British, the insufferable behavior of Carter and F. M. Maxwell, etc., etc. He spoke alternately in Arabic, guttural English and thick French.

Finally when the Minister paused for a moment to collect his thoughts and replenish his lungs, my father rose and approached a low bookcase on the top of which among other things stood a large photograph of a group of seated gentlemen all clad in the broad-striped suits worn by Egyptian prisoners. The photograph had obviously been made in a prison yard, and one of the gentlemen was unmistakably his Excellency.

My father looked at the picture and began chuckling. *"Regardez!"* he said. *"Ce sont les bandits!"*

His Excellency also peered quizzically at the photograph. Suddenly and for the first time he saw himself not as a martyr-hero but as a captured bandit. His belligerency vanished in a mutual burst of hearty laughter. The Minister's mood appeared so friendly and receptive that my father tried once again to win back the tomb for Carter.

Morcos Bey Hanna replied that the government finally and flatly declined to entertain such a proposal. But even more emphatically than he had done on no less than two previous occasions, he now urged my father *himself* to take over the tomb of Tutenkhamon, and in addition offered him any other archaeological concession he might desire in Egypt. "It is of course utterly unthinkable," my father wrote, "that I should accept."

Thus ended the negotiations.

By way of anticlimax, Mr. F. M. Maxwell thereupon informed my father that after thinking over the implications of his letter to Morcos Bey Hanna, disassociating himself from the use of the word "bandit," he—F. M. Maxwell—was contemplating suing him for defamation of character. Finally after further reflection, Mr. Maxwell assured him in writing that he would take no action against him.

"Heaven deliver me," wrote my father wearily, "from ever again attempting to act as peacemaker in a lawsuit over the possession of a royal tomb of ancient Egypt!"

The Egyptian government declined even to acknowledge Sir John's letter, on the grounds that this might have been construed as an admission that the Carnarvon Estate *had* had a claim upon the contents of the tomb, which it had voluntarily renounced. The government did not propose to put itself in the position of accepting from the Carnarvon Estate something which the latter had never owned. The Estate dropped its lawsuit and the issue was never finally decided. My father therefore eventually effected the surrender of Sir John's letter.

Carter returned to England disconsolate and more embittered than ever. It is conceivable that he might never have been allowed to resume his work on the tomb but for the stupid and brutal assassination of the Sirdar, Sir Lee Stack, in Cairo on the following November 20th. As a result of this, England drastically re-established her hold upon Egyptian affairs, the Nationalist party suffered defeat, and while everyone's attention was preoccupied with matters affecting the very destiny of Egypt, the government quietly re-admitted Carter to the tomb, although under conditions far less favorable than those which during the previous spring my father had endeavored to secure for him.

After devoting another year to the many objects in more urgent need of immediate attention, Carter finally sought the body of Tutenkhamon.

"Inside the first coffin was a second one," my father wrote of this final revelation, "over which copious libations of various oils had been poured during the funeral ceremonies. These libations had eventually hardened into a dark bituminous or pitch-like mass which covered the second coffin and was almost impervious even to a steel chisel.

"Within the second was the third and last coffin—of *solid* gold so heavy that four men together could barely lift it!

"The lid of this solid gold coffin, as did that of the outermost one, again represents the King in all his splendid regalia: the face is a portrait; his garments above his crossed arms are encrusted with many-colored semi-precious stones such as carnelian, turquoise and lapis-lazuli; while below his crossed arms he is enfolded by the protecting wings of guardian goddesses whose lovely forms are elaborately graven in the shining gold, and envelop him with a luminous net of golden plumage.

"The lid is again a consummate blend of sculpture, modeling and portraiture, including the art of the lapidary and the skill of the graver. Coffin and lid were wrought out of solid gold equivalent to about $243,000 in bullion. How the portrait-face of the King was executed in the mirror-polished gold of the lid without leaving anywhere even the faintest traces of toolmarks, is a great mystery.

"Within the solid gold coffin lay the jewel-bedecked, mummified body of Tutenkhamon himself—he appears to have been about eighteen years old when he died. The head and shoulders were covered with a magnificent golden mask like a knight's helmet. No other relics of the goldsmith's art surviving from the ancient world, or from Tutenkhamon's tomb itself, can compare with this coffin and mask. I looked upon them with amazement and reverence."

The Egyptian government ignored the suggestion that an appropriate way of rewarding Carter for his discovery and of recognizing his subsequent services and those of his American collaborators would be the presentation to the British Museum and the Metropolitan Museum of duplicate objects from Tutenkhamon's tomb. It gave nothing to either museum.

After the scientific examination of Tutenkhamon's body, and the removal from it of all jewelry, it was replaced in the stone sarcophagus in the burial chamber. The entire contents of the tomb—which did not include so much as a single fragment of the inscribed papyri so eagerly hoped for by scholars everywhere—was taken to the Cairo Museum where most of it was put on display.

The government by way of evincing its appreciation of the work of foreign archaeological expeditions, now decreed that henceforth *everything* found by excavators would belong to Egypt, unless the Department of Antiquities saw fit to make a division. The eventual effect of this was to put a virtual stop to excavations by American and English expeditions—almost the only foreign groups who had been able to resume such enterprises in Egypt after the First World War.

Carnarvon's proposal, repeatedly seconded by Carter, that my father should do the historical section of the eventual comprehensive scientific publication of the discovery, was never formalized or consummated. Carter himself published only preliminary, purely popular and altogether inadequate accounts of his find. Today after a lapse of twenty years, no scientific publication of Tutenkhamon's tomb has yet appeared.

My father felt greatly discouraged over his failure to defend what he called "the rights of science in Egypt" by winning back the tomb for Carter. It augured badly for American scientific enterprise in Egypt. But his spirits quickly rose again as he realized that due largely to the almost incredible popular interest in archaeology aroused by the Tutenkhamon discovery as a whole, the moment he had so long awaited and of which he had so often despaired was at hand when American wealth and scientific leadership and Near Eastern political conditions were convening to make possible the execution of his long cherished plans for the investigation of the origins of civilization.

While the tomb negotiations were still in progress, George Edgar Vincent, then president of the Rockefeller Foundation, paid his first visit to Egypt.

My father personally conducted him through the Cairo Museum, quickly demonstrated to him that here were not only the most remarkable collections of their kind in the world, but that they were housed in a shabby, inadequate, abominably planned and lighted, and actually dangerous building. He told him the sordid story of scandal and graft involved in its design and construction by a French architect and a French contractor; pointed out where the roof leaked in the winter rains, where the plaster of ceilings and walls had crashed down upon and damaged irreplaceable historical items; showed him rooms which had been closed off because they were unsafe, basement storage magazines which were regularly flooded at high Nile. With the Egyptian government hard up because of the low post-First World War price of cotton, there was no prospect that anything would be done toward improving this building in which were already being displayed some of the treasures from Tutenkhamon's tomb.

Vincent was greatly surprised and impressed. "This might greatly interest Junior," he said. "I shall tell Raymond Fosdick about it on my return to New York."

Raymond Blaine Fosdick, then only just turned forty, had already achieved a record of brilliant legal practice and public service, and as one of the most intelligent and enlightened Americans of his generation had become one of Mr. John D. Rockefeller, Jr.'s closest advisers, especially in philanthropic matters, much as Mr. Gates had been to Mr. Rockefeller, Sr. My father once described him to me as "the eyes and ears of his chief in discovering places for the investment of one of the greatest private incomes of modern times, so that it will pay human dividends."

Both Mr. Rockefeller and the trustees of the several Rockefeller boards were now earnestly seeking new fields of human endeavor which they could safely support. Under these circumstances, when a scholar of established scientific standing, endowed with vision, practicality, humility, absolute integrity and great personal charm laid before them a coherent program of logical enterprises in the virtually untouched field of archaeology and the investigation of the origins and development of civilization, it was more welcome than its author at the outset realized.

He soon perceived, however, that ambitious plans involving great sums were more likely to arouse favorable attention than small plans entailing modest expenditures. He became adept at presenting his ideas for new undertakings in concise briefs which while describing their nature, purpose, duration and estimated cost, were often brilliant thumb-nail summaries or appraisals of historical processes awaiting scientific investigation.

Success begot success, one project led to another until with anxiety he saw himself becoming, as George Hale had warned him he might, "a desk functionary with little prospect of ever doing anything but adjust budgets and solicit funds!"

But never had any humanist faced such a golden opportunity to serve science. "I must work at top speed," he wrote, "I am rounding sixty—there is little time left to me, the flow of resources I have tapped might be shut off, the Near East might catch fire again. I must make the most of every moment!"

In the midst of the Tutenkhamon tomb negotiations he had arranged for the construction of a headquarters building for the Luxor Epigraphic Expedition near the Temple of Medinet Habu; had worked out with Professor Harold H. Nelson (see p. 358) its field director, the most accurate method ever evolved for making facsimile copies of ancient wall inscriptions and reliefs, and had laid out a program of publishing the entire vast temple of Medinet Habu in a great series of folio volumes.

"The thousands upon thousands of square feet of historical inscriptions and reliefs carved on the walls of Medinet Habu," he wrote of this undertaking, "reveal to us the contact of Egypt with the tremendous *mêlée* of Asiatic peoples caused by the Indo-European invasion of Western Asia, the devastating overthrow of the Hittite Empire about 1200 B.C., and the great migratory movement that carried the Etruscans out of Asia Minor and the Aegean region into Italy. For the first time these early human records are being accurately preserved for posterity.

"By the conquest of Western Asia in the sixteenth century B.C Egypt entered upon her Imperial Age. Enormous wealth gathered from Asia and Nubia enabled the Pharaohs to glorify their reigns by vast temple buildings which marked a new and splendid chapter in the history of architecture. I felt from the first that the work of the Epigraphic Expedition on the great temple of Medinet Habu was making increasingly clear the character of that imposing building as a human document. To us of the present day it proclaims in terms of great architectural forms the age of imperial conquest. As soon as funds permitted, an Architectural Survey was therefore also organized and associated with the Epigraphic Expedition." *

When he returned to America in April, 1924, his fever had vanished, the arthritis had much abated, and he resumed his accustomed pace.

In the accumulation of correspondence awaiting him on his desk in Chicago he found a letter from Adolf Erman (whose seventieth birthday was to occur on the coming October 31) in which the latter referred with melancholy resignation to the fact that publication of the great *Dictionary of Ancient Egyptian,* the scientific project to which he had devoted his whole career and which he had hoped he might live to see completed, had finally come to a standstill for lack of funds. My father immediately inquired of Fosdick whether he thought Mr. Rockefeller would be willing to help. "Find out how much is needed," was the reply.

Some weeks later he and Fosdick met in New York to "prepare for submission to Mr. R. a constructive plan for improving the Cairo Museum situation," he noted in his journal. "Out of this grew a $10,000,000 project to provide a magnificent new museum building (to be controlled for thirty years by an international commission, this being the period which it was estimated would be required for training a generation of young Egyptians to take over the responsibility themselves); a smaller building alongside the museum to contain administrative offices, a great scientific library and a research laboratory for the study and publication of the museum's collections; and an endowment to maintain all of the foregoing."

When they had agreed on these major points my father mentioned the comparatively insignificant amount needed for completing and publishing the Berlin Egyptian Dictionary. Fosdick answered at once that Mr. Rockefeller "considered it a privilege to be able to assist in such a great scientific undertaking."

"At the period when I was carrying out the commission of the German Academies to copy all the Egyptian inscriptions in the museums of Europe for this Dictionary," my father wrote me later,

* Adapted from *The Oriental Institute,* by James H. Breasted, p. 169 ff.

"Germany was annually pouring out millions of marks for science. Had anyone then told me that I would one day be securing the funds for its completion, I would have thought it utterly preposterous!"

While evolving the plans for a new Cairo Museum and for several other major projects, he tried as best he could despite extended absences abroad to carry on a modicum of teaching. At the same time the University of Chicago was launching a campaign to raise $17,500,-000 of additional endowment funds, and as one of the University's veterans he was called upon for a series of public addresses. "My personal researches are at a complete standstill," he wrote disconsolately, "and I try to find comfort in the belief that the scientific enterprises I am endeavoring to put through will achieve greater and more valuable results than I could ever accomplish single-handed."

Although Mr. Rockefeller had never visited Egypt or any part of the Near East, he showed the keenest interest in the project for a new museum in Cairo, without hesitation accepted the figure of $10,000,-000 as only logical and necessary for the proper execution of such a major undertaking. He proposed that his architect, Welles Bosworth, then his representative in the work of restoring Versailles, Rheims Cathedral and Fontainebleau, should meet my father in Cairo to study the situation and prepare tentative plans for the proposed new buildings. It was agreed that the whole project should be confidentially presented to Lord Allenby, to ascertain whether it would meet with British official approval.

It was also agreed that the most appropriate site for the new buildings would be that of the old Kasr en-Nil Barracks and their parade ground immediately adjacent to the existing Museum. Many years before, the British themselves had condemned these Barracks as no longer fit for human habitation (if they ever were!), and had agreed with the Egyptian government to evacuate them, providing suitable substitutes were erected elsewhere. The Egyptians had kept their part of the bargain, put up much more extensive new ones at Abbassiyeh which the British had promptly taken over without evacuating the old ones. But Kitchener had not regarded the military situation as favorable for the promised evacuation, which had therefore never taken place. Hence it was hoped that both the British and the Egyptians would welcome an American offer to the King of Egypt of a new museum building to be erected on the site of the mooted barracks. Responsibility for the diplomatic negotiation of all this and much else implicit in the Project would rest with my father.

Mr. Rockefeller now also pledged $60,000 for the excavation of the great ancient stronghold of Megiddo in Palestine, on condition that other interested donors should subscribe a like amount annually for three additional years. The problem of meeting this condition was complicated for my father by the fact that the University of Chicago's campaign for additional endowment funds precluded his soliciting the support of Middle Western friends of the University for the work of the Oriental Institute. He therefore sought from the veteran Mr. F. T. Gates "a list of a few names of Eastern men of means who might be interested to finance the Megiddo project."

"I am compelled to say," replied Mr. Gates, "at the risk of whatever esteem you have for me, that I cannot try to help you promote the Megiddo scheme.

"I am in touch as you cannot be with the overwhelming needs of this suffering world, and I know—or think I know—that the money this will cost can and ought to be used for more immediate and exigent needs.

"With the museums of Europe stuffed for years with material that is not even unpacked, much of which can be utilized only by you and your personal staff—with this and other things you already have on hand, enough to keep you overwhelmed with work of the highest importance as long as you live—I cannot find it in my heart to approve anything that can divert you at all.

"What yet lies under Eastern soil if fully disclosed, *cannot* throw any valuable light on the problems that confront the civilization of today. No *important* changes will ever be made in your great book, *Ancient Times*.

"The origin and historicity of the Old Testament is of course fascinatingly interesting, especially to old preachers like me! But it has been a generation since modern men have lived by anything in either Testament but the words of Jesus. Megiddo and all its neighbors are curious, but no longer vital. Civilization can save them up like other choice dainties of its luxurious table, for times of leisure."

"I like your forthrightness," my father answered. "It is obvious that we do not agree, but I am sure that in half an hour's personal conversation I could present a brief in my case which would prove convincing.

"Coming generations will hold ours responsible if we fail to save from destruction the vast body of records which we have inherited from the Ancient Near East, many of which have come down and almost reached our eager fingers, only to be snatched away and to perish at the hands of modern vandalism.

"I am entirely in sympathy with you regarding the need for the alleviation of human suffering. But it is a mistaken assumption that funds contributed for research in the Ancient Near East might be made available for such purposes.

"The boyhood village of Jesus looked directly down upon the Megiddo plain. We shall never know how often his own visions of future peace and brotherhood may have been clouded by contemplation of that great battlefield where the fate of world empires had been decided for thousands of years by the brutal force of physical power, which he proposed to displace by the rule of love. It is the task of those who look back upon his wonderful life to piece together the marvelous development which culminated in his teaching. And we cannot do it without Megiddo."

In January, 1925, my father returned again to Egypt.

"The proposed Museum building," he wrote from Cairo, "promises to be a superb thing. It will be almost 900 feet long, one very tall story in height; and in style a restrained and beautiful adaptation of ancient Egyptian, with great colonnaded halls surrounding four lovely courts.

"I showed Bosworth's drawings to Allenby who expressed cordial interest and promised to forward the entire proposal to the British Foreign Office with his approval and support. We foresaw two difficulties: the clause in the Anglo-French treaty whereby the French hold the director-generalship of antiquities in Egypt,* and the question of demolishing the Kasr en-Nil Barracks. He advised my visiting London to confer directly with the Foreign Office on these points."

When it became apparent that the Cairo Museum Project was to be added to his other responsibilities, my father wrote me in anxiety, pleading his need of help. So once again I left my own work, this time in California, and came to his aid.

His activities following his return from Egypt anticipated the pace of the next ten years.

He hurried to Cornell University, inaugurated the newly established Messenger Lectureship on the evolution of civilization; between lectures conferred with Secretary of State Kellogg in Washington regarding the Cairo Museum Project; and in New York with the offi-

* See p. 143 ff.

cers of the several Rockefeller foundations "on the question of largely increased support for humanistic research as contrasted with the foundations' enormous contributions to natural science." He persuaded Fosdick to review Mr. Rockefeller's conditional pledge for the excavation of Megiddo, and in an hour early one morning in Washington drew up a plan calling for $215,000 distributed over five years, which the donor accepted.

"The hobgoblin that now haunts me," he wrote in his journal, "is the question, Where am I to find the young men to staff the projects for which the funds are coming in so fast?

"On reaching Chicago I found that my dear friend [Ernest DeWitt] Burton [President of the University of Chicago] lay dying of cancer. Instead of conferring with him as I had so eagerly anticipated, I served as one of his pallbearers—a desolating blow in the midst of the exhilarating progress of all the plans he had so loyally supported."

Impressed with his success in raising funds, the University's Board of Trustees now voted that he should be relieved of all teaching in order to give his entire time to the development of the Oriental Institute. While to be sure he had done very little teaching since before his reconnaissance expedition to the Near East in 1919–1920, he found it difficult to realize that henceforth he would never teach again, and that on the eve of his sixtieth birthday he stood responsible, scientifically speaking, only to the research enterprises of his own creation.

On the night of June 5, 1925, we boarded a ship for England, where pursuant to Allenby's counsel he was to confer with the Foreign Office regarding the Cairo Museum Project. In his briefcase my father carried a letter which Mr. Rockefeller had written to him that afternoon from 26 Broadway:

"I am enclosing herewith a draft of a letter to His Majesty, the King of Egypt, expressing my willingness to contribute ten millions of dollars for the purpose of providing and maintaining a new and adequate museum for the housing of the great treasures now contained in the present Museum at Cairo. This letter I am prepared to sign and send you upon receiving word from you that the matter is in shape to go forward."

As we watched the glowing honeycombs of Manhattan receding into the American summer night, and felt the warm land breeze giving way to a cool one smelling of the open Atlantic, my father said, "We've traveled a long, long way since that broiling day in Cairo in the spring

of 1907 when you and I went to the postoffice to mail a letter to
Mr. Gates at 26 Broadway, over there beyond the Battery! I remember
how profoundly disappointed I was when old Mr. Rockefeller, Sr.
turned down the plans it contained. But if he hadn't, the Oriental
Institute might never have been founded, and probably you and I
wouldn't be sailing tonight on a fascinating errand!"

The American Ambassador to St. James, Alanson B. Houghton, was
under instructions to do everything in his power to further the project.
Lord Balfour, at the time President both of the Privy Council and of
the British Academy, and Austen Chamberlain, then Minister for
Foreign Affairs, both strongly favored it.

Lord Allenby was retiring from Empire service and Sir George
Lloyd, whom my father had first met in Bombay (see p. 266), had
just been appointed to succeed him as High Commissioner for Egypt
and the Sudan.

"Lloyd asked me whether our plans would require *immediate*
evacuation of the Kasr en-Nil Barracks," my father stated in his journal. "I smiled to myself as I listened to the incoming British Commissioner to Egypt inquiring of an American citizen when the British
Army would be required to evacuate their Cairo barracks!

"When I recall with what awe I used to ride past these barracks
on my donkey as I went to and from the original Egyptian Museum
(predecessor of the present-day French structure) during my first
visit to Cairo thirty-one years ago, I find it hard to realize that I am
now negotiating for their evacuation and eventual demolition. If I
succeed it will be an achievement hardly less formidable than securing
ten million dollars for a new Cairo Museum!"

While Lloyd professed interest in the Project, his reluctance to
approve evacuation of the barracks was evident from the outset. His
attitude, as later frankly characterized by members of his staff,
remained throughout one of "malevolent neutrality." This slowed the
negotiations; but toward mid-July we received a letter from the Foreign Office "assuring us," my father wrote, "that it was 'not anticipated
that the transfer of the site of the Kasr en-Nil Barracks to the Board
of Trustees of the proposed Museum Project would cause any serious
difficulty.' Its timing was deemed very important, however, and was to
be determined by the new High Commissioner to Egypt. Our proposed
international commission was approved; and it was stipulated that I

need not consult the French until after the project had been accepted by King Fuad."

True to Foreign Office tradition, most of the points on which they had *verbally* committed themselves to us positively and unequivocally had been deftly emasculated in being reduced to writing. But in principle the Project now had the British government's approval, which at this stage seemed enough; and so we returned to America.

George Hale was following the development of the Project with the keenest interest, for just at this same time he had succeeded in persuading Mr. Henry Edwards Huntington to re-define the great Huntington Library and Art Gallery in Pasadena as a research institution, thus placing "it far in advance of the Morgan Library [in New York] and the great Rylands Library in Manchester, in a position beside the British Museum itself."

"It seems to me that the United States embodies much of the spirit —though often crudely expressed—which came into the world with the Italian Renaissance," Hale wrote my father in August 1925. "At any rate, the roots of the civilization of Great Britain and the United States rise from Italian soil, though they reach back to Greece, Assyria and Egypt. If we concentrate at first on the late period, we must ultimately go back to the true origins, not merely through the classic MSS. but also through a study of certain phases of Egyptian and Assyrian civilization, perhaps especially in the fields of art and science.

"I am, therefore, anxious to establish the closest possible liaison with the new Museum and Research Institute in Cairo."

Mr. Rockefeller became more and more interested in the development of the Project.

From its inception, legally speaking, until the keys of the completed building should be handed over to an international commission to be composed of two Egyptian, two American, two British and two French representatives, the Project was to be under the control of a board of three trustees consisting of his old friend V. Everit Macy, Raymond Fosdick and my father, whom he asked to serve as chairman. The J. G. White Engineering Corporation was chosen to do the construction; and at Mr. Rockefeller's request a survey was made of the newest museums in the United States in order that the proposed new Cairo Museum might embody the very latest and best developments in American museum planning.

Finally at noon on October 2, 1925, Messrs. Fosdick, Macy, Chauncey Belknap (the lawyer who had been chiefly responsible for drawing the complicated documents involved) and my father and I were ushered into Mr. Rockefeller's office at 26 Broadway.

"This has been one of the greatest days of my life," my father later remarked in his journal. "While the rest of us sat looking on, Mr. Belknap took from his briefcase four copies of the bulky trust document creating the Board of Trustees and conveying to them ten million dollars. One of these copies was adorned with showy seals and red ribbons and was intended for the King of Egypt.

"In his quick, businesslike way the donor asked a few questions regarding one or two points on which he was not quite clear. He then drew out his fountain pen and methodically signed three of the documents. As he came to the fourth, he paused for a moment with his pen poised, and peering at us over his quaint half-spectacles, he observed dryly. 'This, gentlemen, is rather an expensive signature for me!'

"The Trustees then signed, a notary witnessed our signatures, and the Cairo Museum Project had legally come into existence. It is a very sobering thought to realize that I am now one of three men responsible for the expenditure and proper use of the greatest single sum ever donated for humanistic research."

Mr. Rockefeller also gave to my father the following letter to the King of Egypt:

"The present transition period in the national life of Egypt has necessarily created many new responsibilities which are to be met by the Egyptian people for the first time. Among these there is perhaps none which has aroused wider interest and sympathy among the other peoples of the world than the responsibility for Egypt's marvelous heritage from the past. . . .

"Because of my profound interest in this matter I should count it a privilege to make a gift of ten million dollars to be primarily devoted: first, to the erection of a new and more commodious building for the Cairo Museum and an additional building for archaeological research; and second, to the maintenance of these buildings and collections, with special reference to their educational value and their usefulness as a great treasury of materials for scientific research.

"In proffering this gift to the Egyptian people and to Science, I venture to hope that the program of cooperation which it would permit may prove acceptable to Your Majesty and to the Egyptian Government."

The plan of procedure from this point onward was that my father should secure from Lord Lloyd (as he had now become) a written statement of the British Army's readiness to evacuate the Kasr en-Nil barracks in favor of the new Cairo Museum; and thereupon should present to the King of Egypt Mr. Rockefeller's letter of gift accompanied by an especially bound copy of a brochure describing the Project, the ribbon-embellished copy of the indenture of trust, and a set of preliminary plans for the proposed buildings.

If the King accepted the gift, he or his appropriate representative was to sign a contract (already drawn) between the Egyptian government and the Project's Trustees, covering the construction of the new Museum and its adjacent archaeological research building, and the appointment of an international commission to be responsible for the operation of the Museum for a period of thirty years from its completion. In anticipation of the legal problems inevitably attending negotiation and consummation of so complicated a matter, Mr. Rockefeller arranged for Mr. Belknap to serve as our adviser in Egypt.

When a few days later we sailed again for England, our fellow passengers included Mr. and Mrs. Rockefeller, who in company with the architect Welles Bosworth were bound on one of their periodic visits to France to observe the progress of the rehabilitation of Rheims, Versailles and Fontainebleau; and the eminent brain specialist and surgeon, Dr. Harvey Cushing, on his way to England to confer with Lady Osler regarding the biography he was then completing of her late husband, Sir William Osler. My father had brought with him photostatic copies of the Edwin Smith Surgical Papyrus together with all his pertinent research materials and paraphernalia, now packed in special boxes which enabled him to set up his "workship" on a moment's notice wherever he happened to find a few hours of available time. Dr. Cushing was greatly surprised and impressed when my father showed him, among other things, that this oldest known scientific treatise in the world contained the earliest known occurrence of a word for "brain." All this deeply interested Mr. Rockefeller too, and when occasion offered, he questioned my father closely regarding both his own work and the program of the Oriental Institute. What with scientific discussions, architectural conferences and the generally enlivening exchange between these men, it would have been an exceptionally happy voyage without a characteristic incident which made it for my father unforgettable.

Mr. and Mrs. Rockefeller were disembarking at Cherbourg. As they were leaving the ship, his private secretary took me aside, gave me a sealed letter with the request that I should hand it to my father as we reached London.

Dr. Cushing sat with us during the run from Southampton to London. As the train neared Waterloo Station I gave the letter to my father, who asked us to excuse him while he opened and read it. An expression of embarrassed incredulity came into his face, and without a word he handed me the letter.

"The most important factor in the advancement of the well-being of Mankind," it read, "is men and women, well-trained, with high purpose and fine spirit. . . . You are such an one—unique in your field. . . .

"The contributions which I have made to the Oriental Institute have been based partly upon my interest in the field which it covers —largely because of my belief in you. Clearly your training, your experience and your knowledge can be put to larger usefulness, and with a minimum of added burden to you if additional workers and sums are made available.

"I will be happy to add the sum of Fifty thousand dollars ($50,000) to my present pledge to the Oriental Institute for each of the remaining . . . years this pledge has still to run . . . I should like to have the first draft upon it made to provide such . . . help for you as will reduce to a minimum the manual and detail work which you are now doing. The balance may be used . . . in any other way which in your judgment will add most to the productiveness of your work. . . .

"With the assurance that I count it a high privilege to have even a small part in this extraordinary work which you are doing, and with the hope that you will make the careful preservation of your own health of paramount importance, I am, etc."

My father tried to continue his conversation with Dr. Cushing, but was obviously so distrait that the latter said, "I hope you have not received bad news?"

"On the contrary," my father answered, "the news is so good it overwhelms me!"

The brochure my father had prepared to assist King Fuad in visualizing the Project was printed by the Oxford Press, which functioned with its proverbial efficiency. Toward the end of October we left London for Egypt.

On the morning of our departure there appeared in the *Times* the historic dispatch which had been smuggled out of Beirut and cabled from Cairo, describing the revolt of the Jebel Druses in Syria and the French bombardment and partial destruction of Damascus with 75's planted in the surrounding hills.

This drastic step had been ordered by the notoriously brutal and impolitic High Commissioner and former general, Maurice Sarrail, because the French had no garrison in the city, which had consequently been invaded and pillaged by bands of Druses before troops could be brought in. The dispatch made it clear that had there been French forces stationed within the city, its bombardment could have been avoided. (Many authorities considered it needless despite the absence of troops in the town; and Sarrail was promptly recalled for his actions.)

This incident bore directly on our Project; for apart from the Citadel which overlooked and commanded Cairo, the Kasr en-Nil Barracks were the only ones *within* the city itself. With the grim example of Damascus before them, would the British be likely to evacuate Kasr en-Nil? And without this "trump card" could we still interest the Egyptians in a new Museum?

Upon locating our deck chairs on our ship at Genoa, I found that my father's stood beside one to which had already been affixed a card bearing the name "Professor Eduard Meyer."

I moved away and waited. Presently I saw approaching the same tall, bearded man of my Gross-Lichterfelde childhood, but now aged and obviously less aggressive. As he seated himself, he happened to glance at the card on my father's chair. Visibly startled, he pointed it out to his Rosina who as for at least the past forty-five years was still beside him. His last message to my father, through Erman, had been: "I can have nothing to do with any American!"

My father was standing at the rail in conversation with friends when Frau Meyer approached him and gently touched his arm. He turned. She held out her hand and said in German, "I want to greet you and give you my hand!—and so does my husband! May he also come to you?"

"There were tears in her eyes," my father wrote afterwards. "Meyer was standing in the background. I stepped forward at once and he likewise. He seized my hand in both of his, and his face glowed with his old friendliness. With glistening eyes and all his one-time hearti-

ness he said, '*Es freut mich ungemein Dich wieder zu sehen!*' [It
makes me extraordinarily happy to see thee again!']

"It was the old Meyer, now a kindly, *gentle* old man of seventy-two.
I confess I was deeply touched by the 'Dich' ['thee']. Good Frau
Meyer beamed with joy through her tears. *She* had done it. Well—it
is better so."

When my father sought from Lord Lloyd the written statement of
the British army's readiness to evacuate the Kasr en-Nil barracks in
favor of the proposed new Museum, which the Foreign Office in London had confidently anticipated "would cause no serious difficulty,"
it caused very little else, and there followed weeks of consideration
and discussion between the Residency, the Foreign Office and General Sir Richard Haking, then commander-in-chief of the British army
in Egypt. The French bombardment of Damascus and the revolt in
Syria had produced a serious impression in London, and after weeks
of negotiations and delay Lord Lloyd conveyed to us, with a show
of well simulated regret, the General's flat refusal to give up the
Barracks.

Mr. Rockefeller's attitude was characteristic. "While I have been
keenly interested in this matter [the Museum Project]," he wrote my
father on November 30, 1925 from Cannes, "I shall take it less to heart
than you if its consummation must be delayed or the whole project
ultimately abandoned. Our one purpose is to render service and at
the same time to promote good-will. . . . If these two elements cannot come hand in hand, it were better to abandon the project. Do not
let this situation worry you at all. . . ."

With Mr. Rockefeller's consent the cherished site was now abandoned for the south end of the Gezireh, the lengthy island in the Nile
opposite Cairo; and out of consideration for the British we never mentioned to the Egyptians the fact of our having tried to dislodge the
former from the Kasr en-Nil Barracks.

We first approached King Fuad through Ahmed Bey Hassanein,
one of the finest of the younger Egyptians—a Balliol graduate who
had recently served as first secretary of Egypt's first legation in
Washington, and was now junior royal chamberlain. The Museum
Project, said Hassanein, had "greatly impressed and gratified His
Majesty." The moment appeared to have come for a personal meeting
between the King and my father. Etiquette required, however, that
the latter must first be formally presented by the American Minister.

America's diplomatic representative in Egypt at this time was a retired physician named J. Morton Howell from Dayton, Ohio, whom his old friend President Harding had thus rewarded for political services—and whom the State Department had verbally instructed us to avoid save for inescapable protocol. Hence on the morning of January 4, 1926 my father in full evening dress and top hat accompanied Dr. Howell to the Abdin Palace and was presented to Fuad I, King of Egypt—until recently a penniless prince, whose selection the British had promoted not on account of his ability or fitness but because, as the only extant son of Khedive Ismail Pasha, he was nearest in line for the throne. . . . The King gave no indication of ever having heard my father's name before, and his acknowledgment of the presentation was perfunctory to the point of rudeness. Not until a week later did Fuad grant him an audience at which to deliver personally Mr. Rockefeller's letter of gift.

"The King's conduct was astounding," my father wrote later that day. "He read the donor's letter hastily, barely glanced at a summary of the Project which for his convenience we had prepared in French. He thrust aside with hardly a look the beautifully bound copy of the descriptive brochure.

"He ridiculed the Project as visionary and impossible, said that the sum proposed for the building was not enough; boasted of Egyptian wealth, and remarked on American readiness to interfere in Egyptian affairs as illustrated by ex-President Theodore Roosevelt's speech at the Egyptian University! * It required the utmost self control not to tell His Majesty that I could no longer listen to such insults. My indignation was handicapped by the necessity of speaking French, but I did say to him that there seemed no further reason for continuing the interview, or for making any further efforts to consummate the Project. To my surprise he changed his attitude at once, requested me to bring the matter before Ziwar Pasha (the Prime Minister), and said he himself would instruct the latter to discuss the matter with me.

"He is obviously disgusted that he cannot get a single finger on any portion of the funds, and resentful of a project which took for granted that the Egyptians had nobody who could do this thing. Probably he also realizes that the Americans have discerned a magnificent opportunity of which he himself should have taken advantage. The superb golden coffin and golden portrait mask of King Tutenkhamon, for

---

* Delivered in 1910. In this speech Roosevelt had denounced the recent assassination of the prime minister Boutros Pasha by a member of the Nationalist party.

instance, have just arrived at the Museum, where they have been installed for public inspection in a storeroom filled with packing boxes!"

Under instructions from London to render the project every possible assistance, Lord Lloyd now personally informed the Prime Minister that the British government desired to see the matter favorably consummated. The King tardily endeavored to give the impression that he welcomed the gift, and that its acceptance rested with his council of ministers.

Ziwar Pasha was a genial, remarkably honest (he was partly Circassian), enormously fat man whose obesity was the subject of countless jokes—native café wags were at the moment remarking that Tutenkhamon's solid gold coffin "weighed two and a half Ziwars"— but whose courage was in scale with his size. He had taken office soon after the assassination of Sir Lee Stack, and though several attempts had been made on his own life, he had continued to go about his business in Cairo in an open car unattended by guards.

"He has from the beginning cordially supported our Project," my father wrote of him. "At the end of my first conference with him he followed me to the door and said: 'You know, Egypt has no civilization except what comes to us from Europe and America. We *must* rely on foreign scientists—but I cannot say that in public! Therein lies our chief difficulty in carrying out your project.'"

Mr. Belknap, our legal adviser, now conferred at length with the same members of the Egyptian government's legal department with whom my father had dealt in the Tutenkhamon tomb dispute. After the government had consumed weeks objecting to every constructive suggestion from the American side, he asked that they themselves draft a contract incorporating the conditions to which they would be willing to subscribe. Among those whose counsel was especially helpful at this difficult stage was the late Neville Henderson, then Great Britain's first minister plenipotentiary to the new Kingdom of Egypt.

At last the government lawyers evolved a draft of a revised contract which Mr. Belknap considered acceptable, and which they asked him and my father to transmit to the gentlemen in New York, together with a covering letter from Ziwar Pasha stating that if this document proved acceptable to the American side, he in turn would recommend it to the council of ministers for signature. Mr. Belknap left at once for New York.

By this time the matter was known to so many individuals that rumors of it had reached the press, necessitating our announcement of the offer while Mr. Belknap was still en route. We made the grave error of failing to state in our release that the contractual conditions governing the proffered gift had been drawn by the Egyptian government itself.

Without exception both the foreign and vernacular press of Egypt greeted the offer with the most flowery praise and adulation, and urged the King and his ministers to accept it promptly. Of the approximately twenty-four English, Arabic, Syrian, French, Italian and Greek papers then being published in Cairo, only the editor of the leading French paper approached me to suggest that his enthusiastic editorial approval of the offer surely entitled him to some tangible financial reward. He remained baffled and incredulous when I explained that the donor never *bought* approval of his benefactions.

Because the status of the thirty-year Anglo-French Treaty of 1904 (which as explained in Chapter VI, stipulated that for the effective duration of the treaty the Director General of the Antiquities Department should be a Frenchman), had been rendered somewhat uncertain by Egypt's recent achievement of nominal independence, the British had counselled us to await the King's decision before discussing the Rockefeller offer with the French. Our desire to cooperate in every way with the British led us to follow this advice, by doing which we made a further serious mistake. For long in advance of our press announcement, garbled news of the offer had reached the garrulous and excitable M. Lacau and his French and English staff, all of whom accepted his interpretation of it as a grandiose scheme for ousting them from their posts and bringing the antiquities of Egypt under American control. M. Lacau therefore fought against it tooth and nail, and being in the good graces of the King, did his utmost to antagonize the latter's already prejudiced mind still further against a gift which he claimed would entail the virtual sale of Egypt's ancient monuments to America.

"It is amazing," my father wrote while at Luxor that February, "what an amount of smallness and petty jealousy this Museum plan has uncovered! I am growing very thick-skinned and philosophical, and shall quietly continue to keep my wagon hitched to a star. But it is a great relief to turn again for a brief time to my own researches."

Throughout the weeks of conferences, negotiations and waiting he had continued at every opportunity to work on the Surgical Papyrus, so that on February 8 he was able to enter in his journal: "Finished translation and commentary on Surgical Treatise in Papyrus Edwin Smith. Magical text on verso [a later interpolation written on the backs of certain pages] will take but brief time."

He had also devoted a great deal of effort to the organization of a prehistoric survey of the entire Nile Valley—a fundamentally important item in his great pattern of Near Eastern research which project by project he was now steadily carrying out.

"Two outstanding problems in the career of prehistoric man have long awaited solution," he wrote. "One of these is the genetic and chronological correlation of the remains of prehistoric man in Africa with similar remains, geologically dated, in Europe. (The same problem exists as between Western Asia and Europe.) The second is the correlation of the enormously ancient—presumably very early Paleolithic—remains on the plateau of Northeast Africa with the earliest stages of human development on the alluvial floor of the Nile Valley. . . .

"It is [also] of vital importance for our understanding of man's early career in these regions to know when the overwhelming catastrophe of desiccation overtook him. The correlation of this tremendous transformation with the human career in the Nile Valley, and in the wide plains and plateau of Egypt and the Sudan is now becoming possible.

"I have made arrangements for a systematic survey of the traces of early man in Northeast Africa and in Western Asia, which will correlate these with geological periods, and wherever possible find the leading types of flint implements in stratigraphic deposits. The project will be called the Prehistoric Survey Expedition, and will begin work in the autumn of 1926.*

While he was at Luxor, Mr. Julius Rosenwald, then a trustee of the University of Chicago, arrived there on his first visit. Mr. Rosenwald's philanthropic interest lay chiefly in negro education among our Southern States, and the work of the Oriental Institute held little appeal for him. My father showed him all the important monuments of Luxor and Thebes, and explained to him the nature and purpose of the Epigraphic Expedition, and its need of a larger building. "He stoutly resisted, suggested all sorts of difficulties, said the problem should be put up to the Rockefeller Foundation; and when I finally took him to lunch on his second day," wrote my father, "I felt that he cared little about our problems.

* Adapted from *The Oriental Institute,* by James H. Breasted, pp. 73; 129 ff.

"But after lunch Mr. Rosenwald said, 'Where are the plans of the new building you told me about?' I laid them before him. He asked a few more questions, then said quietly: 'My son William [who had also recently visited Luxor] wrote me that if I did anything for your new building he wanted to give $5,000. I have decided to contribute $25,000—so I will give you my check for $30,000.' Later I persuaded him to increase this to $37,500!"

At about the same time Mr. Abraham Flexner, then secretary of the General Education Board, re-visited Egypt, and at Luxor familiarized himself with the work of the Epigraphic Expedition to which my father desired to add a scientific library that would be open to students and scholars throughout the world. When Flexner returned to America, the General Education Board approved my father's request for $250,000 for the purchase of books and for library maintenance endowment.

"A man like me ought to have nine lives and the strength of a Goliath," my father wrote from Luxor. "I often wonder where I shall land with all these argosies I am loading with such reckless disregard of the fact that there is only one captain for the whole fleet—which means that he is spread out pretty thin and will evaporate in the next ten years, leaving very little behind, especially in the way of junior mariners to bring the fleet into port!"

He was convinced nevertheless that the greatest service he could now render his science was to continue to load as many argosies as the present golden opportunities would permit.

Within ten days after Mr. Belknap's arrival in New York we received a cable stating that Messrs. Rockefeller, Fosdick and Macy had approved the Egyptian government's revised version of the contract without a single change, and had signed and despatched to us a new document drawn accordingly.

While this was on its way we visited Palestine and Syria on Oriental Institute matters. In Jerusalem, with the cooperation of Bernard Flexner and the (Rockefeller) International Health Board, we made the first moves in a campaign against the malarial mosquito on the marshy Plain of Megiddo—a campaign which a few years later was to become a model for all Palestine.

When my father saw the old house in which the Palestine government was then attempting to display and store its share of the antiquities now rapidly accruing from the excavations of the annually increasing number of archaeological expeditions working in Palestine, it occurred to him that in Jerusalem too there existed a great need for a museum building. He found an admirable vacant site overlooking Gethsemane and the Mount of Olives, between the Jericho Road and the Mosque of Omar; and ascertained confidentially that the British Mandate of Palestine, of which Lord Plumer was then High Commissioner, would welcome the gift of a museum and gladly expropriate the foregoing site.

From Jerusalem we drove northward to Beirut to secure from the new French High Commissioner, Henri de Jouvenel (who had succeeded the hated Sarrail), permission to purchase and export to America one of the finest collections of Phoenician sarcophagi in the world, which had been gathered by an astute old American fundamentalist missionary named Dr. George A. Ford during almost half a century's residence at Sidon. We spent a prayer-and-scripture-filled night as his guests; and as we parted from him he solemnly reminded us *not* to travel on the Sabbath as we expected to do on our return.

De Jouvenel remained unmoved by the combined pleas of my father, of American Consul General Paul Knabenshue, of old Dr. Ford himself, and of our oft-time host, President Bayard Dodge of the American University, one of the most respected and the most influential of the Americans in Syria. The collections, said de Jouvenel bluntly, would stay in the country: France had already suffered enough criticism for her administration of the Syrian Mandate without incurring the charge of having permitted historical treasures to be removed from it. Realizing that his efforts were in vain, my father suggested that the collections in the Louvre Museum in Paris hardly constituted a shining example of such a policy. The High Commissioner, unable to make any answer, merely reiterated his regret, and by rising indicated that the interview was ended. It was obvious throughout that he resented the American offer of a museum to Egypt.

So we turned south again, traveling as it happened on the Sabbath. Guiltily we passed through Sidon without re-visiting Dr. Ford whom we suspected of thinking bitter, un-Christian thoughts about the French High Commissioner whose arbitrary decision had deprived him of the $25,000 we would otherwise have paid him for his collection, a sum with which he had hoped to ease his last years of retirement. We were congratulating ourselves on having escaped his pietistical hospitality and were just passing through the historic town of Tyre when retribution overtook us. With the noise of artillery, two of our tires blew out, and to the delight of my father, who had a weakness for such puns, we were forced to wander through Tyre in quest of two new American tires.

We pushed on to the mound of Megiddo where despite vicious malaria and impassable roads, worsened by an exceptionally long rainy season, the staff of the Oriental Institute's new expedition had built a house and had already begun excavation.

The mound of Megiddo was typical of hundreds upon hundreds of similar ancient sites scattered through Palestine, Syria, Anatolia, Iraq and Iran. It was actually a "layer cake" of ancient cities, one built upon another as its predecessor was destroyed, or as houses merely crumbled with age, fell down and were rebuilt—a process which archaeologists call "urban stratification." The modern archaeological method of excavating such a mound is to survey it, laying out upon it a "grid" of, ordinarily, twenty-five-meter squares; and while always retaining the intersection points of this "grid," to expose and record every layer, each of which is of course older as the digging proceeds. The lowest layer of Megiddo might well prove to be a Stone Age settlement—for there was good reason to believe that Stone Age men lived among these hills perhaps a hundred thousand years before the Hebrews entered what is today Palestine.

Here on March 23, 1926, my father wrote the foreword of a forthcoming library edition of his *Ancient Times,* called *The Conquest of Civilization,* the closing paragraphs of which I quote below because they are at once pertinent and in his best vein; and because, since they embody so much both of his own spirit and of his attitude toward the ancient world, I have always loved them:

"As I write these lines, the broad Palestinian plain of Megiddo stretches before me; behind me rises Har-Megiddo, 'the Mount of Megiddo,' or as known to the Western world in its Hellenized form, 'Armageddon.' Towering high over the plain, Armageddon was an imposing stronghold, . . . now deeply covered by the rubbish of thousands of years, green with billowing grain and bright with nodding anemones.

"Our first trenches have been thrust into the vast mound, . . . [and] already . . . [our] workmen have brought out an inscribed block bearing Egyptian hieroglyphs. As I went into the court of our new Oriental Institute house on the slope of Megiddo this morning and the early sunshine illumined the block, it became evident that the fragmentary signs, scarred and weathered until they were scarcely legible, were those forming the name of Shishak, called by the Egyptians Sheshonk, a Pharaoh of the tenth century B.C.

"Instantly there rose before me the vision of a Sunday school in a little church on the far-off prairies of Illinois, where nearly half a century ago a group of village boys with heads together over a Bible were struggling with the difficult proper names of an old Hebrew chronicle: 'And it came to pass in the fifth year of King Rehoboam that Shishak, king of Egypt, came up against Jerusalem: and he took away the treasures of the house of Jehovah, and the treasures of the king's house; he even took away all: and he took away all the shields of gold that Solomon had made' (I Kings 14, 25–26). And today under the shadow of the great fortress mound, it was with some emotion that one of those boys was reading the name of the old Egyptian conqueror, who carried away Solomon's treasure from Jerusalem [sixty miles to the south] nearly 3,000 years ago. . . .

"It is an impressive illustration of the fact that for ages Armageddon has been the gate between two continents, for possession of which the emperors and kings of Asia and Africa have struggled. Through the pass which it commands, the armies of Egypt marched for a thousand years. Its battlements, now covered by the great mound, were black with terrified Canaanitish throngs, who pulled their fugitive king up the walls to temporary safety after the rout of the Asiatic allies by Thutmose III in the fifteenth century B.C. Across the plain to which Armageddon has given its name, swept the battles of Canaanite and Hebrew, of Hebrew and Philistine; and on the walls of Bethshan at its eastern end the Philistines hanged the bodies of Saul and Jonathan, slain on the slopes of Mt. Gilboa, to which our expedition house looks out. At the seaward end of the plain the Crusaders landed at Acre; from the hills of Nazareth on the north, the child Jesus must often have looked down upon this battlefield of the ages. And through this same pass upon which Armageddon still frowns down, Lord Allenby pierced the Turkish line and won the last great battle of Armageddon in 1918.

"The cloud shadows creep slowly across the misty hills of Nazareth eight miles away. For ages they looked down upon scenes of conquest and blood-shed on this plain—ages whose highest gods were divinities of violence and carnage, the delight of such fierce prophets as Elijah; and after the slow eclipse of such bloody gods, there dawned among those hills of Nazareth a God of brotherly kindness—the vision of a Jewish carpenter's son, whose tiny Galilean village lies just beyond the brow of the northern hills so clearly visible from the battlements of Armageddon. Of all the transformations which thrill the modern visitor to this region, there has been none like this from Elijah to Jesus, from Carmel and Armageddon to Nazareth. It was the culmination of that long commingling of ancient oriental civilizations gathering from Egypt and Asia and forming that Egypto-Asiatic culture nucleus which eventually transformed the life of once savage and barbarous Europe. What more fitting scene in which to write the foreword of a sketch which endeavors to trace in its main contours the unfolding life of man—the Conquest of Civilization!"

As our train clattered hour after hour across the desert from Palestine to Kantara at the Suez Canal on our return to Cairo, he was reminded of all that had happened during the five years since he had made this same journey in company with General Waters Taylor at the weary conclusion of the reconnaissance expedition which had signalized the birth of the Oriental Institute. I spoke of the earlier years when he used to think aloud to me his day-dreams, of which so many were now rapidly coming true.

"I can't fully grasp the change," he said. "The reality is wonderful, but the dreams were on the whole much more beautiful and satisfying. I remember my own father's dreams and visions—air-castles that were never built—and now that some of mine have become fact, I no longer regret that he never realized any of his."

Inevitably his thoughts reverted to the Museum Project. "If it fails to go through," he said, "I shan't grieve, for I have about concluded that its consummation would probably mean my extinction as a scientist."

Late that night we drew into the familiar Cairo Station, and on a morning one week afterward the revised contract for the Museum arrived from New York.

I took it at once to Ziwar Pasha, who asked that my father see him that afternoon. When they met, Ziwar appeared agitated and ill at ease. He rose in all his bulk, and holding the contract in one hand while nervously tapping it with the other, said in French:

"We cannot sign this document! The conditions are absolutely unacceptable, they infringe upon the sovereignty of Egypt! My colleagues in the council of ministers decline to consider the matter until the conditions of the contract have been fundamentally revised!"

My father replied quietly: "There can be no talk of any further revision of a contract drawn by the Egyptian government itself. The only alternative to its signature by the council of ministers is withdrawal of the offer. I am leaving in a week's time for New York. If upon my arrival there I find no cable reporting its acceptance, I shall advise Mr. Rockefeller to withdraw the offer."

Wherewith he bade Ziwar good-bye.

The following day there appeared in the Egyptian press a communiqué from the office of the Prime Minister, stating that Professor Breasted had submitted to it a contract embodying the conditions attached to Mr. Rockefeller's offer, and that these were wholly unacceptable to the Egyptian government.

When no message from Ziwar awaited our return to New York, Mr. Rockefeller sent King Fuad a friendly, brief note withdrawing his offer; and so ended the Cairo Museum Project.

Once again I went about my own affairs, this time permanently—I thought.

The failure of the Cairo Museum Project left Mr. Rockefeller with ten million dollars which he had signified his readiness to contribute to the support of archaeology. He soon made it clear that he intended Egypt's loss to be archaeology's gain elsewhere.

When my father late that spring laid before Raymond Fosdick a proposal for a museum in Jerusalem, he was promptly authorized to explore the matter further with the Palestine government. At the same time the Rockefeller foundations, while steadily augmenting their support of the Oriental Institute, were becoming more and more interested in the whole field of Near Eastern and Mediterranean archaeology, toward the development of which they now asked him to draw up large-scale plans.

"The program I first submitted," he remarked in his journal, "totalled over thirty million dollars." Neither the boards nor Mr. Rockefeller appeared to be taken aback by this figure, but simply as a matter of practicality it seemed to them wiser to begin on a more moderate basis. He therefore drew up for their consideration a modified plan, involving an outlay of eleven million dollars.

With only a few changes it proposed what he had been advocating for at least a decade: a new, completely equipped headquarters at the University of Chicago; greatly expanded teaching facilities, with endowment; the establishment of at least one field expedition in every important cultural region of the ancient Near East; the maintenance by these expeditions of racial, cultural and anthropo-geographical researches; the correlation of the resulting discoveries and observations to furnish the basis for the historical reconstruction of the causes of early human development; and, finally, one of the most ambitious publication programs ever undertaken in the field of humanistic research (see Appendix B, p. 419).

Upon his return to New York in the spring of 1927 from another Near Eastern journey (during which he had secured from the Palestine government through Lord Plumer the gift of the land for the new Palestine museum), he received a confidential indication that his proposed archaeological program would in the main almost certainly be approved and financed by the Rockefeller boards. At this point he sent for me, and during one entire day thought aloud to me his vision of what lay before him. As always he drew an exciting and inspiring picture. Finally he said: "I am standing at a forking of my road. I can leave the Oriental Institute at its present stage and devote my remaining years to my own researches and historical writing—or, putting these aside, I can endeavor to make it the leading humanistic research organization in America and perhaps the world. That is where I know my duty lies. But to attempt this I must have help during the next critical years of expansion. The men around me are competent scholars but administratively futile. Your life has trained you for the task, you are the only person to whom I can turn. Is it too much to ask your help again?"

It seemed to me at the time, and I still believe that nothing in my own life then mattered so much as that while he was yet in the fullness of his powers, his argosies should be brought safely home, and from their rich cargoes he should produce the books which he alone could write.

So I answered that far from asking a favor he was offering me a magnificent opportunity which I would be honored to accept providing he would promise me to *continue* his own researches and historical writing, and to confine himself as nearly as possible to the scientific work of the Oriental Institute, leaving its physical expansion and administration to me. I added that if the arrangement proved to be mutually satisfactory, I would undertake to carry on for five years.

He promised, we shook hands on it, and in July 1927 I entered my "new" office in Haskell Oriental Museum—a building crowded with memories of the years I have described in earlier chapters—and dusted out a decrepit roll-top desk once used by my father's departed enemy, Robert Francis Harper.

In its broadest terms, my job consisted of bringing Western man's latest, most efficient methods and devices to bear upon recovering the story of his conquest of civilization in the oldest lands of history. Specifically this meant the unification and systematization of the Oriental Institute to function both as a division of a great Middle Western university accustomed to domestic American routines, and as a research organization whose foreign operations already extended from Anatolia on the north to the Sudan on the south, and were soon to expand eastward into central Iran. It meant journey after journey to the Near East; the construction, equipment and operation of a whole series of expedition headquarters at remote locations (at Persepolis we rehabilitated the harem palace of Darius!); the purchase of supplies and the correlation of transport for units scattered through six oriental countries; the employment, safeguarding, victualing and seasonal movements to and from the field of personnel; the lease or purchase of archaeological sites through third and fourth trustworthy parties in order to keep down their price; the obtainment of permits to excavate them; the cultivation of friendly relations with the frequently changing governments of the countries in which we were working; the balancing of budgets in the face of fluctuating exchanges in some twenty different currencies; and the infinitude of details implicit in the conduct of ramified scientific enterprises operating along a 2500-mile front, 6000 miles from their American base, before the era of two-day air travel between the United States and the Near East.

It was an exciting, challenging, often exasperating job, simply "cut out" for Americans: and precisely therein lay our greatest tribulation. Americans trained in Near Eastern field archaeology were so few at this time that at the outset, as my father put it, "the greatest majority of our field directors and staffs were drawn from Austria, Czecho-Slovakia, Denmark, England, Germany, Holland, Hungary, Italy, Norway, Palestine, Portugal, Russia, Sweden, Switzerland and Syria! It was obvious that the Oriental Institute's responsibility for training a future generation of young American scientists in every phase of oriental archaeology was as important as the maintenance of its field operations."

"The fundamental difficulty which besets me in this work at every turn," he wrote to George Hale, "[is] . . . the lack of personnel.

Well-equipped astronomers are being created by a great many efficient institutions or observatories, but historically minded archaeologists and field research men are not being produced anywhere. The personal equation is so difficult that I sometimes wish I had never dreamed any dreams."

Nevertheless the job was done with the ablest people available, regardless of nationality or temperament.

From 1927 onwards my father's career moved more and more swiftly. That autumn Mr. Rockefeller pledged himself to give two million dollars for the construction and maintenance endowment of a Palestine museum at Jerusalem.* A year later the Rockefeller boards approved his larger plans by appropriating for the work of the Oriental Institute an initial sum of more than seven million dollars.†

He was of course enormously elated by this unprecedented support of everything he had so long championed. But as he contemplated the array of still uncompleted projects in which he was already engaged, and the many others he was now in a position to launch, he could not forget that he was already sixty-three. Again and again he would exclaim, "If *only* I were twenty years younger!"

In January 1929 Mr. Rockefeller, with a family party which he had invited my father and me to join, for the first time visited Egypt, Palestine and Syria. He wanted especially to see the work of the Oriental Institute's expeditions. Long experience had taught him that incautious self-exposure to the enthusiasms of scientific men was too often a costly business, hence before the party sailed from New York he sent his guests through Raymond Fosdick a friendly but frank request to raise no financial questions during the voyage.

My father was greatly amused, for he had planned a much subtler attack upon his host's interest. He brought with him in a special trunk hundreds of glass slides with which of evenings he illustrated informal presentations of the historical significance of the ancient places and ruins the party would soon be seeing. A month's voyage by private

---

* After the retirement of Lord Plumer, who had given it his enthusiastic and most effective support, the Palestine Museum project was side-tracked by British officials in Jerusalem, in favor of a palatial new British residency and other public works. Though my father lived to see the building virtually completed, he died before it was opened, nearly nine years after the funds had been given.

† It was a source of great mutual satisfaction to my father and George Ellery Hale that the boards at this same time appropriated approximately $6,000,000 toward the construction and maintenance of Hale's projected two-hundred-inch telescope.

steamer up the Nile became a vitalized synopsis of his *History of Egypt*, and a motor journey through Palestine and Syria, a vivification of his *Ancient Times*. By indirection he accomplished far more for his science than he would ever have done by direct solicitation.

From the outset it proved to be Mr. Rockefeller himself who continually led the conversation on to forbidden ground. Throughout the three months' journey he plied my father with questions about the work and expansion of the Oriental Institute and its expeditions, and about his own personal researches. As we were nearing New York on the homeward voyage, he reviewed the matters which would require additional support.

The trip had been for my father an exhilarating but very tiring experience. One morning a few weeks after his return, when in the midst of a characteristic swirl of activities he was inaugurating the Flexner Lectures at Bryn Mawr College, his left arm suddenly became enormously swollen and turned purple in hue. But being in no pain he continued his work, and on the following day went to New York at Mr. Rockefeller's request to confer with him about the pending financial matters.

During a long interview with Mr. Rockefeller and conferences with foundation officers, he tried to keep his left hand from being seen "lest a rumor get about," he wrote later, "that I was unwell just at this critical juncture when everything was going so splendidly." He ended an arduous day by "inspecting some Egyptian antiquities for Mr. Rockefeller at a New York dealer's shop," returned late at night to Bryn Mawr to resume his lectures.

Only the following morning did he consult a physician. The latter on discovering his condition rushed him to Johns Hopkins Hospital for complete immobilization, with his arm in a horizontal position and packed in ice. "They called the thing thrombosis," he wrote George Hale, "but I could not [have] cancel[led] the New York engagement, which was a matter of millions."

I hurried to his bedside, found him quietly at work on the Edwin Smith Surgical Papyrus, to resume which he had good-naturedly but firmly defied the foremost medical men of Johns Hopkins, including the late Dr. William Henry ("Popsy") Welch. "I intend to recover promptly and completely," he said to me with a sparkle in his eyes. "But whatever happens, I shall finish this Papyrus if it's the last scientific work I ever do!"

During his subsequent convalescence, Mr. Rockefeller and the foundations between them appropriated another two million dollars for the work of the Oriental Institute. "I cannot suppress my constant amazement," he remarked in his journal that September, "at the confidence these men are showing me."

By 1932 the Oriental Institute was at work at strategic points along the entire Fertile Crescent.

An expedition in central Anatolia and another in northern Syria were excavating groups of city-mounds once inhabited by the ancient Hittites and by peoples who preceded and followed them.

In Iraq a large expedition in three units was clearing cities of ancient Assyria in the north, and of Babylonia in the south.

The Megiddo Expedition in Palestine had laid bare the foundations of the city of Solomon's time, and in probings at the base of the mound had found flint implements of Stone Age men.

The observations and findings of the Prehistoric Survey Expedition in Egypt were completely revising the geological and early human history of the Nile Valley and of northeastern Africa.

The Epigraphic and Architectural Survey Expeditions at Luxor, now established in a new, greatly enlarged permanent headquarters (including the most comprehensive archaeological library in the Near East) on the east bank of the Nile near Karnak, were producing a series of monumental folio volumes which for accuracy and comprehensiveness were setting a standard never before considered possible. In addition, with funds volunteered by Mr. Rockefeller, three enterprises were recording for publication in color the most beautiful wall paintings in Egypt, including the tombs of ancient Thebes, the painted wall reliefs in the superb temple of Seti I at Abydos,* and the relief paintings in the finest masonry tombs at Sakkara, the cemetery of ancient Memphis.

And finally, in Iran, an Oriental Institute Expedition was excavating Persepolis,† capital of the ancient Persian Empire, which Alexander the Great had destroyed in 331 B.C.

The results of these, and of a score of research enterprises being carried on at home, were now converging upon a long work table in a study such as he had never imagined he would ever occupy, in a beau-

* This was a project of the Egypt Exploration Society of England toward acceleration of which together with reproduction of the resulting color plates in a joint publication, Mr. Rockefeller contributed funds through the agency of the Oriental Institute.

† With funds contributed by Mrs. William H. Moore of New York.

tiful new building for which, as he had observed at its dedication and
opening on December 5, 1931, "we would find no parallel . . . in any
other university either in America or abroad, . . . a laboratory devoted . . . to the evolution of . . . civilization." Spread out upon
this table were the latest reports from the field; the manuscripts and
proofs of the newest volumes in the rapidly growing list of Oriental
Institute publications,* piles of correspondence with investigators in
related branches of science throughout the world; the materials for
his own current researches, including the manuscript of a new book
to be called *The Dawn of Conscience,* tracing the first appearance
and the development of higher moral aspirations in mankind, and,
after a lifetime of contemplating human history, summarizing his conclusions regarding the past and his conjectures as to the future of man;
plans for yet more scientific undertakings—a photographic air-survey
of the entire Near East, an expedition to excavate ancient Amathus
on the island of Cyprus, an offer from the Iraq government to give
to the Oriental Institute the entire site of biblical Calah-Nimrud and
everything it might contain in return for one million dollars for a new
museum in Baghdad. . . . And so on, endlessly.

The *Edwin Smith Surgical Papyrus,* which it had taken him ten
years to complete, had at last been published and was already considered a landmark in the history of medicine. A cabinet beside him
was filled with notes on new discoveries and historical data for inclusion in revisions of his earlier books.

Everything he had ever sought for his science was now a reality.

"Whether a man is a creative artist or a constructive scientist, his
ideas are rather like arrows in a quiver," he said to me one day at
about this time, as he stood before the fireplace in his new study. "He
has just so many of them, and when he has used them all, he has
delivered his message. Whatever else he does is iteration. The books
I have written, the ideas embodied in this building"—he made a sweeping gesture with his arm—"are my arrows. When I have finished *The
Dawn of Conscience* and a preliminary volume or two of *The History
of Civilization,* my quiver will be empty!"

With all their success these were years of deepening sadness in his
personal life, and of belated and growing disillusionment in his experience of his fellow men. He watched my mother's strength gradually
waning before the steady advance of some sinister enemy which doc-

* See Appendix B, p. 420.

tors could not identify. He saw the post-1929 depression threatening the permanent endowment of the laboratory he had devoted his life to creating—in a university which had become a huge, impersonal corporation, in a city which had become perhaps the principal cesspool of American politics. He noted anxiously the continuing paucity and with few exceptions the prevailing mediocrity and self-interest of the young men seeking a career in oriental studies. He observed the mounting envy of colleagues not only in other institutions but in his own university who, while deprecating the Oriental Institute as a luxury enterprise, avidly availed themselves of its facilities and results. With philosophical detachment he watched the most ambitious and the least qualified faculty members of his staff already jockeying for position as his successor.

Above all, he saw the nations of Europe, with the negative assistance of the United States, "building," as he expressed it, "the funeral pyre of the civilized world."

It was with an awareness of these and a great many other sobering considerations that in the late autumn of 1932 he completed *The Dawn of Conscience.*

"The more I have worked on the materials, the more I am convinced that the *subject* is the greatest theme that has ever dawned on human consciousness," he wrote me. "Whether the world will realize this or not is a dubious question; and if it does, that will be very good reason for finding *my treatment* of it wholly insufficient. My horizon is not limited, but I am so completely unacquainted with the history of human thought that I am quite unaware whether or not other men before me have had the same ideas and seen the same truths.

"Summed up in a single sentence, the significance of the book lies in that it will furnish the first *historical* demonstration that the evolutionary process which seems to have operated so largely in the rise and development of material forms, has culminated in ideals of human conduct and has thus produced an age of character which we have little more than begun. For the first time our world, if not the universe, is historically demonstrated to possess a value and a meaning.

"If Oswald Spengler had possessed even a glimmering of knowledge of the early Egypt he essays to bring into his picture of *The Decline of the West,* he could not have written the book."

In February 1933 after a four years' absence from the Near East he returned to it with my mother (who never once betrayed what effort it cost her) on the most thrilling journey of their entire lives. In a chartered Imperial Airways plane they flew from Cairo across Palestine, Trans-Jordania, southern Iraq and the Iranian Gulf to Bushire, and over the Iranian Mountains to Persepolis; northward again to Baghdad, and omitting only Anatolia, back into Palestine, and finally up the Nile. In a matter of hours they passed over the wide terrain—the banks of the Tigris and Euphrates, the villages and towns, the desert trails—which, thirteen years before, his reconnaissance expedition had taken laborious weeks to traverse. It was the supreme experience of his scientific career to trace from the air the pattern of the entire Fertile Crescent, and to see his expeditions at work in each of its ancient civilizations.

On the way home to America he re-visited Berlin, saw again the aged Erman, now virtually blind, and Sethe and the other colleagues of younger days. "To my surprise, all these German friends, who in the past abhorred politics," he wrote, "are now deeply interested in Hitler's new leadership, *and are all in favor of him!* If their judgment is to be accepted, Hitler has united Germany—an amazing and ominous achievement!"

This was my parents' last visit to Germany. From Tempelhofer Field, where on a September day forty-two years earlier he had stood beside William Rainey Harper and watched Kaiser William II review the German Army, they now boarded a Lufthansa plane for England.

Soon after their return to America, Hitler furthered his deliberate destruction of the sources and traditions of German higher learning by appointing as *rector magnificus* of Berlin University (the equivalent of our "president") a thirty-five-year old veterinary, who wore the insignia of his once distinguished office over the brown shirt of nazism.

My father saw in this upsurge of barbarous ignorance, with its contempt for the past, an extreme example of that same inclination to discard human experience which, as one of the consequences of excessive materialism, was already dangerously apparent in America.

"The most pressing need of America at the present critical juncture is not more mechanization but more character," he wrote that June of 1933. "Over four thousand years ago the social prophets of Egypt were hurling the same truth regarding their own land at the 'technocrats' who built the pyramids, the greatest feats of engineering ever achieved in the ancient world. The process of mechanization, which America has carried further than any other people, will and of course *should* go on, but shall it go on at the cost of character?"

This he discussed further in his Foreword to *The Dawn of Conscience:* "The most fundamentally important thing in the developing life of man has been the rise of ideals of conduct and the emergence of character, a transformation of human life which can be historically demonstrated to have begun but yesterday. . . . Man began as an *un*moral savage. How did it come about that he ever gained any moral dictates or eventually submitted to the moral mandate when once it had arisen? How did a world totally without any vision of character rise to social idealism and learn to listen with reverence to voices within? . . .

"Like most lads among my boyhood associates I learned the Ten Commandments. I was taught to reverence them because I was assured that they came down from the skies into the hands of Moses, and that obedience to them was therefore sacredly incumbent upon me. I remember that whenever I fibbed I found consolation in the fact that there was no commandment, 'Thou shalt not lie,' and that the Decalogue forbade lying only as a 'false witness' giving testimony before the courts where it might damage one's neighbor . . . when I was much older, I began to be troubled by the fact that a code of morals which did not forbid lying seemed imperfect; but it was a long time before I raised the interesting question: How has my own realization of this imperfection arisen? Where did I myself get the moral yardstick by which I discovered this shortcoming in the Decalogue? When that experience began, it was a dark day for my inherited respect for the theological dogma of 'revelation.' I had more disquieting experiences before me when as a young Orientalist I found that the Egyptians had possessed a standard of morals far superior to that of the Decalogue over a thousand years before the Decalogue was written. . . .

"The fact that the moral ideas of early men were the product of their own social experience is one of profoundest meaning for thinking people of today. Out of pre-historic savagery, . . . [and] his own experience, man arose to visions of character, . . . to a world of inner values transcending matter. . . . Not projected from the outside into a world of unworthy men by some mystic process called inspiration or revelation, but springing out of man's own life two thousand years before the theologians' 'age of revelation' began, illumining the darkness of social disillusionment and inner conflict, a glorious vindication of the worth of man, the dawn of the age of conscience and character broke upon the world. No conception of a spotlight of Divine Providence shining exclusively on Palestine shall despoil man of this crowning glory of his life on earth, the discovery of character. It is the greatest discovery in the whole sweep of the evolutionary process as far as it is known to us. . . . The human adventure has no value or significance except as we see it rising . . . toward . . . the Age of Character." *

While the body of the book was a deeply thoughtful presentation of the processes and stages by which man became imbued with conscience and what is commonly called a soul, the "Epilogue" of the book, from which the following passages have been selected, was also a revelation of the scientist whose story I have tried to tell:

"Ours are the first minds so placed as to realize that the emergence of conscience and the rise of a sense of social responsibility after 3,000 B.C. . . . were events of yesterday. . . . [They] marked our Father Man's approach to the frontiers of a New Country. Today we his children have hardly crossed those frontiers to begin the exploration of the New Country beyond. We stand in hesitation upon its outer margins, the beauty and sublimity of its distant prospects are hidden from us by the mists of human frailty, or blackened by the stifling smoke of greed, selfishness and World War. Blinded and dismayed we have stumbled and faltered with the foothills of the New Country all before us, while beyond them, if we would but lift our eyes, are glorious glimpses of the Delectable Mountains. Towards their still unscaled heights points the long and rising trail behind us, revealing to us, as it has risen from savagery to *character*, an unconquerable buoyancy of the human soul that has somehow issued from the deeps and risen so high.

"In using the words 'unconquerable buoyancy of the human soul' I am not employing a meaningless rhetorical phrase. I first used those words years ago . . . after returning from a journey among the buried cities of the ancient orient,† when I felt as never before the meaning of the great fact that in the life that once pulsed along the streets of those now long vanished cities, man had for the first time risen from the conquest of material resources to visions of social idealism so vital that they have continued to be a power among us who are building

* This concluding sentence is taken from the Epilogue of the *Dawn of Conscience.*

† See p. 316 ff.

Western civilization in the light of the great truths which still shine out of the East.

"That phrase 'unconquerable buoyancy of the human soul' . . . represent[s] a reality, an irrefutable fact in human life, whether past or present, a fact with which such men as Oswald Spengler and all the other pessimists do not deal, for they seem totally unconscious of it. It is a thing as demonstrably present in the spirit of man, as the circulation of the blood in his physical body. What other force has been the driving power in that amazing transformation from savagery to character, the beginnings of which we have been following? What carried the early man from purely material conquest to a recognition of the inner vision and its irresistible attraction? A philosopher like Bergson proclaims something which he calls the *élan vital*; but I am not dealing with philosophical conceptions, for I am not a philosopher. I am discussing the history of man and . . . [of] a force visibly present and operative for several hundred thousand years, . . . which I believe is still at work. No one can define it, or tell what it is, but like the force of gravitation, we can observe what it does. . . . We have only to look around us . . . to realize that the historical buoyancy of the human soul is still with us.

"From that dim and distant day when a human creature struck out the first flint implement, through all the ages until now, . . . the course of human life has prevailingly been a career of material achievement. For several hundred thousand years this Age of Material Conquest has gone on and still goes on. But yesterday, . . . through the dust of an engrossing conflict our Father Man began to catch . . . faintly the veiled glory of the moral vision, and to hear a new voice within, responding to a thousand promptings, old and new. It was interfused of love of home, of wife and children, of love of friends, and love of neighbors, of love of the poor and lonely and oppressed, of love of country and veneration of the Sovereign; and all these which were new, mingling with a vastly older reverence, the love of cloud and hilltop, of forest and stream, of earth and sea and sky, and not least of the earth's green mantle which every year burgeoned with life and nourishment for the children of men.

"Thus the old nature gods were shifted into a new world of social forces and . . . were fused into one with a god of human needs and human aspiration, a Universal Father in whom men began to see all the highest values that their own social experience had revealed to them. . . .

"The surviving [ancient] documents demonstrate historically that the thing which was long called 'the moral consciousness of mankind' has grown up with each generation out of the discipline and the emotions of family life, supplemented by reflection and the teaching of experienced elders. The supreme values which lie within the human soul have therefore, as a matter of historical fact, entered the world for the first time through . . . those gentle and ennobling influences which touch us continually in our family life. Whether in the beginning they were anywhere else out yonder in this vast universe, we shall never know; but they were not anywhere here upon our globe until the life of father, mother and children created them. . . .

"Bertrand Russell . . . tells * us that the most important change which communism would introduce is the abolition of the family and, throwing human experience entirely overboard, he advocates this change. Notwithstanding the revolt of the new generation, human experience cannot be annihilated, nor can the traits it has produced in us be obliterated or ignored. . . . There is one supreme human relationship, that which has created the home and made the family fireside the source out of which man's highest qualities have grown up to transform the world. As historical fact, it is to family life that we owe the greatest debt which the mind of man can conceive. The echoes of our own past from immemorial ages bid us unmistakably to venerate, to cherish, and to preserve a relationship to which the life of man owes this supreme debt.

". . . The life of man . . . has become a struggle between the *new* ideals . . . and the deep-seated passion for power, which is as old as the human race itself. . . . It has thus far been so dangerously victorious over new-born conscience and character that we are faced with the grave question of the survival of civilization. . . . That the vision of the New Past may influence the conduct of the *individual* I am profoundly convinced. Whether *nations* or *mankind as a whole*, realizing this vision, will find in it a really potent influence toward quenching international hatreds, or better still for building up international feelings of brotherhood and generous regard, may seriously be doubted. . . .

"In wandering for years through the ancient lands of the Near East, I have been impressed with this outstanding fact: the insistent monuments now surviving in all these distant lands have been primarily expressions of man's *power*. It is as if his struggle with the

* *Education and the Social Order,* by Bertrand Russell (London, 1932).

forces of nature, . . . which has now been going on for perhaps a million years, had imbued him with a defiant consciousness that he could win only by fighting his way through as he met the opposing forces of the natural world which challenged him on every hand. It was with this same attitude of relentless force that he met his own human fellows when the long struggle for supremacy eventually arose among the earliest nations.

"Today you may enter one of the lonely valleys of Sinai and find there, suddenly confronting you, the tall figure of an Egyptian Pharaoh carved in relief upon the face of the rock wall. There he has been standing since the thirty-fourth century before Christ, the oldest historical monument in the world. With uplifted weapon he is about to crush the skull of an Asiatic captive whom he had thrust down upon his knees before him. A monument of brutal force, it was a declaration of possession by right of conquest, serving imperious notice on the Asiatics that the king of Egypt had crossed from Africa into Asia and had taken possession of the surrounding copper and turquoise mines. Here, then, at the beginning of historical monuments and written records, the conquest of natural resources emerges as a fundamental motive of national action, and the monument which reveals it strikes the note of force which has dominated human history ever since. . . .

". . . In the lands of the Ancient East we . . . look out [today] upon the works of nature and the works of man, and in a New Crusade of scientific endeavor, we are striving to recover the story of both. . . . Already we have discerned enough to realize that . . . the processes of nature and the unfolding life of man are but chapters of the same great story; that . . . the culmination of a developing universe is *character*; [and] that the process of human advance which brought [it] forth . . . is still unfinished, . . . still going on. The possibilities of the future are *unlimited*. . . . Just as the light of character once dawned in a darkness which had never known such light before, so there is no reason to doubt the growth of that light to illumine realms of being that still lie all unrealized in the unfathomed ages toward which our limited vision of today looks out but does not see."

Thus wrote one who for more than forty years had lived in daily contemplation of the unending struggle of man within himself, of the incompatibilities of the human race, and of the inexorable and unaccountable rhythm of the rise and fall of nations.

The air-journey through the Near East had taken my mother's last strength. From the moment of her return she steadily declined; and at last it was found that throughout her life she had been waging a hopeless battle against a fatal malady of the heart.

She was not told, but she knew; and as her physical strength waned, the chains of anxiety, of household responsibilities, of over-conscientious devotion to self-imposed duties in which illness had so long imprisoned her, fell away, and like a sunset after a great storm her spirit emerged in all its beauty and calm fortitude, and for a final strange, timeless period during which she suffered greatly, the magnificent person she had inwardly always been stood forth free and triumphant.

On a morning early in July, 1934, she summoned each of us in turn, and speaking slowly and with infinite gentleness, asked us to forgive her her failures, for which she could never make amends: for though she longed to stay with us now that she had escaped from a lifetime of morbid shadows and had discovered the true beauty of life, she must soon leave us. She wished for us supreme happiness, and bidding us to cherish one another, she quietly said good-bye. Thereafter she fell into a sleep from which she never awoke.

I persuaded my father to take a journey with my sister to regions he had never seen—through the Panama Canal to Alaska, homeward through the Canadian Rockies. From his ship on the Pacific he wrote me:

"Your life now reaches further back into mine than that of any other soul. My world has passed away, and a new and totally different one has engulfed me. With youthful vigor and ambition gone, I am rather blindly and helplessly groping to find a place in this new world to which you belong. But I shall carry on—and, as I begin to do so, I want to tell you that henceforth my needs and my work must no longer keep you from whatever you desire to undertake. I say this with a chilling dread in my heart, yet with inexpressible gratitude for the help you have given me and the beautiful companionship which has been ours."

The momentum of almost half a century of unswerving devotion to his work helped him to carry on; and outwardly his life betrayed no change. He was soon re-absorbed in the scientific progress of his expeditions, in the ever-growing number of their publications filled with new discoveries in every phase of man's Near Eastern career.

Beginning with *Ancient Times*, he set about incorporating this wealth of new material in his earlier books, and laying out the larger pattern of the first volume of his projected *History of Civilization*.

But his talk now turned more frequently to the old days in Europe and Egypt, to the experiences of his boyhood. He found and hung on the walls of his room old photographs of Charles and Harriet, of "The Pines" at Downers Grove, of the Garrison house on The Hill and of Aunt Theodocia's "Pleasant Nook" at Rockford—where, as he had done more and more often of late years, he revisited the family plot in the old cemetery and lingered for an hour of quiet self-communion. "It gives me peace and comfort," he wrote, "to find the fresh green growing over the graves of my father and mother in a spot beautiful with trees that murmur in the wind."

In the midst of this increasing consciousness of his own past, he met again, after a lapse of years, one whose memories of it (as he had for the moment forgotten) reached farther back than mine—Imogen Hart, my mother's younger sister, whom he had first known during his Berlin student days when she was only a child—she whom I had so adored, that far-off summer in Williams Bay. She was gray-haired now, and since that carefree time had come a long and arduous road. But there was about her the same quality of gaiety and unquenchable girlhood, now tempered with wisdom. . . . Almost apologetically, as if gray heads had forfeited the right, they found a happiness together which was beyond words; and in due time they were married. Thereafter they set out for Italy and the Near East.

I bade them good-bye with a deep sense of fulfillment and happiness. Still youthfully vigorous, with his mind never more alive and tireless, with years of his maturest scientific productivity before him, my father was returning *happily* to the far-flung enterprises which together we had set going, and which now were at the peak of their development. I did not begrudge the years it had required beyond our contemplated five to bring all this about; and I was full of gratitude as I turned Westward to resume my own life.

But again this was not yet to be.

"I am as keen as a boy to get back to my desk and to begin the revision of my 'History of Egypt,'" he wrote on November 21, 1935 from Genoa Harbor on his homeward voyage.

In mid-Atlantic a sore throat he had acquired in Italy flared up with a high fever which he mistook for a recurrence of his old malaria, and which the Italian ship's doctor treated as such. When the ship reached New York he was desperately ill with what was found to be a virulent hemolytic streptococcic infection which at this time, before the advent in America of sulfa drugs, was still invariably fatal. Though they marvelled at his magnificent refusal to surrender, the attending doctors, and the Rockefeller Institute for Medical Research which Mr. Rockefeller placed at their disposal, were helpless.

I reached him before he died on December 2, 1935.

His ashes lie buried beside the graves of Charles and Harriet in the cemetery at Rockford; and over them rests a block of rough-hewn granite from the ancient Egyptian quarries at Aswan in Upper Egypt.

APPENDICES

Appendix A

1. The following, in chronological order, are the principal honors which were conferred upon James Henry Breasted:

1907   Prussian Royal Academy of Sciences of Berlin—corresponding life membership.
1918   American Oriental Society, president
1918   LL.D., University of California
1919   American Philosophical Society, member (vice-president, 1927–1933; committee on nominations 1933–34).
1919   Society of Antiquaries of London, honorary membership
1920   Art Institute of Chicago—Honorary Curator of Egyptian Antiquities (lifetime).
1920   National Academy of Sciences, member, Division of Anthropology and Psychology
1922   D. Litt. *honoris causa*, Oxford University
1922   American Geographical Society, corresponding membership
1923   Royal Asiatic Society of Great Britain and Ireland, honorary life membership
1926   History of Science Society, president
1927   American Schools of Oriental Research, trustee 1927–1933
1928   American Historical Association, president; life membership
1929   Chicago Geographic Society, gold medal
1929   LL.D., Princeton University
1929   Rosenberger Gold Medal, for contribution to history of civilization
1930   Ernest De Witt Burton Distinguished Service Professorship (emeritus 1933)
1930   Holland Society of New York, gold medal
1930   Academie des Inscriptions et Belles Lettres, Institut de France, Foreign Membership
1931   American Council of Learned Societies, member of Advisory Board, 1931–34; chairman, 1933 till death
1931   Archaeologisches Institut des Deutschen Reichs, honorary membership, 1931–
1931   Bavarian Academy, honorary membership
1931   Belgian Academy, corresponding fellow
1932   American Association of Museums, member of Council, 1932–34
1933   American Association for the Advancement of Science, member and fellow
1934   American Institute of Architects, Fine Arts Medal, May 16, 1934
1934   British Academy, corresponding fellow
1934   Oxford Society, honorary life membership
1935   Danish Royal Academy, member of historical-philological class

2. He was the author of the following publications (apart from a great number of articles which appeared in scientific journals of Europe and America):

1894 *De Hymnis in Solem sub Rege Amenophide IV Conceptis,* (his doctor's dissertation).
1900 *A New Chapter in the Life of Thutmose* III
1903 *The Battle of Kadesh*
1905 *Egypt Through the Stereoscope*
1905 *A History of Egypt* (German edition, 1911; Braille edition, 1911; Russian edition, 1917; French edition, 1925; Arabic edition, 1929).
1906 *Ancient Records of Egypt* (5 vols.)
1906 *The Temples of Lower Nubia*
1908 *A History of the Ancient Egyptians*
1908 *The Monuments of Sudanese Nubia*
1912 *Development of Religion and Thought in Ancient Egypt*
1914 *Outlines of European History* (jointly with James Harvey Robinson)
1914 *Short Ancient History*
1916 *Ancient Times, A History of the Early World* (translated into Swedish, Arabic, Malay, Chinese and Japanese). Revised 1935
1919 *Survey of the Ancient World* (Japanese edition, 1933)
1920 *History of Europe, Ancient and Medieval* (with James Harvey Robinson)
1921 *General History of Europe* (with J. H. Robinson and Smith)
1922 *The Oriental Institute*—A Beginning and a Program
1924 *Oriental Forerunners of Byzantine Painting*
1926 *The Conquest of Civilization* (a revised, somewhat maturer library edition of *Ancient Times*)
1930 *The Edwin Smith Surgical Papyrus* (2 vols.)
1933 *The Oriental Institute* (Vol. XII of *The University of Chicago Survey*)
1933 *The Dawn of Conscience*

Appendix B

The most lasting monument to James Henry Breasted is not the Oriental Institute Building (now named after him) at the University of Chicago, nor the Palestine Museum at Jerusalem, nor the block of granite from the ancient Egyptian quarries at Aswan in Upper Egypt which guards his ashes in the cemetery at Rockford. It is the following group of scientific publications.

The various series of Oriental Institute publications all appear under the imprint of the University of Chicago Press.

THE ORIENTAL INSTITUTE. *By* James Henry Breasted. xxiii+455 pages, 207 figures, 2 colored plates, 1 map, 12mo, cloth, special binding.

Oriental Institute Communications (OIC)

Illustrated reports describing for the general reader the progress and the results of Institute activities. Royal 8vo, paper.

No. 1. THE ORIENTAL INSTITUTE OF THE UNIVERSITY OF CHICAGO. A BEGINNING AND A PROGRAM. *By* James Henry Breasted (1922). (Out of print.)

No. 2. EXPLORATIONS IN HITTITE ASIA MINOR. A PRELIMINARY REPORT. *By* H. H. von der Osten (1927). (Out of print.)

No. 3. FIRST REPORT OF THE PREHISTORIC SURVEY EXPEDITION. *By* K. S. Sandford and W. J. Arkell (1928). xi+52 pages, 29 figures, 1 map.

No. 4. THE EXCAVATION OF ARMAGEDDON. *By* Clarence S. Fisher (1929). xv+78 pages, 53 figures.

No. 5. MEDINET HABU, 1924–28. *By* Harold H. Nelson and Uvo Hölscher (1929). xv+50 pages, 35 figures.

No. 6. EXPLORATIONS IN HITTITE ASIA MINOR, 1927–28. *By* H. H. von der Osten (1929). vii+153 pages, 160 figures.

No. 7. MEDINET HABU STUDIES, 1928/29. I. THE ARCHITECTURAL SURVEY. *By* Uvo Hölscher. II. THE LANGUAGE OF THE HISTORICAL TEXTS COMMEMORATING RAMSES III. *By* John A. Wilson (1930). ix+33 pages, 18 figures, 3 plates.

No. 8. EXPLORATIONS IN HITTITE ASIA MINOR, 1929. *By* H. H. von der Osten (1930). vii+196 pages, 163 figures, 9 maps.

No. 9. NEW LIGHT FROM ARMAGEDDON. SECOND PROVISIONAL REPORT (1927–29) ON THE EXCAVATIONS AT MEGIDDO IN PALESTINE. *By* P. L. O. Guy, with a chapter on "An Inscribed Scaraboid" by W. E. Staples (1931). ix+68 pages, frontispiece, 61 figures.

No. 10. MEDINET HABU REPORTS. I. THE EPIGRAPHIC SURVEY, 1928–31. *By* Harold H. Nelson. II. THE ARCHITECTURAL SURVEY, 1929/30. *By* Uvo Hölscher (1931). vii+69 pages, 42 figures, 4 plates.

No. 11. ANATOLIA THROUGH THE AGES. DISCOVERIES AT THE ALISHAR MOUND, 1927–29. *By* Erich F. Schmidt (1931). x+165 pages, 213 figures.

No. 12. THE ALPHABET: ITS RISE AND DEVELOPMENT FROM THE SINAI INSCRIPTIONS. *By* Martin Sprengling (1931). (Out of print.)

No. 13. TEL ASMAR AND KHAFAJE. THE FIRST SEASON'S WORK IN ESHNUNNA, 1930/31. *By* Henri Frankfort, Thorkild Jacobsen, and Conrad Preusser (1932). ix+112 pages, frontispiece, 54 figures.

No. 14. DISCOVERIES IN ANATOLIA, 1930–31. *By* H. H. von der Osten, with the collaboration of R. A. Martin and J. A. Morrison (1932). xi+149 pages, 134 figures.

No. 15. EXCAVATIONS AT ANCIENT THEBES, 1930/31. *By* Uvo Hölscher (1932). vii+65 pages, 41 figures, 4 plates.

No. 16. TELL ASMAR, KHAFAJE, AND KHORSABAD. SECOND PRELIMINARY REPORT OF THE IRAQ EXPEDITION. *By* Henri Frankfort (1933). ix+102 pages, frontispiece, 66 figures.

No. 17. IRAQ EXCAVATIONS OF THE ORIENTAL INSTITUTE, 1932/33. THIRD PRELIMINARY REPORT OF THE IRAQ EXPEDITION. *By* Henri Frankfort (1934). ix+92 pages, frontispiece, 83 figures.

No. 18. WORK IN WESTERN THEBES, 1931–33. I. THE CALENDAR OF FEASTS AND OFFERINGS AT MEDINET HABU. *By* Harold H. Nelson, with a chapter by Siegfried Schott. II. THE EXCAVATIONS. *By* Uvo Hölscher (1934). vii+118 pages, frontispiece, 62 figures.

No. 19. ORIENTAL INSTITUTE DISCOVERIES IN IRAQ, 1933/34. FOURTH PRELIMINARY REPORT OF THE IRAQ EXPEDITION. *By* Henri Frankfort, with a chapter by Thorkild Jacobson (1935). xi+103 pages, frontispiece, 107 figures, 1 plate.

No. 20. PROGRESS OF THE WORK OF THE ORIENTAL INSTITUTE IN IRAQ, 1934/35. FIFTH PRELIMINARY REPORT OF THE IRAQ EXPEDITION. *By* Henri Frankfort (1936). xi+108 pages, frontispiece, 85 figures, 8 plates, 1 table.

No. 21. THE TREASURY OF PERSEPOLIS AND OTHER DISCOVERIES IN THE HOMELAND OF THE ACHAEMENIANS. *By* Erich F. Schmidt (1939). xxi+139 pages, frontispiece, 97 figures.

Oriental Institute Publications (OIP)

Scientific presentations of documents and other source materials. Quarto, cloth, except as individually noted.

Vol. I. ORIENTAL FORERUNNER OF BYZANTINE PAINTING. *By* James Henry Breasted (1924). vii+105 pages, 58 figures, 23 plates (4 in colors), 2 maps, 4to, boards.

Vol. II. THE ANNALS OF SENNACHERIB. *By* Daniel David Luckenbill (1924). xi+196 pages, 3 plates, 4to, boards.

Vols. III–IV. THE EDWIN SMITH SURGICAL PAPYRUS. Published in facsimile and hieroglyphic transliteration with translation and commentary in two volumes. *By* James Henry Breasted (1930). I. HIEROGLYPHIC TRANSLITERATION, TRANSLATION, AND COMMENTARY. xxiv+596 pages, 8 plates, 2 tables, 4to, cloth. II. FACSIMILE PLATES AND LINE FOR LINE HIEROGLYPHIC TRANSLITERATION. xiii pages, 46 plates, folio (30×40 cm.), cloth. Sold only in sets.

Vol. V. RESEARCHES IN ANATOLIA. I. EXPLORATIONS IN CENTRAL ANATOLIA, SEASON OF 1926. *By* H. H. von der Osten (1929). xix+167 pages, 242 figures, 24 plates, 1 map.

Vols. VI–VII. RESEARCHES IN ANATOLIA. II–III. THE ALISHAR HÜYÜK, SEASON OF 1927. *By* H. H. von der Osten and Erich F. Schmidt (1930–32).
Part I (vol. VI). xxii+284 pages, 251 figures, 6 colored plates, 22 maps.
Part II (Vol. VII). xi+134 pages, colored frontispiece, 106 figures.

Vol. VIII. MEDINET HABU. I. EARLIER HISTORICAL RECORDS OF RAMSES III. *By* the Epigraphic Survey (Harold H. Nelson, Field Director) (1930). xviii+12 pages, 2 figures, 54 plates (2 in colors), large folio, cloth.

Vol. IX. MEDINET HABU. II. LATER HISTORICAL RECORDS OF RAMSES III. *By* the Epigraphic Survey (Harold H. Nelson, Field Director) (1932). x+2 pages, 6 figures, 76 plates (7 in colors), large folio, cloth.

Vol. X. PREHISTORIC SURVEY OF EGYPT AND WESTERN ASIA. I. PALEOLITHIC MAN AND THE NILE-FAIYUM DIVIDE. A STUDY OF THE REGION DURING PLIOCENE AND PLEISTOCENE TIMES. *By* K. S. Sandford and W. J. Arkell (1930). xv+77 pages, 25 figures, 11 plates, 1 map.

Vol. XI. CUNEIFORM SERIES. I. SUMERIAN LEXICAL TEXTS FROM THE TEMPLE SCHOOL OF NIPPUR. *By* Edward Chiera (1929). xi+19 pages, 126 plates with 256 texts in facsimile.

Vol. XII. THE PROVERBS OF SOLOMON IN SAHIDIC COPTIC ACCORDING TO THE CHICAGO MANUSCRIPT. *Edited by* William H. Worrell (1931). xxx+107 pages, frontispiece.

Vol. XIII. BARHEBRAEUS' SCHOLIA ON THE OLD TESTAMENT. I. GENESIS–II SAMUEL. *Edited by* Martin Sprengling and William Creighton Graham (1931). xvi+393 pages.

Vol. XIV. CUNEIFORM SERIES. II. INSCRIPTIONS FROM ADAB. *By* Daniel David Luckenbill (1930). ix+8 pages, 87 plates with 198 texts in facsimile.

Vol. XV. CUNEIFORM SERIES. III. SUMERIAN EPICS AND MYTHS. *By* Edward Chiera (1934). xi+9 pages, 112 plates with 117 texts in facsimile.

Vol. XVI. CUNEIFORM SERIES. IV. SUMERIAN TEXTS OF VARIED CONTENTS. *By* Edward Chiera (1934). ix+8 pages, 109 plates with 135 texts in facsimile.

Vol. XVII. PREHISTORIC SURVEY OF EGYPT AND WESTERN ASIA. II. PALEOLITHIC MAN AND THE NILE VALLEY IN NUBIA AND UPPER EGYPT. A STUDY OF THE REGION DURING PLIOCENE AND PLEISTOCENE TIMES. *By* K. S. Sandford and W. J. Arkell (1933). xvii+92 pages, 21 figures, 43 plates, 1 map.

Vol. XVIII. PREHISTORIC SURVEY OF EGYPT AND WESTERN ASIA. III. PALEOLITHIC MAN AND THE NILE VALLEY IN UPPER AND MIDDLE EGYPT. A STUDY OF THE REGION DURING PLIOCENE AND PLEISTOCENE TIMES. *By* K. S. Sandford (1934). xxi+131 pages, 25 figures, 39 plates, 1 map.

Vols. XIX–XX. RESEARCHES IN ANATOLIA. IV–V. THE ALISHAR HÜYÜK, SEASONS OF 1928 AND 1929. *By* Erich F. Schmidt (1932–33).
Part I (Vol. XIX). xxi+293 pages, 377 figures, 47 plates (7 in colors), 1 map.
Part II (Vol. XX). With a chapter by Wilton Marion Krogman. xvii+148 pages, colored frontispiece, 198 figures, 11 plates, 4 tables.

Vol. XXI. THE EXCAVATION OF MEDINET HABU. I. GENERAL PLANS AND VIEWS. *By* Uvo Hölscher (1934). xiv+6 pages, 37 plates (3 in colors), large folio, cloth.

Vol. XXII. Ancient Oriental Seals in the Collection of Mr. Edward T. Newell. *By* H. H. von der Osten (1934). xiii+204 pages, 28 figures, 41 plates.

Vol. XXIII. Medinet Habu. III. The Calendar, the "Slaughterhouse," and Minor Records of Ramses III. *By* the Epigraphic Survey (Harold H. Nelson, Field Director) (1934). xvi+2 pages, 5 figures, 62 plates (1 in colors), large folio, cloth.

Vol. XXIV. Sennacherib's Aqueduct at Jerwan. *By* Thorkild Jacobsen and Seton Lloyd (1935). xii+52 pages, frontispiece, 12 figures, 36 plates.

Vol. XXV. Reliefs and Inscriptions at Karnak. I. Ramses III's Temple within the Great Inclosure of Amon. Part I. *By* the Epigraphic Survey (Harold H. Nelson, Field Director) (1936). xix+2 pages, 1 figure, 78 plates, 5 plans, large folio, cloth.

Vol. XXVI. Material Remains of the Megiddo Cult. *By* Herbert Gordon May, with a chapter by Robert M. Engberg (1935). xiv+51 pages, 13 figures, 41 plates.

Vol. XXVII. Researches in Anatolia. VI. Inscriptions from Alishar and Vicinity. *By* Ignace J. Gelb (1935). xv+84 pages, 5 figures, 63 plates.

Vols. XXVIII–XXX. Researches in Anatolia. VII–IX. The Alishar Hüyük, Seasons of 1930–32. Parts I–III. *By* H. H. von der Osten (1937).
Part I (Vol. XXVIII). xxii+283 pages, frontispiece, 281 figures, 10 plates (6 in colors).
Part II (Vol. XXIX). xxii+481 pages, frontispiece, 513 figures, 25 plates (3 in colors).
Part III (Vol. XXX). With contributions by Wilton Marion Krogman and others. xxiv+496 pages, 289 figures, 15 plates (5 in colors), 20 maps, 9 tables.

Vol. XXXI. The Mastaba of Mereruka. Part I. *By* the Sakkarah Expedition (Prentice Duell, Field Director) (1938). xxv+18 pages, 103 plates (4 in colors), 8 plans, large folio, cloth.

Vol. XXXII. The Megiddo Water System. *By* Robert S. Lamon (1935). xii+41 pages, 30 figures, 8 plates, 4to, paper.

Vol. XXXIII. Megiddo Tombs. *By* P. L. O. Guy, with contributions by Robert M. Engberg (1938). xxiv+224 pages, colored frontispiece, 206 figures, 176 plates, 6 tables.

Vol. XXXIV. The Egyptian Coffin Texts. I. Texts of Spells 1–75. *By* Adriaan de Buck (1935). xix+405 pages.

Vol. XXXV. Reliefs and Inscriptions at Karnak. II. Ramses III's Temple within the Great Inclosure of Amon (Part II) and Ramses III's Temple in the Precinct of Mut. *By* the Epigraphic Survey (Harold H. Nelson, Field Director) (1936). xi+2 pages, 47 plates, 5 plans, large folio, cloth.

Vol. XXXVI. Medinet Habu Graffiti. Facsimiles. *Edited by* William F. Edgerton (1937). xi+6 pages, 103 plates (3 in colors), 11 plans, folio (30×40 cm.), cloth.

Vol. XXXVII. Ancient Oriental Seals in the Collection of Mrs. Agnes Baldwin Brett. *By* H. H. von der Osten (1936). xi+76 pages, 20 figures, 12 plates.

Vol. XXXVIII. Khorsabad. I. Excavations in the Palace and at a City Gate. *By* Gordon Loud, with chapters by Henri Frankfort and Thorkild Jacobsen (1936). xv+139 pages, frontispiece, 129 figures, 3 colored plates.

Vol. XXXIX. THE MASTABA OF MERERUKA. Part II. *By* the Sakkarah Expedition (Prentice Duell, Field Director) (1938). xiii pages, 116 plates (9 in colors), 7 plans, large folio, cloth.

Vol. XL. KHORSABAD. II. THE CITADEL AND THE TOWN. *By* Gordon Loud and Charles B. Altman (1938). xxi+115 pages, 12 figures, 91 plates (3 in colors), large folio, cloth.

Vol. XLI. THE EXCAVATION OF MEDINET HABU. II. THE TEMPLES OF THE EIGHT-EENTH DYNASTY. *By* Uvo Hölscher, with contributions by Rudolf Anthes. Translated by Mrs. Keith C. Seele (1939). xvii+123 pages, 96 figures, 58 plates (2 in colors), 3 tables, folio (30×40 cm.), cloth.

Vol. XLII. MEGIDDO. I. SEASONS OF 1925–34. STRATA I–V. *By* Robert S. Lamon and Geoffrey M. Shipton (1939). xxvii+235 pages, 124 figures, 116 plates (1 in colors).

Vol. XLIII. THE GIMILSIN TEMPLE AND THE PALACE OF THE RULERS AT TELL ASMAR. *By* Henri Frankfort, Seton Lloyd, and Thorkild Jacobsen, with a chapter by Günter Martiny (1940). xviii+271 pages, frontispiece, 131 figures, 24 plates.

Vol. XLIV. SCULPTURE OF THE THIRD MILLENNIUM B.C. FROM TELL ASMAR AND KHAFAJAH. *By* Henri Frankfort (1939). xiii+87 pages, colored frontispiece, 5 figures, 116 plates.

Vol. XLV. HITTITE HIEROGLYPHIC MONUMENTS. *Edited by* Ignace J. Gelb (1939). xviii+40 pages, 4 figures, 94 plates, 1 map.

Vol. XLVI. PREHISTORIC SURVEY OF EGYPT AND WESTERN ASIA. IV. PALEOLITHIC MAN AND THE NILE VALLEY IN LOWER EGYPT, WITH SOME NOTES UPON A PART OF THE RED SEA LITTORAL. A STUDY OF THE REGIONS DURING PLIOCENE AND PLEISTOCENE TIMES. *By* K. S. Sandford and W. J. Arkell (1939). xix+105 pages, 23 figures, 30 plates, 1 map.

Vol. XLVII. ANCIENT ORIENTAL CYLINDER AND OTHER SEALS, WITH A DESCRIPTION OF THE COLLECTION OF MRS. WILLIAM H. MOORE. *By* Gustavus A. Eisen (1940). xiii+94 pages, 17 plates.

Vol. XLVIII. MOUNDS IN THE PLAIN OF ANTIOCH. AN ARCHEOLOGICAL SURVEY. *By* Robert J. Braidwood (1937). xi+67 pages, frontispiece, 9 figures, 26 maps, 4to, paper.

Vol. XLIX. THE EGYPTIAN COFFIN TEXTS. II. TEXTS OF SPELLS 76–163. *By* Adriaan de Buck (1938). xiv+405 pages.

Vol. L. THE RISE OF THE NORTH ARABIC SCRIPT AND ITS KURʾĀNIC DEVELOPMENT, WITH A FULL DESCRIPTION OF THE KURʾĀN MANUSCRIPTS IN THE ORIENTAL INSTITUTE. *By* Nabia Abbott (1939). xxii+103 pages, 1 figure, 33 plates, 1 map.

Vol. LI. MEDINET HABU. IV. FESTIVAL SCENES OF RAMSES III. *By* the Epigraphic Survey (Harold H. Nelson, Field Director) (1940). xii pages, 57 plates (8 in colors), 1 plan, large folio, cloth.

Vol. LII. THE MEGIDDO IVORIES. *By* Gordon Loud (1939). xi+25 pages, 8 figures, 63 plates (1 in colors), folio (30×40 cm.), cloth.

Vol. LIII. THE TEMPLE OVAL AT KHAFĀJAH. *By* Pinhas Delougaz (1940). xix+175 pages, frontispiece, 126 figures, 12 plates.

Vols. LIV–LV. THE EXCAVATION OF MEDINET HABU. III–IV. THE MORTUARY TEMPLE OF RAMSES III. PARTS I–II. *By* Uvo Hölscher (1941——).
Part I (Vol. LIV). xiii+87 pages, 56 figures, 40 plates (1 in colors), folio (30×40 cm.), cloth.
Part II (Vol. LV). (In preparation.)

Vol. LVI. KEY PLANS SHOWING LOCATIONS OF THEBAN TEMPLE DECORATIONS. *By* Harold Hayden Nelson (1941). xi pages, 37 plates, large folio, in portfolio.

Vol. LVII. NUZI PERSONAL NAMES. *By* Ignace J. Gelb, Pierre M. Purves, and Allan A. MacRae.

Vol. LVIII. PRE-SARGONID TEMPLES IN THE DIYALA REGION. *By* Pinhas Delougaz and Seton Lloyd, with chapters by Henri Frankfort and Thorkild Jacobsen. (In press.) With 213 figures, 28 plates, 1 map.

Vol. LIX. TALL-I-BAKUN A, SEASON OF 1932. *By* Alexander Langsdorff and Donald E. McCowan (1942), xi+81 pages, 19 figures, 85 plates, 1 table.

Special Publications

ANCIENT EGYPTIAN PAINTINGS. Selected, copied, and described by Nina M. Davies with the editorial assistance of Alan H. Gardiner (1936). Two large folio volumes, each containing 52 plates carefully copied in color from the originals, and one royal 8vo text volume.

FLIGHTS OVER ANCIENT CITIES OF IRAN. *By* Erich F. Schmidt (1940). xxii+104 pages, 119 plates, 6 maps, folio (30×40 cm.), cloth.

Ancient Records

English translations of historical documents of the ancient Near East.

ANCIENT RECORDS OF EGYPT. I–V. HISTORICAL DOCUMENTS. *By* James Henry Breasted (3d impression, 1927). cxlv+1,774 pages, 15 figures, royal 8vo, cloth. Sold only in sets.

ANCIENT RECORDS OF ASSYRIA AND BABYLONIA. I–II. HISTORICAL RECORDS OF ASSYRIA. *By* Daniel David Luckenbill (1926–27). xxviii+801 pages, royal 8vo, cloth.

Assyriological Studies (AS)

Researches based chiefly on cuneiform sources. Royal octavo, paper, except as individually noted.

No. 1 BEITRÄGE ZUM ASSYRISCHEN WÖRTERBUCH. I. *By* Bruno Meissner (1931). vi+92 pages.

No. 2. THE SUMERIAN PREFIX FORMS e- AND i- IN THE TIME OF THE EARLIER PRINCES OF LAGAŠ. *By* Arno Poebel (1931). xi+47 pages.

No. 3. DAS APPOSITIONELL BESTIMMTE PRONOMEN DER 1. PERS. SING. IN DEN WESTSE-MITISCHEN INSCHRIFTEN UND IM ALTEN TESTAMENT. *By* Arno Poebel (1932). viii+86 pages.

No. 4. BEITRÄGE ZUM ASSYRISCHEN WÖRTERBUCH. II. *By* Bruno Meissner (1932). vii+112 pages, 2 figures.

No. 5. HISTORICAL PRISM INSCRIPTIONS OF ASHURBANIPAL. I. EDITIONS E, B_{1-5}, D, AND K. *By* Arthur Carl Piepkorn, with an appendix by Joachim Mayr (1933). xiii+109 pages.

No. 6. PHILOLOGICAL NOTES ON ESHNUNNA AND ITS INSCRIPTIONS. *By* Thorkild Jacobsen (1934). xiv+35 pages, 3 figures.

No. 7. THE CHICAGO SYLLABARY AND THE LOUVRE SYLLABARY AO 7661. *By* Richard T. Hallock (1940). xiv+79 pages, 10 plates, 4to, paper.

No. 8. THE SUMERIAN PREFIX FORMS be- AND bi- IN THE TIME OF THE EARLIER PRINCES OF LAGAŠ. *By* S. N. Kramer (1936). x+29 pages.

No. 9. STUDIES IN AKKADIAN GRAMMAR. *By* Arno Poebel (1939). xxv+196 pages.

No. 10. GILGAMESH AND THE *Huluppu*-TREE. A RECONSTRUCTED SUMERIAN TEXT. *By* S. N. Kramer (1938). x+64 pages.

No. 11. THE SUMERIAN KING LIST. *By* Thorkild Jacobsen (1939). xvi+216 pages, 1 plate, 2 tables.

No. 12. LAMENTATION OVER THE DESTRUCTION OF UR. *By* S. N. Kramer (1940). xii+97 pages, 4 plates.

No. 13. THE SYSTEM OF THE QUADRILITERAL VERB IN AKKADIAN. *By* Alexander Heidel (1940). xvii+141 pages.

Studies in Ancient Oriental Civilization (SAOC)

Monographs dealing with various specific phases of the cultures of the ancient Near East. Royal octavo, paper, except as individually noted.

No. 1. NOTES ON EGYPTIAN MARRIAGE, CHIEFLY IN THE PTOLEMAIC PERIOD. *By* William F. Edgerton (1931). x+25 pages, 1 figure.

No. 2. HITTITE HIEROGLYPHS. I. *By* Ignace J. Gelb (1931). xxii+88 pages, 2 tables.

No. 3. DIE HETHITISCHE BILDERSCHRIFT. *By* Emil O. Forrer (1932). ix+62 pages, 45 figures.

No. 4. ARCHEOLOGY AND THE SUMERIAN PROBLEM. *By* Henri Frankfort (1932). (Out of print.)

No. 5. A NEW INSCRIPTION OF XERXES FROM PERESEPOLIS. *By* Ernst Herzfeld (1932). viii+14 pages, 5 figures.

No. 6. KITĀB AL-ZAHRAH . . . . COMPOSED BY ABŪ BAKR MUḤAMMAD IBN . . . . DĀWŪD. *Edited by* A. R. Nykl in collaboration with Ibrāhim Tūqān (1932). vi+8+v+406 pages.

No. 7. I. PLANO-CONVEX BRICKS AND THE METHODS OF THEIR EMPLOYMENT. II. THE TREATMENT OF CLAY TABLETS IN THE FIELD. *By* P. Delougaz (1933). xi+57 pages, 40 figures.

No. 8. THE THUTMOSID SUCCESSION. *By* William F. Edgerton (1933). ix+43 pages, 5 figures.

No. 9. DIE PÄKHY-SPRACHE. *By* Julius von Mészáros (1934). viii+402 pages, 1 map, 2 tables.

No. 10. NOTES ON THE CHALCOLITHIC AND EARLY BRONZE AGE POTTERY OF MEGIDDO. *By* Robert M. Engberg and Geoffrey M. Shipton (1934). xiv+91 pages, 25 figures, 1 chart.

No. 11. EPIPHANIUS' TREATISE ON WEIGHTS AND MEASURES. THE SYRIAC VERSION. *Edited by* James Elmer Dean, with a Foreword by Martin Sprengling (1935). xv+145 pages.

No. 12. HISTORICAL RECORDS OF RAMSES III. THE TEXTS IN *Medinet Habu* VOLUMES I AND II TRANSLATED WITH EXPLANATORY NOTES. *By* William F. Edgerton and John A. Wilson (1936). xv+159 pages, 4to, paper.

No. 13. THE ORIENTAL ORIGIN OF HELLENISTIC KINGSHIP. *By* Calvin W. McEwan (1934). xiii+34 pages.

No. 14. HITTITE HIEROGLYPHS. II. *By* Ignace J Gelb (1935). xx+37 pages, 2 figures, 1 table.

No. 15. The Kurrah Papyri from Aphrodito in the Oriental Institute. *By* Nabia Abbott (1938). xviii+101 pages, 2 figures, 4 plates.

No. 16. The Monasteries of the Fayyūm. *By* Nabia Abbott (1937). vi+67 pages, 3 figures, 1 map.

No. 17. Notes on the Megiddo Pottery of Strata VI–XX. *By* Geoffrey M. Shipton (1939). xiv+51 pages, 1 figure, 20 plates, 6 charts.

No. 18. The Hyksos Reconsidered. *By* Robert M. Engberg (1939). xi+50 pages.

No. 19. The Coregency of Ramses II with Seti I and the Date of the Great Hypostyle Hall at Karnak. *By* Keith C. Seele (1940). xiii+95 pages, 23 figures.

No. 20. Animal Remains from Tell Asmar. *By* Max Hilzheimer (1941). xiii+52 pages, 20 figures, 8 tables.

No. 21. Hittite Hieroglyphs. III. *By* Ignace J. Gelb. (In preparation.)

No. 22. Hurrians and Subareans. *By* Ignace J. Gelb. (In preparation.)

No. 23. The Comparative Stratigraphy of Early Iran. *By* Donald E. McCown (1942). xvi+65 pages, 18 figures, 1 map, 2 tables, 4to, paper.

Joint Publications of the Egypt Exploration Society and the Oriental Institute

The Temple of King Sethos I at Abydos. *Copied by* Amice M. Calverley, with the assistance of Myrtle F. Broome, and *edited by* Alan H. Gardiner.

I. The Chapels of Osiris, Isis, and Horus (1933). xi pages, 42 plates (8 in colors), large folio, cloth.

II. The Chapels of Amen-Rēᶜ, Reᶜ-Harakhti, Ptah, and King Sethos (1935). ix pages, 46 plates (4 in colors), large folio, cloth.

III. The Osiris Complex (1938). xi pages, 65 plates (13 in colors), large folio, cloth.

Joint Publications of the University of Chicago Press and the Oriental Institute

History of Early Iran. *By* George G. Cameron (1936). xvi+260 pages, 1 map, 5 tables, 12mo, cloth.

A Political History of Parthia. *By* Neilson C. Debevoise (1938). xliii+303 pages, frontispiece, 1 map, 3 tables, 12mo, cloth.

INDEX

INDEX

429

Where the Spirits Ride the Wind

Where the Spirits Ride the Wind

TRANCE JOURNEYS AND OTHER
ECSTATIC EXPERIENCES

Felicitas D. Goodman

WITH DRAWINGS
BY GERHARD BINDER

Indiana University Press

BLOOMINGTON & INDIANAPOLIS

The paper used in this publication meets the minimum requirements of American
National Standard for Information Sciences—Permanence of Paper for Printed
Library Materials, ANSI Z39.48-1984.

MANUFACTURED IN THE UNITED STATES OF AMERICA

Library of Congress Cataloging-in-Publication Data
Goodman, Felicitas D.
Where the spirits ride the wind : trance journeys and other
ecstatic experiences / Felicitas D. Goodman ; with drawings by
Gerhard Binder.
p. cm.
Includes bibliographical references.
ISBN 0-253-32764-4 (alk. paper). — ISBN 0-253-20566-2 (pbk.)
1. Astral projection. 2. Spirits. 3. Trance. 4. Visions.
5. Ecstasy. 6. Experience (Religion) I. Title.
BF1389.A7G66 1990
133.9—dc20 89-45567
CIP

1 2 3 4 5 94 93 92 91 90

To my companions
who traveled the path of the Spirits
with me,
and whose voices speak through me, page after page,
this work is fondly dedicated.

Contents

LIST OF PLATES

PROLOGUE

It was with trepidation, even fear, that in response to the urgent entreaties of many friends here and abroad I began writing this account of our common adventures. Would our spirit friends, the Surpassing Ones, approve of the endeavor, which was bound to reveal much, perhaps too much, about their secrets? And even more important, had I even properly grasped the nature of the kind of reality into which our hesitant steps had taken us?

Then one night, just before the day was about to break, I had a vision. Snowy white against the grey of restlessly seething clouds, I saw the head of the Bear Spirit emerging. But before I could give in to the feeling of happy recognition, it twisted as if agitated by a mighty wind and, dissolving, became one with the hulking mass of a powerfully pulsing white presence. Driven by the storm, that in turn lifted, and from below it, a bundle of taut, vibrating strands streaked with enormous force into the hugely magnified likeness of one of the pebbles that I had found during the summer of my initiation, bearing the face of the Badger. The wind carried that away also, and a delicate fawn cavorted out of nowhere, twisted upon itself, and was gone. Then all was calm, and nothing was left but a slightly tilted, narrow, empty bookcase, carelessly nailed together from short furring strips with some of them missing, floating, as if suspended forever, in the vacuity of the now immobile greyness.

The significance of the vision and its relation to the project I was agonizing over did not become clear to me until a week later, when on a field trip to Yucatán (Mexico) late in 1986, I once more saw Anselmo preach. In May 1970 this young Maya Indian farmhand and barber had had a vision. During the Sunday service of the Apostolic village congregation to which he belonged, he saw some candles being extinguished, and he heard the voice of the Holy Spirit ordering the Brothers to go out and convert everyone, for Christ's Second Coming was close at hand. The hoped-for event was to occur at the beginning of September of that year. After the failure of the prophesy, what was left of the devastated congregation developed along more conservative lines, while a handful of diehards gathered around Anselmo and built their own House of Prayer at the far north end of the village, independent of any church authority or organization.

Anselmo was still the fluent and effective speaker I had known sixteen years before. But as I sat there in the carefully tended small mud-and-wattle building, listening to him speak about a vision of the Prophet Isaiah, it occurred to me that not once did he ever refer to his own many visions of that fateful summer so many years ago. Instead, over and over again, he lifted the Bible high and laid his dark and work-worn hand on the white, open pages. That is where it was, only there. There was nothing else.

There was a sudden chill in the air in that warm tropical night. There had been a time when Anselmo had known the power of seeing. It still gave wings to his words. He had been to where, in-ever rolling waves, religion was in a constant state of being born. He had been propelled during that summer to leave behind the world of a faith in which all was solid, finished, created, safe, and had stepped out into a reality where everything was new and scintillating, a revelation continually rising anew. But timidly, he had stepped back. With compassion I recalled how during that season of visions the Brothers had watched him for many days and nights to keep him from killing himself. He was still fighting that battle, grasping for that security that was destined to elude him. He now knew that whoever had really been "out there" could never have that kind of safety again, the security of the ancient revelations, frozen on the printed page. In front of the altar there stood a man who was mortally afraid.

And suddenly the understanding of my own vision washed over me like a mighty wave. The structure in which I had been raised no longer offered any shelter and protection. I would never again be allowed to flee back to it when the power of the Outside became overwhelming. That finite world was but a fragile, empty hull, like the empty bookcase of my vision, that I could no longer occupy. My small fears were meaningless. For life or for death, I was committed to that mighty realm of which I was shown a brief reminder, the world where all was forever motion and emergence, that realm where the spirits ride the wind.

Section I

THE SEARCH
FOR THE SPIRITS

CHAPTER ONE

The Call of
the Old People

On the eve of my twelfth birthday
I had a severe headache, and it startled me, for I had never had that kind of
a headache before. The next morning, I bled for the first time. I went to my
mother, and she showed me what to do. There was great trust between us,
and because she was not upset, I was not either. When the shock came, it
was in a different guise. My mother took a piece of chalk and drew a little
cross on the bedroom door. "This means," she said, "that we now have an
adult daughter in our house." I puzzled over what that might mean—sex education had not been invented yet—but did not ask her. I always kept the
most disquieting questions to myself.

Very soon I discovered all on my own what being an adult apparently
meant, and confided it to my diary: "The magic time is over." For all of a
sudden and without the slightest warning, I realized that I could no longer
effortlessly call up what in my terms was magic: that change in me that was
so deliciously exciting and as if I were opening a door, imparting a special
hue to whatever I chose. I noticed the curious impediment first with the fresh,
crunchy snow which fell right after my birthday. It was nice, but I could not
make it glow. Bewildered, I began paying more attention to my seeming dis-
ability. The orange glow of dawn streaming through the bedroom window was
the same as before; so was the smell of the horses on the market. But I had
changed.

I believe today that a large part of initiation in the wiser societies, those
small ones that, together with so much else that is worthwhile and beautiful,
are disappearing at an alarming rate in our century, has to do with helping
the adolescent to reconstitute the waning capacity for ecstasy. The harsh stimulation of the nervous system incorporated in many of those rituals, the pain,

the fatigue, the fasting, are designed, I think, to substitute a different, an adult, form for the spontaneous ability to call up that very special trance, the one leading to ecstasy, the passing of which I mourned so deeply as I entered puberty.

Obviously I was living at the wrong place. How gladly I would have submitted to whatever trial if only someone could have told me what it was I was losing, and if there would have been a promise of reconstitution. Actually, I was coming up for confirmation, which was modeled after ancient initiation rituals, but it was cruelly vacuous. I was confirmed in the simple Lutheran church of Nagyvárad, in the Hungarian region of western Rumania, and for some reason I hoped vaguely that it might provide the help I wanted. But after the ritual, the details of which we had had to learn by heart and dutifully performed, there was only a festive meal in the Kispipa, my father's favorite restaurant, and then nothing, absolutely nothing happened. I did not even know what I had expected, but it was very clear to me that I had not received it.

I experienced that frightening emptiness once again when in the convent school I sang in the choir during the induction of a novice into the order. We talked among ourselves about Philomela's hair being cut, and about how she would be given a wedding band that from then on would mark her as Christ's bride. "Then what will happen?" I wanted to know. "Oh, she can't leave the convent anymore." I knew that already, and it was not what I was after. I wanted to find out what sweet miracle would engulf her once she went back to be alone in her cell. But no one had an answer. I imagined Philomela in her lonely, empty room, and the vicarious anguish nearly tore me apart.

The question is, why did I even hope for "something" unimaginably wonderful to happen in conjunction with a ritual? After all, I was brought up in a Western-type society where such expectations were certainly not taught, in school or out. Neither did I have any source of information about other types of tradition—no radio, no television, not even a public library; only a few books borrowed from friends here and there. But that was perhaps how it happened. Everyone had books of Hungarian tales, legends, and myths, which I began reading even before starting grade school. Stealthily, those stories insinuated a knowledge and a yearning into my childish world that were to shape me for the rest of my life.

Because what to me was so precious was inexorably slipping further and further away, I finally came to the conclusion that I had to do something to save what was still left of it. Its fading had clearly been associated with entering adulthood, so I decided that I simply would refuse to become an adult. Wisely, I kept that decision a secret. To everyone around me, I was a normal teenager. I developed strong physically. I was at the head of my class in school. I enjoyed swimming and ice-skating, and I fell in love with a boy whom I had known in grade school and for whom I embroidered a fancy handkerchief. But I had a secret chamber deep within; I could retire to that hidden place, and working with desperate concentration, I could cheat adulthood out of a victim and stay a child and have the familiar trance wash over me once more.

As the years went by, though, the occulted ecstasy became less and less accessible. There was college, professional work, love, and marriage. I bore and suckled three children. The Second World War burned over Europe, and when it was over, I went to America with my family.

I arrived in this country as countless immigrants before me, starving, beggarly, all my belongings in one cardboard box, and deeply scarred by the blood, gore, and death of the war. For years, I woke up at night barely able to suppress the urge to scream. The floor of reality was a thin crust of slag; I had to walk over it ever so gingerly in order not to break through and fall into the merciless darkness of the void below. Caring for my children and my professional work were my only safety, my escape. Do not look left, do not look right, and especially never look up at the sky, for it too was endless and void.

Seven years after my arrival in this country, I had a new baby, the world around me became less threatening, and I began feeling safer. I even started writing again, poetry, and then a novel. Yet I could not escape a feeling of pervasive despondency. This world was entirely different from that of my childhood, where I could always feel the comfort of invisible presences around. All was deserted, empty around here. No matter how wide I opened the gates of my inner being, there was nothing asking to enter.

My new daughter was still quite small when it happened that we took a trip to a national park in neighboring Kentucky. Lying in the grass, I rediscovered the sky. It was dotted with fluffy cirrus clouds, and as I watched, an endless procession of white bundles came drifting across the blue, like Indian warriors laid out for burial, the feathers of their war bonnets trailing behind them in the wind. We later stopped at a historical marker, which spoke of Kentucky as "the dark and bloody grounds," home of the frontiersmen who, I recalled, notched their rifle butts to keep count of the Indians they murdered. Perhaps those cloud biers were of the Indians' spirits, forever reenacting their sorrowful exit after the white men had killed their people and had raped the land. Were the spirits dead now too? There seemed to be no answer, and I felt even more disconsolate than before.

Then in 1960 friends from Ohio State University invited me to spend my vacation with them in their new home in Santa Fe, New Mexico. I had never before been to the Southwest, with its vast spaces and sepia and magenta flat-top mountains, dotted with patches of green junipers and pinyon trees, and alive with a thousand lacy rock carvings created by wind and sand and shimmering golden in the sunlight. Most of the time the madonna-blue sky above the land was brittle and clean. But sometimes, ample cloud breasts would drip the blessing of rain from their nipples on the thirsty earth, and the misty Feathered Serpent humped over the ridges in the morning, celebrating fertility.

There were still other impressions. After walking over the Indian arts-and-crafts markets with their celebration of beauty, so appealing to the senses, I came away with the feeling of having been touched by an almost palpable presence, a special, undefinable quality. Was this the land to which the spirits had fled from the dark and bloody grounds? Nowhere in Europe had I ever experienced being overwhelmed by such a magical quality except when I was very young and still knew ecstasy, and it filled me from the start with an intense yearning. For what I did not know, perhaps for that secret recess of childhood, a world that used to be sweet, holy, and inviolate.

It was the month of August, and my hosts took me to see the Corn Dance that took place every year at Santo Domingo, the largest of the Rio Grande pueblos. The dance is an ancient Indian prayer ritual asking for an ample harvest for all people. Well over a thousand Indian men, women, and children in colorful native attire danced this prayer from the forenoon until sundown to the songs of the men's choir and the rhythm of the large drum, the tone of which resounded in the desert like the heartbeat of the earth. I was totally overwhelmed by the bewildering beauty of this new and strange world.

The night after the dance I had a dream, or more likely a vision. I saw three old Indians in front of the window. They were dressed in the colorful shirts and slit pants of the choir, and one of them carried the big drum. With his drumstick, he knocked on the window, and when I looked up, he waved for me to come along. The experience made me unaccountably happy. I did not know the ethnographic literature about the Pueblos at the time, but it seemed to me that what I had seen was the spirits of the "Old People" of the pueblo I had heard about, and who had come to invite me to this, their land. And so I decided, like a sleepwalker choosing the right corner to turn, that no matter what, I was going to acquire some small piece of land here. Then I would be able to say to those kindly old spirits, "You see, here I am."

The search took nearly three years; land was—and still is—very scarce in the Southwest. Finally, in 1963, my real-estate agent found not the modest five acres that I thought I could afford, but a large spread, nearly three hundred acres, which the Forest Service had rid itself of some years ago, and which its present owner wanted to sell off at a suitable profit. My lawyer counseled adamantly against it: "Don't waste your money on that," he wrote. "We call it the Pojoaque Badlands." But after all, I was not intending to grow alfalfa, and I knew the beauty of the Pojoaque Valley from my previous visit. I was not going to be disappointed.

This "badland" was on all sides surrounded by Indian pueblos, which in part had retained their old Tewa names—Tesuque, Pojoaque, Nambe—and by Santa Clara and San Ildefonso. In the east, the Sangre de Cristo range turned wine-red at sundown. To the west, the property was protected by the fortress wall of the Jemez Mountains, where, according to Indian legend, humans emerged from the crowded and dark third world to this, their fourth one under the arc of the rainbow. Its loose sandy terrain was crisscrossed by arroyos, deep cuts caused by water erosion, but each one a picturesque world of its own. A million years ago, the volcanoes of the Valle Grande, thirty miles away, spewed glinting, many-colored pebbles on its softly rounded hills. Yellow rabbit brush bloomed near a juniper by the fence, and on some barren hillsides Indian paintbrush flamed red among the rocks. At night, the coyotes laughed from across the ancient river bed of the Cañada Ancha, and the spirits haunting the pueblo ruins by the river whispered in my dreams. Of course, I could not make the despoiling of the earth go away that rolled on greedily on the highway down in the valley day and night, or the threat of the final holocaust that glowed in the steely lights of Los Alamos, the "Atomic City" toward the west. But at least here among these gentle hills, the world was still at peace. I signed the contract for the land, and never regretted that the decision committed me to much sacrifice and many years of hard labor.

In the summer of 1965, after days of hiking, we—that is, a helpful relative, my young daughter, and I—located a spot suitable for building. It was like a tongue stretching outward from among the hills, affording a view of the Sangre de Cristo toward the east but surrounded on all other sides by protective ridges. I had a well drilled, and men on horseback brought in electricity from the region's electric co-op. We knew next to nothing about how to build a house from the local sun-dried bricks, the adobes. But if we got stuck, we went to our Hispanic or Indian neighbors for advice, or to the ever-useful builders' supply store. People would make expansive fun of us. "Look at that, here they come again from the Rancho Grande," they would say. But actually, everyone was friendly and helpful, and also curious about what a woman was doing there, homesteading pretty much on her own.

It was hard. We could not use our tent, because scorpions and six-inch orange centipedes with dragon heads made it their home. Besides, it kept collapsing in the violent storms that were our frequent visitors. In the cruel heat of midday we crawled instead into the sparse shade of the junipers. During the cloudbursts of the summer's rainy season, our only safe haven was the cabin of the pickup truck. Our camp stove gave up in the persistent wind, so I had to cook on an open fire. It rained, our firewood got wet, and we had to eat sandwiches. There was no money to hire a backhoe, so armed only with pick and shovel, we dug all the ditches for the foundation. We laid the heavy cast-iron pipes for the rough-in of the plumbing and finally built the walls for our first room.

The summer was nearly over when we finally nailed the tarpaper on the roof and hung the door. I had registered for graduate school at Ohio State University, and two weeks before school was to start, we were finally ready to leave. We loaded everything we had borrowed on our pickup truck, the wheelbarrow and the sawhorses, the scaffolding, and Baba, our faithful goat, to take back to the neighbors in the valley. As we rolled out, I turned back for a last glance. Our flat little house was shrinking into insignificance in the glare of the noonday sun, its adobe walls becoming one with the sand and the clay. Had the Old Ones, the spirits of this land, even noticed that I had come? Did some of them live in these hills or did they have to be invited? I had no idea of how to invite spirits, and after all the big problems and small triumphs and successes of homesteading, it seemed to me that I had left the most important task undone. Perhaps next summer, I thought hopefully. After all, I was now on the right path. I did not realize then how long and arduous that path would turn out to be.

CHAPTER TWO

Getting in Touch
with the Spirits:
The First Discoveries

In the Protestant Christian tradition in which I was raised, it was held that the only way in which a human could communicate with the beings inhabiting the alternate reality was by prayer. But in the view of the vast majority of other traditions, speech, as the mode of communication of ordinary reality, is singularly unsuited for this purpose. It is but a hardly audible knock on the very thick wall separating humans from the spirit realm. In fact, humans have to make a truly heroic effort to be noticed on the other side. Merely talking, falling into a worshipful mood, feeling "transcendent," "numinous," or "oceanic," or whatever other pompous words are listed in the dictionary, simply will not do. Instead humans, if they have the urgent necessity or desire to squeeze through the chinks in that wall, need to change the very functioning of their bodies in the most radical way. The term summarizing these changes is *religious trance*, one of a large group of altered states of consciousness of which humans are capable. It is termed religious because observation shows that it is the one occurring in religious context, that is, when contact is made with the alternate, the sacred, reality. (For the problem of defining "religion," see Goodman 1988.)

Before the worship service on the particular evening in the Apostolic church in Mexico City which I want to describe here, I had only read about this kind of trance; I had never actually seen a person experiencing it. I had come to Mexico City in hopes of finally observing this nonordinary behavior, the presence of which, I was fervently wishing, would clinch a scholarly argument I had advanced in a paper for a seminar in graduate school.

It was the summer of 1968. Around me in the crowded bus there were brown-skinned passengers going home from laboring in offices and factories, girls in fashionable dresses, men in bedraggled work clothes. Women boarded with baskets or shopping bags filled with vegetables and fruit from the market, a mother with her sleeping infant slung across her back in a scarf. My destination was the Colónia Pro-Hogar, a rather poor section of the city, and I had wrapped my tape recorder in newspaper so it would not tempt any would-be assailant. As the bus rumbled and lurched over the narrow back streets of the vast metropolis, burping Diesel fumes, I thought about the circuitous search that had brought me here to Latin America from the classrooms of Ohio State University.

My initial university training, a diploma (master's degree) in translating and interpreting from the University of Heidelberg in Germany, had certainly not prepared me for what I was now interested in. Neither had my professional career in the United States. For many years after immigrating to this country, I earned a living as a multilingual scientific translator in the fields of metallurgy, biochemistry, and medicine. But I was never quite happy in my work. So when my children were old enough and gone the greater part of the day, I decided to go back to school in the fall after we had completed our first building in New Mexico.

This was in 1965. I was fifty-one years old, and the concept of the "mature scholar" had not yet been invented. I recall how shy I felt about having to present my diplomas, which in the meantime had acquired a telltale yellow hue. But I had the good fortune of encountering an understanding dean of admissions at Ohio State University and was accepted into graduate school as a special student. I elected to major in linguistics, for languages were really the only subject I felt I was competent in. Despite dire predictions to the contrary from friends and relatives, studying came easily and after the first quarter, I was upgraded to "regular" status.

As it turned out, it was a propitious time to embark on linguistics. This was no longer the old-time philology, the endless search for roots and relationships of words in musty documents written in long-forgotten tongues. Everything was being questioned, turned upside down, and put together in new and interesting ways. There were the acoustics of speech sounds, the physiology of the way we produced them, and the psychology of language usage. Language behavior was being tied in with human evolution and with culture. Much of it, such as Noam Chomsky's ideas about a deep structure in our mind, which he thought of as a black box full of grammatical rules that "generated" what we said out loud, was new and controversial. It was great to see all this innovation happening right before my eyes. Yet I kept feeling that this was not what I had come to the university for, and as the quarter wore on, there arose an undercurrent of doubt and uncertainty about what I was doing that I could not staunch.

It was in this mood that in the second quarter of my graduate career I registered for a course offered by Professor Erika Bourguignon of the Department of Anthropology, entitled "Religion in Native Societies." I had never been interested in the Protestant philosophy of religion or in theology generally. But there was something in religion as a topic that seemed to tease me. I had read, widely if unsystematically, everything from Robert Graves's *White Goddess* to Bronislaw Malinowski's *Magic, Science, and Religion*. The title of the course seemed to carry a promise, as if to say, "There *is* something to all of this," an allure like the distant jingling of a shaman's staff.

Dr. Bourguignon's lectures began putting some order into the jumbled mass of information on the religious systems of small, non-Western societies that I had gathered on my own, and this alone was most gratifying. But there was an added bonus, for she also introduced us to her own ongoing research. For a number of years she had been heading a project, funded by the National Institute of Mental Health, the aim of which was, as she explains,[1]

> a multifaceted analysis of what appeared to be a widespread psychocultural phe-
> nomenon, about which, however, curiously little of a systematic nature was known.
> The phenomenon with which we were concerned was the religious evaluation . . .
> of a psychological state variously termed "dissociation," "trance," or more recently
> and more generally, "altered states of consciousness." (1973:viii)

I was instantly captivated especially by two lines of thought that Dr. Bourguignon presented. One was that such "altered states of consciousness" or "trances" were entirely normal. I had read my share of learned disquisitions about the psychotic nature of religious experiences, especially of shamans. My reaction had always been one of angry disbelief: a *táltos*, the Hungarian shaman, mentally ill, a schizophrenic, or an epileptic? There had to be an error in judgment somewhere. Here then was someone who agreed with me. The second idea that I found enthralling was that such behavior, which added excitement, color, and drama to otherwise humdrum rituals, was institutionalized in many societies, part and parcel of a large number of religious observances. So this was the magic ingredient, the lack of which I had felt so keenly as a child! All these new insights were not only exhilarating. It was also deeply satisfying to discover that my thinking had all along been in line with bona fide behavioral science. The graduate-school adventure was finally taking on a truly thrilling aspect.

And there was more to come. Soon after I joined Dr. Bourguignon's course, she hired me on as a translator for the foreign-language material to be included in the large-scale statistical study she and her staff were working on. Eventually that study was to provide proof that religious trance behavior was not some oddity reported by a few observers, but was so widely spread that we could find virtually no small society of the kind that anthropologists are typically interested in that did not have some institutionalized form of it. I felt happy and somehow personally vindicated by these findings.

Neither was the linguist in me to go empty-handed. In the course of my work for the project, I frequently came across references in the foreign ethnographic literature to the fact that during religious trance rituals, those participating also uttered a strange kind of speech. It was called *glossolalia* in linguistics and was known also to Christians as "speaking in tongues." It is a vocalization that usually consists of syllables that carry no meaning, such as "lalalalala" or "?ulalala dalala." (The ? indicates a consonant called a "glottal stop," a catch or closure in the throat.) It was often referred to as gibberish by Western observers, "something not worth recording," but to my mind, if it was part of a ceremony, it had to have some significance, and therefore it merited a second look. When, after earning my master's degree in linguistics, I took a course in anthropological linguistics with Dr. Bourguignon, I decided to do a paper on the phenomenon.

Dr. Bourguignon provided me with a number of sound tapes recorded by members of her project during fieldwork with various Pentecostal-type congregations, where glossolalia is institutionalized. A linguistic analysis of the tapes revealed some intriguing features. The people uttering these curious sequences of syllables were all English speakers, although they used a number of different dialects—Caribbean black, Appalachian, and American middle-class English from Texas. But as soon as they switched into "tongues," their utterances exhibited a number of characteristics that certainly were not to be found in these variants of English. This speech was rhythmical, "scanning," as it were, with a continually repeated regular accent pattern, as though it were the recitation of traditional nineteenth-century poetry. In addition, each syllable invariably began with a consonant. Most striking, however, on all the tapes there was the same intonation pattern: It rose to a peak at the end of the first third of the utterance unit and then sloped gradually toward the end. I began measuring the pattern with a stopwatch: there was no mistaking it. Years later I analyzed the same tapes in the phonetics lab using a level recorder, and the electronically traced curves were exactly the way I had heard them during that initial scrutiny.

The agreement struck me as strange, because after all, the congregations which had provided the tapes were geographically distant from each other, so there could have been no imitation, especially in light of the fact that they did not even belong to the same denomination of the general Pentecostal movement. What was even more surprising was the regularity of the pattern. Not even poetry was as regularly accented, and certainly intonation was never that monotonous. In natural language, we vary intonation endlessly in the service of communication. The message conveyed by "*John* is in the garden" is different from that conveyed by "John *is* in the garden" or "John is in the *garden*." Something, it seemed, was interfering with normal speech behavior. Remembering that people spoke in this nonordinary way during religious observances that, as those anthropologists reported, included trance behavior, I speculated that this "something" was certain changes that occurred in the body during trance.

There were some nagging doubts, of course, about the validity of this assumption, as always when one hits on an entirely new explanatory hypothesis. So I sent the first draft of my paper to a Canadian linguist who had published a number of papers on glossolalia. I thought he would find my thesis intriguing, and might perhaps offer some additional conjectures. Instead I got a letter back the gist of which was, now, now, young lady, there is no such thing as trance, and even if it did exist, we would not want to make people unhappy by suggesting that they experienced a weird state of some kind.

It was a stinging reprove, and after getting over my disappointment, I decided to fight back. There had to be a way to counter this man's objections, and the best way to do that, it seemed to me, was to discover whether those curious patterns were peculiar to English speakers only. Did the glossolalia of Spanish speakers, for instance, exhibit the same or possibly quite different characteristics? If what I had discovered occurred also elsewhere, I had a better base from which to argue that this peculiar vocalization behavior was not merely a psychocultural one, but carried within it a hidden factor deriving from biological processes. One could think of them as part of the content of a "black box," different from the grammatical one, but in the case of glossolalia equally acting as a generating "deep structure" in the Chomskian sense. To me, showing that actual physical changes were involved in the religious trance, that it was not all "just imagination," imbued the experience with a never-hoped-for, tangible reality. What I did not realize at the time was that with a search in this direction I was in fact joining a larger movement toward the view that behavior had a biological basis, as well; it was not determined exclusively by psychological motivation. In the decade of the seventies, this movement resulted in a revolution in the treatment of so-called mental illness, away from analysis and toward biological psychiatry.

What I wanted to find out in Mexico City, then, was what the glossolalia of Spanish speakers sounded like. I looked for some branch of the Pentecostal movement, for instance, for the Apostolics, because there, speaking in tongues was expected of every worshiper. It was believed to be the manifestation of the Holy Spirit, of its baptism, without which no one could enter into heaven. The telephone book listed a number of Apostolic congregations, among them one in the Colónia Pro-Hogar, which was not too far away from where I was staying.

The modest rectangular temple was a nondescript building on a side street. Its single room was painted pale blue and was lit by a solitary naked bulb hanging from the ceiling. A podium served as the altar. There were vases with bright flowers and a rostrum with a hymnal and a dog-eared Bible. The worshipers were the same kind of people I had seen on the bus, tradesmen, laborers, maids, washerwomen, housewives, who curiously scrutinized the foreign intruder. But I had explained my purpose to the minister on the phone, so he introduced me and said that I had his permission to record, film, and take notes. Although still uneasy, the congregation settled into the usual routine of the service.

I attended a number of these evening gatherings, hopefully setting up my tape recorder next to me on the yellow wooden bench, but nothing happened.

However, during this particular service, the ice was finally going to be broken. I had arrived earlier than usual and before the service had a long conversation with Juan, a professional soldier and one of the deacons of the church. Turning on my tape recorder, I asked him to describe his conversion and some of his experiences when he had spoken in tongues. He told how he had prayed for years for this "manifestation of the Holy Spirit," but it kept eluding him. Finally one day, the bishop of Juan's church laid his hands on Juan's head and prayed for him:

> And after this Brother prayed for me, I continued praying, beseeching God for this gift. And my tongue locked itself, and immediately I knew nothing, I knew nothing at all, but I did feel this impulse to speak. I wanted to stop talking, but my tongue was in this way impulsed. I have noted since then, on other occasions, that I would be praying, but I would insist that I would not talk. But then I'd hear my own words, but no, I don't understand them, but yes, I do feel my tongue impulsed to speak. Afterward, I felt serene, and well, and all my problems were forgotten.

The minister was occupied elsewhere that evening and had left Juan in charge of the service. As was customary, he was conducting it standing on the podium, behind the rostrum with its embroidered white cloth. The service had gone on as usual, with prayers, hymns, and the reading of Bible passages. Then came the altar call, when people came up to the podium and knelt to pray. The minister had told me that speaking in tongues usually occurred then. "How do you know?" I asked. "Pues, that's easy—it isn't Spanish!" was his surprised answer. But all I had heard until then was a low jumble of voices that I also knew from tapes I had worked with at home in Columbus.

Juan had kept the service rather low-key up to this point, but it seemed to me that at the second altar call, perhaps stimulated by our conversation, he was beginning to "drive" his congregation harder with clapping and occasional loud shouts, addressing God and the Holy Spirit. Then his voice dropped for a phrase or two, and all of a sudden, from the middle range, he went into a rising glossolalia utterance, "sió, sió, sió, sió . . ." My field notes reflect how startled I was:

> On the tape, the onset is easily discernible, but upon hearing, it came upon me as a tremendous surprise, because here I was, right in the middle of a true glossolalia. . . . There was a constant pulsing, curve after curve.

The event was not lost on the congregation:

> As the realization of a true manifestation broke upon the people, the trance swept through them like a fire. Another man went into trance, much less intense than Juan's, but with the same pulse, "sió, sió. . . ." A woman at the right had her hands folded, holding them about breast-high and moving them up and down very rapidly.

At the start of the altar call, Juan had knelt down behind the vases filled with gladiolas, but now he suddenly jumped up.

He had his knees slightly bent forward, his body a bit inclined toward the back, very rigid, his eyes closed tightly, his face extremely tense but not distorted, his arms outstretched, his hands alternately clenching and opening with the rhythm of the pulses. After a steep decline in his voice, his arms dropped, his eyes opened. He happened to catch my glance, and an expression of total, questioning bewilderment passed over his face. . . . Then, practically without a pause, he passed into (natural) language and, calling on the Holy Spirit, knelt down again.

Here now for the first time I had actually seen a man in trance, the tight muscles, the flushed and sweaty face, the light tremor, and the cramped hands. I was to see many more examples, men and women, in the course of that summer, in numerous gradations from hardly noticeable to very dramatic changes involving the entire body. And as I had surmised from the analysis of the soundtracks, they were, just as Juan had been, visibly in trance *while* they spoke in tongues, exactly as I had predicted. As he had said in the interview, "I knew nothing at all, but I did feel this impulse to speak."

I subsequently analyzed Juan's glossolalia and that of many other speakers in tongues, and the patterns I had discovered were once more evident. The next summer, I went on to do fieldwork in Yucatán, with a Maya congregation of the same denomination, and recorded the glossolalia of speakers of this Indian, that is, non-Indo-European, tongue. The results were always the same. In fact, after the publication of my book about speaking in tongues,[2] colleagues sent me numerous other tapes recorded during their fieldwork in such faraway places as Ghana in Africa, the island of Nias in Indonesia, the northern edge of the island of Borneo, and Japan. The busy needle of the level recorder continued to trace the same curve. No matter where people spoke in this nonordinary manner during a religious ritual, their bodies apparently underwent the same telltale changes, a wondrous confirmation of our common biological heritage.

The Canadian linguist continued to insist for years that there were no bodily changes involved in glossolalia. Perhaps his consultants, whom he recorded in his office, I was told, had spoken in tongues so long, the physical changes they underwent during their glossolalic prayers were not readily observable anymore, although the level recorder would still have detected the glossolalia pattern. I analyzed a number of such samples from my own collection, and the telltale curves, although somewhat flattened and elongated, were always there.

In the meantime, since the spring of 1968, I had been teaching linguistics and anthropology at Denison University, a private liberal-arts college in northwestern Ohio. In my lectures, I frequently mentioned my fieldwork, especially my observations on the religious trance, how important it was to uncounted societies, that it was a learned behavior, and how well and happy people felt after a trance ritual. I also showed my students the film documentary I had put together from footage I had taken in Yucatán. In previous decades, the topic might have created no interest. But these students were of the generation of the fabled sixties. They were fascinated by the unusual; they talked of "expanding the mind." They were eager for adventure, for experience. "Could you teach that trance to us, too?" they wanted to know.

I pondered their request for quite a while. It would have been impossible and of course quite inappropriate to try and recreate a Pentecostal service for them. Besides, they obviously did not want to experience glossolalia. Would it be possible to dissect the behavior, as it were, and to induce only the underlying physical changes? I finally decided to abstract what to me seemed the salient features for trance induction, leaving out all those factors that I had observed to lead to speaking in tongues. There had to be the expectation that the nonordinary state of consciousness was available to anyone. From their readings of the anthropological literature and my lectures, my students already knew that. Private space was needed, and rhythmic stimulation. We used a classroom at the end of the hall, and for rhythmic stimulation, I chose a gourd rattle of the kind that I had seen during Indian dances in New Mexico. I told my participants that they should do whatever seemed appropriate to them—walk in a tight little circle, stand, sit, kneel, or lie down. Their only task was to close their eyes and concentrate on the sound of my rattle. Initially, I rattled for ten minutes, but after a bit of experimentation that seemed too short, and I went to fifteen.

Experimentation in this form continued with a number of different student volunteers from 1972 until 1976. The experiences they reported clearly indicated that they had achieved a change in the way their bodies acted and also in their consciousness, their perception. They told about noting an increased heartbeat, of feeling hot, of muscles turning stiff, of shivering and twitching. The sound of the rattle might go away, or it turned into light. They saw various shapes, shadowy figures, or a long-forgotten girlfriend. Afterward they felt joyous excitement and a great need to talk to others about the experience. The world around them looked changed, and when one girl glanced into the mirror after an exercise, she found herself exquisitely beautiful. She was startled; she had not thought of herself as Miss America material. I began noting that their sense of time was off. "Did you really rattle for fifteen minutes?" was an often-heard question. It was also difficult for them to tell things "in the right order." After a trance, experiences would tend to come tumbling out helter-skelter, first things last, last things first, and a jumble in the middle, so to speak. Yet all were lucid, perceptively observing both the physical changes and whatever images came floating past their eyes.

There was one thing, however, that bothered me about what the students observed: Their experiences varied too much. Responding to the same rhythmic rattle sound, should the experience not always be the same? Yet some felt hot, but there were others who became very cold. While there were visions of bright light, these contrasted with the appearance of a black hole. To be sure, I had heard similar inconsistencies when talking with various speakers in tongues. But in their case, their conviction that it was the Holy Spirit that was possessing them provided something like a supporting grid. It did not matter that for one, the Holy Spirit entered through the stomach, for the next it came up the backbone, and that still another felt it like gentle rain on his shoulder. But without an absolute commitment to a mythology, as with my students, there was nothing to give any cohesion to the experiences. Yet I could think of no other manner in which I could proceed with the experiments. I decided there was nothing more to be gained with this approach.

One concern that kept secretly nagging at me, and that I was not even willing to countenance, was whether we had even induced the same physiological changes that underlie an ecstatic experience. Humans are capable of so many different states of consciousness. How could I be sure we had hit on the right one? I could think of no way in which I could test that, other than relying on the similarities I had observed between my students' behavior and that of the speakers in tongues. It seemed a dead-end situation. So to wrap things up and put the matter to rest, I reported the results in 1976 at a meeting of the Ohio Academy of Science. "The trance experience itself is vacuous," I wrote in the conclusion. "If no belief system is proffered, it will remain vacuous. It is a neurophysiological event that receives content only from signals present in the respective culture." Outside the Pentecostal movement and its offshoots, such as charismatic Catholicism, our own main-line culture no longer provided any such signals, and I did not know where else to go.

In the fall of that year, however, a new avenue of research was to open up. Dr. Bourguignon, who had become my dissertation adviser, and with whom I had kept in touch even after receiving my Ph.D. in 1971, had called my attention to an article by the Canadian psychologist V. F. Emerson.[3] He had done research with various meditative disciplines and had found that differences in their belief systems correlated with the fact that during meditation, each discipline employed its own specific body posture. All the functions of the body changed with alterations of posture, Emerson pointed out, the heartbeat, breathing, even the motility of the intestines. This was bound to have an effect also on the psychological level.

I had looked at that article briefly in the spring when I was working on my report to the Ohio Academy of Science. But the full implications of Emerson's emphasis on posture did not occur to me until the fall, when I once more pondered how to go on with my research. Then it hit me like a thunderbolt. How come it had never occurred to me to note that there was this connection? Was it this factor that caused the experience of receiving the Holy Spirit to vary so much? I had recorded the details of how speaking in tongues was taught. But not one of the ministers I had seen in action insisted on any posture. In a few congregations, a special body posture seemed to be preferred, but even in those cases, it was neither taught nor assumed by everyone. I could see why they did not care: All that mattered was that the Holy Spirit put in an appearance. But I wanted to find out something about the nature of the physical changes involved and had to find a reason for why the experiences of my students varied so greatly. I had never even thought to suggest any particular posture to them during our experiments. Obviously, we were all subject to the same blind spot, for neither did I recall any instance in the literature where an ethnographic observer specifically called attention to any particular posture used by the celebrants during a trance ritual.

Here, obviously, a novel way suggested itself for carrying out my experiments. What I needed to do was to teach my subjects distinct postures for use during their trance exercises and then record the variations. But what sort of postures? Luckily I never thought of inventing any. Instead I did what comes naturally to an anthropologist: I turned to the body of ethnographic literature for advice. The authors may not have described any postures, but the many illustrations in their books were bound to contain examples anyhow. I began searching for photographs of native, that is, non-Western, subjects during religious rituals, and when that did not yield very much, I started perusing volumes of aboriginal art, looking for figured representations of a religious nature.

The logic of this new step seems self-evident now. Yet it really was something like the egg of Columbus. According to this anecdote, probably apocryphal, the renowned explorer was sitting at the banquet table at the king's court in Madrid after his famous journey, and one of the grandees challenged him, saying, "I don't think what Vuestra Merced, your grace, did was all that innovative. After all, knowing that the earth is round, anybody could have thought of turning his ships west instead of east to arrive at the Indies." Instead of answering directly, Columbus took a hard-boiled egg from the bowl in front of him and asked, "Who can stand this egg on its tip?" Everyone around the table tried, but no one was able to do the trick. When the egg was handed back to Columbus, he took it and brought it down hard, breaking the shell at the tip. That way the egg could easily be stood upright. There was laughter around the table and shouts that anybody could have done that. "Right," agreed Columbus, "but no one thought of it." The idea of adding a posture when going into trance was suggested by Emerson's train of thought, and taking it from the ethnographic literature was only a hunch, a shot in the dark, much like turning the boat toward the west instead of the east. But it had not occurred to anyone before, and in doing so, I was to rediscover a mysterious, long-lost world.

A brief remark about research methods might be in order here. As will become obvious throughout this account, my approach is not a "positivistic" one, as was described by Rosenthal and Rosnow (1969), for example. According to that paradigm, there are a number of "artifacts" that originate with the researcher and might affect the results, such as the experimenter's expectations and the awareness of the subjects of the experimenter's intent. Intense effort is therefore lavished on keeping the experimenter and the subject separate. However, there was no danger of my producing any such artifacts; except for my expressed expectation that a change in perception would take place, I myself was entirely unaware of what kind of experience might emerge, if any at all. Besides, as an anthropologist, I am much more inclined anyway toward a method that has come to be called the "naturalist" one (see Lincoln and Guba, 1985). In this method the case study is the reporting mode of choice, the experimenter and the subject are "in a state of mutual simultaneous shaping" (p. 38), so that it is impossible to distinguish causes from effects, and the researcher is as much a data-gathering instrument as the subjects. Results are not certain but probabilistic and speculative. Most important, from a philosophical point of view, objective reality is not absolute but relative. Such a method was tailor-made for my present inquiry.

Eventually I indeed found a number of postures that I thought might qualify for my intended research. It was obvious, for instance, that the wood carving of a small shaman embraced from the back by a mighty "Bear Spirit" (pl. 1) represented a religious scene, and the ecstatic smile of the Bear's protégé, so familiar to me from people in trance, seemed to point to the kind of experience I was looking for. Clearly, the late-nineteenth-century Indian carver from the Pacific Northwest had to have seen that entranced facial expression many times to have rendered it so faithfully. And there were a number of other representations of the same quality.

With money from the Faculty Development Fund of Denison University, I

Plate 1

embarked on my new research in the summer of 1977. I recruited some interested volunteers, my two yoga teachers, a number of anthropology graduate students, a sociologist—eight in all. Since they had jobs, they could not all come at the same time, so I decided to work with each one individually, which was desirable anyway, because in this way, they could not influence each other. Instead of taking them to a laboratory, I provided an aesthetically pleasing and sparsely furnished room in my own home. The session started with my showing a drawing I had prepared of the posture, containing no other information. After we practiced it, I once again used a rattle to induce the trance, and afterward, I recorded what each had to tell about what had happened.

I wish I could once more experience that surprise, that exquisite wonder that took hold of me as we began exploring this new possibility. The physical changes still tended to fluctuate, although not as uncontrollably as before. As I was to discover later, a remarkable consistency was indeed there, but at a much deeper level, discoverable only by sophisticated laboratory techniques. But as soon as we controlled for posture, something much more important began emerging: The experiences began falling into place. Within certain generous limits, making allowances for individual style and ability of expression, we found that each posture predictably mediated not just any kind of vision but a characteristic, distinctly different experience. In the one where the Bear Spirit hugged the shaman who held his head back, his hands placed above the navel, and his knees slightly bent, the bodies of the subjects or their heads would split open as if to receive something, a substance, a flow of energy, which was then administered to them. In another one, modeled after a photograph of an African diviner (pl. 2), who sits on the floor with his legs toward the right and leaning on his left hand, his right hand resting close to his left calf, the subjects would start spinning around. This furious whirling would then enable them to "find out" or to "understand."

Let me describe another example a bit more in detail. It concerns a drawing in Lascaux Cave from the Old Stone Age, that is, from about sixteen to seventeen thousand years ago. The cave was discovered near the French village of Montignac in the Dordogne in 1940. It contains a profusion of drawings of animals executed with consummate skill, but also a drawing of a human figure (pl. 3). At a cursory glance, this naked man seems to have fallen over backward, right in front of a huge wounded aurochs. It has usually been assumed that the two images represent an integral composition, that the enormous beast had something to do with the fallen man—that the man was frightened or killed, or perhaps was carrying out some hunting magic. At closer inspection, however, it seemed to me that certain features of the drawing of the man did not fit in with any of these conjectures. In the first place, there was a staff stuck upright into the ground next to the man, crowned not by the semblance of horns, as might be expected if there was a connection to the aurochs nearby, but by a bird. If he had fallen, and it was the intention of the artist to show the accident, would the staff not be lying beside him? Also, the animal and the man were executed in different techniques, the aurochs in color and in exquisite detail, the man in black outline.

Yet there was nothing hurried about how the figure was drawn. His left

Plate 2

elbow was represented as a small circle and that arm was stretched out stiffly, while the right arm was bent; his fingers were longer than his thumbs, and only his left thumb was pointing downward, and he had an erection. He was wearing a bird mask, doubtless an indication of a religious context. Analyzing the drawing with a ritual posture in mind, it occurred to me that in fact it contained what amounted to postural instructions. One of these was to hold the left arm rigid, thumb down and elbow locked. The right arm was to lie in a relaxed fashion, elbow bent, so the thumb would naturally come to be

Plate 3

positioned up. And, very important, something that no one had paid any attention to, the body was not to lie flat on the ground, but was to form one side of a thirty-seven-degree angle.

For our own experiment with this posture, we painstakingly duplicated this thirty-seven-degree angle, using chairs, pillows, sleeping bags, and the like. It was quite comfortable, and my participants expected to have a restful fifteen minutes in that posture. Instead, things quickly became highly dramatic, as the following accounts will illustrate. By the way, as I was to hear innumerable times later, not everyone experienced the entire sequence of events, reminiscent of what happens when a number of people are witness to the same event. Rather, the individual reports frequently needed to be taken together and then formed a cohesive, running description of the total event. The following accounts, all from the initial 1977 experiment, are arranged with that fact in mind.[4]

ANITA: The hand position seemed to indicate polarity to me, and I began to experience that more and more as I went into trance. The left hand that pointed down and was pushing away was getting warm, the right one was cold. This seemed to develop a flow of energy that became circular. The energy wrapped me into a cocoon, and for a while I was floating in this very nice, golden cocoon.

Judy G.: The energy was rushing around in my body, suddenly converged on the genital area, then started rising upward through my body.

David S.: The excitation went through my chest, and the closest thing I can think of is orgasm. It was like an orgasm in my head, like everything was being squeezed out of me, I was being squeezed out through my head. Now I am cold.

Bryan: There was something like a giant cookie cutter that was going to work on me, making duplicates of myself. Then something inside of me wanted to get out; even the hair on my body was rising up as this thing was coming out as an exact duplicate of myself.

Suzanne G.: I saw a path, it took me to a white cloud. Then I was in that cloud and it opened and I came out, flying about in the blue.

In other words, the posture prompted such excitation to arise that in the perception of the participants, a flow of energy was churned, the course of which then became controlled, converging on the genitals; hence perhaps the erection of the Lascaux shaman. From there it started streaming up through the body and into the head, and then, as the astounded participants told so graphically, "I was being squeezed out through my head," or "this thing was coming out as an exact duplicate of myself," and "I came out, flying about in the blue." The agreement with countless tales from around the world was evident. In fact, the conclusion was inescapable: We had rediscovered the ancient art of embarking on a spirit journey.

It took a while before the implications of these discoveries sank in. It was now evident that the altered state of consciousness that was induced by the simple rhythmic stimulation of the gourd rattle was indeed the religious trance, for my participants in the experiment had experienced a spirit journey through the agency of this induction method. Not only that—as a wondrous gift from many nameless native artists, we had begun at the same time to rediscover a system of signals to the nervous system, a complex strategy capable of shaping the amorphous trance into a religious experience. Put differently, *guided by hitherto unnoticed traditional body postures, these "subjects" of a social-science experiment had taken the step from the physical change of the trance to the experience of ecstasy, they had passed from the secular to the sacred.*

The question that soon began to occupy us during these experiments was whether such miraculous perceptual changes could really be brought about simply by physiological signals. "The posture sets the stage," Bryan speculated. "I don't doubt that with some practice I could experience all that even without your rattle helping, just by getting into the posture." As a linguist, I started hypothesizing that perhaps as in a gesture, it was the iconic content, a message that lay hidden in the posture, that my subjects were picking up without realizing it. They had done one posture, of an Australian shaman pointing a bone (pl. 4), in order, according to the ethnographer, to "hit" an adversary with a magic missile, where this might have been a reasonable suggestion. But the iconic interpretation simply would not work, for instance, for the above-mentioned divining posture.

Another idea suggested was that the experiences were structured by arousing the chakras in specific, set patterns. This was the time when all sorts of mysterious experiences were attributed to the influence of those complicated centers in our body conceptualized a thousand or more years ago in India. Their bodily aspects correspond roughly to the thoracic, abdominal, and pelvic plexuses of Western anatomic science, together with the optic assemblage and the brain. I conjectured that perhaps by the postures, my subjects were activating various combinations of chakras, creating, in fact, a different altered state of consciousness for each posture. Mathematically, the full extent of combinatory possibilities would have amounted to 2 to the power of 7 = 128, minus the null set, that is, 127. The conjecture did not seem very reasonable even then, and now, after more than a decade of research, we found only about 30 different postures, not 127, and only a single religious trance. This agrees with the observation of other researchers, e.g., Peters and Price-

Plate 4

Williams, who point out that the experiential aspects of various trance states "are descriptive of *a single dynamic psychological process*" (1983:6, emphasis mine; see also Winkelman 1986).

I should like to anticipate here that I did follow up on my early interest in exactly what happens in the body during the religious trance. The first opportunity for doing the medical research needed arose in 1983, at the Department of Psychiatric Neurophysiology at the Psychiatric Clinic and Policlinic of the University of Munich,[5] under consultation with the head of the department, Professor Johann Kugler. Working with the most modern equipment, we tested four volunteers during the religious trance. The findings were the first comprehensive scientifically obtained body of laboratory data anyone had ever discovered about this type of trance. Other researchers, e.g., Neher (1961 and 1962), concentrated exclusively on processes in the brain.

The instruments registered dramatic changes. In the blood serum, the compounds indicating stress, namely, adrenalin, noradrenalin, and cortisol, dropped, and at the same time, there was evidence that the brain started synthesizing beta-endorphin, the miracle painkiller of the body, which is also responsible for the intense joy felt after a trance. The EEG exhibited not the famous alpha waves, so well known from meditation, but a steady stream of the even slower theta waves, in the range of 6–7 cps, usually seen only in bursts shortly before a subject goes to sleep, or in deep Zen meditation. Most puzzling, blood pressure dropped, and simultaneously, the pulse started racing like a runner's during a hundred-meter dash. Under ordinary conditions, I was told, physicians see this kind of paradoxical behavior of the body only under extreme conditions, such as when a patient bleeds to death or is about to die.

Differences in posture did not affect the results, by the way. The experiments were carried out using two different postures, yet all the parameters examined remained the same. It was gratifying that here at last was the consistency I had been looking for in the underlying trance event. But as to the effect of the postures, the message clearly was that while our instruments could certainly reveal something about somatic processes, this was after all what they were designed to do; they were unable to penetrate the mystery of the ecstatic experience.

In the spring of 1987, I had the good fortune to be able to participate in some additional neurophysiological research. When the behavior was approached from a different angle, its results once more demonstrated the truly magnificent modification the nervous system undergoes during a religious trance. The investigation concerned the extent of the negative charge of the direct-current potential of the brain during the religious trance, and was carried out under Professor Giselher Guttmann at the laboratory of the Department of Psychology of the University of Vienna. With EEG equipment available at only a few laboratories worldwide, which works with direct rather than alternating current, it is possible to amplify a weak signal that the brain gives off during tasks requiring intense attention. Peak values during learning tasks found to date amounted to at most 250 microvolts. With volunteers from my workshops experienced in the religious trance, much higher values, rising to an astounding 1,500 to 2,000 microvolts, were achieved. At the same time, the stream of theta waves continued unabated (Guttmann et al., 1988).[6] Again, however, the results remained unchanged when the posture was varied. For the present, their mystery remains intact.

Returning to 1977 now, the summer's work with the postures had put me into a curiously glowing, magical mood, which continued into the school year, especially as I was writing the paper summarizing our findings. But when I presented it in the fall of that year to the annual meeting of the American Anthropological Association, the polite applause of my colleagues was deeply disappointing. Obviously afflicted by an uncharacteristic attack of megalomania, I think I expected them to throng around the podium, begging also to be allowed to try the marvelous adventure that we had discovered that summer. Instead, they went on to the next lecture, and a mild-mannered young man stopped me on the way out and asked, "Are you now planning to do a structural-functional analysis?" The incongruous question struck me as wildly ludicrous, and I was sorely tempted to slip into the jargon of the sixties and counter, "Hey, man, I was in a magic garden!" But these were no longer the sixties. So I smiled politely and left him standing there. I felt like a sleeper trying to awaken from a profound dream, and somehow the ordinary world of my profession and its concerns was very far away.

CHAPTER THREE

The Old Ones
Remember

Without eager company, even magic gardens can be lonely places. So after returning from the anthropology meeting, I bundled up my notes on the mysterious postures and turned to a different topic. It was still part of the same field of study, the religious trance, but this time it concerned the experience of demonic possession.

My interest in this subject had been triggered by news stories about a German university student by the name of Anneliese Michel, who supposedly died as a result of being exorcized. From the American magazine item that had called my attention to the case, I had learned that the girl insisted that she was possessed by demons, but that her psychiatrists maintained that she was psychotic, most likely an epileptic.[1] From the start, I had the impression that this might well be another one of those cases where a religious experience was confused with epilepsy, just as was often done in descriptions of shamans. The German courts decided that the two priests who carried out the exorcism had contributed to her death, and convicted both them and her parents of negligent homicide, resulting in suspended jail sentences.

I was convinced that there had to be an error in judgment, that this was a miscarriage of justice. Demonic possession is an affliction well known all around the world, not only among Christians, and exorcism is the treatment of choice. There are no reports on record anywhere that somebody died of an exorcism (see Goodman 1988). I eventually wrote to the defense lawyer, and as I studied the more than eight hundred pages of court records she sent me, I felt increasingly sorry for the young girl, whose case to my mind had been so poorly handled. She was only two years older than my youngest daughter, and I kept seeing my own child being treated with thinly veiled contempt by uncomprehending psychiatrists as she pleaded for help against the demons that were plaguing her, and being plied with psychoactive drugs that only made matters worse. I eventually wrote a book about Anneliese (Goodman 1981), and during my 1978 summer vacation I really wanted to go to Italy to visit San Damiano, the shrine where her possession had first become public knowledge. But I had earlier promised some childhood friends back home to visit them, and that was a tug at the heartstrings. So although I felt a twinge of guilt for giving preference to personal pleasure, I decided in favor of Hungary.

When planning the trip, I recalled that my mother had often longingly told how beautiful the journey was from Vienna to Budapest by boat. She did not live to take it again, so I would do it in her stead. I flew into the Austrian capital, spent the night in a hotel, and the next morning took a cab to the dock and bought a ticket on one of the comfortable modern excursion boats operated by the Hungarian travel service.

I was the first on deck, but soon a vivacious Austrian lady joined me. It was a hot day and she was thirsty, but she could not make the Hungarian waiter understand what she wanted, so I acted as her interpreter. She was a journalist, on her way to a meeting of economists in Budapest that she was to cover. We quickly warmed to each other, and eventually the conversation came around to my research. When I mentioned Anneliese's case, which had made headlines in Europe, my traveling companion knew a lot about it and animatedly denounced the "superstitious" priests who had obviously done her in. I took the opposite tack, and we became so engrossed in our topic that I never even saw the beautiful landscape we were passing through. The beaded necklace of narrow green islands adorning the blond Danube as it meandered between Hungary and Czechoslovakia, Komárom, the city stretching over both banks of the river and cut in half by an unforgiving border, the towers of ancient Esztergom, see of the archbishop of Hungary, and the mountains of Visegrad, all would have to wait for another vacation.

As we said goodbye upon landing in Budapest, we agreed to exchange information. She would locate newspaper reports for me about Anneliese. In return, I was to let her have copies of my publications about my research on the religious trance. We both kept our promise. She sent me clippings about San Damiano, which I had not gotten to visit, and I reciprocated with my book about speaking in tongues, and with some recent papers. I thought this would be the end of our contact, but instead, later in the fall of 1978, I received a grateful letter, not from my journalist but from an author and former professor of religious studies at the University of Vienna, Dr. Adolf Holl. He wrote that he had "confiscated" everything I had sent to his friend. It seems that the material was valuable to him, because he was working on a biography of Saint Francis of Assisi at the time,[2] and the details of the trance research had provided him with additional insights into the experiences of this famous medieval mystic. All of this referred to my book about speaking in tongues, and I almost forgot that among the papers I had sent him there was also the one about the 1977 posture research.

This lapse of memory was entirely understandable, for in the 1978–79 school year I had other things on my mind than research. Quite suddenly, and entirely out of the blue, forced retirement loomed as an imminent threat. I had been so wrapped up in the challenges of teaching and fascinating research projects that retirement seemed something that only other people had to face. It had never entered my mind that at the age of only sixty-five, in the very middle of my newfound career, my university might want to cut me off. But talk of retirement would not go away, and that five other colleagues were in the same situation was no consolation. I was beginning to feel like a condemned prisoner on death row, who could not believe that the date would ever be set. I protested, but to no avail, and so the last year of my university teaching career was a forlorn and bitter time. I was at a loss as to how to go on.

It was a dank and foggy evening in late November, the kind of night that held out no hope at all that spring would ever come again, when the Old Ones decided that they had to reach out to me once more. But being Indians, they did not come straight out with it, maybe with a thunderclap from heaven or in a burning bush, as other divine personages are reputed to proceed. As I was to find out later when I came to know them better, they were much less obtrusive but full of gentle cunning and a great deal of humor. On this evening they were clearly intent on testing to see if this unreasonable woman could be pulled out of the mire of despair into which she had maneuvered herself. And they chose a most unlikely object for their purpose.

I had a statue in my bedroom of the Virgin of Guadalupe, the patron saint of Mexico, which I had bought during fieldwork. It reminded me of the be-jeweled Madonna in the glittering chapel of the convent at home where I was raised. There were always candles burning before that statue, and suddenly feeling homesick, I decided to light two beeswax candles before it to make things look right.

I went to the bathroom to brush my hair, and glancing back I thought how pretty the scene was, the statue lit by the soft candlelight and the green sprig of fir I had placed there a few days before. So when I came back into the bedroom, instead of blowing out the candles, I sat on the bed, leaning against the wall, intent on admiring it all. Soon, however, I no longer saw the statue with the candles, but rather the figure of a slender young woman, her dress cinched with a belt, filling out the triangle under the Madonna's folded hands. She was framed by an orange glow that emanated from the space in front of her. I could not see her face, for she was turning away from me, apparently looking out into a room that was lit by that beautiful golden light. I was hoping she would turn toward me, but it did not happen, and eventually the lovely image faded and there was only the light of the candles.

The next weekend, I went to visit my oldest son. The conversation soon drifted to religious experience, a topic of consuming interest to both of us, and I told him about my puzzling vision. Did he have any idea what it might mean? He consulted his I Ching and set up a small altar from the toy box of his son, a fir tree, and beside it a little figure with a big head. As I contemplated it in the flickering light of the candle he had lit, the plastic figure assumed the appearance of a "mudhead," the sacred clown of the Hopis, whose clay likenesses can be bought on the Indian markets of New Mexico.

We waited. I had no idea what I was waiting for; we just sat there. Suddenly there was the sound of wild scratching at the front door, and the family cat jumped up and ran to the entranceway, mewing and spitting. We followed after, and my son opened the door. A black cat jumped off the landing, cut across the street toward the left, and disappeared between the houses. We could think of no reason why that cat should have appeared before the door and demanded that we open it. The family cat was spayed and never had any male suitors. Perhaps, as my son suggested, the spirit whom we had evoked with our modest ritual needed a body in which to respond to our summons, and a cat was all it could find in the middle of a big city.

Like a twinkling light on a distant mountainside, the mysterious experience beckoned to me through the dark months that followed. In an inexplicable way, it carried a message of encouragement. I decided that come what may, I would continue teaching and doing research, perhaps on my land in New Mexico during the summer. In order to be able to carry out these plans, I engaged a lawyer and founded a nonprofit educational corporation, which was registered with the state of New Mexico as Cuyamungue Institute. *Cuyamungue* is the Spanish adaptation of the Tewa Indian name for the large pueblo that once flourished in our valley, and remains of a small part of it were on my land. It was probably deserted after the 1683 Pueblo Revolt.[3] Roughly translated, the name means "where the stones are slipping," referring to the hill across the highway from us, an ancient landmark where large sandstone plates protrude at oblique angles from the softer subsoil.

For my first summer's teaching after retirement, I recruited six undergraduates for a course in comparative religion at Cuyamungue. They were due to arrive in July, and as living accommodations for them I designed a simple wooden building and had it built from part of my university pension money.

It was in the midst of this construction work that I went up to the gate one day to set up the sign of Cuyamungue Institute. It was based on a logo I had composed from Pueblo Indian designs, representing the hills, the mountains, the earth, and the clouds of New Mexico. I had carved it on a board and had nailed it to two cedar posts. The ground was soft and clayey, and in search of some stones to steady the posts, I started walking farther and farther into the rough terrain. All of a sudden I felt a strange tugging, drawing me as if by a powerful lure in among the junipers and pinyon bushes, almost as if whispering, "Come—step closer—still closer—see what is hidden within—come—come. . . ." I followed the call of the still voice, and it led me to an open area which was strewn with numerous rocks. When I looked more closely, I found to my surprise that the rocks were laid out in a pattern. There were a large rectangle, several lines, and a number of small circles. I could feel that it was holy, and I fervently wished I could find out who it was who had left so much of his sacred essence behind. Reverently, I left the site and found the rocks I needed farther away in a wash.

Next day I asked Gilbert, my Hispanic builder, artist, and all-around handyman, to make me some wooden boxes for transplanting the seedlings I had brought from Columbus. He did not get to it right away, but as I walked by the building site, I saw a weathered wooden planter of the kind I wanted, which had not been there before. Gilbert thought that perhaps his dog had dragged it there. But I had fun playing with the idea that whoever inhabited the area of the design up in the hills appreciated my not having taken any stones and instructed the dog to bring me what I had wished for.

That weekend, a cherished friend came to visit, and when he had to leave, I was very sad. Badly in need of consolation after saying goodbye to him, I walked forlornly to the stone design to feel the comforting Presence again, and raised my palms in greeting the way I had seen an old Indian do in one of the pueblos, when he blessed the participants in a feast-day observation. The simple ritual eased me, but when I left, I was still crying.

I went into the house, sat down by the table, and wondered disconsolately what to do next, when all of a sudden a cricket started sounding its silver bell from up in the vigas, louder than I had ever heard it before, insistent and ringing clear and high. It was so loud, I thought at first that a bird had gotten into the house, although I knew of no bird that had that kind of song. The sound came from the ceiling of the next room, and I went to see what it was but could not find anything. Then it occurred to me: It could not be a bird, it had to be a cricket. So obeying a sudden intuition, I said, "Thank you, little cricket, and see, I am not sad anymore." And when I said that, the cricket fell silent. I continued listening for a while, but there was no more sound.

It was thrilling once more to imagine that perhaps it had been the Presence at the shrine that had sent the cricket to console me, and so I began to ponder what I could give this new friend of mine in return. Pollen would be best; I had read that the Navajos made offerings of corn pollen to the Spirits, but I did not have any pollen. So on the way to the shrine I picked some yellow blossoms, the closest thing to pollen I could think of, and put them into one of the circles of stone. Then I sat there for a while like a child waiting for candy. Would this be the end of it, or would I also receive something in return? All the while, of course, I was telling myself that this was merely a game I was playing, inspired by my loneliness. But when I finally left the shrine, right in front of me on the path there was a fluffy, fresh bird's feather of the kind Indian women put on their headdresses during the Corn Dance, and which are said to represent blessing. Deeply moved, I picked it up and profusely thanked the Presence for its gift.

The next day a boy and a girl came to help me, children of Hispanic neighbors from the valley. They had come on foot and told excitedly that on the way up they had seen a large cat: "You know, the kind that looks like it has its tail chopped off. . . ." They described how the bobcat had been sitting at what I secretly thought of as "my" shrine, and had run off down into the Cañada as they approached. By this time, I was entirely ready to accept miracles. To me, this was the message that the spirit who had possessed the city cat was the same as the owner of the shrine.

As June wore on, my Friend of the Shrine had other gifts in store for me. I began finding strange little pebbles. Eventually there were six of these, showing the White Buffalo, the Badger, the Bear, the Snake, Mother Earth, and the Starry Sky. Such stones are well known in the Tewa world. I felt overwhelmed by the kindness shown me and tried to think of how to reciprocate. Since my Friend of the Shrine was obviously a part of Pueblo culture, I went to an Indian woman friend whom I had known for years, and who was living in a pueblo where the old traditions were still alive. I told her how I had encountered my spirit friend, and I asked her if there was anything that she thought I could properly present to him. Would cornmeal be all right? She said I could do that, but also, if I prepared an item of food, for instance bread, I should take a little of that, in the morning when the sun came up, and in the evening when it set. "And in your own language tell him that he should not hurt you, just as you would not hurt anyone." Then she gave me some hand-ground cornmeal from a small clay jar with a black ornamental design. "Give this to him," she said, "and I will also pray for you."

I did as she had instructed me, and puzzled for a while about her cautionary remark that I should ask him not to hurt me. For in my heart of hearts, I was still a child, only now I was playing in sacred precincts without fully comprehending their powerful and therefore of course also dangerous reality. I had been given presents, I had been treated with the utmost kindness; what could possibly happen? So I became presumptuous. Disappointed by a number of books I subsequently perused about the Pueblos, none of which had any answers concerning the nature of the spirit world I sought to understand, I one day reproached my Friend at the shrine that I had no teacher to teach me. After all, Castaneda had his don Juan, so how come I was not meeting anyone like that? I told him I wanted an Indian Holy Man to come up that road right then and there to instruct me in everything that I wanted to know. I was at least figuratively stamping my foot, acting like a very spoiled child. Wisdom does not come automatically attached to greying hair. The Old Ones took one look at me and decided that I needed to be taught all right. But the initiation they meted out to me very nearly cost me my life.

By this time it was August, and I had taken my students to visit Bandelier National Park, only about thirty miles from Cuyamungue. The guide there showed us a plaster cast of two stone lions, the original of which was at a shrine about six miles away from Frijoles Canyon and the Visitors' Center.

She said that it was a sanctuary still in use. Indians frequently offered antlers there, and sometimes the lions had pigment on their faces, like that used by the Indian dancers. Six miles sounded like nothing at all; I often walked that much just visiting friends around Cuyamungue, and I thought the students would enjoy the hike. So we made the proper preparations and early on a bright and sunny day drove to Bandelier once more. We were given a wilderness pass and a map by the rangers, and at about eight-thirty started out on our trek, two young men, four young women, and I. Each of us had two quarts of water, a sandwich, nuts, raisins, and some fruit. I carried a small first-aid kit, salt tablets, bits of salty fried meat, and two tomatoes. And we started up.

I soon realized that this was not going to be a picnic. It was a tremendous climb just to get out of Frijoles Canyon. Then we walked for about two hours across the top of a canyon, along a barely visible path. It was getting very hot. To divert the attention of the students from the exhaustion they were beginning to feel, I pointed out different interesting plants we were passing—several giant yucca, a bush with aromatic colorless flowers being harvested by very aggressive wild bees, Apache feather bonnets, three lovely barrel-shaped cacti ready to bloom—but got very little response except from Sara, who was born and raised in the Southwest. She called out about a wild donkey grazing in the distance and a doe with her fawn slipping noiselessly into the shadows. But no one paid any heed to that either.

The heat, meanwhile, was getting brutal. Elizabeth, the blondest of the bunch, had rushed ahead with bravado but soon got exhausted, although we rested several times in the shade of the junipers. Finally she gave up. "This is ridiculous," she said. "I am enormously thirsty, half my water is gone; I just had better turn back." She had forgotten her head scarf, so I gave her mine and she left.

By this time it was about noon. We had reached Alamo Canyon and were zigzagging downward, alongside fantastic promontories, with junipers growing on stony hillsides as forbidding as Dante's inferno. I pondered whether I should also give up and turn back—I had become unspeakably weary—but the Lions were supposed to be just across the canyon on the other side. And there was Sara, slim, fit, brown, stepping over sticks and stones on her bare feet like a graceful gazelle. I felt ashamed about my temporary loss of nerve. Perhaps I could catch a second wind. So I continued on.

We went down and down. To the right was a sheer rock wall, at least six hundred feet high, its glistening black veins rising toward the merciless sky. As I looked up at the wall, I suddenly saw that the basalt columns had been parted like folds of a curtain, and high among the strands a huge figure was leaning out of a window. He looked like a koshari, the sacred Pueblo Indian clown, aquiline nose over a full mouth, wearing a loose tunic, and with the two dry cornstalks sticking up from his cap like horns. His massive face bore a peculiar expression, half curious, half friendly concern. "My Friend might look like that," I thought, puzzled by the fabulous rock formation. "Do you see that face?" I called to the students. But they were far ahead of me and did not answer. None of them later remembered the face when I asked them, although to me it was as real as the path, the unforgiving sun, and the junipers around us.

We no longer saw the path, but down below there was what looked like a narrow, dark mountain brook. "Water," I thought with elation and relief. Then we reached it, and instead of water, it was composed of sinister ankle-deep and tinder-dry volcanic ash. It crackled and crunched as we waded in it. Then we saw the trail again; it led out of the creek bed up to the right and lost itself among the boulders on the other side. I looked back up at the enigmatic rock face that was still dispassionately watching us from above, and down at that awful flow of ash, and decided to turn back. Still another canyon wall to climb up, and then the same stretch down again on the return trip was just more than I could face. So I left my small bag with supplies and my rain poncho—the rangers had warned about sudden downpours—with the students, keeping for myself only one tomato, a few raisins, and my Yucatecan bottle gourd which was still half full of water. I also gave them my camera. "Take a picture of the shrine and the Stone Lions for me," I asked. Then I started back in that hellish rivulet of ash, always looking for the tracks we had made.

I found the path marker that indicated the start of the trail up, but felt deeply disappointed. Partly, at least, I had suggested the hike for my own sake, hoping to find something at the shrine, a sign, perhaps, that I had not been forgotten. But it was not to be. It was two o'clock. Furtively, I cast an occasional glance at the rock wall, but the face was gone. Was it because of a change in my angle of vision?

I plodded on and up, very slowly chewing on my tomato. It was getting still hotter. All of a sudden, from a distance, I heard the beat of a Pueblo drum. It was very clear and urgent, faster than the pounding of my heart. There was consolation in it and reassurance. The drum fell silent, then started up again, seeming to come from a greater distance, and then it ceased altogether.

I was getting very thirsty, so I decided to start drinking some of my water, timing the sips every fifteen minutes. Occasionally, I sat down in the shade of a juniper. My legs were getting dangerously tired. How was I going to go on? I calculated that I had at least four more hours to hike. I looked around me, and suddenly I dissolved. I was gone, melted into nothingness.

In the days to follow, I was to ponder over and over again what it was that happened to me in that canyon. Sometimes I thought that nothing happened, nothing at all. But then I knew that that was not true. For in that crushing, awesome, total, enormous aloneness, where there was nothing human except the almost obliterated trail, I sank down within myself to the very bottom, deeper than I had ever been before. I was not afraid, I just sank. And when I reached that deepest point in that abyss of myself, that point of death,

I stopped. I was hit by something that was neither in me nor outside of me. It was not light or emotion; it was, if it "was" at all, a coarse-grained vibration. Its touching was faster than when the tip of a streak of lightning hit the summit of those sacred Jemez Mountains. Then I came up again and rose into my conscious self, suspended on a wave of life.

I looked around me. I was still at that same juniper, and before me rose the zigzag path. Bewildered, I took a deep breath and started climbing once more. But I was getting so tired, I was not walking, I was stumbling on. On and up, on and up, endlessly. My tomato was gone. I could feel the burden I was placing on my heart, so I put some raisins in my mouth for their sugar. But chewing them turned them into a sticky paste that tasted like gypsum. I had to sacrifice a few extra sips of water to wash them down.

Finally, the zigzag path ended. It was three-thirty. The illusion that I was almost at the edge of Frijoles Canyon made me more energetic, but only for a fleeting moment. Although I was now on top of the mesa and no longer had to struggle with the erratic path, the trail continued rising, and I knew that no amount of willpower was going to move my numb legs any farther. I had to rest. I gave myself five minutes under the next juniper, but that helped nothing at all. I could hardly get up. If only I could reach the bush after the next one—but it was useless. I collapsed under a juniper close to the trail, and I could not even sit; I just lay there on my side.

I was afraid that I might become delirious and get confused about directions. So from then on when resting I always placed the gourd away from me, toward the direction where I was going. The heat was so intense that the skin on my arms seemed to be crackling. It would give some relief, I thought, if I took my blouse off, or at least opened it in front. But I was afraid of a sunburn, so I kept it on and buttoned. The conventional wisdom about traveling in the desert crossed my mind: Sleep in the daytime and walk at night. Good thought, but in the dark, I would not be able to follow the faint trail. And what about the canyons intersecting the mesa, with their sheer rock walls hundreds of feet straight down? And the snakes and scorpions and mountain lions all prowling at night? I thought about appealing to my Friend, but for reasons I could not understand, that felt flat, superfluous. So I just lay there and fell asleep.

Half an hour later I woke up, feeling just as weary as before. I have to get up, I told myself, teach the kids, run the institute, write that book about the Anneliese Michel case that I was working on. I must not give up now. So I rose, and after a few steps my feet started moving almost on their own. It gave me a clue: I could make it, I just had to take longer rests. So I staggered on and then collapsed again in some shade. I thought of what it would be like if I could no longer move. The students coming up behind me on the trail would find me. Sara would go get the rangers with their mules. I would wake up in the hospital between cool white sheets and be given gallons and gallons of ice tea. There would be a news flash: "Professor, head of Cuyamungue

Institute, sixty-five years old, found unconscious on trail; age limit needed for wilderness permits." That would not do. On to the next juniper. As I lay down, I looked around. Right in front of me in the yellow dust there was the delicate imprint of a small rattlesnake. I did not sleep there. I had to defecate, and intense nausea shot through me. At the next stop, a fire ant got into my jeans. Taking them off and shaking the insect out consumed energy I could have better expended on walking. Where were those kids, anyway?

A cloud covered the sun, and for a few minutes a cool breeze billowed my blouse. It gave me courage. Also, the path was no longer rising, although it was not sloping either. My water was cool in the gourd, and this time I managed to walk for half an hour. Then the blaze of the sun hit again, and I slumped under another juniper. But things were not so harsh anymore. In front of me, I saw Elizabeth's footprints, so I was still on the right track. Most important, for the first time I caught a glimpse of the Sangre de Cristo range through a gap in the mountain wall. Home! I was not sleepy, just weary, and I rested for a while enjoying a pleasant, wildly unrealistic fantasy of a tiled bathtub I would build under a juniper in front of the Student Building with a continuous flow of fresh water from the garden hose.

My wristwatch showed six o'clock. I started walking a bit faster and no longer stumbled, for Frijoles Canyon could not be very far ahead. Across the range, the water tower of Whiterock gleamed between the distant greenery. Soon, there should be the sign that we had seen in coming, giving the direction for the Lions, and down to the comfortable path leading to the Visitors' Center. Well, it was not soon, but I did not have to rest so much anymore. The sun had sunk further down on the horizon, and eventually, shortly after seven o'clock, I did arrive at a sign. Only it did not say "To the Visitors' Center" but "To Headquarters." Whatever, I did not care, as long as it was down.

That it was, zigzagging so steeply that it would have taxed a mountain goat, steps two feet high, the path often choked with big boulders. With my short legs, I usually had to hug the rock wall and carefully ease myself down, hanging my gourd around my neck so it would not shatter against the stones. Halfway down, there was a bench, and there were Elizabeth's tracks again. I rested only briefly, for way down I could see buildings and a paved road, and I was getting impatient. A few more zigzags down, I drank the last of my water. Finally, the headquarters trail ran into another path, and I could not tell where that led. So I cut across a slope to the paved road. To the left, a family was eating a picnic supper. I had to ask them twice for directions to the Visitors' Center; the first time my voice was so husky, they could not hear me.

I had only a short distance to walk, then I was on the parking lot and was hugged in great relief by my entire crew. Everybody talked at the same time. It seemed that Elizabeth had also found the headquarters trail, as I had surmised from her tracks. She had met a hiker at the bench who gave her some water. None of the group had gotten to the Shrine of the Stone Lions. They had wandered about lost and finally reached the Rio Grande. Once there, they took a refreshing dip, drank from a mountain brook, and went directly back to the Visitors' Center, never even attempting to return the way we had come. So this was why they had never caught up with me. We had agreed to meet at the car at six in case we got separated. When I did not show up, they became worried. Sara finally went to the rangers, and they sent a Zuni marathon runner, who was also a ranger, up to the sanctuary. Just before I arrived, he had informed them on his walkie-talkie that he had arrived at the Lions and had not encountered me. He must have missed me because in the meantime I was descending via the headquarters trail. If I had any pride left, it evaporated when I realized that the entire run up had taken him exactly one hour.

I sat down in the car, and Sara wanted to rub my feet, but there was no pain and not even the smallest blister. Everybody had waited to eat, and they were now enjoying the big picnic supper I had prepared, German potato salad, meat patties, watermelon. But I could not eat a bite, only drank many glasses of ice water. They were all very solicitous, suggesting, not entirely altruistically, "Let's cancel classes tomorrow; after all, your hike was twice as long as ours, and that way you can sleep as much as you want to."

I slept very well that night, consciously drinking in the cool air. I awoke at the usual time, took a shower, and went up to my Friend's shrine. I was tempted to ask why I had not been allowed to see the Sanctuary of the Lions, but with a newfound wisdom thought that perhaps sleeping lions had better be left alone. The students stayed in their sleeping bags till noon, got up to eat lunch, then slept again. They were sore and severely sunburned. I put in a whole day's work and had suffered no bruises, no cuts, no burns except for a tiny triangle where my blouse had been open at the neck, and no muscle pain. I had died at that place of power in the mountains. But the Old Ones also awarded their gift of rebirth during that initiation, and it involved all of me, my body as well as my spirit.

In the following weeks it became progressively clear how thoroughgoing the change was that I had undergone. Before, it seemed, I had been on the outside looking in. Now, as I was beginning to learn step by step, I was admitted. There was, for instance, the matter of the memorial mass for old Tom, who had been killed in an automobile accident. Tom was an Indian, and walking up to my gate on the way to the neighbors who were going to take me, I thought of the incongruity that his passing should be remembered in a mass rather than with some native ritual. How painful it must have been for the native societies under duress to make such accommodations to the religion of their Spanish overlords. Passing by the Shrine, I thought in a rebellious mood that my Friend might want to come along to represent the Spirits who had been banished by the mailed fist of the Conquistadores. I was alone, so I said out loud, "Please, my Friend, do come along to comfort the spirit of old Tom. Attach yourself to my left shoulder and be my companion."

Being new to the path of the Spirits, I was thoroughly shaken when there was an instantaneous response. Coming up from behind, a tremendous ball of force hit me squarely on the left side of my body. But bewilderment soon gave way to a sense of companionship and a delicious feeling of conspiracy, which stayed with me as I walked into the valley down the hot and dusty trail.

Friends and family of Tom filled the first few rows of the church, so I sat farther back. I expected the priest in his sermon to comfort them by painting the kind of delightful picture of the heavenly abode that I remembered from my nursemaid in Budapest. Lisi told about a kindly old man in a white beard called Saint Peter waiting for people at the gate of paradise, and beyond it there was a lovely meadow with flowers nodding by a chattering brook. Instead, for unfathomable reasons, the priest had chosen from the Hebrew Bible the story of Jezebel and her unsavory real-estate dealings. I was appalled. I just hoped that poor old Tom was no longer around, but had in the meantime safely found his way down the ladder to the Corn Mothers by the lake in the lower world, where the departed passed their days singing and dancing. Then I noticed that while the priest was monotonously talking away on the pulpit at the left, a steady wind coming from the right began persistently and noisily to flap the pages of the big, ornate Bible on the altar. A window may have been open, but for the wind to come up just at that moment seemed to me a marvelous joke perpetrated by my Friend against the insensitive priest.

And there was another surprise to come. Like fairy godmothers at the cradle of the newborn, the Old Ones had readied a truly precious gift. One night that August, shortly after all the students had left and I was totally alone on the land, I woke up around two-thirty or three A.M. from a startling feeling of a vibration, as if my womb had been touched by a live electric wire. I suffered it for a while, then had the intuition that if I guided that excitation from the depths of my body up to my eyes, I would be able to "see." And that was exactly what happened. Images of lustrous clarity began forming before my eyes, a village street, a garden, all bathed in an orange glow, beautiful, but nothing that I could identify. So I just watched and tried to understand what this was about.

Then back in Columbus, around Christmas of that year, at about the same time at night, there appeared against a dark background with tinges of reddish-orange the face of a man. Just the head, nothing else. He had a white untidy cloth on his head, he was swarthy, and his mouth was open almost to a square, with an expression of violent, intense rage. As I came to, I thought, "*He* does not belong in my world!" A day later, there came news of the Soviet invasion of Afghanistan and pictures of the tribal chieftains opposing the Russians, wearing those untidy-looking white turbans. Soon afterward, early in the new year, I began "seeing," always several days ahead, salient events of the hostage crisis in Iran. Patiently, step by step, my invisible Teachers taught me to trust my visions by using details that could easily be checked against reports in the media. I was being trained as a seer. I understand now the classical Greek tradition that the god Apollo "raped" Cassandra, thereby endowing her with the gift of prophecy. For the experience did start with an arousal around the genitals, and then became conscious as it traveled upward, eventually taking shape as imagery.

It soon became obvious that these visions, although frequently difficult to interpret by someone as ignorant as I, were uncannily accurate, for I kept track of what I saw by writing it down in the morning. They took many different forms. Often, as happened in the case of the hostage crisis, what I saw presaged events to come. Thus, early on October 19, 1983, there appeared a gateway, two uprights and a crossbeam, with a small, triangular, limp banner attached to it. As I watched, a bright round ball something like the sun burst in the exact center. It can't be the sun, I thought, it's more like an explosion, for a rush of air came toward me and made the banner flutter wildly. Looking closer, I saw a cartoon of President Reagan's face on it. On October 23, just four days later, on a suicide mission, someone drove a truck full of explosives into the headquarters of our Marines in Lebanon, and more than two hundred young men died. I wondered afterward whether I should have phoned a warning to someone. But it would have been no use. Old King Priam of Troy did not believe Cassandra either, and he was probably much more intelligent than politicians are nowadays.

It is curious to live in this way. I have gotten used to it by now, although the wonder of it never ceases to amaze me. The river of ordinary life keeps flowing on, yet there is also another one rippling alongside, sometimes hardly visible, at other times foaming up, or glowing as if hit by a sudden beam of light. An Indian friend appeared in my room one night. I did not see her face but recognized her from her skirt, and I was surrounded by the warmest, sweetest, most exquisite love. Then she was gone. A few days later I received a letter from her family: The vision came on the fourth day after she died.

In another case I could not attend the funeral of don Liborio, another special person in my life, who guided me through the maze of Mexico City when I was doing fieldwork there. I did not even know when or where it would take place, but I saw many details of it at the exact time, as if I had been a guest among guests, because I fell unaccountably asleep just then. Except what the guests did not see was that don Liborio was present too. I saw him clearly, floating above his grieving family and friends, wrapped comfortably in a silk cloth, his favorite crunched-up hat on his face, the way he liked to take a siesta. However, one detail I could not understand because I could hear nothing: Why were those present handed grey and broken bones caked with sand? It could not have been food. As I was told later, don Liborio was taken back to his small hometown to be buried there in his father's grave. Unbeknown to the family, apparently some poor people, having no money for a cemetery plot, had lifted the granite slab and interred their corpse in the secure sanctuary. The bones of the stowaway were handed around during the funeral and later replaced.

In still another instance, the grandfather of my host family in Japan died when I was there in 1982. Good old Ojiisan liked to make fun of my figure, because being a size sixteen I looked considerably more ample than the wispy Japanese ladies; he said that I could be a Sumo wrestler. I had helped with his taro and rice harvest and loved to photograph his beautiful old face and slender, nimble hands. While his ashes were still on the altar in his home before burial forty days later, I burned many sticks of incense before it, and kneeling and bowing in the proper manner, I wished him a good journey to the beyond. When I left for America, I was given a beautifully packaged box of bean confection, but with the caution that I alone was to eat it. Gifts tied with yellow and black strings, the sign of mourning, could not be passed on.

Back in Columbus, I soon had a series of strange accidents. I stumbled painfully, a burning piece of wood unaccountably jumped out of my stove and burned a hole in my cherished Chinese rug, a wine glass fell out of the cupboard and shattered on the floor, and there were others. I finally decided that Ojiisan had possibly hitched a ride on the bean confection. Even cherished friends can cause harm once they become restless ghosts. So regretfully I placed the pretty box in the fire and burned it. That night I had a vision. Ojiisan appeared, but he wore a mask, a white hood with holes for his eyes. Reproachfully he said that he enjoyed being with me, and that it made him sad that I was ordering him away. Then he disappeared. There were no more accidents, but sometimes when I think of him, I feel a twinge of remorse.

Not always are the visions concerned with death. My beloved consultant and field assistant in Yucatán, Hermana Us, a wise and motherly old Maya peasant woman who taught me how to survive in the cruel tropics, had to undergo a serious operation. I saw the threat to her life, brief but specific details of the operation, and the happy outcome long before the letter came.

Sometimes it is the life of a total stranger that for a fleeting moment appears in the waves of that ghostly river. Once I "saw" an accident. A young man in tight motorcycle garb, but without a helmet on his black, rather long hair, lay on an incline, sprawling face down on the highway. Weeks later I bought a bag of green peppers from an old man down the street. He had a sign on his lawn: "Jim's Lawnmower Repair." "Are you Jim?" I asked, for our lawn-mower needed an adjustment. No, Jim was his son, but he was in the hospital paralyzed from a motorcycle accident. I did not even connect the remark with my vision until the man began describing the scene of the accident and mentioned that his son had worn no helmet. The young man spent many months in the hospital, but against all odds he finally did recover. He does not know me, but sometimes I see him around his father's house, and it is as if there were a slight breeze coming toward me when I catch sight of him. It makes me wonder: Did I merely see the accident, or did I have a task to perform, perhaps protecting him against being killed? I remember nothing except for that brief scene, so I will never know.

Principally, however, the gift of seeing was apparently intended as a kind of channel so that I could be reached when need be. Remembering the vision under the Virgin of Guadalupe's hands, I think it was surely meant to be a message of encouragement: I was that woman looking out into the mysterious glowing room, the alternate reality that I was soon to enter. And there have been many other instances. The Old Ones showed me how to make a prayer stick that by way of its feathers takes the requests of humans to the spirit world. "Red and green on black," they kept repeating, quite severely, I thought. But then, I had really botched my first prayer stick. And the vision described in the Prologue was another teaching session. The Spirits can be demanding instructors: It took me a long time to puzzle that one out.

The gift of the Old Ones is still with me, but I cannot call it up at will. Neither can I teach it to others, and so it is safe from laboratory probing. In the meantime, however, there was a promising new development concerning the postures. In the summer of 1980 there was a letter from Vienna in the mailbox by the highway in Cuyamungue, from Adolf Holl.

CHAPTER FOUR

A New Path Opens

$\mathbf{T}$he letter from Adolf Holl concerned my paper about the discovery of the trance postures, which had aroused so little interest at the 1977 meeting of the American Anthropological Association, and which had been in the packet I had sent to his journalist friend. Holl asked if I would be willing to repeat those experiments with European participants. He was preparing a miniseries on world religions under contract with the West German educational television system, the so-called Second German Program. My research, he felt, would demonstrate to the viewers the common experiential base that all religions shared.

It had been a source of great regret to me during the intervening time that there seemed to be no way in which to continue working with the body postures and related trance experiences. So I was understandably elated at Holl's suggestion and consented with alacrity. Soon after, however, I was beset by serious doubts. With only one series of experiments, how could I be sure that the same results would be achieved again? What if we would both be embarrassed by failure? But feeling that, after all, I had some powerful friends in my corner, I consented anyway and flew to Germany in April 1981.

The first item on the agenda was a preliminary discussion with the private television firm working for the Second Program in Heidelberg. Patiently the director listened to my requests while his secretary took notes. We were going to work in a hotel, so I wanted a quiet conference room away from hotel traffic, preferably at the end of a hallway. It was to have wall-to-wall carpeting, and all furniture was to be removed. We should have some pillows or mats so we could sit on the floor, and a wall clock. A vase of flowers would be nice on a small table, and perhaps some incense. In other words, I was trying to recreate the conditions that had worked so well in Columbus. I assumed that when we arrived at the hotel, nothing would be in place, and we would have to waste a day trying to create even a semblance of the congenial environment that I considered necessary.

I had seriously underestimated German efficiency. By the time we all assembled around Easter at the luxury hotel on the shores of Lake Starnberg near Munich—Adolf Holl, the participants, the producer and his assistant, the former English and the latter German, and the sound man—everything was in place. Only the flowers were missing. So without much ado one of the girls climbed out of the window of the conference room, which was on the ground floor, and broke a few branches off the forsythia bushes in full bloom in the hotel garden. The little scene made me feel at ease. Obviously, these were not the stodgy young people that I remembered from my own German college days. They were the "alternative," the counterculture, children of the same decade that had shaped my graduate-school career. And indeed, their gay abandon and eagerness for adventure were to carry us easily through our unconventional undertaking. I placed incense in my burner, and we could go to work.

The group of participants that Adolf Holl had recruited consisted of three medical students, Uwe, Irmi, and Ingrid, an advertising copywriter by the name of Franz, who was also a long-time Zen practitioner, Kurt, a psychology student, and Doris, a secretary. Later workshops would show a similar composition: young to middle-aged, from the middle twenties to the early forties, both men and women, medical people, psychotherapists of various persuasions, usually academically trained, and quite generally those people in and out of these professions who had a keen interest in and some experience with what is generally termed consciousness-altering techniques. "We, the seekers," said a young German physician.

Understandably, everyone suffered from considerable performance anxiety. It did not exactly help that Tim, our English producer, kept assuring us, "If nothing comes of this, we can always interview the participants about why they volunteered for a crazy project like this." Actually, I was worried only about the content of the experience, not that "nothing" would happen. I knew there would be trances. After all, I had seen over and over again in fieldwork with what ease people experienced a religious trance, given the expectation and with the right stimulation, provided they concentrated properly.

Actually, concentration was a key issue. There had been one participant in the Columbus group who simply could not do that. Her mind was always on her next shopping trip, on her children, on her new husband, on everything but the task at hand. So she never experienced anything. It is a problem that preachers in Pentecostal churches also have to contend with. Those that I had observed teaching speaking in tongues had often warned that one should "think not of the matters of the world, not of whether the milpa would yield or if there would be enough money for tortillas, but only of the manifestation of the Holy Spirit." As insurance against failure due to lack of concentration,

I therefore introduced an innovation in the form of a breathing exercise. At the outset of the session, everyone was to take fifty relaxed, normal breaths, in and out, in and out. Only during inhalation could one feel the air passing over the septum; it was not perceivable when exhaling. This alternation was what the participants were supposed to observe. It was a natural, soothing rhythm, and I hoped that in addition to putting them at ease, it would also narrow attention to a single signal and thus be a suitable preparation for the subsequent rhythmic stimulation by the beat of the rattle. Experience has borne out this expectation, and we still use the exercise today. As added insurance, I also did the first session before breakfast. Fasting is a time-honored adjunct to the trance experience.

Because this was the first time I had worked with a group, it was a surprise to me how much more intense the trance was than when I had worked with each individual separately in Columbus. In addition, I also saw the participants during the time between the sessions, and we had our meals together. As a result I noticed various aftereffects of the trance that I had not observed before. There was a kind of electric, prickling excitement in the group. No wonder the early Pentecostal congregations that used trance behavior were called "enthusiastic." We laughed a lot and talked with a certain verve, casting aside as if by collusion inhibitions present under ordinary circumstances among casual acquaintances. We began sharing little confidences, experiences not usually told to outsiders. On the second morning, for instance, while we were doing the posture of the *Singing Shaman*, my heart began pounding and I saw the rattle in my hand turn into a hard-working, plump little middle-aged lady, busily bending up and down, "doing her thing," her short skirt flying. It was such a curious experience, I mentioned at breakfast afterward that the rattle had turned into "my aunt," and "aunt" it remained from then on, everybody referring to it that way, with an occasional sly wink.

There developed an urgent need to be close to each other at all times. One afternoon after a session, for instance, there was only one table for four available in the crowded dining room of the hotel. Borrowing chairs here and there, eleven of us simply squeezed around that one small table and thought it a great joke. "The hardest thing to report, though, because it is the most subtle," I wrote in my diary, "is the rapidly blossoming, the almost exploding affection of everyone toward everyone. I truthfully don't think that anybody was excluded. A pattern of hugging and kissing emerged, totally devoid of sexual overtones. It had something innocent, almost childlike, about it. It was like the dawn, the touching of fingertips in the early breeze, the converging and parting of playful waves."

Some of the hidebound and obviously very affluent tourists took offense and complained to the management. But we knew they could not throw us out; we were there on "official" business, and anyway, we did not care. We had rediscovered the exhilaration of the celebrating community, and we would not let anybody take it away. As the assistant producer told me later, when we moved to Munich for the taping, "You know, in that hotel we all lived as if under a protective glass bubble; now I have to break out of it and work, and this is all so different, cold and even antagonistic. I wish there were a way in which I could keep alive some of what we experienced."

I felt that loss also when all was over, and I found myself in the hotel lobby, totally alone again, thinking that the same miracle could not take place a second time. But I need not have mourned its passing. For every time we have a workshop, particularly if we also share meals and living accommodations, as we do at various institutions in Europe and especially at Cuyamungue, we are caught up in the same magic once more.

There was another aspect of the group trance experience emerging that I also had seen evolve in the Apostolic congregations that I knew from my fieldwork. The shared trance shapes a ring around the community, keeping the members in and closing others out. Anthropologists speak of paranoia. But that is not the heart of the matter. The group is forged into one body, as it were, by the heat of ecstasy. We had a demonstration of this when one morning Tim, our English director, instead of merely listening to the tapes in his room as he had done before, accompanied the sound man to our session. We were doing a diviner's posture, and afterward Tim did not just listen but started asking questions. He wanted "media-effective statements," he said. It was a painful intrusion, and by the time we assembled for lunch, those of us in charge had a revolt on our hands. We finally came to the conclusion that we would ask Tim not to come to the sessions again, but to rely on the tapes as he had done before. When the decision passed around the lunch table, everyone broke out into relieved, resounding laughter. We had performed an exorcism.

It was easy to understand why Tim was worried. He did not have a clear understanding of what we were doing and desperately wanted to have some back-up material in case we "fell flat." I had also been worried initially, not about the occurrence of the trance itself but, as mentioned before, about whether the curious regularity would once more appear that I had observed in Columbus, with each posture mediating a different type of experience. However, my anxiety dissolved as I continued listening to the reports during the sessions, for the agreements with what I had recorded in Columbus became more and more evident. As during those initial experiments, the overlap certainly was not restricted to somatic changes only, to the perception of heat during one posture, of cold in another, or to the distortion of time, what one of the Columbus group had called "the total collapse of the time perspective." What was actually even more striking was once more the agreement in the distinctive experiential content of the various postures. Despite a great deal of individual variation, the stability of the general character of each posture was unmistakable.

Of the diviner's posture, for instance, Anita of the Columbus group had said, "The energy went up to my head generating heat in a circular motion and creating a halo effect in the back of my head. . . . It was as if I was trying to pierce a veil, or to see the light at the end of the tunnel." In West Germany now, Ingrid was telling us that "the rattle turned into a mill wheel in my head, and I was a balloon being jettisoned outward from the wheel." The overlap could hardly be more perfect: Anita's "circular motion" as against Ingrid's mill wheel, the halo and the balloon, and wanting to pierce a veil and being jettisoned outward.

Or as another example, during the posture of the *Bear Spirit*, Bryan of the Columbus group related, "Suddenly my heart started pumping, and there was something like a passage opening up in me, a stairway or something. . . . I was just a stairway, I was nothing at all, almost like that was all I was; I wasn't even a body anymore." Compare that with Ingrid finding herself reduced to a small beetle in a very large bottle where she looked up through a narrow neck far above her. The further we progressed in our workshop, the clearer it became to me that the power of the postures was indeed overwhelming.

After three days of strenuous work, on Easter Monday, we had to leave the hospitable shores of Lake Starnberg behind and moved to a hotel in Munich, close to the large studios of the Second Program. When on Tuesday morning we went for rehearsal to the studio, I was taken aback. It was cavernous, drafty, impersonal, cluttered with cameras, platforms, booms, and huge lights dripping from the ceiling. For the television show, Adolf Holl and I had decided to do the posture from Lascaux Cave. I wondered how the ancient shaman, whose presence I had felt so keenly in Columbus, would feel about being transported from the intimacy of his cave to these frigid walls. But when we got to see for the first time the platform that the craftsmen had assembled for our program, I was mollified. We were told that it had cost the studio more than three thousand dollars to construct. It was round, about fourteen feet in diameter, padded with foam rubber, and covered with grey corduroy. While Holl and I introduced the program, the participants would sit on the platform on pink cushions. For the exercise itself, it would be cranked up to the all-important thirty-seven-degree angle.

While Holl and I rehearsed our comments and figured out where we should stand, our "experimental persons"—the "kids" by now—got acquainted with their platform. It was cranked up for them, and instead of using the ladder, they were soon exuberantly climbing all over it like so many monkeys. The footrests were too narrow, but that was remedied while we had lunch in the studio cafeteria, and afterward, we had another rehearsal.

Although the studio by now seemed less formidable, the kids still asked about the incense, which I had always lit during our earlier sessions, and which I had hoped would form a sensory bridge between the conference room and the studio. I took the matter up with the producers. They had extremely sensitive smoke detectors at the studio; smoking was allowed only in certain closed-off areas. But after some arm-twisting, I did obtain the promise that they would turn the equipment off and let us light the incense.

The show was taped the next day. I brought all the incense I had left and arranged it in water glasses on the floor around the platform. I figured the studio was so large, if the kids were to perceive the fragrance, it had to be more massive than in the conference room at the hotel. Then we watched the superb collage of scenes from previous parts of the miniseries that had been prepared by the studio staff, and which was to serve as an introduction to our program. After that, Holl and I taped our own opening segment. We had to do it twice, because there was some disturbing noise on the tape. They finally hooked a new transmitter to my belt under my skirt in the back, which cleared up the problem.

Understandably, there was general apprehension about the trance scene itself. In order not to induce the trance inadvertently, I had simulated the rattle signal by arm movements during the trial runs. But there was a scene after Holl and I finished the introduction where the participants were to demonstrate the other postures. It was visually very appealing, the platform still in horizontal position, the pink pillows, and each one of the young people in a different posture. But they had me rattle for it, and although the scene took not even a minute, some of them started going into trance. Then something went wrong, and we had to repeat the scene. There were also repeated noisy altercations in the studio, because the cameramen kept quarreling with the cable movers. At one point, the entire operation had to be halted for twenty minutes so that, because of a complicated union rule, a man could be called from someplace else in Munich to move a boom.

I had impressed on Tim that we could do the scene only once, that it could under no conditions be repeated except several hours later, that we had to have absolute silence, that no one was to move, open doors, or make any other kind of noise while I was rattling. This was of paramount importance, because although the video was to show only three minutes of that scene, we of course had to go through the entire fifteen minutes, for after a brief recovery period, Holl was going to introduce the experimental subjects and was then going to ask them to report their experiences. The tension was heightened because as before, I had given them no clue whatever about what type of adventure the posture was likely to mediate.

Tim was in charge and worked with marvelous precision. He did not just give his instructions to the crew via earphones. He came down from his perch and in remarkably good German gave a little speech repeating what I had told him, and emphasizing that absolutely nothing could go wrong or else. The platform had been cranked up, and the participants in posture lay very still in their places, an eerie twentieth-century replay of the venerable Stone Age scene. Somebody lit the incense, Tim gave me my signal through the bug in my ear, and we were off.

Half a minute later he had to stop everything. Absolutely no sound came through the equipment. "How long will it take you to fix it?" Holl wanted to know. Tim was noncommittal. "You know how technology works. You get hold of the end of a string and you can't tell how long it is." Luckily, the string was short, and once more I started rattling. It was harder than usual; fifteen minutes is awfully long even under ordinary circumstances, and here I could not see any clock. Doggedly I rattled on. At one point Irmi, stretched out at the apex of the platform, started jerking uncontrollably. Panic swept through me: Would the footrest hold? Kurt, positioned at the lower left, said later that he had perceived that Irmi was in trouble and had tried to "send help" to her. After a while she calmed down. I rattled on and on. Just before I received the signal to stop, Irmi's motions ceased.

Holl bridged the ensuing pause with a few comments on our experimental sessions, introduced the participants, and then asked each one in turn about his or her experience. He started with Ingrid, and I listened with mounting excitement:

> There was a tremendous wave of heat that moved from my feet to my head. When it arrived there, my head turned into a mountain peak. That peak kept growing higher and higher, giving me the feeling that I was the highest mountain peak in the world. The entire world stretched out before me, infinitely far and limitless, and I could see it all. Not only the earth was without boundaries, but also the sky, the entire cosmos, as it opened up above me. Then I could feel the heat no longer, and from the tip of the mountain, I fell into this infinity. A soft wind carried me through the eternal expanse. There was no distance, neither toward the horizon nor into the depth. I could allow the wind to waft me where it pleased, and it was exceedingly beautiful.

What the others had to tell was equally fascinating, each in his or her own way:

> DORIS: I also started out feeling heat, but it did not come from my feet. It started around my kidneys and streamed into my entire body. Then I had the feeling, it can't flow through, it can't get through, it is backed up in my body. I became scared; I thought I could burst. At one point, I must have opened my mouth. After a while I finally had the feeling that the heat was flowing through, and that was pleasant. I can't say that I was streaming out with this warmth, but I sure had the feeling that I was flowing away.

Uwe, apparently, had not discovered the release that opening her mouth had brought for Doris:

> For a while I was very quiet, then my entire body began vibrating very strongly. There was a strange pulling sensation coming from my ears and going toward my mouth, and a severe cramping of my face. Even after the rattle stopped, I had an awful time trying to open my mouth. It seemed to be locked and sealed.

Irmi, on the other hand, felt herself expanding like Ingrid had and then splitting open:

I was as if spread out and stretched. Then I had the impression that the rattle appeared behind me, so that I heard two rattle sounds. This being spread out gave me the impression of great space. When I started moving involuntarily, this was converted into being split lengthwise and growing upward.

For Franz, the change was very subtle but still recognizable:

I experienced entering the trance twice, and the image plane moved behind my eyes. I perceived a milky circulation. The second entry was much more intense. I suddenly heard a second rattle, which had an entirely different tone. And although I had the impression that I had fallen back out, I found myself on a vastly different plane afterward.

And finally, Kurt experienced a clear and impressive exit:

I felt a wave arise in me. It came from the extremities and was blocked here in my chest. It was a tremendous struggle, for I knew it had to rise up into my head. That was what I was struggling with, trying to open this blockage in my neck and get through into my head. I then felt a tremendous pressure in my head, and no longer perceived my body at all, only my head. I began hearing the second rattle noise, which became circular. Suddenly there was this picture; I saw this energy exiting from my head in the shape of a circle. After that, I was totally relaxed.

The cameras stopped rolling. Despite all the problems and the interruptions, the experience had come through crystal-clear. I thought the old shaman might have been pleased, just as he probably had been when so many millennia ago he had taken a piece of charcoal-and-tallow crayon and had with such sparse lines and yet so expertly drawn that figure, saying, "All right, now look here, this is what you'll have to do." And his young apprentices had settled on the hillock and, holding their hands and arms the way he had shown them, had gone on a spirit journey.

I had the urgent desire to hug the kids, but all of a sudden, I found myself surrounded by everyone in the studio, the cameramen, the man on the boom, the producers, the "picture mixer" from upstairs, and even some other technicians usually hidden in the caverns housing the controls. Immediately, right then, they also wanted to try what we had just done. Their disappointment was obvious when I pointed out that, after all, the "experimental persons" had worked with me for nearly a week; they had learned to concentrate, they had had a number of other experiences, all in preparation for this one culminating event. "See, I told you," the woman who had done the picture mixing said, as on a cue from Tim, all went back to their places to tape the concluding section that Holl and I still had to do. "Do you realize," Kurt said to me afterward, "that you just witnessed a miracle? These people here in the studio are a thoroughly jaded audience. You should have heard their snide remarks when we were getting ready to tape. All about one more circus and on like that."

"After that, all was painful dissolution," I wrote in my diary. But our story did not end there. We are still in touch, some as friends, such as Doris and Irmi. Ingrid Mueller organized the medical research in Munich, mentioned before, in conjunction with her medical doctoral dissertation. Franz and Uwe were two of the four subjects who volunteered for those tests. And Kurt's enthusiastic reports brought the first participants to the ensuing workshops which I have continued on a regular basis in Europe every spring.

Going on with more workshops was actually the most important development that came out of our television project. The idea originated with Franz. He was the cofounder of the Buddhist Center in Scheibbs (Austria). On the day before the taping, as we were all walking through Vienna, laughing and munching strawberries, he suddenly turned to me and said, "I'd like you to give me copies of those drawings of the postures that we used. Maybe in Scheibbs I could do a seminar like we just had." Then, before I could even answer, he laughed, put his arm around me, and, switching into his earthy Austrian dialect, continued, "Naw. . . . Actually, why should the little smith do it when we can have the real smith?"

CHAPTER FIVE

The Way of the Spirits

The first workshop that Franz organized in the Buddhist Center in Scheibbs (Austria) took place in 1982. He published the announcement in the schedule of the center, and a few of the regulars became interested. Others had seen the television show. Kurt, also of the television workshop, told friends in Vienna about his experiences, and they came to Scheibbs to find out more. Yolanda of a later Scheibbs workshop was from Switzerland. The next spring, she got some friends together, they rented suitable quarters in a mountain resort, and we did a workshop there. A stop in Switzerland has become an institution since then, part of my yearly spring tour, which at this writing covers five European countries.

In this country, the development of the workshops took off slowly. For several summers in a row, I taught anthropology courses at Cuyamungue Institute. However, with the connection to Denison University, my home institution, weakening with the years, recruiting undergraduates became more and more difficult. Increasingly also, that was really no longer what I wanted to do. It was at this juncture that summer workshops comfortably fitted into the premises already available there.

The participants in both Europe and this country represent pretty much the same groups. For many of them, what they are learning in the workshops is simply yet another step on the path to finding out more about themselves. "Esoteric tourists," as one of my friends calls them, are a characteristic feature of our waning century. Others, especially those in the health-care professions, often make the postures and the trance part of their therapeutic activity. Still others give workshops of their own. But the workshops spread acephalously, as anthropologists would say, that is, without a head. An inexpensive newsletter published by the institute announces my program and reports on ongoing research, keeping the lines of communication open, but there is no organization collecting dues or issuing certificates for teaching activity, which is beginning to blossom in a number of other places. The institute itself is a research-and-teaching institution concentrating solely on trance workshops. For many participants, however, Cuyamungue has developed into something of a place of pilgrimage, and taking a workshop has become a highly prized experience.

The grounds of Cuyamungue are an informal wildlife refuge, open to outsiders only during workshops. The house we built over a number of years is now occupied year-round by members of the institute who act as administrators for the workshops and issue the newsletter. The wooden Student Building that we were working on during the summer of my initiation has served us well ever since. It has a long dining table and benches, showers, and a kitchen corner, a thickly insulated roof, mimicking the bushes and the rocks of the arroyos that dispense such cool, protective shade, and a double wall with cracks between the boards, so the wind can waft in and out and keep it fresh. Tiny flycatchers and bluebirds have come to nest between the boards in the spring, and the big-eyed desert mice have discovered the crawlspace underneath, as has their nemesis, the ever-hungry bull snake. A thieving pack rat, recently moved in, has been less welcome. Some summers ago I had a Dutch visitor, a Shinto priest with a passion for shaving his head every morning. The pack rat stole his razor, and he was reduced to borrowing the small safety razor one of the girls used to shave her legs.

Outside the Student Building, I started a vegetable garden. Its mention brings a resigned smile to the lips of my Hispanic neighbors, who helped me plant the fruit trees, and who are expert gardeners themselves. Whoever heard of letting the weeds intentionally take over a garden? For in my garden, the wild ones are invited in. The chiles and the tomatoes and the leaf lettuce and the variety of herbs without which I cannot cook grow topsy-turvy, doing the best they can between Indian tea and mullein and mountain sage, Mexican hat, primroses and bluebells, and dozens of other plants the names of which I have not yet learned that have settled in, brought by the birds and by the ever-singing, ever-driving wind. And from the moist and sheltered place, their seeds now travel outward and are beginning to recolonize the hills about, cruelly denuded by many decades of overgrazing.

We also have some other structures on the land now, a shaded arbor in the back of the Student Building, a favorite of the hummingbirds who come to suck syrup from the feeder there, a shed built in the Hispanic style we use for storage, and a large rectangular adobe shell, the Library, where we can set up our cots when we need to get out of the rain, and where I present an occasional puppet show to the children of the region. It looks out on the land with its two front windows set high, the masked face of a kachina. But the true heart of the land is the kiva.

I no longer remember when exactly it occurred to me that what I needed as a classroom was a kiva. One day, I simply found the suggestion "in my head," like one would a melody, or a poem, a gift from the other, the sacred side. Since white people are barred from entering these sacred buildings of the Pueblo Indians that are still in use, I went around to prehistoric ruins, trying to figure out how the people of old had created their round, semi-underground structures. And then I designed one like them. Only ours has an entrance from the ground level for the greater safety of the participants, not the traditional one with a ladder through the roof. Just like the traditional kivas, ours has no electricity, getting its light from two windows and the panes flanking the door.

From the start, the kiva was special. One summer a workshop participant swore that when she got up in the Library one dark and starless night to go to the bathroom in the Student Building, the empty kiva was lit from the inside, an orange glow suffusing the entire building.

"Did you look through the window to see what was going on?" I asked.

"Oh heavens no," she said, "I wouldn't have dared."

There are those who like to sleep in the kiva, because it is a warm and closed shelter, and the dreams are mysterious and easily remembered, but not everyone is welcome. A German friend, a writer who shall remain unnamed here, came only to visit and wanted no part of any trance experience. "The idea that you might put me into trance," she protested, "makes my soul roll up in fear like a hedgehog." The first night she slept in the kiva, a big drop of water splashed on her face. She moved her cot, and another drop hit the mark. She moved again, then went back with her flashlight to examine the puddle that should have formed on the floor had there been a leak, but could not find any. Another guest, a relative on a tour of the Southwest, heard a mouse run across the ceiling and then slap noisily on the flagstone floor. "The fall must have broken every bone in its body," he remarked. "But this morning, I could not find any dead mouse."

The most dramatic kiva story happened to my friend Hans Peter Duerr, a German anthropologist and best-selling author, who came to Cuyamungue in June of 1981. He later told about it in a small volume of occasional pieces entitled *Satyricon*.[1] A few days before Hans Peter's visit, I was sitting in front of the Student Building with a friend from Albuquerque. Suddenly we saw a large predatory bird circling over the hills toward the west. As it came closer, we recognized that it was an eagle. I had never seen an eagle in our area, and I marveled at its size and the majestic circles it was now describing directly above us. When Hans Peter arrived, the eagle was still very much on my mind, and it was one of the first things I talked about. To our mutual surprise, he had just had an encounter with an eagle himself, at the Sun Dance of the Cheyenne Indians.

Hans Peter had been invited to the Cheyenne by Dr. Schlesier, a German ethnographer doing fieldwork there. As he was sitting among the guests watching the Sun Dance, he closed his eyes for a moment and suddenly saw a bright light on the horizon. As it came closer, he realized that it was an eagle. It finally stopped directly before him and turned its head as if wanting to look him over. The eagle was so close that Hans Peter saw every detail of the bird's eye as it was steadily scrutinizing him. Startled, he said to Schlesier, "Hey, look what came by!" Needless to say, Schlesier saw nothing, but he suggested that Hans Peter go to the Arrowkeeper, the Cheyenne Holy Man, and tell him about his vision. The Arrowkeeper explained to him that the whistles the dancers were blowing were made from eagle bone and that it signaled great good fortune that the Eagle Spirit had chosen to appear to him. The Eagle Spirit, he said, was very powerful, and it did not matter that Hans Peter was a white man, he would still be blessed.

We both felt that the eagle that my guest and I had seen had announced Hans Peter's arrival, and that indeed, the Eagle Spirit had taken a liking to him. I asked him whether he had properly thanked the Eagle, perhaps by a small gift of tobacco? After all, I argued, Hans Peter being an anthropologist, he should realize that he had been invited into a world of reciprocity with his vision, where each gift merits another one in return. But Hans Peter procrastinated, and I did not press the point.

We spent some pleasant days together; there were guests, we went sightseeing, and the return gift to the Eagle Spirit had obviously been forgotten. On Saturday morning, as always, we were using the adjoining bathrooms of the Student Building, and Hans Peter asked through the thin board wall whether I had removed the lid of his soap dish. He was sure that he had put it on tightly to keep the mice from eating the soap, and several times, he had found it off. I had not been in his bathroom, so I said, "Who knows, perhaps the Spirits are teasing you because there is something important you haven't done yet, like presenting a gift to the Eagle."

This time, to my surprise, he was apparently quite eager to carry out the small ritual. We walked together up to the ridge, where I usually say a blessing before sunrise and after sunset and scatter some cornmeal. He not only offered the Eagle his due, but even had a pinch of meal for my Friend, leaving me still to wonder about the reason for his change of heart. On the way down, he suddenly asked, "Tell me, the kind of rattle you use, is that available locally?"

"Yes."

"Do you have one here?"

"No, I left mine in Columbus and have not gotten around to buying another one yet."

Then the story came out. After our dinner guests had left the night before, Hans Peter had retired to the kiva to go to bed, closing the door behind him. He was wide awake, listening to the concert of the crickets outside. Suddenly he heard a loud rattling in front of the door and thought that I was trying to play a practical joke on him. As he tells in the *Satyricon,*

> I got out of my sleeping bag, opened the door, and checked. I could see the entire area clearly in the bright moonlight, but saw no one, not even a rattlesnake on the

ground. The rattling had stopped, and I crawled back into the sleeping bag. I felt very unwell, and the only thing that I could think of was to "call" the Eagle Spirit. Suddenly, the cot began to jerk violently three times in succession at an interval of several seconds, and I thought, "How in the world am I going to get out of this situation?" Then I had the feeling that the Eagle was there, in the kiva, spreading his wings over me. (1982:84–85)

During all this time, the noise of the crickets had stopped, and there was a deathly silence outside. Just as suddenly, all was over, the crickets went back to their music, and Hans Peter fell asleep. He was quite shaken by it all. "And to think," he writes, "that twenty years ago I officially left the Church!"

I think the reason Hans Peter was treated so roughly in the kiva was that he had shown disregard not only for reciprocity but also for ritual. But why should ritual be so important to the Spirits? Because ritual is the means of communication for them, as important as speech is for us. In fact, there can be no religious ceremony without ritual. This is a simple fact, known to all religious communities the world over. Ritual is the rainbow bridge over which we can call on the Spirits and the Spirits cross over from their world into ours. The question is, of course, why would they even want to? Because they are so much wiser than we. They know something that we in the West all too often forget, namely, that the ordinary and the other reality belong together. They are two halves of one whole. Only their joining will make a complete world, a world worth living in. The existence of humans is empty without the Spirits, but theirs is equally incomplete without involving us, and the world about us. Although they are so much more powerful than we are, in this sense they need us.

As an anthropologist, I of course knew all of this in theory. But being a recent immigrant in an unfamiliar country, I too had to learn many new rules, so to speak, from the bottom up. Dimly at first, as when I asked the Spirit of the Shrine to accompany me to the mass to say farewell to Tom, I began to understand that these Beings were standing ready to be our helpers and our friends. All we had to do was ask them, and they responded instantly and in startlingly tangible ways. I had experienced this many times before, but never more thrillingly than at a workshop I offered at the *Volkshochschule*, an adult education institution in Salzburg (Austria) in the spring of 1984.[2]

It had snowed on this day in April, and the snow continued to fall gently as the group of more than thirty people assembled for a session in the large hall on the second floor. We were doing the posture of the Singing Shaman (see Chapter 11). At my suggestion, the participants started singing to the rattle, and soon the initial open *a* vowel (as in *father*) began to increase in volume under the effect of the trance, and the many voices united in a powerful chorale, with the many pulsing glossolalia phrases rising from it like so many sparkling flames.

That morning, before coming to the session, I had leafed through a new

German publication on shamanism,[3] and I noted a section where the author quoted the Hungarian folklorist Vilmos Diószegi. It seems that during a trip to Siberia, Diószegi visited an old shaman, whom he found lying on his cot, weak and chronically ill. When the folklorist began asking him about his past shamanistic activity, though, the old man became animated and visibly gained strength. At this session now, as the group in front of me was beginning to sway lightly, and some were trembling under the effect of the trance, and I felt the wave of energy that started streaming toward me, I suddenly thought of something. If what I was perceiving had any sort of reality, it should actually be possible to gather it up, to concentrate it like ball lightning, and to dispatch it to an old shaman like the one Diószegi met, to console him and to heal him. So while rattling on, I spoke to my Friend and asked him to be our messenger. Idly I was thinking of the surroundings of a shaman in Siberia, the endlessly undulating low shrubs on the dark and mucky tundra, the snarling dogs, his black felt tent dusted with snow, when all of a sudden I was startled by my rattle slipping in my hand and leaning over to the left. Brought out of my reverie, I grabbed hold of it. But a minute or so later, the rattle did it again, this time jerking noticeably to the right. I was puzzled. Had we actually sent out something and, like an echo, it was being returned to us?

At the conclusion of the rattling, the participants settled down on the rug, and since the group was so large, I did not call on everyone but asked for volunteered comments. I did not mention the favor I had asked of my Friend, or the strange behavior of the rattle. I felt that that was my secret, which I was not obligated to share.

There were the reports expectable for this posture—how they had felt extremely hot, how the muscles of the chest had become stiff, and how the singing had seemed to become independent of volition. Some talked of their hearts beating fast and of weeping. There was nothing that I had not heard before, and my attention flagged a bit as I looked out through the window on the soft snow that in the dusk was continuing to fall, when to my left a young woman started to speak. "Actually, nothing remarkable happened to me," she said. "I think I probably continued in the ordinary state of consciousness all the way through. And then there came this very large yellow butterfly, and it settled here on my left upper arm, and I could feel exactly how its legs affectionately pressed around it."

It all sounded so commonplace that I smiled and answered, "Oh, I see, and all that happened while you were in the ordinary state of consciousness!" Then what she had said sunk in. It took my breath away, and tears came to my eyes. Not only had our missile reached its goal, but we had also received a greeting in return.

A week later I conducted a workshop at the Forum in Freiburg. I had given the introductory lecture, and we had held the first trance session. The meeting room was in the front of the building, and the traffic noise seemed to distract the participants, so their concentration was not as complete as I had wished. At any rate, I was not too happy with the results. That at least was the explanation that occurred to me. Or had the fault been mine? I decided to give it my all during the next session.

Once more, we did the Singing Shaman. I started rattling. Usually I keep my eyes open, because I want to observe the participants. But this time, I closed them in order to be able to concentrate more fully. As soon as I started rattling, something truly surprising happened. As if drawn by a crayon of gold, an old man appeared in front of a wall of fog, but only the upper part of his body. His deeply creased face was serious, inwardly directed. It showed Mongolian features, almond-shaped eyes and high cheekbones. His grey hair, which was short and waved in the wind, hung down on a crumpled collar. He did not look at me but up at the sky, and he held his arms extended as if in prayer. If I could only see him long enough so that I'll remember everything, I thought, as I desperately tried to keep my rattling even. But in an instant he was gone, the image wiped away, and I was left with only that ephemeral sweetness that often followed an ecstasy.

What had been discovered by serendipity soon became a new ritual, namely, always asking my Friend to participate in the sessions. And just as I had done it the first time, I expressed such requests when I started rattling and with the barest movement of my lips. As I became more experienced in ritual matters, it also felt appropriate at the outset of a workshop to invite all the Spirits that I felt were hovering about to come and be our guests, by rattling toward the four directions, as well as toward the earth and the sky, and then to scatter a pinch of cornmeal as an offering of welcome.

That the latter ritual was proper and, in fact, expected was brought home to me some time later. This was in Cincinnati, and I had a group that included several psychiatrists, a Protestant preacher, and a Catholic priest. I felt that it might be tactless under these circumstances to confront the group with something that would be "unscientific" to some, and most certainly "pagan" to some of the others, so I skipped the opening ritual.

After the first morning session I felt unaccountably tired, and in the intermission, I settled down on the rug and tried to sleep. Instead of sleeping, however, I immediately slipped into a brief vision. I was holding a small object and eagerly hid it under my pillow. Touching it gave me an indescribable feeling of joy and yet also yearning. I knew that what I had hidden was something that I needed in order to resolve a situation. But when I came to, I could remember neither what "it" was nor what the problem was that I needed it for. So I went over my notes before the start of the next session, and then I understood. Ordinarily when I invite the Spirits, they announce their presence with a gust of wind that one of the participants feels. Not once had it been reported this time. Obviously, they expected to be invited, and I had neglected to do so. Humbled, I stepped into the center of the room before the next session and went through the requisite ritual. I knew all was well when Jill, the Protestant minister, told about seeing the "Wind Spirits" dance during the following posture.

This particular workshop was a learning experience for me also for another reason. After not carrying out the ritual that was expected of me, I made a second mistake. I taught the group a posture that was unfamiliar even to those who had worked with me before, the *Calling of the Spirits* (see Chapter 11). It is somewhat similar to another one, that of the *Feathered Serpent* (see Chapter 13). For the Calling of the Spirits, I usually ask my Friend to help us achieve the experience. In the case of the Feathered Serpent, I appeal in addition to that mighty source of life and fertility directly. Perhaps because of a brief lapse of attention and the similarity of the two postures, I made the mistake of calling on the Serpent. No sooner had I spoken the wrong request than I noticed it and corrected myself, apologizing to the Venerable Ancient One for troubling her inappropriately.

When it came to the telling of the experience, I called on Diane first. It was a random choice, but this young psychiatrist had done a workshop with me previously, and I knew how gifted she was. I expected her even at the first try to turn into a tree or something similar, as happens during this posture, and to see the Spirits approaching. Instead, this is what she told:

> My mouth became very large and dry, and then snakes started coming out of it, very many snakes, and I don't even like snakes. Then a very large snake followed, and my mouth and throat became white, as if coated· with clay. After that, some Essences arrived and started making a hole in the roof, so that the snakes would be able to leave.

Diane was the only one who saw the Serpent, and she clearly helped to guide the snakes out. The incident taught me an important lesson about the power of a conjuring ritual. I also comprehended once more that this was a gentle world. No lightning struck my stupid head; there was only the indulgent wagging of a finger. I could almost hear my Friend say, "It's all right, but try to be more careful next time."

As far as postures were concerned, I initially taught only those that we had explored in Columbus during my various courses. In fact, I was under the illusion that the postures that I had discovered were peculiar to the particular societies who represented them in their art, the Indian fishermen of the Pacific coast, for instance, or the Nupe of sub-Saharan Africa. Actually, there had been a faint signal that this was the wrong view, but I did not understand it. For soon after we did the TV show, a friend pointed out that the thirty-seven-degree angle was not peculiar to the Lascaux Cave shaman. It appeared in Egypt as well, although about twelve thousand years later. With an altered position of the right arm, which is stretched upward, it is at this angle that the god Osiris rises toward the heavens (pl. 5). According to classical Egyptian tradition, Osiris's twin brother Set dismembered him. His mother, together

Plate 5

with his sisters, put him back together again, and whole once more, he was then ready to join the other gods in their sky home.

The divine twins, the dismemberment, and the reassembly, as well as the spirit journey to the world above, are all shamanic elements, known from the Mediterranean, from Siberia, and from the Americas. We may therefore assume that originally Osiris was a shaman, for the figure contains elements of this role and seems to point to the fact that shamanism in this form once predominated around the Mediterranean, from southern France all the way to Egypt. What is remarkable is that these elements were preserved in northern Africa over such an enormous time span, especially in light of the fact that we are dealing with two different cultural types. The shaman of Lascaux was without a doubt a hunter, like everyone during that period. Osiris, on the other hand, changed into a god of the much more recent agriculturalists on the Nile, without, however, losing his original character. Nor indeed did the Egyptians lose the knowledge about the correct posture, especially about the proper angle for ascending to the sky world.

I took the agreement to be an engaging coincidence and was too dull to look any further. What is even more chastening is that it took me two more years to realize the significance of the fact that here we had a revealing, completely independent confirmation of the experiences reported in connection with this posture. My participants had risen to the sky world, too, without any prior knowledge whatsoever of the connection to Osiris's resurrection, body posture, and angle of ascent.

As to the wide-ranging occurrence of the postures, I was not to remain blind much longer. Friends from various workshops began looking around in museums and in books of "primitive" art, and they realized what I had not seen. A number of the postures we had done also appeared elsewhere, and there were others, perhaps equally potent but unfamiliar to us, that occurred over and over again in various parts of the world. Clearly, we were dealing not with a few curious, isolated local ritual patterns but with a behavior and no doubt an attendant knowledge having a worldwide distribution. Not only that, this very frequent occurrence also meant that most of the thirty-odd postures which we eventually identified had to be extremely old. Actually, we knew this intuitively. I recall hearing the well-known American flutist Herbie Mann speak about playing a three-thousand-year-old Maya flute, and of the thrill he felt as the moisture of his breath activated the fragrance of the ancient clay. That was exactly what we experienced as we went on exploring these various postures. The Old People began to talk to us, awakening anew in the unfathomable depths of time.

Gradually, as I was seeking to put order into the seeming chaos by identifying just which societies were involved in the phenomenon, I began to understand that here was a cultural complex that the ancient hunter-gatherers did not just know about but of course must have invented eons ago. It became apparent that the Lascaux Cave shaman was only the most ancient example we had been able to find of the pictorial or sculptural representation of an important feature of ancient religious rituals, of a way to establish contact with another dimension of reality. It was then brought to full flowering by the horticulturalists, the hunter-gardeners that followed the hunter-gatherers and who gave us so many telling representations of the postures in their art.

For important cultural reasons, there was an occasional crossover between distant cultural types, as in the case of the Lascaux Cave shaman, the hunter, to the Egyptian agriculturalists' god Osiris, illuminating some historical accident, but these instances were relatively rare. Instead, a few postures remained for various reasons the exclusive property of the hunters in the course of historical development, while others passed on to the horticulturalists and there were retained unaltered, as happened, for instance, in the case of the Bear Spirit (Chapter 8) or the Singing Shaman (Chapter 11). Or new ones were enthusiastically elaborated, as in the case of those leading to metamorphosis (Chapter 10). The entire complex vanished with the advent of full-scale agriculture. This insight was very useful; it meant that we were not facing the almost unmanageable task of searching all the records of art, but had to consider only those found in these types of societies.

However, despite the obvious antiquity of the postures, what made work with them so enjoyable from the start was the fact that they mediated experiences that we moderns could relate to. It was easy to celebrate with the Singing Shaman, to go on a spirit journey with other postures, or to open up to healing. One reason, as I saw it, was that we still possessed the same nervous system as those humans that lived so long ago. So basically, although surely not as masterfully, we could do what they were able to accomplish. The other reason was that horticulturalists were cousins to the agriculturalists, from whom we descended. But there were two postures, one that apparently had never made it into horticulture and another one that did, where the cultural gap was so pronounced that when we tried them, we felt like strangers in a strange land.

One of these postures was that of *Bone Pointing* (pl. 4), mentioned briefly in Chapter 2. It is an Australian posture which for obvious geographic reasons could not spread outward from there. The aboriginal societies practicing it believe that only the deaths of young children and of the old are due to natural causes. When mature adults die, it is as a result of murder by "magical" means. Bone pointing is used to take revenge on the murderer by hitting him with an invisible but deadly missile.

In order to carry out this execution, the avenging shaman folds his right leg under him, while his left leg is upright and bent at the knee. His left hand holds the bone, with his arm resting against his left knee, and his right hand touches his left wrist and serves for sighting. My participants, who were generally unaware of the ethnographic context, usually experienced a tremendous flow of energy which seemed to come from the earth, course through their bodies, and explode out of the end of the stick they were holding in lieu of the bone. Othmar, of the 1984 Scheibbs group, related,

> It was amazing how my left hand kept vibrating more and more as if supercharged with energy. Then that stopped, and I saw a small tree with its branches hanging down. They had slender thorns on them. To the left of the tree there was a small being, something like a dwarf, who remained motionless. The landscape was that of a steppe; the ground was brown, and there was a puddle of water which reflected a white skeleton. In the distance, the grass was burning, animals fled by me, and then I saw a man, but only his legs. Then I saw the tree again.

In this experience, Othmar did not just conduct the energy but was himself the invisible spear that emerged through the stick, the surrogate bone, and went in search of his victim. The Australian landscape is surprisingly complete—the color of the plain, the grass fire, even down to the puddle of a water hole and the thorny vegetation—except that it is the Australian outback in the alternate reality, as indicated by the motionless dwarf and the skeleton reflected in the water, foreshadowing the deadly intent. However, Othmar does not have murder on his mind, so when he comes upon his quarry, the attack is aborted; he sees only the legs. Whoever it was he encountered remains unharmed, and he is taken back to the tree. No wonder that Franz, who did the posture several times, eventually refused to repeat it, as he said, because he was afraid that he "might do too much," that is, actually carry out the aggressive act and hurt someone in the alternate reality. We know of many societies where it is believed that such injury can cause illness and even death in ordinary reality.

Plate 6

The second hunter's posture is one frequently represented. Once we started looking for it, we found traces of it on the Northwest Coast (pl. 6), pecked out on rocks in California (pl. 7a), painted on a jar in Cochiti Pueblo (pl. 7b), and cut into a menhir in Sweden (pl. 7c). It was known in prehistoric times in Florida and Peru, in the Sahara, in New Guinea and islands of the South Pacific. Gerhard Binder, an artist from Austria and the illustrator of this volume, and I explored it one summer in Cuyamungue. The posture involves standing with legs apart and knees somewhat bent, although some stick figures also stand straight, which was what we elected to do to make things easier on ourselves. The arms are raised to shoulder height; the elbows are bent, so that the lower arms are nearly at right angles to the upper arms; and the fingers are spread.

The following is my journal entry:

> Cuyamungue, 29 August 1985
> This morning after the sunrise ritual we decided to go to the kiva for a session. We had not done anything for several days, and felt that special yearning of wanting to "go home." I suggested that we do that petroglyph posture that looks almost like a child's drawing in its simple directness, and which neither one of us had tried before. I had taped my rattling, so I was also able to participate.
>
> After the breathing I turned on the tape, assumed the posture, and closed my eyes expectantly. But as soon as the rattle sound started, the tape began behaving so outlandishly that I thought that either the recorder was malfunctioning or the batteries had gone berserk. First the signal was extremely loud and fast, then it slowed down and became almost inaudible, and from then on it kept going up and down like a roller coaster. I wanted to turn toward the tape recorder to see what was going on, but found myself frozen in the posture and unable to move. Finally, the tape settled down, but by that time, the fifteen minutes were nearly over. I had a searing pain in the shoulders which later dissolved. I had not seen anything, but felt as if I consisted of nothing but enormous hot, radiating palms.

Gerhard had also heard the tape acting strangely and described exactly what I had heard, but since he did not feel responsible for the equipment, he simply screened it out, and concentrated on his experience instead:

> The sound of the rattle started off with a bang. A line passed through my body; there was power that entered into my hands. My hands started getting bigger, and that power flowed through them. I felt that I was passing over into a simpler form; a round hole opened in me that reached down to the ground. Then I became amorphous. A sheaf appeared; I embraced it with tremendous force. It was very

bright, yellow, then turned bluish-white. I fell on the ground with it in my arms and rolled on and on over the stubbles on a field that I knew from my childhood. It used to be a field, it isn't anymore. The sound of the rattle was very loud, like a tremendous roll of thunder, and I seemed to be making powerful sounds myself. At that point I started turning toward you. I can still feel it in my belly how strongly my energies were stimulated.

The feeling that we had experienced something extraordinary persisted throughout the day. My hands felt like sieves; they were leaking my life force, energy, I didn't know exactly what.

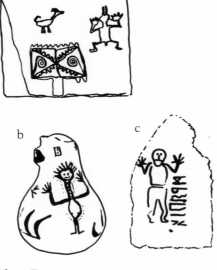

In the evening, we were sitting in the Student Building, and Gerhard was working on a choker of porcupine quills. I had spotted the animal on the shoulder of the highway near the Mescalero Indian reservation some time back. It probably had been hit by a car and was still warm when I pulled out its quills. I used them later to make necklaces for my marionettes. There were some trimmed quills left over when Gerhard had finished the choker, so I said, "Keep those, too, really, I can always get more." I had no idea how; I had not seen any porcupines in our area.

Plate 7

We both felt the urgent need to get some answers about the puzzling posture, so we decided to do the posture of the *Tennessee diviner* (see Chapter 7) before sunup the following day. I woke up before my alarm sounded, and as I lay quietly in my sleeping bag, looking up at the paling stars, I heard a curious sound, "Swush, swush, swush, swush," rhythmical and persistent. Finally it became softer and then fell silent. I was sure there was no insect that sang that way. It was not until I imitated the sound for Gerhard that I realized that I had heard my own rattle. We had had forerunner experiences around here before, where the perception anticipates the event often by an hour or more, so it wasn't so startling, but it still seemed to signal the dawn of a special day.

We went to the kiva, painted our faces as required in this posture, and then assumed it. I had injured my left knee months earlier, but it no longer gave me any trouble. However, unaccountably it now started hurting unbearably. In agony, I tried to change the posture, but at that moment, I reared up and I *was* a wounded animal. It was an unbelievably strong experience, that rearing up, the very pinnacle of ecstasy. Then an overwhelming force pushed me down and I collapsed.

Gerhard had worn the cap of the Tennessee diviner, which I had recreated and which tends to sharpen the images (see pl. 12), and as a result his experience was even more elaborate than usual:

> The cap seemed to make my skull transparent. I saw a bright light when the rattle started and had to turn my head to the right. The kiva had an exit in the back. I was brightly illuminated from the back. Then it turned dark again and I could see myself. That picture dissolved and I asked my question. At the exit the stickman appeared in the posture we had done, except that he had his legs apart and his knees bent. Simultaneously, the sound of the rattle changed. The figure glowed brightly and was gay and pleasant. I climbed into it from the back. In front of me everything was brightly lit, behind me it was dark, and I as the figure was the partition. It all felt very positive, as though I were being saturated with sun energy.
>
> Then I stepped out of the figure, again toward the back. I saw a sphere, and I climbed into that and was being propelled forward like a bubble. I stood on the summit of a mountain and kept calling, "Grandfather Bear, Grandfather Bear." He came and treated me by scratching the inside of my mouth and the nape of my neck. Then the stick figure appeared again; there was a lot of light, but I didn't know if it was day or night. I asked the same question once more and was given to understand that the hunter needed the posture, it was completely clear at the moment why, but now I don't remember it anymore. Then everything turned grey. I was in a teepee at sunrise. An old Indian sat in the tent; he had sparkling eyes, and he wore an animal skin, the skin of a buffalo. Together, we looked out into the dawn. A rug covered the floor of the teepee, once more showing the stick figure, which glowed. He said that he would tell me a story, but then the rattle stopped.

When we stepped out of the kiva, the sky was still pale. The moon had sent all the stars to bed and was making ready to retire herself, but the sun had not yet risen. With Kizzie, my German shepherd, joining us as always, we walked up to the ridge to speak the morning's blessing. Kizzie behaves perfectly during such rituals; she never jumps up on anybody and does not beg to have her ball thrown. She just settles down patiently, her front paws crossed, and waits until we are done. This morning, however, she was restless. She went over the edge of the hill, stopped by a juniper bush down a ways on the other side, and started to growl, her hackles raised. Curious, we followed her, and there under the bush, nearly hidden by the branches, sat a porcupine. It was completely motionless, and as silly as this may sound, I swear it was grinning at us.

I grabbed Kizzie by her collar to save her from harm, for although porcupines do not shoot their quills at attackers as popularly believed, even a sniff at the animal's armor might have turned her snout into a pin cushion. So I took her with me up on the ridge, spoke the blessing, and scattered the meal offering, and then we went down and were afraid to look back for fear that the engaging miracle we had seen would be there no longer. And indeed, when Gerhard went back at noon, the porcupine was gone. Had it been there? We had seen it, but then, we might still have been in a residual trance. However, it was Kizzie who had discovered the animal. What had happened?

Porcupines are no strangers to the Southwest, and being animals that feed mainly at night, it was understandable that I had not seen one on my land before. But the question was, why had it appeared at that particular spot on that particular morning? Going back over what we had experienced, I think that the hunters' posture that we had assumed was one designed to call the animals. We both had stimulated our bodies in trance and broadcast our call through our palms, as an antenna radiates microwaves, so powerfully that it even sent the tape recorder reeling. And we had given shape and direction to that energy by handling the porcupine quills. Perhaps if it had been a deer tail, it would have been picked up by that animal. The porcupine answered our summons, and since it was willing to sacrifice itself, it was probably bewildered and pleasantly surprised that it did not end up on our spit.

Of course, there was, as always, a great deal more that we were taught. For in the trance, we were both hunter and hunted. Gerhard the hunter embraced the sheaf of grain that he had cut as a stand-in for the game and rolled on the earth with it. But Gerhard the kill had a hole in his body and was reduced to a simpler form, and then to the ephemeral state of spirit substance. When we asked the wise old man from Tennessee for clarification by assuming his divining posture, he patiently went over our experience. The wounded animal passes through the ecstasy of dying, he seemed to be saying. The hunter is the partition; before him is the light of life, behind him the darkness of death. But there is renewal of life in the healing power of the mighty Bear. That was the message, as full and round and complete as the bubble that Gerhard stepped into. But the rattle continued on, and our forbearing teacher started the explanation over again, using different imagery this time. In the teepee the stick figure glows on the rug: you see, above it is light, below it one sinks into the darkess of the earth. "We hear you," we are tempted to answer.

Anyone who has read ethnographies of hunter societies[4] cannot help but be struck by how genuine these two trance experiences feel, except that they take us a step further, into the secret heart of the hunter. And indeed I am sometimes asked whether it is not an inadmissible intrusion into occulted secret worlds not our own when we imitate these ancient postures. Obviously, the Spirits do not think so, or they would not have invited us into their world. But these questioners do not know enough history either. For we are not intruding: we are merely trying to find our way home. Once, very long ago, our ancestors were equally hunter-gatherers, part of their habitat instead of its destroyers. Later, someplace along the way, we went wrong and we closed the door on this gentle ancient world. We started conquering the habitat, first by the plow and then by science. That was the Fall. As D. H. Lawrence says in speaking of the Hopi Snake Dance,

> We have undertaken the scientific conquest of forces, of natural conditions. It has been comparatively easy, and we are victors. . . . The Hopi sought the conquest by means of the mystic, living will that is in man, pitted against the will of the dragon-cosmos. . . . We have made a partial conquest by other means. Our corn doesn't fail us: we have no seven years' famine, and apparently need never have. But the other thing fails us, the strange inward sun of life. . . . To us, heaven switches on daylight, or turns on the shower-bath. We little gods are gods of the machine only. It is our highest. Our cosmos is a great engine. And we die of *ennui*. (1934:77)

What D. H. Lawrence could not foresee in 1934 was that in addition to dying of boredom, we may also perish in a nuclear holocaust. Perhaps the secret of the postures was revealed by design. Along with so many other new movements that we see all around us, going in the same direction toward "the strange inward sun of life," it may be one more attempt to turn us around. To that purpose, it seems to me, the postures are uniquely suited. They take us to strange and beautiful worlds. They teach us to divine, to heal, and to celebrate. They comfort us and soothe our fears, better than any of our scientific achievements. And they thrill us with ever-renewed, never-predictable adventure, adding the very stuff of miracles to a modern existence that all too often is drab and unappealing.

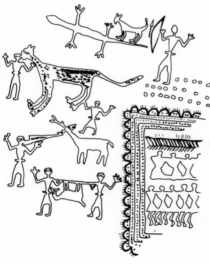

Plate 8

Postscript. After the completion of this manuscript, I received copies of two examples of aboriginal and/or folk art, which in the most surprising way confirm our experiences with the porcupine. The first one is a petroglyph composition from South Africa (Holm, fig. 28). A tall shaman, his arms raised in the characteristic manner, is surrounded by a massive school of fish. The heads of most of the fish point in his direction. To the left beyond the fish there are seven small boats, each one manned by a fisherman armed with a long spear, aiming at the fish. One fish has been speared, and the fisherman is making ready to pull it into his boat.

The second picture (pl. 8) is a wall painting from Saora in the Koraput district of Orissa, India. In Saora, it is customary to hire masters of the art of *Ittal* painting, to paint pictures with rice starch on the clay walls of the houses.

This is done to honor the dead, to conjure up spirits, and as protection against bad luck. Before the master begins his work, he deposits before the picture wall the present he has received for his spirit, so that in a dream the spirit will reveal the subject of the painting. Once the picture is completed, the spirit will through a medium in trance reveal whether it accepts the painting, or whether there are still corrections to be made. Once more, as in the case of the petroglyph from South Africa, there is a close, unmistakable association between the hunters in the "porcupine" posture and the game. All the hunters are shown in this posture. One hunter carries a bow, another one a gun, and they have killed a large reptile, an equally impressive cat, a deer, and several smaller hoofed animals.

Section II

THE POSTURES AND
WHAT THEY HAVE
TO OFFER

CHAPTER SIX

Going on
a Spirit Journey

What happens on a spirit journey? People fly away on birds' wings, peacock clouds spread their shimmering tail feathers, a woman with stars in her hair guards the entrance to the world below, and humans turned into albatrosses alight on the waves of the ocean. These are some of the tales people tell when they come back. There are several postures that are specifically designed to take us either to the sky, to the middle world where humans live, to the lower world, or out to sea. Although brief sallies or "out-of-body experiences" also happen frequently during other postures, those described below have proved to be the ones needed for a prolonged trip.

The Lascaux Cave shaman's posture. How we happened to try the posture, I told briefly in Chapter 2. Let me recapitulate briefly how it is done. You lie down comfortably on the slanted board (37-degree angle), your legs together, and letting your feet spread apart naturally. Somewhat bent at the elbow, your right arm is placed on the board a few inches away from your body in a leisurely fashion. As a result, your right hand rests on its outside edge, and your thumb is up. Although also resting on the board, your left arm is tensed by contrast, very straight, and your left hand is turned so that its back is turned toward your body, and your thumb is stretched stiffly down. You close your eyes, and you are ready to go.

Since the posture requires a support inclined at thirty-seven degrees, some friends have constructed single boards for themselves inclined at the proper angle and find that it works quite well. But the setup is difficult to procure, and so we cannot always do it during workshops. At Cuyamungue, I had individual boards made that can be hooked onto a stand. We can even move the stands outside, and do the exercise under the blue sky of New Mexico, which makes it very special. In Scheibbs the Buddhist Center had several stands and large rectangular plates that could be assembled when needed. They called the setup Felicitas's launching pad, and it was often the subject of light-hearted levity on the part of novices. As we were gathering for the session a few years ago, one of our participants, a psychologist with the Austrian state mental institution at Gugging, decided to try out the "launching pad" by standing on his head on the footrest. During the session, he of course had his feet down like everyone else. He turned into a bird during the trance, and started happily flying around—but belly up.

In many societies, a spirit journey to the sky is considered to be initiatory; the shaman "dies" during his initiation flight and is "reborn" upon returning. In abbreviated form, this is an experience reported by many who take the trip. Soon after the trance is induced, as if in the agony of death, the trancers experience being split or opened: "I broke in half," or "My belly opened up and there was a gaping hole," or "A flap opened at the top of my head." Frequently after considerable struggle, a being emerges like a butterfly from the chrysalis: The trancers give birth to themselves. "It was as if somebody was pressing me out, like a pea out of a pod," or "I was covered by a black box, there was a light toward the top, and I wanted to get out through that spot. Finally I got out and flew low over the land." This new form of one's being is usually associated with birds: "At the first rattle sound, I saw a huge bird," or "I sat in a tree among hundreds of small birds that were all twittering away, the way your rattle sound seems to twitter." Or what emerges is or becomes a bird or a birdlike being. It will be recalled that, entirely in keeping with such experiences, in the cave drawing the stick figure wears a bird mask, and the stave next to him is crowned by a bird. As Eva D. (Scheibbs, 1983) recalled:

> There was a large bird above me, but I was not that bird. It grabbed me with its talons and flew around with me for the longest time; it was fantastically beautiful. But then I wanted to fly all by myself, and it let go of me. I was very small, more like a woodpecker, and being released produced a tremendous physical reaction, making me twirl downward in very tight circles.

Not everyone goes through all the phases of the experience. The entrance especially is often given short shrift during retelling. As one participant said, "It just went too fast, I don't remember much of it." I recall the same rapid transition from my own first spirit journey, which was, by the way, a rather humiliating affair. I did not experience leaving my body at all. I just found myself a fledgling on wobbly wings aiming directly at a tall rosy wall and thinking all the while, "I really must lose those extra pounds!" Luckily the rattle stopped before I came in for a crash landing. The experience of actually flying is so novel that there is confusion: "I saw a tiny rabbit on the ground and couldn't figure out why it was getting bigger." Others take it in their stride, reporting as a matter of course that they saw large brown mountains down in the distance, or other features of the landscape.

The most impressive spirit journey in this posture is the one that takes people up into the blue sky and beyond (as happened to Ingrid in the TV program):

> Isi (Cuyamnungue, 1986): I was afraid because I was feeling so light, and that I would lose touch with the ground. But by that time it had already happened, and I was in the sky. I saw on the ground below me the shadow of a big bird, and when I moved, the shadow moved too, so I knew that I was that bird. I kept somersaulting backward through the clouds, and saw behind them lots of peacocks, spreading their tail feathers. I kept going higher and higher, I couldn't stop. Finally I arrived at a star, it was really a door, and there was a bright light behind it. I went through the door and saw a sculpture, but it had no head. There was a lot of light all around; people were dancing, and they all seemed very happy.

Spontaneously, and without any prior information, Isi in this case experienced what Australian shamans relate, namely, that after climbing the rainbow up into the sky, one arrives at a door and, upon entering it, is in the company of spirits. Such unexpected emergence of myth fragments during a trance is quite frequent. In fact, there are so many such fragments reported all the time that if they are not identified, it is probably simply because we are unfamiliar with them.

That the statue that Isi saw had no head is another example of this fact. Hunter and especially horticulturalist traditions hold that if humans see the true countenance of a spirit, they die. That is why spirits wear masks. There is a faint memory of this also in European myths, especially in classical Greece, which is still very close to its horticulturalist roots. There is a story of a love affair between Zeus, the father god, and a mortal girl called Semele. Semele nags Zeus; she wants to see his true face. When Zeus finally relents, he appears as fire and she burns to death.

Or take the motif of the miraculous egg seen by another participant. Mircea Eliade, the venerable father of shamanic studies, quotes a Siberian Yakut story,[1] according to which the Bird-of-Prey Mother, which has the head of an eagle and iron feathers, lights on a giant fir tree, the Tree of the World. There she lays a number of eggs, from which she hatches the shamans. The following experience is reminiscent of this legend:

> Bente (Cuyamungue, 1986): I was slow starting out, then I began spinning through the universe and did not know where I was. A voice said, "I will tell you a story about children." I was sitting in a nest, and when I pushed a button, a maypole rose out of it. From it streamed guardians, in strands of many colors, who formed a cocoon, like a wasps' nest. It opened and a little white slippery dove came out. She began flying toward the sun, and she dried up as she was flying. The sun touched her heart and her belly. She returned to the solar system, laid an

egg, it opened, and a new earth emerged. The earth was very green, and hundreds of children played on it, children of the sun.

A spirit journey does not always take the participant up into the sky, however; it may traverse the middle world of humans instead:

> ANN D. (Cuyamungue, 1986): I went out through my left thumb, which I felt was very powerful. I did not leave the kiva right away; I hovered over you first, Cynthia, and patted your hair, then I hovered over Krissie. I tried to find Darlene [another participant] but did not see her. So I thought maybe I should go look for my parents, but there was this voice that said, "Don't, they don't need any protection." So I decided to try and find my friend Jeffie. She was in great pain; I hovered over her, trying to touch her, but could not, so I tried to envelop her to comfort her. But I could not stay with her; I knew my time was almost up. So I turned back, but my thumb had collapsed in the meantime. I was in panic, I thought it was broken. I kept rolling over and over in the air, trying to think of a way of how to straighten out my thumb. All my concentration went into that one thing: how to straighten out my thumb so that I would be able to get back into my body. Finally, only four beats before you stopped rattling, I was able to straighten it out and slipped back in.

Ann had to tolerate a great deal of good-natured ribbing about her thumb later, and we took a picture of her contemplating the offending digit.

Although encountering one's spirit guide is usually experienced in the lower world, it can happen during the trip to the upper world, too. Thus Ewald (Scheibbs, 1985) once more came upon his little Dragon:

> As soon as you started rattling, I took off through the window, like a jet engine. But instead of going up, I tumbled down into a hole full of snakes. There was a witch's broom; I took that and fled through the door, and there was my Dragon. We started playing ping-pong together, and I saw you rattling, but your head was that of a white horse.

Lukas (Scheibbs, 1985), a physician, could not avoid his friend the Bear Spirit, the mighty healer, who had taken a liking to him:

> I felt effervescent, as though I were becoming gaseous. My third eye popped open, and the Bear appeared. He nodded to me, saying, "Come along." So I went with him and came to a clearing in the forest. I lay down and saw above me a bright spot. I flew away into that, still feeling the prickling sensation, as though I were boiling all over.

And Yolanda (Cuyamungue, 1984), at home in the Swiss Alps, was accompanied on her trip by her Eagle:

> My head split open and a spring of water issued from it. Then I felt something pulling me, and when I looked up, there was the Eagle holding me in his arms, and I felt his wonderfully soft, fluffy breast feathers. I did not want to fly, so we

Plate 9

walked up the side of a mountain hand in hand and came to the entrance of a cave. We went in, and I saw a hole in the ceiling, and through it the sky, the world, so much brightness. So we flew through that hole. The Eagle had such enormous wings; I felt embraced by those wings and touched once more by his soft breast feathers. Then I became transparent and flew away on my own.

In my notes about this session, there is the following entry: "While rattling, and of course having no idea what it was Yolanda was experiencing, I saw an eagle feather fluttering down beside her. When I tried to look closer, I saw only her shoes."

By the way, being carried away by a huge bird is frequently reported in this posture, and the motif often occurs in ancient art, too. Yolanda's experience, for instance, agrees closely with the one worked into a gold pitcher by an artist at the time the Hungarians entered their present homeland in the Danube Valley about a thousand years ago (see pl. 9).

SPIRIT JOURNEY TO THE LOWER WORLD

The lower world offers a much more variegated range of experiences than the sky world. It is a realm as rich as the entire human universe, with its landscapes and towns, its animals and plants, its history, memories, and myths, its many spirits, and its dead. Just like the sky, it is a real world in which the traveler does not only see and act but is also observed and acted upon. Gerhard B. tells of lying supine in a cave, with an eagle sitting on his naked belly, looking him over. And Jackie was carried through the jungle by a troop of ants that made ready to eat her and were disappointed when at the stop of the rattle she escaped.

In many parts of the world, in Siberia, Australia, and South America, the lower world is a place where healing is taught,[2] or where the shamans descend in order to retrieve lost souls, also a curing strategy. In our work with the postures, we found healing to be more broadly based. It can take place in a number of different postures, as we shall see, and it is principally a gift of the greatest of all healers, Grandfather Bear (see Chapter 8).

A Sami (Lapp) posture. A drawing of the posture used by these nomadic reindeer herders of northern Europe was published in Germany in 1673 (pl. 10). The shaman lies prone on the ground. His arms are stretched out above his head, with his right hand reaching somewhat farther than his left. His feet are crossed at the ankles, with his right foot on top of his left. His drum, on which he "rides" to the lower world, is on his back, its handle up, covering most of his head. An assistant provides the drumbeat for his trip. We had no drum of the right size and shape for this posture and ended up simulating it with a wreath of cottonwood boughs or with a pillow. I also believe that the designs on the drum of both the shaman and his assistant, as well as the shaman's garment, have an important role to play in guiding the traveler. We should remember that those are not just haphazardly applied "symbols," a favorite buzzword of Western observers. They are all revealed in trance, and instead of symbols, they are what we might think of as "holes," entranceways into the other reality. However, those were elements we could not supply.

Despite our incomplete rendition of the Sami spirit journey complex, it still mediated a very intense experience. "I must have gone very deep down,"

Plate 10

I wrote in my field record. The following is Barbara's account (Cuyamungue, 1985):

> The images started coming as soon as I assumed the posture, even before you started rattling. I was in a beautiful landscape, similar to the land around here. There was a wall stretching for miles and an adobe house with a door. As I watched, a black insect crawled out of it, then another one. They were followed by an antelope, and then by many dark-skinned people wearing ornaments on their ankles. Ahead of me, there was a dirt road. I followed it and saw the legs of many light-skinned people. A brightly illuminated human figure came toward me. It startled me, and the figure disappeared. I looked up, and above me I saw a beautiful opening into the sky.

When we did this posture in the Netherlands in 1987, almost everyone in that workshop, obviously for important cultural reasons, ended up having something to do with water, as if they had all been taken by charter bus to the same region in the lower world. "I saw nothing; there was only the noise of golden raindrops," was one report; or "I heard water dripping as in a cave, and there were mushrooms growing out of me"; or "There was an intensely bubbling small waterfall, and through it I saw the sun with tiny rays." And according to another one, "I found myself in water, and felt that I was sinking. Then I started swimming like a dolphin." And according to still another one, "I was in the sea, and saw a big animal. It came from below, and I saw its huge spine." Claudia's report was more elaborate (Utrecht, 1987):

> I felt my head getting very heavy, as if there were too much blood in it, and I had problems with breathing. I was a fish, or maybe a whale, very big and massive, and I was swimming in the sea. Before that, I saw a waterfall; there were salmons jumping, and I had fire in my hands. But my hands were not hands; they were completely out of shape.

Other groups scatter, having many different adventures as soon as they reach the lower world, as did the one in Vienna in the spring of 1987. The trancers still sometimes encounter water, although it does not predominate as it does with the Dutch. Thus we hear from Thomas: "As I listen to the rattle, I feel a prickling sensation under my [simulated] drum, and a force is penetrating from above into my body. A wind comes up, and there is a chorus of voices. A curtain is raised, and I am floating above a forest. There is a spring; I dip my fingers into it, and the water feels cool and fresh. I also drink from it. Then I knew that I had to get into the mountain." Or from Isi: "I slipped out from under the drum and slid into the ground, which felt more like water. I saw a a white transparent woman, and she asked me, 'What do you want?' I couldn't think of anything, but suddenly I was floating in the sky and didn't know what was up and what was down." This Viennese group was relatively large, so we added a drum to the rattle, and for some participants the sound of the drum became the dominating stimulus: "The drum ordered me to leave my body. It was very commanding, so I did leave and wondered what I was supposed to do next."

Animals predominated in the lower world. Sometimes they joined the visitor as companions: "As I arrived below, a hyena joined me and guided me to a cave full of crystals. This was the place where the philosophers' stone was stored, but the hyena said they had no use for it, because they were animals." Or "A raven flew by, and I wanted to fly with it. We flew toward some mountain peaks; they were black, like in the fairytale about the seven ravens." In other instances, the travelers turned into animals themselves: "I was running around on all fours, wondering what on earth I had turned into now. I killed a deer and started feeding on it, but I was not vicious." Or they retained their human shape and wandered about, like curious tourists:

> Sep: I stood on my head, and that way I slipped into the ground. The path led downward, and the noise was always ahead of me. I stumbled over a worm; it was soft and pulled me down into the depths. I ended up in a passageway like in a mine and then arrived in a cave that was a smithy; I could smell coal and iron in the steam.

Or somewhat more ethereally:

> Rosemarie: I fly up to the moon sickle, and on it, I slip down into the swampy earth. I am a being of light and am dancing in the city. There are trees, and I watch them as they are marching out of town while distorted masks stream in.

South American Indian posture. Because of the various difficulties with the intricacies of the Sami posture, we have more experience with a simpler one, suggested by Michael Harner,[3] who presumably saw it used by some of the South American Indian shamans who taught him. The participants lie flat on the floor, face up. The right arm is positioned loosely by the side of the body; the left arm is placed on the forehead in such a way that neither the elbow nor the hand touches the floor. Care must be taken that the forearm puts no pressure on the eyes. As in all postures, the eyes are closed. (See pl. 11.)

With this posture, some people simply find themselves below as soon as the rattling starts. Most of the time, however, there is a clear perception of turbulence at the entrance to the lower world. I was startled when I saw it for the first time: "The entire world was swirling in a massive whirlpool before my eyes," I wrote. It was quite frightening. There is an incident in the Navajo emergence story[4] where the people have fled from the rising floodwaters up into the fifth world, and then, looking down the hole, they see the turbulent water welling and churning below, and they are sorely troubled.

The entrance to the lower world may assume many other shapes also. It may be a cave, and some women see its opening as having the shape of a vulva. For another woman, it was a giant flower. "It had soft petals, and there was a fragrance all about. Further down, it got sticky and dark." An Austrian participant came to a hollow old tree, and there was a girl with stars in her hair sitting at the entrace to the way down. Franz liked to look for "his" bridge.

Once, he told, he could not find it: "I finally decided to visualize it, and it promptly appeared. At the end of it, there was a dark spot, *and then came the real bridge.*" I like to use this example when I am asked about the difference between visualization and a vision of the alternate reality. A visualized image is your own creation; a vision comes about when you see what is "out there," the alternate part of reality.

The way down may lead over a slanting highway, down a flight of stairs, or very frequently through a chute, a tunnel, or a similar passageway. Going down is hardly ever accomplished by simply walking. Some ooze over the earth, "like chocolate," somebody said, or sink into it. There are those who float gently on a magic carpet or a pillow. Others somersault backward and then slip, slide, or tumble downward. Many feel that they are caught in a whirlpool. This is not always comfortable, as we hear in the following account from Judy Ch. (Columbus, Ohio, 1985):

Plate 11

> I felt extreme discomfort, and my arm on my forehead went numb. I heard sounds of spinning, and then I myself was also spinning around in a spiral, rotating faster and faster. I was going in a circle like the clothes in a washing machine. Then I was in a clothes washer, going round and round and hurting all over. I was glad when it was over.

Clearly, Judy never made it down into the lower world in this session, but her pain dissolved with the last beat of the rattle. She laughed with us about her misadventure in the washing machine, and she has been to the lower world uneventfully several times since, although sometimes feeling "like a dull drill bit."

Once down, the travelers pass through fog or, more often, water. Frequently, arrival involves a boat ride, like that taken by the recently dead in Greek myth. "I saw bright circles of light," one told. "I felt a pull in my legs and arrived someplace where there were many dark birds, and I found myself in a boat that was being rowed by somebody." Or "I was in a boat and was slowly traveling into infinity." And "I was lying in a canoe and drifted along. Then I fell headfirst into black water."

Coming back up again is recounted relatively rarely. There are a few reports of floating upward, guided by the sound of the rattle, of suddenly seeing a hole above, or of being back in the kiva and its roof opening up. Some accomplish their reemergence gracefully, as when Fritz E., having assumed the shape of a great white owl, saw the moon through a hole in the rock wall and flew through it into the night sky. But for many travelers the fifteen minutes seem too brief for the journey through the lower world, and they are not quite ready yet to come back when the time is up. Thus there are those who are caught by the cessation of the rattle signal in the midst of preparing for the trip back. Thomas, for instance, had been riding all over that strange world ready yet to come back when the time is up. Thus there are those who are caught by the cessation of the rattle signal in the midst of preparing for the trip back. Thomas, for instance, had been riding all over that strange world sitting on a horse, but facing backward, a situation often described in European folklore. Shortly before the rattle stopped, "something suddenly put me on the horse facing forward." Or in another account, a girl had been hiking about without a head, and when it came time to leave, she put her head back on.

Others do experience emerging, but it is difficult and has to be tried several times, as when Ann B. (Cuyamungue, 1986) tells how, after having turned into an eagle and exploring the lower world,

> I flew into the mountain, and then I was the mountain, I was a dormant volcano storing up energy. Then I erupted, streaming out of the mountain as red energy. Then I was in the mountain again; I erupted, and I was a flame dancing on the rim of the mountain, faster and faster, as the rattle became faster and faster, and I had to watch where I danced, so I would not fall back in again. [By the way, I always keep the rattle signal constant: that it was speeding up was her perception.]

In this posture, too, fragments of folklore keep bobbing up. Thus, in one of Grimm's fairytales,[5] a girl drops her spindle into a well. Afraid that her stepmother will punish her if she loses it, she jumps into the well and finds herself near an oven, where the loaves of bread are done and call out to her, begging her to take them out. She does and later hires herself out to Frau Holle, a principal Germanic deity, whose presence marks the place where she arrived at the bottom of the well as the magical lower world. Ann B. (Cuyamungue, 1986) obviously ended up at the same spot:

> The ground began to shake, then it opened and I fell through, into a world that was green and dark, and there was a fluorescent light everywhere. I went around,

exploring, and came to an oven. I opened it, and the bread inside was done, so I ate some of it.

Those familiar with Greek mythology[6] will in the following tale instantly recognize the entrance to Tartarus, complete with its brooding shadows and its cold fog. Only Hugh (Cuyamungue, 1986) was met not by Charon, the miser who used to ferry the Greek ghosts across the river Styx, but by the generous White Buffalo:

> I was at a cold place; the air was foggy, and there was a dark and eerie light. A White Buffalo was with me, and he came with me when I entered into a boat. On the other side the ground was different, it wasn't solid. I met all sorts of relatives and especially my father. He turned into a bear and we danced, but I felt very cold, so he took me to a fire in a rocky grove, and I began feeling warmer. We danced around the fire, but real slow. Then the White Buffalo came, and we went back.

Here are a few examples of complete reports from this posture. In the first one, the traveler did not make it to her destination, although many different beings, birds, a weeping willow, gnomes, and fish, tried to show her the way:

> MICHELLE (Vienna, 1985): I felt the ground vibrating under me. I became liquid and spread out over the earth. I felt a hot liquid in my abdomen; it opened up, and a golden being rose from it. There were birds above me, and to the left, far above, there was a black hole. It sucked in the birds, but I could not get there. Behind me, I saw a weeping willow; it waved to me. Tiny gnomes emerged from it, and they began dancing on me; it was wonderful. They disappeared in the black hole, too. Then I was in the water; the black hole was the gaping mouth of a fish. Many fish swam toward that black hole. I think I could also have gotten there, but the rattle stopped.

Both here and also abroad, American Indians are often seen in the lower world, as told in this report:

> ELIZABETH R. (Columbus, Ohio, 1985): My face became warm, and I heard a flapping as of wings. I relaxed into that sound and changed into an eagle and was sitting in a tree. There was an Indian family under the tree, a father, a mother, and a small daughter. I flew down to them, and the child gave me part of her meal. In exchange, I gave her one of my feathers, which she stuck in her hair. Then I flew up into the mountains and turned into myself. I came upon an old Indian. He wore traditional Indian clothes; he was small and had snow-white hair, and I instantly fell in love with him. He gave me a necklace made of large green and blue stones. He then took me to the water, and I took off my clothes and stepped in, and it was very cold. He poured cold water over me; I had the feeling that it was a kind of initiation. Then he let me come out of the water, and he wrapped me in furs. There was a brown bear fishing in the water; he gave the old Indian one of the fish. It was night by then. The old Indian made a fire, fried the fish,

and we ate the fish together, and I felt blessed, very grateful, and I began to cry. I asked the old Indian about the pain in my neck. So the Indian and the bear began pulling and shaking me and said that I would be okay. I told them that I did not want to leave, but they said that I would come back again, and that there really was not all that much separation between our two worlds. Then I changed back into an eagle and came flying back, very reluctantly.

Guatemaltecan Indian shamans contend that they possess among their several souls one that is the healer, and during diagnosis and healing this soul enters the patient's body much like the spirit does during a spirit journey. I was aware of this, but it was still startling to hear it being told by a physician in Austria, half a world away, who knew nothing of Central American shamans. Susanna (Vienna, 1985) had not felt well during the session of the previous day, and I did not expect to see her back. But she did come again, and this is what she experienced in this posture:

> I felt the rattle jumping up and down in my belly, and then its beat spread out in waves. Suddenly a tiny green man appeared before me, holding a spear. He jumped into my belly and wandered all about in my body. When he got to my heart, he stuck his spear into it. That felt very good; he had let out all the old air. Then he arrived at my navel and seemed to be pondering what to do next. He slipped out through my navel and became as tall as I. He started wrestling with me, shaking me real aggressively. Then he grabbed hold of my hair from the back and swung me back and forth. He appeared before me, bowed down, then stroked my body from all sides. Then he spread out his arms, gathered up the light, and I found myself floating in that light when the rattle stopped.

While Susanna was given a treatment for what she felt was a bodily ill during her trip to the lower world, Adolf was taught during this spirit journey how to cope with a severe psychological problem, his dread of aging. We all noticed from the start that he had what at first simply seemed like an aversion to elderly women like me, but it soon became obvious that although he was a man in his forties, he was mortally afraid of becoming old. This is what he told:

> My forehead became very hot. Suddenly I found myself in Jerusalem, at the Wailing Wall. Beyond it there was a narrow path among some trees, and I followed that. I did not walk, I was gliding along. Suddenly, I saw next to the path a rabbit sitting in the grass. He looked at me, and I saw that he was a very old rabbit. I was surprised that he did not run away. We were all there together, but we could not see his face.

I never asked him what an "old rabbit" looked like, feeling that a wound was best left untouched, especially when after a number of sessions it was apparently beginning to heal. Two days later we did the *mallam*, the Nupe divining posture (Chapter 2; see also Chapter 7), and I was delighted to hear what Adolf had to tell. It seems that he was taken back once more to the spot he had seen in the lower world:

Once more I saw and heard everything that happened day before yesterday. The path I had seen continued along some fields and then led into the forest. Some lumbermen were at work, cutting down all the old trees. They were even pulling up the roots. It was very sad, because after all, old trees can tell stories to the little trees. I sat down in a clearing, and there were birds around me, and I decided that it was time for me to overcome my sorrow. I looked up and I saw a triangle of light, and from my head, rays of light went in all directions.

After this session, Adolf went for a walk in the forest, and when I came to lunch, he had placed a small bunch of wildflowers in front of my plate. And there were no more snide remarks about elderly women.

Finally I should like to describe a ritual, a combination of makeup and posture that is also a spirit journey, although it has some special and rather curious features. Because of what the women usually experience, we call it the *Albatross adventure*.

In a number of books on American Indian art, I came across photographs of a couple, found in grave C in Etowah, Barlow County, Georgia, made of a marble native to North Georgia (pls. 12 and 13). The man sits cross-legged, his right hand on his knee. His left arm is broken off, but a museum later recovered and reattached his broken-off limb, and he has his left hand on his knee, too. The woman is kneeling with her legs drawn under her body, sitting on them like Japanese women do, but with her knees slightly apart. Her hands are placed on the sides of her thighs, rather close to her hips, and she bends slightly forward. Both figures have protruding tongues, but the man's sticks out farther than the woman's, and both bear traces of striking facial paint.[7] They actually wear greenish-blue painted-on half-masks, the woman's a bit

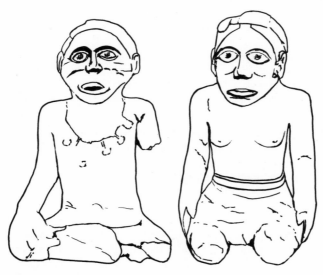

Plate 12   **Plate 13**

shorter than the man's, the lower edge and eyeholes of which are outlined in carbon black.

In April 1985, when I had a group of experienced people assembled in Scheibbs for a masked dance (see Chapter 11), we tried this posture. We painted on the ancient mask, which looked truly spectacular. The following are the experiences of some of the women:

> ILSE S.: I was in greenish-blue cold light, somewhere where there was a lot of ice. I was an albatross and flew over the sea; there were icebergs and much water. I landed on the mast of a wrecked large wooden boat. The crew was gone, and there was no one to steer it. I was being rocked back and forth.

> MICHELLE: I somersaulted backward and changed into a large white albatross. I alighted on an ancient Greek ship, and there was music from somewhere. I jumped into the blue water and became a dolphin, then I myself turned into water; I evaporated and rose toward the sun. I turned into rain and penetrated the plants and the trees. I was quiet water that started to run as a brook, then as a waterfall. I penetrated into the rocks, then came up to the surface again as a spring in the tropics. Then everything started all over again.

> SIGRID: I saw a large number of birds, then my wings began to grow and became longer and longer. I flew up very high into the violet-blue light. Then I descended on the water and began to rock on the waves. That continued for the longest time. The energy began coursing through me; something grew out of my head and began pulling me upward. I became a lake with blooming water lilies.

The presence of water, turning into a bird—sometimes understood to be an albatross—and a rocking motion were quite prevalent. By contrast, the men seemed to be propelled upward by a tremendous force and rushed outward beyond the bounds of the earth:

> FRANZ: I took a very fast trip through a long tube in greyish-white, cold light. When I got out on the other side, I was in space, in a different world, on a distant star. There were crowds of transparent people there, as if of glass; they had pointed ears and wore tall caps, and danced in ocher light. Then I had to hurry on.

> RUDL: My Tiger appeared, but he said I should go to ask help of the Eagle. The Eagle slipped into my body, and I streaked into empty space in a shower of a thousand sparks, in among multitudes of suns and splinters of more suns. I pleaded that I wanted to stay, but I had to fly on, clear to where the universe started curving upon itself, circles upon circles, space after space. I felt that I could stand it no longer, but then I saw all of you, living, dying, living, dying. Then I heard the Eagle screech, and I was back here.

Listening to the men was quite frightening; they seemed to have "overshot" their goal in this posture. I had had everybody assume the female variant of the posture, so I was concerned that perhaps that had been a mistake. However, even when in a later workshop I was more careful and let the men do the male posture, there was still something exaggerated, an aspect of dangerous abandon, in what they experienced. Thus, Hannes (Salzburg, 1987) told how

> the earth began to swirl crazily; we turned into rockets and started rushing through space, racing by the planets, then back to earth again. . . . I am on the edge of a volcano; it explodes, and I am in a boat, paddling down to the ocean in the lava flow. . . . I find myself in Africa; I am in a hammock, and there are hundreds of snakes, all swaying to the music of a flute. . . . I turn into a monkey, into a gorilla, into King Kong. . . . I become a mosquito and return to the mountaintop and watch as an acorn starts germinating and then grows into an enormous tree . . . but this takes many generations.

We are reminded of Rudl's rush into space and then seeing his friends in the workshop living and dying over and over again; that is, he equally witnesses events that would cover several generations. Is there something wrong with the male posture? The archeologists who discovered the couple reported that they found the two figures tossed carelessly into an open space in the grave, and that was how in all probability the man's arm broke off. Perhaps their contemporaries disapproved of the violence experienced by the men in the posture and discarded the figures for that reason. A woman's figure in the same posture and with the same painted-on mask was found also in Kentucky, but apparently there was no male companion.

In conclusion, I cannot resist sharing a special adventure that has something to do with a spirit journey, although not with posture. The story concerns a group of "little men" from Peru, who were our visitors in Cuyamungue in the summer of 1986. Actually, they were clay replicas of ancient *whistling vessels*. Each figure consisted of two connecting chambers, the back one in the shape of a shell that could easily be held in two hands, while the front one was figured. The figures represented fat-bellied, short-legged little men with curious headdresses, who held various objects on their stomachs—
a fish, a parrot, or a lizard (pl. 14).

Plate 14

I am not being facetious in referring to these whistling vessels as though they were personages. They were not simply span-high pieces of pottery, but as we set them up in a circle in the center of the kiva, they exuded a palpable, very powerful presence. So to welcome and to honor them, we hung a tapestry on the wall, actually half of a huipil from a famous weavers' village in Guatemala, intoxicating in its design and riot of colors, and whenever we did a ritual in the kiva, we offered them some cornmeal and the fragrance of burning sage.

These whistling vessels have an intriguing history. They were produced by successive sophisticated cultures in Peru over a period of more than a millennium until the time when the Spanish overran the Inca empire. There are only minimal traces of popular awareness concerning their use or ritual application (see below), so they may possibly have been the property of highly placed priests, who passed on the tradition about them as esoteric knowledge, which was mostly forgotten with the passing of the priestly hierarchy. Archeologists thought of them as water jugs until Daniel Stat, an amateur scientist, bought one at an auction in Pennsylvania in 1972. A careful examination of a number of them, later extended also to broken samples in various museums, convinced him that these various vessels were intended not to contain water but to be blown. He eventually borrowed several other vessels from various museums and worked out a method for duplicating them.

In 1980, Stat and Dr. Steven Garrett of the UCLA physics department ran a number of tests on a sample of sixty-nine bottles and discovered that the high, piercing tone produced on them was confined to an extraordinarily narrow range of frequencies, spanning only half an octave, between 2,000 and 3,500 cps. It was also established that if several vessels were blown simultaneously, a resonance was set up, termed a "difference tone." This tone, although modern physics acknowledges that it exists, cannot be registered by any instrument. It is purely a subjective phenomenon. Speculation is that this difference tone is capable of producing an alteration of consciousness.

Stat carried out a brief ritual with us in the kiva, and owing to the very special acoustic properties of that round subterranean building, the whistle tone was extremely powerful. It seemed to enter into one ear and literally to exit through the other. In addition to the very high, piercing tone, we also heard lower ones that were like a background rustling. As Stat discovered early on, and as others before us who had the privilege of blowing the whistles had found out also, this whistling action did indeed set up a distinct alteration of perception, a trance. As Eva D., one of our Austrian friends present, described it, she felt a strong wind. "It was eerie and filled the entire room. It produced a strange condition, like an intoxication. When we stopped whistling, I continued hearing the whispering and singing for a long while." In a way, we were disappointed, because we thought that with our ample trance experience, we might discover a clue as to what the vessels were used for, but we seemed to have hit a blank wall.

At the time of the visit by the vessels, we were preparing for a masked trance dance (see Chapter 12), and so we did a divination to find out in what way the little men wanted to be involved. We were told that there should be rattling and drumming and dancing. We followed these instructions, and we also made the blowing on the vessels a part of a ritual that we did in the kiva prior to our dance. Apparently, the little men derived some satisfaction from the treatment they had received and, unbeknown to us, had already made preparations to give us a present in return. This is what happened:

As a first part of our masked trance dance, we entered the kiva fully costumed, rattling and drumming, and danced in a circle around the vessels, according to the instructions we had received. After concluding the dance, everyone sat down around the vessels. I fed each one of them a pinch of cornmeal, then handed them to the dancers. I did not notice at the time that Isi, an anthropology student from Vienna, exchanged vessels with Belinda, one of the other dancers. I started rattling, Burgi and David, also of our Austrian contingent, played the drums, and those who had vessels blew on them. Since this was a ritual and not a working session, I did not subsequently ask for a report on what those who had blown on the whistling vessels had experienced. It was not until days later, when we were sitting around reminiscing about the dance, that Isi told what happened to her during that whistling session, and she dictated it to me:

> I found myself in the middle of the desert. It was very dry, there were not even any bushes, and everywhere I saw lizards flitting across the rocks. There was a sound, very soft; it was the sound that they made as they were flitting about. Suddenly there was a house before me, a very simple, low house; it had a rectangular opening, but there was no door. A man was standing in that opening; I could not see him very clearly, but I knew there was a man standing there. He did not fill the entire opening, only part of it, so that I realized it was an invitation, that he wanted me to enter. As I stepped in, I knew that he was a salamander. Once inside, I had the impression of being in a cave. It was very moist, dripping everywhere, and the walls were deeply fissured. Everywhere on the ledges, reptiles lay sleeping peacefully. Then he said, "This is where the moisture comes from for the desert."
>
> Afterward, when we replaced the vessels on the floor, I realized that I had been blowing on the one where the little man was holding a lizard in his hands. Belinda had been holding it first; I thought, it doesn't really matter which one I blow on, but then I had the feeling that that was the one I would like to use. Even before I asked for it, when I just looked at it, at the shape of the little man's hat, which was all I could see in Belinda's hand, there was this feeling of recognition that this was the little man who had whistled a few nights earlier, and that I had a special relationship to him.
>
> During the night of August 1, before we went to see the Jemez Corn Dance [our masked dance started on August 5], I had heard what sounded like a whistle or a flute. When I woke up, I thought at first that it was the chirping of the crickets, but then I heard them very clearly, and I thought, what could the whistling be? There was a difference between the crickets and what I was hearing, which was the sound that we had made when we blew on the whistling vessels, and it came from the kiva. It was three o'clock in the morning—I know because I looked at my watch—and the glowing arc of the Milky Way was above the kiva, and the moon was just rising. I had to go to the bathroom, and when I got up, the sound stopped.
>
> I was really glad that I came to have this encounter with the little man of the whistling vessel. Finally, somebody was friendly to me. Other beings always wanted

to force me to get going; they frightened me when they started pushing me around. This man did not try to make fun of me, not like the birds, who found my petty fears hilarious, like the one that pushed me across the abyss.

We might speculate, then, that in the trance produced by whistling on this particular vessel, the one that the kindly little old lizard man was in charge of, the shaman could journey directly to the cave where moisture was stored. There he could plead for rain to be sent to his village. Duerr (1984:346) notes, by the way, that many Central and South American societies used to carry out rituals asking for rain in subterranean caves.

Perhaps something of a similar nature was true of the vessel where the little pot-bellied man was holding a fish. In that case, possibly, the shaman sets out to the seashore to ask for a school of fish to be sent. What might be involved with the one holding a bird we have no idea, but recently a friend showed me a rather crudely made whistling vessel purchased in a village in Guatemala. It had only one chamber, which represented a woman holding a tiny baby. The purchaser had been told that the whistle served to "call people to come to church." Who knows, this may be a memory, reduced to a faint whisper over the centuries, that at one time the blowing of that whistle afforded access to a special place where a sacred being would grant a woman the desired child.

CHAPTER SEVEN

The Many Faces
of Divination

Divining is as old as humanity. The hunters developed it as a ritual to discover the location of game, a matter of vital importance to them. As other types of societies arose, divination was adapted to the changing circumstances, but it continued to serve important societal goals. It is regrettable that in the Western world divination has been decried as irrational, antirational, or a fraud perpetrated on the ignorant and the superstitious, because divination is not that at all. It is *sooth*saying, that is, revealing the truth. What the diviner does is uncover to his clients some hidden truth about themselves, or about what is going on around them. There are certainly situations in everyone's life where such insights could be of overriding importance. This is why within and outside the Western orbit, divining continues to play an important role, exposing that which is hidden, soothing anxiety, and aiding in decision making.

In Western-type societies, ours among them, quasi-mechanical means such as tarot cards are frequently employed for "fortunetelling." However, the repository of much of divinatory knowledge is the alternate reality, and access to that treasure trove can best be gained in trance, and in the appropriate posture.

In the course of our research, we discovered three very effective divining postures. One of them is that of the Nupe diviner or mallam (pl. 2), recorded in a photograph from sub-Saharan Africa, and which we have not seen represented in any artwork. It was among the earliest postures we explored (see Chapter 2). As we found out in Munich, where it was one of the two postures our experimental subjects assumed during our medical research project, it was accompanied by a powerful trance. The second posture of this nature comes from Tennessee (pl. 15). It shows the portrait of an elderly man, cut in stone

Plate 15

with outstanding skill. Plate 16 seems to be the same posture, equally from Tennessee, but the figure is not well preserved. The third posture (pl. 17), shown by two female figures from Cholula (Mexico), is similar to that of the Tennessee diviners, except instead of half-kneeling, these women are sitting on a low stool.

The experiences mediated by the above three postures have a number of characteristics in common. Most important, they provide visionary insights about oneself and one's social situation not available in ordinary consciousness. In addition, the trancer may also ask questions in all three postures. In fact, on occasion this is even being suggested, as we see in the following account of a trance experience in the mallam posture:

> EVA D. (Vienna, 1985): I was being twirled in this posture with enormous rapidity. I was above you and saw you all. Then I sank down, and I heard someone say, very urgently, "Ask the birds, ask the trees!"

Curiously, we have found that if on the other hand someone poses a question in a posture not intended for divining, this obvious breach of etiquette will simply be ignored, or one is informed, quite summarily, "This is not the time for that," or something to that effect.

However, there are some subtle differences. The mallam addresses principally social relations; the wise women from Cholula and the Tennessee diviner are more interested in personal problems. In seeming contradiction, however, the old master from Tennessee is also an expert in ritual matters. Another difference concerns the preparatory perceptions, to be detailed below, such as a blue light, and others that characterize the mallam posture. These are lacking in the Tennessee and the Cholula diviners' posture, where the matter at hand tends to be addressed directly, as it were, without any introduction. Still another difference is a certain laconic brevity of the message which is often reported for the Tennessee diviner's posture, so that it can

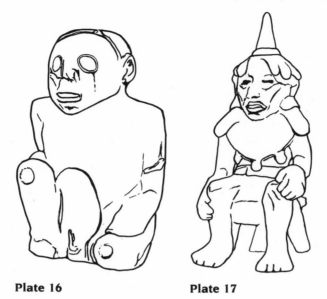

Plate 16   **Plate 17**

happen that if the message is concluded and the rattling is not, the entire vision is replayed, much to the consternation of the questioner.

The Nupe mallam. As described before, this posture requires that we sit on the floor, turning our legs to the right in such a way that the sole of the left foot rests against the right thigh. Because some participants had problems with their knees, we also experimented with a mirror image of the posture, placing the legs toward the left, and it seemed to make no difference. When the legs are to the right, the body leans on the stiff left arm, while the right hand is placed on the lower left leg, at the end of the calf muscle, with all fingers, including the thumb, turned to the front.

Generally, the trancers report the appearance of a vivid blue color in this posture, covering the entire visual field, or more clearly defined in the shape of a light, small spots, or, for Patty, for instance, the vividly blue eyes of a Wolf Spirit. A gyrating motion is experienced, turning on one's own axis, or hearing the "circular motion of the rattle," or the rattle dancing around one; descending into swirling black, orange, and blue colors, or feeling a bright purple light splash on one's face and then swirling; or in minimal form, seeing a white circle of fog, or of arrows. This "cranking up" seems to generate the energy necessary for the successful continuation of the vision. Some then observe how their body or their head splits open, often in the form of a triangle, pointing either up or down. Since many diviners around the world are shown wearing pointed hats (see also the Lady of Cholula, below), we may speculate that this could well be a representation of the triangular split perceived in the divinatory trance, especially because frequently it directly precedes "seeing" or "finding out."

These introductory impressions are usually followed by personal memory content. Thoughts of the past few days flit by, acquaintances, events from childhood or adult life, "like a film." Soon, however, indications of psychological problems may begin to bob up, but significantly for this posture, the personal aspect passes into the societal one. It will be recalled how Adolf's preoccupation with aging, which he had to come to terms with during his trip to the lower world, came up again in this posture. That was how he experienced the importance of the old trees in the forest, because, as he so poignantly observed, they were the ones that told stories to the small ones. Or take the social import of remarks such as "I became sad because I did not seem to be able to reach the people in the room," and this especially wistful comment, "I heard a sound in a canyon but could not find its source." A woman burdened by circumstances at home said, "I saw two figures; they were unsubstantial like fog or smoke. I wanted to rise up, but they kept pulling me softly down." Or from a graduate student who had problems with women, we heard: "I saw the opening to a tunnel; it was pale green, and there was a woman standing in it. She was very delicate, and she was naked, but she wore a shell of hard cold steel; it was like an armor." All of these concern the relationship of the respective person to the social ambience.

Revelations of this sort can on occasion be quite surprising not only to the visionary but also to the group listening to the report. One summer we had a young man by the name of Victor as a guest in Cuyamungue, whom his girlfriend had brought in tow, and who apparently had not been informed that we followed a modified vegetarian diet, using even poultry only minimally, mainly just for seasoning. What we did not know was that for Victor, apparently, red meat was not only a passionately desired food, but its consumption was also a confirmation of his male dominance, which he felt was threatened by our style of eating. All this became clear when we heard him recount his experience:

> There was a warm feeling. I was sitting on the earth outside; there was grass and yellow corn. I walked through it and came to a lonely tree and a rock at the edge of an arroyo. There was a red-and-yellow mountain; I started climbing it and kept going higher; finally I flew. I came to a valley, the mountain was in the middle of that, and in the mountain there was a cave. I flew into the cave and saw a pictograph. There was a man in the cave, he had been hunting, and he had brought in an antelope. He cut the liver out of the antelope and fed it to me. After eating, I flew out of the cave, higher and higher on the mountain; everything became very small, it looked like the region of the Pecos River. I got into another valley; there were bears hunting for fish. I saw a man dancing on a rock. I became that man and carried out a very intense dance. I stopped dancing, went hunting, found an antelope, speared it, took it to the cave, cut out its liver, and ate it. I left the cave, climbed down the mountain, and walked through a cornfield; I got to a creek, drank some water, and started going hunting when the rattle stopped.

Despite the striking repetition of the hunting episode, unusual for this posture, the trance experience did not rid Victor of his preference for red meat, which clearly had deep-seated, socially informed roots. On the contrary, it made his yearning all the more acute and imbued it with trance-borne legitimacy. Since we had no antelope liver for him, or any other part of an antelope for that matter, he drove down into the valley as soon as this was decently feasible, and under the petroglyph of the local Lotaburger, he consumed a fulfilling quantity of the red-and-yellow mountain of his vision.

Usually we do the mallam posture at the outset of a workshop, and as could be expected, various beings whose home is the alternate reality take the opportunity to look over the new intruders, often with the obvious intent of introducing themselves as possible future spirit guides. In fact, they are very anxious for this role, as Patty found out when the big, blue-eyed white wolf she saw at the outset of the divining session kept coming back in the course of the workshop. Some of the spirits are quite cagey, knowing that Westerners have been estranged from animal garb for many centuries, and so take care not to scare them. Yolanda, who was afraid of spiders, felt only a large, warm, and furry round spot on her leg, and it took a while before the true mask of her gentle friend was revealed. A big white she-bear, who became Elizabeth R.'s trusted companion, did not disguise her shape, but reassured her in another way: "She let me smell her fur and see her back. I thought all animal spirits had wings, but there were no wings there, only energy."

Advice in decision making is also something that the mallam posture can mediate. In the summer of 1984, Yolanda was pondering whether she could leave her three young children for a whole month while she came to Cuyamungue. Her husband had no objections, but she was still wavering.

> Being unsure about what to do [she wrote], I did some rattling for myself in the mallam posture. A big bear came and took me on his arms and carried me up a large mountain, then on the backside of the mountain down again on a narrow path. He set me down next to a structure that looked like a very large beehive and then left. Didn't you tell me that the people around there where you are have ovens that look like that?

The vision convinced her that powerful beings of the alternate reality approved of her plans, and the trip to Cuyamungue became a seminal experience for her.

Finally, the following account tells of an unusual application of the mallam posture, and I want to include it here as a teaser. It is an intriguing mix of ancient knowledge and modern technology, showing how much we do not know about the power of ritual and the effect our trance may have on what surrounds us. During the first workshop I held in the Buddhist Center in Scheibbs, two young women of the group, Eva D. and U., decided to tape my rattling so they would be able to hold trance sessions of their own. A few months after the conclusion of the workshop, I received the following letter from U.:

> Soon after coming home, Eva and I started to try out your rattling tape, and things went very well. There was only this thing that we noticed that there were rooms where it was harder to concentrate. So we of course avoided those. . . .
>
> During the last weeks before Christmas it happened a few times that the tape did not function right, and only with intense effort were we able to hear a very weak rattle sound. The first few times we thought—well, it is not supposed to be today—and the following day, the sound was once more clearly audible. Until one day the sound was gone completely, not only that of the rattle tape but *also* [her emphasis] of all the tapes of the trance sessions in Scheibbs that we had copied. This went on for weeks. I kept the cassettes in my apartment with others I own. The sound of those other cassettes was as normal as before. We then tried to play the workshop tapes on different tape recorders, although we suspected right from the start that perhaps the trouble did not have anything to do with a technical defect. But just to be sure, we tried changing equipment. As expected, unsuccessfully. I then took the tapes to Eva's apartment, which did not help either. I had the intuition that we had let the rattling become a method, and besides, it was not really any part of our workaday culture. Eva and I felt simultaneously awed and helpless. We finally hit on the idea that we should carry out a ceremony of sorts, but procrastinated because we really didn't know how to go about it. After Christmas we then sat down together, and suddenly we knew what to do. We sat facing each other in the mallam posture, and between us we placed two pebbles and a hazelnut which I had picked up during a walk with you in Scheibbs. We stayed there for your "quarter-hour." Both of us had the following very intense insight. Our inner attitude became prayerful, and we understood that whatever power it was that wanted to tell us something, it was not inimical, and that the disturbance had nothing to do with our cultural background.
>
> For half a day more, we left the tapes with the pebbles and the nut where they were, and the tapes completely recovered their former sound. We don't rattle quite so frequently since then, and when we do, it is with a different attitude. (March 11, 1983)

The Tennessee diviner. The beautifully worked sandstone figure of this elderly Indian man (pl. 15) was found in a grave in Wilson County, Tennessee, and is estimated to be about seven hundred years old. Such figures used to be placed into wooden temples on top of earthen mounds, but few escaped the iconoclastic wrath of the white settlers. The second example of the posture (pl. 16) was dug up in the same general area.

The man is sitting on his left leg, which is drawn under him. His right leg is bent at the knee and positioned at a right angle to the floor. Both hands are resting on his knees, which makes him look relaxed, but in reality the posture is quite taxing physically. His head is turned slightly toward the right. A black line is drawn from below his earlobe over the bridge of his nose to his other earlobe, and his tongue is visible between his lips. Since he is nearly naked, it is all the more striking that he should be wearing an elaborate cap.

As mentioned before (Chapter 5), I duplicated that cap, and wearing it had the effect of making the visions sharper and their flow richer.

That this was a trance posture was evident from the start, particularly because the man had his tongue clearly visible between his lips. According to a number of Amerindian traditions, on the Northwest Coast, for instance, but also in Asia, especially in Tibet, one receives power from the spirits by way of the protruding tongue. But discovering what kind of experience it might convey was more difficult. What was the common denominator in observations such as "My ears grew bigger and bigger, until I could hear all your thoughts. Then I slipped into an insect and I could hear like an insect"; and "I came to a fence in the forest and it had an open gate. I kept taking one step forward, one step backward, and could not figure out whether I should go in"; or "I found myself in a kettle with steep, reddish walls. Above the rim I saw a violet-colored landscape. I asked myself: What will I do if I cannot get out of this kettle?"

Soon, however, with the help of the training we had received as we worked with the posture of the Nupe mallam, things began to fall into place. Here we had very clear messages about personal traits and problems—the compulsive curiosity of the first one; in the case of the second, the inability to make use of opportunities as they presented themselves; and the lack of self-confidence of the third. In other words, this was also a divining posture, except that in contrast to the auguries received in the mallam postures, these had nothing whatever to do with social relations.

We soon noted another fascinating difference. The Old One of Tennessee came across very much as a distinct personality, which we never experienced with the mallam. Sometimes, he actually seemed a bit testy. When Christian, an Austrian, was a guest in Cuyamungue, he asked him about a posture he had seen in trance. Which foot was he to put forward? Laconically, the answer came, "The right one." The session could have stopped right there. But I did not have any way of knowing that Christian's question had been answered, so I went on rattling. Subsequently it became clear that the venerable Old One felt that he had said what Christian needed to know, and he was in no mood for further discussion. When Christian persisted, he took him to a deep canyon and had him look at some mountain sheep. "And then," Christian told, somewhat bemused, "I melted into a sheep." I wondered how the Old Wise One could possibly have known that for a German speaker, "sheep" is synonymous with "stupid." His irritation carried over to the next day, when Christian assumed the posture once more, with an entirely different question in mind. The first thing he got was a rather annoyed "And now what do you want?"

When we do the Tennessee diviner's posture in a group, I take the short temper of the Old One into account. I always ask my Friend to summon him in the most respectful terms and afterward thank him for his trouble in the same way, as a granddaughter would a venerated elder. Perhaps the old diviner's impatience can be understood, because telling people about themselves is really just a sideline for him. His true expertise is in the area of ritual. When it comes to those questions, he never tires of providing information down to the most minute detail and on occasion even a brief glimpse of the future, if he deems it appropriate. As we shall see later (Chapter 11), it is for this reason that we always call on him when we plan a dance ritual, and on those occasions, he is our most valuable guide and patient friend.

To give just one example, in the summer of 1986 I needed some advice concerning the location of the sweatlodge we were planning to construct for the masked trance dance ritual we were going to carry out the following month. So I asked two gifted friends, Cynthia and Krissie, to consult the Tennessee diviner for me while I rattled. In both instances, what he told them had a similar content. There was some clarification of a personal nature, as if to say, "Only if your thoughts are pure and clear, unclouded by personal trouble, can you carry out a ritual." In a way, this was on the spiritual level the same as taking purgatives and emetics prior to an important ceremony, so prevalent in American Indian culture. And then there were the instructions concerning the place for the sweatlodge and still other matters our old friend considered important for us to know.

After working through some personal concerns, Cynthia went to quite a bit of effort scouting around for the right spot for the sweatlodge:

> I came to the evergreen tree by the Student Building, and wondered if that was where we should put the sweatlodge, but it burst into flame, so I knew that wasn't it. I passed on to where the kiva is, but I was told, "No, not by the kiva." I started spinning around, but that caused me to be pulled upward. I flew over a snowy landscape, and looking down, I wondered what I was doing there. So I descended into the snow; my legs got very cold, and I was afraid. So I called to Felicitas to bring me back. I did come back, flying very low, and then I saw the spot. It was a flat area, and to the right, a hill rose up. Is it here? I asked. And I knew that it was.

This was not the end of Cynthia's vision, however. She saw a large number of formless spirits hovering about, was told that it would be her task to move them through the sweatlodge during that ritual, and was even given instructions about the costume she was to wear during the dance.

Krissie, too, had to dispense with some personal matters first. Then she reported that she saw crystals all lined up:

> We were at the edge of a drop, and the crystals danced in a circle. They were beginning to lose their moisture. I looked down, and I saw the ground swelling up before me, and there was an aura around the mound. The mound changed into a frog; it was quiet and beautiful. It shrank to its normal size. I looked into its eyes and said, "Grandfather Frog, tell me." And he said, "Include me, include me!"
>
> Then there was a lot of light. An eagle danced, then turned into a flower; I saw the setting sun, a mushroom cloud, and it started to rain.

Krissie was also shown the place where the sweatlodge was to be built. It was on the edge of a drop, which was puzzling, because it seemed to contradict what Cynthia had seen. But we later walked over the land and found the location, which was both a flat area near which a hill rose up and at the edge of a deep arroyo. In confirmation that we had found the right spot, we saw as we looked down into the arroyo a clearly marked flat oval area, and on it, as if laid out on a platter, a large number of granite rocks, perhaps the crystals that Krissie had seen, of the size we needed for the sweat.

Again, as in Cynthia's case, Krissie was given more than just the location of the sweatlodge she had been asking for. She had encountered Grandfather Frog, and since he asked not to be left out, we named the sweatlodge for him. But there had also been a brief preview of what was to come. She had seen us dancing by the sweatlodge, and we were indeed instructed later to do that. While this might be viewed as being within the logic of the situation, the subsequent events were certainly not. A cloud did gather during that dance, but most remarkably only above our sweatlodge. We were indeed rained on, and there was thunder and lightning. After that manifestation of the power of the eagle's "dance," and as we stopped dancing, the whole cloud turned delicately pink, and then, to our amazement, a rainbow girded it from end to end. Truly, the eagle had changed into a flower.

The Cholula diviner. There are two little clay figurines extant in this posture, created about A.D. 1350 in Cholula, one of the important pre-Hispanic religious centers of Central Mexico (pl. 17). Their facial features are quite different, as are their earrings, but both are wearing the same pointed hat and a wide collar with tassels on it. Each is sitting on a stool. They have their eyes closed, their tongues between their lips. Their right hands are placed slightly below the knee, clutching the leg; the left hands are somewhat higher.

Whether the Lady of Cholula is also adept at giving advice on ritual matters, we have not explored yet. She is as competent concerning personal problems as her colleague from Tennessee. But there is a touch of femininity in what she reveals, an element of motherly caring, which is absent in the visions provided by the old gentleman from the South. I consulted her a while ago, because I was quite frightened by the results of a medical test. It took a while before I got through to her, but then I felt surrounded by a number of solicitous elderly women, and one of them said, "Remember, you are our daughter." It was wonderfully reassuring, and the test results turned out to be of much less significance than I had feared. To varying degrees, the theme of loving support was equally evident when we tried this posture in Columbus in the fall of 1987. Even diffuse questions elicit a concerned answer, as we see in this example:

NORMA: I asked about myself and the rattle was very loud, like it was in my head. I saw the head of a buffalo and mountains like in the Southwest. The buffalo kicked up a lot of dust, and when I repeated my question to him, he said, "Stay grounded." Then I went to the forest and could feel the forest floor under my feet. I got to the beach; a turtle came out of the water and repeated the same thing, "Stay grounded."

But we found that the Lady of Cholula could also be much more subtle, as when she helped heal old wounds by the visions she gave and then summoned Elizabeth's guide during the same session:

> ELIZABETH: I saw a black panther attacking a man; they killed each other. Then there were scenes from my life, my car slipping on ice; how once I nearly drowned; or how during one delivery I almost hemorrhaged to death. There was a Maya temple and in it an altar for sacrifice, and I thought about just wanting to be comfortable. But my guide appeared and shook me. Did I want to choose death? he asked. "Do you want to sacrifice life?" I said, "No." Then he kissed me.

Problems on the job receive almost practical attention:

> BARBARA: I saw my place of work, and I felt really irritated. There was a stairway and an altar on top. I brought some flowers and put them on that altar. There were two doors on top, and I asked, "May I go through?" No, I was told, there was no more time. Then I saw a raccoon playing with a fish, but it didn't eat it, it let it go. There was a woman flying by wearing a grey crown, and she said, "Stay centered."

Nancy's problems are of a different nature. She works in the health-care field for a large organization of mostly men, and many a day must surely feel lonely and lacking support:

> I saw an electric field that had a lot of broken circuitry. When I started putting the broken ends together, the sparks began to fly. A white buffalo appeared; either she was immense or I was very small, because I nestled in her hair on her head, and her hair was warm and soft. We went from mountain to mountain; I danced on her back. I asked her about what I should do with my clay pipe, and she said, "You'll learn." Then she brought me back, and when I complained, she said, "Stop whining." She kissed me, she did human things, but she was a buffalo.

Belinda and Jan are psychological counselors, and the Lady had some important messsages for them.

> BELINDA: I asked about my health and saw a rusty tube in my throat. Then I heard it said many times, "You push too hard, you push too hard." Bulls came up looking like the astrological figure of Taurus, thousands of them, stampeding. I asked the bulls to stop, and they lay down; all was quiet, and somebody said, "Change the story."

> JAN: My question was, "What about the larger story?" I saw a long caravan that was walking with difficulty. The Bear came and said that with enough energy it

was possible for the caravan to move from country to country, but more helpers were needed. Healing was possible in different countries, but I hadn't paid attention to that, and I wasn't prepared. While we were talking, I saw the instability of ordinary reality, and there were painful memories of the people I work with. Then I saw Belinda in her lion's costume; she was pushing a wheel, and her hands were bleeding. I wanted to help her, but I couldn't do anything. She just kept pushing that wheel, and she was bleeding and I couldn't get to her.

Finally, there was Maxine with her severe health problem, who badly needed encouragement. So the Lady showered presents on her, like an indulgent mother on a sick child:

Things passed before my eyes very rapidly. All was inky black. In the center there was a black opening, something like a tube. I was supposed to go down; it was like a tunnel. When I slid down, I came to a place down in the earth that was lit in orange light. A huge hawk appeared next to me. It had powerful legs and wore a leather saddle on its back. There were a number of tents, seven in all, and the hawk took me to each one in turn. The first one was full of colors, and I chose blue for myself. The next one had feathers in it, and I chose a large black-and-white one. Then came a tent; there was an old woman in it, and I chose old age for myself. In the next tent there was a big pot with meat stewing in it that I took along. Then we came to a tent with many children in it. I said to the hawk, "I don't want any children." But I had to choose one anyway, so I selected a twelve-year-old boy. After that there was one with all sorts of weather in it. I saw a beautiful plain and mountains with a lightning storm, so I chose that. In the last tent there were innumerable eyes looking at me. I chose a clear blue eye, then I put all my things in a sack, and there was the tunnel again, and I was sucked up.

CHAPTER EIGHT

The Gift of Healing

In Chapter 2, I described the posture of the shaman who is embraced from behind by a huge Bear Spirit (pl. 1). It took some time before I recognized that the trance experience mediated was that of being healed. The posture involves a more or less pronounced inclination of the head toward the back and a positioning of the hands very close to or right above the navel. As I began searching for other representations of this posture, I also came across examples where the hands, although in the same general area of the body, seemed to be placed too far apart. At first I thought we were dealing simply with a variant, but experimentation proved me wrong, and the observation eventually led to the discovery of the *birthing posture*. Although not involved with curing per se, historically the experiences it provided may indirectly have led to the development of the healing posture, and so I am going to discuss it here, in the way of an introduction, although it deals with a different topic, that of the fetus at birth.

In the Western world, women are forced to lie flat on their backs while being delivered. It is a most unfortunate development, doing great harm to the mother, as childbirth activists very correctly keep pointing out. Neither was it done that way in past centuries. In a Berlin museum I once saw a "birth stool" a few hundred years old, with a large hole in the center of the seat for the newborn to emerge. Having just gone through a frightful delivery lasting nearly thirty hours, it seemed to me that letting gravity do part of the work was an eminently good idea. And indeed, in other parts of the world, mothers, past and present, assume postures that are much more helpful, as we see in plate 18. This clay jar, of unknown origin, was most likely created by a woman, probably in Bolivia at a time before white contact. As the artist must have seen many times, the mother is seated for delivery, and a helper in front of her receives the infant as it emerges through her vagina.

What fascinated me in this dramatic figured representation of birth was the woman sitting behind the mother. Not only was this companion supporting the mother's back, but she also had her hands on the mother's abdomen. It was, although vicariously, the "anomalous" healing posture that had been puzzling me. Over and over again, around the world and through the ages, figurines clearly marked as female are shown in this posture, sometimes sitting but most of the time standing (see pls. 19–22). Obeying the conventions of their time, they may be highly stylized, like the European Neolithic figure (pl. 19), about six or seven thousand years old, where slits mark the eyes and rosettas the breasts, and the one from the Negev in the Near East (pl. 20), almost that old. Others are quite naturalistic, such as the Olmec one (pl. 21), created about twenty-five hundred years ago, and the nearly modern one from sub-Saharan Africa (pl. 22). Other examples come from Hungary and Crete (both from 5000 B.C.), and from modern times from New Guinea, New Zealand, Polynesia, and numerous ones from Central and West Africa.

Plate 18

The question is, why would a birthing posture be re-created so persistently? My guess was that most probably the purpose was not to demonstrate the right posture for giving birth, which everyone knew anyway. The reason must have had to do instead with a religious observance, the single most important topic of ancient art, always connected with trance. Thinking along these lines, my conclusion was that representing this posture might have had something to do with the fact that, as I have shown elsewhere,[1] the pivotal, the most significant, rituals of the hunter-gatherers and later of the horticulturalists, who created these figurines, centered around the celebration of birth. Some of these figures are quite large and may well have marked the sacred places where such important rites were celebrated.

In such rituals, which can still be observed in surviving societies of this type in Australia, South America, and elsewhere, the central issue is not the birth pangs of the mother but rather the welcoming, strengthening, and nurturing of the infant. This topic is flanked, as it were, quite logically, by an invocation of the ancestors, whose life is continued in the newborn, and by

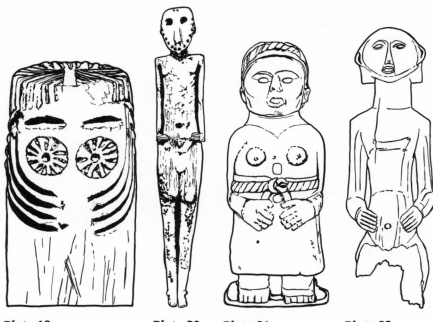

Plate 19   **Plate 20**   **Plate 21**   **Plate 22**

rituals referring to propagation. Surprisingly, when exploring the birthing posture, I found the same to be true of our trance experiences. In fact, the visions
reported by the participants can easily be ranged along the principal sections
of such ancient rituals. The only feature that is more elaborated in the trance
experiences than in the native rituals is the experience of the fetus in the
womb right before and during delivery. Not until that is given its place, too,
the figurines seem to say, not until its sweet mystery revealed in this trance
posture has been intertwined with the communal, the social, celebration, will
the rite be complete.

The posture is quite simple. We did it standing, with our hands flat on
the abdomen, pretty much as shown in plate 20. We tried the posture twice
in 1987, in Cincinnati (C) early in the year, and with a different group at
Camp Agape, Ohio (A), in the fall. The two experiments complement each
other, so I am going to treat them as one.[2] In the analysis, the structure of
ancient hunter-gatherer rituals will serve as our guide. At the outset of such a
large ceremonial, the spirits of the ancestors are invited to participate, and in
the visions, they in fact did arrive. As one of the participants (A) related,
"There appeared faces of old men, with purple beards and white eyebrows."
Or:

> LIBET (A): There was swirling blue light. It moved into the womb; the sound and
> the light became muted. Then the sensation changed. I was in a cave, and there

were seven or eight women around me, wearing dark cloaks and doing some healing. They aged and withered, becoming skulls, but it wasn't frightening. Then there was a lot of movement; they disappeared, but their spirits were still around me.

In the womb, meanwhile—in the "narrow ravine with the winding river" of the umbilical cord—the unborn dream of the world they are about to enter, as it rises from the vapors:

> TERRY (C): I was in a long, narrow ravine, with a winding river, and dense vapors arose from it. I saw lots of clouds; they were light grey. There were also trees and water, but they appeared upside down. The walls of the ravine were cliffs, and along the edge of those walls antelopes could be seen grazing. In swirling colors of purple and black, I saw the eye of a cat, maybe a lion. Lakes with trees appeared, then more eyes, and some more purple. A swan came swimming down the stream, and as I watched, its white color turned to purple. A bear was drinking from the water of the stream. The swan became striped and had strange metallic parts. Then the swan became an eagle, beating its wings. The eagle had totally black eyes, without any pupils at all, and a white stripe down its body. It wanted me to come along, but I couldn't do that. I felt that my head was going to explode, and once more there was that swirling purple and black, and I was it.

As yet, however, birth is not imminent, and the small human-to-be is quite happy inside the womb:

> BARBARA (A): I felt comfortable. I could dimly see a circle of light; it had the shape of a cone, and I could see the rays. I saw the tail end of a manatee; we went swimming with them, we were manatees underwater, and there were caves with double doors. Then something put a necklace on me.

Soon, however, this "underwater" life in the womb is about to end, and the fetus is getting impatient:

> NANCY (A): I felt energy pushing me from my knees to my waist. I was swaying and kept thinking, "I am ready." But there was the answer, "Be patient."

The little being, a bird in the nest, is still confined but will soon be released:

> ANITA (A): There was the image of a huge bird in a huge nest. I felt a strong heat on the left, and that stayed that way. Then the trance became deeper, and I became solid, like a dark column of energy. I was rooted but also wanted to sing. I was pushed to the right, and I became aware of light that was coming from above.

Being born is hard work for the little one in the womb, which is narrow and confining:

> ELIZABETH M. (C): I was in a narrow canyon, walking on and on and feeling very tired. Colors started coming down, black, blue, purple. I felt an arm across my shoulder; there was someone walking with me. I was getting even more tired,

and those colors were still coming down. Then they changed to yellow, and out of it there emerged a human eye. I was so very tired, I was glad when the rattling was over.

Finally, the birth takes place, with the fetus, ready to be expelled, appearing as a blue bud, and then the newborn emerges through the vagina:

> MARIANNE (C): I was down in a canyon, and there was a lot of purple. The purple became black and began to swirl. Then, as if looking at it from a bridge, I saw a blue bud coming up out of the canyon. I saw an eagle's eyes, then a slit appeared in the pupil. I thought the slit looked like a vagina, but then rejected the idea. The slit had white figures in it. Suddenly I was cold, there was cold air swirling around me, and I saw more purple.

> JEANNIE (C): Everything was in a box, purple and black, changing. I saw a V-shaped opening; it closed and became an eye. I swirled around; there were purple colors, coming and going. I had no hands. I wanted to check if that was true when the rattle stopped.

Now the newborn begins to look around:

> LAUREN (C): There were purple and magenta circles of various sizes, and they moved in a rhythm to the rattle. There were presences around the edges of the color, and I was full of apprehension and didn't feel safe. I was standing in front of a column of stone; it was made of coarse material. I saw veils lifting; it felt like layers were being pulled up and back. I touched a mask; it was a painted white cat with whiskers. I was anxious again, my body trembled, but the mask sent a message that I was allowed to go on. So I went behind the cat mask, but no one was there. I was inside the mask, confused, I had no idea what was going on. My body was swirling. I did not want to fall. I wanted to get back into the canyon, but I only had a thin thread of control. I could not do it, and I could feel no answer. I saw the silhouette of a sleeping figure but could not decide if it was a man, a woman, or a child. It was unaware of me but was not resting.

The guests begin to arrive, gathering around the newborn to welcome it: "I saw the face of my white furry bear, and the nose and eye of a cat or a lion," one participant (C) told. They also assume the rule of power animals and impart strength to it:

> VILLIE (C): There was pressure on my neck and shoulders. I went down a black-and-white swirling tunnel, further and further down. I saw the face of a tiger with the light behind him. The tiger was waiting. Then there was blackness again; a point of light appeared, and I felt warm. It might have been the sun. Then I saw the whole tiger.

Next, the newborn is placed at its mother's breast, and the purple circles that are the breasts, the nurture, are everywhere:

> MAXINE (A): I am sitting by the fire. I am in a cave; the light is coming from above, and the smoke goes up. The back of my body feels cold and it aches. I am

surrounded by purple; it is dense, and its edges are black. It comes on as a large purple circle, with several small ones in it. They are all around me, on the fire, above me, and on my feet. A circle of women sits around the fire. Outside the cave, there are overlapping purple circles.

With the newborn safely sheltered by the women in the nurturing purple circles, the ritual now turns to its last act, that of procreation, with the egg entering the body of the woman, and the small fairies, the spirits of other unborn, playing in the "old forest."

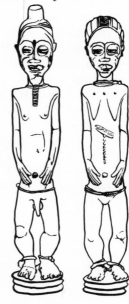

BELINDA (A): I saw a brightly lit hole with antlers on top. I thought it might be the birth canal, but then rejected the idea. There was pressure around my body. I saw an emu swallowing an egg; it went down her esophagus and landed in a nest in her belly. A little fairy came out of the egg and sat on a swing. Then I swallowed an egg. At first a green snake hatched; it came out of my mouth, then it went back in, and I laid it as though I was giving birth to it. I laid an egg through my vagina. I was aware that in the posture my hands were on my ovaries, that is, on my eggs. "What is there to learn?" I asked. The answer was that it wasn't my job to have babies, and I should not be concerned about it. I turned to the right. There was an old green forest. I saw the night and the forest and lots of fairies. They were aware of me because I was different. They were welcoming me, but the rattle stopped, and I knew I would be out of trance, so I asked if I could return. But I was not sure how to get back, because I had lost contact with the fairies at that point.

Plate 23

But the small fairies, "little silver things, containing the memories of the whole race," as Elizabeth R.(A) saw them, have something else on their minds than playing in their secret hideaway. They are hoping for an entrance into a womb, a chamber barred by a gate:

JAN (A): I am riding on the energy of a dying star. When the energy of a star becomes conscious, it can assume form. I am riding on a star, like in a spaceship. Then I am running, racing; my wings are flapping, so I can get through the gate.

The participants quoted for this first session using the birthing posture were all women, but actually there were also three men in the Cincinnati group, and their experiences, although less detailed, materially agreed with what the women told. There were statements such as "Black turned into purple; I was floating and felt like an embryo. I was looking up, through something, and then looking out." Or "There was a muted, generic light and a sense of opening. A wild cat appeared; it seemed coy, rather feminine, brushing its face with its tail." That, in fact, the birthing posture can equally serve as trance posture for men is lent further credence by plate 23, from sub-Saharan Africa, where a man and a woman stand side by side in this manner.

Delivering a woman is essentially a healing. It is quite reasonable, therefore, to assume that in some quantum jump of insight possible in trance, the birthing posture led to the development of the healing one. It is similar, and some of the experiences reported during healing are reminiscent of what happens in the birthing posture. The nurturing purple color appears quite regularly also. However, this is where the resemblance stops, and the sponsorship of the Bear Spirit clearly stamps the healing posture as independent and different.

The healing or *Bear* posture (see pl. 1), as described before, is usually assumed in standing, although there are also some sitting and even kneeling representations (see pl. 24). The feet are about a foot apart, the knees are not locked, the fingers are slightly curled, and the hands are placed on the middle of the trunk in such a way that the knuckles of the index fingers touch at or slightly above the navel.

Judging from plentiful archeological finds, the Bear posture is extremely old and the most widely known of all the postures (see map 1; examples are given in pls. 22–29). In very ancient Europe it seems to be somewhat younger than the birthing posture. However, this impression may be erroneous, given the small number of examples found. That early, representations of it occur exclusively in female figurines. My special favorite is the one created during the brief flowering of horticulture in the fifth millennium B.C. on the Danube near the Iron Gate,

Plate 24

at Lepenski Vir (pl. 24); it is the beautifully abstract representation of an ecstatic woman's face, her head tilted slightly back, her hands in the Bear posture, and the triangle of her vulva like an ornamental design on her lower abdomen. By the third millennium B.C., however, the posture is found in Greece in female figures with a phallus in place of a neck and face, possibly signaling the beginning of male dominance over female ritual activity.

As I told earlier, the posture demonstrated by the shaman with the Bear Spirit (pl. 1) was among the very first we worked with. As we began exploring it, and although I was aware that the Bear Spirit was considered a mighty healer in many regions, I was quite generally blind to the connection between tradition and what my coworkers reported about a particular posture. I thought that perhaps the posture was an early one mediating possession, for so many participants reported having been "opened up." Eventually, however, I understood from fieldwork observations of true possession that the latter requires different strategies, and body posture plays no role. I realized that this "opening" was something needed for the curing power to enter, and I began teaching the Bear posture as a healing ritual. Then, whatever nagging doubts I might still have had finally dissolved when I was myself granted a number of cures by mighty "Grandfather Bear."

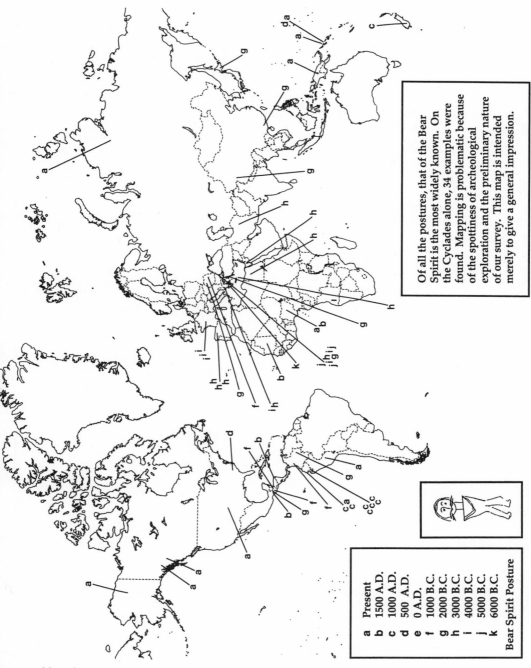

Of all the postures, that of the Bear Spirit is the most widely known. On the Cyclades alone, 34 examples were found. Mapping is problematic because of the spottiness of archeological exploration and the preliminary nature of our survey. This map is intended merely to give a general impression.

a   Present
b   1500 A.D.
c   1000 A.D.
d   500 A.D.
e   0 A.D.
f   1000 B.C.
g   2000 B.C.
h   3000 B.C.
i   4000 B.C.
j   5000 B.C.
k   6000 B.C.

Bear Spirit Posture

Map 1

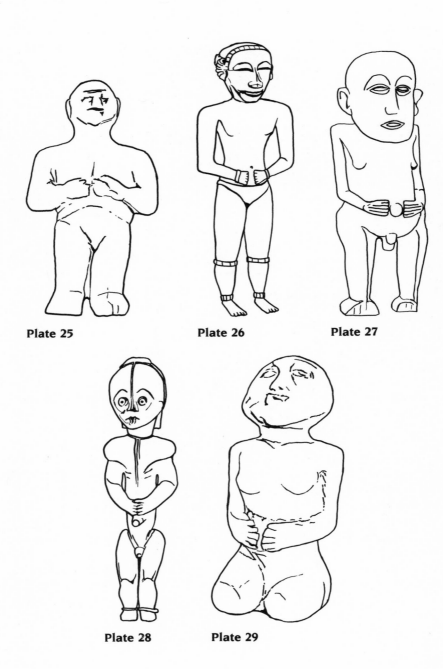

Plate 25   Plate 26   Plate 27

Plate 28   Plate 29

One of these cures involved an aching shoulder. For many years I had been in the habit on my numerous field trips of carrying a heavy shoulder bag made by a Yucatecan village saddler from sturdy deer leather. Finally the maltreated muscles rebelled. Putting anything on that shoulder began to cause excruciating pain; I could no longer sleep on my left side, lean on my left arm, or even turn in that direction. That summer a guest in Cuyamungue noticed that I was suffering and started massaging me. I nearly fainted with pain the first time, but she was quite knowledgeable, and after twelve sessions, when she had to leave, I did experience some relief. She warned, though, that I was not cured by a long shot, that a number of muscles were still bunched into hard knots in my back, and that upon returning to Columbus I should find a masseuse to continue with the treatment.

The massage therapist in the office of my family physician quickly found the same hard muscle knots in my back and after half an hour's work suggested that for those to dissolve I would have to have at least six more treatments. My pain had eased by then, so I foolishly carried a heavy suitcase on my trip to Cincinnati, where I was to do a workshop, with predictable results. By the time I had rattled for fifteen minutes during our first session, I was sure some fiend was gleefully tightening a vise on my left shoulder and pulling on it. We had done the Singing Shaman, and I intentionally slipped into a light trance while rattling, thinking that might give me some relief, but the pain was so fierce, I contemplated calling off the workshop.

At the next session I taught the participants the posture of the Shaman with the Bear Spirit. As I started rattling, I assumed as much of the posture myself as was possible under the circumstances and pleaded with Grandfather Bear to help me. Imperceptibly at first, as though it were stealing away on tiptoes, the pain eased and then disappeared. Nor did it recur during the rest of the workshop.

On the following Tuesday I went back to massage therapy. Try as she might, the masseuse was unable to find those six or seven hard knots that she was going to work on. "I can't understand this," she kept shaking her head, as she worked on me beyond the allotted half-hour. "Obviously you don't need me anymore," she said. "What did you do since the last time I saw you?" It would have been too complicated to tell her about Grandfather Bear, so I lied and complimented her on her good work, while breathing a grateful thank you to my old benefactor. This happened nearly three years ago, and the trouble has not recurred.

An even more dramatic cure happened to me in 1986. I was wearing a pair of lined woolen slacks during my spring trip to Europe. While in Austria, the weather suddenly turned warm, and I began to perspire. The perspiration apparently dissolved the formaldehyde in the lining, to which I am allergic. I developed a burning, itchy skin rash, which soon turned into dermatitis, and I was in agony. So I consulted the Bear Spirit. The attempt was disappointing; I did see his mask, but that was all. Then during the night I heard a voice reverberating through space, "Vinegar water, vinegar water." I was puzzled. Was it a belated message from the Bear Spirit? Besides, where was I going to get vinegar water on a trip? So I did not act on the curious counsel. I gave away the slacks, a physician friend let me have an antihistamine ointment, and in about four weeks, the rash gradually disappeared.

During the early summer, I helped with digging up some plants in Cuyamungue. It was extremely hot, I began to perspire, and as my bad luck would have it, I was wearing a Mexican blouse, which apparently also contained formaldehyde. Within minutes, I was covered with the same rash as before, first where the blouse had touched my moist skin, and soon from my toes up to my neck. As usual, I tried some home remedies first, but to no avail. By evening, I knew what burning in hell was like. To make matters worse, the night was unusually warm. I did not think I would see the dawn. Then I finally remembered that reverberating voice and its strange advice. I went over to the Student Building in the middle of the night, prepared a mixture of vinegar and lukewarm water, and sponged myself down with it. Relief was instantaneous. Within two more days, all traces of the rash had disappeared.

Except in such obvious cases, cures taking place in this posture, performed as we experience it by the Bear Spirit, are difficult to describe, first because, as in all non-Western medical systems, they serve predominantly health maintenance rather than specific cures; that is, they are designed to maintain balance and harmony. So both the body and the soul are treated. Second, the treatments are usually subtle and highly individualized, and frequently concern problems that the patient may be aware of only marginally and the observer even less.

Quite generally, even beginners tend to see their visual field completely suffused with a luminous purple color. They may be supported, shaken, or pushed from behind, gently or quite roughly; they may be caught in a spiraling movement and about to lose their balance. There is heat rising in their abdomens and over their backs, and a heavy weight presses down on their shoulders. They may shrink to a very small size or open up to receive a healing liquid, as we learn from Judy Ch. (Columbus, 1985): "I felt thirsty, so I was instructed, 'Put your head back!' And I felt a nectar of honey trickling down into me." Or from Belinda at the same workshop: "I saw a circular hole and started down. At the end of it there was an enormous glass with ice and a bubbly liquid in it, and that was poured into my head." Some cures are more exotic, as when Jan was fed a generous portion of worms with the assertion that it was good for her.

Without any prompting or prior knowledge, the Bear Spirit readily appears to the participants, visible partially or in his complete mask, either as a furry force holding or warming them from behind, or actually examining his would-be patients, as when Jan's guide took her to a spot in the Big Dipper, where the Bear "assessed my body and energy patterns." In addition, he is often seen to perform cures on others, as when Elizabeth R. watched how, touch-ingly, he made an incision in a woman's eyes "so she would be able to cry like others" (Columbus, 1985).

Let us listen to a few individual reports. The first one shows how physical perceptions keep merging with experiences that are possible only in the alternate reality.

> KRISTINA (Cuyamungue, August 1984): I was taken up into the Bear, but also saw him. We went flying together very slowly; I perceived a spiraling motion of my feet and also of my spine. There were bluish and purple flowers with yellow centers. I was being pushed back and forth by the Bear, then there were subtle movements all over my body. I felt that I was sinking ever deeper into my body, while at the same time dissolving into nothingness. Then I became conscious of my body again, and it felt okay all over.

For Pij (Salzburg, 1987), the hurt caused by an extremely unhappy childhood begins to dissolve:

> The rattle took me back to a happy memory from my childhood, when I used to roll marbles in a bowl. I saw them rolling around and was very sad when the image dissolved. Then I crawled through a tunnel, and my sorrow and pain were gone. I arrived in the midst of a family of bears; there were thirteen tiny bear cubs, and in the distance, I could see the huge mother bear. I left the bears, and felt very strong. There was a white light to the left of me and blackness to the right; I leaned back and was being rocked, and felt sheltered and warm. A green spot appeared before my right eye. I thought that perhaps it really wasn't there, but it wouldn't go away, and it frightened me. But I felt something black against my back, two heavy paws embraced me, and I was told that I should feed the birds. After I did that, the thirteen little bear cubs all started crawling around on me. I received a white bear skin and turned into a bear myself.

Linda (San Diego, 1985) is helped to resolve a conflict of sexual identity:

> My body was filled with a lot of sexual energy. There was a quick change of scenes; woods appeared as at home in Connecticut. I was a young man. A bear appeared and we danced together. Suddenly my spirit shot out of my face, and I saw a lot of fluffy clouds around me; they were like enormous kachinas, benevolent and powerful. Their energy was reassuring, telling me that I was doing fine. I found myself on a clearing. I was now a woman, and the Bear started teaching me how to dance, and I realized that I was also a bear. The dance had the feeling of a fertility ritual about it. Then I gave birth, not to humans but to many bears. The Bear turned into a she-bear, and she helped me nurse the bear cubs.

Eva D. (Vienna, 1985) speaks of overcoming fear:

> I felt very hot in the back, then I saw a bear skin. Suddenly, the Bear spread it all over me, and I became very afraid, thinking, "What is he going to do?" I was walking as if standing on his feet; I stumbled and fell down. But then I felt how from his skin strength was pouring into me. A fire sprang up before me; I walked

into it, and then I was the fire. The fire split into two fire tunnels and I was in both; I shot into them with tremendous speed, then the two tunnels merged. I once more looked into the fire and I understood. Some gnomes flew by; they wore wild, distorted masks, but I was no longer afraid.

Still others endure parts of their body becoming detached or being torn apart. To hear that was truly amazing to me: Without any preparation and entirely spontaneously, modern Westerners apparently were able to experience dismemberment, which for Siberian shamans is an important phase during their initiation as healers.[3] Apparently, the Bear Spirit especially singles out various kinds of healers for this treatment, which ties these experiences in with the Siberian culture complex. I was alerted to this peculiar coincidence in one of my very early workshops in Europe, when Lukas, a recent graduate of the Medical School of the University of Vienna, reported that the Bear Spirit grabbed him, threw him into a kettle, and started stirring the boiling liquid with him as the ladle. Lukas's body dissolved until only his head and his lungs remained, attached to each other by a thin cord. Suddenly, he was whole again. But while to the Siberian shamans the experience means intense suffering, Westerners do not perceive it that way. Christian St. (Vienna, 1985), for instance, paradoxically found that being manhandled this way by a powerful spirit was great fun, and he laughed about it afterward.

> The Bear put his arms around me, and I felt sheltered as in a motherly embrace. But then he began stroking me with his paws and tore off my head. He ripped open my belly, pulled out my intestines, and I felt the healing power of his paws. Then he looked me over with a serious expression, rent open my chest, and placed three masks in it, together with some threads. I had a long black penis and found myself at a black lake; I either walked into it or I fell, I don't remember. Then I saw all of you in this room. I wanted to dance. The Bear was here, too; he pissed on Eva, then he kissed Felicitas on her nose, and he was about to rip my head off once more when the rattle stopped.

At the time this happened, Christian was a graduate student in history, and I thought that perhaps my impression that such initiation experiences were reserved for healers had been wrong. However, only two years later, Christian began taking courses in holistic healing and is now well on his way toward his new career as a healer.

On occasion, the Bear Spirit is helped during curing by snakes, and also by various raptors and carrion-eating birds, a fact known from Pueblo Indian myths. "A snake appeared and knocked three times on my forehead," one participant reported. "An eagle came into my body through my forehead. It opened it up." Or as Sharron told (Columbus, 1985): "There was a flicker of fear. I had black plates on my shoulders, head, and back. Then I saw a bird's face looking at me; it was picking at me and tearing pieces out of me, out of that plate." Here is an experience of a similar nature from Switzerland:

URSULA ST. (Sommerau, 1985): I found myself inside a mountain and felt great pain in my shoulders and my neck. I leaned back and felt something supporting me, not only there but on my sides as well. My abdomen felt warm. Dark figures appeared before me; I heard the flapping of wings. I split in half; rags, ribbons, and colors rose out of my belly; my rigid shell dropped away. I felt wonderful, so light. The birds flew away. I saw an eye above me and embryos floating in the light. One fell into the split in my body and turned. I wanted to keep it in there.

The Bear posture can also be assumed if a cure is to be effected for someone else. During the workshop in Cincinnati in the fall of 1987, Dean, one of the participants, complained about sciatica causing severe pain along her right thigh. To help her, I asked the group, including Dean, to assume the Bear posture. After I had rattled for fifteen minutes, everyone gathered around her and touched her, and I continued to rattle for another three minutes to keep the trance going. Healing rituals of this nature are used extensively around the world. The understanding that trance can heal must be extremely old, for modern hunter-gatherers, such as the Bushmen, guardians of the most ancient human traditions, use the strategy simply to keep everyone in their band well and also to heal. Anthropologists tell of seeing the medicine men inducing the religious trance in themselves by singing and dancing, and then touching everyone in their group to this end. Trance healing has survived as "laying on of hands" in Christianity.

After our ritual, Bernie reported that as he placed his hand on Dean, he felt a resistance, and that he was doing "all the work." It was so strenuous, he thought he might collapse. But then his strength came back, and he was back in equilibrium. Another one felt, "not saw but felt," a bright yellow light traveling down her arm and into Dean; or "I saw a large hand; it had a bluish marble on its fingertips, which changed to white and then passed into Dean, a gift to her"; or "I felt pins and needles streaming out of my arm. They were really shooting out; I thought I was going to electrocute her." Dean later reported complete relief.

I should like to add still another example here, for it demonstrates the great power of the Bear Spirit. In this instance, Belinda called on him for help when her mother was discovered to have uterine cancer. The examining physician was convinced on the basis of his tests that the cancer of this patient was extensive and had possibly metastasized. Belinda was desperate. So she and her friends decided to suggest a healing ritual to her mother, and to Belinda's great relief, her mother consented to try it, although she was unfamiliar with what her daughter was talking about.

Belinda and her helpers had her mother assume the Bear posture lying in bed, so that her hands were above her uterus. They then assumed the same posture themselves. The patient felt her uterus start getting very hot. She began seeing small white mice running around in her body and producing more mice. They were busily gnawing away at her uterus, as though they were intent on consuming the uterine wall. After the conclusion of this part of the ritual, one of the healers handed the patient a large crystal which she was to hold on her abdomen above the uterus. The crystal, which had been clear before, showed grey streaks after the treatment and needed to be cleansed by burying it for a while. Going into trance once more, the group guided the "mice" into a bowl of water. This is not unlike what is done by Australian shamans, who, in a ritual which the Australian psychiatrist John Cawte[4] likens to a sacrament, make the illness visible by "sucking" a small object, a pebble or a fragment of glass, out of the patient, thus facilitating a cure.

The subsequent operation proved the physician wrong. It turned up only a small cancerous nodule within a large benign fibrous growth. When the intervention was so successful, Jan, one of the participants in the ritual, joked, "We should have had another week!" I would not go that far, but certainly at least in this case the ritual of the Bear posture proved to be a valuable adjunct to the surgical procedure.

Plate 30

The Bear posture is so powerful that according to some folk traditions, it can also mediate a cure if the patient is too ill or weak to assume it himself. In modern Siberia, for instance, wood carvings of the Bear Spirit in the healing posture (see pl. 30a) are given to the chronically ill. Such carvings are not objects of worship or "idols." After use, children have been observed playing with them, and if the band moves away, they are often discarded.

Even when large-scale agriculture takes over, which usually means the loss of the knowledge of the postures, this particular one seems to endure. This is true of classical Egypt (see pl. 30e), and also happened in the Aztec empire. The Aztec goddess Tlaelquan was conventionally represented in the Bear posture. She bore the epithet of "eater of contamination" (*comedora de cosas sucias*), because she nourished herself with the faults that humans confessed to her, thus freeing them of sin. In other words, there is a memory about psychological healing and the restoration of harmony attached to this posture.

Because of its relationship to curing and health, the posture in other areas of the world has come conventionally to mean "I wish you good health." This at least seems to be the case with the golden jugs from Colombia created by Quimbaya and Chibcha goldsmiths of pre-Inca time (pl. 26). They are decorated with male or female figures in the posture of the Bear Spirit. Such containers were used to carry lime. In many mountainous regions of South America, lime and coca leaves have always been chewed together, contributing to health and well-being, because above fourteen thousand feet, carbohydrates cannot easily be digested without the aid of the active ingredient in the coca leaf.

CHAPTER NINE

Female Powers
of Healing

T*he forty-one girl knights.*
Although the Bear Spirit may on occasion appear in the form of a female bear, his power seems to be predominantly male. There is another posture, however, which apparently summons a special kind of female energy.[1] The posture first came to my attention early in 1985 in a publication about antiquities from Tennessee.[2] The stone sculpture, created about A.D. 700, represented a woman who had her arms placed on her chest in a special way, so that her right hand came to rest above the left (see pl. 31). Subsequently, I saw the posture also in Marija Gimbutas's book about ancient Europe.[3] The terra-cotta figurine, once more a woman (pl. 32), was much older (5th millennium B.C.), but there was no mistaking the position of the hands. I was anxious to explore the posture, but in neither case was there any indication about the position of the legs, and I was at a loss about what to do about that.

When I went to Europe in the spring, I took my notes about the posture with me, however, in order to have some trained people in Austria see what they could do with it. Given the fact that there were so many standing postures, I suggested that we try it standing upright. Christian St. subsequently saw himself in the midst of clinging plants with strange fruit that started wildly growing about him, and a woman who breathed on his heart. His experience carried a suggestion of healing, but Eva D. provided no confirmation. She even became sick to her stomach, and her legs began hurting. Standing, I assumed, had probably been the wrong choice.

My next assignment was in Budapest. My host, the Hungarian folklorist Mihály Hoppál, showed me a new book which he had edited about Eurasian shamanism.[4] There was no time to read it, but I looked at the photographs, and I was surprised and delighted that one of them showed a modern sha-

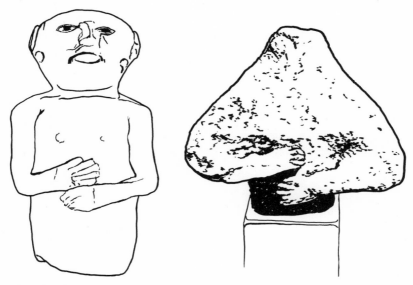

Plate 31   **Plate 32**

maness from Central Asia during a healing ritual in the posture that we had
explored in Austria.[5] She had her arms folded over her chest in the way I had
seen in the above two ancient pieces of art, and she was sitting with her legs
crossed. Here apparently was the answer to our problem.

Once back home in Columbus, I ordered Hoppál's work, and by fall I had
it in my possession. We had planned a working session anyway, and so I put
the new posture on the agenda. On the day of our meeting, I settled down
for a noonday nap but almost immediately woke up again with the curious
feeling that I was not alone. The entire room seemed to be crowded with
joyously excited entities. I thought, well, a few of our spirit friends are aware
that we are going to invite them in this evening, and they arrived here ahead
of time. I had much to do before my guests arrived, but I got out Hoppál's
book anyway to read something about the shamaness shown in the photograph.
But being in a hurry, I could not locate the article in question, so I put the
book away again.

We used a tape, so I was able to participate, too, and there were five of
us. For reasons to be told later, I am going to give here only three of the five
reports:

JUDY M.: Even while we were breathing, I left my body and went outside. I was
floating up high, and looking back into this room, I saw that it was empty. I felt
very light and disappeared. I looked down on a desert landscape; there was a dark
tunnel with a light at the end, and my spirit guide, a huge stag, appeared next to
me. The tunnel ended in a cave with a very high ceiling, and there was a bonfire,

and there were others sitting around it. I stepped into the middle of the fire and started dancing. Then I left the tunnel and became a raindrop; it was wonderful. I smelled the earth and felt all the elements. Then I had to get back into my body, and I didn't like that at all.

JAN: From the start I had the feeling of the room being full of energy. The energy was between my hands; it was so intense, it hurt. Then it became an ear of corn and it burst, and the kernels danced around in a circle. I saw each one of us, living, dying, each one at a different spot. Then we were back in this room. Each of us brought something back; we were a kaleidoscope. Then I went diving down and saw a crystal cave glowing in brilliant colors; I was in the water, then in the air. I shot up to the stars. The energy was still there, so great that my body couldn't take it.

FELICITAS: I was flying rapidly through a glowing, dark-blue world against a night-blue background. To my left, flat images began developing, pitted white surfaces in the dark, like fly-by pictures of the earth taken from a satellite. I reined it in; I didn't want to leave the earth. Then I was sad that I was no longer flying. The vision subsided, and all I still felt was being rocked back and forth and then more energetically sideways by an energy that wouldn't let go of me.

We were struck by the fact that the three of us had all been on a journey to some faraway cold and rainy place. The other two, Belinda and Elizabeth R., equally reported on such a region, and about restlessly dancing, but in addition there were other, curious elements in their tale, something about a totem pole and a white she-bear, and the horns of a mountain goat, which did not fit in with the rest of our experiences. Confident that someday I would understand, I left it alone for the time being. When that understanding finally came, it was one of the biggest surprises of our common journey of discovery, as we shall see later (Section III, The Story of Kats and His Bear Wife). In our discussion we concentrated instead on the dancing multiple energy that had had all of us in its grip, and wondered what its nature might be.

During the following night, shortly before daybreak, I had a vision. A row of curiously shaped masks appeared before a background lightly blushing into rose. They were white and round, delicate like Chinese paper lanterns, yet with their pointed ears they recalled the heads of cats. The place for the eyes was cut out, and inside each one a dark-grey hairy ball was incessantly in motion. Several times I was given to understand emphatically that "we lick blood, we lick blood."

The next morning, I recorded the vision, but except for the restless motion of the grey balls inside the paper lanterns, it seemed to have little to do with what we had experienced during our session the night before. However, that same afternoon, I finally located the report that belonged to the photographs,[6] and I found out that this conclusion was wrong. It seems that in Inner Asia, in the valleys of Uzbekistan, shamanesses ask for the help of a group of spirits called Chiltan when they are called upon to cure. The Chiltan are said to be forty-one young girl knights. No wonder my room had felt so crowded the day before! Their favorite color is white, and in agreement with what I had been told in my vision, the shamanesses smear the blood of sacrificial animals on their tambourines, because the Chiltan spirits like to lick blood.

Now I understood why from the start, even during that first attempt in the spring, where Christian St. was surrounded by clinging plants with strange fruit wildly growing about him, there was the experience of multiple, powerful energy. And in Uzbekistan, obviously, the energy was summoned to aid in healing, as Christian knew when he felt a woman breathing on his chest.

Representations of the *Chiltan posture,* as we are now calling it, have turned up on the Northwest Coast, in Arizona, and with the Olmecs in Central America. In addition to Tennessee, it is known in South America, in ancient Europe, and in modern Africa. A search of the record also turned up a connection between the posture and the cat ears I had seen. It appears that in Colombia, archeologists dug up a tall stone column, about three thousand years old, which shows what appears to be a bearded man in the Chiltan posture (pl. 33). The power animals of the Indian societies of Central and South America, namely, two jaguars with their catlike pointed ears, are carved into the base of the column. The relationship to healing is evident in the snake appearing on the left.

The archeological record also demonstrates that my conclusion about one always having to sit with legs crossed was a hasty one, arrived at with too little experimentation. There are a number of male figures extant that are not sitting but standing in this posture. So in our workshops we now have the men stand, as usual with their feet somewhat apart and their knees soft, while the women sit cross-legged, with the right leg in front.

Experience has shown that the Chiltan spirits can provide a fast surge of energy. In the summer of 1986, for instance, I used the posture to good advantage giving a much-needed boost to a group assembled for the trance dance ritual and tired from working on their masks all day in the unaccustomed heat. Not only did the exercise produce the expected results, but I was once more amazed at how consistently the Chiltan spirits revealed themselves. As during the first time, there was the trip: "I burst forth out of my chest"; "I rode

Plate 33

fast through the forest"; and "A tall woman stood by the kiva door; she motioned for me to follow her, and we flew over the land." We heard the endless repetition of experiencing energy, usually in multiple form: "The energy came in waves"; "Lots of energy was lifting me up"; "Whirlwinds twirled me into a cave"; "Lots of energy went through my body and I was getting dizzy; I felt that it was female energy"; and, similar to what Jan had told during that first session, "I became a green pepper and I exploded." Even the fire kept reappearing, as in "We went across a fire"; or "I sat in the flames and it was healing."

What I found particularly fascinating were the specific references to the blood sacrifice that I had heard about in my vision: "I saw a gorge, in it a river of blood, and a huge sun"; or "I was a leopard. An African warrior threw his spear; he killed me and licked my blood"; and even, "I was covered with the sweet and sticky nectar of a blood sacrifice that the spirits licked off of me." And finally we heard about the militant and possibly dangerous aspect of the girl knights, as in, "We were all spirits in the clouds and were organized like an army."

Here are some examples from other workshops. In rich variation, they play out the different motifs of this posture. One theme, for instance, is the experience of being rocked by the energy of these spirits:

ELLA (Cuyamungue, summer 1987): I saw pictures like of marbled paper, of earth colors. I was floating and saw an eruption; it was red like fire, but it was also like a flower and a river. I felt movement back and forth, like being rocked, or maybe riding, but I didn't know on what. Was it an animal? I couldn't see it. Suddenly I was flying over a canyon, but I saw only one side of it, and next to it a flat-top mountain. I was riding and rocking again. Then there were unclear figures and a triangle of complicated shape.

Another theme is the multiple nature of the energy. It appears in many different forms, as a group of people dancing, a circle of women all looking alike, and in a vivid burst of visual display, as many multicolored snakes and balls:

KRISCHTA (Sommerau, Switzerland, spring 1987): I felt warmth in my abdomen and was whirling around. I was supposed to get dressed, and the rattle was my garment. Suddenly I found myself in a dark forest, and it was the forest that was doing the rattling. I got out of the forest, and in front of me there was a huge beak, and gradually an eagle developed out of the beak and vanished into the ground. There was a light from above, and surfaces started moving into each other. I could feel that but didn't see it. Many people appeared. They danced to the rhythm of the rattle; they kept picking up what, I could not see. Then the rhythm of the rattle was a horse, but I couldn't catch it. I was enveloped in an enormous waterfall; its noise was deafening, and there was much movement. I became a stork and flew away into the distance until I was nothing but a black dot.

KRISTINA (Cuyamungue, summer 1987): There was a lot of talking in the room, and I was wondering what was going on. There was the presence of heavy energy. I was looking down from above, and in the room there were many women; they all looked alike, they were gathered around the fire. The light kept flickering; it got smaller, then larger. I started collapsing and fell to the ground, then I disappeared. I saw a slug or a small snake curling, and I wondered whether I was going to turn into a ring. Suddenly I felt a lot of energy; my spine and my head all became of one piece, and all around me there were peacock feathers.

VRENIE (Sommerau, spring 1987): From my left, there came many multicolored snakes. I landed in a chute. I was very small. I turned into a snake, then into an ant, a flying ant, and flew across a lake. The sun was orange-colored, like a flowerbed. I landed on it and started crawling around; it was very difficult to do, managing the rhythm of the six legs all at the same time. Many green and multicolored balls started coming in from all sides, moving wildly up and down. I fell into a cleft, into a cave, and a multitude of animals started arriving, leopards, deer, snakes, many different animals.

Not only do the Chiltan spirits have energy to give, but they are also healers. Their healing energy may be scattered in the form of gold dust, it may come equally gently carried as honey by swarms of bees, or it may burn as cleansing fire:

JACQUES (Cuyamungue, summer 1987): I saw many animals coming in from all sides, also birds from far away, and many black ravens. They landed and were very strong. A rainbow appeared, and the birds took gold dust and a fan, and scattered the gold dust all over us.

NORMA (Cuyamungue, summer 1987): I became a garden; the earth was moist, there were birds, and bees, and a turtle was sitting on my stomach. There were insects on me; it was pleasant, and the bees dropped honey in my mouth to give me energy. Then the sun became dimmer. It was evening; everything went to sleep, the insects, the birds, and the turtle, too. All were contented.

KATHRIN (Sommerau, spring 1987): For a while, everything seemed to be reversed. Instead of standing, I was lying down, and animals came rushing toward me, a deer, a fox, some birds, many animals, but I could see only their heads. I was a black beetle and could feel my wings in the back, like an armor. Then I was a lion. A white bird emerged from the shadows; then there were many more birds, and their movements seemed to multiply. Finally, a shower of fire rained down on me from the left.

REGULA (Cuyamungue, summer 1987): I saw a wheel turning. I went down into a whirlpool, and masks started coming from all sides and crowded all over me. I heard the drums, and the masks danced around the fire and I with them, and my hands and feet became very warm. Above us, there was a large eagle with its wings spread out, as if standing in the air. Just before the rattle stopped, a large fire sprang up and started burning me.

Finally, the Chiltan spirits are fully capable of taking a novice through a Siberian-type initiation if they encounter a healer worthy of their attention. This is what happened to Hanna, who is a registered nurse:

HANNA (Cuyamungue, summer 1987): I was standing in the desert. As I was looking down on myself, I saw a hand holding a knife that was cutting into my skin. I started objecting; I didn't want to lose my inner parts. But it was useless. The hand took out my heart, my liver, everything; I was left only with my skin, and I started to dance. I was afraid that the hand would cut off my head, too. I said, "Don't do that!" But it happened anyway. I saw myself without a head. The hand put my head into a big pot to boil, and scraped out everything, so my head was completely empty. Then the hand took a totem pole and pushed it through my body. It got bigger and bigger and turned into a medicine man. The medicine man started pounding me into the ground, and I was nothing but rock and sand. The medicine man was an ecstatic dancer; he danced on me, and I was only sand. With every step he took, he began creating me entirely anew; it was like a rebirth. My skin began reappearing, but I was still empty inside when the rattle stopped.

The Couple from Cernavodă. In five- to seven-thousand-year-old arche-ological sites in Europe, but also in much younger ones in Africa, archeologists occasionally come across a male figure seated on a low four-legged stool, his elbows propped on his knees. The folds of his cheeks are pushed up by his hands, which seem to form a fist. He has been called variously the pensive god or the sorrowful god. At one particular dig, however, at Cernavodă near the Danube delta in present-day Rumania, he was found in a seven-thousand-year-old grave together with a female figure, both formed of clay and covered with a brown slip. As luck would have it, the first time I ever saw him was in association with this female companion (see pl. 34). The woman is sitting on the ground. Her left leg is stretched out in front of her, and her right knee is raised. Her hands are resting lightly on her right knee in such a way that her left hand seems somewhat stretched out, while the palm of her right hand is lifted, creating the impression of a paw.

What the man might be experiencing by himself in this posture, if anything, we have not yet investigated. But remarkable things happen when the two of

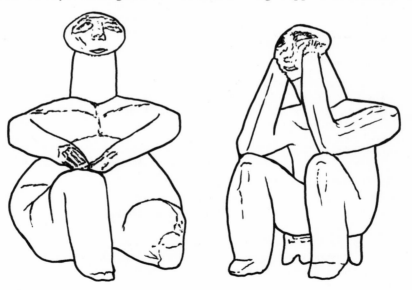

Plate 34

them get together. What takes place, apparently, is a ritual during which it is the female partner who does the shamanizing, while the man's experiences are minimal. Yet he ends up totally exhausted. The reason seems to be that he is the one who provides the energy. "He is the battery," one participant commented.

We tried this combined posture for the first time at a workshop in Switzerland in the spring of 1986. There were only three men facing nine women, and I soon suspected what was going on when I heard the first man complaining that he had felt some shooting pains in his heart, and all he wanted to do when the rattle stopped was to go to sleep. The next one had radiated energy toward the women, which caused him to dissolve, and although he recovered even while still in trance, he was extremely tired afterward: "I started getting nauseated," he said, "and rays issued from my chest, and then I briefly dissolved. After that, I became immensely tall, and there was a lot of light in my head." And Urs R., a physician, recognized the pivotal role of the shamaness when he saw her approaching as a dark mass from which a triangle emerges, which then turns into the navel of the world. However, he struggled in vain to provide the energy needed for her work. That is why he saw the navel of the world, the rounded stone of the *omphalos* at Delphi, under a glass dome:

> I had the feeling that parts of the rattle collected in my cerebellum. I had to let it seep into my spinal cord, then it wanted to escape through the tail bone, but I couldn't let it out. I saw two surfaces, a white one on the right and a black one on the left; they were moving from left to right, and each one had tall doors, which I entered simultaneously. On the other side everything was covered by fog. For a long time, nothing happened. Then a triangle appeared; it turned into an obelisk, then into a rock representing the omphalos. It was covered by a glass sphere. I wanted to enter it, then once more there was nothing.

To be sure, in the end the men, although terribly tired, were glad they had given of their energy. For listening to the women, they too understood that this exercise in psychological archeology had afforded us a glimpse of a lost world, full of wonder and mystery, like a scintillating jigsaw puzzle. But it was clear that there had been too much of a strain on the men. So I decided to do this exercise only if the number of men and women was more or less evenly balanced.

Considering the individual reports of the women now, we find that riding on the power of the men, a shamaness may make daring voyages into the world of legend:

> DOROTHEA: I was in a small boat, and something was pulling me toward the left. I struggled against it, and finally, I was able to stop. I felt something approaching from the right. A strong wind came up, and I struggled to keep from capsizing. Suddenly the wind abated, and I saw a sea serpent approaching; she was green

and very long, a real sea monster. As I watched, her eyes turned green and her tongue red, then her tongue split into three tongues and she had three heads. She kept threatening me, and I needed a lot of power.

The shamaness of old is also a midwife and healer. Her rattles put a young woman into trance to ease the pains of labor, and then she summons the birds to take her through to delivery:

> REGINA: I heard many rattles, and had the feeling that I could breathe deeply and well. I saw a black bird coming from the right, and a white one from the left. They flew over the valley. Then they came back, and one of them carried a small child in its beak, like a stork. He asked me, "Do you want it?" And the white bird said, "If you want it, you can have it." And I said, "All right, I will take it." So the birds left the bundle, and as they flew away, they winked at me.

Sometimes a pregnant woman is seriously ill, and it takes all the skill of the shamaness to save her, taking recourse not only to the succor of the rattles but also to decoctions that can work miracles and ease suffering. In the case that unfolds before our eyes in Kathrin's story, the old shamaness has been summoned to a woman who is ill and pregnant with twins. The shamaness raises her arms to invoke the helping spirits and, as in very ancient traditions, transmits spiritual power to the patient through her tongue. She administers a healing potion. It transports the patient into a soothing dream; the shamaness appears to her as a praying mantis and a horned beetle. As her strength comes back, she sees the dancing moons, and completely restored, she wakes up in the familiar cave and sees the rock walls outside.

> KATHRIN: I saw a mouth. It stuck out its tongue, and a ribbon came out of it and flowed into me. Then there were some disjointed sequences. I saw a praying mantis, then a horned beetle, which turned into a rhinoceros. I was in a waterfall; there were two moon sickles, and they danced with each other. I saw a drake. I ran after it and came to some water, with a child in it. The drake passed right through me. I became a gold ring, and there were two embryos in the ring. A large tube appeared, and from its opening milk flowed into me. Then I was in a cave lit by burning candles, and I lay down and reddish-brown drops fell on me. Suddenly I was outside the cave, and I had the feeling that I was a part of the rock wall.

One of the most important tasks of the shamaness is taking the soul of the deceased in the shape of a cocoon in a boat to the lower world, to the abode of the Spirits of the Dead. Immediately after death, the soul is still heavy with earthly concerns, and so Pij as the shamaness finds that rowing the boat is tremendously strenuous. After a while of rowing upstream, the shamaness loses her strength. The soul, which has not become reconciled yet to being forever parted from the living, takes advantage of the shamaness's waning strength, turns into fish bones, and tries to escape. This must not happen, for the ghosts of the recently dead will bring disease and misfortune to the living. To renew her strength, the shamaness sinks into the depths, the canyon of her childhood. The restful sojourn takes a long time, but finally she rises from the canyon and begins to dance in the street. The magic strategy works, the street turns into the river once more, and the task is completed: the people who had gone along in the boat return without the cocoon. Everyone celebrates, because the deceased has been successfully taken to the home of the departed. But the shamaness has been to the realm of the dead, and she must now undergo a ritual of death and rebirth before she can return to the world of the living:

> PIJ: The rattle immediately split into many sounds, which moved around me wildly in the form of colored waves or snakes. Then the rattle sound became a waterfall, and the water, coming from the left, hit me hard like hail. I was in a canoe rowing but couldn't look behind me. I had the feeling that somebody was sitting behind me, or that I was carrying a load, and that I had to go on rowing. I knew that behind me, someone was lying in the canoe, enveloped like a cocoon, and there were six or eight people with him. I asked, "Where am I supposed to go?" And the answer came, "Upriver." I found it very strenuous; my muscles hurt as I was rowing against the current. I was proud, but also nearly at the end of my strength.
>
> Suddenly the person in the canoe turned into the skeleton of a fish and wanted to get out. Inexplicably, I had some brief images of childhood memories at this point. It seems that I fell off a high wall into a canyon, and was waiting for something, and the rattle sounded very slow. Then I was standing in a street; I had many legs, six, or maybe eight, and had to dance wildly, over and over again. Suddenly the street turned into the river, and the people of the canoe were coming back. The cocoon was no longer with them. I saw people dancing happily in the streets of Luzern. They laid me down on top of a wall. I had the feeling that it was all right, but then again, I had my doubts. I had to lie there for a long time. Many Indians started emerging from my vagina, ants, then also horses. I became very old; the flesh fell off my bones, which were fish bones, or maybe they were a human skeleton. I had the feeling that all was well, and that it had been worth the trouble.

The second time we did the posture of the Couple of Cernavodă was at a workshop in Vienna in the spring of 1987. This time there were almost as many men in the group as there were women, so I hoped that it would not be as strenuous for the men as it had been in Switzerland the year before. We were in a large, rectangular hall, so I had the men and women sitting facing each other. As a result, some of the women afterward commented spontaneously that they had been aware of the men "radiating" toward them.

Once more, the men's experiences were very meager, although their reports did not reflect the extreme exhaustion suffered by the Swiss men. "The trance seemed very short," said one. "There was the snout of a monkey, but all was very unclear." According to another one, "I saw an eye, and I rushed toward it. It had an enormous pupil. I fell into it and dissolved into my elements."

In Othmar's vision there is an indication of the role assigned to the women in this posture when he sees, as Kathrin had in Switzerland, the shamaness ready herself to transmit energy to her patient through her tongue: "I saw very little. I felt sleepy. I saw images that were unclear and disjointed. There was a witch; a red ribbon came out of her mouth, and then I saw a bird." And both Wittigo and Wolfgang distributed power, the latter characteristically perceiving himself as a leaky vessel:

> WITTIGO: I dissolved, then became a hallucinogenic mushroom. I rose as if in a balloon. I was in control of rain and let raindrops fall on the earth. I had small mushrooms, which I cut into pieces and spread on the ground.

> WOLFGANG: I saw purple, blue, and green colors; they seemed to weave back and forth, and I was sending out rings of light that were bright and warm. I was a vessel with a hole in it.

Although by this time I had forgotten the details of the Swiss reports, and no one of the Swiss group had any contact with the rather large one in Vienna, the experiences of the women precisely followed the same general outline. There was the trip to the mythological world beyond:

> ROSMARIE: I came to an iron fence and went through the gate. Behind it there were many dwarfs peeking out from behind the trees. I came to a round lake. There were dwarfs rowing in small boats toward a canal. There they got out; they were now white spirits, moving like marionettes. They began playing with balls on the seashore. Then some whales arrived. They picked up the balls, swallowed them, and took them away. The sea was light blue; it looked like silk, with white seagulls rising from it. I sat on the bank by a hut and I was an old man. I collected the droppings of the seagulls and fed them to the whales.

In the next experience, there is the topic of delivery, although the shamaness is present only by implication. In addition, except for the perception of the constriction in the abdomen, the birth event is experienced from the point of view of the fetus:

> CHARLOTTE: I felt a constriction in my belly. Most images were very unclear. The landscape I saw was pale, but I distinctly heard water rushing by. A black spot appeared, then I saw the sun and in the background a small bird. I was in a pea pod and saw it very clearly from the inside, and then I disappeared.

Or during this second delivery, we are given the impression that the mother died, while the child lived to run and play:

> CLAUDIA: I saw the blood running out of me, and I heard someone say, "Lie down." I refused; it was a woman who said that. I again said, "No," and really hated her. But she prevailed; she slit open my abdomen and examined my uterus. I could no longer hear the rattle. I saw a small being running around, and there was dancing and swinging.

And once more, the shamaness appears as the healer, who is called upon to cure many ailments, as related by Irmgard:

> IRMGARD: I had pains in my upper jaw and in my groin; my arms felt heavy and trembled, and my head kept bothering me. A man appeared, made of shadow; his hair glowed as if with electricity. Out of the shadows, the heads of animals began emerging, of a steer first; that turned into a deer, and then into an owl. Suddenly, I felt water splashing on my head, and it turned light. I was given raw mushrooms to eat. I can still taste them now.

The shamaness may even be able to make the old and sick young again, as in Isi's concluding story. The connection of the shamaness to the power animal becomes evident when, after she brings about a cure, pointed ears start growing from her pelt:

> There was so much energy around, but I still felt that this posture was very strenuous. I was in a snowy landscape. A woman came to me on a sleigh; she wore a white fur coat and a white cap. She made me get into the sleigh and off we went, very fast, because we had to save a woman's life. We arrived at a house and went in. There was an old couple in the house, and the woman was dying. As I watched, the woman started getting younger and younger, and pointed ears started growing from the fur cap of the white woman. Suddenly, I was outside, it was light, and the snow had melted. When the rattle stopped, I noticed that I had a backache.

In the summer of 1987, Thomas, a psychology student and friend of Isi's who had also taken part in the above workshop, came to her for help. On a hike through the Austrian forests, he had picked up some ticks, which may spread meningitis, and he had neglected to get inoculated. Understandably, he was thoroughly frightened and depressed. So he asked her to rattle for him. As she wrote,

> I figured that perhaps a rattle session would give him back some feeling of joy and confidence in himself, and that is exactly what happened. The rattling was so intense, I was completely overcome. What happened was that as I rattled I saw the woman in the white fur coat returning, whom I had come to know in the Cernavodă posture. Except this time she came with bells on her sleigh. She was definitely in the room, and with the tips of her fur, she gave Thomas something like an aura massage, and she pointed out to me exactly where the energy was blocked in his body, especially around his heart. The fascinating thing was that afterward Thomas told that he had felt something like feathers fanning him, and that then those feathers settled protectively on his heart. At first, I used a very bright-sounding Huichol rattle, while I had him stand in the Bear posture. Then I had him lie down for a trip to the lower world and used our [New Mexican gourd] rattle and then a drum. Suddenly I knew that he was not in any danger at all, and I suggested to him that he get in touch with his power animal. It was a wonderful present that afterward he felt so well. He was completely relaxed and full of hope. I could feel your presence too all that time, and you kept saying, "Go on. It's all right." (July 1, 1987)

CHAPTER TEN

Changing Shape—
The Shimmering Game

In a tale of Rabelaisian abandon related by Indian fishermen of the Northwest Coast,[1] their culture hero, the Raven, changes himself into a fisherman in order to make merry with the latter's wife. When the fisherman unexpectedly returns and begins beating the intruder into a pulp, the Raven is constrained to revert to his original shape. The incensed husband ties him up and throws him into the pit of the outhouse. But the Raven, being immortal, eventually frees himself of his bonds and lives to see another day and more adventures of a similar nature.

Traces of such "softness," as one anthropologist calls it,[2] of the boundaries between humans and animals, when matters were in a state of flux between the species, are all about. Egyptian and Celtic and Hindu gods have animal heads or shapes. Echoes of the same tradition abound in the myths of every society of the world. They are known among the Australian aborigines and on the other end of the spectrum among the nineteenth-century Germans who were the consultants of the Grimm Brothers. And they are, of course, equally familiar to the Indian societies of our continent. There is a story current among the same Indian fishermen of the Northwest Coast, according to which a hunter once heard laughter coming from a cave. When he sneaked up to the entrance and peeked in, there were the animals hilariously playing at turning into people. In fact, the Haida Indians of the region recount that in those early times animals used to have both human and animal forms. As the Navajo singers put it, "In those times all the animals were like people. The four-footed beasts, the flying birds, the coiling snakes, and the crawling insects behaved the way that earth-surface people who occupy the world today behave" (Zolbrod 1984:98).

It stands to reason that humans should equally have the capability of crossing the boundaries of their species. In fact, various hunter societies that still exist today have sacred dances in which humans turn into those animals to which they have a special relationship. Modern observers of Australian religious life[3] describe dances where the movements of the respective animal are expertly imitated, until in trance the dancer turns into the being depicted. Similar dances are also known among African hunter-gatherer societies. To the rhythm of the clapping of the women, as we see in an old cave drawing (pl. 35), the Bushman dancers are imitating, we might conjecture, the movements of an antelope, and one of them has changed shape and has metamorphosed down to the waist into that animal.

During our trance sessions, we frequently perform such dances, preferably to the sound of a drum. The ritual has also become an integral part of our masked dance, to be described in Chapter 11. During a workshop the participants do a preliminary breathing exercise, the same as for the posture sessions, and are then asked to move rhythmically and to imitate as much as possible the behavior and motions of the animal whose spirit likeness they encountered in their visions. When I participated in this dance for the first time and danced the movements of the buffalo while doubling over, I felt very clearly that I had horns and large brown eyes and the head of a buffalo. But I was amazed to find that my metamorphosis involved only the upper half of my body, in the same way as I saw it four years later in that Bushman drawing.

Plate 35

The experience produces a surprising empathy with the respective species. One trancer, who danced a snake, told of becoming conscious not only of the feel of the earth but also of the difference in body structure and of being afraid about not having any limbs. Yet she felt strong and supple, and strikingly, "I realized how totally silent I was." At the same dance exercise, another participant perceived how his friend the Bear entered into him, "and my muscles became very strong, but not physically." One participant in a German workshop, a professor of Jungian psychology, recalled with delight his turning into an elephant, and the sensitivity of the protuberances of his trunk that he became aware of as he tore leaves off a tree. And an elderly woman in Amsterdam remarked that she had never known how fresh and green a turtle felt "inside."

While such identification could possibly be explained on psychological grounds, another experience that quite frequently follows a metamorphosis dance cannot. It seems that when a dancer becomes a particular animal, a powerful bond is created between that dancer and the species represented, which breaches the separation between realities. Or perhaps by experiencing another species in trance, we enter a field common to all animate beings, where the barriers of communication erected during our evolutionary history do not exist. When Kristina, after becoming a dolphin during a recent dance in Cuyamungue, went to a marina in California, the dolphins atypically all crowded around the spot where she had stopped to watch. And Walter, a participant in several workshops in the Netherlands, wrote in a letter in 1984,

> [During the metamorphosis dance] I concentrated intensely on being a heron, flying, circling up and down, stopping in shallow water for fishing, landing on a nest, etc.
>
> The next morning my wife and I were sitting in our small garden in the city area of Amsterdam. Within a minute, the crashing sound of a heron filled the air, and the heron for several minutes made low-flying circles above our heads. We have lived about fifteen years here in the city area, and this or something like that never happened before. (September)

The tradition of animal dances continued into the era of the horticulturalists, and their memory is still alive in the deer, eagle, buffalo, and butterfly dances of our own Pueblo Indians. However, while among the hunters the animal dances express the kinship of humans with other species, the complex shifts into a different direction among horticulturalists, i.e., that of postures. Their women were the first to put seeds into the ground, and thus became conscious of the miracle of seeds' turning into plants and yielding seeds once more. Consequently, the central cultural idea in horticulture is that of change, of metamorphosis. Given the propensity of horticulturalist shamans for developing postures to facilitate certain important experiences, it is understandable that they would come up also with the requisite postures for metamorphosis. Or who can tell? Perhaps the experience of metamorphosis and the postures to go with it originated in the alternate reality.

At any rate, postures of this nature do exist, because eventually we rediscovered a few that apparently were designed specifically to facilitate metamorphosis, that is, the change from human to nonhuman form. Such discoveries were made easier by the fact that the softness, the instability of the human shape had become part of our expectation early on, as soon as we started working with the trance postures. The adventures told by the trancers on the preceding pages illustrate this fact over and over again. The shapes assumed without the slightest inhibition covered much of our animate and even inanimate environment, everything from birds, mammals, and insects to clouds, mountains, and sand. In the metamorphosis postures, the same process also occurs, except in more predictable form. What was truly amazing to us, however, was that Ego, the observing person, remained immutable throughout; there was never any of the disturbance in self-concept that psychiatry always expects to see when changes of the state of consciousness of this sort take place.

To date, we have found four metamorphosis postures in prehistoric art. The oldest one, that of a European masked woman of great antiquity and truly magical power, will be discussed in Section III. The other three are all part of the classical Indian cultures of Central America. The postures of the *Prince* and of the *Tattooed Jaguar* come to us from the Olmecs, the most ancient of the classical societies of the region. The latter was known in precontact time all over Central America and as far north as Tennessee. That of the *Corn Goddess* is part of the Aztec heritage.

Plate 36

The Olmec Prince. The figurine is called the Prince by archeologists, because the young man wears an unusual, rather ornate headdress (pl. 36). It is dated from a time between 1100 and 600 B.C. and was found in Mexico, in the present state of Tabasco. The figure sits cross-legged and bends forward slightly, leaning on stiff arms bent at the wrist. The man's hands form fists, which are placed on the floor in front of him rather close together. His tongue is between his lips, and his eyes are rolled up, the sure sign of a very deep trance.

The Olmec Prince came to my attention in 1984, and we tried it for the first time in Cuyamungue that summer. As intimated by Belinda, the iconic content of the posture in this case helps set the stage for the transformation, for one readily feels like a four-footed animal when placing his arms before his crossed legs in the fashion described. This was intentional in Olmec culture, of course, for the jaguar was their most important power animal, a spirit being represented innumerable times in their art. By the way, there is also another male figurine, with a somewhat different head ornament but in the same posture. Belinda was not familiar with it at the time, but it is also part of the Olmec record and comes from the same region and time period. The man represented is shown with his head thrown back, and the human face is replaced by that of an impressively exaggerated jaguar mask (pl. 37). Not being part of that culture, however, Belinda was worried about obeying an external suggestion and rejected the jaguar experience offered to her:

A leopard or jaguar face appeared in front of me, reminding me of one of the gold masks in the King Tut collection. But I recalled feeling so much like a cat in this posture that I dismissed the jaguar as simply suggested by the posture.

Plate 37

Even at this early stage of our experimentation, a few features became apparent that continued to characterize this posture. For instance, achieving metamorphosis, we learn from Belinda, requires the investment of tremendous energy, experienced by her as having her molecules scattered like stars. But the great effort notwithstanding, the transformation is difficult to keep going. In Belinda's experience, no sooner had she become a buffalo than she appeared as an owl, and she could hold on to neither, alternating back and forth until she appeared as a giant bee. The theme of the experience becomes evident in her last impressive image: In metamorphosis, humans come face to face with the life-giving power of the eternal sun; they approach a place between the two worlds, where in infinity the ordinary and the alternate reality meet:

> The image of a galaxy appeared, billions of stars, which I realized were my molecules being pulled apart in order to be reorganized. There was a series of images, going back and forth. First there was a buffalo, standing on the plains in the daylight. It was important that he was part of a herd. The second image was that of an owl, flying in the night, singular and alone. It was back and forth between night and day, upper and lower, flying in the sky and standing on the ground, being singular and being one with the herd. I recall that this went on for a long time. Then there was a final image, which was that of a giant bee. It was golden, and it was flying between two mountains toward an enormous rising sun. My feeling was that the bee was flying toward a place between two worlds.

Others in Belinda's group, and in a subsequent one that summer, reported similar impressions. There was the perception of transformation, as in "I saw layers being pushed into each other," or of its attendant turbulence, as in "I saw lots of images half in and half out of the earth." As Christian St. recounted it:

> A jaguar sat facing me, and then there were many animals in vivid colors, changing into each other; a snake became a bird, the bird turned into a turtle, that became a lynx, and then a puma.

In a more complete sequence, Morgan reacts to the iconic content of the posture. She experienced the heat of the relentless generation of energy, and after turning into a mountain lion, she could not retain it, becoming a stone figure instead:

> The posture reminded me of a cat, and I became a mountain lion. I felt extremely hot, and the sun was painfully bright. I kept climbing and running. Then I saw a snake, and our movements became a dance. I was up on a high plain and saw Indians riding by and buffalos running. Suddenly I was a shrine, like that of the Stone Lions in Bandelier National Park, but I don't know whether I was a stone or not. Then I started running again, and turned into a shrine again, and began chasing things. I became aware of the pain in my legs and I began feeling anxious. I wanted to scream, but at that point I was the mountain lion. The feeling of discomfort was gone, and I started catching fish in a stream.

In Scheibbs, Austria, the following year, there were reports along the same line. We heard the reaction to the suggestive posture:

> MARGIT: I felt thoroughly animallike. I found myself in a shadowy dense forest, and encountered a fox; it had a snout with pointed teeth.

or to the sudden transformation and its instability:

> SARI: I was in the earth and felt like I was part of it, and that was wonderful. It was as if I had been hibernating. Suddenly a ladder appeared in my hole, and I climbed up. There were masked people; I was also wearing a mask, first that of a frog, then of a carnivore. My tongue dripped, and my entire body was covered by armor, or maybe by fur. In that disguise, I danced a fertility dance.

and equally in Cuyamungue in the summer of 1987, when Hanna was able to hang on to being a frog, and experienced the instability instead in the changes of locale, until she lost the struggle and was torn apart by an eagle:

> I was a cat, then couldn't decide whether I wanted to be a lion or a frog. So I decided to become a frog. I had a private pool. I was surrounded by flowers. I caught flies and had a good time. Then I decided to go on a trip. It took me over some flat country, where I met an elephant. We had a nice conversation, and he took me for a ride, back to my pond. Then I was in a small river, and I swam to the ocean and had a great time there, too, only it started drying up, and I became scared. But a wave took me back to my pond, although it was hard going against the current, and things were good again for a while. Suddenly an eagle appeared; it tore me to pieces and fed me to its eaglets. I experienced a sudden shift in perception, and that took me back to being a frog in my pond again and the good times.

The Tattooed Jaguar. The two figurines shown in plate 38 were also found in the old Olmec settlement area, in the state of Tabasco, and are of the same period. In contrast to the posture of the Olmec Prince, the one of the Tattooed Jaguar has no iconic content; that is, the trancer is not subject

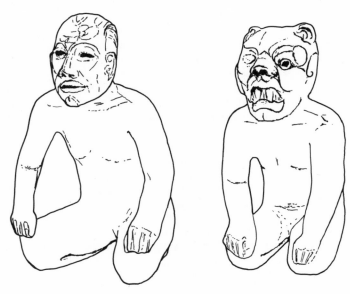

Plate 38

to any suggestion of animalness. Instead, the man depicted kneels with his knees apart and sits on his heels. His hands are on his knees, with the right one somewhat raised, so that his arm is a bit arched, and his left hand is slightly farther back on his thigh and flattened. The two figurines are exhibited in different museums, and in the book on Indian art in which one of my participants discovered them,[4] they were on two different pages. To my mind, however, they clearly belong together. They obviously were created by the same artist using the same model. Both the man's head and the jaguar mask are tattooed, and both are shown in the same posture. But most important, the two figurines taken together are also, as was the case with the two different Princes, a statement about the same experience: "If you go into trance in this posture, you will participate in the power of the Jaguar by turning into him." Interestingly, by the way, the artist was so familiar with what happens in trance that he made a distinction in the way his model holds his right hand, something I too have observed many times. After metamorphosis has been achieved, both the right hand and the arm are relaxed.

Despite the fact that nothing in this posture suggests any metamorphosis, it reliably leads to a change of shape. Without the sponsorship of the Jaguar Spirit, as would be the case in an Olmec ritual, the transformation is not always into its likeness, although it does occur occasionally, especially if the trancer has seen the two figures together, as in the following example:

GERHARD (Vienna, April 1986): The sound of the rattle made me shudder. It penetrated me from the front and pulled me up, then slammed me down with lightning speed. In the distance, the jaguar appeared but then was gone again. I passed under an arc, and in the process something was rubbed off of me and I turned into a jaguar. Behind me I saw a huge figure wearing a jaguar mask as in the figure. He grabbed me by the nape of the neck like a pup and ran away with me and then set me down. Then he fell asleep, and I ran away. At the end I was here in our courtyard, still in the shape of a jaguar. I passed under the arc in the direction of the garden, and then all was gone, as if in a fog.

Here is an example of a clear metamorphosis into a wolf, the mighty power animal of European antiquity:

> URSULA ST. (Sommerau, Switzerland, 1985): I felt a strong pulsing around me and inside of me, and I forgot about my legs. I found myself sitting on red earth and became very long, and I saw a hole in the earth with water in it. I heard something dropping into the water. That made rings in the water that turned into a whirlpool, sucking me in. It kept whirling me around until I myself became the whirlpool. Suddenly my feet, thighs, and belly became hot, and somebody handed me a wolf skin. My face acquired the snout of a dog. I slipped my arms into the wolf skin and put it on that way, and it felt wonderful. I was squatting in this posture, I was fat and had thick haunches, and next to me I saw a being looking just like me, except it was much larger and I called it mother. She lay down and I slipped into her belly. The eddy was like a path; I dissolved and the water was warm. Inside my mother's belly, I was all belly and haunches. I saw other little wolves next to me. Then I was in a passageway; it felt like being born. I was trembling, and I was supposed to help. I had just slipped out of the passage when the rattle stopped, with the feeling, now all was well.

My own transformation was also into a large predator, although it never became clear to me exactly what I was:

> (Cuyamungue, July 1985): As soon as the rattle started, my fingertips got hot and changed into claws; my face protruded, and I had round ears. This was a clear physical feeling. I could feel my thighs turning into muscular haunches, and from the end of my spine, a tail began to grow. It caused me some momentary anxiety, for what was I going to do with a tail later? What I saw was pictures appearing and disappearing, all in orange light, for example, of a jaguar catching and chomping a bird. I saw an orange sky and a green forest below, and some white shapes that I couldn't identify at first. Then I understood that they were pyramids because I smelled the masonry smell typical of Maya ruins. There was a Maya priest who was like a cutout, and as I watched, he turned like a weathercock. I was still thinking how strange that was when I felt my face flattening out, the most extraordinary experience of the posture. My face just became flat, and it was over, while the rattle was still going on.

There is a vague suggestion in the above report that I had momentarily changed into a bird, and that was the reason I saw the pyramids from above. For Pij, becoming a bird was the core of the transformation:

(Sommerau, 1985): A ray came from below immediately as the rattle started and penetrated me, causing circles and eddies in me and around me. I was dancing; I felt so light, I was enveloped in a white light. There was a wind coming from the right, from above and from below, and I felt a presence; I had no idea what it was, but it was bigger than me. I wanted to become something and was vibrating in my shoulders. I wanted to change, and my head started getting narrow. I was being carried along; I was sailing, then I was flying. I wanted to glance upward, but I couldn't do that, I could only look down. Then I flew over the Salzburg castle.

Plate 39

As mentioned earlier, we occasionally come across surprising confirmations of our experiences in tales connected with a certain posture. Such instances are the journey to the sky experienced in the posture and angle of incline of the Lascaux Cave drawing, and its confirmation by the tradition that Osiris rises to the gods in the sky at the same angle, or the many examples of the healing power of the Bear in the posture we know as that of the Bear Spirit. Something of the same order happened also in connection with a metamorphosis posture. According to Aztec tradition, Chalchihuitlicue, "she of the skirt of green jewels," the goddess of water and the consort of the rain god, is represented in the posture of the Tattooed Jaguar, except that she has her legs crossed (pl. 39). This variant is known from seventh-century figures from Tennessee (pls. 40 and 41), and the experiences it mediates are the same as those of the Tattooed Jaguar. Now, it is told of this goddess that she sent a flood to earth and changed humans into fish, so they would be able to move in the water. It is therefore fascinating how often participants report having turned into fish in this posture. The following are two examples:

KATHRIN (Sommerau, 1985): I was surrounded by red, warm light, which issued from two semicircles. They divided, and their center became the sun. I passed through a point in the middle of the sun. It was made of fire. Then I myself also became fire and started burning; the points of the flames danced around me. Then there was a change; I could feel a rainbow, and a man and a woman held out their hands to me. I sank into a white whirlpool and became a fish. I swam through a tube, and encountered some branches and wondered where I had come from.

VRENIE (Sommerau, 1985): My head opened up and something came out of it.

Plate 40   **Plate 41**

I had the feeling that I was being turned inside out like a glove. A wind came up and started whirling me around, which made me close up, and I became a bird. I flew into the light blue, which then turned light green. As I was gliding along, I saw the sun; it was light yellow. I flew into it and then could not escape; its rays kept holding on to me. I kept struggling, and suddenly they let go of me, and I fell down turning like a top, and still whirling around. I found myself at the bottom of the ocean, and I was a fish. Around me there were figures in green scarves; it seems that the sea was part of the lower world.

The Corn Goddess (pl. 42). The Aztecs represented the Corn Goddess as a young woman, and she is always shown in the same graceful pose, sitting on her heels as a Japanese lady would, and resting her outstretched hands on her thighs close to her body, pointing toward her knees. The cat effigy of Key Marco, Florida (pl. 43), has its hands somewhat closer together. Of the three postures discussed here, it seems the most recent, deriving from a time when the Aztecs were in the process of converting to full-scale intensive agriculture. This may be why it is also the weakest of the three postures. It does mediate metamorphosis, but the transformation is characterized by an inherent uncertainty. "Every time I saw something," one participant said, "it disappeared." Some trancers experience nothing but the whirling agitation that leads into the metamorphosis, as in the following example, in which Anne B. is even proffered help by the Bear Spirit, who often undertakes this task, but except for a brief interlude, she is still unsuccessful. So he and his companions disappear; she sees the fire again, with only humans dancing around it:

Plate 42   **Plate 43**

(Cuyamungue, August 1985): I was in a clearing in the forest, and I was dancing around a fire, a wild, frenetic dance. I went around in circles and kept jumping over the fire with others. Then I danced backward, and there were lots of owls watching us, also a circle of animals. The animals joined us, especially many friendly bears. I became one of the bears. A huge bear, I thought of him as a chief or a god, took hold of me and and whirled me around. The bear replaced the fire, or the fire became the bear; we once more danced backward, I became a human, and we humans danced with the animals. Suddenly the fire reappeared, the animals and the owls were gone, and only we humans were dancing.

Some trancers succeed better, but a certain inconsistency remains. We hear of transformations into elephants, wolves, panthers, jaguars, birds, or even snakes:

ELIZABETH M. (Cuyamungue, August 1986): I was a very large cat, chasing animals, and I felt my power, and the dust blowing over my face. Then I was a wolf chasing a rabbit. I encountered a large snake and became that snake, and could feel how different my snake spine was. Then my spirit guide appeared and offered to teach me how one flies as a snake. And he showed me where my feathers were on my body.

CINDY (Cuyamungue, August 1986): I was a grey wolf; my body was sinking down, and the smell was intense. I felt sharp hunger pains and decided that I needed to go and hunt. I made my chest expand, and I started loping over the ground. It felt wonderful to run like a wolf, but then I got tired of it. I saw Elizabeth and asked her, "Are you a wolf?" She left. And I was told, "You need to survive as a wolf to be human."

NYDIA (Cuyamungue, August 1986): I was in a blue tunnel, which was green further down. I saw a jaguar in front of me; we went on together, with me holding on to its tail. We came to a winding river; the water smelled fresh. The jaguar turned into a lizard, or maybe it was a salamander, then back into a jaguar. Then the jaguar became a wolf. It had golden eyes, and its fur felt soft. I was a puppy. The wolf picked me up, and we walked through the snow. The wolf killed an antelope. We licked its blood and ate it.

GABI (Cuyamungue, August 1986): Something pulled me back, and at that instant my mouth turned into the snout of a black panther. I felt very hungry, and I could find nothing to kill. Besides, my feet began to hurt. So I fell asleep. A black tiger came by. He put his paws on my shoulder; that was nice, but quite uncomfortable.

The only feature that appears with more consistency than the above animal shapes during the Corn Goddess posture is plant and insect life, as could be expected with a pose attributed to such a spirit being. Thus I was told during a workshop in Utrecht (the Netherlands), in the spring of 1986, "I am in the dark, we are roots together." Instead of the roots, the cotyledons appear in another instance during the same workshop:

PETI: I could feel how the energy was building up. I could not see anything, but I felt the colors; they were red and brown and swirling. I had two halves, and they were pumping up energy. The cells and patterns were splitting, then there were more colors. I was growing out of my shape.

Breaking through the earth and growing is yet another theme of this type of experience:

ISI (Cuyamungue, August 1986): I was surrounded by earth and sand. I was feeling comfortable, but I tried to make a hole and didn't know why. Then I heard a voice saying, "You're a seed, you are looking for light, for the sun." So I started growing roots, and I felt that I really was a seed. I broke through to the surface and saw the sun, and it was wonderful. I kept growing, and I was a field of grain. I didn't stop growing until I grew up into the sky, and it was a nice difference. At first I had felt the earth; now I was in the sky, and there was nothing but wind. Then I found myself sitting on a branch. I was a big bird, but the branch was small, and I was afraid. I started playing with the wind, and I lost my fear and began flying around in circles with the wind.

Although as always unaware of the origin and name of the posture, Belinda turned into corn when she tried it for the first time. Toward the middle of the trance session, however, as happens so frequently in metamorphosis postures, she ran out of energy and could no longer hold on to being a plant:

(Cuyamungue, August 1985): In the beginning, I felt nothing at all. I was in the earth, not seeing anything. I began moving out, and I realized that I was a corn plant, and I was growing as tall as a mountain. A brown bear came along, tore off my right breast, but it was corn also, and he ate it. So I was in the bear's stomach, and there was a truly foul smell around. The bear was nursing a cub, and I came out of her breast as milk. Suddenly, I felt great pain, and I was flying. I landed in a circular nest, and I looked around to see what was in it. A black statue emerged from the hole; it was in this posture, and as I watched, it turned into white marble. I could feel my legs hurting, and so I was happy that at this point my Lioness turned up. We had a joyful reunion; she let me become a part of her body, and we went back and forth like that until the rattle stopped.

The following August, although Belinda had been a corn plant the year before, she turned into a caterpillar instead:

Immediately, there was the sensation of twirling. I was inside a flower. I saw the stamen; it was like a thick rope. I grabbed hold of it and started climbing out of the flower, and then down toward the ground. I sat at the base of the plant, thinking, what do I do now? I went to another blossom; it was an iris. I could see it, and it was beautiful. Then there was the sensation of whirring and breathing fast. I saw a snake next to the plant, so I got excited and got back into the plant. I started breathing hard, and suddenly I broke open and I was a big yellow butterfly on a field of flowers. I started sucking honey, then flew up into the mountains. I huddled into the branches and saw the landscape, and felt protected by the branches. I saw a strong light, and as I turned toward it, I changed into a cobra.

Belinda's experience is quite similar to one related the following year in Switzerland. During that session, the men did the Tattooed Jaguar and the women the Corn Goddess. Yet in a strange crossover, Urs's experience is more that of the Corn Goddess, although with some masculine features:

Something took me by my hands and whirled me around, then let me go, so that I catapulted away and turned around my own axes. Suddenly I landed on a giant anemone. My feet felt cold, but the sun was shining and felt warm. A bumblebee landed next to me and asked, "Are you also collecting honey?" I said no, but that I wanted to try. The anemone turned into a daisy, and a giant butterfly appeared; it had a red body and white wings with yellow dots. It said, "I like you, would you like to come along?" But I was too slow. I did get out of the flower, but then landed in a cornucopia with transparent golden yellow and orange walls, and I felt compelled to go further and further down into it. Suddenly, there was a blinding light, and the white figure of a woman appeared with outstretched arms, and there was a voice saying, "You will have to pass through the woman to get to your goal." So I passed through her, and did not fall into a precipice. Instead, I was in a Greek temple. In it, there were nine statues arranged in a semicircle, and in the middle of it there was a huge black steer with enormous horns. The statues kept changing their faces, appearing as foxes, dragonflies, and other shapes. I asked what I was suppowed to do in that temple, but then the rattle stopped.

CHAPTER ELEVEN

Celebrations

For the 1985 spring workshop at the Buddhist Center in Scheibbs, our friend Franz announced that we were going to have a masked dance. "Dear Friends," he wrote in his flyer,

> you have all taken part in an introductory course on trance and the religious altered state of consciousness with Felicitas Goodman. For this year, we are planning a more intensive project with Felicitas, to deepen our knowledge about trance and ecstasy and to practice integrating it into our daily lives. This project is not to be as serious as it sounds, however. We want to make it a celebration as it used to be in ancient cultures, a celebration of joy. It is to be a game between the dimensions of the world, a sacred event demonstrating our connectedness with everything that surrounds us.

I arrived late on the first day from another assignment. I had not seen the flyer; we had discussed the matter only in the most general terms, but in no detail, and I knew only that Franz had engaged Rudl, a trained Viennese maskmaker, as an instructor for our project. So I was understandably startled when after greeting the fourteen participants in the upstairs meditation room of the center, Franz turned to me with a confident smile, saying, "All right, Felicitas, so why don't you just describe some native ritual to us, and we'll proceed from there."

What in the world was I supposed to pull from my hat? To gain time to think, I agreed that such rituals could indeed serve as models, but that they were embedded in a social context that we could never replicate, and therefore we had to do something different, something that would be our very own. The question was, what? As I continued talking, born of desperation, an idea was beginning to take shape. This was to be a masked dance, so logically, I suggested, we should first of all discover what kind of mask to make. "Instead of starting with the ritual," I said, "why don't we begin at the other end and think about the masks first?" Remembering that my Friends "on the other side" were always standing ready to help, I added, "So how about going to the lower world? Maybe there we can discover some spirit form to serve as model for the masks."

In other words, instead of choosing a rational path, always the first choice of Westerners in a pinch, my intuition told me that I needed to direct the group to the alternate reality. This novel approach made good sense to people already familiar with ecstatic experience. After all, the masked dance was to be a religious celebration, and so quite correctly we had to entrust the shaping of it to the forces to whom this task properly belonged. Going to the lower world, where every one of us had been before, was a plausible first step. I could see the enthusiasm in the faces of my participants.

And indeed, they were not to be disappointed. Judging from Yolanda's report, who was the first one to recount her experience at the conclusion of the trance, our Friends equally approved. This happens quite often when I am in doubt about a new venture: The first person I call on turns out to be the messenger. The choice seems arbitrary, but in actuality it is guided by a sort of prompting that is as gentle as a puff of wind. In this case, the message transmitted could not have been clearer. For in the cave to which Yolanda was taken, an Indian placed his own mask on her face:

> About me it was night. I flew up to the stars and danced with them. I was among rocks, and water came spouting from them. Then I sank into the earth and I was badly frightened; everything was so dark. I searched for a way out, and the rattle sounded like many shells knocking together. I turned into a bird and flew away together with a raven, who took me to the entrance of a cave. I wanted to rest there, but I was ushered into the cave, and there saw an Indian wearing the mask of a black mountain lion. He placed his mask on my face. Then I was surrounded by smoke, and the Indian disappeared far in the distance.

The other members of the group reported mainly experiences of transformation. That is, encountering the masked spirit being apparently brought about a metamorphosis of the visitors. I was surprised, because, as will be recalled, a visit to the lower world is usually a journey, with changing shape only an occasional secondary feature. I was also delighted, for obviously we were on the right track. This process of transformation was frequently reported from among those societies where masks were used ritually, namely, that the bearer turned into the being represented. My trancers told of changing into a bear, or maybe an owl; into a crow or a cat with black spots; into a tiger, a lion, a snake, and a deer; into a snake or a goat. Gerhard became a panther:

> I took a backward somersault, and as if on roller skates, I slipped down into some sort of room, landing on my back. Something or somebody was dancing

around me. A panther appeared; it slipped into me, and I could feel exactly how that transformed me. I ran up a mountainside, and a man wearing a hat, but without a face, and a bird came with me. Behind the mountain, there was nothing, only indistinct forms, and the three of us jumped into that emptiness. I felt that I was floating, or I was being carried, and placed into a golden liquid, which turned me into a gold-colored panther. I became a horse, then emerged from it, and as a panther I sat on the back of the horse. Then we dissolved completely. The man with the hat carried me over the mountain on his shoulder, then put me down. I slipped through him and found myself back here.

Ewald encountered a dragon:

> I melted into the earth, and there was no air between me and the ground. Then I was at a campfire, and there were people around it. I looked around but could see nothing else. Suddenly he was there, to the right of me, a mere shadow at first, then assuming the shape of a dragon and getting bigger and bigger. The right side of me began tensing painfully. I asked him for help, and I felt it physically how he scraped all that section of my body off, even my eye. It felt great. Then I assumed his shape. I fell into some water, and the rattle stopped.

Fritz found a snowy owl:

> I saw the white head of an owl, like a shadow, and it beckoned to me. Everything else was dark. I was in a black chasm; a river of fire flowed through it, and I became the owl.

We had used a tape for the session instead of my rattling, so that I would also be able to participate, but I was disappointed with my trip. For quite a while nothing happened; then I began to feel a cool and gentle wind brush over me. I saw a few small cometlike streaks of light, then bright green willow branches appeared with dots of yellow sunlight and blowing in the wind. Half hidden by the branches, there were patches of light-brown fur, but I could not make out what that was; the rattling seemed too short, and in the end I merely felt the gentle wind continuing to surround me. Instead of exhilaration, the experience left me with a pervasive fear which I could not place. What was I being told?

The answer did not come to me until the following day. For the first time, it seemed to me, we had not been simply sojourners but had stirred up forces in the lower world when we appealed to them for response, forces that we knew nothing about. Thus, perhaps, my fear. I concluded that we had to turn to ritual now and learn how to deal with those forces, to shape them in some way. In Pueblo tradition, the beings beyond the border of ordinary reality are thought of as "raw." In order to consort with them, we had to translate them into something more akin to our humanness. This, quite possibly, was what ritual had always been about in human history. However, here was the rub: Where were we to find the proper ritual? This time, the answer was readily available. Our trip to the lower world had been richly rewarding, so once again, we should turn to that inexhaustible source of inspiration, ecstatic experience. Because of the nature of our problem, I suggested that this time we appeal to our wise old counselor, the Tennessee diviner.

On this occasion, I chose to be not a participant but simply the recorder. And as I now read once more my cursory notes of that session, I remember again the thrill of seeing the dance ritual unfold before me. With my eyes sharpened by the trance, which had come to me while I rattled, I saw spread out before me an ecstatic, scintillating celebration of spring. "I live a fairytale," I wrote dumbfounded later that day, as I started working out the dance. Simply for the asking, all the details of the ceremony had been revealed. Later on, when we repeated that session several times in order to record it, there were details of the sets, and even such minor instructions as that there should be a fast before the dance. At least this is how we interpreted one of Ewald's experiences with his Dragon. Ewald had seen a table laid with a sumptuous feast, but the Dragon told him that he was not allowed to eat of it. Ewald became obstreperous, whereupon the Dragon took hold of one end of the table and turned it over, spilling all the delicacies. And we were advised to use the soundtrack of the Singing Shaman as music for our celebration. As we see in plates 44–47, this festive posture was a favorite in many parts of the world. It was known in Melanesia and on New Guinea, on the Cyclades Islands five thousand years ago, and surely since that time also in the Americas, from the Arctic Eskimos all the way down to Central America.

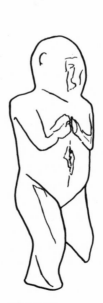

Plate 44   **Plate 45**   **Plate 46**

a   b   c

Plate 47

With faces still marked by the black line of the diviner's posture, everyone trooped down into the large hall on the first floor where the supplies for the masks had been laid out. The fever of creation was upon them. They hardly took time to break for lunch and barely realized that they had stood at the work tables for close to nine hours, shaping the clay, spreading plastic foil on the form, gluing layers of paper and cloth on it, impatiently waiting for the time when they could apply the paint to make their vision plain.

I had initially intended to excuse myself and spend all my time writing the dance. After all, I had not been favored by a vision except for those elusive patches of brown fur that I had seen behind the willow branches. I had no idea what was hiding inside that. But then I could not stand being away from all the exciting activities and the companionship in the work hall, and I decided to give maskmaking a try, too. Since I wanted to save my right arm for rattling,

I started to work on the clay with my left hand. As soon as I did that, my indecision dissolved, and to my amazement and entirely without any conscious effort, a presence emerged from the inert substance. The more I worked, the clearer it became: It was the face of a buffalo dancer, half human, half animal mask, simple and powerful. "Look," I kept saying to those working near me, "this is the mystery, here it is!" No one was interested. They were all busy with their own mysteries.

Rudl, our maskmaker, kept walking around the room and shaking his head. Beyond simple technical instruction, he had given no help whatsoever, for none was asked for. Most of us had never made a mask, and yet under our untutored fingers, such beauty blossomed forth as he had never seen in any of the classes he had conducted before. "What I usually get in my courses are twisted, tortuous faces scarred by conflict and decay," he said.

The following days were occupied with finishing the masks, sewing costumes, and creating the sets. I spent happy hours painting the willow branches that ended up as decoration for my skirt. We also did trance sessions, which kept the excitement high and the miraculous energy flowing. To our surprise they also helped those who were still unclear about details of their masks, providing further instructions. Franz was shown to paint his bear mask half white and half black. Rudl saw his red-and-black tiger clearly for the first time. Instead of a healing experience, which everyone else had undergone when we did the Bear posture, Christian St., who had been absent during our trip to the lower world, unexpectedly was given a terse version of what the Spirits expected of him during the dance:

> I was in a landscape that was teeming with wild boars. There was one, I only saw his head, and he stared at me, and I had the feeling of tremendous power radiating from him. A gaunt figure with a boar's mask stood at my left, or maybe at my right, I can't remember, and placed a bristly skin robe on my shoulders. I began dancing, wearing the boar's mask. When I looked down at my feet, they had turned into boars' hoofs. A herd of seven or eight wild pigs thundered by. An enormous wild boar knocked me down, a sow began suckling me, and then the entire herd started devouring me, and my guts spilled on the black earth. I saw all of us dancing, and the man wearing the boar's mask danced with us.

On the morning before the dance, we took the completed masks upstairs in a festive procession and carefully placed them around the walls. As yet, I felt, they were mere forms, bodies without souls. The question was, in what way could I invite the Spirits to take up their abode in these shells we had created for them? There was a posture named the Calling of the Spirits, the story of which I will relate in Section III. It involves the basic leg posture with knees slightly bent; the head is back and the mouth open, and the hands with fingers spread wide are placed on the line between abdomen and thigh (pl. 48). However, as I remembered, it mediated an experience where the caller turned into the Tree of Life, and the Spirits gathered around it. I was not sure whether it could also be employed for the present purpose. But I had no other choice.

So that was the posture I asked the participants to assume. I closed my eyes as I began to rattle and sent a wordless plea. In response, like shadows blowing in the wind, I saw a procession of Spirits entering and soundlessly slipping into the masks. And indeed, on this occasion, no one turned into a tree, and as we see in the examples cited below, all instead had very clear encounters with their mask and its spirit.

CHRISTIAN ST. (wild boar): I stood next to a tree at the edge of a precipice. I wore the mask, and the mask sucked me out. We all danced with our masks on, they united into one; and like an octopus, its many arms touched us all. My body became the mask.

GERHARD (panther): The rattle entered into me, and I slipped into a hole. We were all in that hole. The Spirits came to greet us and guided us out in a snake dance. I was wearing my mask and felt a great force from behind, which entered into me and overpowered me. This turned me into a panther. I started running and got to a clear stream of water. After drinking from it, I slipped into a tree and rested. After a while, I sat up high in the tree together with the man wearing a hat and a bird, and we started dancing together.

EWALD (dragon): The Spirits gathered in this room, and the Dragon put on his mask. I also turned into a dragon, and we started wrestling together, which gave me a lot of energy. Then the two of us passed through a fog bank, and behind it we encountered another masked figure. But

Plate 48

when I asked the Dragon what that was, he gave no answer. Instead, he guided me across a meadow, and it was getting very dark. We met a black cat, which was quite aggressive, and a masked figure accompanied by a snake. They were about to attack me, but with my fiery breath, I chased them away.

FRITZ (snowy owl): There was a wild circle of shamans dancing, and we in our masks formed an outer circle around them. I saw myself and a dark figure coming toward me, together with some light ones. They slipped into me and I became the owl. I was completely white. I stood still and waited stiffly, uttering not a sound, the female hunter of the night. I was time; I was the passing of the seasons.

ILSE (goat and snake): My goat came jumping from the left, sat down next to me with her front legs crossed in a human pose, and started conversing with me, complaining that I had made her ears too small. We had an animated conversation until I turned into the snake. Five kids appeared, then condensed into the goat. Behind them there were many figures wearing masks and enveloped in smoke, which curled upward. In the end, I changed into the tongue of the goat, which was also the snake.

SUSIE (bird of paradise): An eagle appeared before me and put on its mask. I heard music, and the eagle invited me to come along. We got to a tree trunk, which had a golden door, and we entered, sat down, and ate. All the animals were there, even the goat with her legs crossed. Then they started dancing, and the eagle and I flew away.

YOLANDA (mountain lion): The Mountain Lion stood behind me and put its paws on my shoulders until I lay down. He put some soil and dry leaves on me, dug small holes around me, and placed a light in each. Then he went up the mountain, and a number of lion cubs gathered around me. Then I found myself standing in front of him. He hit me on the head, then scratched my right breast, skinned me, and boiled me in a kettle. The small lions dumped me out of the kettle. Grabbing my hands, the Mountain Lion then lifted me and took me to a cave. He dug a hole and placed fire in it, and the cool wind played around me, and fireflies started gathering about.

Because according to the divination the dance was to be a celebration of spring, I chose a posture of death and rebirth, called the posture of the Feathered Serpent, for the concluding trance session of the workshop on the evening before the dance. This posture will be discussed in Chapter 13. It provided such a satisfactory closure that we have continued to use it in subsequent trance-dance workshops.

So much had happened during the workshop that it seemed as if we had been together forever when the day of the dance finally dawned. We had walked through the entire ceremony only once. The individual scenes were easy to remember, because the principal role in each one was played by the person who had originally experienced it. Franz was in charge of the soundtrack, and my task was merely to provide the cues for the sequence. Obeying the instructions of the Dragon, we had no breakfast, and at an early hour and fully costumed, we assembled in the upper meditation room to take the masks downstairs. We had invited only a few guests, among them Eva D., who was so taken by the beauty of it all that she sacrificed her entire savings and took part in a masked dance in Cuyamungue the following year. I will try to describe the ritual not as I experienced it as a participant but as it might have looked to our spectators.

Imagine a starkly white, rather low room with small windows set into walls of medieval thickness. The first light of the morning is barely sifting through the curtains. All you can see is a small table over to one side with a bowl on it and a large yellow disk hanging from the ceiling in the center, circled along its perimeter by a snake, which appears as a thick dark line in the muted light of dawn.

A door opens behind the columns in the back, and in perfect silence, a line of gowned figures on stockinged feet enter in stately defile, each carrying a mask visible only in outline, and they form an open circle around the table. Each person in turn steps up to the bowl, takes some of the meal, breathes on it for a blessing, scatters it on the mask to feed it, and then puts it on.

Suddenly there is magic in the room, as in rapid succession in the faintly blossoming light tiger and panther, bird, owl, and buffalo, boar and dragon and bear join red and golden beings of fantasy in the line around the goat, whose horns are circled by an orange snake.

Hardly audible at first and sectioned only by the muted beat of the rattle, a chorus of voices starts up, a mere hum at first as if coming from the chasms of the earth, then gathering volume and spreading into a rainbow of harmony like the distant chorale of a Gregorian chant. Now and then bright cadences born of the trance flicker above the somber lines of the base. The masks begin to fall in with the shaking of the rattle, and the unswerving thud of their feet is the thread that to the end will hold together the beaded necklace of the dance.

At the table, the Goat, ancient generative power, hands each mask a small glass bowl, and like the first stirring of life in spring, tiny flames burst under its hand as it lights the candles floating in the water. The masks turn and, following the Goat, dance with the light held high until there is a spiral of flickering flames rotating faster and faster under the disk of the sun. Suddenly, the hands of unseen helpers lift the curtains, and the tiny sparks of the young season melt into the bright daylight of the first day of spring. Then the candles are gone, and with the brilliant colors of the masks awakened, their spiral continues to rotate under the sun disk.

As yet, though, spring has not triumphed over the forces of winter. In the middle of the spiral, the Bird of Paradise appears, its mask a riot of brilliant yellows, blues, and greens. At its signal, the masks dance into the shadows and return, heads bent low, each with a staff on its back, the bond of ice still holding hostage the stirrings of new life. As their circle converges on the Bird of Paradise and becomes ever tighter, its grip seems to choke the blossoming season in the center.

But the new beginning will not be denied. The Mountain Lion takes up the struggle. It breaks out of the line of the dancers, a sleek black streak with bright-blue eyes and the red circle of the sun painted on its palms. The Mountain Lion carries the disk of the new sun in its upstretched hands and, holding it high above its head, dances toward the circle. The new sun's power parts its grip; the line opens and lets the Lion pass. Upon reaching the old sun, it hangs the rejuvenated image over the old tired one, and the snake of renewed life circling its rim now unites both. With the ice on their bent backs, the masks are still tied to the powers of winter, but the Mountain Lion now approaches each one and lifts the staffs. When this happens, each mask straightens up, turns around its own axis, and continues dancing in the circle. A colored scarf appears in their hands; they dance toward the Lion and hand it over as their offering. The Lion gives them staffs in return, which, transformed, will now serve to celebrate the conquering power of life, as each mask, dancing on the spot, marks the rhythm of the rattle by stomping the floor with it. In the meanwhile, the victorious Mountain Lion continues to dance and wave the scarves until, upon a signal, all masks run to one corner and put down the staffs, and the Mountain Lion places the scarves on top, a gift to the earth.

Spring, now fully installed, is the time for initiation. In youthful exuberance, the Black Panther dances to the rim of the circle, where the masks are holding hands. Under their upstretched arms, it dances in and out of the circle, pursued by the Mountain Lion. After slipping through all the openings, the panther runs into the circle, still followed by the Lion. Exhausted, it collapses, and on its chest and back it suffers the initiatory scratches of the Lion.[1] The young Panther is now a full-fledged member of the circle. Guided by the Mountain Lion, it takes over and, breaking the circle of the dancers, leads the masks in a snake dance.

But initiation is not only a triumph of life, it is also descending into death. A golden mask, half man, half beast, wrapped in a black shawl, dances to the front of the masks, which now form a straight line. The dark shawl is heavy; the mask tries in vain to shake its oppressive weight and finally collapses under it as under a shroud. Two Birds of Paradise arrive, carrying a totem pole. One of them holds the pole upright, the other one pulls the shawl off the prostrate figure. The golden mask pulls itself up, holding on to the pole, and finally supports it alone. The Birds return to the line while the sorrowing mask dances holding the pole. It begins knocking it on the floor on the first beat of a four-quarter rhythm. Each time that happens, one of the masks leaves the line, turns on its own axis in the struggle against death, and joins the circle of twirling masks.

In the end life, now complete, emerges triumphant. In the circle, the masks have stopped twirling and have moved on to a pendulum pattern of two steps to the right, then two to the left. Two masks leave the circle, then come back carrying a skeleton. The tall Bear, striking in its yellow-and-sepia gown, goes to meet them, takes over the skeleton, and, while they rejoin the circle, begins dancing by hugging its ghostly partner. The circle of dancers begins to dance to the right, while the Bear with its skeleton dances outside the circle in the opposite direction. After twice repeating the round, the Bear suddenly jumps into the middle of the circle, lifts the skeleton high, and, turning it around, reveals the blooming Tree of Life on its reverse side. Small bells are attached to its blossoms, and they ring out as he shakes it and knocks it on the floor. The Birds of Paradise come fluttering by and pick at the seeds scattered on the ground at the base of the tree.

Night, the time of magic, descends on the scene. The Snowy Owl shoos the Birds of Paradise away and dances around the Tree, ushering in the miracle of transformation. The masks are now what they had seemed, birds and animals of the forest and beings of story, and they stomp, slither, slink, and flutter around the Tree of Life.

Finally the music ends, and the world of fancy subsides with it. The dancers return to the bowl of meal, take some, bless it with their breath, and scatter it as a final offering to the Spirits. The last thing I remember seeing as I sat on the floor exhausted, still half buffalo and half woman, and with the sound of many rattles ringing in my head, is two toddlers over in one corner, a little boy and a girl, children of couples living at the center, crawling over to the Tree of Life lying on the floor and playing entranced with the shiny bells. Spring had truly come.

As I am describing the dance now, several years later, it seems to me that for Sigrid, the golden mask that reminded me of the picture on a tarot card, death under the dark shawl of the dance, had had an additional meaning, something she had no way of understanding at the time. I checked once more what she had told after the divination, and indeed, after describing the scene with the shawl which she later danced, she told how she saw men squatting in a circle in the diviner's posture, and she was told that they would decide and that she should not be afraid.

> Then I turned into a small girl, climbed up an incline, and became a woman. I found myself in a dark passageway and asked where it was leading. Someone handed me a glowing staff. A large bird came, and once more I asked, where does all this lead to? With my staff, I started drawing glowing circles in the air, and then I died.

Soon after the dance, she met a man, her golden figure of the tarot card. They fell in love and got married. A month after the wedding, on a distant California seashore, the young husband climbed up on a rock ledge and exuberantly started to dance. The rock shelf broke off and buried him under the rubble, killing him instantly. Sigrid remained behind, and in the future-past of the masked ritual, she danced her sorrowful dirge with the totem pole.

The format and the approaches developed during the 1985 masked dance in Scheibbs served as a basis for other dances to follow. Altogether, I think, the most important outcome of the masked dances was the realization that here was an opportunity to apply the postures to one particular purpose. It was as if one reason we had been introduced to them was so that we would learn a new way to be joyous, to celebrate in ecstasy, something sadly lacking in our own culture.

Nurtured by the inexhaustible source of the alternate reality, each dance was different, both in theme and in detail, for every time we asked, we received new instructions. We also have a sweatlodge now on the institute grounds in New Mexico, and a sweat has become an integral part of our yearly masked-dance celebration. We continued to experiment with other postures that could meaningfully be integrated into the dance. For instance, while in 1985 in Cuyamungue we used the Chiltan posture to gain extra energy, we later discovered still another posture that produced a similar effect. We call it the *Maya Empowerment posture.* I saw it first in photographs accompanying an article about a Maya sculpture in wood,[2] the only example of such a wood carving in the round from the tropical lowlands of Middle America. A standing variant of the posture was known in classical antiquity in Europe, both in the

Minoan culture at about 2000 to 1700 B.C. and in Mycenae, and in Persia two thousand years later, as well as with bent knees as far in time and place as modern Polynesia (more about this in the Conclusion).

As seen in plate 49, for this posture the male figure is kneeling with legs apart and sitting on its heels. The head is slightly inclined toward the back. As the most salient feature of the pose, the arms are raised to shoulder height and the hands touch. It is not clear how the hands are held. We assumed that the figure has its fingers curled, so that was what we did. We also pressed our index fingers together along the lower joint, which seemed to come close to what the carving shows. In this posture participants report the accumulation of a radiant, "peaceful" energy, experiences such as falling through smoke and heat but then ending up in a refreshing bath, of having access to learning and wisdom, of being "able to do anything," and quite generally, of joy and empowerment.

Plate 49

Since that first masked dance in 1985, we do several every year, and special memories are associated with each and every one. In Switzerland, for instance, we danced the play of chaos and order around the Tree of the World, and we will not forget our tall trickster, who had never seen or heard of his prototype in our own Indian Northwest, and yet shaped his mask in the trickster's image with deer antlers and represented, as Paul Radin put it, "god, animal, human being, hero, buffoon, he who was before good and evil, denier, affirmer, destroyer and creator" (1972:169).

In Cuyamungue during the first dance there, our procession sanctified the land, and our animals came to watch. After the completion of the dance and emerging for the first time that summer, our own big garter snake wound her way down the hill behind the Student Building, wended her way to the garden, and then slithered back up again to her home. Hawks circled overhead, and the shy hummingbirds swooped at us wildly as we sat in the arbor next to their feeder. Another time, as I told before, as we got ready to dance around the sweatlodge on the eve of the ritual, a thunderhead rolled up only above that small spot in the vast land. As we started to drum and dance, rain began to fall, splashing cold and invigorating drops on our shoulders. When our dance stopped, so did the rain; the cloud turned pink in the evening light, and on that rosy cloud, a rainbow formed.

In Cuyamungue in 1987 we were instructed to invite the Spirits of the region to our celebration, and we did so, scattering the sacred meal in the four directions. We had carried out a sweatlodge ritual on the eve of the dance, and afterward some of the participants lingered behind and continued drumming. I thought that was what I heard when I awoke from a deep sleep of exhaustion sometime close to three in the morning. But the drumming was curious; it sounded far away at first and then came closer. Others on the porch where we slept heard it too, and one got up and went to the Student Building to check things out. But no one was using the drum; it was safely on the table, drumstick neatly beside it. Others about the same time smelled tortillas being warmed and bacon frying. No one on the land eats bacon, and so I think the Spirits did arrive, and to make sure that we would know, they brought along a cooking smell we knew could not be ours.

Then there was the last dance we did in Scheibbs, in 1986, before program changes there closed the center to us.[3] In lieu of dancing to the soundtrack of the Singing Shaman, we asked two men of the center staff to drum for us. The weather was pleasant, and instead of performing inside, we danced around a fire under the tall fir trees behind the building. I had been worried about this dance; the center was in a period of transition, and although the core group of experienced trancers worked with great dedication, the attendant tensions inevitably made themselves felt in the quality of the preparations. "Are you with us anyway?" I asked, as I passed into the metamorphosis part of the dance. As if in response, three things happened simultaneously. There was a sudden gust of wind, which caused the fire to crackle and made the sparks fly like tiny stars into the dark branches of the conifers, and one of the two drummers momentarily stumbled in his rhythm. I felt that I had been answered, and I was grateful.

Most of the participants left soon after the dance, but a friend who was going to give me a ride to Vienna in her car had gone for a walk, and I used the time to rest in my room. I was awakened by a knock on my door, and upon opening, there was Guschtl, one of our two drummers, leaning on his broom. "Excuse me for bothering you," he said, with obvious embarrassment, "but I just have to ask you this. Are there any Indians four meters tall?"

I became confused. "I have never seen any," I said, "but why do you want to know?"

He clutched the broomstick. "I don't know whether you noticed it, but at one point I lost the beat when I drummed for you. That was when the fire suddenly crackled. I got confused because I looked up, and standing next to me there was this extremely tall Indian. He wore white pants and a white shirt, and he had long, straight black hair. I couldn't see his face, it was in the shade. He just stood there, and then he disappeared. I can't figure it out; I haven't done any drugs for years. Do you think it was something evil?"

It took a moment before I could answer. "Oh, no, Guschtl, don't worry, he is a friend of mine," I said, and wondered why the young man looked at me rather confused and left in such a hurry. But it was really true. During the very first workshop I did in Cuyamungue, Joseph, an Indian friend from a pueblo to the north of us, had seen him too, looking just like Guschtl had described him, white garment, black hair, towering over the kiva. In his vision, Joseph heard him call to him, and when he went outside, he saw him coming from the direction of the shrine. The tall Spirit then handed him a ritual as a present that he needed in his work with young people. I asked what the apparition's face looked like, and Joseph said, rather perplexed, "Why . . . dark, of course."

CHAPTER TWELVE

The Pit of Death
and the Psychopomp

$\mathbf{T}$he postures we have explored
up till now have all dealt with life in its manifold aspects. They taught us new
insights about spirit journeys and divining, about healing and metamorphosis,
and about celebration. But they had nothing to show us about death. For that,
we need to turn to two other postures that instruct us about the final journey
awaiting all of us at the end of all the "sound and fury."

The trip to the Realm of the Spirits of the Dead. It will be recalled (see
Chapter 9) that there is a posture where the arms are placed on the chest in
such a way that the right arm is up. We called it the Chiltan posture, because
the healing spirits that Uzbeki shamanesses call on for help bear this name.
In scanning the archeological record, however, I found that there was a parallel
series, where instead of the right arm being up, it was the left one. It was
known in Central America and in the thirteenth century in New Mexico (pls.
50 and 51), where it appears in two painted tablets, one a man, the other a
woman, found hidden in a cave. Traces of it occur in sub-Saharan Africa and
Polynesia, and early representations were found in prehistoric Central Europe
and Eastern Anatolia (Turkey) (pls. 52a and b).

There is an especially touching figure of a young warrior from the fifth
century B.C. (pl. 53) shown in this posture, his arms folded on his chest as
though he were cold and apprehensive of his way. It was discovered at Hirsch-
landen in the present state of Baden-Wuerttemberg (West Germany). As archeologists reconstructed the site (see inset, pl. 53), this sandstone figure,
about five feet tall, had been placed on a hill, which was a central grave, ringed
by stone slabs. The youth is naked, and his thighs and erect penis are shaped
in naturalistic detail. However, his chest and arms seem more like a bas-relief.

Plate 50   **Plate 51**

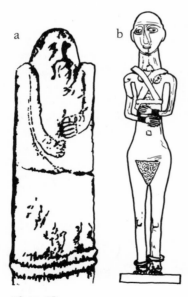

Plate 52

Apparently, the writer of the catalog text remarks, the Hallstatt tradition, of which the statue is a part, allowed the artist some latitude in shaping the lower part of the body, but the representation of the position of the arms was circumscribed by rigid convention. Remnants of sculptures from the same century of young men holding their arms in an identical pose were found also in Istria (northeastern Italy).

No speculation is offered as to the reasons for this curious arm position. Its significance becomes clear, however, if instead of looking at it as a peculiar artistic affectation of the age, we treat it as a trance posture. The following is what Bernie, a sculptor by profession, experienced at a session in Cincinnati in the fall of 1987, when we tried the posture for the first time:

I had a very good experience, very powerful, I felt. From the time I got into the pose and heard the rattle, it just flowed very, very naturally, without too much trouble on my part. I had not been too happy with my performance this weekend. Today I thought I'd take a little more initiative than I had taken in the past, get a little more directness in approaching the postures and without prodding and questioning. And I'll tell you what happened to me.

At first I became alarmed; there was a sudden cold, sweaty kind of a feeling. I was feeling ill, sick, maybe even dead, and being transformed into a corpse. Then I was traveling along a long, cold, horizontal landscape, with the leaves off of the trees, a snowy, breezy roadway, and moving and moving and moving, it seemed like forever along that particular path. Until finally I came to a rack, I guess you might call it, with bones and skin, things of that nature, all piled up as if they had been discarded. And what struck me then was that the entire landscape was being transformed from being a landscape into this rack with bones and skins. And immediately next

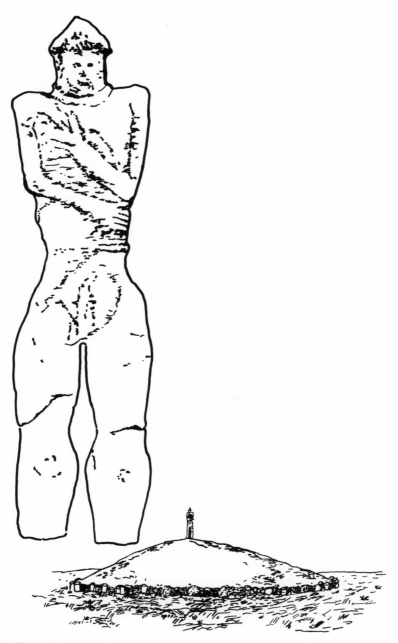

Plate 53

to· that rack was a huge pit, with darkness and individual flickering lights in the darkness, which seemed to be spirits. I recognized it from some past trance experience, and I was very eager to enter that space. And what surprised me was that in order to enter it, I didn't just have to take off my clothes, but all my skin, my flesh, my bones, and everything else to enter this place of the spirits. And it was a very curious thing. But I guess I was very willing to do that.

Once on the inside of the pit—from the beginning of the trance experience I had asked the Bear once more to come back and help me through this—I felt that once I was inside, I was being reconstituted and clothed in the warmth of the Bear, the quality of the Bear, and the image of the Bear; there was this fur and the skeletal structure. And I was given a great sense of power. I guess that was what impressed me the most, this sense of strength, really strength, I guess, of physical strength that I had through this experience. Out of that, then, it seems that we began moving away from that pit back through the cold, and with this big sense of warmth and power and light, different kinds of lights—I can't describe them— and with an overall feeling of well-being. And that was my experience.

In other words, Bernie experienced dying, then traveling to the entrance of the Realm of the Spirits of the Dead in the lower world. There he discarded his human physical attributes and, aided by the Bear, his spirit friend to whom he had appealed for help at the beginning of the session, he experienced a resurrection. With a tremendous surge of power, he was reinvested with a different body and arose to new life in the shape of the bear.

No one else in the group had thought to invoke any spirit help, and curiously, not a single one experienced any return to a new life. The women— and, as we see in plate 52b, the posture is also assumed by women—reported mainly details of the passage. One saw a black statue standing next to the road, with red lips that moved soundlessly. A man's face appeared in a hole and turned into a skull—"he had eyes, but the eyes were the first to go"—and eagles perched on bare tree branches. One of the birds unzipped the earth so Terry, one of the participants, could look inside.

The experiences of the other men in the group were similar in texture. Bob saw an Indian chief wearing a headdress from which colors kept flying off like sparks into the darkness. Michael, whose spirit guide was an Indian girl, was taken away by her over snowy land on a horse that turned into a bald eagle. They encountered a threatening owl, the spirit bird of the night, then ended up at a lake, which is where one arrives upon dying, according to Pueblo Indian tradition. Bill's experience was the most instructive. He found himself in the same black spirit pit that Bernie had described, that is, at the entrance to the Realm of the Dead. However, he had appealed to no spirit helper, and so the animal spirits that he encountered there could not help him. They had no energy to give to him: there was "no breeze, no wind at all." He tried to raise the energy on his own, but he floundered, achieving only a helpless rocking motion, not enough to award him a return to new life:

As soon as the rattle started, I felt a powerful forward movement around my shoulders. It was like flying, and I was a bird. Suddenly a bear, a wolf, and a bison appeared, and many eyes and muzzles. It was dark. There was a hole above me through which I was able to look up into the sky. Around me, there were some earthworks, with a series of holes. The moon was shining, and I saw the grass growing above, but there was no breeze, no wind at all; it was a calm night. I had a strong desire to get out but couldn't. An eye appeared and was going to act as my guide. Almost immediately, I began rocking in rhythm with my breathing. I wanted to stop it but couldn't.

With the Hallstatt youth we are taken back to a time centuries before our era when the horticulturalist tribes, we may surmise, struggling against encroaching agriculturalists, sent their young men, members of the warrior age grade, out against them on the warpath. The shamans, we might imagine, would teach them this posture of the passage to the Realm of the Spirits of the Dead, which then became their hallmark.

Actually, the Hallstatt youth and his contemporaries are not the earliest ones to show this posture. Almost three thousand years earlier, at the time when the waning Neolithic began blending into the new Bronze Age, this posture experienced an intense local flowering on the Cyclades, a group of islands north of Crete. Subsistence was still clearly horticulturalist. People grew some barley, they had a few olive trees, goats, and sheep, but mainly they were fishermen. With the appearance of Minoan culture traits a thousand years later, the art of the Cyclades collapsed.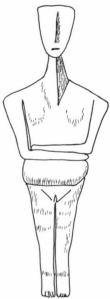

Every grave, it seems, of that particular period, whether of a man or of a woman, contains a characteristic figurine exhibiting this posture (pl. 54). Prehistorians have speculated that we are seeing a good-luck charm, or perhaps a local deity, but recalling the above experiences, a different conclusion suggests itself. I think that what is involved instead is the representation of a psychopomp and a power object. Psychopomps are shamans who have the office of accompanying the soul of the person who just died on its way to the beyond. Although the posture shown by these Cycladic

Plate 54

figurines is always the same, usually with the left arm close to the right arm or in a few instances with the left arm higher up in the manner of the Hallstatt youth, they exhibit individual characteristics. Some are slender and graceful, others are squat like peasant women; one even has a goiter, and two have their infants on their heads. Those figurines, then, are most likely the local shamanesses, women one of whose tasks it was to guide the spirits of the dead over that perilous path to the Realm of the Dead. It was clearly a woman's office; men took it over only under exceptional circumstances. Of the 121 figurines shown at an exhibit in West Germany in 1976,[1] only two are male.

But more important, I think, the small figurines acted as power objects, so that once the soul arrived at the black pit leading to the abode of the dead, it had the strength to return to the living, albeit in a different shape.

Confirmation of this view comes from a totally unexpected source—"London Bridge Is Falling Down" (Hopscotch), a traditional, highly popular children's song game,[2] well known in Hungary and in the German-speaking regions of Europe, and in a somewhat abbreviated form among English-speaking children as well. Manhardt Wilhelm (1859) summarizes the plot of the German variant, called *Brueckenspiel* ("game of the bridge"), as follows:

It seems that there is a bridge that leads to the sun and the moon, to heaven and hell, or to the angels and devils. A golden gate is substituted for the golden bridge in some variants. A group of people desire to cross the bridge. However, the bridge is *broken*, perhaps by the actions of the king, or the goldsmith and his youngest daughter. It can be repaired only with stones or bones. In order to cross the bridge, a toll must be paid, in the form of the last one of the group, or perhaps a golden horse (in Hungary, the toll is a beautiful maiden). This player becomes a prisoner in the *black kettle*, and on the basis of certain rules, it is decided whether he/she is to be apportioned to the sun or the moon, to heaven or hell, etc. In the end, the two groups struggle with each other by trying to pull each other over. Wilhelm notes that the game refers to the passage of the soul over the bridge of death.

The agreement of the game with our experiences is truly remarkable. As we saw in Bernie's case, he had to divest himself of all human attributes; that is, the bridge of life was broken. He ended up in a black pit, the "black kettle" of the game. According to the game, a contest ensues concerning the fate of the soul. Is it to end up with the sun or the moon, in heaven or hell; that is, is it to be forever consigned to the abode of the dead, or is it to enjoy a resurrection? A toll must be paid at this point. We may interpret that as meaning that the soul needs some extraneous power in order to gain resurrection. Bernie had the help of the mighty Bear Spirit, and he reentered life. Without such help Bill had to remain confined in the black pit. This additional power, I think, was what the small marble figurines in the graves of the Cyclades were intended to provide for the dead.

While the role of the psychopomp seems secondary for the shamanesses of the Cyclades during the above posture, it is the focal issue for the next one. We originally called it the mourning posture, although in view of the fact that it made it possible for the shaman to act as a guide to the lower world, this designation was not a particularly good choice. Instead, this is in fact the posture of the *Psychopomp*.

I saw the posture for the first time in a clay figurine created at Cochiti Pueblo about 1890 (pl. 55). The man has his arms lifted and with his fingers touches the upper edge of his earlobe, and his mouth is wide open. The posture is duplicated in sub-Saharan Africa (pl. 56), in a polychrome rattle fragment from the Northwest Coast (pl. 57a), as well as on a totem pole from the same

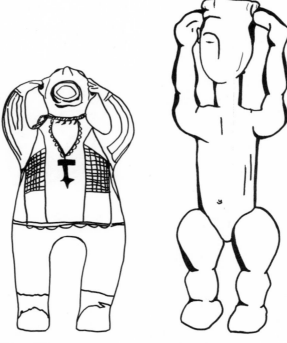

Plate 55   **Plate 56**

region (pl. 57b). The latter was carved a hundred years ago by a Tsimshian artist. It has a hole in its lower part, and the central figure above the hole is clearly tugging at the upper edge of his earlap, in the same way as the Cochiti figurine, and his mouth is equally as open as is that of the face on the rattle fragment. The hole is called a "place of opening," or a "hole through the sky." "Ladders," we are told, "led to this hole on the inside and the outside of the house, so that it could be used during ceremonies; on these occasions the normal entrance to the house was covered over."[3] According to local Indian tradition, those entering the house recreated the ancestral cosmic passage between this world and the other world. I had not seen this totem pole at the time we tried the posture, but the tradition, as we shall see, is once more a telling external confirmation of our experiences.

The first time we tried the posture was with three friends in the spring of 1986 in Vienna. I did not have the Cochiti slide with me, and all I remembered was the position of the arms. Gerhard spoke of a tall figure of light he had seen during the last few minutes of the trance. Christian St. saw a tiny man slipping in and out of his gullet. And Eva D. experienced suffering, "but not the way we understand the word," and a long, stout pole being driven through her as part of a burial rite. The use of the pole was in itself remarkable, for early observers of Pueblo Indian funeral rites speak of a pole being driven

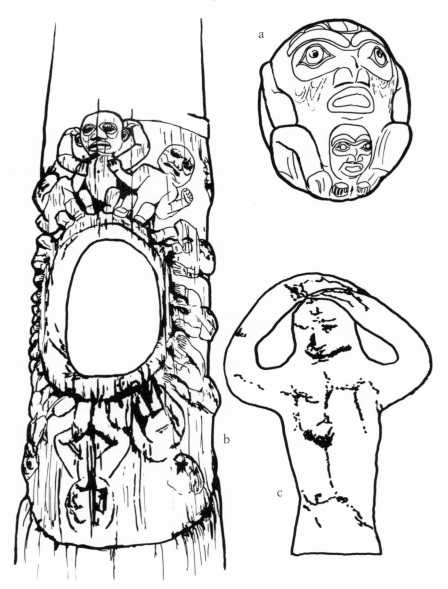

Plate 57

through the chest of the corpse after burial. Besides, we were clearly dealing with a trance posture, so I resolved to explore it further. The opportunity presented itself when nearly a year later we scheduled a research meeting in Columbus. Then, on the day before our meeting, I had the following vision:

(January 20, 1987): I heard the lines of the old song, only the last three words, "[And we won't come back 'til it's] *over, over there* . . . repeated several times, then very loud church bells, which lasted for a while. After a pause white flowers appeared, as if on a grave, and people huddling around it together with a young man on his knees in profile, in a posture that made him look like a rabbit. His hair looked slicked down like that of a movie hero of the twenties; I was surprised to see his face, but it was more like a mask, white and motionless like a cardboard cutout.

Once more, there were intimations of a burial, but other than that, I could see no connection between the posture we wanted to try and what I had recorded about it in Austria. Since my three friends were all experienced coworkers, I mentioned that this might have something to do with a funeral rite, but I did not tell them of my vision. It was not until we actually looked at the slide that I realized that I had made a mistake in Vienna: In addition to the special position of the arms, the figure also had its mouth wide open. That we had not done during the first trial.

Belinda was the first one to talk, and her experience to some degree fitted in with my—much briefer—vision:

> When we started the breathing, there was an image of a brightly colored toucan with a big beak, sitting on a branch, profiled against the night sky in brilliant turquoise, purple, and magenta colors. It was very clear and very bright. When the rattle set in, the branches of a tree appeared with umbrellalike leaves with colors so intense, it was notable for that. I looked beyond to see a beach of white sand curving and waves coming in, and there was no one there. I could see the waves clearly, and on the waves were many little spirits "body surfing," coming in; there was the sense of the spirits coming in on the waves.
>
> Then I was very aware that the posture, with my arms and the way my legs were, and my mouth open, made huge holes in me—and there was the wind blowing through, drying me out like a weathering wooden statue. My mouth was very dry, and saliva was collecting in a dark, deep pool in the bottom of my mouth and filling it up. I was sure I was going to start overflowing with this water.
>
> Fairly quickly then there was a shift, and my arms seemed connected in a straight line, with a circle of light circling right to left and back, again and again. The slow, gradual effect was one of loosening connections until I realized that it was pulling my body apart, and there was a jagged crack right down my body, splitting me in two. The physical pain in my shoulders was terrible, and it intensified the feeling that I was coming apart. Eventually I felt as though my left arm was crumbling, not exactly to dust, but my arms were crumbling apart.
>
> Then there was a decided shift again, and I saw the image of a white plate with a piece of nut pie on it. Then I noticed that the pieces of nuts in the pie looked like teeth. Then it became like a dog's head, with the teeth, and as I focused some more, it became the pointed head of a dog with its teeth gnashing. I, too, became dog-wolflike and interacted with the dog, who I thought must be Cerberus. And I thought that I must try to get past that dog. And then there was a dark hooded

figure with the big staff by a river, and I thought, naw, this is too intellectual, but it wouldn't go away. I did not want to be taken by the boatman; I didn't see a boat or a raft or anything. So I jumped into the inky, oily water and swam the short distance to the other side. It didn't take very long, and when I got to the other side, there was this same hooded figure, but it was much more pleasant on the other side. It was much easier to be there. The figure tossed back its hood, and he had on a white mask, and I could see the back of his head with very short cropped hair. So then he started to walk this path along the river back into a tunnellike cave, and I followed, and then quickly he was no longer leading me and the rattle took over. There was a dancing figure rattling, but I couldn't see the figure. What I could see were these little sparkling diamonds, shimmering starlike things that were shook along the path. My impression was they were souls, they were spirits, the essences of the people. And I followed the figure as it danced along, and it almost brought them to life, there was almost a sound. And as we went into the cave then, there was another change.

All along, the pain in my shoulders was so intense that I thought I could not stand it anymore. And I kept saying to myself to remember the pain of those who had gone before me, and sometimes it helped, and sometimes it didn't. But it was very important to acknowledge those others' pain and to not [reject it]—I could choose to not feel the pain, and it was my choice to keep with this. And I saw a skull with crossed legs, and as it started to crumble, I thought, how can I bear the pain? And then I started convulsing, and as the rattle stopped I was still convulsing a little. I had heard you two making noise, and there was the feeling that I wanted to make noise, to moan and wail. I started to make a little noise toward the end. If I would do it again, I would want to do it from the beginning consciously, as with the Singing Shaman, to allow the sound to come out.

Taking Belinda's experience as a guide to interpreting my own vision, those little spirits arriving on the seashore "body-surfing" seemed qualitatively the same as my people around the grave, souls arriving to be guided to the Realm of the Dead. That this was the reading to be given to my own vision was then further emphasized by Belinda's drying out and beginning to crumble, that is, dying, and by the appearance of a doglike being, something like Cerberus, the dog at the entrance to Hades. Although she had seen a psychopomp at the outset in the guise of a bird, which I had not, we agreed on the details of the external appearance of her second psychopomp: We had both seen his short-cropped hair and his white mask. His posture had reminded me of a rabbit precisely because he was getting ready to descend into the earth, like a rabbit into its burrow. But there were two features of her account that puzzled me: her pain, which she had rationalized as something she shared with the dying, and her intuition that there should be sound, "moaning and wailing," as she said.

Elizabeth's experience, which followed next, can be viewed as having a frame: At the outset, she is in a teepee, created by our composite energies, and is attending a person who has just died. And that is where she once more encounters herself at the end, piling stones on the corpse. This frame holds together what the dying that had just happened was like, the progressive dissolution that is really only a change in the expression of states of energy, as well as the kindly presence of the animal spirits. No psychopomp appears, but once more we hear of the pain:

> During the breathing I was aware of our breathing together, and that intensified the feeling of being together. During the breathing, the Bear came into the room, and my spirit guides and the Lion came in, and the Buffalo came in, and a huge white owl, it was very feathery. I felt very protected during the whole posture. I felt the presence of the Spirits very strongly, and their protection. They even tried to hold my arms up for me. [She laughs.] Our breaths met in the center and swirled together; it was a lot of red energy that just swirled around and then formed a teepee.
>
> Inside, I was leaning over a dead person, and I was with somebody else. And then my shoulder started to hurt really bad. During this whole session I was in excruciating pain, and I couldn't maintain the posture the entire time. I would have to break it and then get back to it again. When we began the posture, the whole thing was really physical for me. Besides the pain, I first noticed that the left side of my head—I would want to say disappeared, but it didn't. It was more like it filled up what it had displaced before it was there; I felt it filling up the room, the energy in the room, so that it wasn't there anymore [in my head]. It was different from disappearing; I don't know how to explain that any better than that. It was a filling-up feeling. But the left side of my head was gone. And then slowly the right side of my head was gone, it was just gone, and I was real aware of the rattle, and of myself, going down a ladder very fast in time to the rattle, down into myself.
>
> I was a little small person inside me, a big person with no head, and climbing down inside myself as fast as I could, in time to the rattle, while parts of me were slowly disappearing above me. And I got down to a level above my solar plexus, and there was a slime, the little green monster that I sometimes have to deal with. This creature that was in my solar plexus wouldn't let me go any further. I felt for minutes very stuck and in a lot of pain and couldn't keep the posture. I would get back in the posture, and finally I called for the Bear to come and help me.
>
> The Bear crawled down inside and asked what was the matter. And this little green monster said, "Well, nobody asked me if this was all right." So the Bear said, "You can ride on my back." That definitely appeased the little green monster. He got on his back, and we went on further down and came to a place where it was very dark blue and pretty uncomfortable. It felt like— you know, when the guides shake me out and the stuff crumbles off—that crumbly stuff was stored in this dark-blue place. It seemed like what we were going to do was clean it out and dust it. We all had little rattle dusters, and we were inside of me, rattling and dusting, and rattling and dusting in time to the rattle.
>
> Then again I was back with the pain and breaking the posture, and then back again in the posture, and I became aware of that same filling and disappearing and going down probably to my lowest part. But then the energy changed, so that I was back into my head, and it was still not there, but it was there in a different form. But I felt at a molecular level that I had changed form, and I was still invisible or not there; there was a lot of light and colors. Then it shifted again, and I was

back in that teepee where the dead person had been, and we were piling stones on top. I thought, this isn't right, this was a teepee and we should be burning him, but it was definitely stones; the person was being buried under lots and lots of stones.

Jan, finally, picked up on the problem of producing sound, and transmitted a stern lecture on our failure to provide it:

> There was a lot of energy ahead of time and with the breathing for me. And when the rattle began and we assumed the posture, it was like I knew from the minute we started that something was wrong, that something was missing, and it was the sound we were talking about. It was like I was being torn apart in the posture because we weren't sounding. It felt like a light trance to me, off and on, although there was a lot of energy building up. Some of the messages that were there were like—this is about guiding, with sound, the energy of the dying, of the spirit, so it can get where it needs to go. When we assume the posture, it's like we are agreeing to be those guides.
>
> And so we were standing here in this posture agreeing to be those guides and listening to the sounds of the spirits which were like wind, that need to get where they needed to go and we weren't doing anything; we weren't doing what we were supposed to do. I was in that conflict the whole time, and it was really difficult. On the intellectual level the conflict was, go ahead and sound, because I knew that was what I needed to do, versus disrupting the trance of the other people. So for the most part I just tried to deal with it myself, and I noticed what I was doing was a lot of movement; I was doing things like tapping my feet to create a rhythm, or using my breath to create the rhythm of a sound that would do the job. Because there were spirits here that needed to go. The times when I was forgetting to open my mouth, and my mouth was closed, there was tremendous energy in my heart center, and it was like taking in all that dying energy and not releasing it. I would open my mouth, and it would be like I could hear myself singing, and it was the Singing Shaman. It needs to be like the Singing Shaman.
>
> There was one point where I remember shifting my arms, and it felt like blood running down my leg. When that happened, the energy shifted, and it felt like you, Felicitas, were on a ladder and you were using the rattle to lift the energy up through my body. The energy at that point became very different; it was a heightened kind of energy. The conflict was still there, and toward the end I did then make a sound. It was like I didn't want to be responsible for being in this posture and not doing some of what we knew we were supposed to be doing; some of it was like I couldn't help it anymore. That was my job.
>
> And it was like the posture and the mourning sound were a signal to the other reality. It was the guide that was making the connection with the guides of the other reality requesting them to come and do their part. When I heard Belinda breathing loudly, my thought was, well, we are all doing something trying to cope with the problem. Right at the end it felt like we got it a little bit, and it was like the spirits understood that we didn't know what we were doing and it was allowed this time, but don't do it this way again.

In our discussion afterward, the lesson finally sank in. I must confess that I was not particularly proud of myself, especially in view of the fact that, as

Jan was given to understand, the sound acted as a signal to alert the guides "on the other side." With that remark, a considerable volume of customs about the "bewailing" of the dead all of a sudden fell into place, as well as highlighting our own total lack of any such mourning behavior. No wonder that the Spirits had been so anxious to make clear that they wanted us to add the sound, first alluding to the song with its suggestive "over, over there" in my vision and then practically hitting me over the head with those bells that I had heard. At one point they had been so loud, I was afraid I would lose the vision and come to. Yet I did not propose singing in trance to my group. We also concluded that had we given voice and thereby acted as proper psychopomps within the confines of this particular posture, there would not have been any pain, either.

The assumption was confirmed when we repeated the posture with a larger group at Camp Agape, Ohio, in October 1987. This time I included the instruction to use the voice the way we do it with the Singing Shaman, that is, starting with an open *a* vowel and letting the tone ride on the trance. This time, there was no pain, and both Belinda and Jan were clearly psychopomps. As Belinda reported, "I was with a group of miners; we were on an expedition and we had to climb up a mountainside, and the sound provided the energy. The sound knew where to go." It is easy to see that the "miners" were the souls traveling to the abode of the spirits of the dead, and it was the sound that made the passage possible.

> JAN: Even before the rattle started I had the clear impression that I did not have any body. Then I was surrounded by white fireworks. The rattle seemed to provide access to unfamiliar ranges. I was a magnet, gathering up energy. I called out to the energies and they took on form, and I started separating them by color. I was directing their traffic by using the tones. The tones and the colors had personality.

Even relatively inexperienced participants not familiar with the posture saw the psychopomp in action, for instance in the shape of a bird—"I looked up and saw the sun rising, and a bird was wrapping its wings around Norma [a participant who had been audibly crying during the session] and lifted her up"—or experienced the burden of the task: "I had to fly over a terrible crevasse, and it was frightfully hard for me. Then I remembered my feather; I screamed and became a hawk, and I flew up and felt strong."

I later became aware also of what I think is another variant of the psychopomp posture, which I saw in a television documentary some time ago. In that report the camera focused on a group of Sudanese women mourning a relative whom the men had gone to bury. The women had their hands on their heads, in a posture identical to one seen in a figure several thousand years old from Azor near Jaffa (in modern Israel) (pl. 57c). In our experiments, however, we have explored only the Indian variant to date.

CHAPTER THIRTEEN

Life Everlasting

In the first of the postures treated in Chapter 12, there was a clear indication that life's story did not end after the vestments of the body were surrendered at the entrance to the Realm of the Dead in the lower world. After arriving there, Bernie received a new form, that of the bear, full of power and joy. This metamorphosis is rather restricted, however. There is another posture, which allows this theme to be played out much more fully. For reasons to be explained further on, we have come to call it the Feathered Serpent posture. It is one of the few postures the origin of which can actually be traced back reliably to our ancient hunter roots.

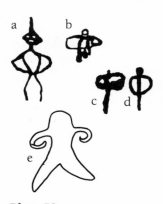

Plate 58

According to traditions still encountered among hunter-gatherers and some horticulturalists to this day, it was the task of shamans to descend into a cave, the womb of the earth. There they created likenesses of the animals surrounding them, and by no means only of those that provided food. They then lifted the soul essences from the drawings and took them up into the world of the sun, thereby helping the Earth Mother in the task of increase, of propagation.

This tradition offers a satisfying explanation for the innumerable pictures of animals our ancestors pecked out, incised, or painted in caves and also on exposed rock surfaces in many parts of the world. Humans are also often represented, dancing and engaging in many other activities, and naturally also in the role of hunter. However, human figures appear in some extremely old representations (pl. 58) which are not engaged in any of these activities. They were created during the fifth to the fourth millennia B.C. and were discovered by Russian archeologists on rock faces all across Siberia.[1] As the authors of that work point out, these human figures, which they tentatively identify as shamans, are usually placed above the animals, exerting, as it were, their power over them.

Of these figures, the one shown in pl. 58a is quite naturalistic. It clearly indicates what to me looks like a specific body posture: This person has slightly bent knees, his hands rest on his hips, and artfully, there is even a minimal indication of the bent wrist shown on the right side. To my eyes, this is an astoundingly articulate "instruction" about a trance posture that we are quite familiar with. It is a deceptively simple posture: We stand straight without locking our knees, as nearly always, and cup our hands, as illustrated best by the African figures (pl. 59), resting them palm up on the waist. The core of the experience is the eternal renewal of life.

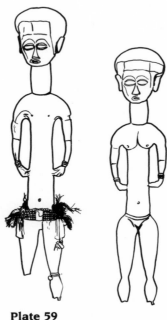

Plate 59

How ancient the knowledge about this posture must be is attested by the fact that plate 58a is the only representation that is this naturalistic. Others, although easily recognizable as treating the same posture, are quite abstract, which means that people drew the figure so many times and it was so well known that eventually, a few sparing lines were sufficient to make the meaning clear. During times of great cultural stability, such as the era of the hunters in fact was, a development of that nature takes a very long time. Thus plate 58b abstractly represents a shamaness according to the Russian researchers, the round hole being her womb, while plates 58c and 58d are so highly abstracted that they seem like an ideograph, communicating in ultimate abbreviation the message that the animals shown will return to life once more because of the action of the shaman.

In this context it is revealing to note that nearly three thousand years later, in the Ganges River valley, people cherished copper objects (pl. 58e) on which the practiced eye of the archeologist was unable to detect any trace of use.[2] This motif is so similar in shape to the Siberian petroglyphs that it may have been brought to India by cultural diffusion. Quite possibly people carried these copper plates because they reminded them of the promise of resurrection.

Plate 60

For the same reason, surely, in the city of Ur, in the fourth millennium, one of the most frequently encountered effigies is a clay figurine of a deity standing in this posture.

However, I saw this durable posture for the first time in a drawing by a modern American Indian shaman. In the 1970s, Gerhard Baer, a Swiss anthropologist, did fieldwork among the Matsigenka Indians of eastern Peru. One of their shamans, Benjamin Sanchez, made him a drawing of the places and beings he habitually encountered on his spirit journeys (pl. 60). Of the three spirits drawn large, whose power is indicated by their facial hair, which is not a moustache but jaguar whiskers, the one on the right was standing in the posture of the Bear Spirit, the middle one in that of the Singing Shaman, and the one on the left in a posture that I was totally unfamiliar with. But soon after I came across the photograph of a clay figurine from a pre-Columbian grave site in eastern Peru,[3] of a man being

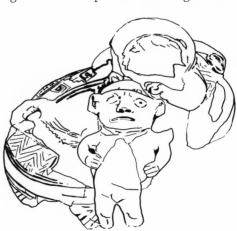

Plate 61

carried aloft by a plumed serpent that grabs him by the head (see pl. 61). His posture was the same as that of the Matsigenka spirit, and in addition provided details not discernible in the above drawing on how to do the posture, which has become one of our favorites over the years. Quite often the trancers in fact do experience the presence of this mighty, ancient being of fertility. For Westerners it is hard to recognize a Feathered Serpent, and it was an occasional source of merriment when participants confessed that they had taken it for "a seal with feathers stuck in" or "an eagle, but maybe more like a caterpillar."

With Judy Ch. and Jan, we are introduced to varying impressions of the actions of the Feathered Serpent. For Judy this is principally the motion of a curving serpentine body, which sometimes is a woman and then again a serpent, while Jan assumes the role of the Feathered Serpent as a giver of fertility, and in fact becomes her.

> JUDY CH. (Columbus, 1985): I felt much movement; I was like taffy being stretched. Somebody behind me put his hands into the holes in me and stretched me and bent me over. I felt tremendous heat pouring out of my chest and rising up, and my eyes began to itch. Then I was pulled again, and I was moving in figure eights. The loops moved into vertical flip-flops; they circled, and started spinning, and were illuminated in a vivid purple color.

> JAN (Columbus, 1985): I was flying over the earth and was cross-pollinating. I was taking seeds and planting them, and that felt like Mother Nature doing it. Then I was shown how life patterns were woven into one and saw all realms dancing. I was moving in a figure-eight pattern, and was asked to be the movement. "You are the dance," I heard, "you are the dance."

In Vienna, Christian St. was really confused about what exactly he had tangled with:

> Something or somebody got hold of me from the back. It was a powerful being, but I couldn't figure out if it was an eagle or a caterpillar. Then I saw the seashore, and at that point I was confused again: Was I a caterpillar? And who was doing the flying? Was I doing it or not? There were strange fish in the sea, and a white dot. There was a lake, and a thick worm was reflected in it, and what seemed to be a butterfly. Then I was standing on a rock ledge. I was supposed to fly, and over my back there was a huge hand, and its fingers reached down on my chest as far as the nipple.

Eva D., in the same session, recognized the powerful feline head of the serpent. She went through dying, when it suddenly turned dark, and also the repose when she watched a spider digging itself into the sand. Finally she is reborn in a number of different shapes:

> I saw the face of a big cat above me, looking at me, then it was gone. It was dark. I started running up toward the bright light. There was a house on the side of the mountain. I was a panther and went into the house, which was very bright inside. A black spider or maybe a scorpion was crawling over the yellow sand and then dug itself in. I became the spider, then a woman, then a ball of light raining golden drops, and then I was inside a bird's body that had a long beak.

Except for the above motifs, there are also a number of other elements that appear during this posture. Thus Jane, a beginner, told at a workshop in Columbus, Ohio, in the spring of 1985:

> I felt my body splitting in half. Then I was being rolled up to a mountain peak. I fell into a foggy, grey, soft light, and instead of stopping when I reached the bottom, I kept right on falling through the earth, through many different layers and

through crevasses right into the center of the earth. After I got there, I rested. Finally I emerged, and that was very comforting.

Jane clearly experienced a sum of the outstanding features of what the posture mediates, being carried aloft, falling into what might be a hollow mountain, resting, and then rising once more. The report also throws sudden light on a symbol carved into the chest of a female figurine shown in this posture and wearing a bird mask, unearthed in central Yugoslavia and dated about 6000 B.C. The marking (see pl. 62) consists of a V, with a line penetrating into it from above. Amazingly, the symbol is an exact representation of the salient experience in this posture.

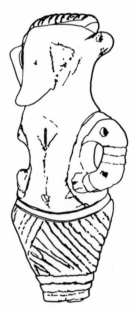

For Elizabeth R., at the same workshop, falling into the mountain passes rapidly before her eyes, and the transformation is touched on only briefly, when, after receiving the crystals, colored rays issue from her head. The important experience for her is the repose under the cozy Eskimo skins on a slab of ice:

> I felt tired; flashes of flowers and animals passed before my eyes, and I did not seem to be able to stop. Suddenly I saw the face of an Eskimo, clothed in a fur outfit. He took me into an igloo. I had to take a step deep down into the ice, and everything was bathed in this bluish-white light. "Do you have any questions?" he asked. But I couldn't think of anything, so he left. In the igloo, it was pretty big; there were other Eskimos, all working on bones and stretching hides. My Eskimo gave me a hat. It was made of the skull of a polar bear. Then he had me lie down on a platform of ice. I should rest, he said, and do nothing. That felt so comfortable, and so restful. A woman was sewing beads on a skin. She came and implanted crystals in my head. After she did that, I could see rays of color coming out of my head.

Plate 62

With Gerhard (Vienna, 1985), we are introduced to some other features of the experience in this posture, namely, the dance that follows the repose of death, and the fire of regeneration in the depth of the mountain, which for him takes on the shape of a glowing circle:

> I felt the rattle in my body. I ran up into the air at an angle and found myself in a dense, swirling fog. I started walking; it was pitch-dark. I saw a circle of black people dancing in a glowing white circle. I slipped into an egg and was alone in a dark landscape. A bird and a shadowy figure took me along up to the crest of a mountain. Then I came to the sea, which was as yellow as gold, and I lay down in it.

We may assume that Gerhard was a bird after emerging from the egg. Eva D., too, had been of a different shape at the conclusion of the experience. In fact, the risen shape is hardly ever human. This aspect of the posture of the Feathered Serpent illustrates a view about animate life that is quite different from our own. It is all a game, it seems to say; you have one shape today, another one tomorrow, and over it all arches the miracle of everlasting life. As the Eskimos held,

> Animals sometimes chose to die because they had grown tired of their present existence and wished to come back as some other form of life. In one Eskimo tale, the soul of a dead human fetus is successively dog, fjord seal, wolf, caribou, dog again, and finally, by slipping into the body of a woman as she bends over a seal, once more a human fetus, eventually to grow into a dutiful son and successful hunter. . . . This is more than transformation, however; each being contains many forms simultaneously, sometimes manifesting itself as one, sometimes as another. (Furst and Furst 1982:141)

In Scheibbs in 1986, Franz was not carried by the Feathered Serpent but was guided by a psychopomp, which assumed, as it had for Belinda (see Chapter 12), the shape of a bird, a motif frequently encountered in folklore. There was no dance at the bottom of the hollow mountain; it was a soccer game instead—also intense motion, in other words.

> A bird appeared before me. It had a black body, a many-colored neck, and wore a little crown. The bird began dancing around me for a long time. I was at a curious mountain; it was hollow inside like a volcano, relatively high. The bird and I started climbing up that mountain, then the bird carried me the rest of the way. Inside the mountain everything was reddish-brown, but in the middle there was a vivid emerald-green spot. Very far below me people were playing soccer. I wanted to see more, but a red layer began to cover the scene, and I was at a loss what to do next.

The basic features—the hollow mountain, in this case a wall formed by slanting pillars, the movement, the fire, and the transformation—are easily identifiable also in this 1986 account from Switzerland:

> VRENIE: We were in a circle, surrounded by slanting pillars. Inside the circle there was a lot of movement by small beings. Above there were many colored ribbons swirling around, and below a fire was burning brightly. Then the rain started falling, and water came rushing in from all sides. The fire dissolved, and I with it. I turned my head upward and saw many orange-red suns. Then I changed into a vessel, which was open toward the top, and in it there was a golden ball. A fragrant liquid kept dropping on my right side. Suddenly, a white feather came floating down, and the fragrant liquid began to spread. I left the vessel and did not know where to go. But a black cloud came and carried me up in a whirl to the brown earth above that was full of life.

Pij's experience during a workshop near Salzburg (1987) has a similar idyllic cast. She mentioned that shortly before the session, she had been to a cemetery and had admired the crocuses growing on a grave. She took their image with her into her trance:

> The light around me was pale green, and the rattle seemed far away. Some soft gold-colored good-luck feathers stroked and tickled me and gave me a feeling of happiness, of harmony. I became a cross on a grave and had to bend down in order to be able to see the crocuses that were growing there. I bent down so low, I began to see their roots. I sank into the earth; it was cool and lovely to be down there. I sat down next to the crocus bulbs and turned into a bulb myself. It was a quiet feeling. I had many layers, I had become a real firm bulb, and I was in the earth for a long time.
>
> Then the light began to dawn, and I figured it was a matter of logic, I would definitely turn into a crocus, and I was looking forward to that. Instead, however, I became an ancient, thick, gnarled tree with spreading branches. This condition lasted a long time. Under the tree, there were tiny snakes wiggling around. The branches had meadows on them with red and yellow flowers, and when Felicitas had to sneeze, all the blossoms closed up. The scene was bathed in a soft green light. My roots sucked water out of the ground; it spread all over and fructified everything. It was beautiful. I saw a Mexican female figurine from a distance. It turned into my mother, and I became a very small child and crawled around through the roots. My mother placed me into a nest with tiny green snakes that had feathers on them. I was in an eggshell, and I had to chew my way out, and it was fun the way the eggshell crunched between my teeth. I was a very tiny child, but then I became a snake, and enormously big, and from high up, I could see the entire earth.

Finally, there was Edeltraut. She had never done any trance before, and unaccountably, the fire of regeneration took on a very special meaning for her during a workshop in Utrecht (the Netherlands) in 1986. She saw herself wearing an ugly mask and being burned at the stake as a witch, and then flying away free with a swarm of white birds.

> I heard insects flying in and out, and it seemed that I couldn't stop the insects from buzzing in my ear. I had a distorted face, and I thought that I was very ugly in this mask, which was like an animal mask, like a caricature. I became an insect, which had big ears; actually I was two insects flying around. I was an insect in the rattle, being battered in between the stones and the seeds in the rattle. Then I had human shape again, and I was hanging forward and was rolling down headfirst into a valley. I straightened up and started dancing. There was light above me. I was naked and felt very hot. There was a fire. I was burning in the fire; I was standing in one place, me, but not me, I was a witch being burned at the stake. I felt my face burning, but there was no pain. Suddenly everything went black. Then I saw a light. It was like an eye, and I wanted to go through that light, up into the sky, up into the air and into freedom. Above me, there were white birds circling, swans, or maybe geese, and I was flying with them. I thought I was a white bird, too, but when I looked at myself, I had no body. I was invisible.

Edeltraut seemed to have gone through a curious, special application of the experience of the Feathered Serpent, and I recall puzzling over it. But other impressions intruded, two years went by, and I more or less forgot about it. It was not until I started working on this chapter and looked through my notes that it occurred to me that possibly there had been a special dimension to Edeltraut's experience which I needed to explore. The more I thought about it, the clearer it became to me that her account actually represented an invitation to the mystic ranges of human myth.

Section III

MYTHS OF THE
ETERNAL PRESENT

My first reaction at rereading my notes about Edeltraut's account of her experiences during the posture of the Feathered Serpent was amazement. Through the magic of the posture, the burning of a witch, the obscene crime perpetrated against uncounted women in centuries past, had here undergone a miraculous, a redeeming transformation. But at closer scrutiny, there seemed to be even more to it. As though witnessed from the inside, the event assumed an eerie reality. Joan of Arc might have experienced her trial this way, the Inquisitors tormenting her like the bothersome insects whose buzzing she could not stop; the distorted mask of the heretic that had been forced on her, and which hid the gentle girl who used to dance around the trees at her father's homestead; the battering of the endless hearings that bruised her day after day. Finally there she is, standing naked at the stake, burning and yet not in pain, and flying through the blackness toward the light, a free spirit at last, an invisible companion of white birds.

It was all so specific, much more than simply a recreation informed by whatever Edeltraut might have read. The question was, had we been listening to Edeltraut, or had it been Joan who told her story? On the one hand, it is Joan's life, obvious to anyone familiar with the tragic fate of the peasant girl who in the fifteenth century raised the siege of Orléans, thus helping to free France from English domination. On the other hand, it is also myth, for we are told how her life triumphs beyond the flames of the pyre.

If we accept this interpretation of what Edeltraut experienced, we will have to rethink what myth is. It may be a fanciful tale about imaginary beings, or a repository for nearly forgotten historical events, or a story invented to give meaning to some ritual. But principally, a myth is a report about events that took place in the other reality and that involved people or beings who straddled the two dimensions. Joan heard and saw and was guided not by a military high command but by spirits whom she did not disguise as saints until she came in conflict with the Inquisition.

The question is, how did Edeltraut come to experience this vision in its vivid immediacy? After all, Joan died in 1431. The extraordinary incident may have something to do with the fact that the alternate reality does not have a dimension of time. Gernot Winkler, the director of the Timekeeping Service of the U.S. Naval Observatory, defines time as "the abstract measure of change, an abstraction of an abstract notion." In order for a flow of time to exist, in other words, there must be constant change. And the more we experience the alternate dimension of reality, the more proficient we become in our travels through those misty ranges, the more we are struck by the fact that such a flow of change does not make its presence felt there. Its absence becomes obvious in such minimal observations as not being able to locate a certain experience in sequence. Was it at the outset of a vision or possibly later on? While in trance, that does not seem to matter, but a correction is quickly made when the trancer tries to recollect the details in the ordinary state of consciousness.

This does not mean that the alternate reality does not change. But the change is not a linear one, not a continuing process, where one event is added to another one like beads on a necklace. Instead, once in a very great while, a shift occurs, in the way the earth occasionally lurches on its elliptical path. The religious philosophy of the Yąnomamö Indians makes this matter beautifully clear.[1] They hold that the cosmos is layered, and humans live on the third layer from the top. The topmost layer is simply there. It has no present function; whatever originated there sifted down to the other two layers a long time ago. The next one is the sky layer. Again ages ago, in a cataclysmic event, a piece of this sky layer broke off and formed the jungle where the Yąnomamö and many other people live today. Then another such event occurred, another piece broke off the sky layer; it crashed through the earth-surface layer and came to rest below it, forming the village of hungry spirits who go after souls because they have no territory to hunt in. The point is that there were really only two such lurches of the world. Essentially, the cosmos is forever suspended in the eternal present of the alternate reality.

An event such as the trial and death of Joan of Arc is a fragment of reality that penetrated into the other dimension not as a part of an "orderly" history, but by virtue of who she was and the spirit company she kept. Once there, it remained, ephemeral yet lasting forever, floating in that mystic space like a rainbow-colored cobweb. That was why Edeltraut could reexperience it in such untrammeled freshness. In order for these fragments to become visible, however, conditions must be just right.

The first of these conditions concerns the behavior of the crack between the earth and the sky on the horizon. According to a tradition known around the world since ancient times, that is the hole, a kind of slit, that leads from our ordinary reality into the alternate one. This gateway is not always open, so the time for attempting a passage must be chosen correctly, obviously when it happens to be ajar. For us, who are so ignorant in these matters, there is no choice; we enter by chance, or perhaps by invitation.

The second condition refers to the intruders. It seems that their bodies, to use a technical simile, must be tuned to the frequency of a particular event for it to become visible. This tuning is accomplished by the posture. Yet paradoxically, most of time the experience seems curiously at odds with what is usually experienced in the respective posture. Edeltraut's was not an experience typical for the posture of the Feathered Serpent. Such incongruity has occasionally been the red flag for me that something out of the ordinary was going on.

The third condition is the most illusive. We might think of it as the angle of vision. There are occasions when only a single person in a group accidentally finds that correct angle. And for that to happen, it does not really matter whether that person is experienced or not. Edeltraut was a complete novice. At other times, as we shall see, several participants may hit it just right, or even an entire group. When all these conditions are met, the perceiver usually turns into the actor, as Edeltraut did in our example. Finally, the event, which is always sketched out in the most gossamery of details, must be recognized. The stock of myths of humankind is infinite, and my knowledge, regrettably, is quite limited. I am sure that many precious tales were alluded to in our workshops that I did not recognize and that therefore escaped me.

The experiences I am going to recount in this section, then, are myths that a favored few among us participated in as present events. They are present in the sense that once they happened, they did not vanish, but became forever suspended in a dimension that has neither past nor future, the true treasure house of our species.[2]

The Emergence Story

Two Indian friends, Rosemary from Taos and Joseph from Picuris, were participants in the first workshop I ever did in Cuyamungue, in the summer of 1982. We had done the postures together that I had worked through for the German television program, and then the question came up whether there were also others that I had not tried yet. So I got out the few examples that I had collected at the time, and we decided on the posture of a man squatting on a carved red sandstone pipe, an exquisite piece of art created about A.D. 1300 and discovered during excavations in Hale County, Alabama (pl. 63). The man is naked except for a cap, perhaps made from strips of hide. He has his tongue between his lips.

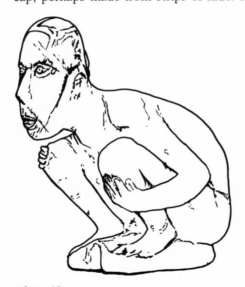

His left hand grabs his lower left leg at an angle, his right hand is on his right knee, but stretching upward on the side of the leg, and his buttocks rest on the ground, a posture extremely demanding physically.

Both Joseph and Rosemary were shaken by what they had seen in the trance using that posture. It was dark, said Joseph, and the earth had burst open, as if an enormous volcanic eruption was about to take place, and the sky was lit up by exploding stars. Rosemary had heard people screaming, sighing, and moaning as if they were about to die. They both said that they would not try that posture again.

Plate 63

Listening to them, I thought that perhaps they were describing the emergence of humans from the third world to the fourth world, which, as I told before, is said to have taken place across the valley from Cuyamungue in the sacred Jemez Mountains. But the modern Pueblo tradition[3] is much gentler than what my two friends had seen. It tells about the third world being dark and crowded, and so the Corn Mothers decided to send out one of the men to examine the earth above if it was solid enough, and after some difficulties were overcome, humans did emerge and started their southward migration.

But there is also another, more harrowing tradition, part of the Navajo emergence story,[4] according to which humans escaped from the fourth to the fifth world. They were moaning and groaning and in fear for their lives because of the threatening floodwaters that were churning below them, which had arisen because of a foolish deed of Coyote. That may have been what Joseph and Rosemary had witnessed, but an event even more grandiose than either tradition describes, with the earth itself moaning and the stars exploding as humans came forth to start their earthly journey. In some brown kiva under the southern sky, we might imagine, men knowledgeable in the art of trancing would sometimes get together for a sacred ritual, light the pipe, and, seeing the crouched figure in the swirling smoke of the tobacco, experience over and over again that marvelous event, the way it truly happened when humans set foot on the dark new world that was to become their home.

$\mathbf{A}$s told by the Navajo singers,
the religious specialists who are the guardians of Navajo oral literature, Coyote
is the child of the sky but was born from the embrace of the sky with the
earth. It seems that one day, the people saw the sky swooping down:

> It seemed to want to embrace the earth. And they saw the earth likewise looming
> up as if to meet the sky.
>   For a moment they came in contact. The sky touched the earth and the earth
> touched the sky. And just then, at exactly the spot where the sky and the earth
> had met, Ma'ii the Coyote sprang out of the ground. (Zolbrod 1984:56)

Thus in his parentage, Coyote bridges the earth and the sky, the ordinary
and the alternate reality. But something else also entered into his makeup, for
his birth happened at the same time the elders were involved in an important
ritual. They were giving a penis to a boy who had come of age, and a vagina
to a girl who had come of age, which they had not had before. Coyote went
to where the people were, and meddler that he was and fascinated by sex
obviously from the time he sprang from the ground, he decided to make the
young people even more beautiful than having a penis and a vagina made
them. And so he blew some of his own facial hair in such a way that it landed
between their legs. However, First Woman, in charge of uncontrolled impulses,
was worried that now the young people had become too attractive to each
other, and so she ordered that they cover themselves.

Here we have Coyote's problems in a nutshell. As the child of the sky, he
wants beauty, but as the child of the earth, he has an unbridled interest in
procreation. And not being accountable to anyone, having no neighbor glancing over his shoulder, no mother to be ashamed of his shenanigans, he is able
to give free rein to his wildest impulses. Yet while he can cause havoc and
even disaster, he has in common with his northern cousin the Trickster (Chapter 11) that he also brings forth much that is new and useful. He is credited,
for instance, with bringing fire to humankind. Other innovations he is responsible for are frequently blessings in disguise, such as death, which came
about because Coyote disobeyed the shadow people and touched his wife after
bringing her back from the Realm of the Dead, a Nez Perce Orpheus tale.[5]
No wonder that, as Zolbrod says, "To this day, Navajos of all ages take great

delight in heaping scorn upon Coyote for his misadventures, yet they maintain a sturdy reverence for him" (1984:355, fn. 22).

Coyotes are much in evidence at Cuyamungue, and enchanted, we listen to their song in our sleeping bags on moonlit nights. One time, we did the posture of the Singing Shaman on the ridge rather than inside the kiva, and to our delight, we heard their answering call from across the Cañada Ancha. But Coyote rarely appears in our trances. The reason may be that in the culture complex to which the trances take us, sexual behavior, although much freer than in the agriculturalist societies to which we are heirs, is still under tight social control, very much a concern of ordinary reality, and that may keep him in check. But he cannot be suppressed forever, and in the summer of 1986 in Cuyamungue there was one girl whom Coyote obviously could not resist, and with conditions being just right, he took advantage of the situation. So this is what happened to one of our participants in the posture of the Feathered Serpent:

> ANN B.: I saw a yellow path to the left, and I started following it. It kept turning and twisting, and finally went spiraling through the clouds. I looked down, and below me there was a lake, and I was startled. Suddenly, a coyote appeared beside me and started leading me along the path, and I was grateful for the company. I finally got on the coyote and started riding it, which went on for quite a while. I was feeling extremely hot and began shaking. We were in the desert; there was a medicine man who was rattling all around me. Then the coyote made love to me, and when it was over, I found myself in some cool mud, and the coyote was gone. But when I turned, there were now two coyotes dancing around me. A rope ladder appeared, and I climbed up toward the sun, getting hotter and hotter.

Ann's encounter with Coyote is admirably in character. He appears, knowing full well that she will be a willing partner. Slyly he offers to help her on the perilous path in the clouds, even letting her ride on his back. To take away what resistance she might still muster, he has a medicine man dance around her and with his rattle benumb her senses. Or was that a shape he himself assumed? It could well be. At any rate, he makes love to her and then disappears.

How right Coyote had been about Ann became clear in a letter I received from her during the following winter. After some personal news, she continued as follows:

> If you remember, my dying/rebirth trance was very special for me. I met a coyote who accompanied me through my journey, and with whom at one point in the sky, I made love. It was most beautiful, and I felt very lucky to have been chosen by the coyote spirit. I told the man I am in love with about this, and he started reading up on coyote. He took out from the library a bunch of coyote tales. They were about coyote man, this trickster, who is constantly on the move, in search of young female spirits. He convinces them to meet him in a remote place, and then he makes love to them. He is supposed to have love-making down to a fine

art and always causes the young female spirits great pleasure. Anyway, I thought that was funny and it makes sense to me. I'm very trusting and always think the best of people. I guess it's naiveté. The coyote knew how to appear to me to charm me. I trust guiding spirits. (Letter, January 3, 1987)

The Man of Cuautla

For years Ursula S., a Swiss painter, had been telling me about a figurine she had inherited from her grandmother. Her uncle had immigrated to Mexico and settled in Cuautla, not too far from Mexico City, and when his new house was being built, the workers came across a perfect little clay sculpture and brought it to him. During a visit to Mexico, Ursula's grandmother saw it in her son's house and liked it so much, her son gave it to her. Ursula was familiar with it from early childhood, and when her grandmother died, she inherited it. She finally brought a photograph of it to our workshop in Switzerland in the spring of 1987 (pl. 64).

The man is sitting flat on the ground, his legs apart and bent at the knees. His right hand is on his knee, the left arm is stretched a bit more than the right, and his left hand is placed somewhat to the side of his knee. He wears a feather crown, and his head is slightly tilted back. His tongue is between his lips.

What the Swiss participants told after we did the posture did not suggest any particular experiential type to me, healing, for instance, or divination. If anything, it seemed to be a spirit journey of sorts, but not a very productive one. Urs R. repeatedly saw three "pointed mountains." Kathrin told about a wall and hearing rocks falling down a stone stairway. Monica had to look down, very deep down, past legs of stone. There were shadows of lions, according to Romana, but they had no manes. She came to a cleft in the earth; it was like a cave, and a shaft of light illuminated two or three more caves. Vrenie turned into a spectator:

> I came to a rock wall. In it there was a circular staircase which I was supposed to climb up, but that was difficult in this posture. So finally I grew wings and was able to fly. The wind current carried me up, and as a bird I came to perch on the banister.

Krischta had been pulled backward into a cave, and in a hall lit from above had seen a woman in white and an altar with sheaves of grain, grapes, and fruit, and when she asked what that was for, she was told that these things should be distributed over the earth as gifts:

Then beings appeared, a tiger, a deer, a man who came from the forest, looking untidy and clothed in leaves and tendrils of plants—I could not see his face—and a large bird, whose wings were hanging down, but they were really arms, and it turned into a woman with the head of a bird, who had snakes curling around her arms.

Ursula, on whom I had called first, had the longest tale:

It was dark. To the left of me there were stones forming a wall next to a ditch. The wall was quite high straight in front of me and to the left. I saw an opening in the floor. But I didn't want to go down into that hole, and I asked, "What does this mean?" As if in answer a black shadow lifted itself out of the opening, slipped back down, then reappeared. The shadow repeated this action several times. I thought it was showing me what to do, so I slipped down after it, past lots of cut stones and down many steps, down and down, sometimes with the shadow before me. We arrived at a stone toad, which suddenly sprang to life. There were also eyes of stone, and they too became alive. Then there were more steps and more stones. The shadow

Plate 64

that guided me now had a red spot in the middle of its chest, which glowed and rotated. I finally arrived in a large hall with a domed ceiling, and at that point, the rattle became quite audible. The stone frogs and also some stone snakes, all wanted to get out, but they had to use the stairs, and they went as fast as the rattle. The air became warm; I saw the sky and the light of the sun, and once more there was the wall and the shadows standing beside it.

The majority, including Ursula, had apparently been someplace underground, among walls, in a cave, in a number of caves perhaps. But it was all quite opaque, and poor Ursula, I think, was disappointed that I could not make more sense out of the experiences mediated by her small treasure.

In the summer of 1987 I had a minor accident in Cuyamungue, which forced me to cut down on physical activity, and so I did some reading instead. One of the books I spent time with was Dennis Tedlock's new translation of the Popol Vuh.[6] This "Book of Counsel" is a remarkable work, an epic collection of Maya myths, written by Quiché Maya priests shortly after the Conquest. And there sudddenly, to my utter delight, and I must confess with a bit of a shiver, I saw spread out before me the context for the experiences of my Swiss friends, connected with the Man of Cuautla.

In one of the Quiché Maya myths, we learn that the four heads of the Quiché patrilineages decided to acquire patron deities to whom they could bring offerings. To this end they went to a great eastern city called Tulan Zuyua, Seven Caves, Seven Canyons. It is a famous incident, and I had read about it in one of the earlier translations of the Popol Vuh. What I did not know was that this place could actually be located geographically. As Tedlock points out,

> [But] in giving Tulan Zuyua the further name Seven Caves, the Popol Vuh preserves the memory of a metropolis much older and far grander than any Toltec town. The ultimate Tulan was at the site now known as Teotihuacan, northeast of Mexico City. It was the greatest city in Mesoamerican history, dating from the same period as the classic Maya. Only recently has it been discovered that beneath the Pyramid of the Sun at Teotihuacan lies a natural cave, whose main shaft and side chambers add up to seven. (1985:48–49)

So that was where the man of Cuautla had taken his charges! The "three pointed mountains" that kept reappearing to Urs were pyramids, having walls faced with cut stone, reliefs of people with "stone legs," effigies of sacred toads and snakes, and the great power spirit, the jaguar, a "lion without a mane," hovering nearby. Entirely within the classical Maya scheme of things, Vrenie turned into a bird that sat on a banister watching. In Maya myth the Celestial Bird has the task of witnessing events for the gods. And Krischta saw offerings of grain and fruit, relating to an account in the Popol Vuh where the Quiché turn against human sacrifice and offer resin and produce instead.

However, the adventure got even more specific. Krischta had actually seen the Quiché lineage elders arriving at the Pyramid of the Sun to pick up their deities. They were not city people, such as the white-clad woman who was expecting them, but men from the forest, dressed in leaves and tendrils. And some of them wore animal masks, because they were hunters and gardeners, people who in their dances turned into animal beings. On a wall painting in Teotihuacan, a priestess bringing sacrifices is shown in a long garment, and some others, also bringing offerings and identified as "tribesmen," wear animal-mask headgear.[7]

Ursula, finally, in return for her love for the ancient figurine, was singled out for the most wonderful gift of all. The guide who took her into the depths of the caves was not an ordinary spirit. He had, as she clearly saw, a glowing red spot on his chest, which kept rotating. In the world where she was taken, that shadow could only be Tohil, the patron deity of several Maya lineages. In the classical Maya period, as we know from inscriptions at Palenque, he bore the name of Tahil, a Cholan word meaning "Obsidian Mirror," and he was always shown with a mirror on his forehead, from which a burning torch protruded. That Ursula saw him with a rotating red disk on his chest may well be the manifestation of a more ancient form, for as Tedlock (1985:365) explains, Tohil was the giver of fire, pivoting in his own sandal like a fire-drill.

A Maya Whistle

In tomb 23 on the Rio Azul in Guatemala, archeologists came across a figurine representing a young man (pl. 65). He is sitting cross-legged and has his arms folded over his chest. The posture is also seen in a warrior from a classical Maya site at Jaina, on the western coast of the peninsula of Yucatán. Two features, however, distinguish the Rio Azul figurine from the Jaina one. The man from the Rio Azul has his tongue between his lips, and the figurine is a whistle.

When we did the posture for the first time in Cuyamungue in the summer of 1986, one participant was advised to heal a split in her body, another one was to guard something, and Isi was told, rather severely, "If you don't have any questions now, come back when you do." Although there were also other kinds of visions, of a hammock, of finely decorated pots, "as if from Mimbres," of potsherds scattered about, we still decided mainly because of Isi's report that the posture was intended for divining. However, when we did the posture once more in Columbus in November 1986 with a rather large group, Belinda was informed emphatically that divination was not what the Spirits had in mind: "No—that won't happen here."

Plate 65

The question was, what was it we were going to be shown? Listening to the subsequent reports took me back on the wings of magic to my own many fieldwork trips to Yucatán, to the warm nights of the rainy season, to the modest pyramids that are still standing choked in weeds outside the village at the end of a road as straight as the flight of an arrow. For a moment or two that basement room of the university building was filled with the intoxicating fragrance of the blossoms of a jasminelike bush the villagers call "Juan de noche." I had the feeling that we had been witness to an ancient funeral, with the soul like a will-o'-the-wisp flitting about among the corn plants and the lanky papaya stalks, looking for a home.

Accounting for my intuition afterward, though, became a frustrating exercise, somewhat like attempting to reconstruct a pot from a thousand sherds scattered over a rough terrain, while being ignorant of what the finished piece was supposed to look like. It was not until a year later that Linda Schele's book *The Blood of Kings* helped me find the basic design.

So here it is. The cracks still show, of course, and the doubters may look in the drawer and weigh the evidence for themselves.[8] Here and there, a piece needed to be created born of intuition and not of fact, but all in all, I have the feeling that the Spirits are satisfied.

A Ghost Says Good-Bye

This is it, this is the official story. It happened, they say, a long time ago, when the Precious Red Stone had barely completed the spiderweb of the order of the world. It was then that Hunahpu and Xbalanque, the Hero Twins, were playing ball. The noise disturbed the Lords of Death in the Underworld, Xibalba, the Land of Terror.

Then the Lords of Death ordered the Twins to appear before them, it is said, and they put them through many frightful trials. Those trials had killed their father and their uncle before them, but the Twins were young and strong and cunning, and they survived. And they decided that they would trick the Lords of Death in turn. So they pretended defeat, allowing themselves to be burned to death and their ashes strewn on the waters. It is said that on the fifth day they rose to new life and traveled the land as entertainers. They showed the people their mastery over death, how they could sacrifice a dog, and even a man, and yet they lived. The Lords of Death were curious. They summoned the entertainers to their court in Xibalba, and thinking they would live again, they let themselves be killed. This is how the Hero Twins gained over the Lords of Death—they did not resuscitate them. Since then, it is said, life is triumphant, and after the soul passes through Xibalba, it will dance to the North Star and join the ancestors and the gods.

Much time went by, and many souls took that road. And then it happened that the crack between the worlds was open, and the story of a young warrior who had gone that way came whispering on the wind:

—We were in among the trees on an errand for our prince, looking for captives that would increase his renown. It was hot, the afternoon rains had not come yet, and the perspiration was burning in my eyes. Suddenly, there was a rustling behind the bushes. I thought it was the army ants and turned to jump across their stream of a thousand vicious stings. But I did not get to vault. Somebody had grabbed my long hair and yanked back my head as the priests do during a sacrifice. I thought—no, not my heart! But it was not to be my heart. I felt the blade slice into my belly; it twisted and turned. My abdomen became transparent, it was on fire; my head opened, and flowers sprouted out. Then I was cool and wet, and the world turned dark.

When I opened my eyes again, I saw my companions, who were carrying my body away. It was night by then, warm and soft, and the fragrance was overpowering. I followed them for a while then slipped away, up a mountainside, in among the tall trees, whose every twist of bark has its own thorn. I laughed, for now I had no skin to bleed and burn. I was among reptiles, I was one of them, and as they crawled up my spine, a fierce pain shot through me. Then they were gone, and up and up I went. I was like a feather, and in my head there was a light, and I flickered among the bushes, a giant lightning bug. Suddenly something tugged at me from the left, and I shrank back. No, not yet, not yet to Xibalba. The terror must wait. I have a right to tarry, four days, the priests used to say, and that I will demand.

Up, up, higher up on the mountainside. A flute sings far away; the forest is moist and warm, and I want to stay. Somewhere in the distance, people are dancing to the drum. The moon has risen, and there is a whisper among the trees. They say it is the memory of the souls that succumbed to the trials and remained in Xibalba, buried forever in the stinking rot of the flesh and the blood. I will go on, I will make it through like the Hero Twins, Hunahpu and Xbalanque. They are in me, facing each other, then they are a chalice. They have the sun on their tongues. But I am not going, not yet.

Over there, to the right, is a man. He is tall, but old and toothless. He sits cross-legged, and as I watch, he pulls out an eye and motions for me to take it. I freeze in terror. A messenger from Xibalba—the jewelry of the Lords is eyes, torn from their sockets. His belly is distended; he is going to fart, and the stench will be about like stinking mist. I turn and flee.

Am I drooling? No, I will not drool, I will not be like the Lords of Xibalba. But perhaps I strayed over by mistake and did not see the passage? No, it couldn't be—there was no water. There must be water; one sinks below it to reach Xibalba. God of my Day, watch over me, let there be no water yet. I stumble and fall backward, and am held as if in my mother's womb. But the womb expands; it is the forest once more.

I see a fire through the trees and men dancing around it. The man over there, he is the one whose knife slipped into my belly. Without that knife in my bowels, we would be the ones dancing now. I could dance with them, but this is not my time. First through Xibalba, through the knives and the cold, and the murderous bats, and the fire. After that, I will dance, dance to the north, all the way to the North Star.

I slink around the dancers to the hut. A hammock is slung from crossbeam to crossbeam. For a moment I rest in it and let the breeze cool my chest. Or maybe I am the breeze now, I don't know. The men bring in a deer. They have cut out its heart. We are the people of the deer, it is said. Outside, the fire has gone out. Uy, uy, I am the breeze. I blow into the embers and the flames leap up. Then I melt back into the trees. I am tired and want to rest. But I need to stay alert. How long has it been since the knife?

I turn and am with my companions. The priest is working with clay; he is making my likeness. He is powerful, that priest. He sees me and there I am, in his clay. It is a cage, and he is rolling me around, crossing my legs, folding my arms, pulling out my tongue. I struggle, but I cannot escape. Then he shapes my back; it is hollow, a whistle, and I am in it, I, the breeze. I expand and expand. Soon I will shoot out, the Twins and I; we will create the sun, and the moon. My body will break into droplets; I will be a newborn star.

And then I saw the water. It was huge and dark, and stagnant, and it had not moved in eons.

The Story of Kats and His Bear Wife

During our exploration in 1985 of the Chiltan posture, the one about the forty-one girl knights whom the Uzbeki shamanesses call on to help them in curing (see Chapter 9), there were two reports that did not seem to fit the picture. One of them was Belinda's:

> Even during the breathing exercise I began seeing bark figures dancing. When the rattle started, I realized that I was flying very high; the ground was very far away. Then I approached a scene that was brown and green. There was a little pool of water that was like a mirror, and in it I did not see my own reflection, but a stick figure in the shape of a Y. There was a tree, and through it flew a little bird. In place of the pool, there was now a nest with three eggs. The little bird invited me to sit on the nest and intimated that to do that was very important. I stayed on the eggs for a long time, feeling intensified. Then I saw a totem pole, and was embraced by it, by the spirit in the wood. On the other side, there was snow, and pine trees. A hand moving a feather was making marks in the snow. An enormous she-bear appeared; she stood upright and we danced together. I grinned because she made me feel so light. She sat down and embraced me from behind, giving herself to me and penetrating me, and I felt greatly moved. My Lioness came and brought some twigs for the fire and then left. There were the horns of a mountain goat; everything felt high and cold.

The other anomalous one came from Elizabeth R., a close friend of Belinda's:

> When the rattle started, I saw all of us with our masks on, and we danced. We had on long flowing robes, and our hair was blowing in the wind. Belinda became a statue, and a bird built a nest in her hand. The colors became very vivid; twigs and leaves grew out of her all over, the life force was in her, she was a magnificent tree. She started dancing on her roots, and then we danced together. As I put my arms around her, I felt her wetness; I knew she was crying, but she was happy. I faced the tree, the sun came up, and I felt so powerful.

I filed them, as I always do, but I had no idea what to make of them. Then for Christmas 1986 I received a book about totem poles in Alaska.[9] Looking for postures on those poles, to my surprise there was a Tlingit pole housed at Saxman Totem Park near Ketchikan, on which one of the carved figures, embraced from the back by a huge bear, stood in the Chiltan posture (pl. 66).

When these poles were assembled and restored, the Forest Service asked the Indian craftsmen about legends they might know about the various poles. And for the pole in question, called the Loon Tree because of the bird perched on top, one of the artists recalled the legend about the man and the bear.

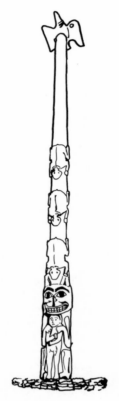

It seems that a young man called Kats, who lived a very long time ago, when humans and animals were still as one, was caught by a grizzly bear. He was supposed to be eaten, but he was saved by the she-bear, who fell in love with him and became his wife. He later returned to his village together with his bear wife and his cub children. His bear wife warned him never to look at his former human wife, but quite by accident, it happened anyway. Upset, his bear wife gave him a shove, meant to be gentle, but the cubs misunderstood and tore him apart.

Generations later, one of Kats's descendants became a powerful shaman. The boy's initiation started when he killed a mountain goat, and after skinning it, he began dancing while wearing its skin over his shoulders, and then he fainted. Over and over again he danced, fell into a dead faint, then danced again, until the multiple spirit powers which his ancestor had acquired from his wife during his sojourn with the bears had passed into him. After becoming a shaman, the young man decided to take revenge on the bears for killing his ancestor. While his grandmother beat the drum, he danced, and in that way he lured the grizzly bears into the large communal house.

Plate 66

Soon the people heard a noise far back in the woods coming closer and closer. They recognized the grunts and growls of grizzly bears, and they all ran out and hid as the bears crowded into the house. Soon there were so many that the old woman was not able to beat the drum. She nodded her head toward it, and the drum continued to beat while the shaman danced. Soon the spirit powers began to leave the boy, and the grizzly bears began to drop over dead. When all his powers had left him, every bear was dead.

It is said that the grizzly bears were the descendants of the cubs born to Kats and his bear wife and that they were killed by the shaman's powers.[10]

Now finally Belinda's experience took on meaning. Perhaps it was the shaman grandson of Kats who was the stage manager, arranging the play so his forebear might once more encounter his beloved bear wife. After all, he signed his creation: Belinda saw the horns of the mountain goat of his initiation. With a few delicate strokes of the hand, marking the snow with a feather, the ancient Indian legend awakens to new life. Like the first roll of the drum calling to a dance, the sign of fate appears reflected in the clear pool, the forked emblem of the Tree of the World. A bird, messenger of the Spirits, invites the stranger to sit brooding on a nest of eggs. Behold, the saga will be of love and procreation. The totem pole appears; its spirit embraces the guest, and she is changed and she is Kats, lending for a fleeting moment her human strength to the sorrowing spirit man. Now the huge she-bear may step on the stage; she embraces her husband, and they laugh as in the old days, when she found him so light, and they melt into each other in loving embrace. Then the play is over, the shadows dissolve, but the cheeks of the human woman are still wet with tears when in her vision, Elizabeth puts her arms around her. In a jubilant finale, she steps across the threshold of magic once more. She turns into a totem pole, and twigs and branches sprout from her in celebration of the power of love.

The Spirits and the Wounded Tree of Life

MYSTERY IN THE MUSEUM
In addition to books on native art, museums often yield tantalizing representations of postures. This presupposes, of course, that what you think you see
on that rack or shelf is actually there. In this business, you cannot always be
sure.

The story I should like to tell next started in a museum. The School of
American Research in Santa Fe had asked me for a luncheon lecture. Afterward
one of the associates of the institution took some of the guests and me on a
guided tour of its private museum, which possesses an outstanding collection
of Amerindian art. The first spacious hall contained a great number of the
most magnificent ollas, large clay vessels no longer made today. This hall had
a door that opened to the right. The other members of the party had already
walked through, when my attention was caught by still another shelf to the
left of the exit. Instead of ollas, this one contained an exhibit of figured pieces,
the likes of which I had never seen on the Indian markets. Always on the
lookout for new postures, I immediately noticed a male statuette in an unfamiliar stance. It was only about five inches high, made of yellowish clay with
red-brick markings, and it stood on a small pedestal which carried the inscription "Calling the Spirits." I carefully noted the posture, how the hands
were positioned on the groin with fingers spread, and how the head was tilted
back slightly and the mouth was open. I wanted to sketch it, but the young
woman who acted as our guide came to close the door, so I quickly jotted
down a brief description and did not even check if the figurine had a number
or some other identifying code.

As soon as I got home, I showed the posture to the group working with
me at Cuyamungue at the time. We made a comical mistake at the first try
because on the basis of the inscription and because the figure had its mouth
open, I thought that one actually had to "call" the Spirits. We assembled on
the ridge, and I had someone else do the rattling. Meanwhile I took up position
outside the circle and started yelling, "Heya, heya. . . ." If there were any
Spirits present watching us that day, they must have had a hilarious time. For
the only thing that happened was that I went into trance and started singing
in glossolalia. Everyone thought it was lovely, so they listened to that instead
of doing what they were supposed to do, namely, go into trance. After that

fiasco, I remembered that Siberian shamans opened their mouth and "yawned," as the ethnographers describe it, when they called their spirit helpers. As soon as we tried the posture without giving off any sound and just keeping our mouths open, things began to make sense. Being helped by the fact that we knew from the inscription what to expect, we soon saw the Spirits approach in manifold shapes, as rolling fog or colored veils, as geometric shapes or eyes, or wearing a mind-boggling variety of masks, everything from Mickey Mouse to all the birds and beasts of the forest and the plains. We also either noted or became some sort of upright form, usually a tree.

The following summer it occurred to me that it would be useful to own a slide of that small statue. So I called the School of American Research and described to the staff member exactly where it was exhibited and what it looked like. She went to search for it but could not find it. So we drove down to Santa Fe. I showed the lady the spot where I had seen it, but the statuette was gone. In its place there was another one, in a similar but not exactly the same posture, and much larger, so it was exhibited lying on its back. It was not yellowish with red markings but grey, and its design was black. Nowhere was there a single figurine standing on a pedestal with an inscription on it. Since I kept insisting that indeed that was what I had seen, I was shown all the slides of the collection, but my small friend had vanished into thin air. He was simply not there. And nowhere in the records was there any hint of the information about calling the Spirits.

It is possible, of course, that the Spirits were making sport of me. They have a very earthy sense of humor. I have vivid memories of being made their plaything and ending up in particularly undignified situations, as the time when they knocked out my sense of place and had me wander around lost in a village that I had known for twenty years. But in this case, that may not have been their intention. I like to think that they really wanted to give me a present.

There are only faint traces of the posture worldwide. It seems to have been known in Europe from the Neolithic on, for instance in the Ukraine, and in more recent times in sub-Saharan Africa, in Melanesia, and especially in New Guinea. Most representations I have seen are from our hemisphere, however, starting from the Eskimos and going south all the way to Central America. Plate 48 is a fine Olmec example. But to me, the most impressive artwork showing the posture is a Salish *tamanus* board from the late 1800s (pl. 67). Little is known about such boards; they were usually deposited at the shaman's grave and left there to disintegrate. The intensity of the face has no peer. That shaman must have seen some pretty mighty Spirits.

As we began working with the posture, we discovered that the Spirits could be asked to come for a number of different purposes. We used it, for example, to invite them to possess the masks during the masked dance ritual, as I told in Chapter 11. Or, as I also mentioned, we can summon them to help with a cure. Not always do they appear invested with power, or in the best of health.

They may, in fact, occasionally need our help, as will become clear from the following little incident, which illustrates what an unholy mess we humans have made of things, in this reality and also in the other one.

Plate 67

A housing development in Austria where I occasionally go visiting is built into an old factory, which used to obtain its power from a turbine, driven by a narrow and very fast river. In the course of modern "development," this river became severely polluted. In a letter, Johanna, one of the members of the settlement, told the following story about it:

> On the 25th of December we held a rattling session and did the Calling of the Spirits. We could not find a tape, so we asked one of the men to rattle for us, and it was very intense but also lovely. We did it by the side of our small river, and we also lit a fire. During the trance Walter saw a bedraggled, down-on-his-luck, and clearly suffering river spirit who was barely alive anymore. If you remember the sad straits our river is in, the condition of the river spirit should not surprise you. So after the trance, each one of us cast an offering into the water. Then we drank a bottle of champagne to the river, and the river got some of it, too.

Enter the Tree of Life

For quite a while, my attention was taken up by the Spirits in this posture, and I paid little attention to the tree around which they assembled. But one summer, as we continued exploring its experiences, Joanne Mc. experienced something extraordinary:

> I saw a tree; it rose high into the sky. Its roots went very deep. I became an ant and went about exploring the roots that penetrated into a cave. There were tunnels,

which were dark, confining, endless. The roots went even further down, and finally, there was an opening into an airy world of light and spaciousness, with whitish, light fog. I ceased being an ant and drifted in the fog. There was a fire glowing, so I turned back into an ant and saw that it was a dragon that was spewing the fire and making amusing noises. The dragon's eyes were green. I began exploring its tongues and crawled around on its underbelly. It was enormous, miles and miles of it, and the dragon was connected to the world above.

Even as Joanne talked, I realized what I had been missing, and I wrote in large letters across the page, *THE TREE OF THE WORLD*. Joanne had seen the *axis mundi*, the axis of the world, Yggdrasil, the mighty ash. She had been down to its roots in the lower world, so huge it made her turn into an ant. She had seen the mighty dragon Nidhogg and heard it gnawing at its roots down there in Niflheim. Legends tell of the Tree of the World everywhere tales are told. Its branches harbor the sun and moon and touch the home of the Spirits of the Sky. As we hear in Hungarian myth:

> There is in the world a marvelously tall tree, which has nine spreading branches, each one vying in size with an entire forest. When these branches begin to twist and rustle, the storms start arising. It is such a marvelously tall tree that not only the moon is hidden in its branches, but also the sun. But only that person can find this tree, only he can discover where it is, who is born with teeth, and who for nine years has taken only milk for nourishment. That kind of a person is a *táltos* [Hungarian shaman]. This marvelously tall tree grows in a special place so that only such a man of knowledge can get to it. Other people merely hear of it but can never see it. (Diószegi 1958:270–271)

The Tree of the World, the Tree of Life, grows at the navel or at the vulva of the Earth Mother, at the stillest place on earth, according to the Siberian Yakut, where the moon does not wane and the sun never sets, where the summer is everlasting and the cuckoo calls incessantly. It is the world pole, the Huichol Indians say, which penetrates the layers of the cosmos, connecting the earth with the underworld and the heavens. Cascades of honey, the Teutons told, flowed down Yggdrasil. We are reminded of the pole that the sacred clowns of Picuris Pueblo climb during their yearly feast, to garner the presents attached at its tip. Shamans make their drums of its wood, and the witches' brooms are its branches. On this Tree of Life, the shamans ascended in their magical flight, and the victims of Maya rituals of sacrifice fell down along its trunk to the underworld.

The mighty tree has many stand-ins. It used to be a fig tree for the Greeks or an oak, and a birch in Siberia. Altaic shamans placed a stripped birch tree in their yurt; its top reached through the smoke hole, and its stem bore nine notches on which the shamans climbed to the world beyond. Yggdrasil was an ash, but many traditions contend that the sacred tree is really a yew.

The yew is a curious tree. It looks like a conifer with glistening dark-green needles, but it has a paperlike bark and it bears red berries. All parts of the tree except the outer part of the berries contain taxine, a poisonous alkaloid, which evaporates in sunlight. A friend and I once suffered its strange effect when we visited a grove of yews near Meggen, a small town in Switzerland. Inhaling it made us feel faint. Our throats became dry, and we were nauseated, and since it is hallucinogenic in minute doses, we became giddy and started chattering and giggling as if we were tipsy. The following tale is about the yew.

A Dutchman's Cure for the Tree of the World

At a workshop near Nieuwaal, a town in the Netherlands, we had done the Calling of the Spirits. "I saw a tree with a hole in it," Hennie, the first one to give her report, started out, "and all sorts of things came out of that hole, like presents." Annmarei had heard a breathing, like the rustling of the leaves in a forest. And Tineke noted that she had been a tree: "It had very big branches, and the branches grew into rainbows." Then it was Ton's turn:

> For a while, it seemed I was simply waiting to see what was going to happen. Then I saw something very tall, maybe a mountain, and out of it oozed a brook of old, coagulated blood. There were many loud noises; then I heard a bird singing a little song. My throat became very dry, and I felt sick to my stomach.

During my subsequent remarks about their stories, I mentioned that in this posture people usually turned into something tall, such as a tree, and Ton volunteered the comment that although he had not gone through that transformation, his experience still had something to do with a tree. It seems that there was a tree in his yard at home, a yew. It had poisonous needles, and so he and his father were going to cut it down. But its wood was very tough. They managed only to cut off some branches, and the resin continued to ooze from the cuts. He thought that the tall dark mountain he had seen might have been the tree, and the coagulating blood the oozing resin.

No one else had seen an injured tree, but we had all heard the "loud noises" Ton mentioned. The sound had been massive, like many feet jumping up and down on the wooden floor at the vacant end of the rectangular meditation room. After the session ended, we went to investigate. Some of the men thought that machinery operating in the basement might have been the source, but there was no basement. We jumped up and down, but the boards were heavy and nailed down solidly and so gave off no sound at all.

The next posture we did was that of the Aztec Corn Goddess, which mediates metamorphosis. For Ton, however, an entirely different experience took center stage:

> A dancer appeared and started using Felicitas's rattle. She came over to me and began pushing me, saying, "Go on, go!" I did not want to leave my place. I started fighting with her, but she was a very exotic girl; she put her arms around me and started kissing me, and dragged me over to where Felicitas was standing. There

she turned into a red female Buddha, and many presences rose from her head. Then she changed into an old man in very poor clothes—I didn't think much of that; and then he became an eagle, and he said to me reassuringly, "Don't worry, everything is all right." He grabbed me and carried me to my house, into the garden with the bleeding tree. There was a pile of bandages, and I started bandaging the tree; there were so many bandages, and I put them round and round the tree. After that, everything was very peaceful in my garden. I saw my wife; there was such peace, and I also saw my dog. He had been sick, but he was fine now. I touched him and he licked me. Then the dog was a deer. I sat on its back, and it took me to the seashore and down to the ocean floor littered with discarded oil cans. Then I came up to the surface and I walked on the water. A big whale appeared, but I knew that I had the power to stop it. Finally I came back here and saw the female Buddha again. She had many arms and was glowing in yellow light.

What had happened? In ordinary reality, Ton had tried to cut down a yew. But when Ton put an ax to the tree in his yard, he also injured the Tree of the World in the alternate dimension, and its agony reverberated through the spirit realm. Injuring the Tree of the World can have disastrous consequences. An Iroquois story tells how the celestial Tree of Life was once carelessly uprooted in the sky world, and the daughter of the chief tumbled down through the hole. Luckily, quick-thinking Mud Turtle dove down to the bottom of the sea and brought up some mud for her to stand on, thereby not only saving the girl but also creating the earth and with it a place for a new Tree of Life to be planted.

Of course, yews are being cut down in many places, continually causing damage to the Tree of Life as well. But at least on this particular occasion, the Spirits saw a chance to do something about it. Here was a group of people in a condition to listen to spirit suggestions, and they were not about to let the opportunity slip by. That tremendous noise they caused in the Dutch meditation hall was only a part of their strategy. Another was prompting the participants to describe the nature of the tree, with one woman seeing a hole in it and presents emerging, and another one hearing the rustling of its leaves and watching how the branches turned into rainbows, all properties of the Tree of the World.

But the principal effort of the Spirits was directed at Ton. After all, he was the one who had wielded the ax. As soon as he became accessible to them, they revealed the frightful emergency he had caused by making the Tree of Life bleed. The problem was that Ton, being a novice, had not been fast on the uptake, and the rattle was about to stop. There was just enough time to give him a quick nudge. His mouth became dry and he felt sick to his stomach, the selfsame thing that had happened to him as he began cutting into the yew tree in his yard.

Worried that time was running out for helping the Tree of the World, the Spirits then decided to take extreme measures. They took advantage of the very next trance, the metamorphosis of the Aztec Corn Goddess, and, not having much faith in Ton, decided to do the changing themselves. One of the Spirits turned itself into a voluptuous girl, knowing of course that Ton, a ruddy, lusty Dutchman in his early forties, would not be able to resist her. And she dragged him to me, the ritual center, for extra power. Since lecturing Ton would not have been effective, and besides is not part of Spirit nature anyway, the Spirit then changed again and assumed the aspect of a "female Buddha," something that Ton, according to the Spirits' alternate-reality intelligence reports, was said to be familiar with. Spirits always wear the mask most acceptable to their human, this being a very effective communications device. The "female Buddha" was Kwannon, the deity of mercy and compassion, identified for Ton by the "presences" emerging from her head, the eleven faces of compassion. And compassion is what was expected of him.

But they reasoned that Ton, so he could grasp the seriousness of the situation, should also be made aware of the fact that the event in which he was called upon to play a role had much more ancient roots, going back long before the birth of Buddha to a time when yews were still venerated as the representation of the Tree of the World. So the Spirit in charge now showed itself as an old man, in tattered, timeworn clothing. It seemed a very clever thing to do, but apparently using sign language did not work out, and only confused Ton. So shrugging their shoulders, the Spirits decided on the direct approach. All right, Ton, forget the old man. No more historical allusions. We made a mistake; he is really an eagle, and look what power *he* has. The eagle took Ton to the bleeding Tree of Life. Now it was Ton's turn, for this is what the Spirits had needed him for all along, and the bandages had been readied and were waiting.

To their great relief, Ton's good heart took over. Round and round he twisted the bandages about the wounded tree, until all the bleeding stopped. Then there was peace in the garden, but also power. His touch healed his sick dog; he got to the ocean and walked over the waters and commanded the whales. And in his own terms then, he was praised for having performed an act of kindness. For as the rattle stopped, he was shown the Kwannon once more, the many-armed Goddess of Mercy, bathed in golden light.

In the Land of Centaurs and Mermaids

In scanning a book recently about archeological finds in Europe,[10] I noticed the picture of a figurine dug up in Thessaly (present-day Greece), about eight thousand years old (pl. 68). It represents a nude, rather full-breasted woman, sitting with both her legs turned toward the right side, her hands resting on her knees. Examining the figure shown a bit more closely, I realized that what at first glance seemed merely an oddly shaped face was really a mask, possibly that of a bird. That was exciting, for wearing a mask among hunter-gardeners or horticultural-ists, as we know from their modern coun-terparts, is always a sign of a religious oc-casion, involving a trance experience as a matter of course. But what was even more intriguing was that in this case, the mask was combined with a totally unfamiliar pos-ture. Ordinarily, the postures that come to

Plate 68

light from such early horizons in Europe are those that are encountered in many other areas of the world as well, of birthing, of the Bear Spirit, of metamorphosis, and so forth. But here was one that was completely unknown in the later record. We had planned a workshop anyway for experienced participants only, to be held in a camp in rural Ohio, so this was an opportunity to try and see what the lady from Neolithic Thessaly had to teach us.

As I rattled in the gathering dusk of the autumn afternoon, I was trying to guess what my friends might be experiencing as they sat unmoving in a circle in that awkward position, their faces drawn inward in the familiar trance expression that artists of bygone days loved to sculpt and carve. Would it be something neutral, divorced from time and space, being healed or resurrected, having a divinatory revelation, going on a spirit journey? I could not know not only that this was going to be another one of those times when the crack between the worlds would be ajar, but also that as a special boon, the Spirit of the posture we had assumed would act as our guide to her ancient world:

> MAXINE: In the beginning, I couldn't close my eyes and watched the rattle until I could feel its beat in my mind. It felt as though the beating was the coursing of the blood through my brain. Before I closed my eyes, I looked to the right and I saw an old woman, and I thought it was Felicitas sitting on the floor, and then I realized that that couldn't be, she was standing and rattling. And I closed my eyes.

I could sense the presence of the old shamaness filling the room, shaping our experiences as she began to spread her lost world out before our eyes with apparent urgency. "Listen to me," she seemed to be saying, "listen to me, you women of another generation, and I will tell you our tale. It is a mighty tale, the tale about our world and how it was. Listen first to the tale about the beginning of things. I learned it when I was a child and had not been to the pool yet, to the pool where you die and are reborn."

> ELIZABETH R.: As soon as the rattle started, I saw lots of light, lots of exploding light, and I was looking at volcanic eruptions. And then all of these scenes played out before me rather rapidly, big chunks of earth falling into the ocean, cliffs, land falling, trees falling, lots of falling earth and clouds.

And the old voice continued, "From the passionate mountains, this was the tale of our mothers, rose Phoenix, the giant bird, soul of the nubile Earth, to search for her mate, the Sun":

> ELIZABETH R.: And as I was starting to be aware of the clouds, I noticed that I was flying, that I was a bird, a big, very large bird, and I flew around for a while, watching all kinds of big earth changes, shifts, things sinking, and other things coming up out of the ocean. It wasn't alarming at all. There was really no emotional attachment, I was just watching it. And I flew higher and higher; I seemed to be drawn to this light that eventually became the sun. As I approached the sun, I could feel the feathers burning and falling away, and then the skin melting and falling away, then the bone getting dryer and dryer, until as I passed through the sun, my bones became dust. As that dust passed on through the sun to the other side, I spent a long time in darkness, as dust, and there was nothing else around; it was very peaceful. I thought this was wonderful.

I heard the Ancient One again. "Then the breath of life rose from the ashes, that was what our mothers told, life and its young laughter, and took on flesh in the nest prepared for it in the Mother's womb":

> ELIZABETH R.: But at that point my right hip was hurting very badly, and I decided that what I needed to do was to lift my right knee up just a little bit. So I shifted the posture ever so slightly to raise my hip, and the pain went away completely out of my hip. What I experienced then was passing back through the sun and coming back to earth and just seeing a nest being formed by real tiny, fluffy, downy white feathers, and this wonderful soft nest being formed was beginning to twirl around. And eventually I changed into a big white bird that had a woman's legs, and I thought, now this was a really bizarre thing to turn into; it wasn't anything

that I had seen on this planet. It had very lovely legs, of course [she laughs], and big white plumes. And I was getting ready to say, well, now what am I up to here? And I became aware that I was really on a different planet, I was not on earth, and I started walking around. And I found this big wall, shiny; I didn't identify it as a gemstone, it was more like marble. It was dark blue, and I slid down it, like on a big sliding board, sliding around on it, having a wonderful time, and the sensation was very good. And then I landed in what I thought was grass. It wasn't; it was these really lush pomegranate seeds, only they were brilliant green. As I walked through them, they would kind of pop under my feet. It was a wonderful sensation.

"Then it was time," the old shamaness continued, "to endow the body of this magical being with the capacity to bear the young, and that was, our mothers told, how women came to have a womb":

> ELIZABETH R.: And then I flew back to the sun, and this time I did fly back to the earth, after I flew through the sun, and I landed in a nest, and my spirit guide came. I was in a huge nest, and my spirit guide and I lounged around in the nest, peeking over the edge, feeling very satisfied with ourselves. This was a real special warm feeling that we had. He reached in and made some adjustment in my second chakra area, and said that he had some more things to teach me, and we were feeling all cozy in the nest and having a wonderful time.

Leaving the happy couple behind, our old Spirit Friend then turned to a new topic: "Of the spirit beings, our mothers told, which roamed the earth, some turned into plants":

> SUSAN: At the outset of the rattling a voice said, "Lose your fears, Susan, lose your fears." And then I saw new green curlicued vinelets growing and starting. Later those vinelets grew and curlicued all around my body, and I budded.

"Of all these things our mothers spoke," the old voice continued, "and we listened, in the gardens as we weeded and while we spun and wove. And when we were old enough, they also taught us to see, these events of the beginning of all things and much more. For that to happen, though, and also many other miraculous things, we had to die in the pool and change, to come to life again":

> BELINDA: Immediately after the beginning, I briefly felt a tingling in my legs. I was swimming with a mask on, and I tried to dismiss that image until I remembered that the woman in the posture was wearing a mask. I was swimming out to a place in the sea, where there were some rocks and a cave. When I got out of the water, there had been a fire built in front of a very black cave entrance. I realized that I felt young, and I knew that while this was a ritual, I was doing it for the first time. I went into the cave. It was completely dark; I knew that I was there to find out about a mystery. The rattle became very loud, and it became skulls on sticks, and there was something in the skulls that made them rattle, and they were being rattled

all around me. I knew it was something about birth and death. The older women—I just felt them, but I knew they were older women—took me and dumped me into a pool. It was oddly like a baptism, except that they kept me down in there. There was a funny little reed in my nose, somehow to help me breathe, but I almost drowned. That was part of the ritual, of almost drowning, like to go into the other realm.

Later there was a sinking sensation of going deeper and deeper into the sea. My mind was thinking about the times when the whales first were there. It wasn't like going to when the earth was first being formed, but in young days. Then it was as though the planet was still Gaea, a consciousness, and she was remembering when she was in her youth, and the land was very fresh; it was formed, but still very fresh. It was almost as if there was a connection with a consciousness. As if the earth was remembering those earlier times of herself, and there was a deep sense of us being connected with her as her daughters.

Then there was a shift, and there were images, dazzling images of sitting on a rock by the sea that was really glistening. And I saw Jan sitting in water up to her bare shoulders. I could see through the water, and beneath the water, she was human above, but below she looked like a sea mammal, a manatee maybe. I looked up and down, and I saw Elizabeth sitting beside her, and she was the same way. And then I saw my shoulders, and all of us, above we were women and below we were manatee. It seemed like we shifted and we became even more like mermaids. It was the same quality, but the lower part of the body was different from a mermaid as we usually think of her. I feel a little mischievous about this, like see? The old Greek stories are really mere remnants of what I just experienced—like now I know what the mermaids really are.

And then the tired old voice continued: "All this happened a long, long time ago, and I can see that I must be patient with you women of so late a generation. Listen how your friend wanted to gain it all in a single gulp, the knowledge of precious things that it took us years to acquire when we were young":

BELINDA: And I knew that I was supposed to find out something in that cave, and I kept asking. Finally it was like these voices said, "But you haven't been prepared!" And they were saying, "You can't just come in on a Friday night and expect to understand the mystery of an entire culture, of an entire process, and the history of it!" And I sit here on a Friday night and just expect that it will happen like that. And I asked, though, "Do you want the ritual known? Do you want it to be practiced again?" Kind of like it has to be retrieved in order to be practiced. But the rattle became very loud, very intense, and then it stopped.

Our old guide was getting impatient. "I must hurry on; there is so much to tell and so little time given to me. You should know that we were a seafaring people; the sea was the skirt of the Mother, and if we wanted to be close to her, that was where we went and sank into the waves. She reveals herself in the sea":

NANCY: I felt a tugging at my right leg. I thought it was the cat. There was only blackness, but there was no sense of fear about it. I had no body form, yet I was not out of my body. There was a sense of changing form. I felt the grace of the swan, the beauty of it; it was being pulled, it was without a spine, without a body, but not being out of my body. I was being pulled to the left, then there was a sharp pain in my eyes. This was repeated three times. From there I went to a dark place of nothingness, with no feeling of joy or sadness. The sound of the rattle changed from soft to hard, and when that happened, the blackness changed from soft to hard too. It got deeper, more intense, then there was a sense of sadness, being in touch with this lack of existence, this form. I was in a place of healing, a sense of healing in nothingness. Going to deeper levels, deeper down, deeper, there was eye pain to the point of burning, and then being pushed back.

The shamaness sighed, "My daughters loved the sea, and longingly, I too remember sinking into the waves":

> NORMA: I saw the sea and the sky, both in different blues. The land is way off. I traveled through dark spaces. Then I bathed in seawater; it streamed through my body in a continuous cycle. It was a cleansing, and I felt the bubbles of the water. My left body side relaxed, but the right side was tense. As the left side began to pull away, the right side begged it not to leave, but I kept saying, "Don't worry, I'll be back." The left side of my body was female, the right side male. I became a white female horse, and I shook off my male side. It really wasn't a mean thing to do; I said that later it could come back. There was a white bird. I melted into the earth, oozing, soaking in.

The Old One nodded. "In the sea, there was much to see for those of us who had learned the ways. The Mother's skirt had seams of emerald, and in it hidden memories of still older worlds, of cities that once bloomed and then sank beneath her folds":

> LIBET: I was traveling through this incredibly lush emerald green. It wasn't like a forest, it was just green with plants; not heavy like a forest, but it was very beautiful. I wasn't walking, but I was just moving. It wasn't conscious walking, it was more like gliding. There wasn't a path—when I looked down I didn't see a path—but there was a path in my body; there was not a path before me. And this wonderful black panther came beside me as a guide to me. Part of the time I rode her, part of the time she was ahead of me, and there was a connection like a leash, but not that formal, like a piece of leather that bound us, and sometimes I would be ahead of her.
>
> We moved through this green, lush space for a long time. Then on my left as I looked up, the entire space to my left was a wall, a precious stone, a clear, precious gem, but it was huge; it was green, sometimes it was red, and bright, shiny, incredibly different colors. And as we moved past that, we continued through this green space; the cat became a bird, and we flew off into the sky, and she was one of those very ancient birds, and we flew over every terrain that could be possible— it was green, it was brown, it was desert, it was mountains, it was glacial, as we rose very high.
>
> We then went down into the water, just kept on moving through water; I was very much aware of the difference between the air and the water, the way it

surrounds your body as you move through it. And we came to this city under the water, and I was just enjoying being there; it was an incredibly developed city. And at one point there was this judge; it was a judge person that was there, that was his role. Then my bird took me right out of the water, up into the sky. And at that point I moved away from the bird and into darkness, but I was still flying, and I didn't have anything on; it was just darkness, and moving through this space of darkness for a long time, there were seemingly no guides, no other things around, but just moving in this darkness, for a long, long, long time.

And then there was a light. I moved toward it, and I perceived that it was a sun, but it wasn't a hot sun, it was a cool light. I moved through. I aimed right through it and into darkness again, and the rattle became everything, the darkness and the rattle was everything, and then the rattle ended.

Again there was the voice. "When our mothers left for the beyond and it was our time to serve, we were called on for advice about many things. We were the women of knowledge; we knew how to heal and when to place the seeds in the ground. We turned and turned and sent our spirits out and spoke to the Spirits of the Above":

JAN: I became aware that there was another part of me right on this spot in another time and space that was just walking around. I wasn't doing very much, and I kept wanting to know what I was doing; it was like that part of me was in a circular room and kept pacing and pacing. Not nervous, just kind of walking, and I perceived that perhaps I was getting ready to do something. And I didn't know what it was. It seemed very normal, and she, that other part of me, seemed very comfortable in what she was doing. I felt like being in my other body that was sitting there in trance, and that was different than this one. I could feel both of them at once, and that my other body was in trance also. I've never had that specific feeling that my trance body was also in a trance state over there.

And then I saw everybody in this room, doing the same thing in their own little room, their own little spaces. And I had on some sort of long robe; that was all I could see, it wasn't very distinct. I was a little uncomfortable in this body, so I shifted a little bit to the left, and as soon as I did that, I felt a wind that came from my left side. It was quite strong, and so I leaned into it, and I found myself shooting through darkness, very fast, but not seeming to go anywhere; there wasn't much there.

And I shifted a little again, and I think I leaned back a bit, and as soon as I shifted, I shot up and exploded. As soon as that happened, I found myself sitting in front of a cave that was totally dark behind me, and I was nude. It wasn't exactly like I was sitting in this posture, I couldn't say that, but I was sitting there and I was very aware that I was performing some rite or ritual, that I had come out of the cave and I was sitting there. The moon was out; everything else was very black. And the wind was just blowing past me incredibly, and the cave was black in my back. I was doing something about contacting, and the words that were there were "Sky people." And this part of my consciousness said something like, "Oh, that's just because she's got a bird mask on." And immediately there were these words, "Be still, you know better than to talk." It seemed to have something to do with finding out what needed to be done, to have a good planting was the word, that it was a night of planting. And if the plants were going to grow in the way they needed to, and have a good harvest, then there had to be certain information that was received and acted on.

And the wind at that point really picked up, and it was saying, "Listen, listen, listen" in my left ear, and "be still." It seemed like it was a metaphor for growth in general, it was like, don't be silly to think that this is just about planting seeds. It had to do with the growth of the culture, or the growth of the community, or something. And that there was very specific information. But right at the time that it seemed that I was going to get some needed information, the rattle stopped.

Our ancient guide then changed course: "But where were the men, you might ask me? Our men, they disliked the backbreaking labor of the gardens and tended the horses instead, and if they wanted to see, to divine, they turned into their shape, man-horse, horse-man, and sometimes into the magic one, the one that had wings and flew up to the moon. I see no man among you, my daughters, so one of you will have to tell what it was like. It is not easy for a woman to assume the shape of a horse, but we too have done it. Go, my daughter, go, see the brown earth and the rock faces of my land, and the shimmer of the sea in the distance, and be one of our youths, in the glory of his manhood and of his braided hair."

ANITA: Our whole group began twirling around in a circle, and the colors became blue and red. We all swirled around and became one by circling around, and that happened at the very first. The first thing I then saw was an Indian on a horse, but it didn't seem like an American Indian—he was shorter and muscular, he had very thick braided hair in strands all around, and I had the sense of maybe an Australian aborigine or an African, I wasn't sure. I had the experience that I was the Indian, but I was also the horse. And that experience kept changing throughout the whole trance. Sometimes I was the Indian and sometimes I was the horse; it got to be kind of funny, because just when I would be reacting as the Indian, I would be the horse, so that was kind of fun.

And the scene was what I picture the American Southwest being, somewhat barren, but plateaus, craggy rocks, and reds and oranges and bluish haze in the distance. While I was on the horse, which was black, I also saw some wild horses, and they came nearer, and they started to fly. And there was one that had kind of an electric silvery mane, and it was silvery, but I only saw that for a moment, and there was this sort of longing in seeing that creature. It was a very mystical sort of creature. And then the horse, being definitely the horse, was extremely tired of the bridle, and there was the sense of wanting to run around, of wanting freedom, and the Indian at this point was not on the horse's back. So the horse threw off the bridle and was experimenting with walking around and running around. And then the horse went over and joined some of the other wild horses that were grazing but also moving as one in one direction and then in another. Then what happened was that I became half horse and half woman, and again the interesting thing was that part of the time the head was the horse, and part of the time the bottom part was the part of the horse. The images kept changing that way.

There was also the sense of seeing, in that there was something I needed to see, but again in the wider sense, and I found myself as this horse-woman creature gazing into the distance and trying to see what it was that I needed to see. I didn't see anything, but there was the sense that I needed to do that.

The Old One agreed. "Listen to her, my daughters. She knows with the horses that the rain is coming. Horses are the children of the moon, and it is from the moon that we receive the blessing of the rain":

> At several points there was a very strong sense of breathing like a horse; I actually felt like a horse, and breathing through the nostrils, and I could hear the breath of the horse in my own ears and experience that. At about the same time, the rhythm of the rattle changed for me, and again on my left side there came something that I imagined to be like drops of water, rhythmically dripping into a canyon, and quite separate from what the rattle was doing. I didn't turn to the left, however, so it remained that way.

"I can feel it too now," sighed our old friend, "the presence of the horses. There is a drought; the land is parched and yearning for moisture, and I can sense the anxiety of the horse. It runs, it wants to outrun its fate, but it cannot. It will be sacrificed to the moon in exchange for the gift of rain."

> MAXINE: My heart is beating at a very high rate, and I feel air moving into my lungs. It is real hot and searing, and when I take a breath, it burns and is uncomfortable, and I am running. I am all alone, and I am aware that I have been running a long, long time, from the time it's dusk until it goes into darkness. I can feel the heat of the sand rising and touching me; I can feel it in my feet, the grittiness of the sand, and I can feel the day's heat rising up through my body and touching my face with every breath. I can feel the dust from the sand hitting my legs as I run, and the air is all full of this dust. And I become aware of my body. I am a young boy, and I am all brown and naked. I can feel the dust embedding itself in my face, in my eyebrows, my eyelashes, and I can feel it in the little hairs above my lip.
>
> As I run across the desert, I become aware that I have four legs, not two, and I can feel the wind through my nostrils; I can feel the tiny hairs in my nostrils as they swell and shrink. And I am running all alone, but then I am in a herd of horses and running amongst them. We are running so fast that I think I am going to be overwhelmed by them, that I am not going to be able to escape. We run for a long time together, and I am completely surrounded and enclosed. But then I break away and head to a mountaintop, and in the darkness I try many paths, but none of them go to the top. Then finally after many tries I reach the top. I am aware that I am extremely thirsty. And I look over to the moon, which is full, and I see myself with the moon reflected across my body. My mane is glistening in the moonlight. And then I jump into the moon, and when I jump into it, the darkness is replaced by silence, and even though I know the rattle is rattling, I can't hear it, all I hear is the silence.

"We women too offered sacrifices," our guide explained, "but ours were for the Sun, the consort of our Mother, and we turned into birds and sent our souls to the eternal flame. But having been consumed, we returned, sleek and black and fresh, in a thousand glistening drops, bringing the renewal of spring. It was a fearful journey; I took it many times and never knew if I would return alive. It took us through the furnaces of the volcano, down to our Mother's womb, and then on, purified, to the fires of the Sun, as He was about to turn toward spring on His path'':

> JUDY CH.: I felt heat in the solar plexus. I was nude, running up a spiral staircase. I was half woman and half bird, white. I was soaring up in a spiral, higher and higher, feeling that I was calling out a warning. I could see a volcano; I went through the lava, into the earth. My feathers burned off. I felt a dramatic change; there was complete darkness. After a long time, I came up again. I became a slick and black bird; there was a definite feeling of acceleration. The speed was so great that I felt I was a rocket or a comet, breaking through a barrier. And when I broke through, there were thousands of stars, each one a mirror; there were millions of mirrors, and I saw the same image in each one, repeating what I had experienced in the beginning, the whole story. There was vibration and heat on the back of my neck. There was a repetition of the vibrations, hard, then soft. There was calmness and silence, and I felt myself going toward the sun. I plunged headfirst into the sun. I was burning, but I was not afraid; all my flesh and the skin burned off, but there was a hand that pulled me through and popped me right up, and there was a feeling of freedom, of darkness, but there was light around my essence. I broke through the earth's atmosphere and became a bird again.

Our spirit guest was gone. The hills outside lay still in darkness, as if holding their breath before the first glimmer of the new crescent would appear in the sky. And I wondered if our spirit caller would have come at any other time.

Epilogue. I believe that the old shamaness who graced our meeting with her presence gave us a true view of her world. Anthropologists are trained to watch for details that others might overlook; to them such minutiae often clinch an entire argument and validate an observation. That Eva D. smelled the putrefaction of the animal sacrifices in the posture of the Greek maiden, as we shall see in the Conclusion, confirmed to me that she had been to the Eleusinian mysteries more than all the other experiences put together that she brought back from the trance. There is a similar "signature" detail also in these reports. Anita tells of the strange hairdo of the rider she had seen, as though he had twisted his hair into many strands or braids. Archeologists unearthed a beaker (Gimbutas 1982:114, pl. 70) from the mid-sixth millennium B.C., found at Tsangli in Thessaly, that is from the time and the home region of our figurine. It has a black-painted design of eyes associated with hair "portrayed like snakes."

Prehistorians propose that the way of life of the Neolithic Thessalians was continuous with the later classical Greek culture.[11] And indeed in our reports we are witness to the emergence of such beings as Phoenix, the magical bird, and of the mermaid. And then there are the horses. There is no clear evidence about when the horse first appeared on the eastern borders of Europe, but it is not supposed to have been in Thessaly at the outset of the sixth millennium B.C. However, our shamaness tells us that at the time she lived, the horse was already there, magical, Pegasus, endowed with flight, and the shamans of her world possessed an important secret: they could at will turn into this most magical of creatures, and then they had the gift of sight.

What was the life of the ancient Thessalians like, who lived close to eight thousand years before the present? There was no writing as yet, only perhaps some ideographs, such as the one on the chest of the figurine from the same region demonstrating the posture of the Feathered Serpent (see Chapter 13). But written into the earth there are clear traces of a horticulturalist way of life. These Thessalians cultivated wheat, barley, vetch, peas, and other legumes in their gardens. They had pigs, cattle, goats, and sheep; they hunted, and especially they were fishermen. Pictures of their sailing boats are incised on their ceramics. They lived in permanent villages and built shrines. As mentioned before, there are indications that they knew a number of postures, mainly those of Birthing, of the Chiltan spirits, and of the Psychopomp, all shown on female figurines. And they knew this unique and special one, the vehicle for the present myth. Through it our old spirit shamaness gave us access to her world, a mysterious one, enshrined forever with all the other treasures of a similar nature in the Eternal Present of the alternate reality. To her and all the other Spirits who took us to that realm, our profound thanks.

The Twilight
of the Spirits

There is no doubt that the societies that used postures in religious ritual highly valued this knowledge. Shamans must have cherished them; that was probably why in a first-century Eskimo grave, three finely incised statuettes were found as grave offerings, carved out of walrus ivory, and clearly created by the same artist (pl. 69). They are (from

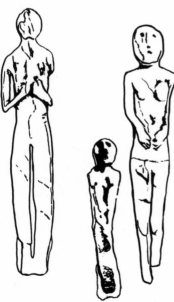

left to right) shown in the Singing Shaman, the Calling of the Spirits, and the Bear Spirit postures respectively. In each instance the hands are placed somewhat lower than we are used to seeing them. Perhaps it was the intention of the artist to indicate that this was the shaman in death. Not only are the postures recreated over and over again in native art, they are also considered attributes of the Spirits, part of their power, as we see in the drawing of the Matsigenka shaman (pl. 60). Going from left to right, the "pure and invisible Ones" are shown in the posture of the Feathered Serpent, of the Singing Shaman, and of the Bear Spirit. And they passed into later traditions as conventionalized characteristics of the gods, as in the Aztec examples (Chap. 10).

The most intricate of these types of inventories comes to us from a temple on Rurutu Island of the Austral Group in Poly-

Plate 69

nesia, carved from ironwood in the eighteenth century and said to represent the god Tangaroa generating gods and men (pls. 70a-d). With beautiful logic, Tangaroa himself is shown in the Birthing posture (pl. 70a). On his right upper arm (side view, pl. 70b), a figure, presumably a human, is in the hunter's Porcupine posture, and the tiny woman under his right elbow uses the Birthing posture. The somewhat larger figure on his upper right thigh is appealing to the Bear Spirit, complete with the ecstatic, inward-directed facial expression, his head slightly tilted back, his eyes closed, and that lightly smiling mouth we know also from the Northwest Coast carving of the same posture (pl. 1).

While these figures are all human, I think we need to consider the four paired figures on the god's back to be spirits (pl. 70c). They use the posture we call Empowerment (compare pl. 49), which makes good sense: Spirits possess, as we know from our experiences, tremendous, highly concentrated energy. They are placed above another human in the Bear posture, supplying the energy for healing. Special care is lavished on the upper torso and head of Tangaroa. The only posture I do not recognize is the one forming his left nipple and his ears. That still needs to be explored. His right nipple is once more a figure in the Bear Spirit posture. The place of his heart is marked by an upside-down figure in the Chiltan posture, right arm up, a reference to the restless, multiple, pulsating energy of the heart. With his eyebrows and the crease between them, the god is the psychopomp (remember Chapter 12, pl. 50, the Chiltan posture with the left arm up), and his cheeks are the seat of power with the paired Empowerment figures on either side. Only his mouth remains a secret. It has a small inset face above the double line of the lips. The Indian carvers of the Northwest Coast used to represent spiritual essence that way, but I would have to know more about the traditional culture of these Polynesian islands before I could come to any conclusion. However, even this way, Tangaroa is certainly a magnificent god.

There are many unanswered questions about the mystery of the postures. Because no observers paid any attention to them, we do not know whether they are still in use anywhere, except in Uzbekistan and possibly among the Matsigenka Indians. Neither do we know what neurophysiological changes might correspond to the differences in experience. These physical shifts are apparently so subtle that to date, at least, we have not been able to pinpoint them in our laboratory research. Still another puzzle is the fact that they were known in many parts of the world, often nearly simultaneously. If we consider in how many different ways we are able to hold our bodies and heads and can place our hands, arms, feet, and legs, it is truly astounding that these roughly thirty specific combinations should appear over and over again world-wide. How could they have spread without any modern communication techniques? We could speculate that they were available in the other reality; we talked about sudden shifts that according to many traditions occur occasionally in that dimension of reality, and religious specialists would have gotten hold of them there. Another mode of propagation is suggested by Rupert Sheldrake.

Plate 70a

Plate 70b

Plate 70c

Plate 70d

He calls his theory the "hypothesis of formative causation." The nature of things, he says, depends on fields he calls "morphic fields." Each kind of natural system has its own field, that is,

> non-material regions of influence extending in space and continuing in time. They are localized within and around the systems they organize. When any particular organized system ceases to exist, as an atom splits, a snowflake melts, an animal dies, then its organizing field disappears from that place. But in another sense, morphic fields do not disappear: They are potential organizing patterns of influence, and can appear again physically in other times and places, wherever or whenever the physical conditions are appropriate. When they do so, they contain within themselves a memory of their previous physical existence. (1987:1-4)

Sheldrake's work awaits further testing, but his hypothesis fits neatly with our observations about the postures. The archeological record, by no means complete, of course, demonstrates that a particular posture will appear at a certain point in time and space, and then unaccountably will spread to other regions as well. This process behaves very much like his morphic fields. When a posture dies, that is, is no longer performed as part of a particular ritual, it does not simply go away. If the conditions are right, as when we began combining the physiological arousal of the trance with a particular way to tune the body in the posture, the entire behavioral and experiential complex reappears.

The greatest mystery of all, however, is the agreement in visionary content. Where we do have evidence in local traditions, it is clear that cross-culturally the postures elicit almost identical experiences, as in the case of the posture of the Bear Spirit or the Chiltan Spirits. This flies in the face of one of the most cherished tenets of anthropology, namely, that the individual cultural system shapes the content of experience. It is supposed to supersede all else, even structuring visual illusions, as Segall et al. have shown in their research on the influence of culture on visual perception. There are those who would argue that the reason for the agreement is that the source of the visions is the body itself: We all have the same nervous system; therefore, everything else being equal, that is, the posture and the religious trance, we of course have the same visions. It seems to me that those holding this view contend, taking a simile from technology, that the source of the radio program is the set. As should be clear by now, I take a contrary position and consider the source of the visions to be the alternate reality. The body is tuned by the posture in the trance in such a manner that we are enabled to experience, to perceive a certain part or aspect of the other dimension.

Others point to the iconic content of the postures that might suggest a certain kind of experience. As I mentioned earlier, we have come across only two postures, those of the Australian Bone Pointing and of the Olmec Prince, where such a process could possibly be construed to take place. So this approach does not lead very far.

In other discussions on this topic, it is sometimes suggested that the visions are merely archetypes which appear because we all have equal access to Jung's collective unconscious. According to this psychoanalyst,

> The creative imagination has at its disposal, in addition to obvious personal sources, also the primitive spirit with its peculiar images, which, although long forgotten and obscured, are expressed in the mythologies of all times and peoples. The totality of these images forms the collective unconscious, which as a potential is transmitted by inheritance to every individual. It is the *psychic correlate* of human brain differentiation. This is the reason mythological images arise anew spontaneously and in complete agreement not only in all corners of this wide earth, but also at all times. They are present all the time and everywhere. (Carl G. Jung, 1938:p.iv; emphasis of the author; my translation)

In refutation of this hypothesis, the German anthropologist Adolf Jensen argues,

> A myth is not the succession of individual images but an integrated meaningful entity, reflecting a distinct aspect of the real world. . . . The individual elements meaningfully refer to one unit of action. . . . We have stated that fundamentally we consider it to be entirely probable that in the psychic realm agreements can be found with the myths of ancient human history. But there will never be a case where such contents of consciousness will be drawn so clearly that with a larger number of experimental subjects the same integral idea could be found, from which one might be able to read one and only one particular myth. (Jensen 1966:115–116, my translation)

As I have shown over and over again, our visions act very much like integrated myths, and our experiences with the postures amply illustrate Jensen's point. Individual, highly fragmented archetypical images simply will not account for what we have experienced.

The question is, of course, why did the postures vanish from the scene in so many instances? Why would a snowflake melt, to refer back to Sheldrake's image? It turns to water when there is a change in the temperature. The same way, we may assume, postures also disappear as a result of change—in this case, of the cultural ambience. Why that would happen, we cannot tell. Is it a development of the human scene? Or did a piece of the sky world break off once more and crash into the world where humans live, as the Yąnomamö might say? All we can observe is that in many areas of the world, the demise of the postures coincides with the intrusion of intensive, open-field agriculture, frequently coupled with animal husbandry.

Such cultural change brings about frightful human misery and pain. Since, for the most part, the societies involved were not literate, we can only intuit what horror the loss of a way of life entailed. In the Nordic myths we hear of Ragnarök, the doom of the gods, of their struggle against enemy forces, and of the eventual destruction of the earth. The Popol Vuh equally tells of murder committed against such men as Seven Makaw, a stand-in for the independent horticulturalists, by the new gods, who then create docile humans entirely of cornmeal, whom they even deprive of the gift of "seeing."

Even when the change takes place in literate societies, we do not often get the entire story. The history of preclassical Greece is a case in point. According to the renowned Greek historian Herodotus, the wise lawgiver Solon of Athens (ca. 638–ca. 558 B.C.) once called on Croesus at Sardis, an important city in Asia Minor at the time. Intent on trying to impress the famous Athenian, Croesus showed him all his magnificent treasures and then asked him, with the proper compliments, whom among all the men he had known did he consider the most fortunate. He expected Solon to name him, of course, but Solon was not only wise but also honest, and so he first nominated Tellus, an Athenian who had seen sons grow up and grandchildren born, and then died with honor on the battlefield. Croesus now hoped that he would at least make second place. But when he pressed his guest further, Solon named a pair of brothers, Cleobis and Bito of Argos.

It seems that these two men, great athletes of their day, wanted their mother to attend a festival in honor of the goddess Hera. But they arrived home late from working in their fields, so instead of spending time going for the oxen, they put the yoke on their own necks and pulled the heavy cart with their mother in it the entire five miles to the temple. Everyone praised the young men for their great strength and for having honored their mother in this fashion. Their mother, overjoyed at the deed and the praise it had won, besought the goddess to bestow on her sons the highest blessing to which mortals can attain. The youths offered sacrifice, took part in the holy meal, and then fell asleep in the temple, never to wake up again. Their countrymen were so impressed by this chain of events, they caused statues of them to be made and given to the shrine at Delphi.

Herodotus interpreted the tale as meaning that death was better than life. But the story of Cleobis and Bito is quite puzzling. Why was everyone so impressed with what on the surface seems an accidental death of two young men brought on by their own carelessness? They had worked in the summer heat in the fields all day, then they had pulled the heavy oxcart with their mother in it over a five-mile stretch of a bumpy dirt road, and in the end they had eaten a greasy meal. The transition from the heat to the cold temple, the tremendous exertion, the heavy meal, and then lying down to sleep could most certainly have caused a sudden physical collapse. Clearly there is something odd about this story.

The fault lies not with Solon, however. In the sixth century before our era, when Greece was still predominantly horticulturalist, we may be sure that he knew what he was talking about. The great boon that Cleobis and Bito had received, their "falling asleep" in the temple and then dying, was their successfully achieving an intense ecstatic experience during initiation. The question is, why would Herodotus misunderstand the tradition in this manner?

The answer lies hidden in the statues that the Argives caused to be made of the youths and given to the shrine at Delphi. Statues of that sort, with both the youth and the girl stereotypically always in the same posture, were made for hundreds of years in Egypt and then were carried to Greece. But as we learn from art historians, a startling transformation occurred in these so-called Kuroi statues by the early fifth century B.C., the time Herodotus was born. The artists began to be concerned with the "visual reproduction of natural forms." Put differently, a fundamental change had taken place in Greek culture; the significance of the posture was forgotten, and interest shifted to the person instead and to "natural" movements. Simultaneously, in the same century, the Greeks also began formulating a theology, something totally alien to the kind of religion characteristic of horticulturalists.

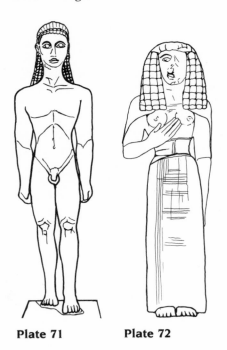

Plate 71   Plate 72

When we started exploring the two respective trance postures, a fascinating difference emerged between the male and female experience. As seen in plates 71 and 72, the youth is standing with his knees locked, resting his weight on his right leg. His arms are hanging straight down, and he seems to be carrying a small object in each hand. We used crystals for that purpose. The girl is standing equally straight; her right hand rests between her breasts, the left hangs straight down in the folds of her skirt.

When we attempted the postures for the first time in Vienna with only three participants, the brief experiences seemed to take us back to early, preclassical Greece. U. found herself in a forest and saw the entrance to a cave. It was outlined in red, and looked to her like a vulva. Eva D. also saw the cave, but she managed to enter, and once inside, she tasted blood in her mouth. She also smelled such an intense stench of putrefaction that afterward, she minutely searched her living room, where we had done the session, to make sure that there was no dead rat someplace in a corner. Christian St., on the other hand, was in a town with gleaming white rectangular buildings. He saw a square hole in the ground, outlined in white, but was unable to get in.

During another visit to Greek antiquity two years later, Eva landed on a sunny seashore, not doing anything in particular, but wondering all the time why she was "outside," instead of in the cave once more as before. U. was no longer in Vienna, and her place was taken by Amitaba, who had done seven years' fieldwork with the Paï Indians in Paraguay. In her trance, she was once more in South America, but more to the north, in a village in the rain forest. "You know how those villages always smell," she said, "of cooking fire and ashes." She saw the Indian villagers and had the premonition that soon a number of them would die. Christian returned to his white town but was in something like a basement, part of what seemed to him a labyrinth. There were many exits, but he could not enter any of them. Instead, he saw a flight of stairs leading upward, and he joined a row of figures wearing white robes who were walking up the steps toward a gilded statue, and all of them bowed before the statue. Then everything disappeared, and Christian held a brown envelope in his hand. He was given to understand that it was important, but when he opened it, it contained a sheet of paper bearing marks that he could not read.

What do these experiences tell us? I think the women in this case found themselves back at a time when the Eleusinian mysteries were still in full swing, a celebration of the return of Persephone from abduction, and in honor of Demeter and Bacchus. Participants were sworn to absolute secrecy, but reconstructions based on a number of sources, for instance by Jensen,[1] show an outline of rituals containing many of the elements reported by U., Eva, and Amitaba. The mysteries involved animal sacrifices—thus the feeling of imminent death that Amitaba noted—especially of piglets to the Earth Mother. These were thrown into crevasses and putrefied there, emitting the stench that so startled Eva. Many of the rituals took place in caves, and the conclusion was usually a bath in the ocean.

It is well known that the women held on to the old rituals longer than the men in classical times.[2] While the women in the trance session knew what was going on, Christian was unable to enter the caves, and was constrained instead *with other men* to bow to a gilded statue in the white city. Yes, the message of the envelope he received seems to say that the mystery is still there, but it is no longer accessible to him. The transition is reflected by the story Herodotus tells. At the time of Solon, everyone knew what the boon was that the brothers had received. That is why the Argives commemorated the event by taking statues of the young men to the Delphi oracle. But in the continuing and separate culture of the men, that knowledge had by Herodotus's time, only two hundred years later, effectively dissolved, causing conflict and sorrow for the women.

Agriculturalist societies also utilize the trance, but it is used for possession, an experience where an alien entity penetrates the body and takes over its functions. The poses of agriculturalist religions, the kneeling, the folding of the hands, the bowing, are not designed to tune the nervous system for specific experiences, for participating directly in events in the alternate reality, but are intended rather to express symbolically such contents as surrender and humility.

Agriculture ushered in the unbounded exploitation of our earth. As a result, the "tribal" societies, the living treasures of humankind, who should be protected and cherished because they still possess an easy access to the spiritual

homeland, are vanishing at an accelerated rate. Their habitats are being destroyed and taken over by developers and exploiters, the vultures of the modern age. Retribution was swift and merciless: the development threatens everything, the earth, the sky, the waters, the plants and the animals, our very existence. As the Navajo creation myth warns, if things are no longer held sacred, the monsters arise and will devour the people.

And, we might add, the Spirits will withdraw, with our spiritual base becoming increasingly narrower. This account is an attempt to demonstrate what riches are hidden in those ranges of mystery. But what is accessible to us is but a meager remnant, and with every myth that vanishes because no one is there to tell it anymore, there is less that we can understand of our trance experiences. In the late 1700s, a Haida carver on the Northwest Coast created a most delicate work of a naked young woman being taken

Plate 73

away by a dogfish (pl. 73). She is shown in the posture of Calling the Spirits, but no one living today can remember why she was carried away. We may have seen the story, but without the legend to give us a hint, we did not recognize it. Extinction is forever.

APPENDIX

Some Practical Points

—If you would like to try any of the postures I have described, you will need rhythmic stimulation. With some practice, you can record a tape for yourself, using either a drum or a rattle. The beat should be even and rather fast. Mine is timed at 200–210 beats per minute, and one session should last about fifteen minutes.

—Familiarize yourself with the posture first, then do a breathing exercise. It consists of fifty light, normal, complete breaths, with inhaling, exhaling, and pause constituting one breath unit. At the conclusion of this exercise, assume the posture once more, close your eyes, and start listening to the beat of the instrument. After a while, you may no longer hear the soundtrack. Do not worry about it. Your nervous system registers it anyway, although out of awareness. If you try to get back to the sound, you may interrupt your vision.

—As soon as the soundtrack stops, and provided you are clinically healthy, you will return to ordinary consciousness. Once in a great while a person does not manage this transition well. For this reason, *a beginner should always have a companion.* If the companion notices that the trancer does not come to right away, the first thing to do is to call his/her name. Gently releasing the trancer's posture is also a good strategy, and providing a glass of water will help, too. As the group leader, you will occasionally go into a light trance yourself. One of my participants told that as she was rattling, her Indian spirit friend appeared before her and rattled along with her.

—Ask your participants to take notes immediately after coming out of the trance. Precious details are sometimes forgotten later, as happens also in the ordinary state of consciousness. As mentioned before, I do not tell a group beforehand what the experience is going to be. With the publication of this text, such secrecy will no longer be possible. Quite often, the "ideal" content of the posture, the basic outline of the experience, is immediately obvious; sometimes it is not. The posture is like the tree of story: You may have to shake it repeatedly before the golden apple drops down. Point out the basic outline where it appears; such teaching is always practiced where visions are a part of the religious ritual. However, extraneous material must not be rejected out of hand. It may appear for a number of reasons: a personal matter must be resolved first; a Spirit anxious to make friends may intrude; the fragment of a myth with some tenuous connection with the posture is unaccountably perceived. Even if the "standard" content is experienced, remember that each posture can be likened to a melody, and no matter how often it is done, there is no end to variations on the basic theme. They are not, however, as easy to recognize as in the case of one friend in Switzerland, who attended my workshop several years in succession and saw a crystal castle the first time she went on a spirit journey. She badly wanted to get in but could not enter. The following year, she arrived at the same castle. It was closed once more, and when she insisted on trying to get in, an invisible antagonist dumped a bucket of cold water on her head. It was not until the third try that she was finally admitted and then found it to be empty.

The constancy and accompanying great variability have stimulated a group of my coworkers to plan a phenomenological study, which will be undertaken in the near future. In the meantime, we have come up with some interesting statistics. From 1982 until the end of 1987 and including the one exploratory project in 1977, I have offered a total of eighty workshops. Of the 890 participants, 592 were women, 298 were men. This number includes repeat attendances of 159 women and 68 men. Subtracting those, we had 433 women and 230 men participating in the workshops.

NOTES

SECTION I

2. GETTING IN TOUCH WITH THE SPIRITS

1. Erika Bourguignon, ed., *Religion, Altered States of Consciousness, and Social Change* (Columbus: Ohio State University Press, 1973).

2. Felicitas D. Goodman, *Speaking in Tongues: A Cross-Cultural Study of Glossolalia* (Chicago: University of Chicago Press, 1972).

3. V. F. Emerson, "Can Belief Systems Influence Behavior? Some Implications of Research on Meditation," *Newsletter Review*, the R. M. Bucke Memorial Society, 5:20–32.

4. Unless obvious from context, speakers are identified by first name, or first name plus initial where necessary, the location of the workshop, and the year. In a few cases I changed the name in order to spare the person unnecessary exposure. In later chapters, the descriptions of the physical trance processes are abbreviated or left out entirely because they are tediously repetitious. The quotations concentrate on the visionary, the ecstatic events instead. Other than that, editing has been minimal, concerning mainly the sequence of episodes in Section II. In Section III the nature of the material called for more extensive editing. I used both copious notes, often checked against the notes of the participants, and tape recordings.

5. This research was originally planned as part of a medical doctoral dissertation by Ingrid Mueller, a medical student at the time at the University of Freiburg, West Germany. For personal reasons, she did not complete the thesis, but I was given the data for publication. A report by Professor Kugler is in preparation.

6. Several students working for an advanced degree are at the moment continuing with this research.

3. THE OLD ONES REMEMBER

1. My research on the Anneliese Michel case resulted in a book, *The Exorcism of Anneliese Michel* (Garden City, N.Y.: Doubleday, 1981).

2. Adolf Holl, *Der letzte Christ* (Stuttgart: Deutsche Verlagsanstalt, 1979); English version: *The Last Christian* (Garden City, N.Y.: Doubleday, 1980).

3. In 1683 the Pueblo Indians revolted against the oppression, the greed, and the religious persecution of the Spanish conquerors. They succeeded in forcing the invaders to retreat to the south. Twelve years later, the Spanish returned with armed might and took revenge. Many Indians were killed, and numerous pueblos were deserted.

5. THE WAY OF THE SPIRITS

1. Hans Peter Duerr, "Fragmente eines Tagebuchs (1981)," in *Satyricon* (Berlin: Karin Kramer, 1982), pp. 77–92.

2. I included this incident, as well as the incident in the Santa Fe museum and the story about Kats and his bear wife, in a collection of tales from the alternate reality entitled "Der Hauch im Spiegel" (Breath in the Mirror), written for an anthology edited by Adolf Holl, *Die zweite Wirklichkeit* (Wien: Ueberreuter, 1987), pp. 109–123.

3. Hans Findeisen and Heino Gehrts, *Die Schamanen: Jagdhelfer und Ratgeber, See-lenfuehrer, Kuender und Heiler* (Koeln: Diederichs, 1983).
4. See, e.g., Colin M. Turnbull, *The Forest People: A Study of the Pygmies of the Congo* (Garden City, N.Y.: Anchor/Doubleday, 1961).

SECTION II

6. GOING ON A SPIRIT JOURNEY

1. Mircea Eliade, *Shamanism: Archaic Techniques of Ecstasy*, Bollingen Series 76 (Princeton: Princeton University Press, 1964).
2. In his 1980 book *The Way of the Shaman: A Guide to Power and Healing*, Michael J. Harner is principally interested in teaching his participants how to heal.
3. See ibid., p. 38. Harner's students encounter their spirit guides in the lower world, as we do frequently also. But their task is to fight with these beings in order to gain power, and this is indeed what many experience, which hardly ever happens to my participants. The difference may be due to the fact that in Cuyamungue we are located, both geographically and culturally, among Pueblo Indians, who have a pacific tradition. Harner, on the other hand, did his fieldwork among the Jivaro, the fierce headhunters of Ecuador. The initiation of their boys involves a fearful struggle with a spirit being. See Michael J. Harner, *The Jivaro: People of the Sacred Waterfalls* (Garden City, N.Y.: Anchor/Doubleday, 1973).
4. Paul G. Zolbrod, *Diné bahane': The Navajo Creation Story* (Albuquerque: University of New Mexico Press, 1984), p. 83.
5. Brueder Grimm, *Hausmaerchen* (Leipzig: R. Becker, n.d.).
6. Robert Graves, *The Greek Myths*, 2 vols. (Baltimore, Md.: Penguin Books, 1955).
7. I had seen this curious painted mask in pictures reproduced in Rudolf Poertner and Nigel Davies, eds., *Alte Kulturen der Neuen Welt,* (Duesseldorf: Econ, 1980), pp. 104–105. When I later obtained colored photographs from the Historic Preservation Section of the Georgia Department of Natural Resources, where the statues are stored, the paint had deteriorated to a few unsightly brown patches.

8. THE GIFT OF HEALING

1. Felicitas D. Goodman, *Ecstasy, Ritual, and Alternate Reality: Religion in a Pluralistic World* (Bloomington: Indiana University Press, 1988), Chapter 10.
2. No one, including me, had any idea, of course, what experience this posture would mediate. As a matter of interest, I am identifying the group to which each person cited belonged. They did not know each other.
3. See my article "Spontaneous Initiation Experiences in an Experimental Setting," in *Proceedings of the Third International Conference on the Study of Shamanism and Al-ternate Modes of Healing*, August 30–September 1, 1986, St. Sabina Center, San Raphael, Calif. (Madison, Wis.: A-R Editions, 1987), pp. 68–73. See also Findeisen and Gehrts, *Die Schamanen*.
4. John Cawte, *Medicine Is the Law: Studies in Psychiatric Anthropology of Australian Tribal Societies* (Honolulu: University Press of Hawaii, 1974), p. 65.

9. FEMALE POWERS OF HEALING

1. The story of the discovery of the Chiltan posture is told in Holl, *Die Zweite Wirklichkeit*.
2. *Tennessee Archeologist* 4, nos. 2–3, n.d.

3. Marija Gimbutas, *The Goddesses and Gods of Old Europe* (Berkeley: University of California 'ress, 1982), pl. 145.

4. Mihály Hoppál, ed., *Shamanism in Eurasia*, 2 vols. (Goettingen: Herodot, 1984).

5. Ibid., photograph on p. 265.

6. V. N. Basilov, "The *chiltan* Spirits," in Hoppál, *Shamanism in Eurasia*, pp. 253–261.

10. CHANGING SHAPE

1. Bill Reid and Robert Bringhurst, *The Raven Steals the Light* (Seattle: University of Washington Press, 1984).

2. Karl W. Luckert, *The Navajo Hunter Tradition* (Tucson: University of Arizona Press, 1975), p. 133.

3. See Jane Goodale, *Tiwi Wives* (Seattle: University of Washington Press, 1974), p. 245; also Richard A. Gould, *Yiwara: Foragers of the Australian Desert* (New York: Scribner, 1969), p. 109.

4. Jill L. Furst and Peter T. Furst, *Mexiko: Die Kunst der Olmeken, Mayas und Azteken* (Muenchen: Hirmer, 1981), pp. 22 and 23.

11. CELEBRATIONS

1. In an Olmec rock relief in Chalcatzingo, Morelos (Mexico), phantom jaguars are scratching the chest of supine humans.

2. Gordon F. Eckholm, *A Maya Sculpture in Wood*, The Museum of Primitive Art Studies no. 4 (Greenwich, Conn.: New York Graphic Society, 1964).

3. Since then, leadership of the Buddhist Center has changed hands, and the programs are more specifically oriented toward Buddhist concerns, which has left no place for us.

12. THE PIT OF DEATH AND THE PSYCHOPOMP

1. From an exhibit catalog: *Kunst der Kykladeninseln im 3. Jahrtausend v. Chr.* (Badisches Landesmuseum, Karlsruhe, 1976).

2. I am grateful to Edith Hoppál for this information.

3. Norman Bancroft-Hunt and Werner Forman, *People of the Totem: The Indians of the Pacific Coast* (New York: Putnam, 1979), p. 39.

13. LIFE EVERLASTING

1. A. P. Okladnyikov and A. I. Martinov, *Szibériai sziklarajzok* (Budapest: Corvina, 1972). Original in Russian; the Hungarian edition enlarged and edited by Mihály Hoppál.

2. Leone Fasani, *Die illustrierte Weltgeschichte der Archaeologie* (Muenchen: Suedwest Verlag, 1978), p. 535.

3. Terence Grieder, *The Art and Archeology of Pashash* (Austin: University of Texas Press, 1978), p. 81, pl. 54.

SECTION III

1. Napoleon Chagnon, *Yąnomamö: The Fierce People* (New York: Holt, Rinehart, and Winston, 1977).

2. In the introduction to Heino Gehrts and Gabriele Lademann-Priemer, eds.,

Schamanentum und Zaubermaerchen (Kassel: Erich Roeth, 1984), Gehrts provides valuable insights into the nature of myth.

3. Alfonso Ortiz, *The Tewa World* (Chicago: University of Chicago Press, 1969).

4. Zolbrod, *Diné bahane'*.

5. Jarold Ramsey, ed., *Coyote Was Going There* (Seattle: University of Washington Press, 1977). "Coyote and the Shadow People," pp. 33–37.

6. Dennis Tedlock, trans., *Popol Vuh* (New York: Simon and Schuster, 1985).

7. G. C. Vaillant, *The Aztecs of Mexico* (Harmondsworth, Middlesex: Pelican, 1960).

8. Background material for this story was taken from Linda Schele and Mary Ellen Miller, *The Blood of Kings: Dynasty and Ritual in Maya Art* (Fort Worth: Kimbell Art Museum, 1986). There are a number of different local Maya religious traditions. See, e.g., Christian Raetsch, ed., *Chactun: Die Goetter der Maya* (Koeln: Diederichs, 1986).

The Rio Azul figurine was created between A.D. 400 and 500. While postures fell into disuse in later classical times, some local traditions still employed them ritually during that century. There is a stele in Copan from the same period on which the priest stands in the posture of the Singing Shaman. Even his mouth is open.

For the record, from the archeologist's drawer in our simile, here are the relevant original reports from the workshop in Columbus, Ohio, on November 16, 1986.

GAYLE: I felt pushed back, and something or somebody was pulling me back by my hair. I became dark and cool and damp. Five rattles were going around, and they danced. At my left, something was pulling me, I could not tell what it was, and a pressure engulfed me. I felt warm and safe. The rattle sound turned into the distant sound of a flute. It was nice. I wanted to stay there.

JACKIE: My body was rocking. It was a special movement; my torso described a circle. I asked, how can I hold this? And I was told, let the body do it and listen instead. There was a whispering. I saw feet and paid attention to the dance. I saw a mountain, it was hot; and I felt a power on the mountain, it felt big. I climbed the mountain, and on the mountain there was a man in this posture, and he was serious. He took out one of his eyes and gave it to me. I looked through the eye; I could see vibration, colors that merged. It was channeling energy.

DIANE: I saw a being holding a child, rocking it to the rhythm of the rattle. The air was warm, it was dark, and a fire was burning. People were celebrating, talking in a foreign language and yelling. Acrobats were jumping into the fire, but they were not hurt. I backed away from the fire and went into the forest or jungle. I went back to the fire and tried jumping into it myself. Then I went to a hut to sleep. A deer came into the hut. I killed it and took out its heart. Then I rekindled the fire. I went back into the dark and walked in time with the rattle. It was like a dance; I was in a chain of people, and the chain was very long.

JUDY: I felt really warm. On a screen I saw a white bird; it had the profile of an eagle. I tried to be the [clay] figure. When I got into it, I saw a huge dark pond; it was very still, stagnant, and had not moved in eons. It was very beautiful and sterile. When I got outside, I fell apart, and that made me feel happy. Something was saying, "Things can start again."

CATHLEEN: I felt the straightness of my spine, the possession of power. I was large and was expanding, and I felt male. Then I bent back; it was like giving birth, and I held back a scream, but nothing came out.

JILL: I thought that the posture would not hurt, but it did. I was with a lot of reptiles, iguanas, like that, and I was one of them. I thought that I will have to look at the world from their perspective. The pain was caused by a reptile going up my spine. I was in an iron cage, and I was being rolled around.

JAN: All was hazy, then things began to clear. I was told, "Don't be afraid to expose your power center, your belly, but watch the heart." Someone was poking a sword into my belly, and that sword in my belly was being turned. My belly became transparent; it becomes fire. My body opens, my head opens, flowers come out of my head. I was no longer in the posture, but was making an X with my arms. I was rejuvenated and was giving the energy back to the universe. We shot out; there were four others with me. We created a sun, then went back into the posture, and this was repeated twice. Very quickly I went through the moon and through the earth, and my body broke into droplets, and this too was repeated. I was a newborn star; it was an incredible feeling.

ADRIANA: All was dark blue; the rattle sounded like fire crackling, and I was being pulled from behind. Afterward I had to struggle. I must not fall asleep, I must stay alert.

SHARRON: The energy was not flowing easily. There was a light in my head. Then there is a twin in me, but we are facing in opposite directions and meet at the tongue. There is a sense of spreading out, of a chalice forming. I am being hollowed out. At the right there is a flower basket. I see the sun through a circle. I am given to understand that that's how the sun rises; we participate in it. My tongue is being pulled outward. We are waiting for the sun to be put on our tongue.

9. Viola E. Garfield and Linn A. Forest, *The Wolf and the Raven: Totem Poles of Southeastern Alaska* (Seattle: University of Washington Press, 1986). Original 1948.

10. Ibid., pp. 31–35.

11. For classical Greek myths, see Graves, *The Greek Myths*.

CONCLUSION

1. A. E. Jensen, *Die getoetete Gottheit: Weltbild einer fruehen Kultur*. Stuttgart: Kohlhammer, 1966.

2. Hans Peter Duerr, *Dreamtime*, trans. Felicitas Goodman (Oxford: Blackwell, 1984).

BIBLIOGRAPHY

Altenmueller, Hartwig. 1982. *Grab- und Totenreich der alten Aegypter.* Hamburg: Hamburgisches Museum fuer Voelkerkunde.

Badisches Landesmuseum Karlsruhe. 1976. *Kunst der Kykladeninseln im 3. Jahrtausend v. Chr.* (exhibit).

Baer, Gerhard. 1984. *Die Religion der Matsigenka: Ost-Peru.* Basel: Wepf.

Baer, G.; E. Ferst; and C. N. Dubelarr. 1984. Petroglyphs from the Urubamba and Pantiacolla Rivers, Eastern Peru. *Verhandl. Naturf. Ges. Basel* 94:287–306.

Bancroft-Hunt, Norman, and Werner Forman. 1979. *People of the Totem: The Indians of the Pacific Coast.* New York: Putnam.

Basilov, V. N. 1984. The *chiltan* Spirits. In *Shamanism in Eurasia,* Mihály Hoppál, ed. Goettingen: Herodot, pp. 253–261.

Bernal, Ignacio. 1969. *The Olmec World.* Berkeley: University of California Press.

———. 1970. *The Mexican National Museum of Anthropology.* London: Thames and Hudson.

Bounure, Vincent. 1968. *Die amerikanische Malerei.* Lausanne: Editions Rencontre.

Bourguignon, Erika. 1973. *Religion, Altered States of Consciousness, and Social Change.* Columbus: Ohio State University Press.

Budge, W. E. E. 1911. *Osiris and the Egyptian Resurrection.* New York: Dover.

Buehler, Alfred; Terry Barrow; and Charles P. Mountford. 1980. *Ozeanien und Australien: Die Kunst der Suedsee.* Baden-Baden: Holle.

Bushnell, G. H. S. 1957. *Peru.* New York: Praeger.

Campbell, Joseph. 1983. *The Way of the Animal Powers.* Vol. 1, *Historical Atlas of World Mythology.* London: Alfred van der March.

Cawte, John. 1974. *Medicine Is the Law: Studies in Psychiatric Anthropology of Australian Tribal Societies.* Honolulu: University Press of Hawaii.

Chagnon, Napoleon. 1977. *Ya̧nomamö: The Fierce People.* New York: Holt, Rinehart and Winston.

Charbonneaux, J.; R. Martin; and F. Villard. 1969. *Die griechische Kunst II: Das archaische Griechenland.* Muenchen: Beck-Verlag.

Cholula, Ciudad Sagrada. 1971. *Artes de México* 18, no. 140.

Coe, Ralph T. 1977. *Sacred Circles: Two Thousand Years of American Indian Art.* Exhibition, Nelson Gallery of Art-Atkins Museum of Fine Arts, Kansas City, Missouri.

Daicoviciu, Constantin, and Emil Condurachi. 1972. *Rumaenien.* Genf: Nagel.

Demarque, Pierre. 1975. *Die griechische Kunst I: Die Geburt der griechischen Kunst.* Muenchen: C. H. Beck.

Diószegi, Vilmos. 1958. *A sámánhit emlékei a magyar népi müveltségben.* Budapest: Akadémiai Kiadó.

Dockstader, Frederick J. 1973. *Indian Art in America.* New York: Promontory Press.

Doebler, Hanns Ferdinand. 1972. *Kunst- und Sittengeschichte der Welt, Magie, Mythos, Religion.* N.p.: Bertelsmann.

Duerden, Dennis. 1974. *African Art.* London: Hamlyn.

Duerr, Hans Peter. 1984. *Dreamtime.* Trans. Felicitas Goodman. Oxford: Blackwell.

———. 1982. *Satyricon.* Berlin: Karin Kramer.

———. 1984. *Sedna oder die Liebe zum Leben.* Frankfurt am Main: Suhrkamp.

Eckholm, Gordon F. 1964. *A Maya Sculpture in Wood.* The Museum of Primitive Art Studies no. 4. Greenwich, Conn.: New York Graphic Society.

Eliade, Mircea. 1964. *Shamanism: Archaic Techniques of Ecstasy*. Bollinger Series 76. Princeton: Princeton University Press.

Elkin, A. P. 1964. *The Australian Aborigines*. Garden City, N.Y.: Anchor/Doubleday.

Emerson, V. F. 1972. Can Belief Systems Influence Neurophysiology? Some Implications of Research on Meditation. *Newsletter Review*, the R. M. Bucke Memorial Society, 5:20–32.

Fasani, Leone. 1978. *Die illustrierte Weltgeschichte der Archaeologie*. Muenchen: Suedwest Verlag.

Feest, Christian. 1968. *Indianer Nordamerikas*. Museum fuer Voelkerkunde, Wien (exhibit).

Findeisen, Hans, and Heino Gehrts. 1983. *Die Schamanen: Jagdhelfer und Ratgeber, Seelenfahrer, Kuender und Heiler*. Koeln: Diederichs.

Furst, Jill L., and Peter T. Furst. 1981. *Mexiko: Die Kunst der Olmeken, Mayas und Azteken*. Muenchen: Hirmer.

Furst, Peter T., and Jill L. Furst. 1982. *North American Indian Art*. New York: Rizzoli.

Gafni, Shlomo S. 1983. *The Glory of the Old Testament*. Jerusalem: The Jerusalem Publishing House.

Garfield, Viola E., and Linn A. Forest. 1986 (original 1948). *The Wolf and the Raven: Totem Poles of Southeastern Alaska*. Seattle: University of Washington Press.

Gehrts, Heino, and Gabriele Lademann-Priemer, eds. 1984. *Schamanentum und Zaubermaerchen*. Kassel: Erich Roeth.

Gimbutas, Marija. 1982. *The Goddesses and Gods of Old Europe*. Berkeley: University of California Press.

Goodale, Jane. 1974. *Tiwi Wives*. Seattle: University of Washington Press.

Goodman, Felicitas D. 1972. *Speaking in Tongues: A Cross-Cultural Study of Glossolalia*. Chicago: University of Chicago Press.

——. 1981. *The Exorcism of Anneliese Michel*. Garden City, N.Y.: Doubleday.

——. 1988. *Ecstasy, Ritual, and Alternate Reality: Religion in a Pluralistic World*. Bloomington: Indiana University Press.

——. 1988. *How about Demons? Possession and Exorcism in the Modern World*. Bloomington: Indiana University Press.

Gottschalk, Herbert. 1982. *Lexikon der Mythologie*. Muenchen: T. B. Heyne.

Gould, Richard A. 1969. *Yiwara: Foragers of the Australian Desert*. New York: Scribner.

Graves, Robert. 1955. *The Greek Myths*. Baltimore: Penguin Books.

Grieder, Terence. 1978. *The Art and Archeology of Pashash*. Austin: University of Texas Press.

Grimm, Brueder. N.d. *Hausmaerchen*. Leipzig: R. Becker.

Guttmann, G.; F. D. Goodman; C. Korunka; H. Bauer; and M. Leodolter. 1988. DC-Potential Recordings during Altered States of Consciousness. *Research Bulletin, Psychologisches Institut der Universitaet Wien*.

Halifax, Joan. 1982. *The Wounded Healer*. London: Thames and Houston.

Die Hallstattkultur: Fruehform europaeischer Einheit. 1980. Land Oberoesterreich, Schloss Lamberg, Steyr (exhibit).

Harner, Michael J. 1973. *The Jivaro: People of the Sacred Waterfalls*. Garden City, N.Y.: Anchor/Doubleday.

——. 1980. *The Way of the Shaman: A Guide to Power and Healing*. New York: Harper and Row.

Holl, Adolf. 1980. *The Last Christian*. Garden City, N.Y.: Doubleday.

——. 1987. *Die zweite Wirklichkeit*. Wien: Ueberreuter.

Holm, E. 1969. *Felsbilder Suedafrikas*. Tuebingen.

Hoppál, Mihály, ed. 1984. *Shamanism in Eurasia*. 2 vols. Goettingen: Herodot.

Jelinek, J. 1972. *Das grosse Bilderlexikon des Menschen in der Vorzeit*. Artia: Prag.

Jensen, A. E. 1966. *Die getoetete Gottheit: Weltbild einer fruehen Kultur.* Stuttgart: Kohlhammer.
Jung, Carl G. 1938. *Wandlungen und Symbole der Libido,* 3d ed. Leipzig.
———. 1980. *Der Mensch und seine Symbole.* 6th ed. Olten: Walter.
Kooijman, Simon. N.d. *Niew Guinea: Kunst, Kunstvormen en Stijlgebieden.* Leiden: Rijksmuseum voor Volkenkunde.
Land, L. K., 1979. *Pre-Columbian Art from the Land Collection.* N.p.: California Academy of Science.
Lawrence, D. H. 1934. *Mornings in Mexico.* New York: Knopf.
Lensinger, Elsy. 1985. *Propylaen Weltgeschichte, Naturvoelker.* Wien: Propylaen Verlag.
Lincoln, Yvonne, and Egon G. Guba. 1985. *Naturalistic Inquiry.* Beverly Hills: Sage.
Lommel, Andreas. 1966. *Vorgeschichte und Naturvoelker.* Vol. 1. London: Paul Hamlyn.
Lothrop, Samuel K. 1969. *Das vorkolumbianische Amerika und seine Kunstschaetze.* Genève: Editions d'Art Albert Skira.
Luckert, Karl W. 1975. *The Navajo Hunter Tradition.* Tucson: University of Arizona Press.
Mair, L. 1969. *Witchcraft.* New York: McGraw-Hill.
Mode, Heinz. 1959. *Das fruehe Indien.* Stuttgart: Gustav Klipper.
Monti, Franco. 1969. *Precolumbian Terracottas.* London: Hamlyn.
Museum fuer Voelkerkunde Wien. N.d. *Voelker der Tundra und Taiga: Schutzgeister der Orotschen und Golden* (exhibit).
Museum fuer Vor- und Fruehgeschichte, Frankfurt am Main. 1983. *Keramik und Gold: Bulgarische Jungsteinzeit im 6. und 5. Jahrtausend* (exhibit).
Neher, Andrew. 1961. Auditory Driving Observed with Scalp Electrodes in Normal Subjects. *Electroenceph. Clin. Neurophysiol.* 13:449–451.
———. 1962. A Physiological Explanation of Unusual Behavior in Ceremonies Involving Drums. *Human Biology* 34:151–160.
Okladnyikov, A. P. and A. I. Martinov. 1972. Hungarian ed. by Mihály Hoppál. *Szibériai sziklarajzok.* Budapest: Corvina.
Oppitz, Michael. 1981. *Schamanen im Blinden Land.* Frankfurt am Main: Syndikat.
Ortiz, Alfonso. 1969. *Tewa World.* Chicago: University of Chicago Press.
Osborne, Harold. 1969. *South American Mythology.* Feltham, Middlesex: Hamlyn.
Peters, Larry G., and Douglas Price-Williams. 1983. A Phenomenological Overview of Trance. *Transcultural Psychiatric Research Review* 20:5–39.
Poertner, Rudolf, and Nigel Davies, eds. 1980. *Alte Kulturen der Neuen Welt.* Duesseldorf: Econ.
Radin, Paul. 1972 (original 1956). *The Trickster: A Study in American Indian Mythology.* New York: Schocken.
Raetsch, Christian, ed. 1986. *Chactun: Die Goetter der Maya.* Koeln: Eugen Diederichs.
Ramsey, Jarold, ed. 1977. *Coyote Was Going There: Indian Literature of the Oregon Country.* Seattle: University of Washington Press.
von Reden, Sibylle, and G. T. Best. 1981. *Auf der Spur der ersten Griechen.* Koeln: Dumon.
Reid, Bill, and Robert Bringhurst. 1984. *The Raven Steals the Light.* Seattle: University of Washington Press.
Rosenthal, Robert, and Ralph L. Rosnow, eds. 1969. *Artifact in Behavioral Research.* New York: Academic Press.
Scheffer, J. 1673. *Lapponia.* Frankfurt.
Schele, Linda, and Mary Ellen Miller. 1986. *The Blood of Kings: Dynasty and Ritual in Maya Art.* Fort Worth: Kimbell Art Museum (exhibit).
Segall, Marshall H.; Donald T. Campbell; and Melville J. Herskovitz. 1966. *The Influence of Culture on Visual Perception.* Indianapolis: Bobbs-Merrill.

Shao, Paul. 1976. *Asiatic Influences in Pre-Columbian American Art*. Ames: Iowa State University Press.

Sheldrake, Rupert. 1987. "The Habits of Nature." Manuscript.

Soustelle, Jacques. 1979. *Die Olmeken*. N.p.: Atlantis.

Striedter, Karl Heinz. 1984. *Felsbilder der Sahara*. Muenchen: Prestel.

Tarradell, M. 1978. *Regard sur l'art ibérique*. Paris: Société Française de Livre.

Tedlock, Dennis, trans. 1985. *Popol Vuh*. New York: Simon and Schuster.

Torbruegge, Walter. 1967. *Europaeische Vorzeit*. Baden-Baden: Holle.

Turnbull, Colin M. 1961. *The Forest People: A Study of the Pygmies of the Congo*. Garden City, N.Y.: Anchor/Doubleday.

Vaillant, G. C. 1960. *The Aztecs of Mexico*. Harmondsworth, Middlesex: Pelican.

Wiesner, Joseph. 1963. *Die Thraker*. Stuttgart: Kohlhammer.

Wilhelm, Manhardt. 1859. Das Brueckenspiel. *Zeitschrift fuer deutsche Mythologie und Sittenkunde* 4:301–320.

Wingert, Paul S. 1970. *African Art*. University Prints, Series N, Section I. Cambridge, Mass.: University Prints.

——. 1970. *Oceanic Art*. University Prints, Series N, Section II. Cambridge, Mass.: University Prints.

Winkelman, Michael. 1986. Trance States: A Theoretical Model and Cross-Cultural Analysis. *Ethos* 14:174–203.

Zenil, Alfonso Medellin. 1966. *Obras Maestras del Museo de Xalapa, Veracruz* (exhibit).

Zolbrod, Paul G. 1984. *Diné bahane': The Navajo Creation Story*. Albuquerque: University of New Mexico Press.

INDEX

Adolescence: magic and initiation rituals, 3–4

Adulthood: puberty and loss of magic, 3, 4–5

Aging: fear of and spirit journey, 82–83

Agriculture: cultural complex and postures, 60–61; survival of Bear Spirit posture, 114; Corn Goddess posture and metamorphosis, 137; modern and demise of postures, 219–23

Albatross adventure: women and spirit journeys, 83–85

American Anthropological Association: lack of interest in author's research, 26, 42

American Indians: author's encounter with spirits in Kentucky, 5; impact of Southwest on author, 5–9; appearance in spirit journeys to lower world, 81–82; Feathered Serpent posture, 170. *See also specific groups*

Angle: Lascaux Cave posture and research, 22; postures and Egyptian mythology, 58; slanted board, 71–72; vision and alternate reality, 181

Animals: spirit journeys to lower world, 78; Nupe mallam posture, 93; shape-changing mythology, 128; dances and imitation, 129–30; masked-dance celebration at Cuyamungue, 152; spiritual meaning of petroglyphs, 168–69. *See also* Metamorphosis; Spirit Guides

Anthropology: author and graduate education, 10–11; author's research and naturalist method, 19; culture systems and postures, 218

Apostolics: author's research on glossolalia in Mexico, 13–15; group trance experience, 45

Australia: divining posture, 24; shamans and healing ritual, 114; dances and imitation of animals, 129

Aztecs: survival of Bear Spirit posture, 114; metamorphosis postures, 131; Chalchihuitlicue and Tatooed Jaguar posture, 136; Corn Goddess posture, 137; postures as characteristics of gods, 215

Baer, Gerhard: Feathered Serpent posture, 170

Bandelier National Park: author's spiritual experience in, 32–37

Bear: trance-dance workshop, 150; Pacific Northwest myth, 195–97

Bear Spirit: author's early research on postures, 19; general character of posture, 46; spirit

guides and sky world, 74; posture and healing, 100, 106, 109–15, 136; predominantly male, 116

Binder, Gerhard: experience with hunter's posture, 62–65

Biology: universal physical changes experienced in glossolalia, 15

Bird of paradise: encounter with spirit of mask, 148; trance-dance workshop, 149, 150

Birds: spirit journeys to sky world, 72; Bear Spirit and healing, 112–13; Tatooed Jaguar and metamorphosis, 135–36; psychopomp, 167, 173; Neolithic Thessaly posture and myth, 212–13

Birth: shamaness and Couple from Cernavodă posture, 126

Birthing posture: culture, 100–101; hunter-gatherer ritual and spirit journey, 102–106

Bito: cultural implications of story, 220–21

Blood: reference to sacrifice in Chiltan posture, 120

Boar: encounter with spirit of mask, 147

Boat: spirit journeys to lower world, 79–80; shamaness and death, 124

Bone Pointing posture: cultural gap between hunters and agriculturalists, 61

Bourguignon, Erika: author and graduate education, 10–11, author and V. F. Emerson, 17

Breathing: exercises and religious trance, 44, 225

Buddhist Center in Scheibbs (Austria): idea for workshops, 50; first workshop, 51; change in leadership, 229n

Bushmen: religious trance and healing, 113; dances and imitation of animals, 129

Calling of the Spirits posture: error in ritual, 58; masked dance and invitation of spirits, 146–47; participation in myth, 198–202

Cancer: Bear Spirit and healing, 113–14

Cap: Tennessee diviner posture, 94–95

Cassandra: Greek mythology and gift of prophecy, 38–39

Cat: author's spiritual experience, 30, 32

Cawte, John: Australian shamans and healing ritual, 114

Centaurs: Neolithic Thessaly posture and myth, 211–12

Central America: metamorphosis postures, 131

Chakras: postures and physiological change, 24

Chalchihuitlicue: Tatooed Jaguar posture, 136

FELICITAS D. GOODMAN, *Founder and Director of the Cuyamungue Institute, taught anthropology at Denison University until her retirement. She has written several books, including* Speaking in Tongues, The Exorcism of Anneliese Michel, How about Demons: Exorcism in the Modern World, *and* Ecstasy, Ritual, and Alternate Reality: Religion in a Pluralistic World.